CONTENTS

W9-ANQ-478

1 Tourist regions described in the guide

Administrative boundaries :

---- regional .... provincial

MOST OUTSTANDING SIGHTS

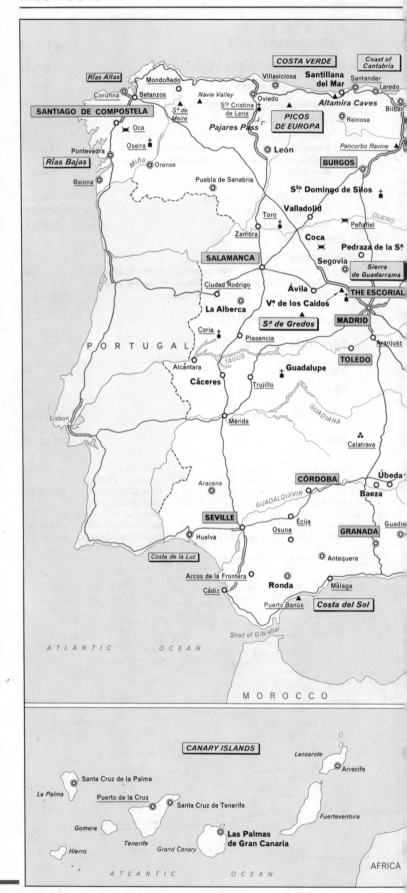

Rías Altas

Corunna
Mondoñedo
Betanzos
Navia Valley

SANTIAGO DE COMPOSTELA
Sª de Meira

Oca

Pontevedra
Oseira

Rías Bajas
Orense

Baiona

Puebla de Sanabria

Toro

Zamora

SALAMANCA

Ciudad Rodrigo

La Alberca

Coria

Alcántara
TAGUS

Cáceres

Lisbon

P O R T U G A L

Trujillo

Mérida

Aracena

SEVILLE

Huelva

Costa de la Luz

Arcos de la Frontera

Cádiz

COSTA VERDE
Villaviciosa
Oviedo
Sta Cristina de Lena

PICOS DE EUROPA

León

Sto. Domingo de Silos

Valladolid

Coca

Segovia

Ávila

Vº de los Caídos

Sª de Gredos

Plasencia

Guadalupe

Osuna
Écija

Ronda

Puerto Banús

Coast of Cantabria

Santillana del Mar
Santander
Laredo

Altamira Caves
Bilbao

Reinosa

Pancorbo Ravine

BURGOS

DUERO
Peñafiel

Pedraza de la Sª

Sierra de Guadarrama

▲ **THE ESCORIAL**

MADRID

Aranjuez

TOLEDO

GUADIANA

Calatrava

CÓRDOBA

Úbeda

Baeza

GUADALQUIVIR

GRANADA
Guadix

Antequera

Málaga

Costa del Sol

Strait of Gibraltar

A T L A N T I C   O C E A N

M O R O C C O

CANARY ISLANDS

Lanzarote

Santa Cruz de la Palma
La Palma
Puerto de la Cruz
Santa Cruz de Tenerife
Gomera
Tenerife
Grand Canary
Las Palmas de Gran Canaria

Arrecife

Fuerteventura

Hierro

A T L A N T I C   O C E A N

AFRICA

4

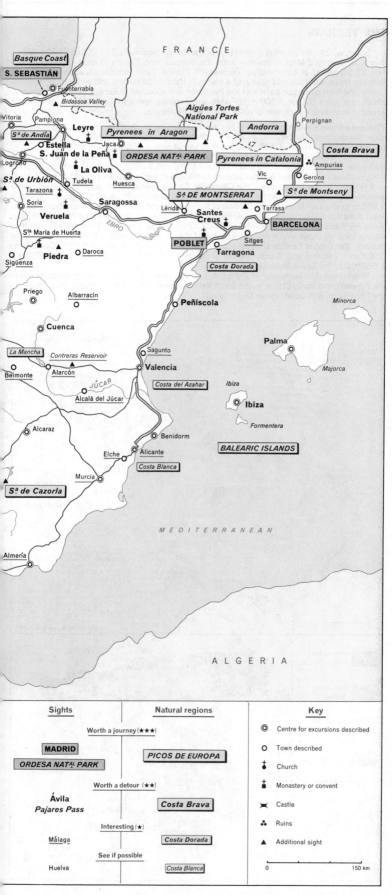

FRANCE

Basque Coast
S. SEBASTIÁN
○ Fuenterrabia
▲ *Bidassoa Valley*

Vitoria ○
Sª de Andía
Pamplona
▲
○ **Estella**
S. Juan de la Peña
La Oliva

Jaca ○
Leyre ✝
Pyrenees in Aragon
▲
ORDESA NATᴬᴸ PARK

Aigües Tortes National Park
▲

Perpignan ○

Andorra

Costa Brava

Vic ○
✣ Ampurias
Gerona ○

Logroño ○
Sª de Urbión
▲
Tarazona ✝
Soria ○
Veruela
Tudela ○
Huesca ○

Saragossa ○
EBRO
Lérida ○
Sª DE MONTSERRAT
▲
Tarrasa ○
Sª de Montseny ▲

Santes Creus ✝
BARCELONA

Sigüenza ○
Sᵗª María de Huerta ■
Piedra ▲ ○ *Daroca*

POBLET ○
Sitges ○
Tarragona
Costa Dorada

Priego ○
○ *Albarracín*

Cuenca ◎
Peñíscola

Minorca

La Mancha
Contreras Reservoir
Belmonte ○
○ *Alarcón*
JÚCAR
Alcalá del Júcar

Sagunto ○
Valencia ◎

Costa del Azahar
Ibiza

Palma ◎
Majorca

Alcaraz ○

○ Benidorm
Elche ○ ○ Alicante
Murcia ○
Costa Blanca

◎ **Ibiza**
Formentera

BALEARIC ISLANDS

▲
Sª de Cazorla

M E D I T E R R A N E A N

Almería ○

A L G E R I A

Sights	Natural regions	Key
Worth a journey (★★★)		◎ Centre for excursions described
MADRID	*PICOS DE EUROPA*	○ Town described
ORDESA NATᴬᴸ PARK		✝ Church
Worth a detour (★★)		✣ Monastery or convent
Ávila	*Costa Brava*	✕ Castle
Pajares Pass		✣ Ruins
Interesting (★)		▲ Additional sight
Málaga	*Costa Dorada*	
See if possible		0 150 km
Huelva	*Costa Blanca*	

5

INTRODUCTION TO THE TOUR

THE TERRAIN

Spain, which occupies the largest part of the Iberian peninsula (581 000km² - 224 325sq miles), is the third largest country with the Balearic and Canary Islands (505 000km² - 194 930sq miles) in Europe after Russia and France. Geographical situation and natural features make it unique and have had a marked effect on its history and civilisation: isolated behind the high mountain barrier of the Pyrenees, it is attached to Europe only by an isthmus which is a mere 500km - 300 miles wide and extends south to within 15km - 9 miles of Africa; between are contrasts of relief, extremes of climate...

The mountain dividing lines. — For average land height Spain comes second in Europe after Switzerland. The highest peak is the **Mulhacén** (3 482m - 11 424ft); one sixth of the country is over 1 000m - 3 280ft and the average altitude is 650m - about 2 130ft.

The peninsula's dominant feature is the **Meseta,** the immense plateau at its centre. This Hercynian base of between 600 and 1 000m - 1 968 and 3 280ft inclines slightly westwards. It is practically surrounded and has access to the sea as well as Spain's neighbours, Portugal and France. To the northwest is the **Cantabrian Cordillera** which joins up with the last of the westerly Pyrenees and in which the greatest heights are the Picos de Europa at 2 648m - 8 688ft; to the east is the **Iberian Cordillera** (Sistema Ibérico), which runs in a southeast-north-west direction (Moncayo, 2 313m - 6 589ft) and forms the south side of the Ebro Valley; lastly the **Sierra Morena** in the southwest (1 323m - 4 341ft). These ranges were all caused by Alpine folding; those which rise directly out of the Meseta are relics of the original, ancient massif: the **Central Cordillera,** made up of the **Somosierra** (2 127m - 6 976ft), **Guadarrama** (2 429m - 7 969ft) and **Gredos** Sierras (2 592m - 8 510ft), the **Peña de Francia** (1 732m - 5 682ft) and the **Toledo Mountains.**

The peninsula's extremes — the loftiest ranges, the widest depressions are at its edge: the **Pyrenees** and **Baetic Chains** — the **Sierra Nevada** forms part of the southeast coast chain — the Ebro Basin and Guadalquivir Depression.

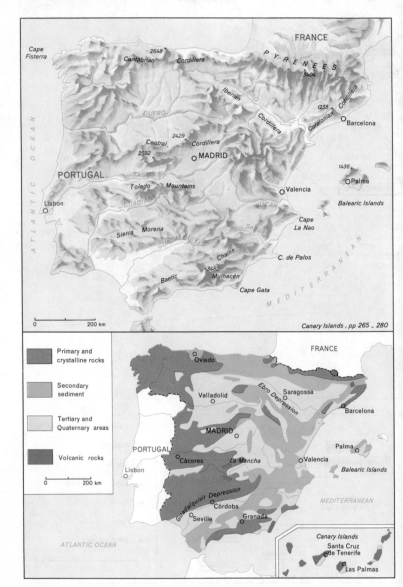

Canary Islands, pp 265 - 280

Primary and crystalline rocks

Secondary sediment

Tertiary and Quaternary areas

Volcanic rocks

Three distinct climates. — The major area of Spain, the Meseta, cut off from modifying maritime influences by the *sierras*, has an extreme, more or less **continental**, type of climate, resembling, in many respects, that of central Europe. The temperature variation is considerable: the summer heat is cruel, the winters are long and rigorous — a situation Castilians describe as "nine months of winter and three of hell". The lack of water, which has increased the general aridity of these poorly endowed regions, results in their often being referred to as **"Dry Spain"**.

The Pyrenean Provinces, Navarre, Huesca, Lérida and Gerona, on the other hand, are known as **"Wet Spain"**; their humid, temperate climate, is the exact opposite of that of the Meseta, the area being open to the Cantabrian Sea and the Atlantic. There are no extremes of temperature, humidity falls frequently as mist inland and fine drizzle on the coast but the sun also shines and the landscape, therefore, is green and lush.

The east and the south coasts, including the south Atlantic provinces of Huelva and Cádiz, and the inland plains of Andalusia, enjoy a typically **Mediterranean** climate. These regions, which represent about a third of the land area, are protected from the cool winds of the Meseta by the *sierras*. Where they comprise only narrow strips between the *sierras* and the sea, they have a particularly mild climate, with temperatures remaining relatively high throughout the year and virtually no winter season — in the southeast the thermometer registers between 13 and 15 ºC - 55 to 60 ºF in January and February. The extreme south is the hottest, particularly in the Guadalquivir Depression. There is a certain amount of humidity along the coast of Catalonia but elsewhere the lack of rain, as on the Meseta, gives rise to an arid bleakness.

Water courses are usually dry, their beds only filling after the heavy rains which fall mostly in autumn. These rains, however, can also be disastrous as in 1957, 1973 and 1982 when all efforts in the Valencian area were fruitless to control exceptional floodwaters and damage was extensive.

The provinces of Murcia and Almeria are so dry that they have been described as having a **sub-desert** climate but, though such heat may be unfavourable to agriculture, it has become an attraction to sun-worshipping tourists, Spanish and foreign alike, who in recent years have taken to journeying all the year round to bask on what is now considered, a privileged coastline.

The great natural regions. — Great natural regions exist in the peninsula outside those areas especially distinguished by climate and relief.

Northern, "Wet Spain", has a green and lush countryside of meadows and fields of maize bordered by trees and hedges. Roads and tunnels cut across the landscape. Cantabria is Spain's apple orchard. The terrain is hilly with valleys tucked away between lower slopes and mountain ranges which, in the Pyrenean area particularly, are covered with conifers, spruces predominantly. The land is closely cultivated even to quite high levels and divided into small acreages, particularly in Galicia where the system known as *minifundio* is practised *(p 141)*. The existence of water and the difficulties of communications have given rise to communities being formed and houses built in widely separated places, small towns often being grouped at the bottom end of a valley, farms scattered over the countryside.

Features similar in many ways to this northern landscape reappear in certain mountain areas of the Meseta and Andalusia even, where the ranges are high enough to catch the rain; the Serranía de Cuenca, the Albarracín, Gredos, Guadarrama and Cazorla Sierras are all densely covered with trees — pines, beeches...

The Meseta itself is totally different: its horizons appear infinite with only here and there a brown, rock coloured, village clustered at the foot of a castle or the distant outline of a low ridge of *páramos* (limestone heights bare of all vegetation). In spring and autumn the vast areas of brown earth turn brilliant with young cereals or grain ready for harvesting. In this austere world, La Mancha *(p 210)* is perhaps the most extreme area, with immense properties or *latifundia*, still, as in the Middle Ages, belonging to single landowners.

(After Hürlimann photo. Zurich)

Landscape in Castile (The Duero)

Mediterranean crops grow along the east and south coasts and in Andalusia: almonds in the mildest areas, vines in Andalusia (Jerez, Málaga, Montilla) and Catalonia (Penedés) where they produce rich harvests. Olives grow everywhere, particularly again in Andalusia where they form the staple crop. This Mediterranean vegetation also extends beyond the narrow coastal belt over parts of the Meseta: La Mancha is a great wine region, olive trees cover vast tracts of land as far north as Toledo.

Irrigation is beginning to transform some of the most desert like regions although the age old distinction still remains between *tierras de secano (p 187)* and *tierras de regadío*. In what would at first appear as paradoxical, regions which, climatically, are among the less well favoured have for long had the greatest output — the Ebro Valley, to an even greater degree the *huertas* of the Levant region *(p 157)* and, in a different way, Elche and Orihuela where the palm groves are unique in Europe. In each case results are due to irrigation.

Finally there is the sea — or rather there are the Atlantic and the Mediterranean. Two thirds of Spain's perimeter is seaboard: it has a coastline of nearly 4 000km - 2 475 miles. There could scarcely be a greater contrast than between the Cantabrian and Galician coasts, washed by the Atlantic and the east and south coasts, lapped by the Mediterranean and more southerly Atlantic; maritime influence extends inland, while the shores, individual in character and climate, attract the passing and remunerative tourist.

The five great rivers of Iberia. — Four of Iberia's five major rivers drain into the Atlantic because of the peninsula's inclination to the west *(see above)*; the Ebro is the only major water course to flow east into the Mediterranean. Other rivers, south of the Iberian Cordillera, which acts as a watershed, do exist in the east — the Turia, Júcar and Segura — but all are relatively short and their flows far from regular.

Three of the major rivers rise in the mountains: the **Duero** (2 060m - 6 759ft) in the Sierra de Urbión *(p 248)*, the **Tagus** (1 620m - 5 315ft) in the Montes Universales, the **Guadalquivir** (1 500m - 4 922ft) in the Cazorla Sierra *(p 38)*. Two others have sources at lesser altitudes on the Meseta: the **Guadiana,** which has only a poor supply of water, in the Ruidera Lakes *(p 212)* at 840m - 2 756ft and the **Ebro,** of which the main source appears at 881m - 2 890ft at the foot of the Cantabrian Cordillera *(p 122)* but which is joined by tributaries from the Pyrenees.

While all five are remarkable for their length (the Tagus is more than 1 000km long - 625 miles), none has a consistent flow, lacking the regular rainfall of the smaller Cantabrian and Galician water courses. In addition those that cross the Meseta and Andalusia, besides not being replenished by summer rains, lose a considerable quantity of their volume through evaporation. This applies particularly to the Guadiana. The Ebro is the same but is massively augmented in winter and spring by mountain waters from the Pyrenees — a factor which contributes to the variation in its flow from season to season and even from year to year. None of the rivers is navigable along more than a brief stretch of its course: the Ebro below Tortosa, the Guadalquivir above Seville...

Flora and fauna. — Spain was once densely wooded and rich in game. It still offers good hunting country although the forests have been reduced over the centuries by landowners, the seasonal migration of stock from the lowlands, to the uplands, lumbering and war. Some areas, which are of little economic value, have turned to scrub and are known as the *matorral* (thicket) or *monte bajo*.

Afforestation. — The state, through the Patrimonio Forestal del Estado, has undertaken an extensive programme of reafforestation since the Civil War. New plantations in the national parks and areas especially planted by growers, for which they receive a subsidy, now amount annually to some 95 000ha - 235 000 acres.

The surroundings of manmade reservoir lakes have been considered especially carefully: trees retain moisture besides enhancing the landscape and they have been planted, therefore, to increase local humidity in the atmosphere, to reduce erosion of the soil which has a tendency to accumulate at the bottom of reservoirs, and to add to the general amenity of the surroundings. Conifers have been used predominately — spruce in the mountains, pine at lower levels and the sea or parasol pine in Cantabria. Eucalyptus is being grown successfully now in Cantabria and Galicia.

Aigües Tortes National Park

The National Park. — The first national park to be designated in Spain was the **Covadonga Mountain Park** *(p 112)* in 1918 — twelfth hundred anniversary of the battle. In the same year, a second park was inaugurated at **Ordesa y Monte Perdido** *(p 67)* in the Aragon Pyrenees. To these have been added **Doñana** in Huelva province *(p 41)*, **Aigües Tortes** in Lérida *(p 76)* and **Las Tablas de Daimiel** in La Mancha, making five parks on the mainland and **Cañadas de Teide** *(p 276)*, **Caldera de Taburiente** *(p 279)*, **Timanfaya** *(p 271)* and **Garajonay** in the Canaries on Tenerife, La Palma, Lanzarote and Gomera.

All are largely in mountain areas. They are traversed by rough tracks, often made by the animals, many of them rare, which, with the flora, the park were established to safeguard. Among the species to be seen are chamois, brown bear, wild boar, red and roedeer, grouse, and the indigenous *capra hispánica* goat. The animals in Covadonga and the birds, especially, in Ordesa are preserved; if you fail to see them on the hoof you will find specimens well displayed at the Riofrío Museum of the Chase *(p 247)*.

There are trout streams in some of the parks which may be fished with permission in certain stretches at specified times *(apply to the National Tourist Office in Madrid)*.

THE ECONOMY

Population. — Spain's population was 37 746 260 in 1981 (population of Great Britain 55 870 000). Large areas are uninhabitable, in some areas the average density is 15 : km^2 (6 : sq mile) such as in Huesca and Cuenca while in Barcelona it is 500 : km^2 (116 : sq mile).

Agriculture. — Included in the cultivation of cereals is rice, which is the major crop. The yield at 60 to 70 quintals per hectare (48 to 56 hundredweights per acre) is the highest in the world (to compare with 25 quintals per hectare - 20 hundredweights per acre in tropical countries).

Olives and vines flourish in Spain's dry regions; the country is ranked first in world production of olive oil and ranks third (after France and Italy) in wine production.

Citrus fruits (from the Levant *huertas*) are the most profitable crop, particularly for export.

Fishing. — Mostly done on the Cantabrian and Atlantic coasts, the catch supplys the country with a major item in the Spanish diet. The Spaniard consumes about 20k - 45lbs of fish per year. The balance of the catch is canned in factories around the Galician coast.

Industry. — Industry in Spain has been revolutionised since the foundation in 1941 of the INI — National Institute for Industry — which has produced plans, encouraged investment, granted subsidies... Specialisation and skill have been encouraged by the inauguration of Professional Industrial Training Centres (for manual workers), Institutos Laborales (technical schools) and Universidades Laborales *(p 114)*. Foreign capital, largely invested in real estate, is being sought for light industry. The large industrial areas are located in northern Spain (Avilès, Gijon, Mieres-Bilbao-Barcelona).

Tourism plays a major role in the Spanish economy, most likely due to a good hotel system, a constantly improved road network, and beaches offering good facilities. The well-known **paradores,** comfortable state-owned hotels, are often located in historic castles or old monasteries *(see Michelin Red Guide España Portugal)*.

CHRONOLOGICAL TABLE

11-5C BC	**Phoenicians** and **Greeks** from Asia Minor land around the coast of the peninsula, already peopled in the east by Iberians, and found trading settlements (Gades or Cádiz; Ampurias *p 76*). The **Celts** invade Spain and intermingle with the **Iberians** forming the Celtiberians.
3 and 1C BC	The **Carthaginians** conquer southeast Spain (Cartagena *p 161*). Hannibal's capture of Sagunto *(p 170)* leads to the 2nd Punic War (218-201 BC). **Rome** triumphs finally (resistance of the Warrior Viriatus, Numantia *p 248*, Sertorius *p 64*), occupies and develops economically the larger part of the peninsula, renamed Iberia or Hispania; Córdoba is founded to become the centre of Roman administration (151 BC).
1C AD	Christianity spreads throughout Spain.
5-6C AD	The **Visigoths** conquer the Swabians (northwest) and Vandals (Andalusia *p 31*) and establish a powerful monarchy over the greater part of the peninsula: Toledo becomes capital of the kingdom *(p 214)*.
711	Battle of Guadalete: the **Moors** invade and conquer the kingdom *(p 11)*.
778	Charlemagne's campaign south of the Pyrenees ends in disaster at Roncesvalles.

THE CATHOLIC MONARCHS (1474-1516) AND THE UNITY OF SPAIN

1474	Isabel, wife of Ferdinand of Aragon, succeeds Henry IV of Castile. Her rights as sovereign contested until 1479 by the Beltraneja *(p 245)*.
1478	Isabel institutes the **Inquisition** in Castile and subsequently throughout Christian Spain. Torquemada appointed Grand Inquisitor 1483. The court, directed against Jews, Moors and later Protestants, continues until 19C.
1479	Ferdinand becomes King of Aragon; Christian Spain united under one crown.
January 1492	**Reconquest of Granada** *(p 44)*.
August 1492	Expulsion of all Jews who refuse to be baptised.
12 Oct 1492	**Christopher Columbus** discovers the New World *(p 11)*.
1496	Juana the Mad, daughter of the Catholic Monarchs, marries Philip the Fair, son of Emperor Maximilian of Austria.
18 Dec 1499	4 000 Moors baptised at Toledo on the orders of Cisneros, grey eminence of the Catholic Monarchs.
1504	Death of Isabel. Ferdinand rules in the name of Juana the Mad; in 1516 he becomes regent during the minority of his grandson, Charles (b 1500).

THE HABSBURG HOUSE OF AUSTRIA (1516-1700)

The climax: Emperor Charles V (1516-1556) and **Philip II** (1556-1598).

1516	On the death of Ferdinand, his grandson becomes Charles I of Spain (through his mother he inherits Spain, Naples, Sicily, Sardinia and overseas territories); Cisneros governs until the arrival of the new king (1517, *p 127*). On the death of Maximilian of Austria, 1519, Charles is elected Holy Roman Emperor: **Charles V**; Germany, Austria, the Franche-Comté and the Low Countries are added to his dominions.
1520-1522	Charles V quells revolts of **Comuneros** *(p 245)* and **Germanías** in Valencia and Majorca.
1521-1556	He wages war five times against the French; prevents the advances of François I (captured at Pavia 1525 and brought to Madrid, *p 200*) and Henri II. He captures Milan.
1555	In Germany, after failing to suppress the Reformation, he agrees to compromise: the Peace of Augsburg.
1556	Charles V abdicates in favour of his son and retires to Yuste *(p 136)*, Philip II becomes King of Spain and the Spanish col-

The Emperor Charles V by Titian (El Prado Museum)

	onies, the Kingdom of Naples, Milan, the Low Countries and the Franche-Comté. Germany and Austria ceded by Charles to his brother, Ferdinand I (1558).
1568	Revolt of the Protestants in the Low Countries. 1598 Philip abandons the Low Countries to his daughter Isabel Clara Eugenia, wife of Archduke Albert of Austria, whose forces under the command of his half-brother Don Juan of Austria win the
1571	Battle of **Lepanto** against the Turks, giving Spain mastery of the Mediterranean.
1580	On the death of the King of Portugal without an heir, Philip II invades the country and is proclaimed King (1581).
1588	The defeat of the **Invincible Armada** *(p 144)* destroys Spain as a sea power.
1598	Philip II, at his death, leaves an immense kingdom which, in spite of vast wealth from the Americas, is crippled by debt after 70 years of almost incessant war and the erection of monumental buildings such as the Escorial.

The decline. — Spain coasts along. **Philip III** (1598-1621), **Philip IV** (1621-1665), **Charles II** (1665-1700) lack the metal of their forefathers.

1609	**Expulsion of the Moors;** the Low Countries obtain their independence.
1640	Catalonia rises in revolt (June). The Portuguese proclaim the Duke of Braganza, King John IV. Portuguese independence, however, was only recognised in 1668.
1618-1648	Spain wastes her strength in the **Thirty Years War;** in spite of major victories (Breda, 1624), the defeat in the Netherlands at Rocroi (1643) signals the end of Spain as a European power. The Treaty of Westphalia recognises the independence of the Netherlands.
1659	The Treaty of the Pyrenees ends war with France: Philip IV cedes Roussillon and part of Cerdaña, Artois, part of Luxembourg and strongpoints in Flanders; his daughter, María Teresa is promised in marriage to Louis XIV *(p 114)*.
1667-1697	Defeat in the **War of Devolution** (1667-1668) against Louis XIV, loses Spain further strongholds in Flanders; in the Dutch Wars (1672-1678, Treaty of Nijmwegen) the Franche-Comté goes to France and 12 strongholds in Belgium are recovered under the Treaty of Ryswick which concluded the third war against the French (1688-1697).

THE BOURBONS - THE WAR OF INDEPENDENCE (1808-1814)

1700 — Charles II dies leaving no heir. He wills the crown to Philip, Duke of Anjou, grandson of Louis XIV and María Teresa. Displeasure of Emperor Leopold who had renounced his rights to the Spanish throne in favour of his son, the Archduke Charles.

1701-1714 — **War of the Spanish Succession:** France opens war on the Holy Roman Empire and its allies — most of the sovereigns of Europe, Catalonia, followed by Valencia and Aragon side with the Archduke. Spain becomes the battlefield for the war (1705). On the death of Joseph I (who had succeeded his father, Leopold, in 1705), Archduke Charles becomes Emperor (1711). England fearing that Spain would again become part of the HRE halted the war. By the Treaty of Utrecht, Spain forfeits Gibraltar (which had passed under British suzerainty in 1704), Minorca, Luxembourg and Flanders, her Italian possessions, Sicily and Sardinia. **Philip V** is recognised as King of Spain (1714).

1759-1788 — **Charles III** reigns as an enlightened despot and, assisted by competent ministers, the Counts of Floridablanca *(p 167)* and Aranda, promulgates economic reforms.

1788 — **Charles IV** ascends the throne. An impulsive weakling, he allows the country to be ruled by his wife, María Luisa, and her favourite, Godoy *(p 133)*.

1793 — Spain declares war on France on the death of Louis XVI.

1801 — Godoy, under pressure from Napoleon, invades Portugal. Spain receives Olivenza as the outcome of the War of Oranges *(p 138)*.

1804 — Napoleon crowned Emperor. Godoy negotiates a Franco-Spanish *rapprochement*.

1805 — Spain assists France in war against England. Spanish naval power decimated at the Battle of **Trafalgar** *(p 36)*.

1808 — The Aranjuez Revolt *(p 191)*. Napoleon arrests Charles IV and his son Ferdinand VII, in whose favour the king had abdicated, and nominates his brother Joseph, King of Spain. The Madrid rising of Dos de Mayo *(p 200)* presages the start of the **War of Independence** (The Peninsular War). After the victory of the Spanish over the French at **Bailén** (1808), Napoleon takes command personally of the French, reinforced by troops from Germany. The war continues with sieges and assaults in campaigns led by both British (Wellington) and French (Suchet) generals.

1812 — Liberals, faithful to the cause of Ferdinand VII, draw up the **Constitution of Cádiz** *(p 36)*. Napoleon recalls troops from Spain to reinforce the Grande Armée, decimated by the Russian Campaign; the Anglo-Spanish forces gain the ascendancy.

1813 — The South American colonies take advantage of the war to declare their independence: Buenos Aires, Uruguay, Paraguay, Chile, Colombia.

March 1814 — Ferdinand is freed by Napoleon, returns to the Spanish throne, abolishes the constitution and so reigns as an absolute monarch.

THE 19C DISTURBANCES

1820 — The liberals, in opposition to the king's absolute rule, are ruthlessly suppressed at each uprising until **Riego** leads a **liberal revolt** at Cádiz *(p 36)*.

1833-1839 — On the death of Ferdinand VII, his brother Don Carlos disputes the right to the throne of Isabel II, daughter of the late king and queen, María Cristina. The Carlists, for the most part Basque and Navarese extremists, hold the liberal supporters of Isabel II at bay for 6 years before the latter win the **First Carlist War** (Vergara *p 127*).

1835 — Minister Mendizábal gets measures passed to suppress the religious orders and confiscate their property *(desamortización)*.

1840 — A pronunciamiento forces the regent, María Cristina, into exile; General Espartero takes her place.

1843 — The **Narváez uprising** *(p 170)* forces Espartero to flee. Isabel II is declared of age. A constitution is promulgated in 1845.

1847-1849 — The **Second Carlist War,** formented by Carlos Luis, son of Don Carlos, breaks out. Isabel is recognised as the sole heir but her reign is troubled by rivalry between the progressives and the moderates which results in *coups d'état* and insurrections.

1868 — Finally a revolt led by General Prim succeeds; Isabel goes into exile. General Serrano is appointed regent. A highly progressive constitution is proclaimed the following year which, however, envisages the establishment of a monarchy. The offer of the Spanish throne to a cousin of the King of Prussia is one of the causes which leads to the Franco-Prussian War of 1870. Amadeo of Savoy is finally chosen.

1872-1876 — Don Carlos disputes the right of the new monarch: the **Third Carlist War.**

1873 — Amadeo of Savoy abdicates on finding himself unable to keep the peace. The First Spanish **Republic** is proclaimed.

1874 — A pronunciamiento restores the line of Queen Isabel in the person of her son Alfonso XII: the Bourbon **Restoration** opens a long period of peace.

1885 — Death of Alfonso XII (at 28). His widow, María Cristina becomes regent.

1898 — **Cuban Independence** at the end of the Spanish American War marks, with the loss of Puerto Rico and the Philippines, the end of the Spanish overseas empire.

1902 — Alfonso XIII, at 16, takes over the throne.

1912 — North Morocco becomes a Spanish protectorate.

THE CRISIS IN THE MONARCHY — THE REPUBLIC (1931-1936)

1914-1918 — Spain remains neutral throughout the First World War but growing financial difficulties and the instability of the government arouse popular discontent. Strikes, notably in Catalonia, are severely punished, in particular that of 1917.

1921 — Revolt in Morocco. In 1927 Spain occupies North Morocco.

1923 — **General Miguel Primo de Rivera,** with the concurrence of the king, establishes a **dictatorship.** Order is restored, the country becomes wealthier but opposition increases among the working classes.

1930 — In the face of hostility from the masses, Primo de Rivera goes into exile. The king nominates General Berenguer to replace him as dictator.

1931 — The Republicans seize power in several towns in Catalonia. The king abdicates and leaves Spain to avoid civil war.

June 1931 — Election of a constituent Cortes produces a socialist republican majority: under the Constitution promulgated in December, certain regions are granted provincial autonomy; far reaching anti-clerical measures proposed. Agrarian reform, voted the next year, was found difficult to put into practice.

1933 — Founding of the **Falange** by **José Antonio Primo de Rivera,** son of the former dictator. The group opposes regional separation; right wing opposition grows; the military plot against the regime.

October 1934 — In the face of majority conservative opinion, Catalonia proclaims its autonomy and a revolutionary insurrection breaks out in Asturias *(p 116)*; the insurrection is brutally suppressed.

February 1936 — The Popular Front wins the elections which precipitates a revolutionary situation which the right immediately opposes.

July 1936 — The Civil War begins *(details p 12)*.

For the historic details of Spain Today see p 12.

THE MUSLIM OCCUPATION: THE RECONQUEST (718-1492)

711: Muslims from North Africa landed in Spain and annihilated the Visigoth monarchy *(p 215)*. In a short time the Moors occupied the entire peninsula (they were only repulsed in Poitiers in 732). The resistance of **Pelayo** at Covadonga in 722 *(p 112)* marked the opening of the 700 year Christian War of Reconquest (La Reconquista) against the Moors.

Muslim Spain: grandeur and decline. — Muslim Spain comprised a number of emirates under the Damascus Caliphate until Abdu'r-Rahman I founded an independent emirate at Córdoba in 756 which Abdu'r-Rahman III raised to a caliphate in 929; **Córdoba** entered a golden age *(p 38)*. Al Mansur *(p 38)* ravaged Spain: the Muslims seized towns in the north (late 10C). Troubles over the succession caused the division of the caliphate in 1031 into *taifa* kingdoms (*taifa:* faction) — the most brilliant of these was **Granada** *(p 44)*, under the rule of the Nasrids (1232). The *taifa* kings, opposing the offensive of Alfonso VI who by the recapture of Toledo in 1085 had pushed the Christian front south of the Tagus, were compelled to call for assistance on the **Almoravids.** In a short time this tribe had overrun the divided areas of Christian Spain — the Kingdoms of Castile and León, Aragon, Navarre and Barcelona County. Following victory over the Moors at Ourique in 1139, Portugal declared its independence. The **Almohads,** also from Africa, defeated their co-religionists and expelled them from the peninsula. The victory of **Alarcos** *(p 195)* in 1195 by Yacoub Al Mansur brought greatness and prosperity to **Seville** *(p 55)*. The Almohad domination was shortlived, however, and ended in the defeat of Las Navas de Tolosa in 1212. Dissension among the *taifa* kingdoms assisted the campaigns of the military orders *(p 132)* and of the great monarchs of the reconquest, Ferdinand III of Castile and James I of Aragon.

The rivalry among the Christian kingdoms. — By the death of James I in 1276, the Muslims ruled only the Kingdom of Granada. Castile had taken possession of the Basque provinces (1200 and 1379), León, Asturias and Galicia (1230), Murcia (1266) and a part of Andalusia; Aragon has annexed Catalonia (1137), the Kingdom of Valencia (1253). Navarre existed as a small independent kingdom in alliance with France. In each kingdom from the end of the 12C, the people were represented by a **Cortes** *(p 64)* before which the monarch swore to respect the **fueros** or charter, granted each community at the Reconquest.

1492: the recapture of Granada by the Catholic Monarchs reduced the last Muslim bastion in Spain — now Christian and united under a single crown since 1479.

THE DISCOVERY OF AMERICA: THE CONQUISTADORES

The year the Reconquest was completed was the year America was discovered. Spain, freed from the Muslim yoke, could turn her attention abroad; crusading against the infidel was succeeded by colonial expansion and renewed battles for Christianity.

The reign of the Catholic Monarchs (1474-1516); the explorers and the search for spices. — While the first step in subduing the **Canaries** had been undertaken by a Frenchman, **Béthancourt,** in 1402 on behalf of the King of Castile *(p 265)* and the most intrepid navigators of the time were Portuguese, it was in Spain that the obstinate Genoese, **Christopher Columbus** ① *(pp 49, 267)* ultimately found royal backing for his project of a journey westwards to the Indies — the Portuguese had so far contented themselves with following the coast of Africa and jour-neying east. Columbus first sighted land (in the Antilles) on 12 October 1492 so giving Spain first claim to the New World. This situation was duly recognised by the **Treaty of Tordesillas** in 1494 *(p 249)*. In 1499, **Alonso de Ojeda** voyaged along the northeast coast of South America; in 1500, his companion, **Juan de la Cosa,** produced the first map of the New World; in 1513, **Núñez de Balboa** ② *(p 137)*, in search of gold and silver, crossed the Panama Isthmus and saw before him the Pacific Ocean. The search for spices gave way to a quest for fabulous jewels and precious metals which the new continent seemed to promise. Spain, enriched by untold treasures from America, became one of the great powers of Europe; **Seville,** with its port and official ex-change, the **Casa de Contratación,** founded by Isabel the Catholic *(p 55)*, through which all the New World trade had to

pass, became one of the most prosperous cities in the peninsula. In 1511 a **Council of the Indies** was established to administer the new possessions, now renamed after the explorer, **Amerigo Vespucci** *(p 55)*.

The reign of the Emperor Charles V (1516-1556); the opening up of America by the Conquistadores. — In 1519, the Portuguese, **Magellan,** *(p 55)*, set sail westwards for Asia with a fleet of 5 Spanish ships; by 1521 he had discovered the strait and reached the Philippines, but there he was killed fighting the natives — the circumnavigation was completed by one of his companions, the Basque pilot, **Juan Sebastián Elcano** *(p 107)*. In the same period the saga of the *conquistadores* was opening with the voyages of **Cortés** ③ *(p 137)* to Mexico, the country he named New Spain and whose capital he seized in 1521; **Pizarro** ④ *(p 139)*, **Diego de Almagro,** who conquered Peru (Cuzco 1533) and brought back the riches of the Aztecs and the Incas to multiply the royal treasure of Spain; **Francisco Coronado** ⑤, who explored the course of the Río Grande and the Colorado Grand Canyon (1535); **Hernando de Soto** ⑥, companion of Pizarro, who took possession of Florida (1539); **Pedro de Mendoza** ⑦, who in South America colonised the Río de la Plata area (1534); **Pedro de Valdivia** ⑧, who founded the city of Santiago, Chile, in 1541 and **Francisco de Orellana** ⑨ *(p 139)*, who set out from Peru to explore the vastnesses of the Amazon basin in 1542.

By 1545 Charles V was financing his unceasing wars in Europe with Bolivian silver; by the end of his reign the continent had come to be known as Hispanic America.

THE CIVIL WAR (1936-1939)

On 13 July 1936, the monarchist leader, Calvo Sotelo was assassinated by Republican supporters. To restore order, the military announced the establishment of an organisation to be known as the **Movimiento Nacional** (18 July). Resistance by individuals and whole regions, however (the Basques, Catalonia, Madrid, Castile-La Mancha, the province of Valencia, and almost all of Andalusia), brought about division and ultimately civil war. The Movimiento, supported by the Church, took on the air of a holy crusade. On the death in a plane accident (20 July 1936) of the leader designate, General Sanjurjo, **General Franco,** who had already sailed from the Canaries (p 276) to Morocco, took command of operations in the south. Simultaneously, to an agreed plan, Franco's troops crossed the Strait of Gibraltar, under Italian air cover, while General Mola formented a military revolt in Navarre.

Summer 1936: the Nationalist linkup. — Franco arrived at Seville on 6 August. General de Llano assists Franco by having already gained control of Seville (p 55). The "Nacionales" aim of linking up with General Mola's forces in the north, was achieved in August with the capture of Badajoz. The taking of Irún by General Mola on 15 September, blocked communications between Republican forces in the north with Catalonia by way of France. On 27 September the Alcázar at Toledo was relieved (p 216).

Nationalist held areas (July 1936)

Autumn 1936: the Battle of Madrid. — The Nationalists began their siege of Madrid, which had sided with the Republicans, on 27 September. On 6 November the government moved to Valencia and the resistance began which was to go on until the end of the war by the people, the Republican forces and the International Brigade. On 1 October Franco was proclaimed Generalísimo and Head of State (p 229) and formally established an administration in Salamanca. Primo de Rivera (p 10) was executed by firing squad in an Alicante prison in November.

1937: Cantabria attacked. — In April, Franco united the Falangists and Carlists in a single party. Guernica was bombed (p 114) by German planes, then Durango. General Mola died in a plane accident (June) near Alcocero (Burgos). The Nationalist campaign in the north brought about the fall of Bilbao (June), Santander (to the Italians in August) and finally Gijón (October), to give them control of the north.

End of 1937-1938: the Levant front. — The Republican Government moved from Valencia to Barcelona in November 1937. The capture of Teruel by the Republicans in December brought relief from encirclement to Catalonia. In January 1938 the Franco political junta declared itself the government in power; the war continued in the Levant region: Teruel was recaptured by the Nationalists in February, Vinarŏs on 15 April, cutting the Republican forces in two. To regain contact the Republicans launched an offensive in July which produced few results except the long and bloody Battle of the Ebro (p 100).

Early 1939: the fall of the capitals. — The fall of Barcelona to German tanks and planes on 26 January brought about the transfer of the Republican Government once again to Valencia and the flight of refugees in vast numbers to France (about 400 000). Great Britain and France recognised the Franco regime on 27 February 1939 although Madrid and Valencia continued to hold out for another month (28 and 30 March respectively).

SPAIN TODAY

Spain, devastated after the Civil War, had a very hard time building itself up again due to the international blockade, the necessity to rebuild what had been destroyed and the lack of raw materials. That time is still remembered by those Spaniards over 40.

Franco's regime was a monarchy with himself as Head of State.

Legislation was in the control of Las Cortes, an assembly inaugurated in 1942, which passed laws although the Head of State had the right of veto. Las Cortes was made up of deputies who met twice a year.

Administratively speaking, at the head of each province was a civil governor (gobernador) appointed by the government.

In the municipalities the governor appointed the mayor except in the provincial capitals where they were appointed by the Head of State.

The influence of syndicates or unions in the nation's affairs was considerable, since they were represented at every level: Council of State, Cortes and town councils.

When in 1955, Spain became a member of the United Nations, she once again became diplomatically involved.

On 20 November, 1975 Franco died and Don Juan Carlos became king.

In 1978 a new constitution was passed establishing Spain as a democratic country and 1 January 1986, Spain became a member of the European Economic Community.

The fifty Spanish provinces are completed by Ceuta and Melilla on the coast of Morocco.

Join us in our never ending task of keeping up to date.

Send us your comments and suggestions, please.

Michelin Tyre Public Limited Company
Tourism Department
Davy House - Lyon Road - HARROW - Middlesex HA1 2DQ.

ART AND ARCHITECTURE

FROM PREHISTORY TO THE MOORISH CONQUEST

The civilisations which succeeded one another in the peninsula from the Palaeolithic Age to 711 AD, have left remarkable imprints, even visible remains:

Prehistoric art. — Dolmens at Antequera, paintings at Altamira, *talayots* and *navetas* in the Balearic Islands *(p 261)*.

First millenium BC. — Celtiberian sculptures (the Guisando bulls, Córdoba lions and in the Archaeological Museum of Madrid the Dama de Elche).

Roman civilisation. — The Romans, as they did throughout their dominions, constructed roads, bridges and aqueducts, built towns and erected monuments: the Mérida theatre, Italica and Ampurias mosaics, Segovia aqueduct, Tarragona triumphal arch...

The Visigoths. — The Visigoths were Christians: their churches were small buildings of roughly hewn stone, constructed without cement, ornamented with low relief friezes carved with geometrical motifs, scrollwork and Christian symbols. The absidal plan and the outlines of the arches were often horseshoe shaped.

Sumptuous jewellery, in which both Byzantine and Germanic traditions are apparent, was presented to the churches and was also placed in the burial tombs of the great: gold votive crowns *(illustration p 208)*, fibulae and belt buckles.

HISPANO-MOORISH ARCHITECTURE

Hispano-Moorish architecture divides into major phases corresponding to the reigns of successive dynasties over the Muslim held territories in the peninsula.

Caliphate or Córdoba architecture (8-11C)

The Caliphate has left us the monuments of Córdoba (the Mosque, the Medina Azahara) and Toledo (Cristo de la Luz) in which, besides the ubiquitous horseshoe shaped arch which became virtually the hallmark of Moorish architecture, other characteristics developed such as the use of brickwork in relief as a form ornament, cupolas supported on ribs, turned and cut modillions, arches with alternating white stone and red brick keystones, polylobed arches and the custom of surmounting doors with blind arcades. Many of these features were to continue, being subsequently incorporated in Mudejar and Romanesque churches throughout Spain and even in some areas of France.

(After Fco. Catalá Roca photo, Barcelona)

The Mosque at Córdoba

The Umaiyads brought from Syria a taste for profuse decoration. The Koran forbade the representation of the human form or even animals and Muslim decoration, therefore, it was based on three themes, which could be infinitely varied and repeated:

Calligraphy. — Inscriptions were made to run horizontally across a wall, frame a doorway or opening. The Umaiyads employed only Cufic script in which the line is angular and of uniform thickness (Cursive is flowing with both thick and thin strokes).

Geometry. — Ornamented brickwork and the interlacing effect of the *claustra* (pierced marble screens) produced an interplay of lines, polygons and stars.

Plant motifs. — A conventional flora, not necessarily lifelike, was depicted over friezes and panels. From an upright central stem, branches would extend symmetrically in flowing interlacing, to end in flowers and palm leaves. The whole effect was enhanced by being delicately carved on varying, light reflecting planes.

Almohad or Seville architecture (12-13C)

Almohad architecture is characterised by brick construction, highlighted only by wide bands of decoration in relief as on the Giralda in Seville. The style was later used in the Mudejar architecture of Aragon. Features appearing at this time also include *artesonado* ceilings and *azulejos (p 18);* arches of alternate brick and stonework disappeared, rounded horseshoe shaped arches became pointed, the multilobed arch developed a curvilinear feature which provided an interplay of curved and straight lines as in the Aljafería of Saragossa. Calligraphic decoration included Cursive as well as Cufic script to which floral motifs were added to fill the spaces between the vertical lines.

Nasrid or Granada architecture (14-15C)

This period of high sophistication produced less innovation in actual architectural design than in decoration and ornament. Stucco and ceramics particularly, were used to cover external walls; surrounds to doors and windows, already the focal points in every room's design, were further emphasised by the positioning of perfectly proportioned panels between them; arch outlines were simplified — the stilted round arch became widespread — as ever more detailed lacework "collars" were placed around them *(pp 45-46)*.

Mudejar architecture

Mudejar art, in the strict sense, is Muslim work executed according to their own traditions and techniques while under the Christians yoke. It occurred at different dates in different regions between the 11 and 15C, depending on when areas were reconquered. Some features, however, such as *artesonado* ceilings, continued for centuries as Spanish decorative themes.

"Court Mudejar" (at Tordesillas, in the Alcázar at Seville and the synagogue in Toledo) was an extension of the contemporary Almohad or Nasrid style; "popular Mudejar", produced by Muslim workshops, used accepted formulae *(p 215)* modified to local taste: in Castile (Toledo, Arévalo, Sahagún), walls were decorated with blind arcades; in Aragon *(p 62)*, belfries were faced with *azulejos* and geometrical strapwork.

(After Archivo MAS photo, Barcelona)

Artesonado ceiling with stalactite decoration *(p. 16)*

CHRISTIAN ARCHITECTURE FROM THE 8 TO 15C

Asturian architecture

A highly sophisticated architecture *(details p 103)*, characterised by ascending lines, developed in the small kingdom of Asturias between the 8 and 10C.

Mozarabic architecture

The Mozarabs, Moorish influenced Christians left churches in Castile *(see map pp 222-223)*; these edifices brought back long forgotten Visigoth traditions (horseshoe shaped arches), which they enriched by Moorish features such as ribbed cupolas and cut modillions.

Romanesque period (11-13C)

Catalonia, the first home of Romanesque in Spain. — Catalonia, largely closed to Mozarabic influence but with close links with France and Italy, developed from the 11C, an architectural

Catalonian Romanesque church : Sant Climent, Taüll

style, strongly Lombard influenced, which was to continue to the 13C in the Pyrenean Valleys, often isolated from the more travelled pilgrim and trade routes *(pp 75, 94; map p 77)*. Usually smooth, interior walls were decorated only with frescoes; on the outside, Lombard bands and single engaged pilasters adorned the façade and east end, where lancets allowed the light to filter through to the altar.

A "European" Romanesque style along the Ways to Compostela. — Northwest Spain opened its gates to foreign influence early in the 11C in the reign of Sancho the Great of Navarre: Cistercian abbeys were founded, French merchant adventurers allowed to live in the towns. It was, however, the great surge caused by the pilgrims to Santiago de Compostela *(p 152)* and the fever to build along the pilgrim ways, which brought about a set style in which French influence was clearly marked — Poitevin and Burgundian characteristics such as plentiful sculpture on portals and capitals and also the Mozarabic. The acknowledged masterpiece of this style is the Cathedral of St James at Santiago: the plan is that of French pilgrimage churches (emphasised transept, ambulatory and radiating chapels) which replaced the simple ground plan of flat transepts and three apses in extension of the aisles of Frómista. Beneath the roof are modillions carved to the full fantasy of the artist craftsmen, as are the capitals at windows, portals and crowning the interior columns.

The European prototype produced local variants such as the churches around Segovia which are flanked by lateral galleries *(p 245)*. In the Zamora region, an indigenous style developed, coloured by Mozarabic features, including multilobed arches and quartered, rounded, cupolas covered with shell shaped tiles *(p 252)*.

(After Archivo MAS photo, Barcelona)

Multilobed doorway
Puente La Reina - Santiago Church

The Gothic period (the 13C onwards)

The Gothic style as brought from France was not generally accepted in Spain except in Navarre which from 1234 had a French royal house. It was the Cistercians who adapted the ogivally arched transept crossing to traditionally unadorned naves to inaugurate what came to be known as the **Transitional style**. The result was that throughout the 13C, while techniques became Gothic, the concept of the beautiful remained Romanesque.

At the same time, bishops in several cities in Castile (León, Burgos, Toledo) were sending abroad for cathedral plans, and for artists and masons. In the Catalan states (Catalonia, Valencia, the Balearic Islands), on the other hand, an original church style developed without a transept and only a single aisle or, where there were side aisles, these would be of equal height to the nave and covered, like it, with pointed stone arcs or a wooden roof on diaphragm arches. The unadorned walls enclosed a large, homogeneous space in which there was a minimum of carved decoration and purity of line supplied a dignified elegance. Civil architecture followed the same pattern, had the same geometrical feeling for space, used often with rare skill *(see Montcada, p 85)*.

The influence of artists from the north such as **Johan of Cologne** and **Hanequin of Brussels,** brought about the flowering during the 14 and 15C in Castile, of a style approaching Flamboyant Gothic. This, as it adapted to Spain, developed simultaneously in two totally different ways: in one, decoration proliferated to produce the Isabeline style *(see below)*, in the other, structures were simplified into an equally typical church and cathedral style which remained in favour until the mid 16C (Segovia and Salamanca).

The last of the Gothic cathedrals. — On the model of Seville, cathedrals became vast. Aisles, almost equal in size to the nave, increased the nave's volume in which pillars, though massive, retained upward sweeping lines. A new plan evolved in which the old *"crescendo"* of radiating chapels, ambulatory, chancel and transept was superseded by a plain rectangle, a vast space in which, between the *capilla mayor* and the *coro (plan p 16)* only the transept crossing (emphasised by a lantern) remained of the traditional cruciform plan. In contrast to the severe design, typically Gothic decoration accumulated around portals, on pinnacles and in elaborate star vaulting.

The Isabeline style. — The prestige of the royal monarchs and grandees in the reign of Isabel the Catholic (1474-1504) provided a perfect context for the emergence of a new style in which decoration covered the entire façade of civil and religious edifices in supple free form, arcs, lace-like carving, heraldic motifs and every fantasy that imagination could devise *(p 250)*.

The diversity of inspiration was due often to artists or their sons, who had come from abroad — **Simon of Cologne,** son of Johan, **Juan Guas,** son of Pierre, **Enrique Egas,** nephew of Hanequin of Brussels.

THE RENAISSANCE and CLASSICAL PERIODS (16C)

At the dawn of its golden age, Spain was swept by a deep sense of its own national character: Italian influence became acceptable only when Hispanised. The great architects of the period were Spanish: **Rodrigo Gil de Hontañón** (career 1523-1577), **Alonso de Covarrubias** (d 1570), **Andrés de Vandelvira** (1509-1576), **Diego de Siloé** (d 1563).

The Plateresque style. — Plateresque was the name given to the style of the early 16C in which buildings were given a lavish decoration so finely chiselled that it seemed reminiscent of a silversmith's rather than a mason's work (*platero:* silversmith). Although close to the Isabeline style in its multiplicity of sculptural forms and extension over entire façades, ornamental themes were Italian (grotesques, scrolls, medallions, pilasters and cornices) as, more importantly, was the effort to achieve symmetry and balance.

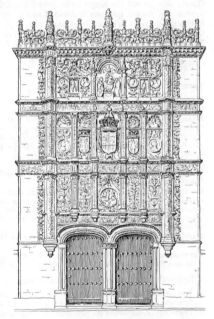

(After MTTC photo, Madrid)

The Plateresque style
Salamanca University

Simultaneously a less ornate Renaissance style, closer to the Italian, was developing; in this, antique forms predominated, including rounded arches, columns, entablatures and triangular pediments. This evolution, which began under **Pedro Machuca** (d 1550) and **Bartolomé Bustamante** (1500-1570), was taken up by Herrera under whom it evolved, inevitably, into a truly Classical style.

Juan de Herrera (1530-1597). — Herrera, favourite architect of Philip II, had a talent perfectly suited to realise his royal patron's desire that his palace, the Escorial, and his churches (Valladolid Cathedral) should symbolise orthodox religion and the Counter Reformation and that they should also possess serene grandeur worthy of sovereign majesty.

The architects of the 16C and their greatest masterpieces

Simon of Cologne: Burgos — *Cathedral: Constable's chapel.* Valladolid — *St Paul's: façade.*

Juan Guas: Toledo — *St John of the King's Monastery.*

Enrique de Egas: Granada — *The Chapel Royal.*

Rodrigo Gil de Hontañón: Alcalá de Henares — *University.*

Andrés de Vandelvira: Jaén — *Cathedral.*

Alonso de Covarrubias: Toledo — *Cathedral: New Kings' Chapel.*

Diego de Siloé: Granada — *Cathedral,* Úbeda — *San Salvador.*

Pedro Machuca: Granada — *Charles V's Palace.*

Bustamante: Toledo — *Tavera Hospital.*

BAROQUE (17-18C) and NEO-CLASSICISM (18-19C)

Architecture in the 17C continued in the two earlier styles of Classical and Plateresque. The first aimed at majesty, although on occasion it fell into cold monumentalism. Its most successful exponents were **Juan Gómez de Mora** (d 1597) with the Plaza Mayor, Madrid and the Clerecía, Salamanca, the Jesuit, **Francisco Bautista** (1594-1679) with San Isidro Church, Madrid and **Francisco Herrera, the Younger** (1622-1685), with the Basilica of the Pillar, Saragossa. In their constructions these men included the domes, the orders and all the decorative features of true Classicism.

The second, Plateresque style, which triumphed in the 18C, became the perfect vehicle for the exuberant decoration so beloved of the Spanish. The interplay of volume, light and colour created a seductive decoration highly propitious to the renewed religious fervour; lines became more sinuous, pediments were broken, planes complicated with intricate hollowing. A new feature, the **camarín**, was introduced: at first simply a passage behind the high altar providing access to the retable niche containing the statue venerated by the faithful, it soon developed into a richly ornamented chapel. Baroque architects often concentrated the style's superabundant decoration on the façade or in the interior, thus enabling an older building to be brought up to date at minimum cost.

The Churrigueresque style. — The desire for sumptuousness resulted, in the 18C, in a style overburdened sometimes to excess in surface ornament. One of the first examples, typified by the use of *salomonica*, or barley sugar columns, entwined with vines and *estípites*, or pilasters in an inverse pyramid, is the altarpiece by **José Churriguera** (1665-1725) at the St Stephen Monastery, Salamanca. Although the style took the architect's name, he was, with his brothers **Joaquín** (1674-1724) and **Alberto** (1676-1750) but its instigator; successors were to push the style to far greater extremes: **Andréas García de Quiñones** (1755: Clerecía Cloister, Salamanca), **Pedro de Ribera** (1720: portal of Madrid Municipal Museum), **Narciso Tomé** (1721: the Transparente, Toledo Cathedral) and **Ignacio Vergara** (Palace of the Marquess de Dos Aguas, Valencia).

Regional variations. — Baroque was popular in the provinces where it flourished independently of the fashions imposed by the Bourbon court. It developed differently according to local tradition: in **Galicia,** where the hardness of the granite precluded delicate carving, baroque was translated into bold lines in the decorative mouldings. Most monasteries were given new flat façades, flanked by lofty towers in which upward sweeping lines were counterbalanced by the horizontal emphasis of superimposed cornices *(map p 142)*. The most ornate example of this style and the undoubted masterpiece of its designer, **Fernando Casas y Novoa,** is the façade of Santiago de Compostela Cathedral (1750).

In **Andalusia** undulation characterised façades in the 18C on palaces (Écija), cathedrals (Guadix by **Vicente Acero**), and the portals of countless churches and grandees' residences (Jerez). The most successful exponents of the style were **Leonardo de Figueroa** (1650-1730) and his sons in San Telmo Palace in Seville, **Francisco Hurtado** (1669-1725) in the Sagrario Carthusian Monastery, Granada and **Luis de Arévalo** in the sacristy of the same monastery.

Neo-Classical style. — With the excavations of Pompeii and Herculaneum (1748), the excessive baroque style was repudiated and the pure Hellenistic style was developed. During this period the kings embellished the cities and especially the capital's buildings: fountains (Cibeles), gardens (botanical) and gates (Alcalá and Toledo). The artists belonging to this period were: **Ventura Rodríguez** (1717-1785) façade of Pamplona Cathedral, cupolas of Our Lady of the Pillar in Saragossa and **Juan de Villanueva** (1739-1811) façade of Madrid Town Hall, the Casita del Príncipe at Escorial and the Prado Museum.

Architectural terms

Terms proper to Spain

Ajimez (pl. ajimeces): paired window or opening.
Alfiz: rectangular surround to horseshoe shaped arch.
Artesonado: a marquetry ceiling in which raised fillets outline caissons in the shape of stars. This particular decoration, which first appeared under the Almohads, was generally popular also in Christian Spain, particularly in the 15 and 16C *(illustration p 14)*.
Azulejòs: glazed, patterned, ceramic tiles *(p 18)*.
Churrigueresque: in the style of the Churrigueras, an 18C family of architects. Ornate baroque decoration.
Mocárabes: stalactite stucco or wood work *(illustration p 14)*.
Mozarabic: the work of Christians living under Arab rule after the Moorish invasion of 711. On being persecuted in the 9C they sought refuge in Christian areas bringing with them Moorish artistic traditions.
Mudejar: the work of Muslims who remained under Christian rule following the Reconquest.

Ajimez and alfiz

Plateresque: a term derived from *platero:* silversmith, and used to describe the first style of the Renaissance which was characterised by finely carved decoration *(p 15)*.

A Spanish church: plan and furnishings

① **Coro:** chancel where the carved stalls *(sillería)* are occupied by canons or religious.
② **Trascoro:** wall enclosing the *coro*. Richly decorated it serves as the background to the altars.
③ **Capilla mayor:** the area of the high altar, often surrounded by magnificent iron grilles.
④ **Retablo mayor:** high altar retable which often rises to the roof.
⑤ **Trasaltar:** back wall of the *capilla mayor* before which there is frequently an altar or monumental tomb.
⑥ **Coro alto:** tribune or gallery sometimes occupied by the choir (stalls).
Presbiterio: chancel in the English sense or space before the altar.
Camarín: see above.
Púlpito: pulpit.
Sagrario: tabernacle or chapel containing it, often situated behind the high altar.
Crucero: transept.
Girola: ambulatory.

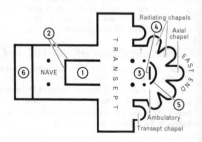

CASTLES IN SPAIN

Castles in Spain are so numerous that they have given their name to an entire region at the heart of the peninsula — Castile. Within the generic term there are several distinct types: there are castle fortresses which had a purely military function, the **alcazabas** of the Moors, the **castillos** of the Christians, there are town citadels or **alcázares** and there are residential palaces.

At the Reconquest

Alcazaba. — The *alcazaba* was the keystone in the Moorish defence system. It was built on a mound as an integral part of a town's ramparts with additional perimeters of its own, crowned with pointed merlons and dominated by the Torre de la Vela or watchtower; the gates, at the end of labyrinthine paths, were defended by massive square towers. The still impressive ruins of several *alcazabas* can be seen in Andalusia *(map pp 32-33)*.

(After Ed. García Garrabella y Cía photo, Saragossa)

The Alcazaba in Málaga

Castillo. — These castles, often of brick, were constructed at strategic, frequently isolated points crowning a mound. They can be seen from a distance on the Meseta, their massive keeps (Torres del Homenaje) standing out squarely against the skyline. Sentry turrets flank the main tower which is protected by a lower perimeter and wide, open ditch *(map pp 222-223)*.

Alcázar. — Few Moorish *alcázares* have outlasted the centuries and the kingdom's unending wars — the Alhambra at Granada is an outstanding exception *(p 46)*. It is known, however, that their construction centred around square *patios* and that they stood in beautiful gardens outlined by straight paths and embellished with fountains, pools and ornamental basins *(see Generalife p 47)*.

Christian *alcázares,* such as those of Toledo and Madrid, built in a hollow square around a central court, canted with pinnacle turreted towers, had a severe appearance by comparison which even recent remodelling has not succeeded in disguising.

The Bourbon Palaces

The French King, Philip V and his Italian Queen, Elizabeth Farnese, wishing to endow their court with greater dignity and splendour than could be achieved in the existing, austere Spanish palaces, brought artists from their respective countries to fulfil their ambitions. These sought to recreate neither Versailles nor Rome, but to ally French Classical harmony and Italian grace with the natural genius of Spain; their respect of Spanish style is evident in their frequent adoption, among other characteristics, of the hollow square ground plan traditional to the *alcázar*.

(After MTTC photo, Madrid)

La Granja de San Ildefonso

Monastery Castles

Monasteries, which in Spain were so often royal foundations, frequently became the residence of an itinerant court, a prince's retreat, the refuge of a widowed queen or a ruler wearied of power. Royal largesse benefited the majority at some period.

It was in this way that Martin the Humane, King of Aragon and Sicily, came to reside at times at Poblet; that the Mudejar Palace at Tordesillas, built by Alfonso XI in the 14C became, on the death of the king, the Convent of Santa Clara, but in 1506, reverted to its original function when Juana the Mad, daughter of Ferdinand and Isabel, took up residence on the death of her husband and continued to live there for more than forty years; it was to the monastery of Yuste that the Emperor Charles V retired to end his days.

State apartments and royal bedrooms, richly decorated with tapestries and other hangings, with frescoes and fine furniture were, therefore, not out of place; apartment plans were also frequently modified, complicated and remodelled, as each royal personage determined to leave his imprint on a building.

Monasteries and convents also, on occasion, became royal pantheons as in the case of Las Huelgas, convent of queens and princesses, in which the members of the ruling families of Castile and Asturias-León were buried between the 12 and 13C.

The most outstanding example by far, however, of a palace with a plural destiny is the Escorial. It was also the last such palace to be built and is considered by many to be the greatest ever erected, for this monument of Philip II was designed from the outset by the king's own vow, as palace, royal necropolis, and Hieronymite monastery. Today, it attracts for its contents as well as its architecture.

THE DECORATIVE ARTS

Furniture. — The most typical items of furniture are **chests,** either decorated with ironwork or chased steel or covered in the Córdoba style with embossed or possibly dyed leather, and **bargueños,** portable desks in the form of small chests which were placed upon a table. The door let down to form a writing flap, revealing a lavish marquetry interior including ivory and mother of pearl inlays in the Mudejar style and fillets designed as decoration and also to disguise drawers, inner drawers and secret cavities.

Tapestries and embroideries. — The majority of Gothic and Renaissance **tapestries** decorating churches and palaces were French, Flemish or Brussels work. They were woven in wool and silk, with gold and silver thread occasionally introduced for added effect. The 15C compositions are often somewhat confused with several religious or allegorical themes depicted on the same panel (Vices and Virtues etc.); in the 16C, wide decorative borders were added and the scenes, by this time often historical or mythological, illustrated in perspective as in contemporary painting. The following century, quantities of tapestries were obtained from Brussels where they were being woven to themes after Rubens. Only in 1720 did Philip V establish in Madrid the **Santa Bárbara Tapestry Workshops,** for which Bayeu, Goya and other artists were soon drawing cartoons. The resulting tapestries illustrated typical contemporary scenes or popular adventure stories: *Young Man with a Guitar,* the *Straw Doll, Don Quixote.*

The 12C so called *Tapestry of the Creation* at Gerona is, in fact, an embroidery. **Embroidery** began soon after to be widely used to ornament liturgical objects such as altar-fronts and chasubles and from the 14C onwards, the date of the oldest still extant, had become virtually needlework pictures illustrating the Gospels or the lives of the saints. The work became ever more elaborate, effects being highlighted with gold and silver thread and embossing into a glittering mass.

Gold, silver and ironwork. — **Monstrances** *(custodia)* in the 16C, fashioned into high pointed shafts, decorated with columns, statues and precious stones, became gigantic in size, often exceeding 3m in height and 150kg in weight - 10ft and 3cwts. For more than a century a family which had moved from Harff near Cologne to Spain, specialised in producing this single vessel: **Enrique de Arfe** (c 1470-after 1545) made the Gothic Toledo monstrance; his son, **Antonio,** (d 1566) the Renaissance one at Santiago de Compostela, and his grandson, **Juan** (1535-1603) the one of Seville.

(After Archivo MAS photo, Barcelona)

Wrought iron screen - Chapel Royal, Granada

Wrought iron screens and grilles have always been outstanding in Spain. Those to be seen today in the *patios* in Seville, edging the balconies in Ronda, are worthy successors to the grilles covering the windows of the House of the Scallop Shells of Salamanca. The most wonderful work, however, has always been in the screens which enclose chapels and *coros.* In the 15 and 16C artist craftsmen were forging iron in such a way that their work appeared both massive and as fine as a lace curtain which they then highlighted with bright colours and gold leaf: **Fray Francisco de Salamanca** and **Juan Francés** produced screens for Toledo and Ávila, **Master Bartolomé** for Jaén and Granada *(illustration above),* **Francisco de Villalpando** and **Domingo de Céspedes** for Toledo.

Ceramics. — The early potteries, working to methods brought by the Arabs, who, in turn, had adapted oriental techniques, were established in the 10C at Elvira near Granada and in the 11 and 12C in Málaga. From the start the metal lustre decoration and moulded relief, which became the hallmark of the Mudejar style, covered bowls, ewers, pots and plates. Some pieces were outstandingly beautiful — the famous blue amphora to be seen in Granada, for instance. *Azulejos* were produced in the same potteries.

Arabic plate

Azulejos — glazed pottery tiles — appeared first, it is said, under the Almohads in the 12C in Triana, Seville. The tiles, which were used to face walls both inside and out, were designed with geometrical motifs, the colours being kept apart by a strip of manganese *(cuerda seca)* or they were given a marquetry appearance by parts of already glazed surfaces being cut away *(alicatados, p 46).* In the 16C, Mudejar decoration was abandoned for a style in which each tile bore the same flower motif in relief, producing a dense effect. Another process was to paint and glaze tiles by the Italian majolica method — first practised by the Pisan, **Francisco Niculoso** for the Alcázar oratory, Seville (1504).

The principal mediaeval ceramic workshops were manned by Moorish craftsmen and were at **Paterna** (13C, *p 173),* **Valencia** and **Teruel,** in the 14C. **Manises** *(p 175)* became famous for its iridescent lustreware, at first designed with Muslim motifs (plants and Cursive script) but soon with Christian themes and incorporating the words **Ave María. Talavera** *(p 213)* was at its greatest in the 17C when the spirit of the Renaissance even entered the design of ewers and bowls. The **Alcora** factory, founded by Philip V in 1727, produced rococo tiles in blues and yellows and, from 1750, porcelain groups. Its glory was shortlived, however, for in 1760 Charles III founded the **Buen Retiro** which produced the ceramics for the famous porcelain saloon in Aranjuez Palace.

PAINTING

Pre-Romanesque and Romanesque periods.
— Illuminated manuscripts provide the earliest known
examples of Spanish mediaeval painting (10C).
Because the illuminations were frequently executed
by Mozarabic monks on copies of the Apocalypse or
Beatus *(p 97)*, they frequently include such Moorish
features as horseshoe shaped arches and Arabic
dress. The **wall paintings** which decorated churches
in the 11 and 12C especially, had heavy black outlines, the superimposed frieze composition, lack of
perspective and rigidity of stance of Byzantine
mosaics. But the addition of realistic or expressive
details transforms the paintings into something
Spanish to the core. In Catalonia, subjects remained
in the Byzantine tradition (Christ or the Virgin in
Majesty in a mandorla); in Castile artists drew on
everyday events. **Altarfronts** of painted wood illustrated the same subjects in disparate ways *(p 81)*.

(After MTTC photo, Madrid)

Romanesque fresco (Catalonia)

Gothic period (14-15C). — This was the period
of the great polyptyches and altarpieces which, in
some cases, exceeded 15m - 50ft in height. The
Primitives, painting traditionally on gold backgrounds, were influenced by the gentle modelling of
the Italians, the French, whose so called International
style became widespread between 1375 and 1425
and the Flemish, who were known for their depiction
of rich materials with broken folds and their meticu-
lous detail; yet as they sought for expressive natu-
ralism and telling detail their painting emerged as distinctively Spanish.

Intense artistic activity developed in the states attached to the Kingdom of Aragon: in
the Vic, Barcelona and Valencia Museums are works by **Ferrer Bassá** (1285-1348), influenced
by the Sienese, Duccio by his successor, **Ramón Destorrents** (1346-1391); the **Serra** brothers,
Destorrents's pupils; **Luis Borrassá** (1360-after 1425) who had a very Spanish sense of the
picturesque; **Bernat Martorell** (d 1452) who gave special importance to landscape; **Jaime
Huguet** (1415-1492) and by **Luis Dalmau** (*c* 1400-after 1445) and **Bartolomé Bermejo** (d after
1490), who were both influenced by Van Eyck

In Castile, French influence predominated in the 14C, Italian in the 15C until about 1450
when Flemish came in with the arrival of Roger van der Weyden. By the late 15C, **Fernando
Gallego** had become the main figure in the Hispano-Flemish movement in which **Juan of
Flanders** (d *c* 1519) had the most appealingly delicate touch *(p 240)*.

The Renaissance. — Under Italian Renaissance influence, there appeared in 16C Spanish
painting, a mastery of perspective, a marked taste for lighter colours.

Luis de Morales *(p 132)*, a Mannerist, worked widely throughout the country.

In Valencia, **Fernando Yáñez de la Almedina** and **Fernando de Llanos** brought in the style of
Leonardo da Vinci to which **Vicente Macip** added that of Raphael. His son, **Juan de Juanes,** has
left harmonious Mannerist paintings *(p 170)*.

Alejo Fernández (d 1545), is remembered for his *Virgin of the Navigators* in the Alcázar,
Seville; **Pedro de Campaña**, born in Brussels in 1503, for his use of chiaroscuro. In Castile the
great figure of the late 15C is **Pedro Berruguete** (*c* 1450-1504) whose personal style was
enriched by every influence which had reached his country. His successor, **Juan de Borgoña**
specialised particularly in landscape and architecture. Portrait painting became the fashion
under the hand of the Dutchman, **Antonio Moro** (1519- 1576) and his disciple, **Alonso Sánchez
Coello** (1531-1588). **El Greco**, who by this time had arrived from Italy, but could find no
success in Madrid, settled in Toledo *(p 215)* where Philip II was summoning Italian or Italian
trained artists to paint pictures for the Escorial (late 16C).

The Golden Age. — Spanish 17C painting bears the imprint of Caravaggio — stern
realism, strong contrasts of light and shade. Painters took up portraiture and still life
(bodegón); lighthearted vanities were transformed into moralities in which wealth and death
were shown symbolically as closely allied. The 16C schools flourished on:

In Valencia, **Francisco Ribalta** (1565-1628) painted a striking *Vision of St Francis* and **José
Ribera** (1591-1652) his uncompromisingly realistic *Martyrdom of St Bartholomew (p 166)* —
both now in the Prado.

In Andalusia, besides the **Seville School,** made famous by **Murillo** and **Zurbarán** and **Valdés
Leal,** there was **Alfonso Cano** (1601-1661), painter, sculptor and architect, working in Granada
painting the slightly remote, other worldly Virgins, typical of his period. The Castilian painters
of the century — **Vicente Carducho** (1576-1638), **Carreño de Miranda** (1614-1685) and **Claudio
Coello** (1642-1693), who were all very good indeed, pale, however, before **Velázquez** *(p 55)*.

18C. — The Bourbon court took pains to attract the greatest painters and bestow on them
official positions; in 1752 Ferdinand VI founded the Academy of San Fernando where it was
intended that artists should learn the rules of painting and study the Italian masters. The
leaders of the time were **Anton Raffael Mengs** from Bohemia who stayed ten years (1761-1771),
the Italian **Gian Battista Tiepolo** who stayed from 1762-1770, the Spanish **Francisco Bayeu**
(1734-1795) and, eclipsing all, **Francisco Goya** (1746-1828) *(pp 207 and 208)*.

19 and 20C. — By the late 19C **Joaquín Sorolla** (1863-1923), a Valencian was painting light
filled beach scenes, **José Gutiérrez Solana** (1886-1945) and the Basque, **Ignacio Zuloaga**
(1870-1945), scenes of everyday life; **J.M. Sert,** vast frescoes *(p 101)*.

Spain's major first half of the 20C painters were all members of the Paris School. They
include the Catalans, **Juan Gris** (1887-1927), **Joan Miró** (1893-1983) and **Salvador Dalí** (b 1904
at Figueres) and **Pablo Picasso**. Picasso was born in Málaga in 1881 and studied in Barcelona
before going to Paris where his participation in every *avant-garde* movement was illustrated
to some degree in each of his successive periods: the "blue" of 1901 (clowns, harlequins,
sick children), the "rose" of 1904, the "cubist" of 1906, the "analytical cubist" of 1912-1914,
the "surrealist" of 1929-1935. The Spanish Civil War and in 1937, the picture, *Guernica,*
marked the beginning of the purely personal style which continued, though constantly
changing, throughout the vast outpouring of canvases until his death in the south of France
in 1973.

SCULPTURE

Romanesque carving. — In so called European Romanesque *(p 14)*, sculpture was characterised by a certain rigidity of posture, robe folds more decorative than realistic and hair on heads and chins always meticulously braided — an obviously Byzantine derivation. The only relief came through a certain vivacity and movement which are immediately attractive.

Portals illustrated Biblical scenes and the labours of the months; Christ in Majesty or the Last Judgment were carved on tympana. Church and cloister capitals fall into one of two groups: the historiated, illustrating scenes from the Gospels or the Old Testament; or those rich with interlaced plant motifs and fantastic oriental beasts.

Romanesque capital
San Juan de la Peña

Gothic carving. — Sculpture, like architecture, became more sophisticated and more delicate. Faces became individualised to the point where recumbent funerary statues clearly resembled the deceased. It became customary also to surmount statues with a pierced canopy, to surround doors and decorate cornices and capitals with intricate plant motifs. Influences from abroad, French in the 13 and 14C, Flemish in the 15C, enriched the art which evolved ultimately into a purely Spanish style, the Isabeline *(p 15)*.

Portals followed the general lines of French design. **Tombs** were, at first, uniformly reminiscent of sarcophagi, decorated with armorial bearings, sometimes surmounted by a conventional figure with a peaceful expression and hands joined. As masons became more skilled at representing in marble the richness of brocades, the suppleness of leather, greater attention was given to costume. In the 15C sculptors were emboldened to produce lifelike figures, kneeling or even in such nonchalant attitudes as the remarkable Doncel in Sigüenza Cathedral. **Altarpieces** comprised a predella or plinth, surmounted by several registers of panels and finally a carved and pierced canopy; **choirstall** backs were decorated with Biblical or historical scenes or carved to resemble a screen.

The sculptors. — Although many works of the period were still anonymous it is known that in the 15C, **Pere Johan** carved the St George medallion on the Diputación, Barcelona, and the St Thecla altarpiece in Tarragona Cathedral, **Egas Cueman**, brother of Hanequin of Brussels, tombs in the Guadalupe Monastery, **Juan Alemán**, the Lion Door of Toledo, Cathedral, **Rodrigo Alemán**, the choirstalls, **Juan Guas**, St John of the Kings, Toledo, **Mercadante de Bretaña**, the free standing figures for the two doors of Seville Cathedral and that **Gil de Siloé**, a native of Antwerp who settled in Burgos, became the most characteristic sculptor of the Isabeline style, endowing with marked sophistication the royal mausoleum at the Miraflores Monastery and Juan de Padilla's tomb *(p 230)*.

Sculpture in the 16 and 17C. — Sculpture in Spain reached its climax in the 16 and 17C. In the 16C, choirstalls, mausoleums, and particularly retables, were still being produced in quantities in alabaster and wood, when they would be painted by the *estofado* technique in which gold leaf is first applied, then the object is coloured and finally delicately scored to remove the colour and reveal the gold beneath where highlighting is required. From this period also dates the framing of carved altarpiece panels in Corinthian architraves and pilasters.

Damián Forment (*c* 1480-1540), working in Aragon at a time when both Gothic and Renaissance styles were current, proved himself equally brilliant in either. **Felipe Bigarny** (d 1543) and **Diego de Siloé** (apprenticed in Naples) both contributed outstanding work to Burgos Cathedral.

The Valladolid School became notable for its lyricism: **Alonso Berruguete** *(p 238)* sought beauty less than strength of expression, his tormented forms equalling in power those of Michelangelo (St Sebastian statue in Valladolid); **Juan de Juni** (d 1577;

(After MTTC photo, Madrid)

Juan de Juni : Entombment

probably from Champagne), whose art was already baroque in style, made his figures strike theatrical attitudes to express sorrow. Among his works, greatly prized by the public and much copied, are the Virgin of the Seven Knives in Las Angustias Church, Valladolid, and Entombments in Valladolid Museum and Segovia Cathedral.

In the 17C free standing groups proliferated, including many *pasos (p 26)* and figures in the round. Those in polychrome wood were made with inlaid stone eyes and tears of crystal. **Gregorio Fernández** (or **Hernández**) (1566-1636), sculptor in the Juni line, worked in Valladolid and Madrid — his Recumbent Christ for the Pardo Capuchin monastery was widely acclaimed and extensively copied; in Seville, **Juan Martínez Montañés** (1568-1649) specialised in carving pathetic *pasos* groups; **Alonso Cano** *(p 44)* became famous for the grace and feminity of his Immaculate Conceptions, and his disciple, **Pedro de Mena** *(p 45)* for the subtlety with which he suggested rather than openly portrayed his models'emotions — the Magdalen (Valladolid Museum), St Francis (Toledo Cathedral).

Baroque altarpieces. — As the size of altarpieces increased until, in some cases, they reached the roof, they began to be designed by architects *(p 16)*. By the 18C every church in Spain had been invaded by immense wood, marble and jasper by Churrigueresque constructions surrounding a central tabernacle. Their overly ornate gilding and other decoration included *salomonica* or barley sugar columns and *estípites* or pilasters in inverted pyramids *(p 16)*. When altarpieces threatened to shut off a chapel completely from the main body of the church glazed sections or **"transparents"** were incorporated.

MUSIC

Spain, since the Middle Ages, has had two streams of music which have evolved simultaneously: a remarkable, rich folk music and a sophisticated and equally rich repertory.

During the Reconquest, as towns were recaptured by the Christians, the drama of events began to inspire musical expression in the form of liturgical chants, dramatic representation in churches *(autos)* like the **Elche Mystery** *(p 165)* which is still performed, and poetry such as the **Cantigas de Santa María** by **Alfonso the Wise**. Music's association with religion was strong and was to remain so for several centuries, although from the 11C minstrels and troubadours were being encouraged away from the church to the court where they founded a new musical-poetical tradition. At the beginning of the 16C, the dramatist **Juan de la Encina,** showed himself to be also an excellent musician. Music at that time also began to benefit from the general prosperity and patronage of Habsburgs. Organs had been invented and become the invariable accompaniment to sacred music; profane airs were first played on the *vihuela,* a sort of guitar with six double strings, then by the lute and eventually the five string **guitar,** said Spanish guitar. In 1629, Lope de Vega wrote the text for the first Spanish opera. Pedro Calderón de la Barca (1600-1681) was the creator of a musical play with spoken passages, songs and dances, the **zarzuela** (1648) which in the 19C became a musical play based in plot and music on popular themes.

At the end of the 19C, the Catalan, Felipe Pedrell, inaugurated a new era as the first to associate with classical form Spain's traditional airs containing, as they did, melodic element from church modes introduced by early Christians and eastern rhythms brought by the Moors. As French composers, indulging in fashionable Hispanism, wrote evocative works (Ravel: *Bolero;* Bizet: *Carmen;* Lalo: *Symphonie Espagnole;* Chabrier: *España),* Pedrell's prolific compositions influenced a host of Spanish composers in using traditional themes as the basis of their inspiration. Their work rapidly became known throughout Spain and elsewhere: **Isaac Albéniz** (1860-1909) became famous with *Iberia,* **Enrique Granados** (1867-1916) with the *Goyescas,* **Joaquín Turina** (1882-1949) for the *Seville Symphony* and **Manuel de Falla** (1876-1946) *(p 37)* for *La Vida Breve, Nights in the Gardens of Spain, Love the Magician* and the *Three Cornered Hat.*

Andrés Segovia is the best known classical guitar player of our own day. He and his younger contemporary, Narciso Yepes, have sought to show that this most Spanish of instruments can also interpret a wider variety of music. The greatest cellist, possibly of all time, was also a Spaniard, Pablo Casals (1876-1973) *(p 75).*

LITERATURE

Roman Spain produced famous Latin authors: **Seneca the Elder,** his son the philosopher, **Lucius Seneca** *(p 38),* Quintilian *(p 236),* the satirist Martial, the Poet **Lucanus** *(p 38).*

The Middle Ages. — The Reconquest provided events in plenty for the epic poems of wandering minstrels. By the 12C the first milestone of Spanish literature had appeared in the form of **El Cantar de Mío Cid,** an anonymous poem in Castilian, inspired by the adventures of the Cid *(p 228).* In the 13C, Gonzalo de Berceo, drawing on his experience as a religious, wrote well observed "clerks poems" of *Mester de clerecía.* Alfonso X, the Wise *(p 215),* a lettered man who wrote poetry in Galician, decided that Latin should be replaced as the official language in his kingdom by Castilian, an act subsequently followed throughout Spain except in Catalonia where Catalan remained the written as well as the spoken language. In the 14C, prose narrative appeared in the cautionary tales of **Don Juan Manuel** *(p 187)* while Juan Ruiz, **Archpriest of Hita,** composed a brilliant satirical verse work, full of gusto, entitled **El Libro de Buen Amor.**

The Renaissance. — In the 15C Italian influence encouraged **Jorge Manrique** *(p 238)* and López de Mendoza, **Marquess of Santillana** *(p 198)* and others to write lyric poetry. At the same time, publication of the totally different **Romancero,** a collection of romances in epic and popular vein, perpetuated the mediaeval style until the 16C when there appeared (1508) what was to be the model for numerous romances of chivalry, the **Amadís de Gaula.** Only with **La Celestina** by Fernando de Rojas, a subtle study of passion and easy going villainy presented in novel dialogue form, did the tone change.

The Golden Age. — Spain enjoyed its greatest literary flowering under the Habsburgs (1516-1700). In that period there were lyric poets such as the gentle **Garcilaso de la Vega,** adept at the Italian verse forms which he transformed into personal poetry, the religious, **Fray Luis de León** *(p 192)* and the sonorous, **Luis de Góngora** *(p 38)* known for his subtle imagery and obscurity. Pastoral and historical Moorish novels became popular (Cervantes, Lope de Vega), the most famous of the former being **Diana** by the Portuguese, Montemayor and the latter, the **Guerras Civiles de Granada** by Pérez de Hita in which the life of the Moors is described with colourful verve. The most popular novel form, however, was the **picaresque,** of which the first to appear in 1554 was **Lazarillo de Tormes,** an anonymous autobiographical work in which the hero, an astute rascal *(pícaro)* suffers the ways of the church and society with racy humour and detachment; later followed Mateo Alemán's **Guzmán de Alfarache,** a vivid tale of a young man's downfall and repentance and its parody, El Buscón in which were displayed the talents of the poet, pamphleteer and satirist, **Quevedo** (1580-1645).

The genius of the Golden Age, however, was undoubtedly, **Cervantes** *(p 189)* and his masterpiece, the universal, **Don Quixote.** At the end of the 16C, *comedia* appeared to which **Lope de Rueda** had already shown the way: dramatic authors proliferated, the greatest who did much to perfect and enrich the art form, being **Lope de Vega** (1562-1635). This phoenix of the mind, as he is known, wrote more than 1 000 works, although most have disappeared, touched on every subject and in **Fuenteovejuna** even illustrated the universality of the inherently Spanish code of honour. His successor, **Calderón,** in historical and philosophical plays *(La Vida es Sueño; Life's a Dream),* reflects clearly the mood of Spain as a nation in decline at the end of the 17C. Finally **Tirso de Molina,** a prolific dramatist, left his impression of **Don Juan** for posterity and **Guillén de Castro** set down the youthful adventures of the Cid in **Mocedades del Cid** (Corneille's source).

The chroniclers of the conquest of America were writing also at this period: **Cortés, Bartolomé de las Casas...** the moralist, **Fray Luis de Granada** and the mystic writers **St Teresa of Avila** and **St John of the Cross (Spiritual Canticle)** *(p 219).*

18 and 19C. — Criticism and even the scientific approach found expression among essayists such as **Benito Jerónimo Feijóo** and **Jovellanos** *(p 113)* — who was also a poet; elegance dominated the theatre of **Moratín** while **Ramón de la Cruz** delighted the populace with his **Sainetes,** short witty scenes with lively dialogue. The great Romantic poet of the 19C was **Bécquer** *(p 74),* the social satirist, **Larra,** the literary critic **Menéndez y Pelayo** *(p 125)* and the political and moral analyst **Ángel Ganivet.**

Realism, introduced to the Spanish novel by **Alarcón** in **The Three Cornered Hat** and the provincial writer, **Pereda** in his **Peñas Arriba**, was fully accepted by **Pérez Galdós** *(p 200)*, who began to write novels vividly coloured by his human sympathy.

20C. — The generation of '98, deeply saddened by defeat in the Spanish American War and attendant losses of Cuba, Puerto Rico and the Philippines, mused philosophically on the character of essential Spain, became preoccupied with human destiny and the future of their country in particular. The atmosphere was reflected in the work of essayists such as **Unamuno** *(p 108)* **(The Tragic Sense of Life)** and **Azorín**, the novelist **Pío Baroja**, the philologist **Menéndez Pidal** and the aesthete **Valle Inclán**, creator of elegant poetic prose. Other 20C writers include the dramatically skilful and witty **Jacinto Benavente** (1866-1954), the novelist **Blasco Ibáñez** (1867-1928) *(p 171)*, the poets **Juan Ramón Jiménez** (1881-1958) *(p 49)* who abstracted experience into the essences of light, water and absence and whose portrait in poetic prose of himself as a boy with a donkey **(Platero y Yo)** has become a children's classic, **Antonio Machado** (1875-1939) descriptive poet of Castile, and **Rafael Alberti** (b 1902). **Federico García Lorca** (1899-1936) *(p 45)*, equally great as poet or dramatist **(Bodas de Sangre)**, Andalusian through and through was, perhaps, the most fascinating echo of the Spain whose mystery the essayist and philosopher, **Ortega y Gasset** (1883-1925) spent his life trying to explain and describe.

Postwar writing. — Writing arose from the ashes of the Civil War after some years with remarkable essays by **Américo Castro**, plays by **Antonio Buero Vallejo**, **Alfonso Sastre** and outstanding novels concerned with social problems by **Camilo José Cela**, **Juan Goytisolo**, **Ramón Sender** and **Antonio Ferres**.

The 18 Spanish speaking countries of Latin America are now making a contribution to Spanish literature (Jorge Luis Borges, Gabriel García Marquez, José Lezama Lima, Pablo Neruda, Miguel Ángel Asturias).

BOOKS TO READ

There are literally hundreds of books on Spain, ranging from the large format volume with wonderful photographs and secondary text to treatises filled with statistics on the economy.

The selection below, is non-political; and there are many authors not listed below, which, however, should not be forgotten, for they provide fascinating glimpses of their time — Washington Irving, Somerset Maugham, Walter Starkie, Arturo Barea, Hemingway. Bibliographies will be found in most of the books cited, several are available in paperback and virtually all at the larger public libraries.

General

Imperial Spain (1469-1716) - J.H. Elliott *(Pelican)*
Living in Spain in the 80's - John Reay Smith *(Robert Hale)*
The Spaniards - John Hooper *(Viking)*

Travel

Contrasting Spain - Charles Moore *(Colin Venton)*
Madrid and Southern Spain - A. Launay and M. Pendered *(B.T. Batsford)*
South from Granada - Gerald Brennan *(Cambridge University Press)*
A Visit to Spain - Hans Christian Andersen *(Peter Owen)*
Iberia - Spanish Travels and Reflections - James A. Michener *(Secker & Warburg)*
Spain - Jan Morris *(Perguin Travel Library)*

Art - Literature

Spanish Short Stories 1 ed by Jean Franco *(Penguin)*
As I Walked Out One Midsummer Morning - Laurie Lee *(Penguin)*
A Rose for Winter - Laurie Lee *(Penguin)*
The Prado - Sánchez Cantón *(Thames & Hudson)*
Velasquez - Joseph Emile Muller *(Thames & Hudson)*
Picasso - Timothy Hilton *(Thames & Hudson)*

SPAIN : The Michelin Regional Map Series (1 : 400 000)

When choosing your lunchtime or overnight stop
use the above maps as all towns listed in
the Red Guide España Portugal are underlined in red.

When driving into or through a town
use the map as it also indicates all places with
a town plan in the Red Guide España Portugal.

Common reference numbers make the transfer from map to plan
easier.

DAY-TO-DAY LIFE IN SPAIN

EVERY DAY SIGHTS AND SOUNDS

The visitor, after he has noted the later mealtimes, the unaccustomed hours at which entertainments begin etc *(p 28)*, will be struck by the importance, in the life of the Spanish people, of communal activities and their ritualised, and in some cases, even daily performance, in specific public places.

The Plaza Mayor. — There is no town, large or small, no village in Spain, without its main square, lined, in nearly every case, by a covered arcade. Even where, as in Madrid and Salamanca, the square was designed with an eye to symmetry, it is as the community forum and rarely if ever as a main crossroads that it functions. It is enclosed and accessible from adjoining and converging streets only through arches beneath one or more of the surrounding houses; it acts as the forecourt of the town hall, should this stand upon it, and it is the setting for public festivities and great occasions. In the 18C the entrances would be blocked and the square serve as a bullring — a practice still observed in villages without an arena but determined to have a *corrida*.

The street. — Spaniards, like most Mediterranean folk, are able, because of the climate, to enjoy a good gossip in the street, make new acquaintances and watch others go about their business — the streets, therefore, remain lively until very late. Every town, every quarter has its local personalities, but common to all are the slowly pacing guardia civil in their peculiarly shaped black patent leather hats, the shoeshine boys at corners and around cafés and lottery ticket sellers. The occasional compliment, made by a man to a pretty girl will be heard — a **piropo,** usually the single word *guapa !* or *bonita* but in Andalusia, a longer allusive phrase. The acknowledgement, however, everywhere will be the same — a silent smile.

The street festival, though, is the evening **paseo.** As the sun begins to set everyone steps out onto the main street which gradually becomes filled with people walking slowly up and down; one walks *(pasear)* to enjoy the last light and the cool of the evening; girls dress for the occasion, young men smarten up for it and then they slowly process in segregated groups, eyeing one another; the boys bandy remarks to the girls and among themselves, while parents, grandparents and friends look on from the pavement cafés.

The café. — The aperitif **(chateo)** is a well established tradition in Spain. At about 1pm one goes to a bar where one meets one's friends, drinks a glass of wine, picks at the **tapas** which may be anything from olives to seafood to chips with mayonnaise. After work comes the **tertulia** or virtually informal club hour when men gather and, over a glass, set the world to rights as they talk over politics, the latest news and football and tell stories *(chistes)*. The end of the afternoon is the time when women often take a cup of chocolate or, in summer, a **horchata de chufas,** a refreshing cold drink extracted from earth almonds, and **churros,** delicious twisted fritters, thick as a stick of barley sugar. Black coffee is **café solo;** white **café, cortado** or **café con leche.**

Sport and entertainment. — The cinema is the most popular entertainment but the *zarzuela (p 21)* and the *flamenco (p 31)* also have keen supporters. **Verbenas** or fun fairs exist only in the largest towns, notably Barcelona and Madrid (amusement parks).

A few regional sports such as the Basque *pelota,* sailing and water sports at the northern summer regattas have their devotees, cycling and skiing also since the 1972 Olympic Games and, bullfighting, the spectacle which is unique to Spain, half entertainment, half sport and a tradition *(p 25)*. Nevertheless, nowadays, the national sport is football. Local matches and the games of Real Madrid and Atlético absorb the community and provide common ground for talk between rich and poor, bosses and workers as nothing else. Betting on match results is made through a tote, the **quiniela.**

National holidays. — **Christmas** is a religious, family holiday when "cestas de Navidad" are given between friends or by firms to their employees — traditional willow baskets or hampers, containing bottles of wine, hams, sugared almonds, *turrón* (sweetmeats) and marzipan. **New Year's Eve** sees everyone out of doors: in Madrid the crowds gather at the Puerta del Sol to eat a grape at every stroke as the clock strikes midnight — a custom you will find followed in every Spanish home. At **Epiphany** there is a family exchange of presents and the Twelfth Night cake or *roscón* is eaten.

What to bring back from Spain

An official craftsmen's centre shop, an ARTESANÍA, will be found in each provincial capital (ask the local tourist office for the exact address). The list below gives a general idea of local craft and gastronomic specialities (1).

1 – ANDALUSIA — **Córdoba:** embossed leather, filigree jewellery. — **Granada:** lace, carpets and rugs, copper ewers, marquetry. — **Níjar:** *tela de trapo* (rustic weaving — *p 33)*. — **Seville:** mantillas, shawls, wrought iron.

2 – ARAGON — **Fraga (圓圓圓 16 and 17):** figs.

3 – CATALONIA — *Porrones* (carafes with long pointed spouts from which to drink direct without touching it with the lips).

4 – THE CANTABRIAN COAST — **Éibar (圓圓 7):** damascene ware. — **Vitoria:** chocolate truffles, playing cards.

5 – EXTREMADURA — **Guadalupe:** copper and terracotta ewers.

6 – GALICIA — **Camariñas:** pillow lace. **Pontevedra:** willow baskets.

7 – THE LEVANT REGION — **Alcoy:** sugar almonds. — **Alicante:** turrón (almond and honey sweetmeat). — **Murcia:** gourds, esparto grasswork.

8 – NAVARRE — **Pamplona:** caramels *(pastillas de café con leche).*

9 – MADRID — CASTILE-LA MANCHA — **Albacete:** knives. — **Almagro:** lace. — **Lagartera:** embroidery. — **Puente del Arzobispo** and **Talavera de la Reina:** ceramics and pottery. — **Toledo:** damascene ware, marzipan.

10 – CASTILE AND LEÓN — LA RIOJA — **Ávila:** *Yemas de Santa Teresa (p 225)*. — **Logroño:** caramels. — **Salamanca:** charros or local jewellery.

11 – BALEARIC ISLANDS — **Felanitx (圓圓圓 42):** ceramics and pottery. — **Manacor (圓圓圓 42):** pearls and, from all the islands, glassware, embroidery, wrought iron, esparto grasswork.

12 – CANARY ISLANDS — Drawn thread embroidery, baskets, Guanche traditional pottery.

(1) Places not described in the Guide are located by Michelin map references (no and fold).

PRINCIPAL FOLKLORE AND RELIGIOUS FESTIVALS

The selection of festivals below attract the greatest crowds, are the most colourful or the most characteristic. Spanish Tourist Offices have annually revised calendars of attractions which include festivals — check places and times locally!

DATE AND PLACE	TYPE OF FESTIVAL
Week before Lent. . . . . **Cádiz - Sta. Cruz de Tenerife**	Carnival festivities: processions.
12-19 March . . . . **Valencia**	"Fallas" *(p 170)*.
3rd Sunday during Lent. . . . . **Castellón de la Plana**	Feast of the Magdalen: *Corridas*, local dress processions.
Holy Week . . . . **Cartagena** **Cuenca-Granada-Murcia-Seville** **Valladolid-Zamora**	Solemn processions *(p 26)*.
First week after Easter . . . . **Murcia**	Spring festival *(p 168)*.
April . . . . **Seville**	April fair *(p 55)*.
22-24 April . . . . **Alcoy**	St George Festival: "Moros y Cristianos" *(p 158)*.
Sunday after 25 April (St Mark's Feast Day) . . . . **Ujué**	*Romería* (pilgrimage) starting at midnight from Tafalla *(p 185)*.
Last Sunday in April . . . . . **Andújar**	Pilgrimage to the Virgen de la Cabeza. On the Saturday different brotherhoods go up to the church in a long procession of decorated carts.
Late April-early May . . . . **Jerez**	Horse show *(p 50)*.
Mid-May . . . . **Córdoba**	Decorated *patios* and *flamenco* competitions *(p 38)*.
15 May . . . . **Madrid**	St Isidore Festival: a fortnight of festivities.
Whitsun . . . . **El Rocío** (Huelva) map ▦▦▦ fold 15	Famous gipsy pilgrimage to the Nuestra Señora del Rocío Sanctuary. The gipsies come from Huelva and Seville along the dusty road either in flower decorated carts or riding horses saddled and bridled in Andalusian style.
2nd Thursday after Whitsun . . . . **Camuñas** (Toledo) map ▦▦▦ fold 27 - **Sitges-Toledo**	Corpus Christi: Camuñas — mimed mystery play in costume: the struggle of Virtue against Vice; Sitges — streets carpeted with flowers *(p 97)*; Toledo — Solemn Procession at 11am *(p 26)*.
3rd Thursday after Whitsun . . . . . . **La Orotava**	Corpus Christi: streets carpeted with flowers *(p 275)*.
21-24 June . . . . **Alicante**	St John Festival *(p 158)*.
23 June . . . . **Barcelona**	Day before St John's Festival: at night local dancing in the Pueblo español; games in the Montjuïc gardens.
24-29 June . . . . **Segovia**	St John's and Peter's Day Festivals with local dancing and costumes.
29 June . . . . **Lekeitio**	St Peter Festival: Kaxarranka (symbolic dance by the fishermen's guild).
30 June . . . . **Irún**	Commemorative military parade *(alarde) (p 114)*.
Late June-early July . . . . . **Granada**	International music and dance festival.
6-14 July . . . . **Pamplona**	"Sanfermines": famous *encierros* and *corridas (p 182)*.
15-31 July **Santiago de Compostela**	St James' Festival: processions, fireworks.
17-31 July . . . . **Valencia**	St James' Festival: battles of flowers, *corridas*.
Early August . . . . **Málaga**	Fair, *corridas*, etc.
1-17 August . . . . **Elche**	Assumption: Elche Mystery Play *(p 165)*.
4-9 August . . . . **Vitoria**	Festival of the White Virgin *(p 128)*.
14-25 August . . . . **Betanzos**	Festival of St Rock: ancient brotherhood dances.
15-16 August . . . . **La Alberca**	Assumption *(p 223)*.
August . . **Corunna, San Sebastián, Gijón, Bilbao**	Semana Grande: sporting events, cultural activities, *corridas*.
September . . . . **Jerez**	Wine Harvest Festival *(p 50)*.
Week of 21 September . . . **Oviedo**	St Matthew's Festival; America Day - 19 September: *corridas*, dancing, processions of carts and floats.
23-24 September . . . . . **Tarragona**	St Thecla Festival: human pyramids, *sardanas*.
24-28 September . . . . . **Barcelona**	Festival of Our Lady of Mercy: *corridas*, folk and general festivities.
Week of 12 October . . . **Saragossa**	Pilar Festival *(p 70)*.

THE SEASONS

The average daily temperature is shown on the Michelin maps of Spain.

Spring and Autumn are the best seasons for a general tour but there is a region in Spain for every season:

Spring. — Andalusia, Castile (except high in the mountains), the Balearic Islands, the Mediterranean coast.

Summer. — *By the sea:* Basque Country, Cantabrian Coast, Galicia; *in the mountains:* Pyrenees, Picos de Europa, Sierra Nevada, Sierra de Gredos, Sierra de Guadarrama.

Autumn. — Central area, Andalusia, Mediterranean coast.

Winter. — Mediterranean coast, Balearic and Canary Islands, winter sports centres in the Pyrenees, Sierra de Guadarrama and Sierra Nevada.

Except where otherwise stated, all recommended itineraries in towns, are designed as walks.

THE BULLFIGHTER'S ART

Bullfighting on horseback was an honoured pastime among the knights of Spain from the Middle Ages to the 18C. The Bourbons, however, had no stomach for such entertainment, and tauromachy ceased to be a noble sport. It passed to the common people and the art of one man on foot fighting a bull, was born. The **Romero** family *(p 53)* were the first to lay down rules of combat; **Costillares** (1748-1800) invented the *verónica* and the *estocada a volapié;* **Francisco Montes "Paquiro"** (1805-1851) confirmed the dominant role of the *matador* on foot over the mounted *picador*. The contest had its formal and final style. Bulls at that time were aggressive, fully grown 5 year old beasts weighing 600kg - 12 cwt; **Juan Belmonte** (1892-1962) altered this to 4 year olds weighing 450kg - 9 cwt — to make the contest livelier and greater test of the *matador's* skill.

Famous toreros. — **Pepe Hillo** (1754-1801) created the spontaneous Seville as opposed to the solemn and less spectacular Ronda style *(p 53);* following him came the Cordobans, **Lagartijo** (1841-1900), renowned for his elegant passes and **Guerrita** (1862-1941), who remained supreme in the ring until 1899. This century there have been the Sevillan, **"Joselito"** (1895-1920), rival of Juan Belmonte, killed in the Talavera de la Reina ring and **Manolete**, born in Córdoba in 1917, killed at Linares in 1947, famous and greatly admired for his moments of dramatic stillness in the ring and his clear cut gestures. Among those fighting today, the favourite, although criticised by purists, is the spectacular **El Cordobés** (b 1936). (An Englishman, H.O. Higgins, has recently made the grade.)

The stock. — Fighting bulls are raised on vast ranges by the Guadalquivir in Andalusia and on the plains of Castile between Salamanca and Ciudad Rodrigo. Selection for the ring and for breeding is based on the **tienta** or bravery a bull shows in the domain's trial ring, and provides the form to be analysed on the day by **aficionados.**

The corrida. — The programme, which starts promptly at 5pm, is made up of two kills each by three *matadores.* The action begins, to the tune of a *paso-doble* with a **paseo** or grand entry led by two mounted *alguaciles* (servants of the *corrida* president) in 17C costume. These are followed by the *toreros* or ring contestants: the three **matadores** (*matar:* to kill) each in his costume of lights leading his **cuadrilla** or team. The contests **(lidia)** are divided into three acts **(tercios),** marked by trumpet calls; by the last, the *matador's* domination of the bull should have reached its climax.

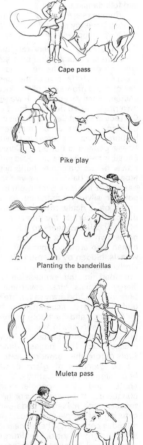

Cape pass

Pike play

Planting the banderillas

Muleta pass

The estocada

1 — Arrival and estimation of the bull

The cape *(capea).* — *Peones* or foot followers begin by attracting the bull's attention and concentrating its attention on the cloak; the *matador* enters and plays his wide red cape before the bull to gauge its intelligence and swiftness of turn. This exercise also gives the *matador* the opportunity to display his style and perform formal figures such as the *verónica* in which the cape sweeps as close to the bull's head as St Veronica's veil did to the face of Christ.

The pikes *(varas).* — *Picadores* on their heavily padded horses, wait with pikes at the ready for the bull to charge, when they thrust their weapons into its withers; this breaks its speed and reveals its prowess. If the bull appears cowardly, the president by waving a red kerchief, can ordain that the *banderillas* which are placed next shall be an ignominious black.

2 — The banderillas

To allow the bull to regain his wind and rouse him further, *banderillas* plant pairs — usually 3 — of beribboned darts in his withers, skilfully avoiding his horns as they do so.

3 — The kill

La faena de muleta. — This, the deft work with the *muleta,* the small red cloth bound to a stick, opens the last act in the drama. The *matador* salutes the president, dedicates *(brindar)* the bull to a particular person or the crowds, throws aside his hat, and faces his adversary. With his sword in his right hand and his *muleta* in his left, he plays the *bicho* (insect), winning applause for the grace, originality and boldness of his passes.

The estocada. — Finally the bull stands still, head lowered. The *matador* advances, his sword straight before him, and aiming between the shoulder blades thrusts to the bull's heart as his body brushes the right horn of the animal still fascinated by the *muleta.* The *estocada a volapié,* when the *matador* throws his weight onto the standing animal, is the more common action; the other, more difficult feat, is the **estocada a recibir** when the man receives the full force of the bull's last charge upon his sword.

The trophies. — A particularly brilliant *faena de muleta,* a courageous and swift *estocada,* will be greeted by the crowd with rapturous applause and the bestowal on the *matador* of one or both the bull's ears and, very occasionally the tail also. If the man makes a poor show with the *muleta* or fails to stop the bull for the kill, the president may wave his green kerchief, imposing the insult of letting the bull leave the ring alive. The blue kerchief salutes the bull's prowess and signals the mules to drag the carcass on a lap of honour.

Other types of fight. — **Capeas** are the popular festivals at which young amateurs match their skill against bulls in village squares — the Ciudad Rodrigo contests in February are the best known; **novilladas** are when 3 year - old bulls, *novillos,* are fought by apprentice toreadors, *novilleros.* The **rejoneador** is a mounted toreador similar to the Portuguese *cavaleiro (see Michelin Green Guide Portugal)* who fights in an ordained, three act, Spanish style. The *rejón,* a barbed lance which breaks when implanted, serves as the pike, the *banderillas* are set from on horseback but the *estocada* is sometimes accomplished on foot. The performance is considered less a contest than a display of horsemanship.

RELIGIOUS FESTIVALS

Religious festivals throughout Spain are imbued with the fire of deep conviction and the ability of the people freely to express their faith; added to this is the natural love of spectacle and a devotion to tradition. The festivities, which vary according to the region, tend towards the bucolic in Galicia, the reserved in Castile and exuberance in Andalusia. Popular joy or fervour are, in the main, everywhere given free reign at some point. Intermingled with the secular celebration in the most natural way in the world, will be local folklore and purely profane rejoicings: every festival is accompanied by a *corrida*, parades in local costume; incessant fire crackers and fireworks.

Bands, songs, dancers in local dress attend the ceremonies so that each is quite distinct in character: in Galicia it is the *gaita*, in the Basque country the dances, accompanied with the *txistu*, in Catalonia the *tenora* which marks the rhythm for the *sardanas* danced in the street, in Andalusia the *flamenco* strutting to the sound of castanets. There may even be sporting contests as with the human pyramids of the Tarragona area *(see details under different regions, pp 33-282)*.

Agricultural fairs *(ferias)*, picturesque and noisy, are held in some places in conjunction with a festival.

The whole town, led by the council and local personalities, joins in on these occasions, which usually include a procession or *romería*.

Romerías. — *Romerías* are pilgrimages made to an isolated church or hermitage by a large crowd in procession. The people are grouped in brotherhoods or guilds or by town quarter or may even consist of a whole village together.

Most *romerías* are to chapels to the Virgin, frequently situated on a hillside.

The chapels are known throughout Spain for their images or statues which are usually held in deep veneration and at the same time are so popular that girls are often named after them; Rocío, Pilar (the patron of Saragossa), Montserrat, Guadalupe.

Pilgrims may dress in local costume and sing folksongs along the way; elsewhere at Ujué for instance, the procession is at night by lantern light and in total silence, elsewhere again, in the northern *rías*, it takes the form of flower garlanded boats sailing out to sea. After the religious ceremony the pilgrims cast off their solemnity and celebrate with picnics and folk dancing.

Romerías are particularly popular in Navarre, along the Cantabrian coast, in Galicia and no less fervently in Andalusia, where they make their way, to the Virgen de la Cabeza *(p 24)* and to the most widely known sanctuary in Spain, El Rocío *(p 24)*.

Processions. — Every religious occasion is accompanied by a solemn procession whether it is a great Christian festival or the feast day of the patron saint of the local church. Each event will have its own ritual: on 16 July, the feast of **Our Lady of Mount Carmel** (Virgen del Carmen), patron of all mariners, harbours will be crowded with flower garlanded boats; on **Corpus Christi**, streets will be carpeted with flower petals, balconies hung with tapestries or banners, to await the passing of the Holy Sacrament in a gold or silver monstrance *(p 18)* borne on a richly carved cart. At **Burgos,** the cart, to the amazement of every child, appears to advance on its own — a trick performed by a man who crouches between the wheels, hidden by an embroidered cloth. The Burgos monstrance is preceded in the procession by clergy, officials, local government personalities, the army in full dress uniform and is accompanied by a fanfare and school-children. After the service, to the sound of tambourines and castanets, boys dressed as 15C pages, dance *jotas* before the cathedral, watched by *gigantes* or giant pasteboard figures of the Catholic Monarchs and the people they conquered, and *cabezudos* or grotesques with massive heads cari-

(After Diario de Barcelona photo)

Holy Week in Seville

caturing the people of Burgos, who thus bring a touch of local history and the profane to the religious ceremony. The procession at **Toledo** is incredibly splendid when, in the beautiful city setting, clergy in the richest liturgical vestments set out, the officiant wearing the magnificent humeral veil incrusted with emeralds, with the famous monstrance by Enrique de Arfe gleaming massively. Accompanying the progress are the city's many brotherhoods, each in brilliant traditional uniform.

Holy Week is the festival which inspires the most fervent demonstrations of devotion, however, throughout Spain. It begins on Palm Sunday with the blessing of the great fronds which will remain for the rest of the year attached to the ironwork of many balconies; there follow demonstrations of mourning: sumptuous church ornaments are veiled in black while the Passion is taken to different sectors of the town in the form of **pasos** or floats bearing groups of lifesize statues carved in polychrome wood — every scene is shown from the Last Supper and the Garden of Olives to the Descent from the Cross with the sorrowing Virgin weeping crystal tears.

Of the slow, sad Holy Week processions, the most spectacular are those held in Seville *(p 55)* accompanied by hooded penitents. In Catalonia the villagers themselves act the Passion, entering into their parts so completely that more than one amateur Christ has suffered flagellation.

TOURING PROGRAMMES

GRAND TOUR
About one month (approx 5000 km) (approx 3100 miles)

★★★ SAN SEBASTIÁN

FRANCE

★★★ BURGOS

Jaca

Ordesa Nat¹ Park

Sª de Montserrat

Gerona ★

★ Valladolid

Santo Domingo de Silos ★★

★★★ Poblet

★★★ BARCELONA

Duero

Ebro

★★★ SALAMANCA

★★ Segovia

Alcañiz

Tarragona ★★

ATLANTIC OCEAN

★ Ávila

The Escorial ★★★

MADRID ★★★

Teruel

Tortosa

PORTUGAL

Tagus

Toledo ★★★

★ Valencia ★★

★ Cáceres

Guadalupe ★★

Guadiana

Júcar

MEDITERRANEAN

★★★ CÓRDOBA

★ Murcia

Aracena

Úbeda ★

Guadalquivir

★★★ SEVILLE

★★★ GRANADA

★ Málaga

— Suggested routes
— Variants or reductions in distances
— Cross country or approach routes

★ Cádiz

Balearic and Canary Islands
(see pp 253-280)

CANTABRIAN SEA

★ Corunna

Oviedo

★★ Santillana del Mar

Santander ★

★★★ Picos de Europa ▲

SANTIAGO DE COMPOSTELA ★★★

Altamira Caves ★★

★★★ SAN SEBASTIÁN

Miño

★★ León

Ebro

Pontevedra

Vigo

Orense

▲ Lake Sanabria

★★★ BURGOS

Esla

PORTUGAL

NORTHWEST
About 2 weeks (approx 2500 km) (approx 1550 miles)

★★ Valladolid

Duero

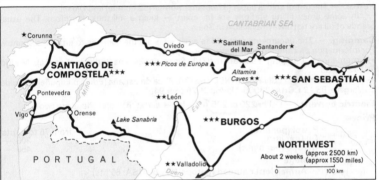

★ Pamplona

★★★ Ordesa Nat¹ Park

FRANCE

★★★ Aigües Tortes Nat¹ Park ▲

★★ Santo Domingo de Silos

Jaca

Duero

Soria ★

Ebro

★ Ripoll

Cadaqués

Saragossa ★★

Sª de Montserrat ★★★

SALAMANCA ★★★

★★★ Poblet

BARCELONA ★★★

Segovia ★★

Tarragona ★★

★ La Alberca

★★ Ávila

The Escorial ★★★

MADRID ★★★

Tortosa

▲ ★★ Sª de Gredos

Aranjuez ★

Cuenca ★★

Tagus

Toledo ★★★

★★ Valencia

NORTHEAST AND CENTRE
About 3 weeks (approx 3000 km) (approx 1800 miles)

Júcar

Virgen de la Cabeza ▲

Úbeda ★★

★★★ CÓRDOBA

★ Baeza

▲ Sª de Cazorla ★★

Murcia ★

Guadalquivir

Jaén

Mar Menor

SEVILLE ★★★

★★★ GRANADA

Guadix ★

Cartagena

Aguilas

★★ Ronda

Málaga ★

★ Almería

THE SOUTH
About 2 weeks (approx 2000 km) (approx 1250 miles)

★ Cádiz

Puerto Banús ★

27

PRACTICAL INFORMATION

Tourist Offices. — For all tourist information apply to the Spanish National Tourist Office:
MADRID   : Princesa 1 Torre de Madrid ℡ 241 2325
LONDON   : 57/58 St. James's St., SW1 ℡ 499- 0901
NEW YORK   : 665 Fifth Ave., 10022 ℡ 759- 8822
PARIS   : 43 ter Av. Pierre I de Serbie, 8 ℡ 47 20 90 54

Some Spanish towns (provincial capitals, main tourist and frontier towns) have official offices (Ministry of Transportation of Tourism and of Communication) *(for local addresses see individual towns in the Michelin Red Guide España Portugal);* most of the remainder have local tourist offices with the sign "Turismo" painted on the outside. Offices in larger towns are usually able to supply English speaking guides to the town and its major monuments.

Access: by air by British Airways or Iberia Airlines to Madrid, Barcelona, Seville, Valencia, Bilbao, Alicante, Málaga and Palma (Balearics); by sea (car ferry) to Santander from Plymouth; by sea and land through France by car, coach or train. For Gibraltar *see p 43.*

Exchange. — The rate is liable to variation; apply to your bank or travel agent.

Entry. — A valid passport is required and for drivers, an international driving licence. Cars need the regulation GB or other applicable nationality plate.

Insurance. — Minor changes frequently occur in administrative and customs formalities. We advise readers to join an automobile club or other specialised association which will be able to give up-to-date information.

The motoring organisations, the AA and RAC, advise tourists, whether taking their own cars or hiring in Spain: a) to take out a Green Card with a special endorsement for validity in Spain; b) and to take out the so called Bail Bond to avoid any possibility of arrest on the spot in case of a traffic infringement. All these papers can be obtained from the RAC or the AA or your insurance company.

Free medical assistance is offered to British tourists covered by the British National Insurance scheme.

Safety measures. — Motorists must wear seat belts, and be in possession of an officially approved breakdown triangle. Do not forget to give way to traffic coming from the right.

Petrol. — The petrol sold is super (97 octane), normal (92 octane) and Diesel.

In some areas filling stations are far apart — keep a full tank, therefore. The usual brands of oil are not always available in Spain.

Camping. — The documents required to enter sites are the same as to enter the country. For information on camping and caravanning apply to:
— International Camping Federation (IZV), Plaza de España (Edificio España), Madrid ℡ 242 10 89
— Spanish Camping Federation (ANCE and CV), Plaza de España (Edificio España), Principe de Vergara, 85 - 2 DCHA, 28006-Madrid ℡ 262 99 94.

Electric current. — Either 220 or 225 AC volts — ask at the hotel. Plugs are two pin.

Prices

Petrol (per litre)	from 76 to 82 pts
Oil (per litre)	306 —
Garage (per night)	450 —

Postage
    Airmail letter abroad (Europe: 48 pts; USA: 66 pts)
    Airmail postcard abroad (Europe: 40pts; USA: 50pts)

Glass of beer	60 —
Cup of coffee	80 —
"Tapas" *(p 23)*	60 —
"Paella" (in a restaurant)	800 —
Cigarettes — Spanish dark tobacco Ducados	42 —
Cigarettes — Spanish light tobacco Fortuna	100 —
Cinema ticket (average price)	400 —
Corrida ticket (average price)	2000 —
An evening of Spanish dancing in a typical setting	2000 —
Theatre ticket for performance of Spanish dancing and singing	1000 —

Tipping. — Hotel, restaurant and café bills always include service in the total charge. Nevertheless, the boy who carries your bags, stops the traffic to help you as you come out of a parking place or renders other small services will generally appreciate a tip (between 5% to 10%).

Public holidays. — 1 and 6 January, 19 March, Maundy Thursday and Good Friday, 1 May, Corpus Christi (2nd Thursday after Whitsun), 25 July, 15 August, 12 October, 1 November, 6, 8, 24 and 25 December. In addition each town celebrates the feast day of its patron saint.

Differences in time and timings. — Spain is one hour ahead of GMT.

The Spanish keep very different hours from either British or Americans. **Meals** are served in restaurants from 1 and 9pm but Spaniards prefer to arrive for the most part any time after 2 and 10pm. **Shops** and **offices** respectively usually open from 9 or 10am to 1 or 1.30pm and from 3 or 3.30pm to 7.30 or 8pm; **banks** 9am to 2pm (1pm saturdays); **monuments** and **museums** 10am to 2pm (where they open in the afternoon it is not usually before 3 or 4pm). **Entertainment,** including theatres, sports etc, have matinées which begin at approximately 4.30pm on Sundays and holidays and 7pm on other days; evening performances start at 10 or 10.30pm.

Hunting and fishing. — Permits are obtained in the capital of each province.

To **hunt** in the Reserva Nacional de Caza ask at ICONA (ICONA SCE., Informacion Turistico - Cinegetica Para Cazadores Extranjeros, Gran Via de San Francisco, 35 — Madrid; ℡ 2. 66.42.02.

*Each year the **Michelin Red Guide España Portugal**
presents a multitude of up-to-date facts in a compact form.
Whether on a business trip, a weekend away from it all
or on holiday take the guide with you.*

VOCABULARY

GENERAL WORDS

For words and expressions used in hotels and restaurants see the current Michelin Red Guide España Portugal.

Terms of address

yes, no	**sí, no**
good morning	**buenos días**
good afternoon	**buenas tardes**
goodbye	**hasta luego, hasta pronto, adiós**
please	**por favor**
thank you (very much)	**(muchas) gracias**
excuse me	**perdón**
I don't understand	**no entiendo**
sir, mr, you	**señor, Usted...**
madam, mrs	**señora**
miss	**señorita**

Correspondance

post box	**buzón**
post office	**Correos**
telephone	**Telégrafos, Teléfonos**
letter	**carta**
post card	**(tarjeta) postal**
poste restante	**lista (de Correos)**
stamp	**sello**
telephone call	**conferencia**
tobacco shop	**estanco**

Time

when?	**¿cuándo ?**
what time ?	**¿a qué hora ?**
today	**hoy**
tomorrow morning	**mañana por la mañana**
tomorrow afternoon	**mañana por la tarde**

Shopping

how much	**¿cuánto (vale) ?**
(too) expensive	**(demasiado) caro**
much, little	**mucho, poco**
more, less	**más, menos**
big, small	**grande, pequeño**
all	**todo**

On the road, in town

a la derecha	on the right
a la izquierda	on the left
obras	road works, repairs
peligroso	danger, dangerous
cuidado	beware, take care
dar la vuelta a...	to go round, tour
después de...	after, beyond
girar	to go round, to circle

SITES AND SIGHTS

See also architectural terms p 16

where is ?	**¿dónde está... ?**
may one visit ?	**¿se puede visitar ?**
key	**llave**
light	**luz**
sacristan	**sacristán**
guide	**guía**
porter, caretaker	**guarda, conserje**
open, closed	**abierto, cerrado**
no entry, not allowed	**prohibido**
entrance, exit	**entrada, salida**
apply to	**dirigirse a...**
wait	**esperar**
beautiful	**bello, hermoso**
storey, stairs, steps	**piso, escalera**

alcazaba	Muslim fortress
alcázar	Muslim palace
alrededores	environs, outskirts
ayuntamiento	town hall
azulejo	ceramic tile
audiencia	audience, court
balneario	spa
barrio	quarter
belén, nacimiento	crib
bodega	wine cellar, store
bodegón	still life
cabo	cape, headland
calle	street
calle mayor	main street
camino	road, track
campanario	belfry
capilla	chapel
capitel	capital
carretera	main road
cartuja	Carthusian monastery
casa	house
casa consistorial	town hall
castillo	castle
castro	Celtic village
ciudad	town, city
claustro	cloister
colegio, colegiata	college, collegiate church
collado, alto	pass, high pass
convento	monastery, convent
cruz	cross, Calvary
cuadro	picture
cueva, gruta	cave, grotto
desfiladero	defile, cleft

embalse	reservoir, dam
ermita	hermitage, chapel
excavaciones	excavations
finca	property, domain
fuente	fountain
garganta	gorges
huerto; huerta	vegetable, market garden
iglesia	church *(p 16)*
imagen	religious statue
lago	lake
lonja	merchants' exchange
mezquita	mosque
monasterio	monastery
mirador	belvedere, viewpoint
museo	museum
nacimiento	source; birthplace
palacio (real)	(royal) palace
pantano	artificial lake
paseo	avenue, esplanade, promenade
paso	sculptured figures: the Passion
pazo	manorhouse (Galicia)
plaza	square
plaza mayor	main square
plaza de toros	bullring
portada	portal, west door
pórtico	portal, porch
presa	dam
pueblo	village, market town
puente	bridge
puerta	door, gate, entrance
puerto	pass, harbour, port
río	river, stream
romano; románico	Roman; Romanesque
santuario	church
siglo	century
soportales	portico
talla	carved wood
tapices	tapestries
techo (artesonado)	(coffered) ceiling
tesoro	treasury, treasure
torre	tower, belfry
torre del homenaje	keep
valle	valley
vega	fertile plain
vidriera	window: plain or stained glass
vista	view, panorama

KEY

Sights

*** Worth a journey
** Worth a detour
* Interesting

Italic type indicates natural sights

Town plans		Maps				Town plans

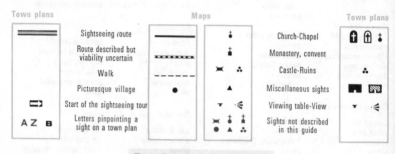

	Sightseeing route
	Route described but viability uncertain
	Walk
	Picturesque village
	Start of the sightseeing tour
A Z B	Letters pinpointing a sight on a town plan

| Church-Chapel |
| Monastery, convent |
| Castle-Ruins |
| Miscellaneous sights |
| Viewing table-View |
| Sights not described in this guide |

Roads and Railways

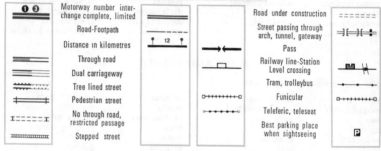

	Motorway number interchange complete, limited
	Road-Footpath
	Distance in kilometres
	Through road
	Dual carriageway
	Tree lined street
	Pedestrian street
	No through road, restricted passage
	Stepped street

| Road under construction |
| Street passing through arch, tunnel, gateway |
| Pass |
| Railway line-Station Level crossing |
| Tram, trolleybus |
| Funicular |
| Teleferic, teleseat |
| Best parking place when sightseeing |

Miscellaneous

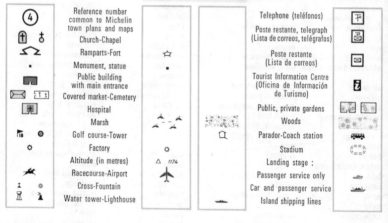

	Reference number common to Michelin town plans and maps
	Church-Chapel
	Ramparts-Fort
	Monument, statue
	Public building with main entrance
	Covered market-Cemetery
	Hospital
	Marsh
	Golf course-Tower
	Factory
	Altitude (in metres)
	Racecourse-Airport
	Cross-Fountain
	Water tower-Lighthouse

| Telephone (teléfonos) |
| Poste restante, telegraph (Lista de correos, telégrafos) |
| Poste restante (Lista de correos) |
| Tourist Information Centre (Oficina de Información de Turismo) |
| Public, private gardens |
| Woods |
| Parador-Coach station |
| Stadium |
| Landing stage : |
| Passenger service only |
| Car and passenger service |
| Island shipping lines |

D	Provincial Council (Diputación)	U	University (Universidad)	T	Theatre (Teatro)
G	Prefecture (Gobierno civil)	M	Museum (Museo)	Real	Shopping street
H	Town Hall (Ayuntamiento)	POL.	Police (Policía) (In large towns : Jefatura)	E	" European " road
				N 230, C 151	Road number
					Provincial capital

Plan or tourist area		Overall town plan and surrounding area
Detailed design showing entire street system and reference points		*Sketch plan showing main arteries and general layout only*
Dark brown		Light brown

1 Andalusia

Andalusia comprises Spain's eight most southerly provinces, a region of 90 000 km² - 34 700 sq miles — bordered by the Sierra Morena, the Atlantic and the Mediterranean. It shares a brief frontier with Portugal.

Geography. — The **Sierra Morena,** to the north, is rich in minerals; the **Guadalquivir** opens broadly onto the Atlantic, its coastal mudflats occupied only by the vast ranges on which fighting bulls are raised; inland, the cereal growing depression penetrates far to the northeast. The **Baetic Cordillera,** which parallels the south coast further east, includes the Sierra Nevada and the peninsula's highest peak, the Mulhacén (3 482m - 11 424ft).

This coast range has a considerable effect on Andalusia's climate which is generally mild in winter and hot and dry in summer; the Guadalquivir depression (near Córdoba) has torrid summers, the Aracena and Cazorla Sierras on the other hand, are high, humid and forested. The Sierra Nevada — the Snowy Range — remains snow-capped all the year round.

Irrigation is being extended to enable the region's traditional cereal and olive crops to be replaced by fruit and early vegetables. Vines are grown extensively around Málaga and Jerez; in the valley, rice (grown at the mouth of the Guadalquivir), cotton and sugar beet have been planted. The Sierra Nevada and Morena mines, worked since Antiquity, are still supplying copper in Minas de Riotinto *(p 35),* Tharsis and El Cerro, lead in Linares and La Carolina and iron in Alquife.

History. — The Romans colonised the region, named it Baetica after the Baetis, the former name of the Guadalquivir, and grew wheat, wine and olive oil on its fertile soil. The name Andalusia would appear to be a corruption of Vandalusia, the land of the vandals, or to come from ''Al Andalus'', the Muslim name for all territory in the peninsula brought under the control of Islam. This area was, in fact, the longest occupied — 800 years in the case of Granada - and has retained more Moorish traditions than elsewhere: terraced roofs, ancient crafts and place names - Gibraltar is from Djbel Tarik, ''the hill where Tarik landed'' in 711, the first syllable of Guadalquivir is a corruption of the Arabic for river, ''Oued''.

The **Umaiyads** (756-1031) developed a brilliant civilisation which continued to the 15C despite the division of the kingdom into *taifas (p 38),* incursions by the **Almoravids** (1086-1143), **Almohads** (until 1184) and **Marinids** (1275-1291), rival Maghrib dynasties. These sought advantage in the destruction of the unity of Al Andalus.

The Christians, meanwhile, from 1212 when they won the decisive Battle of **Las Navas de Tolosa,** began to gain ascendancy until by the end of the 13C only the Kingdom of Granada (approximately the present provinces of Málaga, Granada and Almería) remained Islam.

Habitat, folklore and gastronomy. — The characteristic white walls and cool *patios* adopted from Roman and Arab forbearers are altogether enchanting. The **cortijo,** the vast solitary farmhouse in its own domain or *finca* is equally typical.

The **flamenco** of gypsy and Arabic source, is a display of the true soul of Andalusia. The origin is the **''cante jondo''** or deep song which describes in ancient poetic phrases the performer's profound emotions. Seville, Málaga and Madrid are the places to see the best *tablaos* or performances of *flamenco.* The Andalusian costume, which is always worn by dancers, consists of brilliantly coloured dresses, and heeled shoes and, for the men, short jacketed suits, wide flat hats and heeled boots.

Gazpacho is the gastronomic speciality. It is a cold tomato and cucumber soup.

(After Diario de Barcelona photo)

Flamenco dancers

ALGECIRAS (Cádiz)

Michelin map 446 fold 29 — Pop 86 042
See town plan in the current Michelin Red Guide España Portugal

The Bay of Algeciras has always served the dual purpose of safe anchorage and vantage point overlooking the Strait of Gibraltar. The 14km - 9 mile wide channel, the shipping highway between the Atlantic and the Mediterranean, is yet narrow enough for the opposing shores to have been the bridgehead between Europe and Africa - the Ancients situated the columns of Hercules on either side, Mount Calpe - the Rock of Gibraltar - to the north and Abyla - either Mount Hacho or Jbel Musa, near Ceuta to the south. It is from across Algeciras Bay that you get the world famous **views★★** of the Rock.

The Arabs arrived in Algeciras from Africa in 711 and remained until 1344, naming the town Al Djezirah, the ''Island'' after the Isla Verde, the Green Island, now joined to the mainland.

Annually about 3.5 million passengers and 250 000 vehicles pass through the port. Passengers on the ferries from Tangier and Ceuta give a cosmopolitan character to what would otherwise be a small fishing port. When the frontier between Spain and Gibraltar *(p 43)* was closed, the government applied the policy of setting up local industries to provide employment as at San Roque where there is now a refinery.

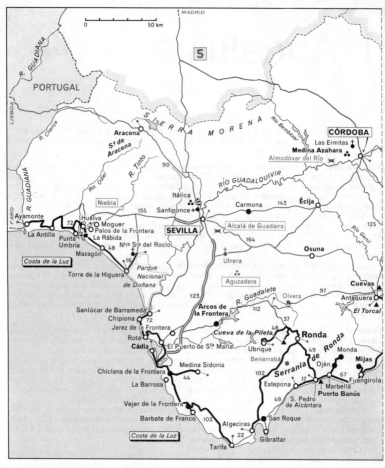

ALHAMA DE GRANADA (Granada)

Michelin map **446** south of fold 20 — Pop 5 839

Alhama, at the centre of a rolling, cereal covered plain, is scarcely more than an overgrown village. The twisting streets and alleys leading to its golden stone church are lined with white walled houses roofed with brown tiles.

Alhama's outstanding feature, which can be seen from the esplanade below the public garden, is its cliff face **site★★**.

The houses are built into the steep rock at the foot of which the Río Alhama pours through a cleft, driving a waterwheel.

Outside the village, a path *(3km - 2 miles)* runs beside the ravine to a sparkling bathing beach in in the heart of a mass of greenery.

ALMERÍA ★ P

Michelin map **446** fold 35 — Pop 140 946
See town plan in the current Michelin Red Guide España Portugal

In the 11C, Almería was the principal city of a *taifa (p 38)* ruled by Motacín, a well read man, protector of poets and scholars, patron of Ben Obeïd Bekri, author of a dictionary of geography which was also a compendium of contemporary knowledge. Under the Almoravids, Almería became the lair of pirates who raided as far abroad as Galicia; Alfonso VII, determined to wipe them out, captured the town in 1147; on his death, however, only ten years later, it fell to the Moors, who occupied it for the next 300 years.

The port exports fruit (Ohanes grapes, which have big pips, and Benahadux oranges) and minerals (iron, lead and copper).

The especially mild climate and nearby sand beaches make Almería a pleasant place to stay, particularly in winter.

Life in the town centres on the **Paseo de Almería,** an elegant tree-lined avenue bordered with luxury shops, banks and cafés; the **Parque de Nicolás Salmerón** skirts the harbour beneath shading palms.

The old quarter, the **Almedina,** which lies at the foot of the Alcazaba and St Christopher's Castle, was originally enclosed by the city ramparts. The **Chanca,** to the west, is the fishermen's quarter where the houses, each with its own terrace, stand in uneven lines like so many coloured cubes set into the living rock.

Alcazaba★. — *Open 10am to 2pm and 4 to 8pm; 9am to 1pm and 3 to 7.30pm in winter; 50pts.*

The Alcazaba, an Arab fortress dating back to the 8C, was badly damaged during the earthquake of 1522. Its high, ochre coloured walls, however, still dominate the town's white houses.

A long wall, vestige of the old ramparts, links the fort with a second hill, the Cerro de San Cristóbal, which was formerly crowned by a castle.

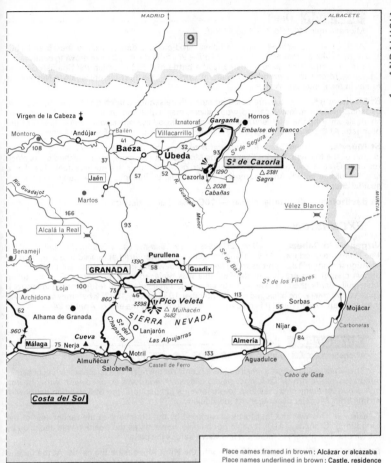

MADRID ↑   ALBACETE

9

Virgen de la Cabeza ‡
Montoro   Andújar   Bailén   Iznatoraf   *Garganta*   Hornos
108   Villacarrillo   *Embalse del Tranco*
41   32   93   S^a de Segura
Baeza   **Úbeda**   S^a de Cazorla   7
37   52   Cazorla   *1290*   △ 2381
Jaén   57   R. Guadiana Menor   Sagra
Martos   △ 2028   Cabañas
Río Guadajoz   166   Vélez Blanco
Alcalá la Real   93   MURCIA
Benamejí   S^a de Baza
Purullena
GRANADA   *1390*   **Guadix**
58
Loja   100   Lacalahorra   S^a de los Filabres
Archidona   73   860   113
62   *3398*   **Pico Veleta**   55   Sorbas   Mojácar
Alhama de Granada   SIERRA NEVADA   △ Mulhacén 3482   Carboneras
960   S^a del Chaparral   Lanjarón   Níjar   84
Cueva   Las Alpujarras
Málaga   75   Nerja   Motril   **Almería**
Almuñécar   Salobreña   Castell de Ferro   133   Aguadulce
   Cabo de Gata

| Costa del Sol |

Place names framed in brown: Alcázar or alcazaba
Place names underlined in brown: Castle, residence

Public gardens★ have been laid out inside the first perimeter: flowers, rivulets and streams where once there were fortifications. Excavations within the second wall, on the site of the royal apartments, have uncovered sculpture and specimens of Arabic calligraphy (now in the small museum). Immediately alongside is the former mosque, surmounted by a watch tower (Torre de la Vela). The keep with its forbiddingly thick walls was built by the Christians in the 15C.

The ramparts command the town, the surrounding hills and the sea.

Cathedral★. — *Open 10am to noon and 5.30 to 7.30pm.* The cathedral was built in 1524 to replace the former mosque. Continuing raids by Barbary pirates, however, dictated the construction of a fortified building — a rare necessity at such a date. In spite of its military character, the cathedral has two well designed portals and, at the east end, a delicately carved sunburst.

The spacious interior is homogeneous: the high altar and pulpits of marble and jasper marquetry are 18C, the choirstalls date from 1560, the jasper screen or *trascoro* with three alabaster statues is again 18C. The axial chapel contains the recumbent statue of the bishop who built the cathedral.

EXCURSIONS

The Almería countryside has a distinctive, desert-like appearance.

The road west. — *13km - 8 miles along the N 340.* From the road as it skirts the edge of the cliffs plunging steeply into the sea, you can look back over Almería, the bay, the sheltered harbour, and the fortress. **Aguadulce** beach appears like a vital outpost in this lonely stretch of the Costa del Sol.

The road northwest. — *71km - 44 miles along the N 340 and N 324.* The road goes through the Andarax depression, Almería's vegetable garden, up to Guadix. The landscape of hills cut by great gorges is grandiose but monotonous except where a small green valley, *vega,* planted with lemon trees, orange trees, or vines suddenly relieves the scene. The vines produce a large sweet grape over a long season - it is the Spanish custom on 31 December for everyone to eat a grape at each stroke of the midnight chime.

The road northeast★. — *55km - 34 miles along the N 340.* A tableland of sand dunes stretches for miles between Benahadux and Tabernas — it was used as the setting for the film *Lawrence of Arabia.*

Beyond Tabernas, the land is red and sterile, providing material for pottery making in the surrounding villages. **Sorbas** has an amazing **site★** as its houses cling to a cliff, circled below by a loop in the river course.

Níjar. — *34km - 21 miles to the northeast.* The old village, carries on the traditional craft of *tela de trapo* or the weaving of thick coverings or hangings in pale colours. The wefts in the process are made of strips of already woven material *(trapo).*

33

ANDÚJAR (Jaén)

Michelin map **446** fold 8 — Pop 34 946

Andújar still possesses many old houses and chapels dating back to the 15 and 16C. The region, with Martos *(some 55km - 34 miles south)* is the major olive growing centre.

Bailén, to the east, gave its name to the battle of 1808 in which the Spanish General Castaños forced the surrender of General Dupont - the first victory against Napoleon's forces in the Peninsular War.

St Michael's*. — The ochre coloured stone Renaissance church dominates the Plaza de España. Inside a massive carved wood **door*** marks the end of the former 17C *coro* or chancel; covering the intervening area is a carved wood ceiling surrounded by figures of the prophets. At the end on the north side is a chapel grille dating from Bartolomé's time *(p 18)*.

St Mary's. — *Open 11am to 1pm and 6 to 9pm; closed 15 November to 10 April.* The church of the Martyr's Square (Plaza de los Mártires) can be easily distinguished by its clock tower. El Greco's painting *Christ in the Garden of Olives* hangs in a north chapel, closed by a fine Bartolomé **grille***. An *Assumption of the Virgin* by Pacheco can be seen in the north absidal chapel.

St Bartholomew's (San Bartolomé). — 16C. Beautiful sacristy door.

EXCURSION

Virgen de la Cabeza. — *32km - 20 miles north. Take the Las Viñas road by the Hotel del Val.* There are good **views**** from the corniche road. The Virgin appeared to a shepherd on an August night in 1227 on this rocky head *-cabeza-* where not long afterwards a commemorative chapel was erected. In the 16C this was replaced by a monastery. Four centuries later, civil guards, their families and a thousand Nationalists sought refuge on the lonely rock spike where they were besieged from September 1936 to May 1937; when they surrendered the sanctuary was in ruins. It is now a popular pilgrimage at the end of April *(p 24)*.

ANTEQUERA (Málaga)

Michelin map **446** south of folds 18 and 19 — Pop 35 171

The white walled town, a small industrial centre at the heart of a fertile valley, successfully integrates old and new buildings: paved alleyways, windows covered with wrought iron grilles and its many churches help to preserve its atmosphere, the St Sebastian belfry with its fine brick Mudejar decoration, its individuality.

Castle. — This was the first fortress captured by the Christians in the reconquest of the Kingdom of Granada (1410). It could not be held, however, as the position was encircled by the Moors. The towers command a fine **view*** across the plain.

Sta María. — Go through a 16C arch onto the Plaza Alta beside the castle. At the far end stands the church dating back to 1514 which has a façade decorated with cleverly composed geometrical motifs. Inside, note the attractively decorated Mudejar ceiling.

El Carmen. — *Closed for restoration.* The interior decoration of the church is entirely baroque: the *artesonado* ceiling, the wall scrollwork and altarpieces.

EXCURSIONS

The dolmens* (Cuevas). — *On leaving town, turn left off the Granada road.* These prehistoric constructions of 2500 BC take the form of funerary chambers beneath tumuli.

The Menga and Viera Chambers. — *Open 10am to 1pm and 3 to 6pm (2 to 5pm in winter); closed Wednesdays; 50pts.* Both chambers are constructed of Cyclopean size boulders. The larger Menga Chamber is oblong and is divided by a line of pillars; the Viera Chamber has a narrow opening.

The Romeral Dolmen. — *Ask for the key at the sugar refinery, 4km - 2 miles along the Granada road. Turn a sharp left on leaving the factory then take the first path to the left after the railway line (50 yds). Lightswitch.* The dolmen is paved inside with large stones similar to the Menga and Viera Chambers but the walls are constructed of small flat stones so laid as to produce a trapezoidal section in the corridor and domes over the chambers.

El Torcal*. — *16km - 10 miles south. Leave Antequera by the Málaga road; bear right after 12km - 7 1/2 miles for El Torcal.* Paths lead to the chaos of strangely shaped rocks *(red arrows: 3 hours; yellow: 1 1/2 hours).* For information apply at the El Torcal Refuge. The most monumental group of strangely shaped rocks can be seen near the hotel.

Antequera to Málaga road*. — *62km - 39 miles south along the N 342, N 331, C 340 and C 345.* The pleasant well laid out road, always within sight of majestic hills, affords splendid **views**** beyond the Lion Pass (Puerto del León, 960m - 3 150ft) of the Mediterranean, Málaga and its harbour.

ARACENA (Huelva)

Michelin map **446** fold 3 — Pop 6 328

Aracena is an attractive town built in tiers on a hillside crowned by the remains of a Templars' castle; the tower abutting the church is a former minaret and is decorated on the north side in the style of the Giralda of Seville *(p 56)*.

The Marvellous Caves** (Gruta de las Maravillas). — *Guided tours (1 hour) 10am to 6pm; 250pts.*

Underground rivers below the castle hollowed out these vast caves which mirror their size in limpid pools. Some of the chambers are very narrow but high, as they follow the line of rock faults. They are known as the Marvellous Caves for the variety and beauty of their concretions - draperies, pipes and coral formations coloured by iron and copper oxide or brilliant white calcite crystal as in the first chamber discovered and known as the Snow Well - El Pozo de la Nieve.

■ ARACENA SIERRA★

35km - 22 miles south. The western part of the Sierra Morena is refreshingly green, the cork oak and eucalyptus being especially pleasant; the road from Aracena passes through a dense pinewood to reach Minas de Riotinto which lies near the Campofrío reservoir.

Approaching **Minas de Riotinto,** the opencast pyrite and copper mines come into view — the Sierra Morena produces 53% of the copper and the totality of the pyrites mined in Spain. The N 435, as it goes south overlooks the winding course of the upper Odiel River.

Serrano ham, which comes from this area, especially that from Jabugo, is considered a delicacy in Spain.

ARCOS DE LA FRONTERA ★ (Cádiz)

Michelin map 446 fold 28 — Pop 24 902

Arcos has a remarkable **site★★** at the top of a rock spike, circled at its foot by the Guadalete. The best views are from the narrow road which links the Bornos and El Bosque roads and crosses the dam to the east of the town. The old town, right at the top of the rock, stands close against the grimly crenellated castle walls and those of the two churches. The Holy Week processions are known for their fervour.

Go up the narrow alleys to the Plaza del Cabildo and park the car.

The **view★** from the main square, one side of which overhangs the deep river cleft, extends across the olive groves on the plain to the green waters of the Guadalete.

The south face and tall square belfry of **Sta María,** one of the town's two churches, stands on the square; the **west face★** is a good example of Plateresque. The Callejón de las Monjas leads off north from the square beneath the church's flying buttresses; other alleys pass below an arch, before an attractive gateway or afford a glimpse of the plain. **St Peter's** with its 16 and 18C tower stands at the far end of the cliff.

BAEZA ★★ (Jaén)

Michelin map 446 fold 9 — Pop 14 799

Baeza, which stands peacefully surrounded by olive groves on the borders of Andalusia and La Mancha, was once a prominent frontier town. Numerous seignorial mansions and other edifices of golden stone give an idea of its days as a *taifa* capital *(p 38),* of its importance as the first town to be reconquered in Andalusia (1227) and its position as a march in the Kingdom of Castile until the 15C. Peace allowed the city to develop, intellectual interests to emerge: in 1595 a university was founded (disbanded in 19C), in 1551 a printing press was established.

■ ARCHITECTURAL CENTRE★★ *time: 1 hour*

Route marked on plan.

Lions' Square★ (Plaza de los Leones) (17). — The **fountain** at the centre, from which the square gets its name, is an antique in a new setting; the **former abattoir (A),** on the left, is a building of noble appearance considering its function (1550-1962); the blason over the first floor portico is the imperial coat of arms. The decorative windows and medallions on the **Casa del Pópulo (B)** (former court), at the end of the square are Plateresque. The six doors opened on six notaries' offices; court hearings were on the first floor. A quarter circle balcony projects onto the **Jaén Gate (C),** which, with the Villalar Arch were dedicated to Charles V.

The Jaén Gate was erected to mark the emperor's passage on his way to Seville for his marriage to Isabel of Portugal on 12 March 1526; the **Villalar Arch,** was dedicated as a gesture of submission to the king after his suppression, in 1521, of the ''Comuneros'' *(p 245)* which the town had supported.

Plaza Santa María (22). — On the left the walls of the 1660 Seminary are covered with inscriptions — the ancient custom having been to inscribe in bull's blood one's name and date on graduation. Behind the **Santa María fountain,** a triumphal arch adorned with statuesque male figures, is the Gothic façade of the **Casas Consistoriales Altas (F)** emblasoned, between two windows, with the arms of Juana the Mad and Philip the Fair, parents of the Emperor Charles V (King Charles I of Spain).

BAEZA		Córdoba (Puerta de)	9
		Gaspar Becerra	12
San Francisco	20	General Quadros	14
		Generalísimo (Pl. del)	15
Agúa	2	José M. Cortés	16
Baldomero Rubio	3	Leones (Pl. de los)	17
Barbacana	4	Matilla	18
Callejón	5	San Felipe (Cuesta)	19
Cardenal Benavides (Pasaje)	6	San Gil (Cuesta de)	21
Compañía	7	Santa María (Plaza de)	22
Conde de Romanones	8	Ubeda (Puerta)	25

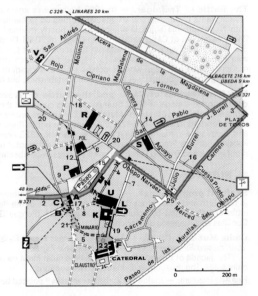

BAEZA★★

Cathedral. — The **interior★** was almost entirely remodelled by Vandelvira and his followers between 1570 and 1593. Some chapels are outstanding: the Gold Chapel has a delicate Italianate relief; St James', a fine antique setting; St Joseph's which follows, is flanked by caryatids. Opposite, framed with scrollwork and angels' heads, is the graceful door to the sacristy; closing the first bay in the nave is a monumental iron grille by Bartolomé; at the end of the sacristy, behind another beautiful grille, a gold and silver monstrance (1668) and, at the transept, a pulpit of painted beaten metal (1580). The cloistral arches are from the mosque.

Jabalquinto Palace★ (K). — The palace's **façade,** a perfect example of the Isabeline style, is best seen in the morning. The **patio,** constructed in about 1600, is of more sober style, the only informal feature being the two lions guarding the approach to the great baroque stairway.

Opposite the palace is the Romanesque Church of **Santa Cruz** (L), the only one to remain of those constructed immediately after the town's reconquest.

Former University (U). — Built between 1568 and 1593 with a plain façade and elegant *patio*. A fine Mudejar ceiling can be seen in the large amphitheatre.

Former Corn Exchange (Alhóndiga) (N). — A frontage of arches and porticoes (1554).

Casas Consistoriales Bajas (P). — The building was erected in 1703 as a gallery for officials attending celebrations held in the square.

Town Hall★ (H). — The façade of the former prison stands transformed by magnificent Plateresque windows, armorial bearings and a wide cornice embellished with portrait medallions.

■ ADDITIONAL SIGHTS

St Andrew's★ (V). — Delicate Plateresque sculpture ornaments the south entrance. The sacristy contains a group of nine Gothic **paintings★**.

Ruins of St Francis' (R). — Only the vast transept and apse, with majestic stone altarpieces, sculptures in themselves, remain to give an idea of the beautiful 16C church.

Montemar Palace (or Palace of the Counts of Garcíez) (S). — Beautiful Gothic windows and an almost Plateresque style *patio* adorn this early 16C nobleman's residence.

CÁDIZ ★ ℙ

Michelin map **446** fold 27 — Pop 157 766

The age old city's bastion **site★** on a rock platform above the waves and still girdled, in places, by mediaeval ramparts, is best viewed from the sea. It is attached to the mainland by a sand isthmus just wide enough to carry the road but now being developed as a holiday beach and lined by hotels. The town, so long the guardian of the deep, well sheltered bay is, today, Spain's major shipyard and naval base. **Rota,** on the north bank, is an American naval air base. Fishing and local saltpans at **San Fernando** also provide employment. On one side of the isthmus lies a long stretch of sandy beach bordered by hotels; this is Cádiz's seaside resort.

A 3000 year old port. — Cádiz' safe inner harbour attracted first, Phoenician merchants from Tyre who founded the city as a trading post in 1100 BC, then Carthaginians, Romans, under who the city grew rich, Visigoths and Moors, who used it as a port of entry. The discovery of America in 1492, the ensuing trade and its position as headquarters of the Spanish treasure fleets soon made it the wealthiest port in western Europe and consequently the favourite point of attack for Barbary corsairs and enemies of Spain such as **Sir Francis Drake,** who in 1587 burned the ships at anchor in the bay, that Philip II intended to send as an **Armada** against England; **Essex** and **Howard,** who in 1596 sacked the town and destroyed 40 merchant vessels and 13 warships at anchor. Rebuilt, the city repelled subsequent British attacks in 1626, 1656 and 1702 before going on to acquire monopoly trading rights with Spanish America (1720-1765) and again becoming vastly wealthy. The end of the century saw the beginning of the blockade by the British of Napoleon's ports including Cádiz (February 1797-April 1798) and bombardment by Nelson (1800).

The Battle of Trafalgar. — In 1805 Nelson was again off Cádiz with the Spanish and French fleets under Admiral Villeneuve, bottled up in the harbour. Villeneuve, out of favour with Napoleon, his ships ill-equipped and poorly manned but outnumbering the British, finally sailed out of Cádiz harbour on the night of 20-21 October. At 5.50am the French and Spanish vessels were sighted against the dark sky off Cape Trafalgar; at 11.35 the signal was hoisted. "England expects...; at 11.50 the French fired the opening broadside; by 4.30pm victory had been won, Napoleon's hope of invading England had been quashed for ever, England's supremacy at sea had been established, but Nelson was dead.

The Constitution of Cádiz and the Battle of Trocadero. — During the French occupation and siege of 1812 Spanish patriots convened the Cortes which promulgated the famous liberal constitution of March 1812. This was promptly rejected by Ferdinand VII on his restoration in 1814. In 1820, the town rose under **Riego** to re-establish the constitution and succeeded in maintaining it for three years. In 1823 Ferdinand was invited to Cádiz and imprisoned. The French, however, came to his aid, capturing the Trocadero headland in a night attack and freeing Ferdinand who then resumed absolute rule.

■ SIGHTS

Seafront promenades★. — The south and west promenades look out over the sea, those to the north and east across the bay to the far shore of the Bay of Puerto de Santa María, the latter are also lined with colourful public **gardens★** (Parque Genovés, Alameda Marqués de Comillas and Alameda de Apodaca).

Cádiz Museum (CY M). — *Temporary access by the Calle Antonio López. Open 10am to 2pm; closed Saturdays, Sundays and holidays; 75pts.*
The façade of this building overlooks the quiet Plaza de Mina with its gardens shaded by palm trees. The museum is divided into two sections:

Fine Arts Museum. — Inside are **Zurbarán canvases★** painted between 1630 and 1640.

Museum of Archaeology and Art. — Phoenician exhibits confirm the town's antiquity; note especially the 5C BC sarcophagus discovered during excavations in 1980.

Historical Museum (BY M¹). — *Open weekdays 9am to 1pm and 5 to 8pm (4 to 7pm 1 October to 31 May); weekends 10am to 2pm; closed Mondays and holidays.*
Outstanding **model★** in ivory and mahogany of the town in Charles III's reign (18C).

St Philip Neri (BY A). — *Open during service. If closed apply at the presbytery in the south side aisle.* It was in the oval shaped interior of this church that the Cortes gathered in 1812 to proclaim the constitution. Above the altar is a Virgin by Murillo.

Cathedral (CZ B). — *Restoration in progress. Enter through museum. The cathedral, museum and crypt are open 10am to 2.30pm; closed Sundays and holidays; 125pts.* The church, to designs by Vicente Acero, took from 1720 to 1838 to erect. The **collection of plate★★** in the **museum** includes a processional cross by Enrique de Arfe, a monumental silver tabernacle, and the more recent "million monstrance", so called since its decoration is said to comprise nearly a million jewels. **Manuel de Falla,** the musician whose music was very much inspired by Andalusian folklore *(p 21)*, is buried in the crypt (1876-1946).

CARMONA (Sevilla)

Michelin map 446 fold 16 — Pop 22 779

Beneath the ancient city walls which rise up on the edge of the plateau overlooking the vast cereal growing plain of Guadalquivir in 206 BC, Scipio defeated the armies of Hasdrubal, the Carthaginian and Massinissa, the Numidian.
The **Seville Gate,** its double Moorish arch a striking contrast to the baroque tower of St Peter's Church opposite, opens onto the old town where every white walled alley has a stone gateway leading to the *patio* of a former noble residence.

Plaza San Fernando. — The square is lined by 17 and 18C houses.

Town Hall. — *At the beginning of the Calle de San Salvador.* There is a large Roman mosaic in the *patio* of the town hall *(apply to the usher)*.

Santa María. — *Calle Martín López.* The church is preceded by the old mosque's ablutionary courtyard; the interior is covered by lofty 15 and 16C white **vaulting★.**
The Calle Santa María de Gracia continues to the **Córdoba Gate** which was built into the Roman wall in the 17C diametrically opposite the Seville Gate. It overlooks the plain.

Santa Clara Convent. — In the church, the walls of the nave are hung with portraits of 17C women.

Roman Necropolis. — *Access to the site is indicated on the road to Seville. Open 9am (10am Sundays) to 2pm and 4 to 6pm; closed Sunday afternoons and Mondays all day; 150pts. The ticket is also valid for the Archaeological Museum in Seville.* Some 250 of the 800 tombs have been excavated. Most comprise a vaulted funerary chamber with niches for the urns, surmounted now infrequently, by a mausoleum.

The Elephant Tomb. — Three dining rooms with running water and a kitchen have given rise to the belief that priests must have performed a banqueting ritual. The statue of an elephant at the tomb entrance is perhaps a memento of the Carthaginians passage.

The Servilia Tomb. — The tomb, the size of a patrician villa has a central piscina surrounded by a double portico. At the end of the entrance passage, the funerary chamber is covered by vaulting resting on buttresses designed as ogive arches.

CAZORLA Sierra ★★ (Jaén)

Michelin map **446** folds 9 and 10

The Baetic ranges in this area tower more than 2 000m - 6 562ft above the surrounding plain. Springs rise in abundance, among them one which eventually becomes Andalusia's greatest river, the Guadalquivir. At first the stream flows northeastwards before, at length, finding a passage west and finally south to the Atlantic. Altitude and humidity produce an upland Mediterranean type vegetation — thyme, lavender, etc.

The Cazorla Sierra is a game reserve. The forest, the most extensive protected woodland area in Andalusia, is open to the public along marked paths *(the offices of the Agencia del Medio Ambiente-AMA of the Junta de Andalucía distribute maps showing the paths).*

NORTH TO SOUTH ACROSS THE SIERRA

110 km - 68 miles including the ascent to the parador; 4 hours along winding roads.

9km - 6 miles north of Villacarrillo the road enters the Guadalquivir **gorges★**, from which it emerges at the Tranco Dam, which controls Andalusia's biggest reservoir; this, in turn, provides water for the irrigation of the Úbeda region. When you come within sight of the picturesque **setting★** of the perched village of **Hornos,** turn right into a road which skirts the lake and from which you will get good **views★★** of the mountains and, at certain times of the day, of deer drinking at the water's edge.

The Sierra del Pozo can be seen on the horizon.

Road up to the parador★. — *8km - 5 miles.* The uphill road through the pines leads to the *parador* which is popular with hunters who favour its isolated position.

From a belvedere a little further on there is a good **view★★** of the Upper Valley of the Guadalquivir. An impressive mountain crest section precedes the Las Palomas Pass (1 290m - 4 232ft) which marks the dividing line between fertile green mountainsides and ochre hills covered by acre upon acre of olive groves.

La Iruela. — Turn right in the village square for the **belvedere road★** *(an unsurfaced but car worthy forest track)* from where, after three successive viewpoints, there are fine **views★★** over the mountain circus.

Cazorla. — The town's steep and sometimes stepped alleys are full of character as are its two large squares, framed by old houses.

CÓRDOBA ★★★ P

Michelin map **446** fold 6 — Pop 284 737

See map of the built-up area in the current Michelin Red Guide España Portugal

Córdoba stands at the halfway point on the right bank of the Guadalquivir where the mines, ranches and farmlands of the Sierra de Córdoba plateau to the north meet the wheatlands and olive groves of the southerly Campiña plains. The city owes its fame to the brilliance of the civilisations which it has twice fostered and which each time raised it to the position of capital. It could live on its past but it has chosen to develop modern industries on its outskirts and maintain its longstanding crafts of silver filigree and tooled leatherwork in their traditional setting in the heart of the city. Mid-May is festival time, with competitions in decking crosses, *patios,* windows and balconies, streets and squares with flowers until the end of the month when the fair brings celebrations in Andalusian costume and *flamenco* dancing.

Between Montilla and Lucena, approximately 50km - 30 miles south of Córdoba lies a wine region where the limestone soil and the dry and sunny climate produces a very sweet grape. The area, known as **Montilla-Moriles,** produces excellent wine and spirits (their sherry can be compared with that of Jerez: *p 50).* The blending of the grape is done by the *solera* system which this region maintains it invented.

The Roman town. — Córdoba, capital of Baetica, was the birthplace of **Seneca the Rhetorician** (55 BC - 39 AD), his son, **Lucius Seneca** (4 BC - 65 AD), philosopher and praeceptor to Nero who made him consul and subsequently ordered him to commit suicide, **Lucanus** (39-65 AD) companion to Nero in his student days and author of the poem *Pharsilia* which recounts the war between Caesar and Pompey.

The early Christian period was marked by the episcopacy of **Ossius** (257-359), counsellor to Constantine, protagonist of orthodoxy against Arianism and reorganiser of the Church in Spain.

The Córdoba Caliphate. — Emirs from the Damascus Caliphate established themselves in Córdoba as early as 719. In 756 **Abdu'r-Rahman I,** sole survivor of the Umaiyads of Damascus who had been annihilated by the Abbasids, arrived to found the dynasty which was to rule over Muslim Spain for 3 centuries and bring untold prosperity and fame to Córdoba; in 929 **Abdu'r-Rahman III** proclaimed himself Caliph and Spain independent. In the 10C a university was founded which won high renown. On the accession, in 976, of the feeble Hisham II, power fell into the hands of his minister, the ruthless but remarkable **Al Mansur** (the Victorious); his descendants, however, in spite of support from the Berbers, failed to prevent Al Andalus fragmenting into small warring kingdoms, the **reinos de taifas.** Córdoba itself, in 1070, became incorporated in the Kingdom of Seville under which it remained until it was reconquered by the Christians in 1236.

Political decline in no way diminished intellectual life, however. There lived in the city from 1126 to 1198 the Moor, **Averroes,** a universal scholar — physicist, astrologer, mathematician, doctor and philosopher — who, although he was prevented from teaching by the doctrinaire Yacoub Al Mansur *(p 55),* who opposed his theories, did much to bring the learning of Aristotle to the west. Averroes' contemporary was a Jew, **Maimonides** (1135-1204) who was famed for his learning in medicine, theology and philosophy.

It was in Córdoba that Columbus finally obtained Queen Isabel's commission for the voyage west which led to the discovery of the New World.

The city's prosperity waned from the Reconquest to the 16 and 17C when Córdoba leatherwork, embossed, tooled and coloured, became the fashion for wall and seat coverings. Among the city's sons are the **Gran Capitán,** Gonzalo Fernández de Córdoba (1453-1515), general to the Catholic Monarchs who distinguished himself in the Reconquest and afterwards in Italy where he captured the Kingdom of Naples (1504) and **Luis de Góngora** (1561-1627), major descriptive poet known for his love of colour, sonority and word play.

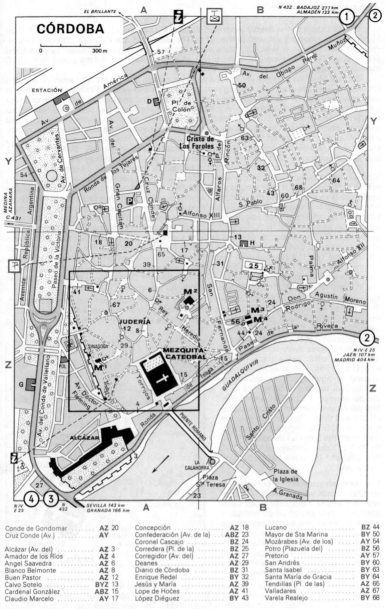

CÓRDOBA

0   300 m

N 432 : BADAJOZ 277 km
ALMADÉN 133 km

EL BRILLANTE

MEDINA AZAHARA
C 431

ESTACIÓN

Cristo de
Los Faroles

JUDERÍA

SINAGOGA

MEZQUITA-
CATEDRAL

ALCÁZAR

LA CALAHORRA

Plaza St Teresa

GUADALQUIVIR

PUENTE ROMANO

N IV-E 25
JAÉN 107 km
MADRID 404 km

N IV E 25

SEVILLA 143 km
GRANADA 166 km

N 432

■ SIGHTS

Mosque★★★ (Mezquita-Catedral) (AZ). — *Open 10.30am to 1.30pm and 4 to 7pm (3.30 to 5.30pm 1 October to 31 March); closed 1 May, during the festival in May and 25 December; 200pts.*

History, in superimposing two faiths on one site and erecting two oratories, one within the other, has produced a heterogeneous edifice where each element must be admired separately.

The Mosque. — *Illustration p 13.* The forest of pillars, the red and white Moorish arches extending apparently endlessly in all directions, are unique but the overall plan is the traditional Muslim one of a crenellated square perimeter enclosing a forecourt with a basin for ritual ablution, a covered gallery and a hall for prayer in which the wall facing Mecca, the **qiblah,** is hollowed out in one place in the form of a sacred niche or **mihrab** (2). In Córdoba the perimeter is entered through the later, 14C, Mudejar **Pardon Door** which is faced with bronze.

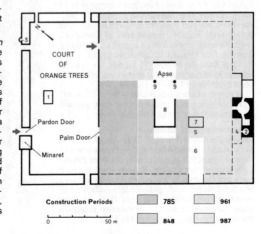

COURT OF ORANGE TREES

Apse

Pardon Door

Palm Door

Minaret

Construction Periods

0   50 m

785   961
848   987

39

CÓRDOBA★★★

A small chapel to the deeply venerated **Virgin of the Lanterns** (3) has also been built since Muslim times, abutting the wall to the north. The courtyard, the Court of Orange Trees — Patio de los Naranjos — which contains the Al Mansur basin (1) is overlooked by the **minaret** *(267 steps, 10pts; fine views),* from the top of which the **muezzin** called the prayer. In the 17C the minaret was enveloped in a baroque tower.

The first Muslims to arrive in Córdoba were content to share a place of worship with the Christians. Soon, however, increasing numbers determined Abdu'r-Rahman I (756-788) to purchase their part of the site from the Christians. He razed and built the church in one year (785), saving only the Roman and Visigothic marble pillars which had previously been taken by Christians from even earlier buildings. These pillars, he incorporated in the splendid mosque, which became famous for an architectural innovation: the superimposition of two tiers of arches to give added height and spaciousness. This feature was repeated by successive rulers as they enlarged the mosque: Abdu'r-Rahman II in 848; El Hakam II in 961 and Al Mansur who, in 987, nearly doubled the area to give it its present size.

It was the Caliph, El Hakam II, mindful of his capital's prestige, who bestowed upon the mosque its greatest jewel, at the end of the main aisle he built the superb, gleaming **mihrab★★★**, preceding it with a triple **maksourah** (4) or enclosure reserved for the caliph. The enclosure is roofed by three ribbed domes which rest on a most unusual series of apparently interweaving multilobed arches, as strikingly decorative as are the cupolas themselves which are faced with mosaics against a background of gold. The first bay, a little before the maksourah and also built by El Hakam II, is constructed in the same way (**Villaviciosa Chapel** or Lucernario) (5). Decoration throughout adds to the richness of the architecture. Conversion of the building to Christian use brought certain physical alterations: the aisles were walled off from the court; a few columns were removed and pointed arches substituted for the Moorish ones in the 13C when the first cathedral was constructed (6) — fortunately nothing was done which destroyed the mosque's vistas. Finally the **Chapel Royal** (7) was decorated in the 14C with Mudejar stucco which harmonised with the whole.

The cathedral. — In the 16C the cathedral canons desired more sumptuous surroundings. They began by cutting away the centre of the mosque roof to erect loftier vaulting. The Emperor Charles V, was far from pleased with the result "You have destroyed something unique", he said, "to build something commonplace". In the search for grandeur and richness every style had been employed: Gothic in the transept and apse (1523-1547); Renaissance for the decorative figures and medallions in the apsidal vaulting (1560); Italian in the dense stucco crowded with cherubim which decorates the nave vaulting (1598) and the coffered dome over the transept (1600). Additional enrichments are the baroque **choirstalls★★** (8) by Pedro Duque Cornejo (*c* 1750) and two **pulpits★★** (9) of marble, jasper and mahogany.

Old Jewish quarter★★ (Judería). — Narrow streets, white walls spilled over with brilliant flowers, doors half open onto cool green *patios,* delicate window grilles, a lively crowd, bars where a group of Córdobans may burst into song to the accompaniment of a guitar, snapping fingers or sharp handclaps — such are the features of the old Jewish quarter northwest of the cathedral.

[Map: JUDERÍA — 0 100 m, showing streets including Pl. San Juan, Pl. Angel de Torres, Leiva Aguilar, Averroés, Pl. C.ª Salazar, Pl. de Maimónides, Calleja de las Flores, MEZQUITA CATEDRAL, PUERTA DEL PUENTE, PUERTA DE ALMODÓVAR, and labels A, B, C, F, M¹, M²]

Synagogue (A). — *To visit apply to the caretaker. Open 10am to 2pm and 4 to 7pm; closed Mondays and Sunday and holiday afternoons.* Córdoba and Toledo synagogues are the only two major synagogues which remain in Spain today. This one dates back to the 14C and consists of a small square roomwith a balcony on one side for the women. The upper parts of the walls are covered in Mudejar stucco.

Not far away is the **Zoco** or souk (**B**), where craftsmen work around a large *patio* which on summer evenings is gay with *flamenco* dancers.

Municipal Museum (M¹). — *Open 9.30am to 1.30pm and 5 to 8pm (4 to 7pm 1 October to 31 May); 100pts.* The museum, in a former Andalusian mansion and devoted almost exclusively to bullfighting, includes mementoes of Córdoba's most famous matadors: Lagartijo, Manolete, Guerrita, Machaquito, El Cordobés (*p 25*).

The **Casa del Indiano** (F) façade, its ground floor in Mudejar style and first in Isabeline, is a good example of 15C city architecture.

From the **Calleja de las Flores** (Alley of Flowers), a picturesque small street further east, you will get a unique view of the cathedral tower.

Archaeological Museum★ (M²). — *Open 9am to 2pm and 6 to 8pm (5 to 7pm 1 October to 30 April); closed Mondays and weekday holidays; 150pts.* The museum is in the Páez Palace, a Renaissance mansion. Several Iberian stone lions can be seen in the *patios,* Roman mosaics and pavements with geometric motifs in coloured marble inside. The first floor galleries trace the development of Andalusian sculpture and decorative arts from the 8 to 15C.

Calleja de Las Flores

Alcázar★ (AZ). — *Open 9.30am to 1.30pm and 5 to 8pm (4 to 7pm 1 October to 31 May); 100pts. The gardens are floodlit in summer from 10 to 12pm.*

The Alcázar of the Umaiyads stood at the centre of magnificent gardens facing the mosque on the site of what is now the bishopric. The present buildings were erected in the early 14C by Alfonso XI.

Of this palace there remain attractively cool Moorish *patios* with ornamental basins and pools, baths and a few rooms with Roman **mosaics★**, also a 3C **sarcophagus★**. From the towers the **view** looks down on the gardens, the Guadalquivir and the Roman Bridge with the Calahorra Tower built to defend its approach. The **gardens★**, in Arabic style, are terraced and refreshed with pools and fountains, and cypresses. The vegetable garden, still cultivated, dates back to before the caliphs.

Plazuela del Potro (BZ 56). — On Colt Square, named after its fountain's statue, stands the inn *(posada)* Cervantes described in *Don Quixote*. In the inn are displayed Cordovan leather and silver.

On the far side are the **Julio Romero de Torres Museum** (BZ M³) with works by the early 20C Cordoban who painted portraits of beautiful women and the **Fine Arts Museum** (BZ M⁴) with a few paintings by Goya and Carreño.

Christ of the Lanterns (Cristo de Los Faroles) (ABY). — The Calvary surrounded by wrought iron lanterns in a silent, austere square, is well known throughout Spain.

Corredera Square (BZ 25). — The 17C arcaded square was formerly used for bullfighting.

EXCURSIONS

Medina Azahara★. — *Leave Córdoba by the C 431 (west on the town plan). After 8km - 5 miles bear right into a road (3km - 2 miles) which ends on an esplanade. Open 10am to noon and 5.30 to 7pm (3.30 to 5pm 1 October to 31 May); closed Tuesdays; 75pts.*

The excavations have recreated this delightful palace built by Abdu'r Rahman III (936: construction began). Hardly had the caliphs had time, however, to complete the undertaking before it was sacked in 1013 by the Berbers, grown angry after aiding Al Mansur's descendants who had not granted them power as expected. The edifice was a veritable township extending upwards in three tiers - a mosque below, gardens at the centre, and an alcázar, at the top of which two wings have been restored, allowing the incredible floral decoration which once covered walls, arches and capitals, gradually to be reconstituted; whereas displayed on the floor are admirably carved stucco and marble pieces.

The **view★** from the mound above the palace extends along the Guadalquivir Valley.

Las Ermitas. — *13km - 8 miles on the El Brillante road (northwest of the town plan).* As far back as the 6C, hermitages stood on this site. Lovely views of Córdoba.

COSTA DE LA LUZ (Huelva and Cádiz)
Michelin map **446** folds 13, 14, 15, 27 and 28

The Spanish coast from the Portuguese frontier to the Strait of Gibraltar is edged with beaches of dazzling white sand which are cooled by the mildest of sea breezes. The atmosphere is translucent: it is known as the Coast of Light.

THE HUELVA COAST
From Ayamonte to Nuestra Señora del Rocío Sanctuary
150km - 93 miles - allow 1 day

A vast sanded up area backs the Gulf of Cádiz from the mouth of the Guadiana to that of the Guadalquivir. Sand bars, formed at the river mouths, protect small saltmarshes; sand dunes, anchored by pines and eucalyptus trees fringe the endless beaches.

Ayamonte. — Ayamonte, a picturesquely alleyed fishing port at the mouth of the Guadiana, bustles with cars crossing into Portugal *(ferry crossings about every 1/2 hour; time: 10 minutes; fare: 424pts for car and driver and 50pts for each passenger).* The *parador* on the hill looks out over the estuary and the plain behind the town.

Isla Canela. — *7km - 4 miles.* A new and elegant resort with a good sand beach.

Isla Cristina. — The old village is on a peninsula attached to the mainland by a 3km - 2 mile long road across the saltmarshes. The villagers live off fishing and salting fish. There are a few hotels on the beach.

La Antilla; Punta Umbría. — Of these two new towns, the second with its villas surrounded by gardens, is the largest.

Huelva. — *Description p 49.*

Mazagón. — Mazagón ends at a *parador* which overlooks the sea from a somewhat isolated site.

Torre de la Higuera. — The resort has been built on the edge of the **Doñana National Park,** (Parque Nacional de Doñana) a vast reserve for flora and fauna amidst the dunes and saltmarshes, where, rare birds (imperial eagle for example) of Europe and Africa and other almost extinct species such as the lynx find shelter *(to visit apply in advance to Cooperativa Marismas del Rocío. Parque Nacional de Doñana. El Rocío. Almonte-Huelva. ℡ (955) 43 04 32; 1200pts.*

Nuestra Señora del Rocío Sanctuary. — Famous for its Whitsun *romería (p 24).*

THE CÁDIZ COAST
From Sanlúcar de Barrameda to Tarifa
237km - 147 miles - allow 1 day

South of the Guadalquivir the landscape is more regular, held by Secondary and Tertiary subsoils which, however, emerge frequently to dominate the coastline. North of Cádiz the road runs through a countryside of large, rich vineyards; south it traverses Baetic ranges and foothills to reach Tarifa.

Sanlúcar de Barrameda. — The fishing port of Sanlúcar is the home town of Manzanilla, a sherry matured like Jerez "Fino" *(p 50)* but which the sea air gives a special savour. The vast cellars *(bodegas)* are in the old quarter of the town. The **Church of Sta María de la O** on the Plaza de la Paz has a beautiful Mudejar **door★**; that of **Sto Domingo★**, in the lower quarter on the Calles Ancha and del Mar corner, has golden stone walls crowned with a stone balustrade, a well composed portal, perfectly allied to its interior coffered vaulting, and the generally noble proportions of a Renaissance building.

Chipiona. — Quiet family resort with a good sand beach.

Rota. — The old town inside the ramparts has an almost mediaeval atmosphere in the streets leading to the castle and the church. Beautiful beaches extend northwards.

El Puerto de Santa María. — Fishing (the harbour is on the north bank), sherry shipping (from the south bank) and the cellars of a well-known sherry make up the town's principal activities. A palm shaded promenade, overlooking the quays along the north bank, leads to St Mark's Castle, once the seat of the great Dukes of Medinaceli.

Cádiz★. — *Description p 36.*

Chiclana de la Frontera. — A typical Andalusian fishing village; immense beaches.

Medina Sidonia. — Seen from this hill top town are fine views of the surrounding country-side. The village includes a Gothic church, Sta María, a ducal palace and seignorial mansions.

South of Cádiz there are good beaches at **Barrosa** and **Conil de la Frontera.**

Vejer de la Frontera. — Vejer is one of the prettiest "white towns" of Andalusia. It stands perched on a rock spike, a favourite habitat of storks; the approach is along a *corniche* road from the south. There is a **view★** from the car park at the north end of the town, down into the winding Barbate Valley.

Barbate de Franco. — A large fishing village (canning factories).

Tarifa. — *Description p 59.*

COSTA DEL SOL ★★ (Málaga, Granada, Almería)

Michelin map ▨▨▨ folds 29 to 35

The Sunshine Coast extends along Spain's Mediterranean shore from Tarifa in the Strait of Gibraltar to Cape Gata, east of Almería. Protected from the extremes of the inland climate by the Serranía de Ronda and the Sierra Nevada, it enjoys mild winters (12 ºC – 54 ºF), hot summers (26 ºC – 79 ºF) and sufficient rain (mostly in winter and spring) to allow subtropical crops to grow in the small alluvial plains. The small beaches, narrow strips of grey sand and shingle, are eroded moraine from the nearby mountains.

THE WESTERN COASTLINE★★
From Estepona to Málaga — *100km · 62 miles — about 1/2 day*

Large private houses, set in their own gardens and with such amenities as pools and tennis courts, have recently begun to be built on the strip of land of varying width between the mountains and the sea. Where the houses form enclaves, however, they are now beginning to be invaded by tourist hotels, holiday villas and small houses.

Estepona. — The most westerly of the large resorts. Fishing port and pleasure boat harbour. Nearby are the ruins of the Salduba aqueduct.

San Pedro de Alcántara. — Not far from San Pedro — lovely beach and Roman ruins — is the resort of Nueva Andalucía with its splendid pleasure boat harbour, **Puerto Banús★.**

Marbella. — Marbella is the oldest and traditionally the most aristocratic of the Costa del Sol resorts. It lies at the back of a bay, at the foot of often blue tinged mountains; it has a long sand beach, a pleasure boat harbour and an old quarter with white walled houses and narrow streets.

Ojén. — *8km · 5 miles.* Ojén is on a spur between two deep, green valleys.

Monda. — *18km · 11 miles.* A typical Andalusian village with white walled houses.

Fuengirola. — The town bristles with high rise blocks; it has a harbour.

Mijas★. — This village of appealing white houses decorated with iron grilles, which often turn out to be restaurants or bars, is a market centre for Andalusian crafts (pottery, basket-making, weaving). There are attactive **views★** from the upper terraces and the road back to Fuengirola, over the undulating countryside towards the sea.

Torremolinos. — The town's name has become a by-word for holidays.

Málaga★. — *Description p 51.*

THE EASTERN COASTLINE★
From Málaga to Almería — *208km · 129 miles — about 1/2 day*

This, at times, beautiful coast is punctuated along its entire length by the ruins of Moorish towers — defences built by local inhabitants after the Reconquest against the Barbary pirates who continued to ravage the coast until the 18C. Villages were hidden inland, in the mountains; these conical towers were erected at every strategic point. The Granada section of the coast is marked by economic activity in agriculture (sugar cane, bananas, sweet potatoes and early vegetables on the coast and vines on the mountain slopes), industry (sugar refining) and exports (the aforementioned products and iron ore from the hinterland).

Rincón de la Victoria. — The Malagans' weekend beach.

Torre del Mar. — The long beach of grey sand ends at this new resort.

Nerja. — *Description p 53.*

Road from Nerja to La Herradura★. — This wide road follows a russet and purple mountain-side. The old road offers delightful **views★★** of the coastline.

Almuñécar. — The amenities of this cosmopolitan resort include a palm shaded promenade, skirting its pebble beach. The small alluvial plain *(hoya)* behind the town is cultivated to produce custard apples, bananas, medlars and pomegranates.

Sierra del Chaparral. — *60km - 37 miles from Almuñécar to Suspiro del Moro (p 44).* The road rises for approximately 20km - 12 miles after Otivar to a **corniche★★** overlooked all the while by impressive limestone mountain ranges (Monte Herrero 1 501 m - 4 925ft) before reaching the plateaux which become part of the Granada Plain and the Suspiro del Moro.

Salobreña. — Salobreña is a white walled village which stands on a rock at the centre of a sea of green sugar cane. The larger **scene★** is equally beautiful with mountains in the background, the plain in the middle distance and the sea in the foreground.

Motril. — The extent of the sugar cane and avocado trees grown on the Motril *hoya* is best appreciated from the Granada road. Motril port is kept busy handling products from the local sugar refineries and produce from the upper Genil Plain.

Calahonda to Castell de Ferro road★★. — The *corniche* road follows every inlet in the coastline as it skirts minute rocky creeks and pushes out to small headlands from where there are picturesque **views** of the bare mountains.

Almería★. — *Description p 32.*

ÉCIJA ★ (Sevilla)

Michelin map 446 fold 17 — Pop 34 619

Écija, which was founded by the Greeks, has a mild climate except in summer when it becomes so hot that it is known as the Furnace of Andalusia. Its baroque belfries, decorated with ceramic tiles, can be seen from a distance pinpointing the town's extent in the Guadalquivir depression. The San Juan, San Gil and Santa Cruz belfries turn out to belong to churches now in ruins; Santa María forms an integral part of the square of the same name lined by old houses.

St James'★ (Santiago). — The church is preceded by a pleasant 18C *patio.* Inside, the Mudejar windows of an earlier building were retained when the nave and side aisles were rebuilt after cavingin, in 1628. The carved and painted predella of the Gothic **retable★** at the high altar illustrates the Passion and the Resurrection.

Benamejí Palace. — A large gateway provides the focal point in the baroque façade.

Valdehermoso Palace. — The palace's Renaissance front stands near San Juan Church.

Peñaflor Palace. — The palace's concave frontage is covered with paintings in false relief. A quirk of this decoration is the treatment, beneath an apparently endless wrought iron balcony, of the stable windows as the noblest part of the edifice.

GIBRALTAR

Michelin map 446 fold 29 — Pop 28 339
See town plan in the current Michelin Red Guide España Portugal

Access. — The border with Gibraltar is open 24 hours a day. Air lines calling at Gibraltar: British Airways (BA); GB Airways, Air Europe. Shipping lines: major lines according to season.

Documents. — Visitors must be in possession of valid passports or other acceptable travel documents. Visas are not required.

Currency. — United Kingdom coinage, Gibraltar Government notes (the Gibraltar pound is equivalent to the pound sterling). Gibraltar is a free port.

Geographical notes. — Gibraltar, a lofty rock headed out into the straits has an incredible landing strip which bisects the narrow isthmus 3km - 2 miles long linking the colony geographically to mainland Spain. By day and even more by night, when the lights can be seen twinkling from a distance and the Europa Point lighthouse beam is shining, Gibraltar is the focal point of the magnificent Bay of Gibraltar (Bahía de Algeciras).
The **Rock** is 6.5 km² in area - 4 500m long by 1 400m at its widest point (2 1/2 sq miles - 4 931 X 1 531 yards). The highest point is Mount Misery at 423m - 1 388ft — although several others top 400m - 1 312ft. The east side presents a sheer rock face plunging into the sea; the west is less abrupt and with reclaimed land at its foot, forms the site of the town with a main shopping street and narrow alleys, the Alameda Gardens, the service base and the naval and commercial ports — trade is chiefly transit and refuelling.
The **Straits,** a channel 58 km - 36 miles long — connecting the Atlantic and Mediterranean, are 27 miles wide at the west end, 8 miles at their narrowest and 15 miles between Gibraltar and Almina Point near Ceuta. Africa is clearly visible on a fine day.

Historical notes. — The history of Gibraltar, the antique pillar of Hercules *(p 31),* begins in 711 AD with the invasion of the Moors under **Tarik-ibn-Zeyad** who seized the Rock, named it Gibel Tarik (the mountain of Tarik) after himself and constructed a castle upon it — now in ruins, but still known as the Moor's Castle. It was recaptured by Spain on 20 August 1462, feast day of St Bernard, who was thereupon created patron of the town. In the War of the Spanish Succession *(p 10),* the British, in alliance with Holland, Austria and the Holy Roman Empire, captured Gibraltar with a naval force under **Admiral Rooke** (1704), an action formally recognised under the Treaty of Utrecht signed in 1713. The citadel, commanding the straits and key to the Mediterranean, has remained in British hands ever since, in spite of Spanish and French attacks, notably the Great Siege of 1779-1783, when the garrison under General Elliot resisted all efforts to starve or bomb them into submission.
The colony, which was granted a considerable measure of internal autonomy in 1964, voted in a referendum, held in accordance with a UN resolution, in 1967 by 12 138 to 44 in favour of retaining its connection with Britain. In 1973 Gibraltar became part of the European Economic Community as a British dependent territory in Europe, but was excluded from the Customs area of the community, the Common Agricultural Policy, and the requirement to introduce Value Added Tax.

The Barbary Apes. — The origin of the apes is unknown. Legend has it that the British will remain as long as the apes survive; when there seemed a danger of their becoming extinct in 1944 Churchill sent a signal ordering reinforcements. The colony has flourished ever since. The apes are actually tailless monkeys and are the protégés of the Gibraltar Regiment. The two packs number about 60.

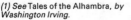

GRANADA ★★★ P

Michelin map **446** folds 20 and 21 — Pop 262 182
See map of built-up area in the current Michelin Red Guide España Portugal

Granada has everything: prestigious and exceedingly beautiful Moorish buildings, luminous skies and a luxuriantly green **setting★★** over which the city, built on three hills at the centre of a wide plain or *vega*, looks out to the snow-capped Sierra Nevada on the horizon. From the hills, the Albaicín, Sacromonte and Alhambra, there are also infinitely varied views, particularly from the first, of the red walled Alhambra.

Religious festivals are full of life, especially those held in Holy Week and at Corpus Christi. The city also holds an annual International Music and Dance Festival *(15 June to 15 July)*.

Provincial capital in the time of the Caliphs of Córdoba, capital of the kingdom created by the Almoravids who overran the city in the 11C, Granada came to its full glory with the advent of the Nasrids from the 13 to 15C. It continued to flourish even in the Renaissance which followed the Reconquest. Only during the ruthless suppression of the Las Alpujarras revolt *(p 51)* did the city's fortunes suffer an eclipse.

A kingdom of 1001 nights. — After the recapture of Córdoba by the Christians in the 13C, the Córdoba Muslims sought refuge in Granada, adding to the city's already considerable prosperity. In the 14C, as Gothic art spread throughout France, as painting and sculpture rose to new heights in Italy before the advent of Classicism, Granada reached the climax of an artistic period which had been in being for 500 years. Its citizens constructed the most prestigious monuments of which, unfortunately, only the Alhambra survives *(1)*.

The Moors continued under the Nasrid dynasty to hold power in Spain for a further century after the fall of Córdoba, although, they were slowly losing hold of parts of their kingdom to the Christians. In the 15C a quarrel in the royal harem inadvertently assisted the Christians: the Caliph became enamoured of a Christian girl, brought to him by a *rezzou* and considered repudiating his queen, Aïcha, by whom he already had a son, Boabdil, for Zoraya, his Morning Star. Aïcha fled with her son but soon returned, to depose the infatuated monarch and set the Boy King — El Rey Chico — upon the throne. As the great Moorish families divided in allegiance, Ferdinand of Aragon seized the opportunity to capture the young king and force his submission. Intrigue and sieges followed during several months; the powerful Abencerrajes, accused of desiring the downfall of Boabdil and of having sold themselves to the Christians were one of several families to see 36 of their leading members massacred at a palace reception *(p 47)*. By 2 January 1492 the Catholic Monarchs had entered Granada; Boabdil had given them the keys of the city and gone into exile (the first, for he subsequently led more than one revolt). As he looked back on Granada from the Motril road his mother is said to have rounded on him: "You weep like a woman for what you could not hold as a man"; the spot remains the Moor's Sigh — Suspiro del Moro. After 781 years the Moorish domination of Spain was ended.

Great Granadines. — Alonso Cano (1601-1667), architect, sculptor, painter, was the moving spirit behind the blossoming of art in 17C Granada. His art, eschewing Renaissance tradition turned towards Classicism; he banished pathos from his sculpture.

(1) See Tales of the Alhambra, *by Washington Irving.*

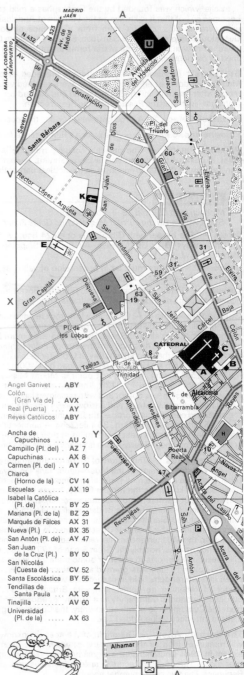

In favour of restrained emotion; in his painting, however, he retained the Renaissance love of lively and harmonious colour. **Pedro de Mena** (1628-1688), his follower, carved the famous Mary Magdalene now in the National Museum of Polychrome Sculpture *(p 250)*.

Eugenia de Montijo, future wife of Napoleon III (Empress Eugénie: 1853) was born in Granada in 1826, daughter of a grandee and, on her mother's side, granddaughter of William Kirkpatrick, Scots by birth, American by nationality and consul at Málaga.

Federico García Lorca, poet and dramatist, talented musician, friend of Dalí and Buñuel, was born 20km - 12 miles from Granada in Fuentevaqueros in 1899 (d 1936).

■ THE ALHAMBRA AND THE GENERALIFE★★★ *time 1/2 day*

The architecture of Granada. — Muslim architecture *(p 13)* reached its climax in Granada where it evolved as the pure expression of a sophisticated civilisation at its moment of decline. The Nasrid princes always built for the present not posterity: beneath the fabulous decoration are ill assorted bricks, plaster, rubble; each sovereign razed the monuments of his predecessor to provide a site for his own new palace which would retain only the architectural principle of grouping all rooms round a central *patio*. **Decoration** was the prime factor and although wall hangings and carpets have disappeared, the sculpture everywhere covering walls and ceilings reveals an art never since surpassed.

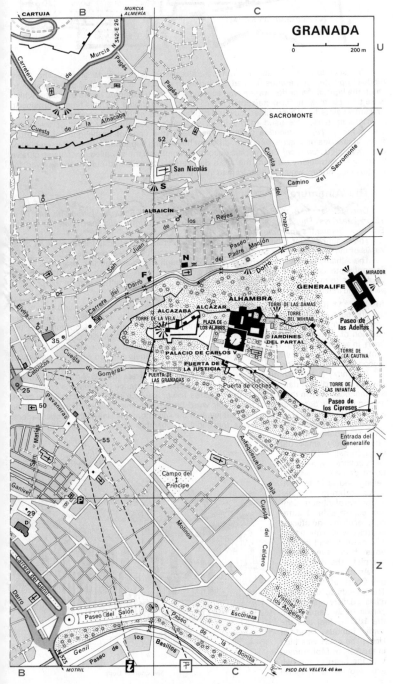

GRANADA

GRANADA★★★

ALHAMBRA (ALCÁZAR)

This sculptural decoration is, in fact, stuccowork, both outside and in. The finely modelled plaster, sometimes pierced, is worked in patterns in a low relief of flat planes to catch the light; another decoration was accomplished by building up layers of plaster which were then cut away to form stalactites *(mocárabes: illustration p 14)*. This type of ornament, brilliantly painted and even gilded, covered capitals, dados, arches and pendentives.

Ceramic tiles were used to provide a geometric decoration for most of the walls: *alicatados (p 18)* produced a colourful marquetry, the lines of arabesque motifs often forming star designs; *azulejos* colour, different hues being separated by a thin raised fillet or a black line *(cuerda seca)*. Calligraphic decoration employed the so called Andalusian cursive which was particularly elegant; the more decoratively complicated cufic was reserved for religious aphorisms which appear framed in scrollwork.

The Alhambra★★★ (CX)

Open 9.30am to 8pm (8.30pm Tuesdays, Thursdays and Saturdays); floodlit visits 10 to 12pm Tuesdays, Thursdays and Saturdays only; ticket (350pts) valid for Generalife and the Emperor Charles V's apartments.

The beautiful Calat Alhambra must be one of the most remarkable fortresses ever built. Views of the town, the bleak Sacromonte heights, nearby hillsides and gardens.

The Alhambra outer perimeter is entered through the Puerta de Las Granadas or the Pomegranate Gateway built by the Emperor Charles V. A footpath leads through the **shrubbery★** to the massive **Justice Gate ★**(Puerta de la Justicia), built so that its tower forms part of the inner ramparts defending the castle terrace.

Alcázar★★★ (Casa Real). — The Alcázar was erected in the 14C. Its richness and variety and the originality of its decoration defy description. The tour begins in the **Mexuar,** the former council chamber, transformed after the Reconquest into a chapel and lengthened by the addition of an oratory from which there is a good **view★** of the Albaicín. Cross the **Mexuar Court,** in which the south wall, protected by a wide, carved wood cornice, may be taken as a sample of Granada art: wall openings are surrounded by panels covered with every variety of stucco and tile decoration.

Adjoining is the beautiful oblong **Court of the Myrtle Trees** (de los Arrayanes) where, banked by myrtles, a narrow central pool emphasises the distance between the colonnades at either end; that on the left abuts the Comares Tower in which are the **Barca Gallery,** a name arising from the deformation of the Arabic word *barakha,* meaning benediction and used as a decorative motif on the walls, and that jewel of the Alhambra, the Hall of the Ambassadors.

The **Hall of the Ambassadors** was the audience chamber of the Moorish kings whose throne faced the entrance.

The relatively small but very lofty hall — 18m - 60ft — is covered by a magnificent domed cedarwood ceiling and is lit by windows offering remarkable views of the surrounding countryside. Lustreware *azulejos* and stucco, impressed with more than 150 patterns and inscriptions from the Koran, complete the decoration.

Another opening off the Court of the Myrtle Trees leads to the **Mocárabes Gallery** (stalactite ceiling badly damaged in the 16C by fire) and the justly famous **Court of Lions.** The court was built in the 14C by Mohammed V at the heart of the palace around a massive

The Court of Lions

lowlying fountain. This he surrounded by deliciously delicate arcades supported on slender single and paired columns. State apartments ring the court; the **Abencerrajes Gallery,** so called after Boabdil had ordered the family massacre and piled the heads into the room's central basin, has a stalactite ceiling and a splendid star shaped lantern cupola; adorning the end of the **Kings' Chamber,** are alcoves containing vaulting painted to illustrate the pastimes of Moorish and Christian princes - the style is so untypical that it is not known whether the artist was a Christian working for the sultan before the Reconquest or later; the **Hall of the Two Sisters,** named after the two identical large white marble slabs in the pavement, and known for its stuccowork and particularly its honeycomb cupola vaulting. Beyond are the **Ajimeces Gallery** and the **Mirador de Daraxa,** both equally resplendent. A gallery beside the green and silent Daraxa Garden, leads to the **Window Grille Court** from which steps go down to the **baths,** bright with azulejos and coloured stucco.

Cross the Daraxa Garden to the Partal Gardens (Jardines del Partal).

Gardens and perimeter towers★★. — Spreading to the east of the royal palaces are the terraced **Partal Gardens** which descend to the gracefully porticoed **Lady Tower** (de las Damas). From this early 14C building, which is as ornately decorated inside as the Alcázar, there are views of the Darro directly below and of the Sacromonte. The Mihrab Tower (right) is a former Nasrid oratory — a rarity since the princes were not notably pious. The Captive's and Infantas' Towers (respectively Torre de la Cautiva and Torre de las Infantas) are sumptuously decorated inside.

Enter Emperor Charles V's Palace from the Partal Gardens.

Emperor Charles V's Palace. — The Nasrid Alcázar was not considered sufficiently majestic to serve as the imperial residence and Pedro Machuca, who studied under Michelangelo, was charged in 1526, with the design of a suitable palace to be financed from a tax levied on the Moors. Their uprising in 1568 *(p 51)* interrupted construction and the palace has only recently been completed.

This purely Classical style building, always thought one of the most successful creations of the Renaissance period in Spain, is the only construction of Machuca's to remain. Although the contrast with the Alcázar may at first appear unfortunate, the palace soon acquires precedence, so perfect are its lines, so dignified its appearance, so simple its plan of a circle within a square. It holds two museums:

Hispano-Moorish Museum. — *Ground floor. Open 10am to 2pm; closed Mondays; 75pts.* Outstanding among the objects from the Alcázar (fragments of sculpture, perfume pans, braziers, vases) is the famous blue **amphora★,** 1.32m high - 52ins — the Nasrid masterpiece, which stood for years in the Hall of the Two Sisters.

Fine Arts Museum (Museo de Bellas Artes). — *First floor. Same opening times as the Hispano-Moorish Museum.* Religious sculpture and paintings of the 16 to 18C predominate: Diego de Siloé, Brother Juan Sánchez Cotán, Vicente Carducho, Alonso Cano, Pedro de Mena.

Alcazaba★. — The Alcazaba has existed since the 9C and is by far the oldest part of the Alhambra. The two towers overlooking the Cistern Court (de los Aljibes) date back to the 13C.

The lofty Watch Tower (Torre de la Vela) commands a magnificent **panorama★★** of the palace, the Generalife, Sacromonte, Granada and the Sierra Nevada.

The Generalife★★ (CX)

Same opening times as the Alhambra.

The 14C Generalife, the summer palace of the Kings of Granada, is particularly enjoyable for its cool and green, terraced water gardens.

The Cypress (los Cipreses) and Oleander Alleys (de las Adelfas), which are at their best in July and August, lead to the palace, a building of modest dimensions surrounding an elongated court, its axis marked by a narrow slit of water. This Canal Court (Patio de la Acequia), bordered by roses, has a graceful pavilion at either end. Linking these pavilions are, on the left, a gallery and on the right, the palace apartments. The *mirador* overlooks Granada and the Darro Valley.

■ THE CATHEDRAL QUARTER *time: 3/4 hour*

Chapel Royal★★ (Capilla Real) (AX C). — *Open 10.30am to 1pm and 4 to 7pm (3.30 to 6pm in winter); 75pts.*

The Catholic Monarchs decided to be buried on the site of their victory and ordered the construction by Enrique Egas. It was begun in 1506 and completed under the Emperor Charles V in 1521. The unity of style, richness of decoration and the art objects it contains, give a unique interest to the chapel.

To enter *(by the south door)* cross the courtyard of the old **Exchange (Lonja) (AXY A),** also designed by Egas. The chapel's south front has an elegant Renaissance façade of two superimposed arcades with turned columns; opposite is the former early 18C **Town Hall (AXY B)** in Granada baroque.

Every conceivable decoration of the Isabeline style is to be seen in the chapel: ribbed vaulting, walls emblasoned with the arms of the Catholic Monarchs, the yoke and fasces (revived in 1934 by the Falange), a monogram of the initials of their first names and the eagle of St John. Beautiful wrought iron grilles close two chapels. The chancel, closed by a **screen★** *(illustration p 18),* by Master Bartolomé, contains the **mausoleums★★** of the Catholic Monarchs, on the right, and of Philip the Fair and Juana the Mad, on the left. The first was carved in Genoa by Fancelli in 1517, the second, which is magnificent in proportion and workmanship, by Bartolomé Ordoñez in 1519-1520 (the sarcophagi are in the crypt). The high altar **retable★** (1520) is one of the first to be free of all Gothic influence; the lower register of the predella has been used to depict the siege of Granada. In the north transept is the famous triptych of the Passion by Thierry Bouts.

Queen Isabel's personal art collection, which includes outstanding 15C Flemish, Spanish and Italian paintings, hangs in the **sacristy★★.**

Cathedral (AX). — *Same opening times as the Chapel Royal.*

The cathedral illustrates the development of architecture in Granada between the 16 and 17C. Construction, in this case, was entrusted in 1528 to Diego de Siloé and continued after his death in 1563 to his plans, apart from the façade (1667), overlaid by three tall arcades, which is by Alonso Cano.

GRANADA★★★

The **Capilla Mayor★** is the first thing you notice inside, for its plan and decoration are surprising. Siloé designed a rotunda circled by an ambulatory, the whole cleverly linked to the nave and four aisles of the basilica. The rotunda combines two superimposed orders, the uppermost providing a setting for paintings by Alonso Cano of the Joys of the Virgin and beautiful 16C glass in paired windows. Marking the rotunda entrance on twin facing panels, are the figures at prayer of the Catholic Monarchs by Pedro de Mena and, in a medallion by Alonso Cano, those of Adam and Eve. The **organ** dates from about 1750 and was made by Leonardo of Ávila. The finely sculptured Isabeline doorway in the south transept is the original portal of the older Chapel Royal.

Alcaicería (AY). — The area, which has been reconstructed and is now a tourist precinct with craft and souvenir shops, was a silk market in Moorish times.

■ ADDITIONAL SIGHTS

Carthusian Monastery★ (**Cartuja**) (BU). — *Open 10am to 1pm and 4 to 7pm (6pm in winter); 75pts, Sunday mornings free.*
Go through the cloister into the **church,** exuberantly decorated with baroque stucco in 1662. At the back of the apse, across a windowed bay is the circular, early 18C Holy of Holies (Sancta Sanctorum) inlaid with multicoloured marble; beneath the cupola, painted in false relief, is a marble Sagrario which contains the Tabernacle.
The **sacristy★★** (1727-1764) is an outstanding example of late baroque. The magnificent door and cedarwood furnishings are by a Carthusian religious.

St John of God★ (**San Juan de Dios**) (AV K). — *Open 10am to 1pm and 3 to 6pm; closed Sundays and holidays.* St John's is one of Granada's most important baroque churches - note the area immediately inside the entrance and the tribune. Behind the central gold and silver door in the massive Churrigueresque altarpiece of gilded wood, is the tomb of **St John of God,** founder of the Order of Knights Hospitallers and the hospital nearby.

St Jerome's (**San Jerónimo**) (AX E). — *Open 10am to 2pm and 4 to 6pm; enter by the monastery;* 50pts. Renaissance sculpture decorates the east end of the 16C monastery church.

Albaicín (BCV). — The quarter, on the right bank of the Darro, covers a slope facing the Alhambra. It was here that the Moors built their first fortress and to Albaicín that they retreated when Christians reconquered the city. The alleys are lined by white walled houses with few openings or long walls enclosing the luxuriant gardens of prosperous town houses or *cármenes*. Go to **St Nicholas'** *(open only during services)* terrace (CV S), *(access by the Cuesta del Chapiz),* if possible at sunset, for a really beautiful **view★★★** of the Alhambra and the Generalife.

Moorish Baths (**Baños Árabes**) (BX F). — *Open 9am to 6pm.* Star pierced vaulting decorates a room surrounded by columns in these ancient (11C) baths.

Royal Hospital (**Hospital Real**) (AU U). — *Open 8am to 3pm.* The hospital, now the university, was founded by the Catholic Monarchs. The plan of a cross within a square provides four spacious courtyards. Of interest are the Renaissance windows in the façade and on the first floor and the *artesonado* chapel cupola over the transept crossing

Sacromonte (CV). — The hillside opposite the Generalife, is covered by a network of paths which lead past clumps of Barbary figs to the gipsies' caves.

Casa Castril (CX N). — Behind the great Renaissance gateway, the **archaeological museum** displays Greek and Roman sculpture, coins and alabaster amphorae. *Open 10am to 2pm; closed Mondays;* 75pts.

■ SIERRA NEVADA

The Sierra Nevada lines Granada's horizon to the south: often snow-capped, massive, beautiful, and in season, preceded by a wave of pink almond blossom. There is skiing in winter around Solynieve and the *parador*.
A road *(46km - 29 miles),* which winds through an arid mountain landscape before it climbs to an altitude of 3 398m - 11 148ft, a feat which has earned it the name of the highest road in Europe — brings you to the **Pico de Veleta★★.** The circular panorama is wonderful, extending north to the Baetic range, northeast to the Sierra de la Sagra, east to the wall of lofty summits dominated by the Mulhacén and Alcazaba and south to the Mediterranean. Finally in the west lie the jagged outlines of the Tejeda and Almijara Sierras. *Access to the Pico de Veleta also by cable-car.*

GUADIX ★ (Granada)

Michelin map **446** fold 21 — Pop 19 860

Guadix stands where the irrigated plain meets the dry plateau, its soft stone has been deeply ravined into fantastic shapes by erosion.
The town's origins go back to prehistoric times; it became important under the Romans and the Visigoths, when it stood at the juncture of the Granada to Murcia and Almería roads. Under the Moors it was allowed to remain Christian but was overrun several times, nevertheless, before being finally recaptured in 1489.
Guadix' peaceful air, as its inhabitants tend the land, belies its turbulent history which, however, is recalled in the cathedral, the Plaza Mayor, which dates from the reign of Philip II and the 15C Moorish fortress.

Cathedral★. — The baroque façade★ (1713) with its undulating lines draws the eye even more than the Renaissance belfry. The interior with its star vaulting recalls the Almería Cathedral *(p 33).*

Troglodyte quarter★. — *Continue to the end of the road which leads to Santiago Church.* Dwellings have been hollowed out of the soft tufa stone, rocks round the entrances whitewashed and conical chimneys constructed to emerge on a level with the paths from which you can also hear grain being flailed on the cave roofs in this fascinating quarter.

EXCURSIONS

Purullena★. — *6km - 4 miles northwest.* The **road★★** winds through tufa rocks to reach the **troglodyte village★** of Purullena; it then rises in a *corniche,* affording wide **views★** over the plateau, cut by deep canyons. Finally the road enters a wild landscape to reach the Mora Pass.

Lacalahorra★. — *18km - 11 miles southeast.* Lacalahorra is a typical Andalusian village, not far from the Alquife iron mines on the vast plain which lies between the Sierra Nevada and the Sierra de Los Filabres. Crowning the top of the hill is the **castle★** *(park the car in the village and walk up the steep path)* which encloses a delightful Renaissance **patio★★.** The design of the arcades and balustrade, the Italian style carving surrounding the windows and the skilful proportions of the staircase convey a highly sophisticated artistic style.

HUELVA ⓟ

Michelin map 𝟺𝟺𝟼 fold 14 — Pop 127 806
See town plan in the current Michelin Red Guide España Portugal

The port of Huelva lies in the joint delta of the Odiel and Tinto Rivers and has developed through shipping copper mined in the hinterland. It is a fishing port with canneries and it handles chemicals; its tonnage amounting to over 10 million makes it Spain's 8th largest port. The town is very old but its buildings were destroyed in the earthquake of 1 November 1755 which largely destroyed Lisbon.

Huelva and the New World. — By the 16C the Tinto River had become one of the Conquistadores principal anchorages. Such a fate had come about by chance: the Prior of La Rábida, the learned Juan Pérez, believed Christopher Columbus' theory put to him by the Geonese in 1484, that the world was round, that it was therefore possible, and would even be shorter than rounding the Cape, to sail to the Indies by a westerly route. The prior's support, where merchant adventurers had been too cautious and the church too disbelieving, finally won Columbus the necessary commission from the Catholic Monarchs. On 3 August 1492 he set sail *(see below)*; he landed on San Salvador (Bahamas) two months later, on 12 October, a day still celebrated annually throughout Spain as the Day of the Hispanidad *(p 135).*

EXCURSIONS

La Rábida. — *9km - 5 1/2 miles. Open 10am to 1pm and 4 to 8pm (6pm October to April); closed Mondays; a religious accompanies.* Within the monastery, amidst pleasant gardens, are vestiges of a 15C church and its frescoes. An interesting small museum contains models of the three ships of Columbus' first voyage *(p 267),* navigation charts and old books.

Palos de la Frontera. — *13km - 8 miles.* The harbour from which Columbus sailed in 1492 (he returned in 1493), is now silted up. It was also from this port that Hernán Cortés *(p 139),* conqueror of Mexico, set out in 1528. The 14C **St George's Church** has a Mudejar north portal and fine vaulting over the chancel and transept *(ask the priest for the key).*

Moguer. — *19km - 12 miles.* Moguer was another port from which expeditions ventured to the unknown. Alabaster **tombs★** of the discoverers who founded the St Clara Convent can be seen before the altar or underneath the Isabeline and Renaissance style niches in the church. In the main street, now named after him, a plaque marks the birthplace of the poet and 1956 Nobel prizewinner, **Juan Ramón Jiménez** (1881 - 1958) *(p 22).*

JAÉN ⓟ

Michelin map 𝟺𝟺𝟼 fold 20 — Pop 92 429
See town plan in the current Michelin Red Guide España Portugal

Jaén came under the domination of the Carthaginians, grew to importance under the Romans and, in the 11C, became a *taifa* capital *(p 38).* It stands open on one side to the plain covered with olive trees, has the Sierra de Jabalcuz rising behind it and St Catherine Hill (Cerro de Sta Catalina) actually dominating it. The **view★** from the Alameda de Calvo Sotelo (gardens) embraces the town and the surrounding mountains.

Provincial Museum★. — *Open 10am to 2pm and 4 to 7pm; closed Mondays and Sunday and holiday afternoons; 200pts.* Of the museum's collections of fine arts *(first floor),* and **archaeology★** *(ground floor)* the last is particularly interesting, since there are such rare items as a fine Roman **mosaic★** of Thetis and Iberian carvings. In another building is the Museum of Contemporary Engravings.

Cathedral. — The architect most typical of the Renaissance in Andalusia, **Andrés de Vandelvira,** failed to take into account the narrowness of the streets, the smallness of the squares and the scale of the existing old town when, in 1525, he designed to such classical proportions the cathedral's immense façade. Behind the high altar is a chapel containing the Santo Rostro relic, one of the veils used by St Veronica to wipe Christ's face and brought, according to local legend, to the cathedral by St Euphrasjus, first Bishop of Andújar. *The relic is exposed on Fridays after mass at 11am and 5pm.* The **choirstalls★** are richly carved in the Berruguete manner.

Museum★. — *Open Fridays, Saturdays and Sundays 11am to 1pm; 50pts; enter through the south transept.* The cathedral treasure, displayed in two underground chambers, includes antiphonaries, paintings by Ribera and a delightful Flemish Virgin and Child. The most original pieces are great bronze candelabra modelled by Master Bartolomé.

St Andrew's Chapel (Capilla San Andrés). — The **Chapel of the Immaculate Conception★★,** with a minutely decorated drum supporting its star vaulting, is a masterpiece of Plateresque art. The gilded wrought iron screen which hangs before the chapel as delicately as a curtain of gold lace is by **Master Bartolomé** (16C), a native son of Jaén.

San Ildefonso Church. — The north portal is Renaissance in style.

St Catherine Castle (Castillo Sta Catalina). — *4,5km - 2 miles west.* The approach **road★** affords views of the blue tinged slopes of the Jabalcuz Sierra; the castle, now a *parador,* commands a vast **panorama★.**

JEREX DE LA FRONTERA (Cádiz)

Michelin map **446** fold 27 — Pop 176 238

Jerez produces Spain's sherries. The town's proximity to the sea was one of the factors which brought about its rapid development in the 18C when English shippers were searching for alternatives to French wines. The name sherry, from the former English spelling of the town's name, Xeres, was first used in England in 1608.

Sherry. — Sherry is divided into four main types: **Fino** or extra dry, the lightest in body and strawlike in colour with a fine bouquet; **Amontillado** or dry, fuller bodied, deeper in colour with a more rounded bouquet; **Oloroso** or medium, fragrant, full bodied and golden; and **Dulce** or sweet.

Sherries are blended and, therefore, have no vintage years; uniformity in a house's wines depends on the grapes, their sunning, crushing, fermentation and subsequent treatment and maturing in the cask. Continuity of wine style is produced by the *solera* system by which wines of identical type are kept in groups of casks in ascending grades — usually 4 — of maturity. The blender draws off wine from the oldest stock, replacing it with a similar amount from the second oldest cask and so on through the group so that the wine moves forward progressively. **Fino** casks, unlike the others, are only seven-eighths filled allowing room for the 'flower' or yeast to develop in the air at the top of the cask and so impart a special flavour to the wine; **Oloroso** matures in changing temperatures and humidity in full casks made from American oak which adds colour and savour; **Dulce** is made by running wine 'must' — juice undergoing fermentation — into casks containing sufficient brandy to arrest fermentation at the desired 9-10º. It is blended with Oloroso to make a dessert wine. A visit to a sherry **bodegas★** (AZ) (above ground wine store) is interesting *(open every morning except Saturday, Sunday and 1 month in summer)*.

Folklore. — Horses are no less important than sherry in Jerez and, in the region, locally bred mounts are equally famous. The Andalusian School of Equestrian Art is located here. Annually in early May there is the **Feria del Caballo** or Horse Show at which time there is racing as well as dressage and carriage competitions. In early September there is a **Wine Harvest Festival** which includes a cavalcade and a *flamenco* festival; the *cante jondo* is particularly alive in Jerez.

St James' (Santiago) (AY). — The church has a finely carved Isabeline **portal★**.

Collegiate Church (AZ B). — The monumental 16 and 17C church has well balanced Renaissance and baroque decoration, and is given added dignity by being placed at the top of wide baroque flights of steps. The transept crossing is covered by a dome.

Former Chapter (BZ M). — The Chapter's Renaissance front is the principal ornament of the small and pretty Plaza de la Asunción. Inside there is now a modest **archaeological museum** *(closed temporarily)* which displays a remarkable 7C BC Greek casque.

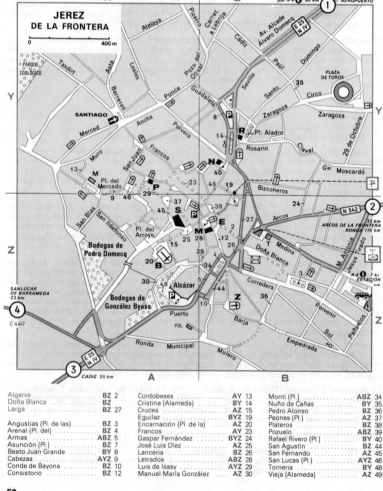

San Dionisio (BZ E). — The Mudejar church has Gothic vaulting above the altar and an *artesonado* ceiling over the nave.

Alcázar (AZ). — Gardens now surround the walls of the old Moorish fortress.

St Michael's (San Miguel) (BZ Z). — Beautiful Isabeline portals in the side walls. The high altar retable was made by Martínez Montañés and José de Arce.

Seignorial residences. — Marquess of Bertemati's Palace (AZ S), Pérez Luna Palace (BY N), Casa de los Ponce de León (AY P), Casa Domecq (BY R).

LANJARÓN (Granada)

Michelin map 446 fold 33 — Pop 4 094

Lanjarón is a reputed spa in a lovely hill **setting★**. Basket makers can be seen at work along the main street which is cut by numerous picturesque alleys. Its ferruginous springs cure liver and digestive troubles and produce a table water, as well.

Las Alpujarras. — The Alpujarras, a mountainous region between Lanjarón and Ugíjar is watered by the Guadalfeo, which is skirted on either side by a road. The last Moors left in Spain after the reconquest of Granada were subjected to obligatory baptism and other humiliations. They fled to this area, where they united and revolted (in 1568) only to be crushed in 1571 by Don Juan of Austria and finally expelled by Philip III in 1609.

MÁLAGA ★ P

Michelin map 446 fold 31 — Pop 503 271
See map of the built-up area in the current Michelin Red Guide España Portugal

Arriving from the north (④ *on the map)*, you will look down on Málaga lying at the foot of a hill at the mouth of the Guadalmedina: the port, the gardens and avenues for which the town, with its distinctive quarters such as Caleta (to the east), is known.
Ferries leave for Melilla in Africa.

Málaga wine. — The town produces the sweet, full bodied wine, known as Málaga, from grapes from local hillside vineyards which can be served either as an aperitif or dessert wine. Since its popularity has fluctuated grapes are now also dried for sale as currants.

■ CATHEDRAL QUARTER

Cathedral★. — The building begun in the 16C, even now is incomplete as its south tower lacks its full elevation. The three aisles of the vast hall church are covered inside with cupolas studded with palm fronds, shells and other motifs but are supported on classically ordered Corinthian columns, entablatures and cornices. The decoration includes 17C choir-stalls with figures by Pedro de Mena, pulpits of rose stone and an 18C organ.

Museum. — *Entrance: by the fourth chapel of the north aisle. Open 10am to 1pm and 4 to 6.30pm; 50pts, free Saturdays, Sundays and holidays.*
The chapterhouse, on the 1st floor, has an *artesonado* ceiling, beautiful wooden chapel screens and a tabernacle door with Arab motifs.

Bishopric (CY A). — On the cathedral square, behind the bishopric's baroque façade, are a succession of *patios*. The third *patio*, which is accessible from the Sta María alley, contains a museum of sacred art *(open 10am to 1pm and 4 to 7pm; closed Saturday afternoons, Sundays and holidays; 50pts, ticket valid for the bishopric)*.

Sagrario (CY B). — This curious rectangular church was originally a mosque. The north **portal** is Isabeline in style.

Fine Arts Museum★ (Museo de Bellas Artes) (DY M). — *Open 10am to 1.30pm and 5 to 8pm (4 to 7pm in winter); closed Sunday afternoons, Mondays, Christmas and 1 January; 50pts.*
The former Moorish palace serves as the setting for interesting collections by local artists. A gallery contains works by **Picasso,** who was born in Málaga in 1881 (no 15 Plaza de la Merced (DY) is his parents' home), and another one is dedicated to one of his teachers, Muñoz Degrain.
Displayed amidst Andalusian furniture, in another *patio,* are paintings by Ribera, Murillo, Morales, Cano and Jordán.

Museum of Popular Art (Mesón de la Victoria) (CY M[1]). — *Open 10am to 1.30pm and 5 to 8pm (4 to 7pm in winter); closed Sunday afternoons, Mondays and holidays.* Located in a 17C inn (restored), this museum displays on the ground floor objects recalling the past : agricultural implements, a sardine fishing boat and tools used for wine making.
On the first floor note the collection of statuettes in 18 and 19C costumes.

■ ALCAZABA and GIBRALFARO

These two fortresses made Málaga one of the major strongholds of Al Andalous.

Alcazaba★ (DY). — *Open 10am to 1pm and 5 to 8pm (4 to 7pm in winter); Sundays and holidays 10am to 2pm; 50pts.*
The winding approach is decorated with the ruins of the Roman amphitheatre unearthed at the foot of the fortress. Inside the final gateway, Christ's Door (Puerta del Cristo) (DY C), where the first mass was celebrated on the town's reconquest (1487), are Moorish gardens. The ramparts command a view of the harbour.
The former palace, inside the inner perimeter, is now a **museum★** of Moorish art. There are two *patios* with Arabic decoration from the 11 to 15C *(p 13)* and a room with an *artesonado* ceiling and models of the Alcazaba and part of the cathedral.

Gibralfaro (DY). — The **view★★** from the 14C ramparts which crown the so-called Lighthouse Hill, includes the town and its setting. The gardens inside are open to the public.

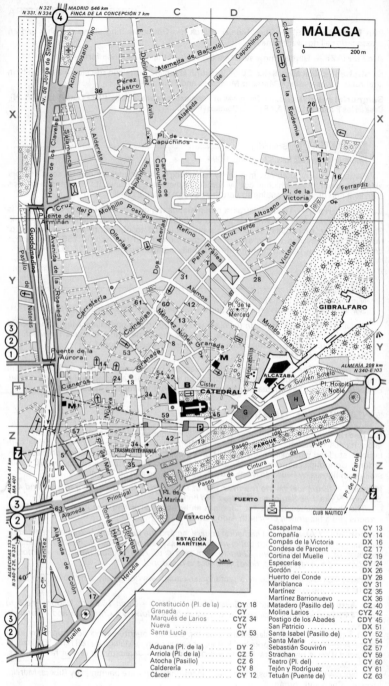

MÁLAGA

0   200 m

GIBRALFARO

EXCURSION

Finca de la Concepción*. — *7km - 4 miles north. Open 9am to 5pm (noon on Saturdays); closed Sundays and holidays.*

Leave by ④ on the map and continue straight ahead. The gardens and shrubbery are mainly made up of tropical species. The domain includes Roman remains and, amidst the cypresses, a *mirador* overlooking orange and lemon groves in an otherwise arid valley.

Michelin Guides

The Red Guides (hotels and restaurants)

Benelux - Deutschland - España Portugal - main cities EUROPE - France - Great Britain and Ireland - Italia

The Green Guides (beautiful scenery, buildings and scenic routes)

Austria - Canada - England: The West Country - Germany - Greece - Italy - London - New England - New York City - Portugal - Rome - Scotland - Spain - Switzerland and 7 guides on France

MOJÁCAR (Almería)

Michelin map 446 fold 24 — Pop 1 581

Mojácar, on its rock spike, overlooking both the plain and the coast has a splendid **site**★. Its architecture and urban planning evoke the town's Moorish past. On the eastern Andalusian coastal side between Cape Gata and the province of Murcia (Costa Blanca) tourism has not yet developed, and yet along the rocky southern coast towards Las Negras and San José there is excellent underwater fishing.

Mojácar to Carboneras road. — *22km - 14 miles.* The road first skirts the shore before turning inland to climb the pyramid-shaped mountains by way of serpentine bends. There are beautiful **viewpoints** before it drops to Carboneras beach.

NERJA (Málaga)

Michelin map 446 fold 32 — Pop 12 012

Nerja, one of the larger resorts on the Costa del Sol *(p 42)*, is known for its "balcón de Europa", a palm shaded terrace-promenade washed on either side by small sea inlets.

Nerja Cave★★ **(Cueva).** — *Access: off the Motril road, 4km - 2 miles from Nerja near the village of Maro. Open 1 May to 15 September 9.30am to 9pm; 10am to 1.30pm and 4 to 7pm the rest of the year; 150pts. Time required: 1 hour.* Traces of paintings, the discovery of weapons and tools, jewels and bones, indicate intermittant habitation since Paleolithic times. Concretions and rocks, water worn into strangely complex shapes are highlighted to full advantage. Individual chambers include the Cascade, which serves as the setting for an annual **festival of music and dance** and the Cataclysm which still retains the atmosphere of when, thousands of years ago, an enormous column fell from the roof to shatter in monumental pieces and a final chamber, blocked by a pillar nearly 18m - 58ft in diameter.

OSUNA ★ (Sevilla)

Michelin map 446 fold 17 — Pop 15 668

Osuna is an elegant Andalusian town with a beautiful **monumental ensemble**★ *(follow thes signs Zona Monumental)*, inherited from its former status as a ducal seat. The dukedom was created in 1558; the house of Osuna remains one of the greatest in Spain.

Collegiate Church. — The vast western portal is harmoniously sculptured. There are four fine paintings by Ribera set in the Churrigueresque high altar retable.

Ducal Sepulchre★. — *Guided tours (time: 20 min) 10am to 1.30pm and 4 to 7.30pm; 10am to 1pm and 3.30 to 6.30pm 1 October to 30 June; closed Mondays and Good Friday; 100pts.* The first crypt is approached through a delightful *patio* with marble decorated arcades in the Plateresque style; it is a church in miniature. The ceiling roses, once gilded, are now black with candle smoke. Above, a second crypt (1901) contains the coffins of the major grandees.

Walk in the town. — *Mainly around the Plazas del Duque and España.* The lines of the straight streets are punctuated by swirling baroque façades; massive wooden doors, darkly shining and copper nailed, reveal, when opened, fine wrought iron grilles and cool *patios*. Note the Chapterhouse (Cabildo Colegial), the Former Law Courts (Antigua Audiencia), the Palace of the Marquess de la Gomera, St Dominic and St Augustin Churches as well as, near the Collegiate Church, the Former University (1548) which has a lovely interior *patio*.

You will find an index at the end of the guide
listing all subjects referred to in the text
(monuments, picturesque sites, points of interest,
historical or geographical items, etc.).

RONDA ★★ (Málaga)

Michelin map 446 fold 29 — Pop 31 383

The town was built at the edge of the Serranía de Ronda on a platform **site**★ cut by the Guadalevín Gorges. The **Tajo** (ravine) actually divides Ronda into two: the **Ciudad** or old town and the Mercadillo, now extended by the modern town. An impressive bird's eye **view**★ from the bridge (Puente Nuevo) down the rock face includes the road (Camino de los Molinos) to the power station, which passes along the foot of the cliffs from where there is another good **view**★ — this time up the ravine cut by the bridge.

The cradle of bullfighting. — Born in Ronda in 1698, **Francisco Romero,** laid down the rules of bullfighting, which until then had been only a display of audacity and agility, and who by his introduction of the cape and *muleta* became the father of modern bullfighting. His son Juan introduced the *cuadrilla* or supporting team and his grandson, **Pedro Romero** (1754-1839), became one of Spain's greatest bullfighters. He founded the **Ronda school,** known still for its classicism, strict observance of the rules and *estocada a recibir (p 25)*.
The Ronda **bullring,** built in 1785 and one of Spain's oldest, has an elegant entrance.

Picturesque streets. — The Carrera de Espinel has a surprising birdcage-like balcony (Y **S**), the Calle de la Virgen, a chapel with modern carved columns on the site of an old gibbet (Y **V**).

■ **LA CIUDAD**★ (Z) *time: 1 1/4 hours*

The old town, an enclave of narrow alleys and white houses with ironwork balconies, lies behind walls remaining from the Moorish occupation (until 1485).

Collegiate Church (Z **R**). — The church's rounded apse, the belfry — an old minaret crowned in the 16C — and the sacristan's house, with its street level arcades, group together attractively. The Renaissance chancel, inside, abuts oddly with the Gothic nave but the profusely decorated baroque stalls are interesting.

RONDA★★

Mondragón Palace (Z B). — The imposing stone face is surmounted by twin turrets. A view, from the terrace, overlooks the ravine and the plain.

Palace of the Marquess of Salvatierra (Z E). — Note the window decorated with two "savage" couples, the iron balcony and detailed low reliefs.

Moorish Baths (Z K). — *Apply to the caretaker.* A reminder that Ronda was a *taifa* capital.

EXCURSIONS

Serranía de Ronda★★. — The deeply eroded *sierra* has a largely stony appearance; its altitude is surprisingly high, its village sites hidden.

The famous, native pines, *pinsapos,* grow on the heights but otherwise vegetation is sparse except in the west which is humid.

Ronda to San Pedro de Alcántara Road★★. — *49km - 30 miles southeast by the C 339 — about 1 hour.* For 20km - 12 miles the road travels through a bare mountain landscape; it then climbs steeply into a **corniche★★** above the Guadalmedina Valley and its smaller tributary valleys.

Ronda to Algeciras road★. — *102km - 63 miles southwest by the C 341, C 3331 and N 340 — about 2 1/2 hours.* The Ronda-Gáucin section is particularly interesting when the road climbs steeply to overlook the Genal Valley and one crosses the small villages of Atajate, Benadalid, Algatocín.

Ronda to Ubrique road★. — *48km - 30 miles southwest by the C 339, C 344 and C 3331 — about 2 hours.*

The lonely road has a certain grandeur as its cuts through the grey or rose countryside, deeply scoured by erosion into fantastic shapes reminiscent of the El Torcal range *(p 34).* **Ubrique** itself is an industrial leather tanning town.

Pileta Caves★. — *27km - 17 miles: time: 1 hour plus 1 1/2 hours sightseeing. Leave Ronda by the northerly, Seville road; after 14km - 9 miles when in sight of a rock amphitheatre, turn left.* Beyond a cork oak wood, you come upon the Montejaque Dam and a striking **view★★.**

Just before Montejaque, bear left and after 1km - 1/2 mile turn right. Continue for 5km - 3 miles, the road passes above Benaoján and affords **views★** of the Guadiaro Valley.

The Pileta Caves *(guided tours 9am to 2pm and 4 to 7pm (6pm in winter); number of visitors limited; 200pts)* are interesting archaeologically: black and red drawings described in simple outline and antedating those of Altamira, indicate that the caves were inhabited at least 25 000 years ago; skeletons and weapons also discovered show that it was still inhabited in the Bronze Age — 1500 BC. Although the Sanctuary Cave has a fine display of many different types of animal, Pileta is known particularly for its drawing of a giant fish measuring 1.25m - 49 inches.

Ceramic remains in the cave, calcified in some instances, date back to the Neolithic period (3rd millenium), making them the oldest known pottery specimens in Europe.

RONDA

0   300 m

Espinel (Carrera de)	Y		Marqués de Salvatierra	Z 9
			Merced (Pl. de la)	Y 10
Campillo (Pl. de)	Z 2		Nuñez	Z 12
Carmen Abela (Pl. de)	Y 3		Ruedi de Gameros	Z 13
Ciudad (Pl. de la)	Z 4		Santa Cecilia	Y 14
Córdoba	Y 5		Santo Domingo	Z 15
España (Pl. de)	Z 6		Setenil	Y 16
González Campos	Z 7		Tenorio	Z 17

SEVILLE ★★★ SEVILLA ℗

Michelin map ⁴⁴⁶ fold 16 — Pop 653 833
See map of the built-up area in the current Michelin Red Guide

Seville, a town humming with life, a tourist city, the capital of Andalusia, an industrial centre, appears to give its all to the passing tourist in just a few days. But Seville is a city of many moods and facets. It has a working class quarter in Triana (AX) on the right bank of the Guadalquivir, an upper class area in Santa Cruz (CV) and the bustling shopping district around the Sierpes (BUV), San Pablo (BV), and Méndez Núñez (BV) streets. The great festivals, when vast crowds flock to the city from all over Spain and overseas, reveal the provincial capital in many guises.

Seville at festival time. — The **Semana Santa** or **Holy Week** festival in Seville is unforgettable. Cathedral services and *pasos* processions *(illustration p 26)*, organised nightly in each city quarter by the rival brotherhoods are equally unusual. *Pasos* are great litters on which are mounted pious, polychrome wood statues, fantastically bejewelled and garlanded with flowers; these constructions are borne on between 25 and 60 men's shoulders in slow procession, interrupted by an occasional kind of rolling dance, through the narrow streets at night to the plaudits of the crowd. Accompanying the holy statue are penitents, hidden beneath tall pointed hoods and each carrying a long lighted candle. There is, also, always a fife and drum band which only pauses in its playing when an unknown singer in the crowd raises his or her voice in a *saeta*, an improvised religious lament based on *flamenco* music.

Holy Week is followed by the April Fair when the city becomes a fairground with parades of horses and carriages in the morning, illuminations at night, bullfights, music and dancing, for Seville is the home of the *Sevillana*, a local air and dance as well as being the great centre of *flamenco*. The *tablaos* or tableaux are excellent *(p 31)*.

Art and architecture in Seville. — The ramparts on the north side of the town, the lofty Alcázar, the Gold Tower (Torre del Oro) (BX) — built in 1220 on the banks of the Guadalquivir to guard the port which could be closed by a chain stretched across the river to another tower, since vanished, on the far bank — and finally, the Giralda, are all reminders of Seville's Moorish occupation.

But Seville was, in fact, Christian at the time the Nasrids were building the Alhambra in Granada and use of the **Mudejar style,** that mixture of Moorish and Christian, long after the reconquest of the town in 1248, was through pure delight in Arabic design — as exemplified in the Alcázar erected under Peter the Cruel, the Casa de Pilatos *(p 58)*, the Palacio de las Dueñas (CTU — *open 10am to 1pm)*, and the San Marcos belfry (DT).

Statues, many the work of the 17C sculptor, Martínez Montañés, are dispersed throughout the city's churches.

The best known are the **Christ of Great Power** (Cristo del Gran Poder) by Juan de Mesa in San Lorenzo (BT P) the **Cachorro** by Francisco Antonio Gijón in the Patrocinio Chapel, Calle Castilla (AV), named after the gipsy who served as the sculptor's model and the **Macarena Virgin,** the most popular figure in Seville, which stands, when not in procession, in a special chapel (CT S). *Open 8am to 1pm and 5 to 9pm (9.30am to 12.30pm and 5.30 to 7.30pm for the treasure); 50pts for the treasure.*

In Spain's Golden Period, the Seville school of painters also brought renown to the city.

Three generations of artists corresponded to the three reigns: under Philip III (1598-1621) Roelas and **Pacheco,** portraitist and Velázquez' master; under Philip IV (1621-1665) Herrera the Elder, who had a violent technique but an epic touch, and **Zurbarán** (1598-1664) *(p 132)* who after having studied in the city remained here, portrayed still figures with rare spiritual intensity. Finally under Charles II (1665-1700) there was **Murillo** (1618-1682), a baroque artist, author of numerous gently radiant Immaculate Conceptions and, also, of brilliantly depicted every day scenes, particularly those including young women and children and characters who must have been common to every town and village, such as the water carrier. Also of this period was **Valdés Leal** (1622-1690) whose best work can be seen in the **Hospital de la Caridad** (BX L — *open 10am to 1pm and 3.30 to 7.30pm; 75pts).*

Velázquez (1599-1660) was born in Seville; entered Pacheco's Academy in 1613 and became his son-in-law in 1618. He visited Madrid in 1622 and became court painter in 1623, where he spent the rest of his life doing portraits of the royal family. Velázquez paid careful attention to the character of the individual and was fascinated by the use of light on his canvas.

HISTORICAL NOTES

Seville's history from prehistoric times to the 13C is neatly summed up by the lines carved long ago on the Jerez Gate: "Hercules built me; Caesar surrounded me with walls and towers; the King Saint took me". Seville, an Iberian town, was chief city of Roman Baetica and before Toledo was granted the privilege, capital of the Visigothic Kingdom. In 712 the Moors arrived; in the 11C, on the fall of the Cordoban caliphs, the city was created capital of a prosperous Almohad Kingdom, under the rule of Sultan **Yacoub Al Mansur** (1184-1199), victor over the Christians at the Battle of Alarcos (1195) and builder of the Giralda.

On 19 November 1248, King Ferdinand III of Castile, the Saint, as he was known and is referred to in the lines above and who was cousin to St Louis of France, delivered the city from the Moors.

The discovery of America in 1492 brought prosperity to Seville. Expeditions to the New World set out from the port: **Amerigo Vespucci** (1451-1512), the Florentine who determined to prove that Columbus' discoveries were not the Indies but a new continent to which his own name was ultimately given; **Magellan,** who set out in 1519 to circumnavigate the world and whose journey was completed for him by his companion, Juan Sebastián Elcano. By 1503 the city's trade with ports far and near had become such that Isabel the Catholic created the **Casa de Contratación** or Exchange to encourage and also to control all trade with America. This monopoly lasted until 1717 when the silting up of the Guadalquivir brought about the transfer of the Casa concession to Cádiz and precipitated the economic decline of Seville.

A stroke of sheer audacity on 18 July 1936 put Seville into the hands of General **Queipo de Llano** and three other officers, enabling it to be used at the start of the Civil War as a bridgehead by the Nationalist forces on their arrival from Morocco two days later.

Today Seville is the fourth largest town in Spain; it is an important industrial centre (textiles, food processing, metallurgy) and the only river port in Spain.

■ MAIN SIGHTS *time: 1 day*

Giralda★★★ (CV). — *Open 10.30am to 1pm and 4 to 6.30pm (6pm 1 October to 28 February); closed Sunday and holiday afternoons; 100pts.*

The Giralda — 98m - 322ft high — was once a minaret; its name, literally weather vane, is called after the revolving bronze statue of Faith at its summit. The minaret is late 12C, the top storey and lantern, 16C. The delicate ornament is typical of the style of the **Almohads,** a dynasty of strict religious belief, opposed to ostentation, whose members created monumental grandeur in exact accordance with their ideals of utter simplicity. A gently sloping ramp, interrupted at intervals by steps, leads to a platform at 70m - 230ft from which there is an excellent **view**★★ of the town.

The **Orange Tree Court (Patio de los Naranjos)** also remains from the ancient mosque; the Pardon Gate on the court's north wall, built in 1522, is Mudejar, as is the Granada Chapel backed against the Giralda.

Cathedral★★★ (CV). — *Tour: 1 hour; Dress accordingly.* "Let us build a cathedral so immense that everyone on beholding it, will take us for madmen", the chapter is said to have declared in 1401 when they were knocking down the mosque. They succeeded for Seville Cathedral is the third largest in Europe after St Peter's in Rome and St Paul's in London.

The **exterior** is massive. As one of the last to be built in the Gothic style, the cathedral shows obvious Renaissance influence. The principal portals are modern though harmonising with the whole, however, the Nativity (on the right) and Baptism (on the left) doors, on either side of the west door include beautiful terracotta figures by Mercadante de Bretaña or Brittany (*c* 1460) while the Gothic, Los Palos and Las Campanillas Doors, on either side of the rounded Chapel Royal (1575) at the east end, have Renaissance style tympana in which Master Miguel Perrín (*c* 1520) has made full play of perspective in true Renaissance style. The **interior** is striking in size and richness. The massive column shafts, supporting huge arches appear slender because they are so tall; the vaulting rises 56m - 184ft above the transept crossing.

The **Chapel Royal** (Capilla Real), left on entering, opens through an arch so high that the decoration can only be appreciated from a distance. The chapel, which is covered by an elegant, richly ornamented dome, is Renaissance: on either side are the tombs of Alfonso X of Castile (d 1284) and his mother, Beatrice of Swabia; at the centre of the high altar is the robed figure of Our Lady of the Monarchs patron of Seville, given, according to legend, by St Louis of France to his cousin St Ferdinand of Spain who lies buried in a silver gilt shrine below the altar. The chapel screen dates from 1771.

The **treasury** *(same opening times as the Giralda; 100pts)* is in 16C rooms - one displays copes, another antiphonaries and lecterns; the sacristy contains the cathedral plate and Tenebrario or Plateresque candelabrum with 15 branches used in Holy Week, and the so called Chalice Sacristy.

The 16C **chapterhouse** has an elliptical dome. The **sanctuary** is unbelievably rich. Splendid Plateresque grilles (1518-1533) precede the immense Flemish altarpiece, profusely but delicately carved and gleaming with gold leaf (1482-1525). In the intervening space the *Seises* — a group of choristers in pages' costume — dance at Corpus Christi, the Assumption and on 8 December, perpetuating a secular tradition of unknown origin. Opposite, but partly hidden by a grille (1519-1523) by Brother Francisco of Salamanca, are magnificent 15 and 16C **choirstalls.** The **trascoro** *(p 16)*, a screen of multicoloured marble, jasper and bronze, is 17C. Colombus' tomb is in the south transept; the 19C monument shows the discoverer's coffin being borne by four kings symbolising León, Castile, Navarre and Aragon.

Numerous works of art are displayed in the periphery chapels: the tomb of Cardinal Juan de Cervantes in the St Hermenegild Chapel (south side) and paintings by Murillo, Jordaens and Valdés Leal in that of St Anthony (west side).

Alcázar★★★ (Reales Alcázares) (CX). — *Open daily 9am to 12.45pm and 3 to 5.45pm; Saturdays, Sundays and holidays 9am to 1pm; closed 1 January, Good Friday, Corpus Christi and 25 December; time: 1 1/2 hours; general ticket: 125pts.*

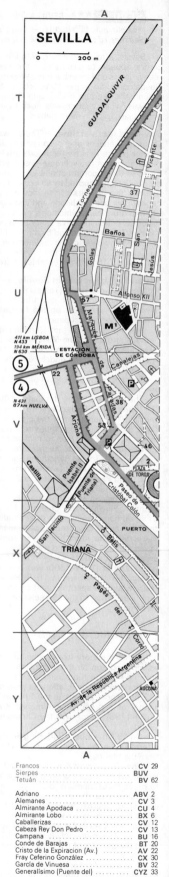

SEVILLA

Francos	CV	29
Sierpes	BUV	
Tetuán	BV	62

Adriano	ABV	2
Alemanes	CV	3
Almirante Apodaca	CU	4
Almirante Lobo	BX	6
Caballerizas	CV	12
Cabeza Rey Don Pedro	BV	13
Campana	BU	16
Conde de Barajas	BT	20
Cristo de la Expiracion (Av.)	AV	22
Fray Ceferino González	CX	30
García de Vinuesa	BV	32
Generalísimo (Puente del)	CYZ	33

Make life easier by using

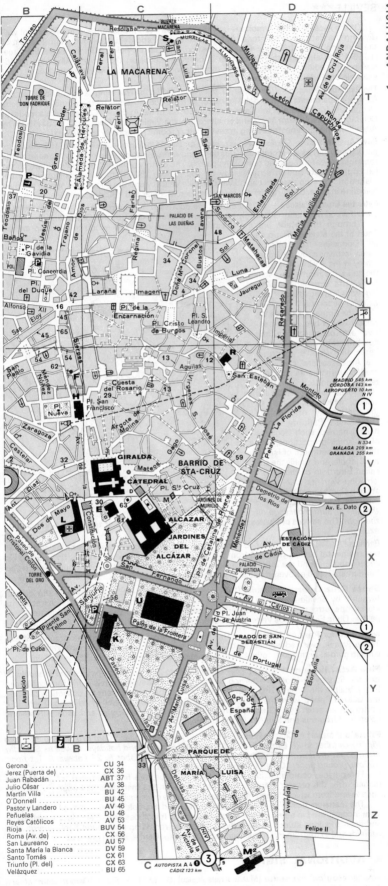

MADRID 545 km
CÓRDOBA 143 km
AEROPUERTO 10 km
N IV

N 334
MÁLAGA 209 km
GRANADA 255 km

AUTOPISTA A 4
CADIZ 123 km

Michelin Maps with your Michelin Guide.

SEVILLE★★★

Of the Alcázar of the Almohads only the Patio de Yeso *(not open)* and the section of wall dividing the Patio de la Montería (A) from that of the Patio del León (B), remain. The rest of the building dates from the Christian period, the palace being built by Peter the Cruel (1350-1369) although the decoration is based in detail on that of the Alhambra *(p 46)*, making the edifice, in spite of later modifications, one of the purest as well as a great example of Mudejar architecture.

The Exhibition Wing. — *Right side of the Patio del León.* The wing is also known as the **Admiral's Apartments** (Cuarto del Almirante) as it was constructed by the Catholic Monarchs as quarters for officers of the Casa de Contratación. In the Audience Chamber are a model of Columbus' vessel *Santa María* and an altarpiece, the **Virgin of the Navigators★** (1531-1536) by Alejo Fernández. Tapestries hang in several other rooms *(temporary exhibitions)*.

Royal Apartments. — *1st floor; access: at the far end of the right wing.* A grand, 16C staircase, particularly remarkable for its *azulejos* dado and *artesonado* cupola, leads to the apartments the most repeatedly altered part of the palace. The oratory of Isabel the Catholic (left, on the landing) is decorated in a novel way for the period, 1504, with *azulejos* illustrating the Visitation; the stone arches carved with lacelike delicacy and the gilded iron screen are pure Isabeline in style. Other rooms alternate between Mudejar and 19C decoration.

Peter the Cruel's Palace. — *At the end of the courtyard.* The narrow façade, protected by a carved wood overhang, is strongly reminiscent of the Mexuar Court at Granada.

Through the façade are the beautifully proportioned and exquisite Moorish arched **Court of the Maidens** (Patio de las Doncellas) (D) unfortunately crowned by an upper storey in the 16C. Surrounding the court, the rooms are especially attractive and interesting with carved stucco and *azulejos* decoration. These include the Emperor Charles V's saloon which has an impressive *artesonado* ceiling, the apartments of María de Padilla, Peter the Cruel's mistress, the Ambassadors' Hall, covered by a remarkable, segmented cedarwood cupola (15C); afterwards follows Philip II's saloon, which leads first to the delicately ornamental Doll's Court (Patio de la Muñecas) named such because of its small proportions, and then to the bedroom of Isabel the Catholic and, finally the so-called Bedroom of the Moorish King with its blue toned stucco. *Come out of the palace into the Patio del León and through a vaulted passage on the right.* The **saloons of Charles V** house a magnificent collection of tapestries and beautiful *azulejos*.

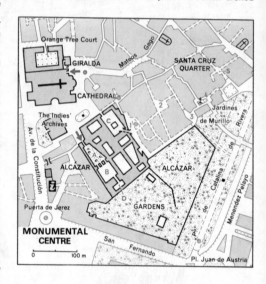

Gardens★★ (CX). — The terraced gardens, planted with exotic trees and shrubs and cooled by ornamental basins, descend from a 17C terrace to the **Charles V pavilion**, finely domed in cedarwood. Beyond are informal gardens. Leave the Alcázar by the Flag Court (Patio de las Banderas) (C) and a covered passage which leads to the old Santa Cruz quarter.

Santa Cruz Quarter★ (Barrio) (CDV). — This former Jewish quarter was the quarter favoured by Seville nobility in the 17C; it remains well worth visiting for its character, its workshops, streets, wrought iron grilles, *patios* and squares shaded by orange trees and palms - Doña Elvira (1), los Venerables Sacerdotes (2), Alfaro (3), Santa Cruz (4), las Cruces (5).

María Luisa Park★★ (CDYZ). — The 19C park, which once formed the grounds of San Telmo Palace, was redesigned in 1929 at the time of the Ibero-American Exhibition as a sunken garden with pools, fountains and *azulejos*. Several exhibition buildings remain.

Fine Arts Museum★★ (AU M¹). — *Open 10am to 2pm and 4 to 7pm; closed Mondays all day and Sunday and holiday afternoons; 150pts.* The museum which is in the former Merced Friary, built in the 17 and 18C around a cool cloister, has an excellent art collection covering the Golden Period with special reference to Seville's own school of painting. There is a portrait of an artist by El Greco, a number of paintings by Velázquez and especially several splendid Zurbaráns and Murillos (in the sacristy).

Pilate's House★★ (Casa de Pilatos) (DV R). — *1st floor is open 10am to 1pm and 3 to 7pm (6pm 1 October to 28 February); 1st floor closed Sundays and holidays as well as Saturday afternoons; ground floor is open 9am to 8pm (7pm 1 October to 28 February). 1st floor: 100pts, ground floor: 100pts, combined ticket: 200pts.*

The palace, completed in 1540 by Don Fadrique, the first Marquess of Tarifa, was named after the praetor's house in Jerusalem which the marquess had seen on a trip to Judaea and from which he had features copied for his own residence.

The mansion, however, is also a particularly good example of the vitality of the Mudejar style incorporated in a Renaissance period building. It includes remarkable lustre **azulejos★★** and finely moulded stucco in the *patio*, outstanding rooms on the ground floor, *cuerda seca azulejos* and extraordinary Gothic vaulting in the chapel and a domed grand staircase.

■ ADDITIONAL SIGHTS

Archaeological Museum (Museo Arqueológico) (DZ M²). — *Open 10am to 2pm; closed Sundays, Mondays and holidays; 150pts.*

The **Roman department★**, with mosaics and antique statues from Itálica, is outstanding.

The Indies Archives (Archivo General de Indias) (CX E). — *Guided tours 10am to 1pm; closed Sundays and holidays.*

The building, dating from 1572, was designed by Juan de Herrera as an Exchange *(lonja)*. It now houses a unique collection of documents on America at the time of its discovery and conquest including maps and charts, plans of South American towns and their defences, the autographs of Columbus, Magellan, Cortés and others.

St Joseph's Chapel (San José) (BV F). — The profusely gilded, baroque chapel, gleams especially at night by the lights of evening service. The overpowering altarpiece, organ and ornate galleries are typical of the period (1766).

Town Hall (BV H). — The hall's east face, dating from 1527-1534, is attractively Renaissance in style with delicate scrollwork decoration. Star vaulting covers the vestibule.

San Telmo Palace (CXY K). — The palace (1682-1796), once a naval school and residence of the Dukes of Montpensier and now a seminary, has a baroque grand entrance, three storeys high, by Leonardo de Figueroa.

University (CX U). — The University with its harmonious baroque façades and elegantly laid-out *patios*, is in the old, 18C, tobacco factory.

EXCURSIONS

Santiponce. — *8km - 5 miles by* ⑤. The monastery church of **St Isidore in the Fields (San Isidoro del Campo)** contains an altarpiece by Martínez Montañés, with, at the centre, an expressive figure of St Jerome. There are also the alabaster tombs of the founder of the monastery, Guzmán the Good, his wife and a son, brother of the boy killed by the Moors at Tarifa *(see below: Guzmán the Good's Castle)*.

Itálica. — *9km - 6 miles by* ⑤. *Open 9am to 6.30pm (5.30pm 1 October to 28 February); Sundays and holidays 9am to 4pm; closed Mondays; 150pts.*

This large Roman town was the birthplace of the emperors Hadrian and Trajan and the poet, Silius Italicus. You see the ruins of the amphitheatre, the network of streets covering the hillside and at the top of the hill, mosaics, and a **view★** extending miles across the vast Guadalquivir Plain. On the far side of the old road (SE 182) is the Itálica theatre *(excavations underway)*.

*The **Maps**, **Red Guides** and **Green Guides** are complementary publications.*
Use them together.

TARIFA (Cádiz) ────────────────────
Michelin map **446** fold 28 — Pop 15 220

Tarifa watches the Straits of Gibraltar from the most southerly point on the Iberian peninsula: the coast of Africa is only 13.4km - 8 miles away. Morocco, however, is only visible when the breeze drives away the sea mist. It has become an ideal spot for windsurfing.

The town is old with cobbled streets and white walled houses, tightly packed within the mediaeval ramparts, which are pierced in one place by an impressive, ivy covered gateway.

Guzmán the Good's Castle (Castillo de Guzmán el Bueno). — *Guided tours (time: 1/2 hour) Fridays and Saturdays 9.30am to 1pm.*

The castle (now a barracks) was built by the Moors as a fortress. In 1292 it was taken by the Christians but soon afterwards besieged by the Moors who captured the son of the fort commander, Alonso Pérez de Guzmán. The young hostage was brought before the ramparts by his captors who threatened his death unless the town capitulated; Alonso, however, threw the Moorish leader his dagger, shouting: "If you need a weapon to murder my son, here is my knife".

The tour includes the octagonal tower from which Guzmán defied the enemy and the south wall which commands an interesting **view★** of the Straits of Gilbraltar and the coast of Africa.

ÚBEDA ★★ (Jaén) ────────────────────
Michelin map **446** fold 9 — Pop 28 717

Úbeda was, at one time, very prosperous. It was recaptured from the Moors in 1234 and became a base in the Reconquest campaign. It is now one of the best examples in Spain of homogeneous construction, dating principally from the time of the Renaissance. Craftworkers (pottery, ironwork, esparto grass) are to be found chiefly in the Calle Valencia, in the gipsy quarter.

The Good Friday evening procession, local in character, is deeply fervent.

■ MAIN SIGHTS *time: 1 1/2 hours*

Plaza Vázquez de Molina★★ (B). — The square, the monumental centre of Úbeda, is lined with old and historic buildings.

Casa de las Cadenas (B H). — The mansion, now the town hall, named after the chains round the forecourt, was designed in 1562 by Vandelvira *(p 51)*. The majestic but not overly ornate façade is relieved by alternating bays and pilasters and decorated above with caryatids and atlantes.

The *patio*, bordered by slender arcades, opens onto the Plaza de los Caídos.

On the second floor the façade of the archives is decorated with *artesonado;* there are views of the square and town *(apply to the Inspección de la Policia Municipal in the patio, 9am to 2pm)*.

Sta María (B F). — The church's architecture is varied: the main and Consolada doors (left side), are 17C, the cloister 16C. The **chapels★**, set in sculptured surrounds, are closed by beautiful **grilles★**, most of which were wrought by Master Bartolomé *(p 51)*.

ÚBEDA★★

El Salvador★★ (B V). — *If closed apply at the first door on the right, Calle Francisco de los Cobos.*

Diego de Siloé designed the homogeneous and somewhat sumptuous church in 1536, including in its massive façade the most characteristic ornamental motifs of the Renaissance. The **interior★** is frankly theatrical: the nave has vaulting outlined in blue and gold and is closed by a monumental wrought iron grille. Beyond, the Capilla Mayor forms a kind of rotunda in which an immense 18C altarpiece serves also as a baldachin and is crowned with a sculpture by Berruguete of the Transfiguration. The **sacristy★★**, by Vandelvira, is ornamented with coffering, medallions, caryatids and atlantes with all the splendour of the Italian Renaissance style.

St Paul's★★ (San Pablo) (B). — The church is a harmonious mixture of Gothic architecture as seen in the west door and the Isabeline style to be seen in the **south door★** (1511). The **chapels★★**, adorned in several instances with fine wrought iron grilles, are the church's chief interior feature: the Heads of the Dead Chapel was designed by Vandelvira; that of Las Mercedes is in Isabeline style and richly carved.

Montiel Palace (B A). — Monumental gate flanked by twisted columns.

Bishop Canastero's Mansion (B B). — Among the figures decorating the mansion's diamond pointed stone façade are two soldiers bearing the owner's coats of arms.

Tower Mansion (Casa de las Torres) (A C). — The mansion front, closely flanked by two square towers, is profusely decorated in the Plateresque style, with delicately carved sculpture.

Marquess of Contadero's Mansion (B E). The late 18C façade beneath a gallery, shows how long the Renaissance style remained in favour in Úbeda.

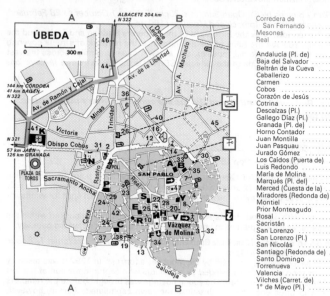

■ ADDITIONAL SIGHTS

St James' Hospital (A K). — A high relief of St James Matamore stands over the entrance. Inside are an arcaded *patio* and a grand staircase with multicoloured vaulting (1562-1575).

St Isidore's (A N). — Beautiful north and south Gothic portals.

La Rambla Palace (A P). — The portal includes the figures of soldiers bearing the palace's coat of arms.

St Dominic's (B R). — The church's south door, overlooking a picturesque small square, is a delicate Renaissance feature decorated with scrollwork and roses.

La Vela de los Cobos Palace (B S). — The palace's distinguished façade, surmonted by an arcaded gallery, is most unusually L-shaped.

The Savages' House (Casa de los Salvajes) (B Y). — Two very odd "savages", dressed in animal skins held together with belts of blackberry branches, may be seen on the façade, supporting a bishop's arms.

The **Michelin Green Tourist Guide Portugal**

Picturesque scenery, buildings
Scenic routes
Geography
History, Art
Touring programmes
Plans of towns and buildings

A guide for your holidays

2 Aragon

Aragon was forged into a kingdom by its struggle against the Moors in the early Middle Ages. It extended, from north to south, over what are now the three provinces of Huesca, Zaragoza and Teruel — an arid region by tradition and yet its scenery is brilliant and widely contrasting in colour and varied in relief. It is also the region where an original art form, the Mudejar, emerged from the fusion of Christian and Moslem traditions.

Landscape. — Upper Aragon (Huesca) corresponds geographically with the Central Pyrenees, an area of both grandiose and enclosed countrysides, dashing spring waterfalls, hidden valleys and small piedmont plains, of villages of rough stone houses with slate roofs.

In the centre lies the **Ebro depression** (Zaragoza). The terraces rising on either side of the river bed are deeply ravined, a feature even more pronounced in the **Monegros** desert where saline outcrops also occur. In contrast, irrigation has transformed the lower valley into a vast green *huerta*. **South Aragon** (southeast of Zaragoza and Teruel), which extends far further, is part of the Spanish *cordillera*. Clay slopes·beside the Ebro around Piedra, Daroca and Alcañiz bear vines and olive trees; brick built villages, such as Nuévalos, merge into the tawny, deeply scored hillsides; bleak, windswept high plateaux surround the city of Teruel. These plateaux form part of the massive spread of the Montes Universales, one of Spain's great watersheds where the Guadalaviar, Turia, Júcar and Tagus rivers rise.

The climate is harsh as a result of the lack of maritime influence: winters are long and hard with snow sometimes falling in November; summers can be burning. The **cierzo,** a prevailing, cold northwest wind brings rain to both the Pyrenees and the Montes Universales but other areas such as Saragossa get only 350mm - 14 ins a year.

The Kingdom of Aragon (1035-1469). — Aragon developed from an obscure Pyrenean kingdom by clever marriages and the commercial acumen of the House of Barcelona into a Mediterranean state whose power reigned from the Roussillon in France to Murcia, from the town of Montpellier in France, to the Balearic Islands, Naples and Sicily. Ambition went further and political alliance against France was even sought with England by the marriage of Catherine of Aragon to the heir to the throne.

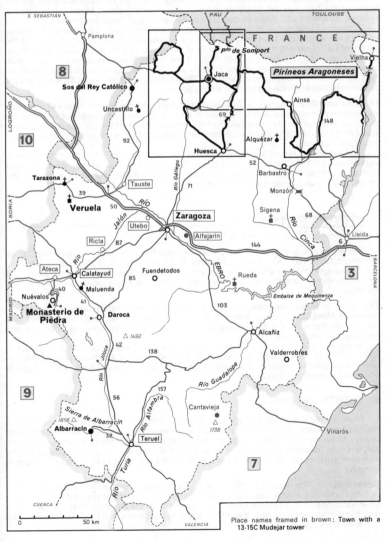

Place names framed in brown: Town with a 13-15C Mudejar tower

Mid-9C: Louis the Pious establishes Aragon as an independent county.

1035: **Ramiro I Sánchez** declares the county a kingdom with Jaca as its capital.

1076: Navarre unites with Aragon (until 1134). Saragossa, reconquered from the Moors in 1118, is promulgated capital.

1137: On the marriage of the Infanta Petronila with Count Ramón Berenguer IV the **House of Barcelona** takes over the Aragon throne (1137-1412).

1213-76: The reign of **James I the Conqueror,** marks the Golden Age of Catalan-Aragon expansion: the dynasty, established in Roussillon and Cerdaña, occupies Majorca (1229), Valencia (1238) and Murcia (1266).

1282: Following the Sicilian Vespers, the French are dispossessed of the crown by the Sicilians who offer it to Pedro III.

1412: With the **Caspe compromise,** the Infante Ferdinand of the Castile Trastamara line is established on the throne of Aragon — prelude to the unification of the two kingdoms.

1442: **Alfonso V,** King of Sicily, enters Naples and founds the **Kingdom of the Two Sicilies** which remains Spanish until the 18C.

1469: Marriage of Ferdinand II of Aragon and Isabel of Castile.

1501: Catherine, daughter of Ferdinand and Isabel, sails to England to marry the heir apparent (1501: Arthur, Prince of Wales; 1509: Prince Henry, future Henry VIII).

From the 15C the princely rivalries tearing apart southern Italy and Barbarian piracy in the Mediterranean, gave the lie to the power of the Aragon "empire" and political ambition returned to peninsular politics where Castile was supreme.

The kings of Aragon were always held in check by a nobility which stubbornly defended its privileges, by provincial assemblies **(Cortes)** jealous of their prerogatives and by municipalities with numerous franchises and liberties **(Fueros).** As early as the 12C a higher magistracy **(Justicia Mayor),** elected and inviolate, had been constituted to defend communal freedom against overbearing royal or seignorial edict. Only in 1591 did it lose power when Philip II had **Juan de Lanuza** beheaded for opposing him.

Art. — **Romanesque Aragon** is limited to the Pyrenees which, freed early from the Moors, became, from the 9C, strongly monastic and deeply influenced by France. Pilgrims to Santiago de Compostela in the 11 and 12C *(p 152)* added further impetus and contacts. Masons, following the Master of San Juan de la Peña, developed a distinctive style, carving capitals with figures which uncannily reveal their souls through disproportionate heads and bulging eyes and a sense of the sacred in gestures with hands outstretched.

Mudejar Aragon (13-16C) covers the rest of the province: architecture is in brick with Moorish style marquetry and blind arcade ornament. The most beautiful examples are the **belfries** of the Zaragoza and Teruel provinces. Gothic painting shows Moorish influences in costume, strapwork and gilded stucco (Daroca, Maluenda and Teruel altarpieces).

Renaissance sculptors were sometimes overly exuberant in their adornment of religious interiors but what should not be missed are the excellent works in alabaster including the figures at Calatayud and the Santa Engracia at Saragossa and the many altarpieces. These usually treat a major subject in high relief at the centre and have a number of densely crowded scenes in miniature on the predella. Artists in alabaster included **Gabriel Joli,** an exile from Picardy who worked in Teruel (1538), the Elder and Younger **Gil Morlanes,** and the outstanding **Damián Forment** at Huesca and Saragossa.

Folklore and Gastronomy. — The **Jota** is a bounding, leaping dance, beloved by the men and women of Aragon since the 18C, and in which the *baturro* or peasant can express his native joy and impetuosity to the full. The fast, whirling rhythm of the couples dancing to the music of the *rondalla* (stringed instruments) is broken only for the occasional brief singing of a *copla* by a soloist.

Food and drink in Aragon depend primarily on the region's own excellent products: fresh vegetables from the Ebro basin, heavy red or full-bodied white wines from Cariñena, oven roasted kid *(ternasco).* Poultry and meat are usually served in *chilindrón,* a tomato and pepper sauce found elsewhere in Spain, but at its best in Saragossa.

ALBARRACIN ★ (Teruel)

Michelin map **444** fold 17 — Pop 1 068

The Albarracín Sierra, inhabited, as can be seen from the local cave paintings, since prehistoric times, has, since the Middle Ages, had a city perched on this particular hillside site. The original defence afforded by the circling Guadalaviar was supplemented as early as the 11C by the wall which goes up the hill behind the town. It was rebuilt in the 14C by the Christians.

The spirit of independence. — Albarracín has twice been independent. In the 11C the Almoravid Aben Razín dynasty, from which the town took its name, established a small *taifa* kingdom on the spot. A defensive wall was constructed against Almohad incursions and help sought from Navarre.

In the mid-12C the town was ceded to the Azagras, Christian nobles from Estella in Navarre. This second period of independence, when the lords of Albarracín refused submission to the powerful Kingdom of Aragon, lasted 50 years until James II was able in 1300 to bring the fief within the royal domain.

■ **SIGHTS** *time: 3/4 hour*

From the narrow, steep and winding, paved streets you get a different aspect of the town at every corner. Many houses with rough stone ground floors have overhanging upper storeys faced with rose coloured roughcast to which fine woodwork balconies, wrought iron grilles at the windows and the occasional coat of arms on a façade add character. The high roof galleries on the houses are quite different from those to be found elsewhere in Aragon.

Cathedral. — The square belfry, crowned by a smaller hexagonal lantern marks the cathedral standing slightly south of the town centre. In a chapel off the vast 16C nave, is a small altarpiece of wood (1566) carved with scenes from the life of St Peter. The **treasure** in the chapterhouse includes **tapestries★** (16C Brussels) recounting the life of Gideon and gold and silver work.

ALCAÑIZ (Teruel)
Michelin map **443** fold 27 — Pop 11 639

Alcañiz, set amidst orchards and fertile olive groves, produces high quality olive oil and also makes a speciality of almond paste sweetmeats (known as *almendrados*).

The memorable façades of the *Lonja*, where a market was held beneath the tall Catalan Gothic arcade, and the Renaissance town hall, meet at one corner of the **Plaza de España.** Both buildings are crowned by the typical Aragon gallery with overhanging eaves.

Collegiate Church. — A rhythmic interplay of vertical lines and curves marks the upper part of the façade of the church, rebuilt in the 18C, while below is an exuberantly baroque **portal★**. The spacious interior is divided by massive columns.

Castle. — This castle built at the top of a mound was, in the 12C, the seat of the Aragon commandery of the Order of Calatrava. Most of the buildings *(parador)* remaining are 18C.

At the far end of the courtyard are the Gothic chapel, its single aisle covered with tiers-point arches, and the keep (1st floor) with 14C interior wall paintings.

ALQUÉZAR (Huesca)
Michelin map **443** fold 5 — Pop 297

The mountain village of Alquézar, straggling and delightful with narrow streets bordered by shady arcades and emblazoned façades has, in addition, a beautiful **setting★★** overlooking the canyons through which flow the Río Vero and its tributaries. *Walk along the alley signposted Téléfonos.*

Collegiate Church. — *Open 10am to 1pm and 4 to 7pm (6pm 1 October to 30 April); 100pts.* The Moors built an *alcázar* on this site which, however, soon fell to the Christians. In the late 11, early 12C the still visible walls were constructed together with a church (rebuilt *c* 1530). The north side of the small **cloister** remains from this earlier period, with, on its **capitals,** illustrations carved in pungent archaic style of the Sacrifice of Isaac, Balaam and his ass, Adam and Eve, the Last Supper...

BARBASTRO (Huesca)
Michelin map **443** fold 16 — Pop 15 182

Barbastro lies at the centre of the Somontano, a fertile plain at the feet of the Pyrenean foothills from which two long and rugged valleys descend. The first provides a rough roadway down from the Ordesa Park *(p 67)*, the second includes the Ventamillo defile *(congosto - p 69)*. The town was already an important market centre at the time of the Moorish invasion.

On 11 August 1137 Barbastro was the setting for the marriage of Princess Petronila and Ramón Berenguer IV, a match sealing the union of Aragon and Catalonia.

Cathedral. — The cathedral is the typical Spanish hall church of the 16C but with a slenderness in its columns, scarcely noticeable capitals and, yet, in complete contrast, ornate network vaulting liberally embossed. The side chapel doors are decorated in Churrigueresque style with an incredible quantity of stucco. An altarpiece by Damián Forment decorates the high altar; the first north chapel contains a fine early 16C painted altarpiece.

CALATAYUD (Zaragoza)
Michelin map **443** fold 13 — Pop 17 941

Ayub the Moor built a castle in this spot which, when it grew into a community, was called after him: Kalat Ayub. The town's houses, built up against the arid hillside, blend into the greyish rock with only the minaret of the old mosque rising above the glazed tile roofs.

The ancient Bilbilis. — Excavations east of Calatayud have uncovered Bilbilis, a Roman city on the imperial Saragossa-Mérida road. Reputed for its arms, it was also the birthplace of **Martial** (*c* 40-104AD), author of the *Satires* in which, with a malicious but honest pen he described high society in Rome. His wit brought him close to those in power who paid as richly to ensure his silence as his plaudits! The poet retained his affection for his native countryside and finally returned to end his days in Bilbilis.

Collegiate Church of St Mary Major (Santa María la Mayor). — The brick built church, typically Aragonese in appearance, has an octagonal **belfry★** which is one of the most harmonious in the region. The regular geometric decoration of the tower shows clearly the persistence of Moslem influence in the 16C architecture of Aragon. Spanish Renaissance influence is clearly apparent in the alabaster sculptures of the **portal★**. The wooden door panels have a delicate decoration of foliated scrollwork, masks and figurines. Inside are an ornately baroque chancel grille, a 17C retable at the high altar and exuberantly baroque chapels behind the chancel.

St Andrew's (San Andrés). — Look up at the wonderfully elegant Mudejar **belfry★**.

DAROCA ★ (Zaragoza)
Michelin map **443** fold 24 — Pop 2 540

Daroca, set amidst pine scattered hillsides, looks, from the main road, the N 330 which partly encircles it, like a jewel in its case. Belfries rise above the red roofs of the city still enclosed by a crumbling but massively impressive wall. Daroca, so picturesque with narrow alleys and attractive house fronts, was a famous craftsmen's centre in the Middle Ages.

The miracle of the Holy Altarcloths. — According to tradition, in 1239 the Christian settlement was attacked by the Moors just as mass was being celebrated. The consecrated hosts were hidden between two altarcloths; when these cloths were taken from their hiding place it was seen that the hosts had left bloodstained imprints on the linen. Three towns claimed the precious relic: Teruel, Calatayud and Daroca. To settle the dispute the holy cloths were placed upon a mule which was then set free. It made for Daroca, dying, however, as it entered the Lower Gate (Puerta Baja).

DAROCA★

■ **SIGHTS** time: 1 hour

Walls. — The town appears somewhat lost within the long perimeter (3km · 2 miles) which encircles the neighbouring crests. Built in the 13C and originally defended by more than a hundred towers, turrets and bastions, it was constantly under repair until the 16C since its original construction material was a friable stone. There were two gates, both fortified, the one in the west being known as the Lower Gate (Puerta Baja) and bearing the arms of the Emperor Charles V.

St Mary's Collegiate Church (Colegiata de Santa María) (A). — The church, built in the Romanesque period as a repository for the holy cloths was transformed in the 15 and 16C. In the north wall beside the belfry is a Flamboyant Gothic portal.

Interior. — The late Gothic nave includes such Renaissance features as a cupola above the transept crossing.

The **south chapels,** partly faced with locally manufactured 16C *azulejos,* contain a series of interesting altarpieces. To the right of the entrance is a 15C **altarpiece★** in multicoloured alabaster which is believed to have been carved in England — note the anecdotal detail. Gothic tombs stand on either side of the nave. The **Holy Relics' Chapel★** (15C) is on the site of the original Romanesque apse. The altar, preceded by a kind of Flamboyant roodscreen and framed by scenes of the miracle on the walls, includes a shrine containing the holy altarcloths. All around stand statues carved out of multicoloured alabaster in delightful, mediaeval poses. The Gothic **retable★** is dedicated to St Michael.

Parish Museum★. — *Guided tours 9am to 1pm and 4 to 8pm; 50pts.*

Among the paintings on wood are two 13C panels and **altarpieces** to St Peter (14C) and St Martin (15C). All the gold and silver plate was made in Daroca except for the **reliquary** which formerly held the holy altarcloths, which was made by the 14C Catalan, Moragues. The figures are of gold, the foundation of silver. Most of the **chasubles,** many of them very old, were woven in the town. The display also includes 17C Mexican robes.

St Michael's (San Miguel) (E). — This church, equally outstanding in its fine appearance for the purity of its Romanesque east end and its 12C portal, has recovered its original design. The 13C wall paintings in the apse have somewhat faded. The brick lantern is in the Mudejar style as is the well restored belfry in nearby **St Dominic's (Santo Domingo) (S).**

Avoid visiting a church during a service.

▇FUENDETODOS▇ (Zaragoza)

Michelin map ▇▇▇ fold 14 — Pop 166

Goya's house. — *Open 10am to 1pm and 4 to 8pm (3 to 6pm 1 October to 30 April); closed 1 and 6 January, 23 to 26 August, 24 and 25 December.*

Francisco de Goya y Lucientes was born in this modest house in this lonely village in 1746.

The main room and kitchen have been left poorly furnished, as they were during the artist's childhood. The chinaware is 18C, the roughly carved chairs are the same as the ones you will see today in many Lower Aragon farmhouses. On the first floor there is a fascinating **display★** of transparencies of the painter's works.

▇HUESCA▇ ★ ▣

Michelin map ▇▇▇ fold 4 — Local map p 68 — Pop 44 372
See town plan in the current Michelin Red Guide España Portugal

Huesca, the capital of Upper Aragon, has a tranquil provincial appearance, richly belying its turbulent historical past.

Marius' officer, **Sertorius,** sought refuge in the town when threatened by Sulla and his followers and then established it as the centre of an independent state. He founded a school (in 77BC) of Latin and Greek for the sons of officers and rich Italian immigrants but in 72BC was assassinated at a banquet by one of his lieutenants.

In 1096 **Pedro I of Aragon** reconquered Huesca, by then an important Moorish bastion, after a long and difficult siege. Having killed four Moorish kings in the struggle, Pedro included four heads in the Aragon coat of arms — a feature still to be seen in the Saragossa device. Huesca itself became the provincial capital but only briefly for in 1118 Alfonso I, the Battler, freed Saragossa and accorded it the privilege of provincial supremacy.

"Resounding like the bell of Huesca" is a Spanish description of a dire event with far reaching effects. The saying goes back to the 12C, when the King, **Ramiro II,** the Monk, angry at the insolence of his nobles, convoked them to his palace ostensibly to watch the casting of a bell which he promised would be heard throughout Aragon. The lords assembled, the king had the most rebellious beheaded — thereby making the fame of the bell indeed resound throughout his kingdom.

During the Civil War, Huesca was besieged unsuccessfully by the Republicans from September 1936 to March 1938. The devastation suffered by the upper part of the city can still be seen in spite of rebuilding around the cathedral.

■ **SIGHTS** *time: 1 hour*

Cathedral★. — The façade is elegant, ornate Gothic and is divided unusually by a gallery and a typical, Aragon, sculptured overhang. A narrow gable encloses a small rose window and the portal covings, where the statues carved out of friable limestone are weatherworn. In relief on the tympanum are the Magi and Christ appearing before Mary Magdalene.

The Late Gothic (15-16C) square ground plan is divided into a nave and two aisles and covered by star vaulting. Above the high altar of beaten silver, is a 1533 alabaster **altarpiece★★**. In this masterpiece, Damián Forment, placed in high relief, three scenes from the Crucifixion. In each the figures are on differing planes to give an impression of milling crowds: on the intricate predella are the Apostles and scenes from the Passion; below, in medallions on either side of the altar, a self-portrait of the sculptor and another of his daughter. The **choirstalls** are in later, Renaissance style.

Facing the cathedral is the town hall, a tastefully decorated Renaissance town house. Ask the usher *(on the 1st floor; daily 8.30am to 2.30pm and 4 to 6pm)* to see the macabre painting of 1880 of the **Bell of Huesca.**

St Peter the Old (San Pedro el Viejo). — *Entrance: Calle de los Cuatro Reyes. Open only during services.*

Although restored, the **cloister★** of this former 11C monastery remains a major example of Romanesque sculpture in Aragon *(p 62)*. On the side facing the church, the tympanum of the cloister doorway has an unusual Adoration of the Magi with all the emphasis on the giving of gifts. The capitals in the east gallery are the least restored. Leading off the cloister are funerary chambers of the Aragonese kings, Alfonso I the Battler, Ramiro II the Monk, where, in one case, a 2C marble tombstone has been installed to serve a second time!

Provincial Museum★. — *Open 10am to 2pm; closed Mondays; 75pts.* The museum is in the old university on an attractive old square. The university itself was built in 1690 as a series of eight halls round a fine octagonal *patio.* Parts of the former royal palace were incorporated in the building, including the gallery in which the Huesca Bell massacre took place. The museum, has a rich **collection★** of Aragonese Primitives (altarpiece of the Coronation of the Virgin by Pedro de Zuera).

There are also late 13C frescoes from the village of San Fructuoso de Bierge and a late 15C Annunciation.

EXCURSIONS

Río Gállego and Jaca★. — *Round tour of 207km - 125 miles. See below.*

Barluenga. — *14km - 9 miles northeast along the N 240.*

The ruins, on the left, are of the Monte Aragon Monastery, originally a fortress built by Sancho I Ramírez when investing the Moorish stronghold of Huesca.
Turn left after 7km - 4 miles after Huesca.

At the entrance to Barluenga, in the cemetery, stands the small Church of St Michael; *to visit apply at the presbytery.* The paintings in the interior date back to the 13C: the wooden framework is covered with a geometric pattern; at the end of the apse framing the window, are Christ in Majesty and the Archangel overcoming the devil; the upper part of the south wall illustrates the episode in the Golden Legend in which Gargan, seeing a bull leave his herd and seek shelter in a cave, tried to kill the beast with a poisonous arrow which was miraculously deflected by the Archangel to the archer's own forehead.

JACA (Huesca)

Michelin map **443** fold 4 — *Local maps pp 66 and 68* — Pop 13 771

Jaca, a small garrison town built on a terrace site in the Río Aragon Valley and overlooked by the Peña de Oroel, remains proud to this day of the part it played in repulsing the Moorish invasion from the 8C onwards. In May, a pilgrimage of historic figures and local dancing commemorates the courage of the women and girls in defence of the town. After this victory a county of Aragon was declared although it only extended over a few upper Pyrenean valleys; in 1035 this was raised to the status of a kingdom with Jaca as its capital.

Jaca today, at the end of the Somport road, serves as a gateway north to the Pyrenees, south to the rest of Spain and as a stopping place in its own right.

Cathedral. — The cathedral, built in the 11C, is one of the oldest in Spain. Its sculptured decoration was to influence the Romanesque craftsmen who worked on the churches on the pilgrimage road to Santiago de Compostela. Outside note the **historiated capitals★** of the south portal and behind it, the south door where great attention has been given to the draperies on the figures in the Sacrifice of Isaac and in King David and his musicians.

Gothic vaulting, regrettably embellished with ornate keystones in the 16C, covers the aisles which are unusually wide for the period. The apse and side chapels are profusely decorated with Renaissance sculpture but the cupola on squinches over the transept crossing has retained its original simplicity.

An episcopal museum in the cloisters and adjoining halls contains Romanesque and Gothic wall paintings (Masters of Bagüés and Urries, Osia church apse) and Romanesque paintings of the Virgin and Christ. *Open 10am to 2pm and 3 to 5pm.*

EXCURSIONS

Huesca and the Río Gállego Valley★. — *Round tour of 189km - 117 miles. Leave Jaca by the C 134; at Sabiñánigo turn into the C 136 going south.*

Lake Arguis★. — The artificial lake *(embalse)* at Arguis, deep green in colour and sparkling against its mountain background, is the star attraction of the Sabiñánigo - Huesca road over the Monrepos Pass (alt 1 262m - 4 140ft). There are frequent open views from the hilly **road★** which, beyond the lake, enters a narrow gorge necessitating numerous tunnels. Boulders block the river course.

Huesca★. — *Description p 64.*
Continue along the N 240 to Ayerbe.

Loarre Castle★★. — *The 4km - 2 1/2 mile castle road is narrow and has hairpin bends.* As you approach this **aerie** the sheer beauty and peace of the place becomes ever more compelling. It was Sancho Ramírez, King of Aragon and Navarre, who had this impenetrable fortress constructed at 1 100m - 3 609ft in 1096 and then installed a religious community within it. The walls, flanked by round towers, command a vast **panorama★★** of the Ebro depression. After the massive keep and fine covered stairway, turn to the church which was completed only in the 12C. Standing over a crypt are a tall nave, a cupola and an apse adorned with blind arcades, all in the purest Romanesque style. The capitals with formalised floral motifs are exceedingly elegant.

Return to the N 240 and turn right.

Beyond Ayerbe the road becomes more enclosed.

The Río Gállego soon comes into view, banked by tall crumbling cliffs, red ochre in colour.

The **Mallos★**, as they are called, are a formation of rose puddingstone, highly vulnerable to erosion which has here created sugar loaf forms — the most dramatic group stands to the right of the road, its flamboyant mass completely dominating the small village of **Riglos.**

Agüero. — *5km - 3 miles excursion off the N 240.* The setting of this village with rose tile roofs is made spectacular by a background pointed by a single upstanding Mallo. 1km - 1/2 mile before Agüero, a road leads off, right, to the Romanesque church of St James where the three aisles are covered by three separate stone roofs. Look at the carvings on the tympanum (Epiphany, Joseph Asleep) and the covings (Salome's Dance, left). *Ask in the village.*

Further up the enclosed Gállego Valley is the artificial **Lake Peña,** encircled on all sides by mountains reflected in its green waters.

Bear left at Bernués for San Juan de la Peña.

San Juan de la Peña Monastery★★. — *Description p 72.*

Take the N 330 to Jaca.

Roncal and Ansó Valleys★. — *Round tour of 137km - 85 miles — about 4 hours.* These high valleys have for a long time lived self-sufficiently. They played an important part in the resistance of the small kingdom of Aragon to the Moors and even today celebrate religious festivals, whenever possible, in local costume.

Sheep, grazed on common pastureland, provide the economic mainstay: Roncal cheese is well known. *Leave Jaca by the C 134 going west along the Río Aragon Valley. Continue between the arid marl hills for 45km - 28 miles.* Turn right into the C 137 which goes up the **Roncal Valley★** often steeply enclosed but always green and watered by the Río Esca. A narrow humpbacked bridge precedes your arrival in **Burgui.**

1km - 1/2 mile south of Roncal, birthplace of the tenor Gayarre (1840-1890), turn right into the Garde to Ansó road. When it drops down towards Ansó, this spectacular **road★** with high *corniche* sections affords a good bird's-eye view of the town and church (interesting ethnological museum; *75pts*) rising from a cluster of brown tile roofs. *To return south, the road follows the winding Río Veral Valley.* Often, at nightfall, great herds of cattle can be seen being driven along by cowherds in small, black hats. The river flows for 3km - 2 miles through the Veral's narrow gorge known as the **Hoz Biniés★.**

Santa Cruz de la Serós★. — *14km - 10 miles southwest of Jaca along the Pamplona road.*

This famous convent, founded late in the 10C, was richly endowed by royal princesses. Doña Sancha, daughter to the first King of Aragon bequeathed it all her worldly wealth on her death in 1095. The religious abandoned the convent in the 16C.

Only the **Romanesque church,** surrounded by small houses, remains. The stout belfry, crowned by an octagonal turret abuts on the lantern tower. The portal with its Chi-rho (Sacred monogram) decorated tympanum recalls that of Jaca Cathedral. Inside, a column and capitals from the now vanished cloisters, have been assembled to form an unusual stoup. Stairs lead to a vaulted chamber in the tower. **San Caprasio,** the small church at the entrance to the village, has been restored to its original simplicity. The nave, adorned with Lombard bands, and the small low apse, are typical of the 11C, the square belfry, pierced on every side by a paired window is late 12C.

MALUENDA (Zaragoza)

Michelin map 443 fold 13 — Pop 1 196

Maluenda will give pleasure to anyone who appreciates Mudejar art and Gothic painting. To reach it you pass through a landscape, between Calatayud and Daroca, of windswept clay hills flamboyant in their harsh red brown and typical of Lower Aragon.

St Justa and St Rufina's. — *The priest accompanies.* The church (15C) shows in its decoration of tall windows and stucco, the continuing influence of Moslem art in regional Gothic architecture.

The church's many altarpieces make it a museum of painting on wood; that at the high altar (16C) is late Gothic and shows the influence of Bermejo *(p 19).*

St Mary's. — Facing one another in the centre of the nave, rebuilt after a fire in 1940, are two altarpieces painted in the 15 and 16C in the local style.

ORDESA Y MONTE PERDIDO National Park ★★★ (Huesca)

Michelin map 443 folds 3 and 4 - *Local map p 68*

The Ordesa Valley, south of the Monte Perdido Massif, was declared a national park in 1918 (expanded in 1982) to safeguard its incomparable natural beauty, the variety of its flora and the richness of its fauna. It is a grandiose canyon cutting through vast, couched limestone folds. The escarpments which rise nearly 1 000m - 3 280ft from the valley floor, are divided into steel grey or red ochre strata. In spring, snow covers the peaks and as it melts cascades down the vertical rock face.

Along the valley bottom, the Río Arazas, a turbulent trout stream, rushes on beneath flourishing beeches and giant poplars. Growing up the lower slopes are pines, larches, firs — some 25m - 80ft tall and a carpet of laurel, sweet briar, heather and broom.

(After MTTC photo, Madrid)

Ordesa National Park

TOUR

The park must be visited between May and September, snow making it inaccessible by car in winter. At the start of the park road you can get a general view of the reserve from a *mirador* and a little further on, from a second, a look at the 60m - 197ft high **Tamborrotera Waterfall** ①. *The three walks below are feasible for the average walker with a good pair of shoes.*

The Soaso Circle Tour. — *Start from the Cadiera refuge; time: 7 hours.* This is the walk providing the best and most complete tour of the park.

From the Soaso Circle path you see, in succession, the **Fan (del Abanico)** ②, the **Strait (del Estrecho)** ③ and the **Cave (de la Cueva)** ④ Waterfalls, which are the park's most beautiful. There follow the **Tobacor** ⑤, 80m - 262ft high and a tributary of the Arazas, the **Gradas de Soaso** ⑥ or Soaso Steps and the 70m - 230ft long **Horse's Tail (Cola de Caballo)** ⑦. The path continues by the **Faja de Pelay,** overlooking the canyon to a depth of 2 000m - 6 500ft at the foot of the Sierra de las Cutas. From the **Calcilarruego Mirador** ⑧ there is a general view of the park and the Gallinero and Tobacor Falls. Return along the **Huntsman's Path (Senda de los Cazadores)** ⑨.

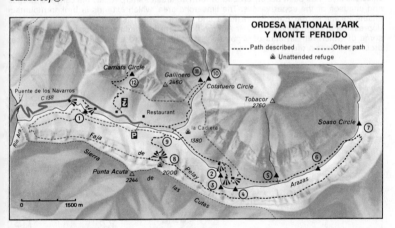

**ORDESA NATIONAL PARK
Y MONTE PERDIDO**

------ Path described ------ Other path
▲ Unattended refuge

Cotatuero Circle. — *Start from the restaurant; time: 4 hours.* On the park's northern border are the **Cotatuero** ⑩ and the **Tufts of Wool (de los Copos de Lana)** ⑪ falls with a drop of 250m - 820ft (dry in summer).

Carriata Circle. — *Departure from the Information Centre; time: 4 hours.*
The walk is worth doing in spite of the *clavijas* or mountaineering peg track which is not recommended to those who suffer from vertigo. The 100m - 328ft — **Carriata** ⑫ waterfall dries up in summer.

*Drive through Spanish towns using the plans in
the **Michelin Red Guide España Portugal**. Features indicated
include:*

- throughroutes and by-passes

- new streets

- car parks and one-way systems

All this information is revised annually.

PIEDRA Monastery ★★ (Zaragoza)

Michelin maps **443** folds 12 and 13 and **442** fold 28

Approach the monastery, if possible, by way of Ateca or the spa, Alhama de Aragón; the roads from each cross the arid, red earth countryside before joining in a final *corniche* section along the mountainside above the Tranquera artificial lake *(embalse)*. Scarcely visible, high up against the tawny hillside, is the village of **Nuévalos**.

The site. — Hidden in a fold of the dried out plateau is a green oasis fed by the Río Piedra. It was discovered, and, as was their way, settled by Cistercian monks from the Abbey of Poblet in Tarragona, who established a monastery on the spot in 1194. This was rebuilt several times before largely disappearing in the 19C. The conventual buildings have recently been reconstructed as a hotel.

The park and its waterfalls★★. — *Open 9am to sunset; 275pts; time: 2 hours.*

Roaring waterfalls and dancing cascades are to be found in the heart of the forest by walking along the marked paths *(follow the red signposts to go and the blue signposts to return)*, steps and tunnels laid out last century by Juan Federico Muntadas have transformed an impenetrable wilderness into a popular park. The first fall is the **Horse's Tail (Cola de Caballo),** a torrent of 53m - 174ft. This you first look down on from a *mirador* and come on again at the end of your walk if you descend the steep and slippery steps into the beautiful **Iris Grotto,** when you will see it from the back.

Diana's Bath (Baño de Diana) and the romantic **Mirror Lake (Lago de Espejo),** cupped between tall cliffs, are both worth halting at on the route which ends at the monastery ruins. The kitchen with its numerous chimneys, the refectory and the cloisters have been restored.

The towns and sights described in this guide
are shown in black on the maps.

The PYRENEES in Aragon ★★ (PIRINEOS ARAGONESES) (Huesca)

Michelin map **443** folds 2 to 5

The northern part of the province of Huesca, the Central Pyrenees, includes the highest peaks in the chain: Aneto (3 404m - 11 169ft), Posets (3 371m - 11 060ft) and Monte Perdido (3 355m - 11 008ft).

The foothills are often ravined and covered only with a sparse vegetation; the landscape at the heart of the massif, accessible up the river courses, is on a different scale altogether. The valleys whether wide and lush or narrow and gorgelike, lead always to mountain circuses well worth exploring.

Structure and relief. — The geological division of the Pyrenees into vast longitudinal bands can be clearly seen in this region. The **axis** of Primary terrain and granite rocks corresponds to the Maladeta, Posets, Vignemale and Balaïtous Massifs, where there are still remains of the Quaternary glaciers.

There follows the Pre-Pyrenees or Monte Perdido area where the deep secondary **limestone** layer has been deeply eroded to form an area of sharp relief: the canyons, gorges and circuses of the upper valleys. The limestone area, which extends in broken mountain chains as far as the Ebro Basin (Peña and Guara Sierras) is divided at Jaca by a long depression through which the River Aragon flows. Tertiary sediment accumulated into hills, some of which remain bare of vegetation, affording a weird blue soil landscape like that around the Yesa artificial lake.

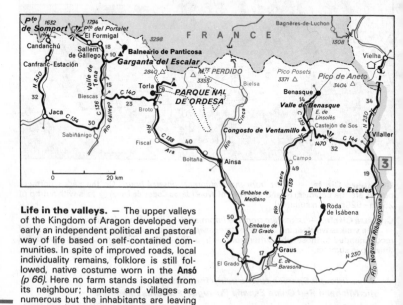

Life in the valleys. — The upper valleys of the Kingdom of Aragon developed very early an independent political and pastoral way of life based on self-contained communities. In spite of improved roads, local individuality remains, folklore is still followed, native costume worn in the **Ansó** *(p 66)*. Here no farm stands isolated from its neighbour; hamlets and villages are numerous but the inhabitants are leaving their slate covered cottages to work in Saragossa, Pamplona and Barcelona. The farming of mountain sheep is in decline though still important; cattle raising is increasing.

Industry is represented by chemical and aluminium works at Sabiñánigo.

Major hydroelectric undertakings are bringing life to certain valley areas, artificial lakes are lapping in previously barren valleys: the **Yesa** in the Aragon, **La Peña** in the Gállego, **El Grado** in the Cinca, the **Canelles** and the **Escales** in the Noguera Ribagorzana.

From Vielha to Vilaller — *See Pyrenees in Catalonia pp 92-94.*

From Vilaller to Castejón de Sos — *35km - 22 miles — about 1 hour*

A route linking the Noguera Ribagorzana and Esera Valleys.

Lake Escales★. — *22km - 13 1/2 miles.* The road, with a layout like a switch-back and by means of numerous tunnels, traces its course along the mountainside, affording as it does so, a good view of the vividly green lake below.

After the fork to Castejón, the road winds through fields and along valley floors before again rising up the mountainside. Once over the Fadas Pass (alt 1 470m - 4 823ft), you begin to get **views★** of the snow covered Maladeta peaks.

Benasque Valley★. — *14km - 9 miles from Castejón.* The Esera, in its upper course, is a clear torrent streaming over light coloured granite rocks in an open valley, lush and green in spite of its altitude. **Benasque,** at 1 138m - 3 734ft and somewhat overshadowed by the formidable granite mass of the Maladeta, serves as a base for walkers, climbers (ascending the Aneto) and skiiers (after 5km — 3 miles is Cerler mountain at alt 1 505m to 2 858m — 4 938ft to 9 377ft). The town itself has narrow streets and winding alleys, lined with old seignorial mansions.

From Castejón de Sos to Ainsa — *116km - 72 miles about 4 hours*

The road follows the most enclosed section of the Esera Valley, the **Congosto de Ventamillo★,** a defile of 3km - 2 miles — in which one is ever more amazed at the sheerness of the limestone rock walls. Where these diverge, the rocks are more friable and the river vanishes into a new course.

Below Campo, the Esera Valley opens out among ravined hills, where in an otherwise arid countryside the irrigated areas planted with vines and fruit trees around the Joaquín Costa and El Grado Lakes stand out clearly.

Graus. — The Esera and Isábena Valleys debouch onto the Cinca Plain close by Graus, a village supported by passing travellers. These, however, never see the village proper unless they get off the main road where they will discover an irregular shaped square, the Plaza de España, lined with old houses possessing carved and painted beams and brick arcades.

Roda de Isábena. — *25km - 16 miles from Graus.* The village looks down on the road from a delightful mountain **site★** from which there are views, looking north of Mount Turbón, and east and northeast of the enclosed Isábena Valley and the green Sierra de Serradúy. The paved cathedral square is stepped and overlooked by the façades of ancient buildings including the former bishops' palace. The cathedral itself is 11C with Lombard bands at its east end. In the crypt beneath the chancel is the **tomb of San Ramón★** with polychrome low reliefs; off the 12C cloister is a chapel with 13C frescoes.

Ainsa. — Ainsa stands on a promontory still girded by a wall, commanding the juncture of the Cinca and Ara Rivers. In the 11C the town was the capital of Sobrarbe, a kingdom established by García Jiménez following his successes against the Moors. The town has a certain attraction with country style rough stone houses, an arcaded main square and Romanesque church belfry.

From Ainsa to Ordesa — *49km - 30 miles — about 1 1/2 hours*

Between Boltaña and Fiscal, the river course has uncovered uneven earth strata which now rise out of the water curiously like dorsal fins. From Broto the great mass of the Mondarruego (alt 2 840m - 9 318ft), closing the Ordesa Valley to the north becomes the distant focal point in a spectacular **landscape★★** in which the small village of **Torla** can be seen massed against the western slope of the Ara Valley.

Ordesa y Monte Perdido National Park★★★. — *Description p 67.*

The Portalet Road — *65km - 40 miles — about 3 hours*

Beyond Torla you get views down the Ara Valley as far as Boltaña as the *corniche* road climbs to Linás de Broto. It continues across a fertile basin from which you can see, up the valleys to the right, the rock escarpments of Sierra de Tendeñera.

The **Tena Valley** is at first narrow and boulder strewn but widens out majestically at Saqués where it is filled by the vast Búbal reservoir lake.

Balneario de Panticosa★. — *10km - 6 miles.* The **Escalar Gorge★★ (Garganta del Escalar)** is so narrow that the sun seldom penetrates to the Gállego tributary running through its depths. The stream hollowed out a bed first through limestone and later through lamellar schists and granite whose boulder rubble now blocks the current. The **road★,** showered with spray from waterfalls when the snow melts, cuts down the west slope by long ramps and tight hairpin bends to an austere mountain cirque and spa (alt 1 639m - 5 378ft). The resort, known for its pure air and the health-giving properties of its six sulphur and radioactive springs *(season: 15 June to 15 September),* is hemmed in by steep slopes, dominated in the east by the Vignemale peak. The hotels are surrounded by greenery in pleasant contrast to the bare hillsides. There is a trout stream in the spa establishment grounds. *Apply to the management for fishing permits.*

After the Panticosa fork, the road becomes enclosed and hilly, rising in a *corniche* through pine trees and a tunnel beyond which the rocky point of the Foradada hides from view the snow-capped peaks of the Balaïtous Massif.

Sallent de Gállego. — Alt 1 305m - 3 297ft. Sallent, a mountain town at the confluence of the Gállego River and the Aguas Limpias torrent, is a frontier post and also a centre for trout fishing and mountaineering.

El Formigal. — Alt 1 480m - 4 856ft. Formigal, a new ski resort 4km - 2 1/2 miles above Sallent on the pass road, is equipped with 13 ski-tows, 4 chairlifts and a cable-car going to a high altitude restaurant (alt 1 890m - 6 201ft) and to the ski runs.

Portalet Pass. — Alt 1 794m - 5 886ft. The pass lies between the Portalet Peak and the sharply pointed Aneu summit to the west. The view northwest extends towards the Aneu cirque and the Pic du Midi d'Ossau in France (alt 2 884m - 9 466ft).

The PYRENEES in Aragon★★

Somport Road — *95km · 59 miles — about 3 hours. An easier road to the frontier but possibly crowded in the holiday season.*

South of Biescas, the Gállego Valley begins to widen as it approaches Jaca.

Jaca. — *Description p 65.*

The N 330, a major trunk road, follows the course of the Aragon Valley as does the railway which, however, ends at the international station of **Canfranc-Estación.**

Candanchú. — Alt 1 560m - 5 118ft. The most well-known ski resort in Aragon is in an open and sunny setting, 1km - 1/2 mile from the Somport Pass. Present equipment allows access to the ski runs at 2 020m - 6 627ft.

Somport Pass★★. — Alt 1 632m - 5 355ft. The Somport is the only pass in the Central Pyrenees which generally remains snow free all the year round. Its history as a thoroughfare goes back to the Romans who built a road over it which was trodden by Pompey's legions, Saracen hordes and later cohorts of pilgrims on their way to Santiago de Compostela. Climb the mound to the right of the monument commemorating the road's construction for the widest panorama there is of the Spanish Pyrenees.

SAN JUAN DE LA PEÑA Monastery ★★ (Huesca)

Map 443 folds 3 and 4 — 28km - 17 miles southwest of Jaca — *Local map p 66*

The monastery of San Juan de la Peña, symbol of the continued existence of the Christian faith in the Pyrenees at the time of the Muslim invasion, was chosen as their pantheon by the kings and nobles of Aragon-Navarre.

The community was founded in the 9C in a secluded site. In the 11C the order adopted the Cluniac reform and built an upper church in early Romanesque style exactly above their earlier church; the carved decoration of the cloister was only completed in the late 12C. All this while generous royal donations attracted many monks, some foreign, to the house. By the 17C, after several fires, it was decided to rebuild the monastery higher up the mountainside. This building, however, was sacked by the French in 1809.

Access and site. — Leave the car by the upper monastery which stands surrounded by firs and beeches and walk, right, along the outer wall to a shaded alley. Bear right at a fork following the signs *Mesa de Orientación* to a table from which there is a **view★★** across to the highest peaks in the Central Pyrenees.

Return to the car and descend the mountain's other slope by a steep and stony but passable road to the lower monastery. This appears minute, half-embedded in the rock wall. The **site★★** itself is spectacular.

Lower Monastery. — *Guided tours (time : about 3/4 hour) 10am to 2pm and 4 to 7pm.*

The monastery plan, because of its age and extraordinary site lodged in the side of the mountain, is unique. The lower storey, which is partially underground, is believed to have been constructed in the time of King Sancho Garcés in about 922.

Council Chamber. — The chamber, known also as the dormitory, has a massive style.

Lower Church. — This, the original church which later served as a crypt, is one of the rare Mozarabic constructions existing in the region. It consists of two adjoining aisles divided by wide arches and ending in twin niche-apses hollowed out of the living rock. Traces of mural painting can be seen on the walls and on the undersides of the arches. Mounting some steps, still within the church, one reaches the upper storey and an open court.

Pantheon of the Aragon nobility. — 11-14C. Funerary stones line the left wall of the court in surrounds of moulded billets or pearls, each emblasoned with a coat of arms, Chi-rho or a cross with four roses, emblem of Iñigo Arista, founder of the Kingdom of Navarre.

Upper Church. — Late 11C. Rock roofs part of the single aisle, while the three absidal chapels, decorated with blind arcades, are hollowed out of the cliff face. The **royal pantheon,** in which for 500 years the kings of Aragon and Navarre were buried, opens off the north wall. The present décor is 18C.

Cloister★. — 12C. The cloister, cornered between the precipice and the cliff face, which provides an unplanned roof, now consists of two galleries only with historiated capitals and a third gallery in a poor state of preservation. The original column arrangement, alternating single, double and quadruple columns is reproduced in miniature between the capital abacci and the arch billets. The mason who carved the **capitals★★,** probably aided by an apprentice, developed a personal style and symbolism, as he worked on his chronological survey of man from the creation to the coming of the Evangelists, which was to influence sculpture throughout the region for years to come *(illustration p 20).*

SARAGOSSA ★★ ZARAGOZA P

Michelin map 443 fold 14 — Pop 590 740
See map of built-up area in the current Michelin Red Guide España Portugal

Saragossa is a warm brown brick agglomeration lying between its two cathedrals and spreading down into the Ebro basin of which it is the metropolis. It occupies a privileged position at the centre of the vast depression, once an arid desert and now a fertile plain, watered by the three rivers which meet upon it and the nearby imperial canal now used only for irrigation. Sugar refining and textiles are staple industries in the local economy which is being developed and diversified.

The city was largely rebuilt in the 19C after the War of Independence and although not especially striking, pleases on account of the bustling life of its broad streets and the coming and going of travellers to Madrid and Barcelona.

Saragossa is both a major university and religious centre, veneration of the Virgin of the Pillar (Virgen del Pilar) making it the first Marian sanctuary in Spain.

The "Pilar" festivals. — In the week of 12 October, Saragossans extol "their" Virgin with incredible pomp and fervour: on the 13th at about 7pm the **Rosario de Cristal** procession moves off by the light of 350 carriage borne lanterns. Other festivals during the week include the **Gigantes y Cabezudos** procession (cardboard giants and dwarfs with massive heads), *jota* dancing and the famous bullfights.

HISTORY OF THE TOWN AND ITS MONUMENTS

Caesaraugusta. — Salduba, well situated at the confluence of the Ebro and its tributaries, the Gállego and the Huerva, became, in the year 25BC, a Roman colony named after the Emperor Caesar Augustus — traces can still be seen along the Via Imperial of the fortified Roman perimeter **wall.** On 2 January in AD40, according to tradition, the Virgin appeared miraculously to St James, leaving as proof of her apparition the pillar around which came to be built the **Pilar Basilica.** In 3C the city is said to have suffered persecution at the hands of Diocletian — it still honours from that time the memory of the Uncounted Martyrs, interred in the crypt of **Santa Engracia (Z V).**

Sarakusta. — Four centuries of Moslem occupation would appear to have left the city, renamed Sarakusta, with but a single major heirloom. From the brilliant but shortlived *taifa* kingdom established under the proud Benihud dynasty in the 11C, there remains the **Aljafería,** a palace, built by the first monarch of the line and a unique and very precious example of Hispano-Moslem art.

Saragossa, capital city. — The Aragon kings, after freeing the city from the Moors, proclaimed Saragossa, the great agricultural town on the Ebro, as capital. The city, however, jealous of its autonomy, voted itself the most democratic *Fueros* in the whole of Spain *(p 62)* and increased its prosperity through wise administration and establishment of a **commercial exchange.** Tolerant by tradition, it protected its Moslem masons, so that the Mudejar style could be used to embellish its churches: (the **Cathedral** apse, **San Pablo (X S)** and **Magdalena** towers **(Y E).** Houses in the old town give a good idea of the city's prosperity in the 16C.

Two heroic sieges. — Saragossa's resistance before Napoleon's army in the terrible years 1808-9 shows the Spanish people's desire for independence and the determination of those of Aragon in particular. In June 1808 the city was invested for the first time by the French, the siege only being lifted on 14 August after news of the French defeat at Bailen in the far south. The exultant Saragossans sang "The Virgin of Pilar will never be French". Alas! On 21 December General Lannes appeared with 18 000 men who remained until the town capitulated on 20 February. Under their General, **Palafox,** the citizens fought off open assaults so that it was only by mining house after house that the French were able to take the town. By the end, combat, famine, epidemics, had accounted for half the inhabitants — some 54 000 were dead. From that appalling siege there remains the French General Lannes' tribute "The brutes certainly knew how to fight" and the shrapnel pitted **Carmen Gate (Z).**

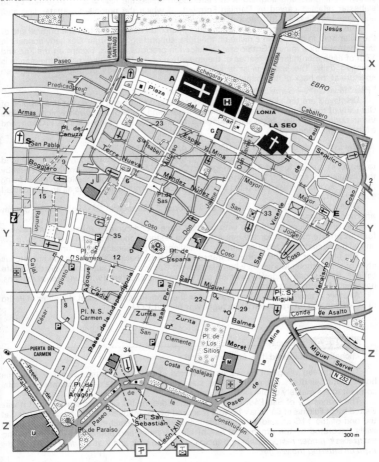

SARAGOSSA★★

■ **SIGHTS** *time: 2 1/2 hours*

The Seo★★ (X). — *Under restoration.* The Cathedral of Saragossa, the Seo, includes all decorative styles from the Mudejar to the Churrigueresque, although it is basically Gothic and remarkable for its size. Added in the 17C was the tall belfry which harmonises with those on the Pilar nearby; and in the 18C it was the baroque façade.

Walk into the Calle del Sepulcro to see the Mudejar decoration at the **east end**.

The interior is impressive with its five aisles of equal height. Above the high altar is a Gothic **retable★** with a predella carved by the Catalan, Pedro Johan, and the three central panels of the Ascension, Epiphany and the Transfiguration by Johann of Swabia (the stance of the figures and the modelling of the faces strike a German note).

The **chancel closure (trascoro)** and some of the side chapels were adorned in the 16C with sculptured groups, clear evidence of the vitality of Spanish carving during the Renaissance. Other chapels, ornamented in the 18C, show the all too excessive exuberance of the Churrigueresque style; exceptions are the **Parroquieta**, a Gothic chapel containing a 14C tomb influenced by the Burgundian style and to a greater extent the **cupola★** in the Moorish style in polychrome wood with stalactites and strapwork (15C).

Museums open: 9am to 2pm and 4 to 6pm; 100 pts, ticket valid for the "Pilar" Museum.

Treasure★. — *In the sacristy.* Exhibited are paintings, an enamel triptych and religious objects.

Tapestry Museum★★. — The cathedral's 60 tapestries of which 16 are on display, form an outstanding collection of Gothic hangings. All were woven at Arras or Brussels; titles include the *Sailing Ships,* the *Crucifixion,* and the *Passion.*

The Exchange★ (Lonja) (X). — *Open only during temporary exhibitions.*

Saragossa, like the other major trading towns of Valencia, Barcelona and Palma in the Kingdom of Aragon, founded a commercial exchange as early as the 16C. These buildings, in a transitional style between Gothic and Plateresque, include some of the finest examples of civil architecture in Spain. In this instance the hall is divided into three by tall columns, their shafts ornamented with a carved band of grotesques. Coats of arms supported by cherubs mark the start of the ribs which open out into star vaulting.

The **town hall (ayuntamiento)** (X H) has been rebuilt in traditional Aragon style with ornate eaves. Two modern bronzes stand at the entrance.

Our Lady of the Pillar★ (Nuestra Señora del Pilar) (X A). — Several sanctuaries have been built successively on this site to enshrine the miraculous pillar. The present edifice, Saragossa's second cathedral, was designed by Francisco Herrera the Younger in about 1677. It takes the form of a buttressed quadrilateral lit by a central dome. The lanterned cupolas whose ornamental tiles may be seen reflected in the waters of the Ebro, were added in the 18C by Ventura Rodríguez.

The interior, divided by giant pillars with fluted pilasters into three aisles, is partly covered by cupolas decorated with frescoes, some of which were painted by Goya.

Highly ornate chapels surround the main area which divides into three: the **chancel**, closed by a grille and adorned with Plateresque stalls; the **high altar** surmounted by an alabaster **retable★** carved by Damián Forment, of which the predella is outstanding and, lastly, the **Lady Chapel**, (18C) decorated by Ventura Rodríguez.

The chapel is, in fact, virtually a miniature church on its own, built on the original site of the pillar now to be seen in a niche on the right, supporting the Virgin. Our Lady appears in this instance as a minute Gothic statue, haloed in precious stones. Except on the 2nd and 12th of each month (anniversaries of the apparition of the Hispanidad, *p 137)* the mantle is changed daily. The jasper pillar is kissed each year by crowds of pilgrims through an aperture at the back of the chapel.

"Pilar" Museum★. — *Same opening times as the Seo museums.*

Displayed are the sketches of Goya, González Velázquez and Bayeu for the cupolas of Our Lady of the Pillar, a model by Ventura Rodríguez and some of the jewels which adorn the Virgin during the "Pilar" festivals. Among the most ancient ivory pieces are an 11C horn and a Moorish jewellery box.

Aljafería★. — *Access by the Calle Conde de Aranda* (Y 15).

The Aljafería, a Moorish palace, built in the 11C by the Benihud family, was rearranged to serve as a palace for the Aragon kings and Catholic Monarchs before being taken over by the Inquisition and later converted into barracks. The enormous building *(now being restored),* so closely resembling the Moorish palaces of Andalusia, comes as an unexpected surprise so far north.

Open 10am to 2pm and 5 to 7pm (4 to 6pm 1 October to 31 May); closed Sunday afternoons, Tuesdays and holidays.

The ground floor is Moorish with delicate tracery and carved capitals. The **musallah,** a form of private mosque, for the emirs, has been restored complete with the mihrab *(p 39)* and all the accustomed Moorish fantasy of multilobed arches and floral decoration.

The first floor and the staircase, transport the visitor back 400 years to the sumptuous style of the Catholic Monarchs when Flamboyant Gothic reigned supreme. Only the ornate **ceiling★,** its caissons divided by geometric interlacing and decorated with pine-cones remains, however, of the throne room.

Another *artesonado* ceiling can be seen in the room in which **St Isabel,** daughter of Pedro III of Aragon and future Queen of Portugal, was born in 1271.

SIRESA (Huesca)

Michelin map **443** fold 3 — *Local map p 66*

The Pyrenean village of Siresa, lies clustered at the end of a narrow valley, its stone houses with windows outlined in white, slate roofs and mountain-type chimneys, a total contrast to the majesty of San Pedro Church.

The monastery of San Pedro was founded before the 9C since we are told that it was visited by **St Eulogus of Córdoba** who was martyred by the Infidels in 859; it was reformed at the end of the 11C and admitted Augustine monks. The **church★** has a fine elevation, its walls decorated by the ornamental use of blind arcades and buttresses. The interesting **altarpieces★** *(under restoration)* are principally 15C *(to visit apply at the first house on the right on entering the village).*

SOS DEL REY CATÓLICO ★ (Zaragoza)

Michelin map 443 folds 2 and 3 — Pop 1 120

It was in this town in the **Sada Palace** *(guided tours)* that Ferdinand the Catholic, who was to unite Spain, was born in 1452. The houses, walls and doorways which line the narrow cobbled streets and alleys leading to the keep and the church give the town a mediaeval air.

St Stephen's★ (San Esteban). – *If closed apply to the priest.* From a passage beneath the church, you can see into the 11C **crypt** dedicated to Our Lady of the Pardon. Two of the three apses are decorated with 14C wall paintings.

The statue columns at the **main door** have the stiff and noble bearing of those at Sangüesa. The **church** itself, built in the Transitional style to the same plan as the crypt, only larger, has a beautiful Renaissance **gallery★** with **stalls★★** dating from 1556 carved by Juan de Moreto.

TARAZONA ★ (Zaragoza)

Michelin map 443 fold 13 — Pop 11 195

Tarazona groups its houses, each a different tone of brown, in tiers above the quays which line the Río Queiles. In Roman times the city drew wealth from the Moncayo iron mines. In the Middle Ages, it was for a time, the residence of the Aragon kings — round the former royal mansion, now a bishops' palace, a picturesque old quarter still remains with narrow streets and tall façades.

Cathedral★. — This Gothic church was largely rebuilt in the 15 and 16C. The Aragon Mudejar style can be clearly seen in the belfry and lantern tower. The portal, which is Renaissance, is flanked by unusual caryatids due to the mixture of styles — Classical Antiquity and Christian tradition. An allegory of charity is carved on the keystone.

The blind arcades of the triforium in the transept have an *ajimeces* air. Walk left around the ambulatory to the second **chapel★** which contains the delicately carved Gothic tombs of the two **Calvillos** cardinals from Avignon. The late 14C altarpiece depicts, in miniature, scenes in the Sienese manner, the martyrdoms of several saints.

Cloister★. — The cloister bays are filled with 16C Moorish plasterwork tracery.

TERUEL ℙ

Michelin map 443 fold 25 — Pop 28 225

The capital of Lower Aragon occupies, at an altitude of 916m - 3 050ft, a tableland separated from the surrounding plateau by a wide divide through which flows the River Turia. A landscape of ravined brown ochre heights, visible on all sides from the *rondas* circling the town, provides a unique **setting★**.

Teruel suffered terribly in the winter of 1937-8 when the temperature fell to -18 °C or -0.4 °F and Republicans and Nationalists took it in turn to attack the town. The great richness of Mudejar architecture in Teruel arises because Christians, Jews and Moslems all lived together in the town until the 15C — the last mosque was closed only in 1502.

The Lovers of Teruel. — In the 16C the discovery in the same grave of the bodies of two young people, **Isabel de Segura** and **Diego de Marcilla** who lived in the 13C, gave rise to a legend of tragic love. Diego sought to marry Isabel, who loved him, but her father, having chosen a rich suitor, refused his consent. Diego thereupon went to the wars to win honour and riches. The day of his return, five years later, was Isabel's wedding day to his rival. He died before her in despair but the following day at the funeral Isabel was overcome with grief and died in her turn. This drama was immensely popular in Spain and inspired many 16C poets and dramatists including Tirso de Molina and Hartzenbusch.

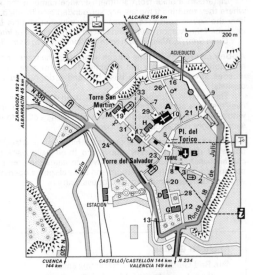

■ SIGHTS time: 1 hour

The triangular **Plaza del Torico** in the heart of the town, is the traditional local meeting place. The square lined with rococo style houses, gets its name from the small statue of a bull calf on a pillar at its centre.

The Mudejar Towers★ (Torres mudéjares). — There are five in all. They were erected between the 12 and 16C in each case to a three storey plan: at the base an arch provided access to the street; the centre, pierced only by narrow Romanesque lancets, was decorated with Moorish influenced ornamental brickwork and ceramics, while at the top was a belfry, pierced by bays in pairs below and quadruples above. The two best examples, the **St Martin** and **Saviour (Salvador)** Towers, are both 13C.

TERUEL

Cathedral (A). — The edifice, originating in the 13C with the tower, was enlarged in the 16C and further increased by a lantern and ambulatory in the 17C. The tower and lantern remain as authentic examples of the Mudejar period. The late 13C *artesonado* **ceiling★**, hidden in the 17C beneath Gothic star vaulting and so preserved, has now once more been revealed, to show caissons, beams and consoles painted with decorative motifs: people at court and hunting scenes. It can be seen up close from the upper gallery at the top of the stairs.

In addition, the cathedral possesses a 15C **altarpiece** of the Coronation of the Virgin (north transept) in which the architectural background in scenes depicted along the second band are shown in perspective suggesting Flemish influence. The **retable at the high altar**, carved in the 16C, is by Gabriel Joli *(p 62)*. Joli was known for his skilful portraits and his way of illustrating movement by a turn of the body but in this piece he is poorly served by wood which is too dark, blurring the details.

St Peter's (San Pedro) (B). — In spite of 18C reconstruction, the church has kept its original Mudejar style in its tower and east end. The 16C altarpiece illustrates many themes similar to those in the cathedral.

A **funerary chapel** for the Teruel Lovers adjoins the church *(open 9am to 1pm and 5 to 9pm; if closed ring at No 1 Calle Matías Abad)*.

The lovers are shown in an alabaster relief by Juan de Ávalos (20C), symbolically reaching out to touch hands. Through the glass walls of the tomb, also in the chapel, can be seen the lovers' actual skeletons.

UNCASTILLO (Zaragoza)
Michelin map **443** fold 3 — Pop 1 862

An unusual 14C belfry ornamented with machicolations and operatic scenery type pinnacle turrets dominates the Romanesque Church of St Mary. But what is truly outstanding is the **south portal★★** where the rich and delicate carving, so well preserved, makes it one of the finest doorways of the late Romanesque period. The church **gallery** with Renaissance **stalls★** and the 16C **cloister★** have a particularly ornate decoration.

VALDERROBRES (Teruel)
Michelin map **443** fold 27 — Pop 1 847

The view of the town from the humpbacked bridge over the river, appears picturesquely foreshortened: crowning all is the tall outline of the mediaeval castle *(under restoration)*, flanked by the polygonal belfry of Santa María; below are the round tiled roofs of the houses and lastly, commanding the bridge, the machicolated gateway in the old city wall.

The façade of the **Church of Santa María** is remarkable for the purity of its deep Gothic west doorway. Great elegance derives from the lines of the bare covings meeting in a pointed arch beneath a crocheted gable and setting off perfectly the great Flamboyant rose window above.

VERUELA Monastery ★★ (Zaragoza)
Michelin map **443** fold 13

Cistercian monks from southern France came in the middle of the 12C to this spot where they founded a monastery, surrounded by a fortified perimeter wall. Seven centuries later the Seville poet **Bécquer** was to stay while writing his *Letters from my Cell* in which he described the Aragon countryside much in the manner of later guide books!
Open 9am (9.30am in winter) to 1.30pm and 4 to 8pm (3 to 6pm in winter); 50pts.

Abbey church★★. — The church, erected in the transitional period between Romanesque and Gothic, has a sober but attractive façade of a single oculus, a narrow band of blind arcades strangely lacking a base line and a doorway decorated with friezes, billets and capitals.

The interior, with pointed vaulting, is an amazing size. The transverse ribs are broken over the nave and horseshoe shaped over the aisles and ambulatory. A Plateresque chapel with a multicoloured carved door was built in the 16C onto the north transept. Opposite, the sacristy door is in a surprising rococo style.

Cloister★. — The cloister is ornate Gothic. At ground level the brackets are carved with the heads of men and beasts; above are three galleries with Plateresque decoration. The **chapterhouse★**, in pure Cistercian style, contains the tombs of the monastery's first fifteen abbots. Housed in the storeroom and several rooms opening onto the cloister is a museum with works by contemporary Aragonese painters.

Michelin Guides

The Red Guides (hotels and restaurants)

Benelux - Deutschland - España Portugal - main cities EUROPE - France - Great Britain and Ireland - Italia

The Green Guides (beautiful scenery, buildings and scenic routes)

Austria - Canada - England: The West Country - Germany - Greece - Italy - London - New England - New York City - Portugal - Rome - Scotland - Spain - Switzerland and 7 guides on France

3 Catalonia

See general map pp 76-77

This province of industry and leisure, ancient history and present activity has accrued material wealth from its labour and artistic riches from its long and lively past.

Geography. — Catalonia, a triangle bordered by the French Pyrenean frontier, Aragon and the Mediterranean has a varied landscape. In the north, at the eastern end of the Pyrenees it is green and wooded, and the watershed of the rivers Ter, Llobregat, Segre and the Nogueras tributaries of the Ebro keep the region well irrigated. The coast, in the north, is rocky, dividing into bays and inlets along the Costa Brava or Gerona shore but flattening out further south into miles of golden sand along the so called "Costa Dorada" which enjoys a dry and sunny Mediterranean climate. The hinterland, divided from the coast by the Catalan *sierras*, is more arid and has to endure harsh winters. The countryside, broken up by Pyrenean foothills, alters in the south to green hills sloping down to an intensively cultivated triangular plain around the lower Ebro. Although fertile (cereals, vines, olives and market-garden produce), Catalonia is primarily an industrial region centred on Barcelona, Spain's major port. The province, already densely populated, attracts labour from other areas.

History. — Catalonia's position on the Mediterranean brought it trade but also made it liable to invasion: in the 6C BC the Greeks arrived, to be followed in the 3C BC by Carthaginians, Romans, who made Tarragona the capital of a large part of the peninsula, and in the 8C AD by Arabs. Christian Catalonians called on Charlemagne who freed the country from the Moors but attached it to his own empire as the **Spanish March.** Only in the 9C, under **Wilfred the Shaggy** was this imperial yoke thrown off.

The province grew prosperous in the Middle Ages from the sea, even sending traders to the Far East. In the 12C Berenguer IV, Count of Barcelona, became King of Aragon *(p 62)* creating the joint kingdom of Aragon-Catalonia which was both powerful and vast, extending across the Pyrenees *(p 61)*. The proclamation of Ferdinand of Aragon's wife, Isabel, as Queen of Castile in 1479 was the first sign of provincial supremacy giving way to a desire for national unity although less markedly than elsewhere in Catalonia. Its separatist ideals were to involve it in revolt in 1640 against Philip IV — the king who by the **Treaty of the Pyrenees** in 1659 was to hand over the Roussillon to France and establish the frontier as it is today — and, in the 18C, it supported Charles, Archduke of Austria in the War of Succession. In reprisal, Philip V on his ascension, dissolved the Catalan *"fueros" (p 62)*.

Finally, in the 20C, Catalonia, by now Republican but still separatist, having obtained provincial autonomy under the 2nd Republic in 1932, became a Civil War battleground. It was on the losing side, however, and in 1939 its provincial autonomy was abolished by the Nationalists. However, in 1977 this provincial autonomy was reinstated.

The Catalan tongue. — Spain's official language is Castilian; Catalan, deriving from the French Langues d'Oc has been recognised by the new constitution as the official language in Catalonia (Catalan is also spoken in French Catalonia). It is a rich language which has always had a living literature.

The Arts. — Catalan **Romanesque art** developed particularly in the area between the Arán Valley and the River Ter where every Pyrenean valley had its simply designed church, frequently with a free standing bell tower. The interiors were rich in frescoes and altarfronts, now displayed in the museums of Vic and Barcelona. La Seo de Urgel Cathedral, the monastery churches of Sta María of Ripoll and Sant Pere of Rhodes are the best examples of the style.

Gothic flowered in Catalonia in a particular way: the pursuit of simplicity admitted no additional sculptured ornament; the elevation of three aisles of equal height *(p 15)* fulfilled the desire for spaciousness.

Catalan art was reborn last century: among the highly original figures to appear were the architect Gaudí *(pp 84-85)* and the painter **José Marí Sert y Badia** (1876-1945). Early this century Barcelona became the meeting place for a group of young artists who later found fame abroad: Joan Miró, Pablo Picasso *(p 19)* and the sculptor, Pablo Gargallo. **Pablo Casals** (1876-1973), the cellist, was born in El Vendrell, Tarragona; his home in the Sant Salvador quarter is open *(11am to 2pm and in summer only 5 to 8pm as well; closed Mondays; 100pts).*

(After Archivo MAS photo, Barcelona)

The Valls Xiquets

Folklore. — The **Sardana** is danced in a circle in main squares on Sunday mornings, to the accompaniment of fife and drum . Corpus Christi processions are most brilliant, particularly in Sitges where the procession walks on carpets of flower petals. At festivals at El Vendrell and Valls the **Xiquets** form human pyramids.

AGRAMUNT (Lérida)
Michelin map **443** fold 18 — Pop 4 562

The church has an early 13C **portal★** : geometric motifs on the covings resemble those on Lérida Cathedral and other nearby churches. The central group, presented by the master weavers of the town in 1283, is slightly later.

AIGÜES TORTES Y LAGO DE SAN MAURICIO
National Park ★★ (Lérida)

Michelin maps 🎱🅖 fold 12 or 🍱🍱🎱 folds 6-7 — *Local map pp 92-93*

The park, which extends for 102km² - 39sq miles between the Noguera de Tort and Noguera Pallaresa Valleys, lies on a plateau at an altitude of 1 500m relieved by heights of up to 3 000m - 5 000-10 000ft. The terrain, which was glacially eroded, now affords a varied landscape of hollowed out valleys and lakes, snow covered ranges and peaks such as the Colomés (2 932m - 9 620ft) which forms the park's snowcapped perimeter to the north. Chamois, Pyrenean wild goat and ibex have found sanctuary among the peaks, wild boar and capercaillie (becoming extinct) in the woods.

Roads to the park are not practical for family cars. Apply in advance (half a day) in Caldes de Boí, Boí or Espot to hire a jeep or go on a tour.

From Caldes de Boí, to the west, one enters into the National Park, whose name *Aigües Tortes* means winding waters *(illustration p 8)*, as the stream twists amidst pastures; eastwards, the Espot road leads to Sant Maurici Lake which reflects the peaks of the Sierra dels Encantats. Walkers can cross the park *(1 day)* from either Caldes de Boí or the Espot track by passing by the Llong Lake and the Portarró de Espot Pass (2 423m - 7 949ft) from which there is a view down both sides of the mountain.

◼ AMPURIAS ★ ───────
EMPÚRIES (Gerona)

Michelin map 🍱🍱🎱 fold 11

In the 6C BC, the Phoceans founded Emporion on the then small offshore island now joined to the mainland and occupied by the village of Sant Marti d'Empúries.

A century after the foundation of the "old town", known as **Palaiapolis** (B) a new town, **Neapolis** (A), was established on the mainland opposite the island. In about 49 BC Caesar installed a colony of veterans on the slopes above the old Greek village. Emporion continued to develop — at one time it was even a bishopric as the basilica ruins (7) discovered in Neapolis prove — but in

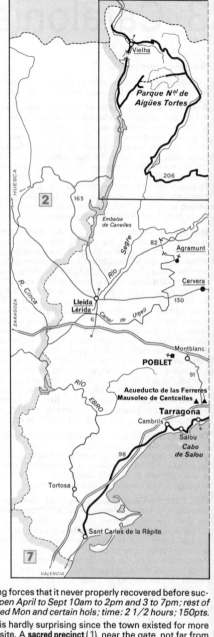

3C AD it suffered so severely from invading forces that it never properly recovered before succumbing finally to the Moors in the 8C. *Open April to Sept 10am to 2pm and 3 to 7pm; rest of the year 10am to 1pm and 3 to 5pm; closed Mon and certain hols; time: 2 1/2 hours; 150pts.*

Neapolis. — The piling up of the ruins is hardly surprising since the town existed for more than 1 000 years on the same restricted site. A **sacred precinct** (1), near the gate, not far from the **Temple of Aesculapius,** god of medicine, contained altars and statues of the gods.

Nearby stood the **watch tower** (2) and, at its foot, drinking water cisterns for the quarter (a **filter** (3) has been reconstructed). On the far side of the gate was the **Temple of Zeus Sarapis,** (sun god and also a lord of healing and fertility) (4), surrounded by a colonnade.

At the other end of the main street was the **Agora** (5), general meeting place and heart of the town, where the bases of three statues remain. A street ran from the *agora* to the sea, bordered on its left by the **stoa** (6) or covered market. Beyond the *stoa* with its double alleyway of shops are the clearly distinguishable ruins of a **palaeochristian basilica** (7) with a rounded apse.

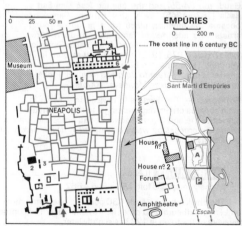

Place names framed in brown :
Museum of mediaeval art
Place names underlined in brown :
Romanesque church

Museum. — A section of Neapolis is displayed together with models and finds from the excavations, including a small mosaic of the sacrifice of Iphigenia.

The Roman town. — Cross the road and climb the hill to the city founded by Caesar overlooking the earlier Greek town and Roses Bay. This geometrically laid out upper town was of vast size.

House No 1. — The entrance on the **decumanus** or north-south street, opened onto an *atrium* or inner courtyard where a basin stood to catch rainwater. To the left were reception rooms paved in black and white mosaic; to the right, at the house's north end, the owner's private bath and, opposite, the residential apartments, all of which faced onto a peristyle or colonnaded court from which the Spanish *patio* derives.

House No 2. — In addition to the rooms which are still paved with mosaic, one, near the *atrium,* has been reconstituted by the original rammed earth method, so that its mud walls now appear standing on the uncovered stone foundations.

Forum. — The great rectangular square, lined along its sides by porticoes and to north and south respectively by temples and shops, was the centre of civic life in the town.
A street led to the city gate and beyond the walls to the **amphitheatre** which is still distinguishable.

Each year
*the **Michelin Red Guide España Portugal***
presents a multitude of up-to-date facts in a compact form.

Whether on a business trip, a weekend away from it all
or on holiday take the guide with you.

CATALONIA

ANDORRA ★★

Michelin map 🗺 folds 14 and 15 — Pop 42 712

Andorra, which has remained curiously apart from its neighbours, Spain and France, attracts visitors by the beauty of its scenery and the picturesqueness of its villages.

Documents; currency; customs. — A valid passport and, for a car, a green card and papers indemnified as for Spain are required for entry. Spanish pesetas and French francs are accepted equally. There are customs' formalities on the frontiers with Spain and France.

Geographical notes. — Andorra, which has a total area of 464km² — 179 sq miles (about 1 1/3 times the size of the Isle of Wight) lies in the heart of the Pyrenees and is made up of two main valleys, the Valira del Orient and the Valira del Nord. The river waters converge to form the Gran Valira which flows south into Spain where it joins the River Segre, a tributary of the Ebro.

The country is separated from France by a ring of summits which vary in altitude from 2 500 to 3 000m - 8 000 to 10 000ft; the road between the two has to scale the Envalira Pass (2 407m - 7 897ft). Communications with Spain down the Segre Valley through Cerdaña, are easier and remain open through all seasons.

It has only been in the past 50 years that Andorra has been accessible to the outside world - the first surfaced roads were opened on the Spanish side in 1913 and only in 1931 on the French side. Since then modern residential and commercial complexes have opened in the Gran Valira Valley. However, the old Andorra can still be found on the high plateaux or the smaller neighbouring valleys, accessible by mountain roads *(excursions by cross-country vehicles)*.

There are 42 712 Andorrans; mostly Catalan speaking they live in 7 parishes or communes each of which comprises several small villages and hamlets.

The daughter of Charlemagne. — "Charlemagne the great, my father, will deliver me from the Arabs" begins the Andorran national anthem, and continues "Alone, I remain the only daughter of Charlemagne, Christian and free for eleven centuries, Christian and free I will remain between my two valiant masters, my two protecting princes".

Andorra has been an independent principality since the Middle Ages; governed by two neighbouring lords who jointly defined their powers and their rights on a territory considered their fief. Particular to Andorra is that the two lords because of their geography and history, became by nationality foreign to each other. However, in accordance with feudal law, Andorra kept its status as a jointly owned territory. It was never found necessary to write down a constitution as customs and rights governed the municipality. Nevertheless, during sessions of the General Council (supreme administrative body - no legislative power), the *Manual Digest* (1748), a record of Andorra's legal and social traditions, is consulted. The dual allegiance to two co-princes was established in 1278 by the Bishop of Seo de Urgel and Roger Bernard III, Count of Foix. However, while the Bishops remain co-prince, the Counts of Foix passed their lordship on to France (when Henri IV Count of Foix and Bearn became king - 1589) and thus to the President of the Republic. To represent him in the valleys each co-prince appoints *veguers* (permanent delegates and judges) responsible for public order, and the judge of appeal who, with the *veguers* forms the *Tribunal de Corts* - the supreme court for criminal justice.

LIFE IN ANDORRA

A taste for liberty. — Andorrans pride themselves above all on being "avid, proud and jealous" of their liberty and independence. A longstanding system of representative government and eleven centuries of peace have given them little incentive to alter the country's administration. Local administration is carried out at the level of each parish (Parròquia). Every two years each Parròquia elects half the total members of a parish council (comù). The Principality is governed by the General Council (called before 1866 Consell de la Terra), which holds session once a month at the Casa de la Vall *(see below)*. This supreme administrative body is made up of 28 General Councillors (four from each Parròquia) and, they, themselves, elect the chief representative — Síndic General — and Sub-Síndic General. The ordinances decreed by the General Council, have the status of decrees, edicts, laws and orders. In 1981 the co-princes agreed to create the Government of Andorra. This government is presided by the head of government and his councillors (varies from 4 to 6 ministers). The Andorrans are not taxed nor do they have military service; postal services are supplied by both the French and Spanish governments. Private property, oddly enough, is minimal due to the large amount of land owned collectively.

Daily life. — Andorran life, patriarchal by tradition was still largely stock rearing and crop cultivation; smuggling had been regarded for centuries as a national skill. Between the high pastures and the hamlets and villages are the *cortals* or groups of barns (bordes) built on the lower slopes. Sun exposed slopes have been terraced in many areas and are closely cultivated. Tobacco, is planted to an altitude of 1 600m - 4 248ft and is the major crop in the San Juliá de Lória valley. Factors revolutionizing the traditional way of life are the development of hydro-electric power and tourism.

Our Lady of Meritxell. — The country is deeply religious and devoutly believes itself to be under the "maternal mantle of Our Lady of Meritxell" patron and protector of the principality. Annually (8 September), the pilgrimage to the Meritxell chapel takes place; this day is also the national holiday of Andorra.

ANDORRA LA VELLA - Pop 16 524

The capital of Andorra, huddled on a terrace (alt 1 209m - 3 967ft) above the Gran Valira Valley tends to be a bustling commercial town in the summer, although once away from the noisy main axis, the heart of Andorra la Vella has kept its peaceful narrow alleyways.

The town is linked to **Les Escaldes**, (alt 1 105m - 3 625ft) a tourist centre, spa and active commercial and industrial town by a bridge over the torrential Gran Valira, which splits into two — northern Valira and eastern Valira — enclosing the village on a plain.

Car parks. — *We recommend that you leave your car in one of the car parks.*

Casa de la Vall. — *Open 9 to 10am and 3 to 4pm; closed Saturday afternoons and all day Sunday.* The Casa is both Andorra's Parliament and Law Court and where the General Council *(p 79)* holds its sessions. It is presided by the Síndic General and Sub-Síndic General. This massive 16C stone structure was restored in 1963. By the main doorway one passes under large, long archstones.

78

On the façade the coat of arms symbolises the government of the co-princes; to the left — the Bishop of Seo de Urgel's mitre and crook and the 4 pales (red) signify royal Catalonia, while to the right — the 3 pales (red) represent the Count of Foix and two roaming cows of the Bearn. Inside, the ceiling and wainscoting decorate nobly the rooms. On the 1st floor 16C mural paintings adorn the reception room, formerly the refectory. The council chamber contains the famous "cupboard with seven keys". Each key is held by one of the country's seven parishes and each turns a different lock; inside are the national archives.

VALIRA DEL ORIENT VALLEY★
From Andorra to Pas de la Casa — 30km - 19 miles — about 1 hour

Envalira Pass (Puerto de Envalira) can be closed due to snow but is usually cleared within 24 hours.

Opening up after Les Escaldes the road climbs amid the rugged valley. In the background is the Radio Andorra complex flanked by an astonishing Neo-romanesque belltower. After Encamp by a steep rise over the threshold is **Les Bons**, a village built on a rocky spur, whose **site★**, is below castle ruins — it formerly defended the passage — and San Roma Chapel. To the right stands Andorra's national shrine, the chapel of Our Lady of Meritxell *(p 78 same opening times as the Casa de la Vall)*, rebuilt in 1976.

> **Canillo.** — Pop 506. The church, is topped with the highest bell-tower (27m - 88ft) in Andorra. The white charnel house, closeby, has cells holding burial vaults.
>
> **Sant Joan de Caselles.** — *If closed apply at the parish house.*

This church with its three-storey bell tower is a good example of Romanesque Andorran architecture. Inside, behind the picturesque wrought iron grille is an altarpiece (1525) by the Master of Canillo; the Life of Saint John and his apocalyptic visions. During the 1963 restoration a Romanesque **Crucifixion★** in stucco was found and replaced in its original location, where paintings of the Calvary were also found.

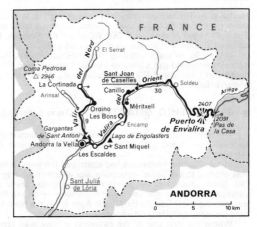

The road makes a wide curve in the Incles Valley.

> **Soldeu.** — Pop 265. This hamlet located at an altitude of 1 826m - 5 991ft is popular with skiers.

While climbing the road up the Envalira Pass one discovers, to the southwest, the Pessons glaciary amphitheatre; to the right is the Grau Roig ski resort.

Envalira Pass★★. — Alt 2 407m - 7 897ft. From the Envalira Pass (Puerto de Envalira) one of the highest passes in the Pyrenees, there is a **panorama**. The pass marks the watershed between the Mediterranean and the Atlantic (the Ariege).

The descent towards the Pas de la Casa (alt 2 091m - 6 861ft) offers spectacular views of the **Font-Negre pond and circus**, where the Ariege River takes its source.

> **Pas de la Casa.** — Pop 1 295. Alt 2 091m - 6 861ft. This high village marks the frontier with France (customs office). It is now also a ski resort.

VALIRA DEL NORD VALLEY★
From Andorra la Vella to La Cortinada
9km - 6 miles — Local map see above

This fresh and agreeable valley has kept much of its ancient atmosphere and character.

> **Sant Antoni Gorges (Gargantas de Saint Antoni).** — From a bridge across the Valira del Nord, you can see, over to the right the old humpbacked bridge, formerly used by muleteers.

The valley narrows, before opening out radiantly against a background of arid mountain slopes. In the distance beyond the Arisinal Valley, you can see the peaks of Como Pedrosa.

> **Ordino.** — Pop 523. *Leave the car in the village square near the church.* Wander through this picturesque village along the alleyways below the church.
> The church has beautiful wrought iron gates. Another example of art metalwork is found near the church; this 18m - 59ft balcony belonged to the Don Guillem residence, the former property of the master smith.
>
> **La Cortinada.** — A pleasant location among tobacco fields. Below the church and charnel house is an attractive house with exterior galleries and a dovecote.

The road continues northwards.

LAKE ENGOLASTERS
9km - 6 miles - and 1/2 hour on foot Rtn — Local map see above

Leave Les Escaldes eastwards on the road to France turn right at the outskirts of the village, onto the Engolasters mountain road.

On this plateau of pastureland — the sports annexe of Andorra la Vella — stands the fine Romanesque tower of **Sant Miquel.**

At the end of the road, cross the crest under the pines and start down *(on foot)* to the dam, which has raised the level (10m - 33ft) of the lake (alt 1 616m - 5 272ft). In the distance, opposite, stand the Radio Andorra aerials.

BAÑOLAS BANYOLES (Gerona)
Michelin map 🗺443 fold 10 — Pop 13 378

This delightful, picturesquely arcaded, town stands beside a bright blue **lake★** full of carp, which once a year is the setting of a water sports contest. A road 8km - 5 miles long circles the water passing, on the left bank, before a 12C church at **Porqueres**. Inside a triumphal arch has on the capitals and the upper parts of the columns most unusual carved human figures.

Besalú. — *14km - 9 miles northwest by the C 150.* Besalú was the capital from the 9 to the 12C of a county which extended from Figueres to the Ter Valley. At the town entrance, spanning the Fluvià, is an impressively carved, fortified bridge. In the town, the Romanesque Church of Sant Pere has a fine lion supported window and, what is rare in the area, an ambulatory. The streets at the centre look and feel old; the houses reveal attractive paired windows.

BARCELONA ★★★ 🅿
Michelin map 🗺443 fold 20 — Pop 1 754 900

Barcelona, the capital of Catalonia, Spain's second largest city and principal port is big, beautiful, rich, and commercial. Dominated by Montjuïc, with its fortress, Vallvidrera and Tibidabo hills, it has extended far beyond the bounds of its early Gothic kernel.

The modern town is cut by magnificent avenues: the **Avinguda de la Diagonal** which is nearly 10km - 6 miles long, the shorter Gran Via de les Corts Catalanes and Passeig de Gràcia and the popular **ramblas.**

History. — The city was founded by the Phoceans. In the 3C BC the Carthaginians gave it the name of Barcino or the town of Barca, the family name of the ruling house of Cartagena. The port began to develop in 201 BC under the Romans. By the Middle Ages its wealth equalled the power of the county of Catalonia *(p 75).*

In the 19C, although suffering frequent insurrections, Barcelona grew as its commercial interests extended and it became a major European port. Throughout the Civil War, until its capture on 26 January 1939 by the Nationalists, it was the seat of the Republican Government and an active revolutionary centre.

■ THE GOTHIC QUARTER ★★ (Barrio Gótico) (MR) *time: 3 hours*

The Gothic quarter, so named on account of the number of buildings within it constructed between the 13 and 15C, is, in fact, far older — traces of the Roman settlement even remain.

In the 4C, after barbarians had destroyed the town, a massive **perimeter** 9m - 30ft high was erected to enclose a rectangular site which could only be entered through one of the four gates situated at the points of the compass. These gates were flanked, like other vantage points upon the wall, by watch-towers — on the Plaça Nova are the towers which guarded the West Gate. In the Middle Ages when the town expanded beyond the walls, this gateway was converted into a house.

Where the east end of the cathedral is now, was formerly the site of the **Temple of Augustus** — four columns can still be seen at no 10 Calle Paradís (MR A).

Excavations beneath the cathedral revealed traces of a 4C basilica and further on of a Visigothic palace — walls from the latter are now in the Museum of the City of Barcelona.

Cathedral★★ (MR). — *Open 7.30am to 1.30pm and 4 to 7.30pm.* The present cathedral was built to replace a Romanesque church (late 13C-1450). The west face and spire are modern reconstructions of the original designs made in 1408.

The appealing **interior** has an outstanding elevation even for a Catalan style church *(p 14).* The nave is clearly lit by a fine lantern above the first bay but the vista is unfortunately broken by the chancel. In order to get a good view of the sweep of the apse advance to the choirstalls.

The **chancel** *(coro: 15pts)* contains double rows of beautifully carved and painted 14-15C stalls and a white marble **choirscreen★**, sculpted in the 16C after drawings by Bartolomé Ordóñez. It illustrates the death of the 4C virgin and martyr, St Eulalia, born in Barcelona and patron of the town. Her relics are in the **crypt** in an alabaster sarcophagus carved in the Pisan style in the 14C.

The **side chapels,** rich in Gothic altarpieces and marble tombs, include retables to St Gabriel (central ambulatory chapel), the **Transfiguration★** (St Benedict's Chapel, 2nd south chapel) and the Visitation (3rd south chapel).

The **cloister** *(access through the south transept),* completed in 1448, is light and airy; it has immense bays.

The **museum** *(open 11am to 1pm; 15pts),* located in the chapterhouse, off the west gallery, displays a *Pietà* by the Córdoban, Bermejo (1490) and altarpiece panels by the 15C Jaime Huguet. Facing the St Yves cathedral north door is the Frederic Marés Museum.

Frederic-Marés Museum★★ (MR). — *Open 9am to 2pm and 4 to 7pm; closed Mondays and Sunday afternoons; for holidays inquire locally; 80pts, Sundays and holidays free.*

Offered to the city by the sculptor Frederic Marés, the museum is in the Royal Palace, the residence of the counts of Barcelona, who were crowned kings of Aragon in 1137. The collection of polychrome wood statues which is exhibited on three levels gives a good idea of the development, continuity and variety of this peculiarly Spanish art.

— **basement:** 10 to 16C stone sculpture — shown in particular Arabic, Romanesque and Gothic capitals.

— **ground floor:** bronze Iberian ex-votos, Punic terracottas, and a **collection★** of polychrome wood sculpture (12-14C) of Crucifixes and Calvaries with the Virgin and St John at the foot of the cross movingly depicted in attitudes of sorrow or resignation. The statues are from Catalonia, Castile and León.

— **1st floor:** a historical continuation of the sculpture: 14 to 19C, including particularly a 16C **Entombment★** of six separate figures, and a 17C **Adoration of the Magi** by the sculptor, Pedro de la Cuadra.

— **2nd and 3rd floors:** a collection of nostalgia (keys, pipes, playing cards...).

Museum of the City of Barcelona (MR M[1]). — *Open 9am to 1.30pm and 3.30 to 8.30pm; closed Mondays, and Sunday afternoons; for holidays inquire locally: 80pts, Sundays and holidays free.* This museum, concerned with the development of Barcelona from its founding by the Phoceans to the 19C is situated in: the Casa Padellás, a magnificent 16C home (which was moved to the Plaça del Rei at the corner of Calle du Veguer), in St Agatha (Sta Ágata), a 14C chapel in the Catalan Gothic style formerly part of the Royal Palace, in the royal antechamber and in the 14C Throne Room (MR B) known as the Tinell.

King's Square (Plaza del Rei). — The square is bordered by the Throne Room, St Agatha Chapel, the Casa Padellás and the Vice Regal Palace, a Renaissance building which contains the archives of the Royal House of Aragon (MR C).

The **Plaza de Ramon Berenguer el Gran** stands at the eastern limit of the Roman city wall which was incorporated in the palace precincts.

Provincial Council★ (Palau de la Generalitat) (MR). — *Open Sundays only 10am to 1pm.*

Among the features of this vast 15 to 17C edifice are a fine early 15C medallion of St George above the gate in the side wall bordering the Calle Bisbe Irurita, a harmoniously styled Gothic inner courtyard with an elegant staircase and, in the shadow of the clock tower, its first floor Orange Tree Patio, attractively framed by Gothic style buildings. The St George's Chapel façade is a good example of Flamboyant Gothic. A Neo-Gothic covered gallery (19C), over a star vaulted arch, spans the Calle Bisbe Irurita to link the Provincial Council building with the canons' residence (the actual residence of the Provincial Council president).

Town Hall (MR H). — *Open 9.30am to 1.30pm and 4.30 to 7.30pm; closed Sunday and holiday afternoons and from the 2nd Sunday in December to the 2nd Sunday in January.* The front overlooking the Calle de la Ciutat is 14C; the Chronicle Chamber was decorated by the painter José María Sert *(p 75)*.

■ **MONTJUÏC★** (BCT) *time: 3 hours*

When the citizens of Barcelona rose in revolt against Philip IV in 1640 they built a **fort** (CT) on the hill (213m - 699ft). The castle terraces still command extensive **views★** of the harbour and the city. Inside is a military museum *(open 10am to 2pm and 4 to 8pm (7pm October to May); Sundays 10am to 8pm (7pm October to May); closed Mondays, for holidays inquire locally; 50pts);* on the grounds are a large **amusement park** (CT) and several museums:

Museum of Catalonian Art★★ (Museo de Arte de Cataluña) (CT M[2]). — *Open 9am to 2pm; closed Mondays and related holidays; 175pts, Sundays free.*

The museum is in what was the Spanish exhibition pavilion. The **Romanesque and Gothic departments★★★** contain beautiful items from many small churches in Catalonia.

Romanesque period (rooms 1 to 34): a highly expressive popular art of extraordinary maturity *(illustration p 19)* developed in the 12 and 13C, particularly in the Pyrenean Valleys as can be seen in the **frescoes** from Pedret (10), Boí (3 and 4), Santa Maria and Sant Climent of Taüll (14 to 16) *(p 94)* and Santa Maria of Aneu (10). The chapterhouse of Sigena Monastery (Huesca) has been reconstituted in room 26 to display realistically the extraordinary pre-1250 paintings in which the stance of the figures is almost Byzantine and the obviously true portraiture, Romanesque. The **altarfronts** of wood, an economic device in place of the gold and silver work to be seen in the Church of San Miguel de Aralar *(p 185)* and in Burgos Archaeological Museum *(p 230)*, divide into two main types: those painted on a single panel like that from the cathedral at Seo de Urgel (4) and those carved in relief, such as that from Santa Maria de Taüll (15). The early ones were inspired by absidal themes (Christ or the Virgin in Majesty), the later ones by the Lives of the Saints.

Gothic Period (rooms 40 to 64): from the 14C, **altarpieces** increased in size and number. Painting, at the time, was strongly influenced by the Italian style (Santa Coloma of Gramenet altarpiece by **Juan of Tarragona**); relief also began to be used increasingly. By 1400 Catalan art had become a mainstream on its own, assimilating foreign influences and with its own leaders such as **Luis Borrassá** (painting c 1400) and his followers, **Raimundo de Mur** (painting c 1400-1415) and the detailed and poetic **Bernat Martorell** (c 1430-1450). Flemish naturalism eventually predominated, as can be seen in the Retable of the Councillors (1445) by Luis Dalmau, ultimately reaching with a supreme elegance in works by such painters as **Jaime Huguet** *(p 19)* and **Bartolomé Bermejo.**

Painting in the succeeding centuries, is represented by Tintoretto, El Greco, Zurbarán and Ribera. Room 72 is devoted to the Catalan artist, Antonio Viladomat (1678-1755).

Ceramic Museum★. — *1st floor.* A diverse collection affords a panorama of Spanish ceramic art from the primitive pots found in the Balearics to the copper coloured arabesque decorated dishes of the 15C *(illustration p 18)*, as well as from 18C *azulejos* to modern works.

Archaeological Museum★ (Museo Arqueológico) (CT M[3]). — *Open 9.30am to 1pm and 4 to 7pm; Sundays 9.30am to 2pm; closed Mondays; for holidays inquire locally; 100pts.* The museum is remarkable for its presentation of megalithic civilisation in Spain, its Roman and Hellenistic collections excavated at Ampurias, the antique "Barcino" and Badalona. Other exhibits include a rotunda (room 21) painted with motifs from Greek mythology after the Centenario's House in Pompeii and the mosaics entitled *Circus Games* in the central gallery.

Spanish Village★ (Pueblo Español) (BT E). — *Open 10am to 8pm (7pm October to May); closed 25, 26 and 31 December, 1 and 6 January in the afternoon as well as Good Friday; 100pts, 50pts Sundays and holidays.* The village was erected for the 1929 exhibition to illustrate different styles and local features in Spanish architecture. As you walk through the streets and squares you will see regional craftsmen at work. A popular festival is held annually on the evening of 23 June.

Joan Miró Foundation★ (CT F). — *Open 11am to 8pm (2.30pm Sundays); closed Mondays; for holidays inquire locally; 200pts.* The foundation presents 290 works which Miró (1893-1983) produced between 1914-75 as well as 3 000 drawings.

The Montjuïc fountains are illuminated Thursdays, Saturdays and Sundays 9pm to midnight in summer and 8 to 11pm in winter.

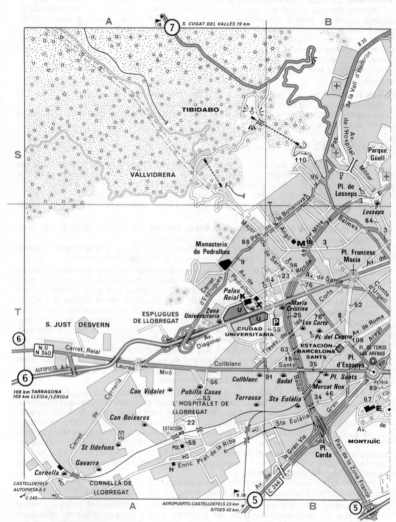

■ LA CIUDADELA

The citadel, constructed in 1716 on the orders of Philip V to enable a closer surveillance to be kept on Catalan rebels, was razed in 1868 and replaced by public gardens. The **Natural History and Geological Museum** (Museo Martorell) (KV **M⁴**) *(open 9am to 2pm; closed Mondays and certain holidays; 80pts, Sundays free)* are at the northwest corner of the park.

Zoo★ (Parque Zoológico). — *Open 10am (9.30am May to August) to sunset; 195pts, 85pts children.* The larger African animals can be seen in natural surroundings in the main zoo while dolphins *(dolphin show: 170pts, children; 65pts)* and other marine species are found in the Aquarama.

Museum of Modern Art (CT **M⁵**). — *Open 9am to 7.30pm (2pm Sundays and holidays); closed Monday mornings; 100pts, Sundays free.* The museum of Catalan painting of the 19 and 20C has canvases by Fortuny, Regoyos, Zuloaga, Gargallo, Dalí, Miró and Tàpies.

■ TIBIDABO★(AS)

From the top of the 532m - 1 745ft hill approached by picturesque roads affording attractive glimpses of the city and the sea, or by funicular, there are excellent **panoramic views★★** of Barcelona, the Mediterranean and the hinterland.

Pedralbes Palace (AT **K**). — *Open weekdays 10am to 1pm and 4 to 6pm (5 to 7pm in winter); Saturdays and Sundays 10am to 2pm; closed Mondays; for holidays inquire locally. General ticket 60pts; for the palace only 45pts and for the museum only 30pts.*

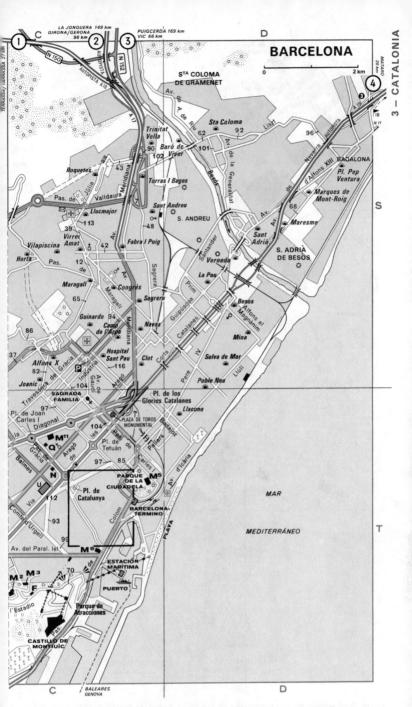

Between 1919 and 1929 the city of Barcelona erected, not far from the private houses set in their own gardens of the Sarriá quarter, a residence for King Alfonso XIII. The palace was inspired in design and decoration by the *palazzos* of the Italian Renaissance and its contents and art objects were in great part brought from Italy (tapestries, furniture, Murano chandeliers). There are temporary exhibits.

There is a **Carriage Museum** *(same opening times as the palace; 30pts)* in the park *(open all day)*.

Pedralbes Monastery (AT). — *Open 10am to 1pm and 4 to 6pm; Sundays 9am to 1pm; 60pts.*

The 14C buildings form a pure Catalan Gothic style group, which includes a single aisle church and three storey cloister *(open 10am to 1pm; closed Mondays; 80pts)* on the wall of St Michael's Chapel are murals by Ferrer Bassá (1346), a Catalan stongly influenced by Italy. The cells kitchen and infirmary can also be visited.

■ ADDITIONAL SIGHTS

Maritime Museum★★ (Atarazanas y Museo Marítimo) (CT M⁶). — *Open 10am to 2pm and 4 to 7pm; closed Sunday afternoons, Mondays; inquire locally for holidays; 100pts.*

Great sailing ships built in the old, 14C, royal naval dockyard stand in a perfect setting beneath a timber roof supported on rounded stone arches. Among the models of mostly Catalan sailing and steamships of every period, is the lifesize copy of the *Real*, Don Juan of Austria's galley which he sailed to victory at the Battle of Lepanto (1571).

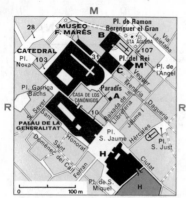

BARCELONA

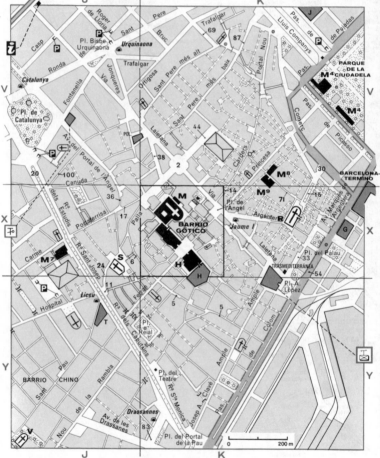

In the harbour, on the other side of the Plaça Portal de la Pau, is a reconstruction of Columbus's, *Santa María, (p 267) (open 9am to 3pm and 4pm to sunset; 100pts).*

Cambó Collection★ (Palacio de la Virreina) (JX M⁷). — *Open 9am to 2pm and 4 to 8.30pm; closed Monday mornings and Sunday and holiday afternoons; 80pts, Sundays and holidays free.* On the second floor of the gracefully designed palace of the former vice-reine of Peru (1778) hangs a small but very precious collection of paintings by the greatest Italian artists Raphael, Botticelli, Tintoretto, Titian and Tiepolo, by the French artists Fragonard and Quentin de la Tour, the Dutch Rubens and Van Dyck and the Spanish Goya, Murillo, Zurbarán and Pantoja de la Cruz.

Gaudí's Works. — Antonio Gaudí who was born in Reus in 1852, studied architecture in Barcelona. He remained detached, however, from current ideas, preferring to draw on his own, almost surrealistic imagination.

Church of the Holy Family★★ (Sagrada Familia) (CT L). — *Open 8am to 9pm; 9am to 7pm in winter; 200pts (includes a visit to the museum and the model). Slide show of Gaudí's work; 75pts.* Gaudí began the construction of this most unique edifice in 1883, modifying (see model) extensively Francisco P. Villar's plans. He completed the crypt *(open 8 to 10am and 7 to 9pm; enter by Calle Provença)* and the absidal walls but was unable to complete the building (runover by a tram in 1926).

Work was restarted in 1940 but has been greatly hindered because Gaudí had left no plans or notes concerning the church. Nearing completion are the east (Nativity) and west (Passion and Death) façades. From the top of the east tower *(50pts Rtn, elevator)* there is a view of the work still to be completed and the city.

Güell Park (BS). — *Open 10am to 6pm.* The intention was to build a garden city of 60 dwellings to demonstrate Gaudí's ideas on town planning. The architect's sudden death reduced the project to the construction of two houses, a few covered walks, and the park entrance which includes a mosaic made from everyday materials in brilliant colours.

Casa Batlló and Casa Milá. — These two blocks of luxury flats, both on the Passeig de Gràcia (nos 43 - CT **N** - and 92 - CT **Q**) and both begun in 1905 are good examples of Gaudí's highly personal style.

Güell Lodge (AT X). — This porter's lodge and iron grille in the Avinguda de Pedralbes date from 1885.

Santa Maria del Mar (KX R). — Santa Maria Church was originally outside the city walls in a quarter resided in by the nobility, ship builders and merchants.

The present church is 14C. The walls are flat and the west front decorated only by a portal gable and the buttresses flanking the large Flamboyant rose window. The interior appears spacious since only slender, canted pillars divide the three lofty aisles.

Santa Maria del Pi (JX S). — The 14C Catalan church has a beautiful rose window.

Calle Montcada (KX 71). — The street is lined with Gothic mansions in which originally the aristocracy and then, until the 18C, the richer *bourgeoisie* lived. Some of the residences are open to the public. Behind the unadorned façades are minute *patios,* their pure lines conforming perfectly to the golden rule of mediaeval Catalan architecture. Along one side, a single flight of steps, supported by a rampant arch, leads to the first floor, often with the added elegance of a slenderly arcaded gallery.

Picasso Museum★ (KV M⁸). — *Open 9am to 2pm and 4 to 8pm; closed Sunday afternoons and Monday mornings; inquire locally for holidays; 175pts, Sundays and holidays free.*

The old, 14C, Berenguer de Aguilar Palace and the Barón de Castellet Palace contain drawings, engravings and etchings by Picasso, dedicated, in most cases, to his friend, Sabartés. Among the few early paintings (in a gallery on the first floor) are *The Sick Child* from the Blue Period (1904) and *Harlequin* (1917). The series *Las Meninas,* Picasso's liberal variations painted in 1959 of the famous Velázquez picture, hang apart, in a separate gallery. Also exhibited are ceramics given to the museum in 1982 by Jacqueline Picasso.

Textile and Costume Museum (KX M⁹). — *Open 9am to 2pm and 4.30 to 7pm; closed Sunday afternoons, Mondays and certain holidays; 80pts, Sundays and holidays free.* The 14C Palace of the Marquess of Lió provides an impressive background to displays of costume and accessories from the 16 to 20C.

Music Museum (CT M¹¹). — *Open 9am to 2pm; closed Mondays and certain holidays; 80pts.* In the Cuadras mansion, an elegant art nouveau building, are exposed 16-20C musical instruments.

St Paul in the Fields (Sant Pau del Camp) (JY V). — The church, built as part of a Benedictine monastery at the end of the 10C contains a part of its original pavement. The minute and quite delightful **cloister★** *(to visit apply at no 101 Calle Sant Pau)* dates from the 11 and 12C.

Clará Museum (BT M¹⁰). — *Open 9am to 2pm; closed Mondays and certain holidays.*

The works displayed in the home of the Catalan sculptor, José Clará, (1878-1958) demonstrate his considerable talent also in draughtsmanship and painting.

BERGA (Barcelona)
Michelin map 443 fold 8 — *Local map p 95* — Pop 14 249

Berga, a town at the foot of the Queralt Sierra, has been devoted to the textile industry since the 18C when the Farguell brothers set up their first loom. Nevertheless, the centre of the town remains mediaeval in character.

The feeling for history and the past comes to the fore in the great folk festival known as the *Patum,* celebrated at Corpus Christi *(Wednesday and Saturday 8pm, Thursday and Sunday noon and 9pm),* when good combats evil and the wars against the Moors are mimed before the crowds.

Our Lady of Queralt Chapel (Nuestra Señora de Queralt). — *4km - 2 1/2 miles west.* Approach along a winding road. A magnificent **panorama★** opens out from the chapel situated at 1 024m - 3 360ft nearly at the top of a rock wall.

CARDONA (Barcelona)
Michelin map 443 fold 19 — Pop 6 561

Approached from the south, along the Suria road, the outstanding setting of the collegiate church is seen to full advantage: the apse, circled by Lombard bands and surrounded by citadel-like walls, stands perched on a brown rock cone dashed with lighter patches of mineral outcrop. (Mineral specimens are displayed in Solsona Museum, *p 98*).

To visit the church, apply at the tourist information centre. Guided tours 10am to 1.30pm. Once through the 18C perimeter you enter a small Gothic arched courtyard.

The **collegiate church,** which was consecrated in 1040, has several features from the Lombard style current in Catalonia *(see Ripoll p 95)* such as smooth, unadorned walls, the elevation of the nave and a total mastery of several styles of vaulting in the same building. The keynote is utter simplicity, relieved only by the placement of the absidal niches.

CERVERA (Lérida)
Michelin map 443 fold 18 — Pop 6 406

Cervera is built on a hill through which a tunnel has since been bored to allow the direct passage of the Barcelona-Saragossa road.

The town itself is worth a visit for its former 18C university and old houses (note the unusual head consoles supporting the town hall balcony). The churches are interesting as well: **Santa Maria** (inside admire the carved tombs) by its large octagonal belfry, and, from the former sentry path, **St Peter the Big (Sant Pere el Gros),** built in the 11C.

COSTA BRAVA ★★ (Gerona)

Michelin map **443** folds 11, 21 and 22

The Costa Brava or Wild Coastline, named after the steep cliff of ancient, twisted rocks which runs its entire length, is bounded inland by the Catalan mountain ranges. It forms the coastline of the province of Gerona. The intensity of the coast's colours, the ruggedness of the rocks and the scent of the plants combine in its attraction.

THE ALBERES COASTLINE ★
From Portbou to Roses — 52km - 32 miles — about 4 hours

The last of the Alberes foothills form huge, enclosed bays, like those of Portbou and El Port de la Selva.

Sant Pere de Rhodes ★★. — 15km - 9 miles from Llançà then 1/4 hour's walk; open 10am to 2pm and 4pm to sunset; 100pts. The monastery ruins stand in a remarkable **setting ★★** at the foot of the San Cristóbal crest from which the full sweep of the coast from Cerbère (France) to Cape Creus can be seen. Of the conventual buildings erected by the Benedictines between 979 and 1022 and protected by massive defensive walls surmounted by two tall towers, but abandoned and pillaged in the 18C, the church remains best conserved. It consists of three aisles, and an ambulatory — a rare feature in 11C Spain. The capitals show Cordoban and Byzantine influence in the strapwork and acanthus leaf carving. Stairs from the north transept lead to a watch path built into the thickness of the walls.

El Port de Llançà. — A good flat beach but a north facing harbour with little shelter against offshore winds or sudden Mediterranean storms.

El Port de la Selva. — This, the only harbour to offer boats shelter along the coast, lies at the back of a great bay, facing into the setting sun.

Cadaqués. — Last century Cadaqués was a simple fishing village; "discovery" by 20C writers and artists spread its name abroad (Salvador Dalí built a house in Portlligat creek). Though popular it remains delightful with arcaded white houses along the narrow main street. Standing on the shaded main square is the parish church, which in contrast to its sober exterior, contains a richly decorated baroque altarpiece.

Roses. — This fishing village dates back to the ancient Greeks who founded a colony named Rhode on the site. In the 11C the port developed when the port at Castelló d'Empúries (see below) became silted up by the Fluviá. Go up to Super Roses for a full view of the bay.

THE EMPORDÀ PLAIN
From Roses to Begur — 58km - 36 miles — about 3 hours

The Costa Brava here gives place, geologically, to the low lying fertile Empordà plain.

Castelló d'Empúries. — **Sta Maria Church** was built in the 13C, when Castelló was at the height of its glory. Flanked outside by a Catalan tower and endowed in the 15C with an imposing portal, it contains inside, at the back of the apse, an unusual, conically pinnacled 15C alabaster **altarpiece ★** carved with scenes of the Passion.

A rock formation between the Rivers Fluvià and Ter divides upper from lower Empordà and forms the flat, though indented **coast ★** of Roses Bay.

L'Escala ★. — Two small promontories shelter the harbour and provide an attractive setting for the village which is popular with swimmers.

Empúries ★. — 2km - 1 mile. Description p 76.

Torroella de Montgrí . — James II, Count of Barcelona, built this fortress in 1294 which still dominates the town. Then it was a large port at the opening of an estuary; by the 14C, however, the river had begun to silt up and Torroella found itself at the centre of a fertile plain which called for a new port to be built at L'Estartit.

L'Estartit. — The port lies where the northern rock coastline, on which it actually stands, meets the long gold stretch of Pals beach facing the Medes Islands. These were once the lair of the pirates who for centuries ravaged Mediterranean shores.

Pals. — Pals has a mediaeval quarter.

THE CORNICHE ROAD ★★
From Begur to Blanes — 78km - 48 miles — about 4 hours

Begur. — The 17C castle commands a good view out to sea.

A continuous swathe of sand around Begur has produced a succession of beach resorts from Aiguafreda to Aiguablava. Beyond, the resorts — **Tamariu, Llafranc, Calella** continue southwards. The resorts and the Cape Roig Botanical Gardens can only be approached by a road from Palafrugel.

Cape Roig Botanical Gardens ★★. — An unsurfaced road goes from Calella to a farm at the entrance to the gardens. Guided tours 9am to 9pm (6pm in winter); closed January and February; time: 1/2 hour; 100pts. Mediterranean shrubs and rare plants are to be found in the garden of shaded paths and terraces built out of the living rock, sheer above the sea.

Palamós. — A large resort occupied in the manufacture of cork.

S'Agaró ★. — S'Agaró is an elegant resort with luxurious villas in the middle of a pine forest. **Views ★** from the seaside promenade.

Sant Feliu de Guíxols. — Sant Feliu lies encircled by hills at the end of a bay. The resort with its cafés and bullring is one of the most popular on the coast. Originally, in about the 10C, the site was that of a Benedictine monastery — a few traces can still be seen on the way out on the Tossa de Mar road. By the main square, marked at its centre by the 17C St Benedict Arch, and abutting the old town wall, is the church. The interior was remodelled in the 14C but the Romanesque front was untouched, preceded by a curious arcade, Mozarabic in style below, Romanesque above.

Lay-bys enable one to enjoy the **corniche road ★★★** from Sant Feliu to Tossa de Mar which alternately skirts the sheer cliff top or descends into pine and cork oak shaded **coves ★**.

Tossa de Mar★. — This major resort has a horseshoe shaped sand beach which extends round to the promontory on which stand the lighthouse and the 12C walls of the Old Town, the Vila Vella. This quarter, principally of fishermen's houses, makes a pleasant stroll, affording glimpses of fishing boats at anchor in the curve of the bay.

The **corniche road★★** continues to Playa Canyelles, where it drops down the hillside finally to the beaches. The beach at **Lloret de Mar** is bordered by a sea promenade.

Blanes★. — The breakwater shelters the pleasure and fishing boat harbour. The **Marimurtra Botanical Gardens★** *(open 9am to 6pm April to October; the rest of the year 10am to 5pm - 2pm on Saturdays, Sundays and holidays; closed Christmas Day, 1 and 6 January; time: 1 hour; 75pts)* where more than 3 000 types of Mediterranean and exotic plants are to be seen beside the paths, overlooks Blanes harbour and affords from each path a **view★★** of the coastline.

COSTA DORADA ★ (Barcelona-Tarragona)

Michelin maps **443** folds 19, 20, 28 and 29

The magnificent band of fine golden sand, from which the coast gets its name, extends almost without a break along the coasts of the Barcelona and Tarragona provinces. This coupled with a particularly mild climate, makes it a paradise for sun and sea bathers.

LA MARESME★
From Río Tordera to Barcelona — *64km - 40 miles — allow 2 hours*

The coastal plain of La Maresme, which widens out considerably in places, and the flat expanses surrounding small coastal streams are highly fertile; the soil is suitable for market gardening in the low lying areas; with cereals, vines and olive trees growing on the higher ground. For this reason it is known as Barcelona's vegetable garden. The coastal towns were, in the Middle Ages, mostly fishing villages built inland to escape the raids of hostile pirates. As these declined, the towns moved to the coast where they expanded, establishing boatyards and initiating trade with South America. By the end of the 19C, textile and chemical industries had been developed in conjunction with those of Barcelona.

Calella. — The town, like Canet de Mar, grew rich at the beginning of the century through the hosiery trade. It got its name of "small cove" *(cala)* from an inlet which formerly existed between the Roca Grossa and Cape Aspre and has since silted up to become a series of small beaches between the rocks.

Arenys de Mar. — Roman pottery found testifies to its long habitation but it was only in the late 18C, when trade began with America and in the 19C with the shipyards and naval officer's school, that Arenys really began to develop. It is now the major pleasure boat harbour on the Catalonian coast and an international regatta centre.

Mataró. — Mataró, is an industrial town which is also well known for its horticulture (its carnations, like those of **Premià de Mar,** are sent all over Spain).

El Masnou. — The resort's 3km - 2 mile long beach is popular with Barcelonans.

Barcelona★★★. — *Description p 80.*

THE TARRAGONESE COASTLINE ★★
From Barcelona to the Ebro — *193km - 120 miles — allow 1 day*

Castelldefels. — The beach, backed by pine covered slopes, is a favourite with Barcelonans.

After Castelldefels the *corniche* road skirts the **Costas de Garraf★,** a series of picturesque creeks.

Sitges★. — *Description p 97.*

Vilanova i la Geltrú. — *Description p 102.*

Tarragona★★. — *Description p 98.*

South of Tarragona is **Cape Salou★,** amidst a peaceful **setting★** of pinewoods.

Salou. — Salou, a large resort, is invaded on summer weekends by the citizens of Tarragona. Modern blocks are rising fast behind the sea promenade bordered with palm trees and flower beds.

Cambrils. — The fishing boats carry lights *(lámparos)* for night fishing.

The Costa Dorada ends at the Ebro Delta, densely cultivated with ricefields, olive groves and market gardens.

Sant Carles de la Ràpita. — King Charles III (1759-1788), an enlightened despot, intended to establish a model port at Sant Carles. The town, at the mouth of the Alfaques Bay, a natural roadstead of 150km² - 37 000 acres retains a grid like street plan as a memento of the king's unfulfilled intention.

ESTANY L'ESTANY (Barcelona)

Michelin map **443** fold 20 — Pop 382

The 12C village church was built with a Romanesque tower over the transept but this collapsed in an earthquake in 1428 which is why the church now appears with a truncated belfry and strong buttresses to support the nave. There are surprising **capitals★★** among those surmounting the double row of columns in the adjoining cloisters: the north gallery is Romanesque and narrative in style (New Testament); the west, decorative with palm fronds and gaunt griffons; the south, geometrical and interlaced although the sophisticated execution and heraldic positions of the animals indicate a later date; the east is profane with wedding scenes and musicians after ceramics from Paterna *(p 173)* which, in turn, drew on Arabic patterning for their design.

*Europe on a single sheet: **Michelin Map** no **920***

GERONA ★ GIRONA Ⓟ

Michelin map **443** fold 10 — Pop 87 648

Gerona has a privileged site on a promontory at the juncture of the Ter and the Onyar and on the highway from the French town of Le Perthus to Barcelona. The historic buildings stand on the hillside, the industrial city spreads out below on either side of the river.

"La ciudad de los sitios". — Throughout history Gerona's strategic site has been so coveted that it has become known as the "city of a thousand sieges". Its ramparts were built and rebuilt by the Iberians, the Romans and throughout the Middle Ages and still mark the old city limits to the north and east.

Charlemagne's troops are described, in the *Song of Roland*, as assaulting the city; in 1809, Gerona resisted for more than seven months attacks by Napoleon's troops, the citizens under **Álvarez de Castro's** command formed themselves into regular battalions before capitulating (commemorative monument in the Plaça de la Independència).

■ **THE OLD TOWN** ★ (Ciudad Antigua) *time: 3 hours*

From the footbridges over the Onyar (Y), there are Sant **views**★ and reflections of ochre-coloured buildings along the river banks, the cathedral tower and the spire of Feliu.

The city alleys. — The alleys, narrow, winding, stepped, punctuated by wrought iron grilles where the sun has trouble penetrating, have, nevertheless, the charm of age. As you wander, endeavour to pass before the palace of the Agullana's (Z B) where an arch spans an adjoining flight of steps, and from there make for Sant Domènec Square, the site of a university in 1446 (Y E). The lively Calle Força (Y), which leads to the cathedral, was the main street of a flourishing Jewish quarter in the 13C.

Cathedral★ (Y). — The cathedral stands at the top of a majestic 17C flight of 90 steps, its baroque façade pierced by a single huge oculus. The rest of the edifice is Gothic: the chancel (1312) is surrounded by an ambulatory and radiating chapels; early in the 15C the decision was taken to add only a single **aisle**★★ but to make it outstandingly spacious and light. The building's two parts are in a similar, powerful, unadorned style, decoration having been restricted to the chapel arches, triforium niches and windows.

In the chancel, beneath a silver canopy symbolising the sky, is a silver-gilt 14C **altarpiece**★, highlighted with enamelwork, which retraces the life of Christ.

Among the chapels, many of which contain works of art, that of Sant Pau (1st north chapel), is outstanding for the tomb, in a Gothic niche, of Bishop Bernard of Pau (d 1457).

Treasury★★. — *Open 1 to 15 March 10am to 1.30pm; 16 March to 30 June 10am to 1.30pm and 3.30 to 6.30pm; 1 July to 15 September 10am to 7pm; 16 September to 3 November 10am to 1.30pm and 3.30 to 6.30pm; 4 November to 28 February Saturdays and holidays only 10am to 1pm; 100pts, valid also for the cloister.*

The second gallery, the richest, displays sumptuous 14 and 15C gold and silver plate; in the third gallery Mozarabic caskets and seven sculptures by the 15C Lorenzo Mercadante of Brittany are shown. Among the manuscripts are a Bible of Charles V of France and a copy dated 975 of **Beatus' Commentary on the Apocalypse**★ *(p 97)*.

The end room shows finely embroidered 12 to 15C altar fronts and the **Tapestry of the Creation**★★ — a unique work dating from about 1100 which shows Christ in Majesty in a circular area at the centre, surrounded by the stages of creation. The four winds fill the corners.

Cloister★. — The cloister's double line of columns is overshadowed by the 11C, Charlemagne Tower, relic of an earlier, Romanesque cathedral. The friezes on the pillars at the gallery corners and centres, in most cases, illustrate scenes from Genesis.

GIRONA GERONA

Álvarez de Castro		Z 2
Ballesteries		Y 3
Calderers		Y 5
Calvet i Rubalcaba (Pl.)		Z 6
Carril (Traves.)		Z 7
Ciutadans		Z 8
Cort-Reial		Z 9
Ferran Puig (Ronda)		Y 10
Independencia (Pl.)		Y 15
Marquès de Camps (Pl.)		Z 18
Sant Joan B. La Salle		Z 21
Sant Domènec (Pl.)		Y 22
Libertad (Rambla de la)		Z 16
Nou		Z

Art Museum★ (Y M¹). — *Open 10am to 1pm and 4.30 to 7pm; closed Sunday afternoons, and all day Monday; inquire locally for holidays; 75pts.*

Installed in the Episcopal Palace, this noble edifice houses part of the works which had been in the Archaeological and Diocesan Museums. Presented is a comprehensive collection of art covering the Romanesque to the 19C periods.

Note especially the Romanesque (a serene Virgin) and Gothic (Calvary by Maestro Bartomeu, altarpiece from Sant Miquel de Cruilles by Luis Borrassá *(p 19)*, the Sant Feliu altarpiece, which marks the transition between Gothic and Renaissance, and the works of the Gerona-born painter Pere Mates who adopted the more innovative Renaissance style) works.

"Sobreportes" Gate (Y N). — The gate at the end of the Calle Força was a kind of fort lived in by a noble family entrusted with keeping the watch on the city wall.

Former Collegiate Church of Sant Feliu (Y R). — *Open during services.* The church outside the town wall must originally have been a martyrium erected over the tombs of St Narcissus, Bishop of Gerona, and St Felix, patrons of the city. A Gothic church was later built on the Romanesque foundations. In the apse are eight sarcophagi let into the walls, of which two have outstanding carvings — on the right, the abduction of Proserpine, opposite, a dashing **lion hunt★**.

Arab Baths (Baños árabes) (Y S). — *Open 10am to 1pm; and 4.30 to 7pm; closed Sunday and holiday afternoons and all day Monday, 1 and 6 January, Easter Sunday and 25 December; 75pts.*

The late 12C baths consist of a **frigidarium,** an area with a pool surrounded by columns and lit by an unusual lantern; a **tepidarium** or warm room; a **hypocaust** for steam baths and a **caldarium** or hot room.

Paseo Arqueológico (Y V). — Steps opposite the baths lead to gardens at the foot of the ramparts from which you can look along the Ter Valley.

Sant Pere de Galligants (Y Y). — *Same opening times as the Art Museum.* Not far from Sant Nicolau, with its clover leaf apse, stands the portal of Sant Pere, a Romanesque church repeatedly fortified since it was first built so that its east end appears embedded in the town wall and the belfry served as a watch tower. The small cloister contains interesting 12C historiated capitals.

The church and cloister house the **Archaeological Museum,** which is devoted to the archaeological finds of the province.

Displayed in the upper part of the cloister are prehistorical and Iberian objects and 13-14C Hebrew memorial plaques. In the former sacristy, which contains Roman art from Ampurias *(p 76),* is the magnificent tomb from Las Estaciones (4C).

EXCURSION

Figueres. — *37km · 24 miles by* ①. A **Salvador Dalí** museum *(open 10.30am to 1pm (12.30pm 1 October to 30 June) and 3.30 to 7pm; closed Mondays 1 October to 30 June, 1 January, Good Friday and 25 December; 200pts)* is installed in the former theatre of the town where the surrealist artist was born in 1904.

LÉRIDA ★ LLEIDA P

Michelin map 443 fold 17 — Pop 109 573
See town plan in the current Michelin Red Guide España Portugal

Lérida is now an industrial city at the centre of a vast expanse of market gardens which owe their prosperity to an efficient irrigation system. Lérida was once a citadel, built on a mound to command a point where communications crossed. Caesar's and Pompey's legions stormed it savagely; the Moors occupied it from the 8 to 12C; the French attacked it during the Wars of Succession (1707) and Independence (1810).

The ancient fortress, the **Azuda** or **Zuda,** sited like an acropolis and occupied in the 13C by the Counts of Catalonia, was destroyed by artillery fire in 1812 and 1936 but the fortifications which surrounded it remain. The glacis has been transformed into gardens. From the **terraces** there is an extensive view.

Old Cathedral (Seo Antigua). — The cathedral dominates the city from inside the walls. It was constructed between 1203 and 1278 on the site of a former mosque: Philip V converted it into a garrison fortress in 1707. The tall, octagonal belfry adjoining the northwest corner of the cloister is late 14C. Efforts are being made to restore the edifice to its original appearance.

Cloister. — The cloister's unusual situation in front of the church serves as a reminder that the site was formerly that of a mosque which would have been preceded by a forecourt. Although the galleries were completed during the 14C, the **decoration★** of the capitals is partly Romanesque. The **view** from the bays extends to the open plain.

Church. — The outstanding decoration in this transitional style church occurs in its **capitals★★** in which Moorish influence can be clearly seen particularly in the carvings of the Children's Portal (dels Fillols), off the south aisle, and in the Annunciation Portal, in the corresponding transept. Above is a lovely rose window.

Sant Llorenç. — A tall, octagonal belfry distinguishes the church, now sadly dilapidated outside although the inside remains harmonious. The 12C nave is covered with wide semicircular vaulting; altarpieces abound: at the end of the apse is a particularly fine **altarpiece to St Lawrence,** in the north transept are others to Sts Ursula, Lucy and Peter.

Former hospital of Santa Maria. — An elegant Catalan *patio* remains from the 15C. The **Archaeological Museum** is on the ground floor.

MONTBLANC (Tarragona)

Michelin map 443 fold 18 — Pop 5 244

The Montblanc ramparts and impressive east end of the Church of Santa Maria appear before you in truly mediaeval style as you approach along the N 240 from Lérida. The town, founded in the 12C, received its patent of nobility. in 1392 when the title of Duke of Montblanc was created for the heir apparent to the Aragon throne. The walls were heightened and 34 crenellated towers added. The narrowness of the fortified mediaeval gates has compelled 20C main roads to bypass the town, allowing it to retain a delightful calm. Among the Gothic houses are a small **museum** and the old **Hospital de Santa Magdalena** where the attractive *patio* has Gothic arches at ground level and Renaissance basket handle arches above. The main street leads down to the 14C bridge.

Santa Maria. — The church, which crowns the hilltop with its massive outline, was begun in 1352. After two centuries, however, construction was halted never to be resumed, although the building has the beauty of a completed edifice. A baroque doorway opens into the single **aisle★**, relieved by tall windows and chapel openings in each bay.

MONTSENY, Sierra de ★★ (Barcelona-Gerona)
Michelin map **443** fold 20

The Sierra de Montseny, one of the mightiest spurs of the Pyrenees, extends into the heart of Catalonia, where it appears as a vast granite dome above the beeches and cork oaks. The range's two highest peaks are the Matagalls (1 700m - 5 578ft) and Turó de l'Home (1 712m - 5 617ft). The dampness of the climate and the impermeable rock face are favourable elements for sources.

From Tona to Sant Celoni by the northern road. — *60km - 37 miles — about 1 1/2 hours*. The **road★** goes through pine and beechwoods and the delightful village of **Viladrau** before beginning a gradual descent with views off to the right.

> **Alternative route by Sant Hilari Sacalm.** — *Extra distance: 23km - 14 miles*. Sant Hilari Sacalm, a regional excursion centre known locally as the Catalan Switzerland is a pleasant resort. It has been a popular spa since the 18C.

The view opens out onto the steep Montseny slopes as the road continues its hillside descent. After the attractively sited **Arbúcies**, it skirts the river for a distance before turning off for **Breda**, dominated by a beautiful Romanesque tower, and Sant Celoni.

From Sant Celoni to Santa Fé del Montseny. — *22km - 14 miles — about 3/4 hour*. This **drive★★** into the heart of the mountains is the most interesting. Beyond Campins, the road rises in hairpin bends, affording **views** of the coastal plain; it continues in a magnificent **corniche** *(2km - 1 mile)* which ends at Lake Santa Fé (alt 1 130m - 3 708ft). The road goes on up *(7km - 4 miles)* to the Sant Marçal Hermitage (alt 1 260m - 4 134ft), perched on the side of the lofty Matagalls ridge.

From Sant Celoni to Tona by the southern road. — *43km - 27 miles — about 1 hour*. You get good views of the *sierra* from the **route★** across the plain irrigated by the Tordera. Beyond Montseny the road rises, reaching a wild area, before descending to Tona past the Romanesque church in **El Brull** and the tower of **Santa Maria de Seva**.

MONTSERRAT, Sierra de ★★★ (Barcelona)
Michelin map **443** fold 19

The Montserrat Massif has a grand **atmosphere★★★** and was, in fact, used by Wagner as the setting for his opera, *Parsifal*. The range is composed of hard eocene conglomerates, which stand solidly above the more eroded surrounding rock formations. The piling up of the ruiniform boulders into steep cliffs, crowned by weird pinnacles, produces a serrated outline from which it has been nicknamed the "sawtooth mountain". It is the principal religious and cultural centre of Catalonia, its Marian shrine attracting thousands of pilgrims.

Access. — The best approach, by far, is from the west. There are excellent **views★★** all the way along the monastery road. Access to the cable-car at Montserrat (**1**) is best by the Barcelona-Manresa road. Good **views.**

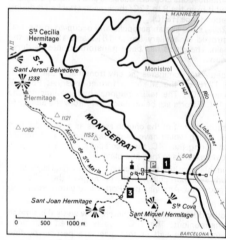

1 Cable-car to Montserrat

2 Funicular to Santa Cova Chapel

3 Funicular to Sant Joan Hermitage

Monastery. — *To visit the sanctuary apply at the information office.*
The history of Montserrat begins in the 9C with the arrival of Benedictines from Ripoll. In 1025 Abbot Oliva *(p 95)* founded a priory on the site which grew rapidly in importance, until by the 13C the Romanesque buildings had to be greatly enlarged. It continued to flourish and in 1409, as an abbey, declared its independence of Ripoll. It had become powerful; its monks were learned — Giuliano della Rovere, the future Pope Julius II, savant and artist, patron of the Italian Renaissance, was an abbot; the community was rich; pilgrims were fervent and numerous. Every century saw additions making the monastery an anthology of masterpieces of every architectural style. In 1812, however, disaster befell, the monastery was sacked by the French. The present buildings, therefore, are 19C. At the end of the dark, overly ornate church (16C) candles burn ceaselessly before the sanctuary to the Virgin.

The Black Madonna. — This is a polychrome wood statue said to date from the 12C; the seated figure of the Infant Jesus was restored in the 19C. According to legend, the figure, now in a glass niche above the high altar *(approached up the monumental staircase)* and venerated annually by thousands of pilgrims as the patron of Catalonia, was found by shepherds in a cave on the mountainside *(see opposite)*.

The services are known for the high standard of the singing: concelabratory mass 11am; vespers at 6.45pm; special services at Christmas and in Holy Week.

The **Escolanía**, one of Europe's oldest boys' choirs — its foundation dates back to the 13C — may be heard at morning mass *(Sundays and feast days at 11am)* at the Salve *(1pm)* and at the end of vespers *(7pm)*.

Hermitages, belvederes. — *Access: mountain roads, cable-cars, funiculars (see map).*

Sant Jeroni. — From the belvedere (1 238m - 4 061ft) there is a **panorama**, on a clear day, from the Pyrenees to the Balearic Islands.

Santa Cecília. — Until the 16C Santa Cecília was a Benedictine monastery like Santa Maria from Ripoll, but lacked its influence. The Romanesque **church,** which is 11C, has a most attractive exterior with an east end circled by Lombard bands, a roof which spreads over the nave and an asymmetric, free standing belfry.

Santa Cova. — *1/2 hour's walk.* According to the legend, it was in this cave that the statue of the Virgin was discovered. Views of the Llobregat Valley.

Sant Miquel. — *1/2 hour's walk from the monastery; 1 hour from upper terminal* ▣. General view of the monastery.

Sant Joan. — *20 minutes from upper terminal* ▣. Beautiful panorama.

OLOT (Gerona) ————————————————————————————————————
Michelin map 🆊🅰🅱 fold 9 — *Local map p 93* — Pop 24 892

Following a geological upheaval which brought about the subsidence of the Empordà plain, the Olot basin became exposed to eruption which is why there are several ancient volcanic cones not far away from the city. The craters are, however, largely hidden from view by lush vegetation. Basalt piles punctuate the landscape, like the astonishing **site★** on which **Castellfollit de la Roca** is poised.

The best general view of the Olot basin and its volcanic formations is from the picturesque Olot-San Juan de las Abadesas **road★**.

In this agricultural area, known chiefly for its cattle fairs, two traditional crafts are still practised: the carving and painting of sacred multicoloured wood figures and the manufacture of Catalan red caps.

Garrotxa Regional Museum. — *Closed temporarily, rearrangement in progress.* Collections of arms and volcanic rocks; geological sections illustrate local configurations.

POBLET Monastery ★★★ (Tarragona) ————————————————————————
Michelin map 🆊🅰🅱 fold 18

It was the Reconquest which brought Poblet into existence, for after Ramón Berenguer IV had recaptured Catalonia from the Moors he gave thanks to God by founding the monastery. By 1150 twelve Cistercians, sent from Fontfroide Abbey near Narbonne in France, had begun to construct the buildings and till the soil for the future community.

The Kings of Aragon maintained a patronage of the monastery which with Santes Creus, became a favourite halt on kingly progresses between the two capitals of Barcelona and Saragossa. It also became a place of royal religious retreat — the abbot was the royal almoner. Finally the monastery was given the supreme honour of being selected as the royal pantheon.

It began to decline at the end of the 16C, suffered particularly during the Napoleonic Wars and in the so-called Constitutional Period (1820-1823), when religious orders were suppressed and riches sold (1835). A century later the buildings were restored and in 1940 a community was re-established. In spite of all its vicissitudes, the monastery remains a rare example of mediaeval monastic architecture.

TOUR

Guided tours (time: 1 hour) 10am to 12.30pm and 3 to 6pm (5.30pm in winter); church closed Good Friday in the afternoon, and monastery closed all day on Christmas Day; 175pts.

An outer perimeter 2km - 1 mile long protected the peasants and workmen employed by the abbey, a second, inner wall, incorporating the 15C **Golden Door (Puerta Dorada)** which owes its name to the gilded bronze plates which covered it, enclosed the conventual annexes. A third wall, 600m - 1 698ft long, erected at the end of the 14C by Peter the Ceremonious, surrounds only the monastery. Inside, on the right, is the baroque entrance to the church built in about 1670 which was flanked fifty years later by two lavishly ornate windows. The **Royal Door (Puerta Real),** between two massive machicolated towers, opens onto the conventual buildings.

Parlour. — The late 14C vaulting in the lay brothers' dormitory forms one with the walls.

Cloister★★. — The cloister's size (40 x 35m - 131 x 114ft) and solemn lines give some indication of the monastery's importance. The south gallery and huge **lavabo** with 30 taps are in pure Cistercian style; the other galleries, built a century later, have a floral motif tracery; beautiful scrollwork adorns the **capitals★** throughout.

Kitchen and refectory. — The kitchen and refectory are 12C. The reader's lectern can be seen strategically placed overlooking the long refectory tables.

Library. — Columns supporting the 13C fan vaulting add interest to the design.

Chapterhouse. — The delicacy of the small columns and capitals show them to be 13C. Tombstones of eleven of Poblet's abbots can be seen inlaid in the pavement.

Church★★. — The spacious church is typically Cistercian, with pure architectural lines, broken cradle vaulting over the nave, two storeys in elevation and unadorned capitals. The only decorative note lies in the windows and wide arches joined beneath an arch which dissolves into the piers of the engaged columns. In contrast to the lack of ornament, the church had to incorporate numerous altars because the community numbered so many and the apse was therefore ringed by an ambulatory and radiating chapels.

Royal Pantheon★★. — The church's major ornament and its most original feature, are the immense shallow arches spanning the transepts on either side of the crossing, surmounted by the royal, alabaster tombs. These were constructed in about 1350 to provide a repository for the Kings of Aragon, buried at Poblet between 1196 and 1479. The sepulchres were desecrated in 1835 but were restored by the sculptor F. Marés.

POBLET Monastery★★★

High altar retable★★. — Damián Forment was commissioned in 1527 to carve this monumental Renaissance altarpiece in which figures in shell shaped niches in four superimposed registers can be seen glorifying Christ and the Virgin.

A wide flight of stairs leads from the north transept to the monks' dormitory.

Dormitory. — Massive central arches support the ridge roof above the vast gallery.

Palace of King Martin the Humane. — The sovereign had sumptuous apartments, which included carved tracery in the windows, constructed for his own use in the monastery in about 1400.

Museum. — Early in the 15C a dormitory for "old brothers" was constructed above the storeroom. It now contains documents on the monastery at the time it was abandoned.

PYRENEES in Catalonia ★★ PIRINEOS CATALANES (Gerona-Lérida)
Michelin map **443** folds 6 to 9

The mountain chain, continuing the crest lines which cross Aragon *(p 68)*, forms an almost unbroken west-east barrier from Maladeta to the Mediterranean. The final range, as the chain drops from the Pico d'Estats (3 141m - 10 305ft) in the west of Catalonia, to Puigmal (2 913m - 9 558ft) in the centre, is the Alberes which plunges finally into the sea from a height of 700m - 2 297ft at Cape Creus. Advancing south from the granite axial ridge are the Cadí, Boumort and Montsec Sierras.

The most travelled route over the mountains is the Perthus Pass on the direct road from France to Barcelona. The mountains elsewhere are deeply cut by valleys such as those of the Segre and Nogueras Rivers and the Vallespir, Cerdaña and Vall d'Arán basins. Lacking intercommunication, each has become a region on its own with an individual tradition, evident, for instance, in the local Romanesque churches, often decorated, as at Taüll, with unique and, in this case, now well-known frescoes *(p 94)*.

From the Ares Pass to Puigcerdà — 106km - 70 miles — about 3 hours

The Ares Pass **road★**, which links the French Vallespir (Amélie-les-Bains) with central Catalonia (Ripoll, Vic), avoids the frontier post of Le Perthus, which is always crowded in summer, and has the additional advantage of taking in a long isolated mountain region. Once past the high mountain pastures on either side of the Ares Pass (Collado de Ares — altitude 1 610m-5 250ft), the road enters the lush and winding Upper Valley of the Ter.

Molló. — The 12C Romanesque church has a beautiful Catalan belfry.

Camprodon. — Camprodon is a proud Pyrenean village with picturesque old houses and a steep hump-backed bridge. All around are woods, lush meadows and mountain streams. The Romanesque Church of **Sant Pere★** has a Cistercian simplicity with a portal decorated only with a double tori, a nave with robust pillars and broken cradle vaulting, and a flat east end *(to visit apply to the priest)*.

Sant Joan de les Abadesses. — *Description p 96.*

Ripoll★. — *Description p 95.*

The valley becomes enclosed and ever greener.

Núria. — *Access by the rack railway from Ribes de Freser and Queralbs; for departure schedule enquire at the station ☎972 72 70 31; journey: 3/4 hour; 790pts Rtn.* The journey up the mountainside affords a series of magnificent **views★**. Núria, itself — at 2 000m - 6 562ft — is a winter sports centre overlooked by snow-capped peaks. It is also a famous pilgrimage with feast days and folklore festivals.

The *corniche* road from Ribes de Freser to Puigcerdà lies nearly always high up the mountainside far above the wooded slopes of the steeply enclosed valley. Beyond the pass the road winds continuously.

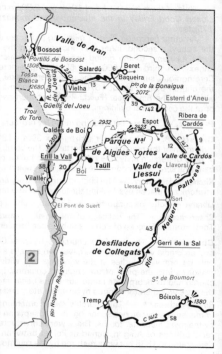

La Molina. — *6km - 4 miles.* The sunny, wide Molina Valley contains two winter sports centres - Molina and Super Molina (respectively 1 436m - 2 537m — 4 711m - 8 323ft).

There are further spectacular views from the *corniche* road of the **Cerdaña,** before it descends to the lowland plain. The Cerdaña basin, owes its existence between the Andorran massifs and the Sierra del Cadí to subsidence and its fertility to the irrigation provided by the Río Segre, a tributary of the Ebro. Since 1659 the Cerdaña (French Cerdagne) has been divided, the northern part, now known as the Cerdagne, going to France under the Treaty of the Pyrenees *(see Michelin Green Guide Pyrénées Roussillon — in French only).*

Puigcerdà. — The town built on a morainic mound, overlooks the Cerdaña of which it was once the capital and remains the centre. It is an attractive place to wander around with old streets and balconied houses. Local boating lake, north of the town.

Llivia. — *6km - 4 miles.* The little town owes its status as a Spanish enclave in French territory to a grammatical nicety. When thirty-three villages in Cerdaña were ceded to France in 1659, Llivia, being classed as a "town", remained Spanish. Lying at the foot of an isolated hill, the former capital of Cerdaña has picturesque alleys and a fortified church. Housed in the **local museum** *(open 10am to 1pm and 3 to 7pm - 6pm in winter-closed Mondays; 50pts)* is an old apothecary's shop which operated from 1415-1926!

From Puigcerdà to Tremp — *140km - 87 miles — allow 1/2 day*

The road drops all the way to Coll de Nargó, travelling through a fertile countryside.

Bellver de Cerdanya. — The town of steep streets and houses with mostly wooden balconies, is perched on a rock overlooking the Segre Valley.

Prullans. — A mountain village where the narrow streets are bordered by houses with steeply pitched roofs.

Lles road★. — *18km - 11 miles.* The road rises rapidly up a tributary valley. As you climb the hairpin bends, glorious panoramas open out of the peaks on Spain's northern frontier and the massive rock barrier of the Sierra del Cadí to the south. The **view★** on all sides from the village itself (alt 1 471m - 4 826ft) is of the surrounding mountain circle which stretches away particularly to the east.

La Seu d'Urgell★. — *Description p 97.*

The road continues to follow the course of the Segre, sometimes at water level, sometimes high on the hillside. The scenery alters from mountain pasture land scattered with outcrops of deep red rock *(puzzolana)* as around Els Hostalets, to narrow grey limestone gorges, the **Garganta de Tresponts★.**
A new opening suddenly reveals a small green basin with poplar edged fields in the heart of the mountains.

Grau de la Granta★. — *12km - 7 miles to the Oliana Dam.* The lake lies enclosed and as narrow as a river, between grey walled cliffs enlivened, in the spring, by leaping waterfalls — the effect is wonderful from the *corniche* road. Returning towards Coll de Nargó you will get glimpses of the towering Coscollet cliffs.

The road passing below the spur crowned by Coll de Nargó, enters a series of canyons, crossing from side to side, sometimes following the line of a pine or evergreen covered slope, sometimes that of the stony face below the yellow or pink rock crests. The landscape is often fantastic particularly around the Bóixols Pass.

Take especial care beyond the pass as the road is steep and narrow.

You emerge into a wide glacial valley where terrace cultivation stretches to the foot of the glacial bolt on which stand perched the church and few surrounding houses which go to make up the village of Bóixols.
The road continues to descend the valley which finally merges into the vast Tremp depression.

From Tremp to Vielha — *147km - 91 miles about 4 hours*

Noguera Pallaresa Valley★. — The road climbs first past timeworn limestone cliffs behind La Pobla de Segur and then, in the **Collegats Defile★★** (Estret de Collegats), past great vertical clefts cut by urgent streams through the soft red, deep ochre and grey rocks.

Gerri de la Sal. — The saltpans below the road are fed by a stream (salt-water) which rises just north of the village.

The scenery becomes more mountainous and more luxuriant. Tributary valleys, inhabited by isolated communities, increase in number.

Llessui Valley★★. — A fresh green valley of smoothly rounded, grass covered hillsides. It is a winter sports centre (1 280 - 2 900m — 4 199 - 9 514ft).

Cardós Valley★. — *9km - 6 miles.* A cool gorge deep in the mountains. The site of **Ribera de Cardós** is highly picturesque. The resort is also known for its trout fishing.

Espot road★. — *6km - 4 miles.* A delightful narrow, shaded road, close to rustling streams, climbs by way of hairpin bends to Espot, at the entrance to the Aigües Tortes y Lago de San Mauricio National Park *(p 76).* The village, spread along the banks of a stream lively with fish, has a circular backcloth of high rocks over which mountain torrents cascade when the snows melt.

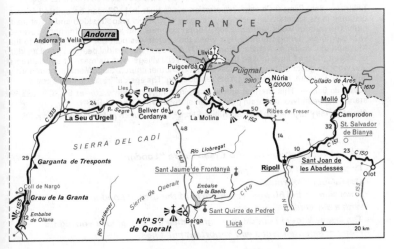

93

PYRENEES in Catalonia★★

The Aran Valley★★. — Beyond Esterri d'Àneu, the *corniche* road rises through impressive mountain scenery to the Bonaigua Pass (2 072m - 6 798ft), gateway to the Aran Valley. The pass is encircled by jagged summits from which the eye strays, left, to a magnificent glacial cirque.

The Upper Valley of the Garona. — Garona is the name of several small rivers in the Aran Valley. The largest, the Río Garona de Ruda, rises near Mount Saboredo (2 764m - 9 071ft), southwest of the Bonaigua Pass. It is fed by tributaries, the largest of which is the Río Garona del Joeu which rises in the heart of the forest at Güells del Joeu and rushes to join the mainstream down a series of 30m - 100ft cataracts. The stream is a resurgence — a fact long suspected and proved in 1931 by the French speleologist **Casteret** in a striking experiment using coloured dyes. On the basis of land configuration, the waters on the north side of the Maladeta should flow into the Esera, a tributary of the Ebro and then debouch into the Mediterranean. In fact, due to the limestone rocks, these waters of melting ice and snow disappear at an altitude of 2 020m - 6 628ft — into the Bull's Hole (Coll del Toro) and, after flowing underground for 4km - 2 1/2 miles — beneath the limestone crest of the Tusse Blanche, reappear on the northern slope and debouch into the Atlantic.

The long isolation. — The Aran Valley on the northern side of the Pyrenees, has belonged to Spain since the 13C. Difficulties of communication with the world outside brought about the development of a community with its own traditions and language, Aranais (Catalan, French and Spanish are also spoken). Only in 1925 was a car-worthy road built over the Bonaigua pass and in 1948 a tunnel was constructed to connect the valley capital to the Lérida road. These two roads have brought changes in the local economy and an increase in population: pasture is being replaced by arable, fir and beech trees are being felled for timber and mineral and water resources (for hydro-electric power) are being exploited. But nothing alters the beauty of the mountain scenery and the brilliant green fields, blotched occasionally by a blue-grey mass which closer inspection reveals are the slate roofed cottages of one of the valley's 39 villages, in many cases clustered around a Lombard Romanesque style church.

Baqueira Beret. — Well-equipped winter sports centre.

Salardú. — Schist and granite houses, a delightful arcaded main square and a 13C parish church with a tall belfry, distinguish this delightful village. In the church is a stylised, but for its 12C date, surprisingly anatomically detailed, wooden Crucifix.

Vielha. — Alt 971m - 3 186ft. The small Aran Valley capital now stands close to the frontier at the juncture of two Pyrenean roads and bustles with passing traffic. The parish church has an octagonal belfry and a 13C doorway. Inside there are 18C paintings in the first two chapels and a retable painted in the 15C at the back of the high altar. In a chapel to the left note a 12C wooden sculpture (all that remains of a Descent from the Cross) of the **Mig Aran Christ★**, a long, handsome face framed by an intricately carved head of hair and beard. The *parador* above Vielha has a wonderful setting: in the distance is the snow-capped circus which closes the Aran Valley to the south and on the right, the formidable spurs of the Maladeta Massif.

Bossost. — *16km - 10 miles northwest of Vielha.* 7km - 4 miles after Vielha a turning on the right leads up to **Vilamòs** *(6km - 4 miles),* a village 400m - 1 312ft above the valley: fine **view★** of the green Garona del Joeu Valley and in the distance of the snowcapped mountains. Bossost itself possesses one of the valley's best preserved Romanesque churches. A nave and two aisles, divided by rounded pillars support the cradle vaulting for the massive roof; there are three Lombard banded apses and a north door with a tympanum archaically carved to show the Creator surrounded by the sun, the moon and the symbols of the Evangelists.

From Vielha to Caldes de Boí — *58km - 36 miles — about 1 1/2 hours*

The road cuts through the Maladeta range by way of a 6km - 4 mile tunnel which ends in the lovely upper valley of the Noguera Ribagorçana. There the river can be seen flowing down a wide boulder strewn bed, providing the water for several power stations.

Vilaller. — The small attractive village has a church with an unusual round belfry.

7km - 4 miles further on turn left into the Boí road.

The Noguera de Tort Valley contains the most beautiful Romanesque churches in the Pyrenees: built to a small irregular plan with stone roofs, they can be distinguished from a distance by their square belfries which abut the nave. They are decorated with double or triple arcades and Lombard bands. A typical example is the church at Erill la Vall. The road goes up the pleasantly picturesque Boí Valley. There are mauve coloured rock outcrops.

Taüll★. — **Sant Climent Church★** *(illustration p 14),* built in 1123, can be spotted from a distance in its spectacular setting by its **belfry★,** which is smooth sided and six storeys high. The interior walls *(entrance fee: 15pts),* columns and apse were formerly covered with paintings, dating from the time when the church was built but now removed to the Museum of Catalonian Art, Barcelona *(p 81).* A copy of the apsidal painting gives an idea of what it must all have looked like originally. Taüll village, with its maze of small streets and wooden galleried houses, clusters around another church, **Santa Maria,** contemporary with Sant Climent, but suffering from remodelling. The apsidal fresco is also a copy.

Caldes de Boí. — This thermal spa with springs flowing with water at 56 °C - 135 °F stands between two mountain peaks at an altitude of 1 470m - 4 823ft.

Aigües Tortes y Lago de San Mauricio National Park★★. — *9km - 6 miles. Description p 76.*

When visiting London use the **Green Guide ''London''**

- *Detailed descriptions of places of interest*
- *Useful local information*
- *A section on the historic square mile of the City of London*
  with a detailed fold out plan
- *The lesser known London boroughs - their people, places and sights*
- *Plans of selected areas and important buildings.*

RIPOLL ★ (Gerona)

Michelin map **443** fold 9 — *Local map p 93* — Pop 12 055

This small Pyrenean town has been known for centuries for its Benedictine monastery. It was founded in the 9C by Count Wilfred the Shaggy. He maintained his interest in the community and was buried there, beginning a tradition which was followed by the Counts of Barcelona, Besalú and Cerdaña until the 12C. Only the tomb of Berenguer III, the Great (d 1131), however, is left of the royal pantheon (south transept) as well as the remains of Wilfred the Shaggy and his son Radulf (north transept).

The monastery as a centre of learning. — The library at Ripoll was one of the richest in Christendom: not only did it possess texts of the scriptures and theological commentaries but also works by pagan authors such as Plutarch and Virgil as well as scientific treatises. The learning of Antiquity was restored by the Arabs, who treasured and disseminated the works of the Greeks which they discovered when they captured Alexandria and, with it, its incredible library. Ripoll, previously overrun by the Moors, became, under Abbot Oliva, a link between Arabic and Christian civilisations, a centre of culture, ideas and exchange to which came such men as Brother Gerbert, the future Pope **Sylvester II** (999).

Abbot Oliva. — Oliva, son of a Count of Cerdaña and Besalú, a learned man, and a born leader, held the appointments simultaneously from 1008 of Abbot of Ripoll and St Michel de Cuxá in the French Roussillon and from 1018 also of Bishop of Vic. He died only in 1046 and thus had time to impress his mark deeply on the region both intellectually and as a great builder. He favoured the basilical type plan with prominent transepts and a dome over the crossing as in the Collegiate Church at Cardona *(p 85)*.

■ FORMER MONASTERY OF SANTA MARIA ★

Open 9.30am to 1pm and 3 to 6.30pm (6pm in winter).

Church. — The 9C monastery church soon had to be enlarged; by the end of the 10C, Count Oliva Cabreta was constructing a third church, consecrated in 1032 by his son, the famous abbot. This majestic edifice, jewel of early Romanesque art *(p 14)* had a nave and four aisles, cut by a great transept on which, in highly original style, seven apses abutted. An earthquake in 1428, remodellings and a fire in 1835, destroyed the edifice leaving only the portal around which yet another new church was erected.

Portal★★. — The 12C portal is weather worn in spite of the late 13C overhang, and the figures are difficult to decipher. They cover not only the doorway but also the surround.

A — Vision of the Apocalypse

1) The Eternal Father enthroned
2) Angels
3) Winged Man, the symbol of St Matthew
4) An eagle, the symbol of St John
5) The 24 Old Men of the Apocalypse
6) A lion, the symbol of St Mark
7) A bull, the symbol of St Luke

B — Exodus

1) The crossing of the Red Sea
2) Manna descending from Heaven
3) Flight of quail guiding the People of God
4) Moses bringing forth water from the rock
5) Moses keeping his arms uplifted to ensure victory for his people
6) Foot soldiers and cavalry in combat

C — The Book of Kings

1) David and the musicians
2) Transporting the Ark of the Covenant
3) The plague of Zion
4) Gad (standing) speaks to David (seated) before the crowd
5) David declares Solomon his heir
6) Solomon riding David's mule, is proclaimed by the people
7) The judgment of Solomon
8) Solomon's dream
9) Elijah rises to heaven in a chariot of fire

D — David and the musicians
E — Monsters fighting
F — St Peter
G — St Paul
H — The life and martyrdom of St Peter (left) and St Paul (right)
I — The story of Jonah (left) and Daniel (right)
J — (at the arch centre — reading simultaneously right and left) - at the centre, the Creator - two angels — above ; the offering of Abel and Cain — below the killing of Abel ; the death of Cain
K — (inner sides of the doorway pillars): the months of the year

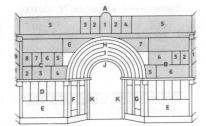

The portal design has been compared to that of a triumphal arch. In this case the carving is seen to illustrate the glory of God and his people, victorious over his enemies (Passage of the Red Sea), a symbol of special significance at the time of the Reconquest.

Cloister★. — *Closed Mondays; 25pts.* Of the vast quadrilateral lined with paired columns, only the gallery abutting the church dates back to the 12C. It was the only gallery until the 14C when the others were added, their later date being betrayed only by the carving of some of the capitals.

SAN CUGAT DEL VALLÉS SANT CUGAT DEL VALLÉS (Barcelona)

Michelin map **443** fold 20 — Pop 31 184

The town is named after the Benedictine monastery established in the Middle Ages on the site of an earlier chapel. This had been built very early to contain the relics of St Cucufas whose throat had been cut in about 303 AD by Diocletian's legionaries on this spot 8 Roman miles along the road from Barcelona.

Monastery★. — The old wall encloses the monastic chapel, cloister, bishopric and conventual buildings abandoned in 1835 which now serve as the parish church and school.

Church. — The 11C belfry decorated with Lombard bands, is the oldest part of the building. Originally it lacked lantern turrets and was free standing but in the 15C it was incorporated in the main building when the chapels were constructed. A chancel had already been added in the 12C. The façade was completed in 1350. The flat, crenellated wall supported by thrusting buttresses, was relieved by a radiating rose window as vast and ornamented as the doorway below, with smooth covings and flowing lines, was plain.

SAN CUGAT DEL VALLÉS

There are three apses, polygonal outside and with engaged pillars inside; the central one was given radiating vaulting, a feature which was to mark an alteration in style, reflected in the ogival vaulting in the lantern and above the three aisles.

Cloister★. — *Access, left of the church. Open 9am to 1pm and 4 to 7pm; Fridays, Sundays and holidays 10am to 2pm and 4 to 8pm; 100pts.*

The cloister is one of the largest Romanesque cloisters in Catalonia. Early in the 13C a double row of columns (144 in all) was erected around a close; in the 16C an upper gallery was added above a blind arcade decorated with sculpted modillions. The skilfully carved capitals are Corinthian (acanthus leaves), ornamental (strapwork), figurative (birds) and historiated (Biblical scenes), these last ones are grouped largely in the south gallery which abuts the church. The most interesting of all, however, is the one over the northeast corner column on which the sculptor, Arnaud Cadell, first carved a self-portrait and then cut his name.

SAN JUAN DE LAS ABADESAS SANT JOAN DE LES ABADESSES (Gerona) —
Michelin map 443 fold 9 — *Local map p 93* — Pop 4 241

The ancient Abbesses' Town has discovered coal resources and with these has founded modern industries (cement, textiles).

The first abbess, in the late 9C, was Emma, daughter of Wilfred the Shaggy, founder of several monasteries *(Ripoll p 95)*. The community, however, was superseded and it was for canons that the present church was consecrated in 1150.

St John's (San Juan). — *Access through the Cloister. Open 1 July to 15 September 10am to 7pm; 16 September to 31 October and April to June 10am to 2pm and 4 to 7pm; November to March weekdays 11.30am to 2.30pm and Saturdays, Sundays and holidays 11am to 2pm and 3 to 6pm.*

The east end has stepped vaulting and the central chapel, the most remarkable, arching and carved capitals to the columns, recalling those of southwest France.

Originally the single aisle led to an elaborate east end with an ambulatory and radiating chapels, again French influenced, but this disappeared when an earthquake destroyed the chancel roof. Local masons repaired the church by prolonging the nave, placing columns where previously the ambulatory had been.

The decoration of the apses echoes that of the chevet, the motifs on the carved **capitals** those of oriental fabrics.

In the south transept is a lovely 14C Gothic altarpiece in alabaster.

Descent from the Cross★★. — The group in polychrome wood in the central apse was carved in 1251. The artist departed from the traditional scene by introducing additional figures and greater realism — note St John's sad gestures, the Virgin receiving her son. In 1426 an unbroken host was discovered in the Christ figure's head which has made the statue an object of particular veneration.

Cloister★. – The present delicate, sweeping arches and slender small columns replaced those of an earlier Romanesque cloister in the 15C.

Former bishopric. — Opening off the small square in front of the church is the attractive bishop's **patio** in which the carved capitals have a graceful form.

Michelin maps to Spain (1: 400 000)

441 *North West*	445 *Central and Eastern*
442 *Northern*	446 *Southern*
443 *North East*	447 *Western and Central*
444 *Central*	

SANTES CREUS Monastery ★★ (Tarragona) —
Michelin map 443 folds 18 and 19

The monastery, pendant to Poblet *(p 91)*, was founded shortly after the latter, in 1157. It was placed in the care of Cistercians from Toulouse, came under the protection of the great families of Catalonia and into the favour of the Kings of Aragon who appointed the abbot royal chaplain. The splendours of the Middle Ages were followed, as at Poblet, by the ravages of the 19C with the difference that worship never ceased in the church as peasants, who had taken over the former conventual buildings, made up the congregation in place of the banished community.

TOUR

Guided tours (time: 3/4 hour) 10am to 1pm and 3.30 to 7pm (6pm in winter); closed 25 December; 100pts.

The monastery plan is similar to that of Poblet in that it has three perimeter walls. A baroque gateway leads to the principal courtyard framed on all sides by houses. To the right is the former bishopric with its attractive *patio*, which is now the town hall and local school; at the end stands the 12-13C church. The façade is plain apart from a central, rounded doorway, a large Gothic window and battlements added a century later.

Great Cloister★★. — The **Royal Gate** on the south side of the church opens onto a cloister with Gothic bays which, although much restored, still has carving full of life and tracery infilling showing a first hint of the Flamboyant style. In contrast, the transitional style of the **lavabo,** which incorporates a large basin, appears almost clumsy. Carved tombs of the Catalan nobility fill the gallery niches.

Chapterhouse★. — The chapterhouse openings enabled lay brothers to follow services without entering the church proper. Abbots' tombstones have been inlaid in the pavement.

Dormitory. — Stairs next to the chapterhouse lead to the dormitory, a long Catalan gallery divided by arches supporting a timber roof.

Church★. — The church, begun in 1174, closely follows the Cistercian pattern of a flat east end and overall austerity; a characteristic square ribbed ogive vaulting, replacing the more usual broken cradle vaulting, does nothing to soften the severity. The lantern, from about 1300, the stained glass in the great west window and the superb absidal **rose window★**, partially hidden by the high altar retable, do, however, relieve the bareness. Gothic aedicules at the transept openings contain the **royal tombs,** on the north side beneath a canopy (c1295) of Peter the Great and on the south, of his son James II, the Just, and his Queen, Blanca of Anjou. The Plateresque decoration below the crowned recumbent figures in Cistercian habits, was added in the 16C.

The Infirmary Cloister★. *Access through the Great Cloister, right of the dormitory staircase.*

The infirmary stood to the north of the cloister also known as the Old Cloister from its archaic appearance. The arcades resemble those of a village main square and indeed the whole design is simple with a central fountain and four cypresses in the close, imparting a cool contemplative atmosphere.

To the right of the entrance is the monks' cellar containing two tuns still permeated with the smell of wine.

The next passage leads to the kitchens and refectory and beyond to the **royal palace** where the second half of the 14C **patio★** has upward sweeping lines, pleasing proportions and a beautiful staircase.

SEO DE URGEL ★ LA SEU D'URGELL (Lérida)
Michelin map **443** fold 7 — *Local map p 93* — Pop 10 681

This onetime city of prince-archbishops, stands in a peaceful countryside where the Valira, which rises in the mountains of Andorra, joins the River Segre. Since 1278 the duties of the archbishop have included those of joint ruler of Andorra *(p 78).*

The former county capital now lives on trade and agriculture which includes stock farming and dairy produce — its cheeses are widely known in Spain.

Sta María Cathedral★★. — The cathedral, dating from the 12C, is a majestic reminder of the city's former greatness. Lombard influence is clear, particularly in the decoration of the façade and the transept towers; sculpture was kept to a minimum, line and proportion, giving the building all its beauty.

The **façade,** framed by twin towers, is clearly divided into three parts, corresponding to the three aisles inside, and into three superimposed registers. A most effective twin arched gallery decorates the east transept wall and circles the apse. Inside, the elevation is spectacular, the nave rising on cruciform pillars, surrounded, in the French style, by engaged columns.

Cloister★. — *Entrance through the Diocesan Museum. Son et Lumière certain evenings in August.*

The cloister is 13C, although the east gallery had to be rebuilt in 1603. The granite capitals were carved by masons from the Roussillon whose most outstanding achievements, among the generally successful series, are the human figures at the gallery corners. A door at the southeast corner opens into the 11C **Church of Sant Miquel,** the only building remaining constructed by St Ermangol.

Diocesan Museum. · — *Open July 9.30am to 1.30pm and 3.30 to 8pm; August 9.30am to 8pm; September 10am to 1pm and 4 to 7pm; closed Sunday and holiday afternoons; 150pts.*

The jewel of the cathedral treasure is an 11C **Beatus★,** one of the rare examples of St John's Commentary on the Apocalypse written in the 8C by the priest, Beatus of Liébana *(p 119).* The manuscript is beautifully illuminated.

SITGES ★ (Barcelona)
Michelin map **443** fold 19 — Pop 11 850
See town plan in the current Michelin Red Guide España Portugal

The picturesque small town of Sitges, with its long sand beach, is a favourite resort with wealthy Catalan families who have built elegant houses on the old town outskirts along the Paseo Marítimo or sea promenade.

Rising from the breakwater, sheltering the fishing boat harbour, is the rose-coloured façade of the parish church. All around are the streets of the old town lined with white walled houses, their balconies brilliant with flowers. Local museums contain canvases from the late 19C, when Rusiñol and Miguel Utrillo (official father of the French painter) painted in this quarter.

Sitges is known for its flowers: the national carnation show — the national flower of Spain — is held in the town in late May, early June; and at Corpus Christi a 9pm procession passes through streets spectacularly decorated with carpets of flowers *(p 24).*

"Cau Ferrat" Museum. — *Calle del Fonollar. Open 10am to 1pm and 5 to 7pm (4 to 6pm 1 October to 30 June); Sundays 10am to 2pm; closed Mondays; inquire locally for holidays; 100pts.*

The former home of the painter and writer **Santiago Rusiñol** (1861-1931) contains, wrought iron works, crystalware, ceramic arts as well as the artist's collection of his own works including drawings by Ramón Casas, Juan Llimona, Miguel Utrillo and two paintings by El Greco.

Casa Llopis. — *Same opening times as the "Cau Ferrat" Museum; ticket valid for the Casa Papiol at Villanueva y Geltrú (p 102).*

The Casa Llopis, a bourgeois house built at the end of the 18C in the then new part of the town *(at the corner of the streets Sant Gaudenci and Sant Josep),* gives a good idea of the life of the middle and upper classes at that date. Dioramas on the ground floor supplement the picture with scenes of private, social and popular activities. Note the mechanical devices and musical boxes. Also in the museum is the **Lola Anglada Collection.** This outstanding collection of 17, 18 and 19C dolls from all over Europe are made of wood, leather, *papier mâché* and china, and served as toys, fashion mannequins or collectors' pieces.

SOLSONA (Lérida)

Michelin map 443 north of folds 18 and 19 — Pop 6 230

Picturesque streets with the occasional mediaeval house in the shadow of the castle ruins, give an idea of the town's age.

Corpus Christi is the occasion for young men, dressed in the clothes of earlier times, to parade through the streets firing salvoes from blunderbusses, for giant pasteboard figures to appear and children to dance the "Ball de Bastons" in the streets.

Cathedral. — Only the apse, decorated with Lombard bands and carved modillions, remains of the Romanesque church, the rest is Gothic with baroque additions such as the portals and the Lady Chapel off the south transept. The latter was designed to shelter within its ornate marble walls the **Virgin of the Cloister★**, a beautifully carved, 12 or 13C Romanesque figure.

Diocesan and Regional Museum. — *Open 10am to 1pm and 4.30 to 7pm (4 to 6pm 1 October to 30 April); closed Mondays (except holiday Mondays), 1 January and 25 December; 100pts.* The Romanesque and Gothic style **paintings★★** in the museum housed in the episcopal palace, are excellent examples of Catalan art. The **fresco collection** includes a painting from Sant Quirze of Pedret (near Berga in the Pyrenees), discovered beneath an overpainting done 100 years later. The archaic style of this fresco shows God, with arms outstretched, in a circle which represents heaven, surmounted by a phoenix symbolising immortality. The narrative talent of the 12C Master of Pedret can be seen in the theme of the Apocalypse, painted in a style obviously Byzantine influenced in a reconstituted Mozarabic apse. Totally different are the thinly outlined, elegant 13C paintings from Sant Pere de Casserres (near Vic) and the already Gothic style, 14C works from Cardona.

The museum is also known for its collection of **altarfronts** which includes a frontal from Sagars, in which all decoration is omitted to heighten the symbolism of the scenes illustrated, and a realistic painting of the Last Supper by Jaime Ferrer I (15C).

The prehistory gallery, on the first floor, has interesting displays of **pottery.**

The **salt museum**, another department, is possibly unique. Everything displayed has been carved out of blocks of salt from Cardona *(p 85):* the table, the setting, the repast and the weird, pinnacled centrepiece.

Ethnographical Museum. — *Apply at the Tourist Information Centre. Open 11am to 1pm and 5 to 6pm; 25pts.* The old feudal mansion, complete with its own well and silo, now houses items from the everyday life of earlier times, including a honey press, the drum from which lot numbers were drawn for military service...

*The Maps, **Red Guides** and **Green Guides** are complementary publications. Use them together.*

TARRAGONA ★★ P

Michelin map 443 folds 18 and 29 — Pop 111 689
See map of the built-up area in the current Michelin Red Guide España Portugal

Tarragona, a city rich in reminders of Antiquity and the Middle Ages, is a modern metropolis of wide avenues and prosperous commercial streets. Its seafront is one of the most attractive along the coast rising in tiers up the cliffside and brilliant with flowers. The promenade skirts the old city and circles the Palace of Augustus, before following the line of the perimeter enclosing the cathedral and antique Tarragona.

Capital of Tarraconensis. — Tarragona goes back a very long time. The imposing ramparts built of enormous Cyclopean blocks of stone, indicate that it was founded by peoples from the eastern Mediterranean early in the first millenium BC. In due course it suffered occupation by the Iberians. The Romans, who by 218 BC had control of the larger part of the peninsula, developed Tarraconensis into a major city and overseas capital. Although it could never equal Rome, it enjoyed many of the same privileges as the imperial capital and Augustus, Galba and Hadrian did not disdain to live in it. Conversion to Christianity, it is said by St Paul, brought it appointment as a metropolitan seat, its dignitaries, the primacy of Spain, an honour it retained throughout the Barbarian invasions of the 5C and the devastations of the Moors in the 8C but lost finally to the ambition of Toledo in the 11C.

■ ROMAN TARRAGONA *time: 2 1/2 hours*

The best preserved monuments lie outside the city limits; the Centcelles Mausoleum *(p 100),* Ferreres Aqueduct *(p 100),* Scipios Tower and the Berà Triumphal Arch.

Archaeological Museum★★ (BZ M). — *Open weekdays in summer 10am to 1pm and 4.30 to 8pm; in winter 10am to 1.30pm and 4 to 7pm; Sundays 10am to 2pm; closed Mondays, 1 January, 24 June, 11 September and 25 to 30 December; 100pts. ticket also valid for the paleochristian necropolis; Tuesdays free.*

The exhibits are all from Tarragona or its immediate environs; most date from the Roman period. There are beautiful mosaics, including the **Head of Medusa★★** with its penetrating stare, statues which once adorned public buildings and squares; friezes, carved cornices and medallions from the Temple of Jupiter (which stood on the cathedral site) and the Temple of Augustus. There is also a ceramics department.

Adjoining the museum is the 1C BC **praetorium,** considerably restored in the Middle Ages but interesting not least as traditionally the place in which Augustus stayed and Pilate, future praetor of Judea, was born, during his father's term of office in Tarraconensis.

(After Archivo MAS photo, Barcelona)

Head of Medusa

TARRAGONA

Nova (Rambla)	ABZ	Baixada de Misericòrdia	BZ 3
Sant Agustí	BZ	Baixada Roser	BZ 4
Unió	AZ	Civadería	BZ 5
		Enginyer Cabestany	AZ 10
Baixada de Toro	BZ 2	López Peláez	AZ 15
		Pau Casals (Av.)	AZ 18
		Pla de la Seu	BZ 19

Pla de Palau	BZ 20
Portalet	BZ 21
Ramón y Cajal (Av.)	AZ 25
Roser (Portal del)	BZ 27
Sant Antoni (Portal de)	BZ 28
Sant Hermenegild	BZ 29
Sant Joan (Pl.)	BZ 31

Paseo Arqueológico★ (BZ). — *Open in summer 9am to 8pm; in winter 10am to 1.30pm and 3.30 to 5.30pm; closed Sunday and holiday afternoons and Mondays; 50pts.*

It was the Scipios, according to Livy and Pliny, who constructed Tarragona's city walls in the 3C BC. They were erected on existing Cyclopean bases, held in position by the sizes of the boulders of which they were composed. They were so massive that they were for a long time thought to have been "barbaric" or pre-Roman. The mediaeval inhabitants extensively raised and rebuilt the ramparts; the 18C citizens remodelled them but still left us with walls bearing the marks of 2000 years of history. A pleasant walk has been laid out through the gardens at the foot of the walls. The outer perimeter was erected in 1707 by the English during the War of Succession. Catalonia and the Balearics were among the last strongholds of the Holy Alliance to capitulate to the Bourbons.

Near the Rosary Gate (BZ 27) can be seen the remains of a Roman **forum** (BZ F).

Palaeochristian necropolis (Necrópolis paleocristiana) (AZ). — *Access: Ramón y Cajal Avenue* (AZ). *Same opening times and same ticket as for the archaeological museum.*

All the different types of tile-covered tomb and amphorae including sarcophagi and a family vault can be seen in this 3 to 6C cemetery of the early Christians of Tarragona. Some of the sarcophagi in the museum, in the centre of the garden which contains the most interesting finds, make it evident that they had previously served as pagan tombs. The so called **lion sarcophagus★** is simply but powerfully carved.

Arena ruins (BZ R). — The arena was built beside the sea, using the natural slope of the hillside for the tiers.

It was here that in 259, Bishop Fructuosus and his deacons, Augurius and Eulogius, suffered martyrdom by fire. Traces of the commemorative basilica have been discovered in the Romanesque walls of the Church of Sta Maria del Miracle which replaced the original basilica in the 12C and is itself now in ruins.

■ THE MEDIAEVAL CITY *time: 1 hour*

Cathedral★ (BZ). — It was erected on the site of the Roman Temple of Jupiter. The 12C apse could still be called Romanesque in style but the greater part of the edifice is Gothic, although of different periods; from the transept to the west front and in the side chapels one sees in succession Flamboyant Gothic, Plateresque and baroque ornament.

Amidst this interior richness are many works of art: the Chapel of the Virgin of Montserrat itself (2nd chapel, north aisle) and particularly its 15C altarpiece by Luis Borrassá; the baroque **St Thecla Chapel** (3rd chapel, south aisle) in Tarragona marble (1760-1775); the Dels Sastres Chapel with intricate Gothic vaulting.

In the place of honour in the central apse, is the **altarpiece of St Thecla★★**, patron of the city, converted, according to legend, by the preaching of St Paul. The unconverted, among whom was her mother, persecuted the convert cruelly but each time she was saved from death by divine intervention. The altarpiece, carved in about 1430 by Pere Johan completely fills the apse, two Flamboyant doors on either side allowing one to pass through to the chevet. The detail and ornament become ever more intricate the nearer they are to the predella which is as finely worked as a piece of goldsmith's filigree. An earlier Romanesque style low relief, dating from the first half of the 13C on the **altar** before the retable, again illustrates the saint's life. The tomb to the right of the high altar is that of the Infante Don Juan of Aragon. The carving is 16C Italian work.

TARRAGONA★★

Cloister★ (BZ N). — *Guided tours 10am to 1pm and 3.30 to 7.30pm (6pm November to April); closed holidays in winter; 100pts. Access through the north transept.*

The cloister is very unusual and large — each gallery is 45m - 147ft long. It was built in the 12 and 13C and the portal, arches and geometric decoration are clearly Romanesque, but the vaulting is Gothic, as are the supporting arches which divide the bays into groups of three. Moorish influence is evident in the *claustra* of geometrically patterned and pierced panels filling the oculi below the arches, the line of polylobed arches at the base of the cathedral roof and decorating the lantern which can be seen from the northeast corner of the cloister. Inlaid in the west gallery is a *mihrab* like stone niche *(p 39)*, dated 960, and perhaps a trophy captured and brought home by a victorious Christian expedition.

The **diocesan museum** in the south gallery contains more than 50 **tapestries** dating from the Gothic period to the 17C; the finest hangs in the **chapterhouse.**

EXCURSIONS

Las Ferreres Aqueduct★. — *Leave by Rambla Nova. 4km - 2 1/2 miles from Tarragona you will see the Roman aqueduct up on your right.* You can walk *(1/2 hour)* through the pines to the base of the two tier structure.

Centcelles Mausoleum★. — *5km - 3 miles by Ramón y Cayal Avenue (take the Reus road; bear right after crossing the Francolí). Turn right in Constantí into the Calle de Centcelles; continue a further 500yds along an unsurfaced road. Just before the village of Centcelles make a 90° turn to the left.*

The mausoleum, which now stands in a vineyard, takes the form of two monumental buildings faced in pink tiles. They were erected in the 4C by a wealthy Roman near his summer residence which was also vast and included a private bath. The first chamber in the mausoleum is covered by an immense cupola (diameter: 11m - 36ft), decorated with **mosaics★** on themes favoured by the early Christians such as hunting scenes, Daniel in the lions' den etc. The adjoining chamber, which is the same size only square, has an apse on either side.

The group of buildings is obviously outstanding although its symbolism remains unexplained.

TARRASA ★ TERRASSA (Barcelona)

Michelin map 443 folds 19 and 20 — Pop 155 360

Tarrasa is a large industrial town which specialises in spinning and weaving, but which has, nevertheless, managed to preserve monuments from the ancient city of Egara.

The City of Egara★★. — A Roman town, then an important episcopal see under the Visigoths, Egara has preserved within a perimeter wall, 3 historic churches (9-12C) of exceptional archaeological importance.

St Michael's (Sant Miquel). — St Michael's, a former Carolingian baptistry, is, of the 3 churches, the one with the most unity. The dome above the font is supported on eight pillars, each different in shape and each of a different marble. Alabaster windows in the apse provide a filtered light by which to see the ancient paintings. Below is a crypt, abutted by three small apses beyond horseshoe shaped arches.

St Mary's (Sta Maria). — The church is a good example of the Romanesque style. Before the façade is a 4C mosaic. Inside there are 11C paintings on the absidal vaulting, a wall painting (13C) in the south transept illustrating the martyrdom of Thomas Becket of Canterbury and superb 15C reredos particularly in the north transept where there is one especially outstanding by Jaime Huguet of **Sts Abdon and Sennen★★.**

St Peter's (Sant Pere). — The church has, in the apse, an unusual stone altarpiece.

Textile Museum★. — *Open 10am to 1pm (2pm Sundays and holidays) and 5 to 8pm; closed Sunday and holiday afternoons and Mondays when not a holiday; 60pts.*

Oriental materials, Merovingian fabrics and brocades provide a panoramic history of textile manufacture.

TORTOSA (Tarragona)

Michelin map 443 fold 28 — Pop 31 445

Tortosa, for centuries the last town before the sea, was charged in those times with guarding, from the heights overlooking the Ebro, the region's only river bridge. Today it is a peaceful agricultural town prospering from the olives planted high on the chalky hillsides, terraced and divided by low drystone walls, and from the early vegetables, the maize, oranges and peaches sheltered from the sea wind by lines of cypresses and flourishing in the rich alluvial soil brought down by the Ebro.

The Ebro Delta. — The river collects quantities of alluvium from the Cantabrian mountains, the Pyrenees and the Aragon plateaux and deposits it in the vast delta which, in consequence, extends a further 10m a year into the Mediterranean. In the 19C a new system of controlled irrigation and drainage enabled rice to be grown for the first time on the delta plain.

Historical notes. — Tortosa, like its neighbour Tarragona, was first Roman then Visigothic; in 714 it was seized by the Moors who built the Suda, of which the ruins still dominate the town. It was reconquered in 1148 by Ramón Berenguer IV.

For several centuries Catalans, Moors and Jews lived peacefully and prosperously together, providing a wonderful setting in which different cultures flourished together.

Whatever its past Tortosa's most ferocious contest occured this century when on 24 July 1938 it became the scene for the **Battle of the Ebro.** The Republicans, who controlled Catalonia, attempted an attack on the rear of the Nationalist forces which were advancing on Valencia. They crossed the Ebro at Tortosa but could proceed no further; for four months they remained stuck in trenches before being repulsed with the loss of 150 000 dead. A monument (Monumento) rising out of the Ebro commemorates the Nationalist victory.

■ **SIGHTS**   *time: 1 1/2 hours*

Cathedral★. — *Open during services.*
　　The never completed baroque façade conceals a cathedral built in pure Gothic style even though construction, begun in 1347, continued for 200 years! In Catalan tradition the lines are plain, the arches high and divided into two tiers only in the nave. The chancel is framed by radiating chapels, which, it was originally planned, should be divided by fenestration like that at the north entrance to the ambulatory. Next to the axial chapel is a large wood **triptych★** painted in the 14C, illustrating the Life of Christ.
　　The two stone **pulpits★** in the nave, which date from the second half of the 15C, are carved respectively left and right with the Evangelists and their symbols and the Doctors of the Roman Church, Saints Gregory, Jerome, Ambrose and Augustine.

Chapel of Our Lady of the Belt (Nuestra Señora de la Cinta). — The chapel which opens off the south aisle is almost a church in itself. It was built in the baroque style of the 18C and is decorated with paintings and local jasper and marble; at its centre is the relic, the belt of Our Lady *(services of special veneration: first two weeks in September).*

Font. — To the right of the chapel stands a stone basin said to have stood in the garden of the antipope Benedict XIII, **Pedro de Luna** *(p 169).* The arms of Papa Luna, as he was known in Spain, and allusions to the Great Schism of the West in which he was so deeply involved, appear in the carvings decorating the basin. On the other side of the Cinta Chapel is the 14C cathedral **cloister (A).**

Bishop's Palace (B). — The fairly large, 14C Catalan *patio,* is memorable for the straight flight of steps which completely occupies one side and the arcaded gallery, lined with slender columns. The Gothic chapel, entered through a carved doorway from a well-proportioned ante-room, has ogive vaulting in which the ribs descend on to figured bosses. The final decorative touch is given by the false relief windows built into the walls on either side.

TORTOSA

0　　100 m

Generalitat (Av. de la)	
Agustín Querol (Pl.)	2
Angel (Pl.)	3
Catedral (Pl.)	4
Ciudad	6
Colón (Av.)	7
Constitución (Pl.)	9
Cruera (Pl.)	10
Dr Vilá	12
España (Pl. de)	13
Montserrat (Pl.)	15
Obispo Aznar	18
O'Callagan (Pl. de)	19
Paz (Pl. de la)	20
Pintor Gimeno	22
Puente Piedra (Pl.)	23
Santo Domingo	24
Taules Velles	26

St Louis College (Colegio de Sant Lluis or Sant Matiés) (E). — *Open 10am to 1.30pm and 4 to 8pm; closed Saturdays, Sundays and holidays.*
　　The college was founded in 1544 by the Emperor Charles V for Moorish converts. The attractive **patio★** of three superimposed arcades is decorated between the ground and first floors, with a frieze of Renaissance medallions carved with likenesses of the Kings of Aragon.

VIC ★ (Barcelona) _____
Michelin map 🔢 fold 20 — Pop 30 057

　　Since ancient times there has been at least a village on the site now occupied by the commercially and industrially thriving town of Vic (leather, food processing and textiles). Vic sausages have long been well-known in Catalonia.

Cathedral★. — *Open 10am to 1pm and 4 (5pm Sundays) to 7pm (6pm in winter); 150pts.*
　　The elegant Romanesque belfry erected beside the nave and the crypt, constructed in the 11C by Abbot Oliva *(p 95),* are all that remain of the present church's forerunners.
　　The cathedral was built in the Neo-Classical style between 1781 and 1803. In 1930 the famous Catalan artist José María Sert y Badia decorated it with wall paintings which were lost when the church was set on fire at the beginning of the Civil War in 1936. Sert took up his brushes again and by 1945, when he died, the walls were once more covered with vast murals.
　　The **paintings★★** have an inner fire, a power reminiscent of Michelangelo and also a profound symbolism. They evoke the mystery of the Redemption (chancel) awaited from the time of Adam's original sin (transept) and prophesied by the martyrs (nave). Three scenes on the back of the west door illustrate the triumph of human injustice in the Life of Christ and in the history of Catalonia: against an architectural background which includes the cathedral in ruins after the fire, Jesus chases the moneylenders from the temple (right) but is himself condemned to crucifixion (left), while (in the centre) Pilate washes his hands and the crowd hails Barabas, symbol of the vandals of revolution. The monochrome tints and browns in the murals, tone with the fluted stone columns, the scale of the murals with the vastness of the nave.
　　The high altar **retable★,** at the end of the ambulatory, is a 15C alabaster which escaped the cathedral's many restorers. Its twelve panels, divided by statues of the saints and mouldings, are devoted to the glorification of Christ, the Virgin and St Peter. Opposite, lies the canon who commissioned the retable in a beautiful Gothic **tomb★** by the same unknown sculptor.

Cloister. — Wide tracery filled 14C arches surround the small close in which stands the monumental tomb of the philosopher, **Jaime Balmes** (1810-1848), native of Vic.

In a cloister gallery one can see the tomb of the painter J.-M. Sert, surmounted by his last and unfinished work, a Crucifixion, intended by the artist to replace that in the cathedral.

Episcopal Museum★★. — *Open weekdays 10am to 1pm and 4 to 7pm; Sundays and holidays 10am to 1.30pm; closed afternoons 1 November to 30 April and 25 December; 100pts, free first Sunday of the month.*

The museum next to the cathedral, contains works from local churches. Its rich collections, particularly of Romanesque altarfronts painted on wood and Gothic altarpieces, provide a comprehensive survey of the development of Catalan art.

Room 1 (11, 12, 13C). — The exhibits include crucifixes and statues of the Virgin in polychrome wood, frescoes — notably a Last Supper from Seo de Urgel — and a series of altarfronts which show a clear evolution in style from the hieratical Byzantine manner to a more personal, narrative approach.

Room 2 (14 and 15C). — Sculpture became more lifelike as perspective and detail increased after **Bartomeu** (c1300). Besides the beautiful French and Italian influenced statues of the Virgin, the outstanding object in this room is the alabaster altarfront of the Life of Christ carved by B. Saulet in 1341 for San Juan de las Abadesas.

Remaining Rooms. — The remaining rooms are devoted to Gothic painting and include works by several great artists: **Ferrer Bassá** *(p 19)* and **Pedro Serra** (1356-1405) who introduced the Italian style; **Raimundo de Mur** (1402-1435) who added a personal note and a sense of the picturesque. After canvases by the Master of Cardona and Jaime Ferrer I (15C), there is a room with paintings by **Luis Borrassá** *(p 19),* a clever colourist who introduced the International Gothic style and another with those of **Bernat Martorell,** his successor, and **Jaime Huguet** *(p 22),* who reveals the first signs of the spirit of the Renaissance which was to appear clearly in Juan Gasco's Holy Visage (late 15, early 16C) which hangs in the last room.

VILLAFRANCA DEL PANADÉS VILAFRANCA DEL PENEDÉS (Barcelona)
Michelin map 𝟺𝟺𝟹 fold 19 — Pop 25 020

As introduced by the huge 16C press, standing at the town's entrance by the Tarragona road, Villafranca has always been a wine town.

Penedés. — The region produces a wine with a high alcoholic content used by blenders elsewhere to fortify less strong varieties; it also produces in its own right, table wines, dessert wines and liqueurs which require a long time to mature *(some cellars are open to the public).* A sparkling wine is fermented at **San Sadurní d'Anoia** *(12km - 7 miles northeast of Villafranca).*

Royal Palace and Wine Museum. — *Open 10am to 2pm and 4.30 to 7.30pm (4 to 7pm 1 October to 31 May); closed Mondays except holiday Mondays and Good Friday and 30 August in the morning and 25 and 31 December; 125pts.*

Beside the church stands the palace of the Kings of Aragon, built in the 14C when they presented their former residence to Santes Creus Abbey, the latter on the far side of the square now being a museum.

The ground floor is devoted to wine: dioramas illustrate the harvest, wine making and its enjoyment from the time of the Egyptians and Romans to the 19C. Presses and bottles complete the exhibition. On the first floor *(access through an attractive Catalan patio)* are geological and prehistorical exhibits and excavation finds from the region.

VILLANUEVA Y GELTRÚ VILANOVA I LA GELTRÚ (Barcelona)
Michelin map 𝟺𝟺𝟹 fold 19 — Pop 43 560

Villanueva has an attractive site on a bay edged by a beach of golden sand framed by rocks. Olive trees and clusters of palms provide a dappled shade. The town developed rapidly in the 18C, when *Indianos (p 103)* returned from the Antilles with fortunes which they invested in the local cotton industry which remains the principal source of prosperity.

Casa Papiol★ (Museo Romántico). — *At the north end of the town. Open 10am to 1pm (2pm Sundays) and 4 to 6pm; closed Sunday and holiday afternoons and all day Mondays; time: 3/4 hour; 100pts; ticket also valid for the museum's other departments: the Casa Llopis, Sitges (p 99).*

The house's interest lies in the picture it presents, complete and perfect in every detail, of the every day life of a well to do family in the early 19C. It was built between 1790 and 1801 by a rich landowner, Francisco Papiol. The owner's apartments on the first floor include reception, music and billiard rooms and bedrooms filled with every imaginable luxury including "modern" inventions such as gas lighting. The decoration effectively combined Pompeian, Empire and Isabeline styles. Suchet's apartment, so called as the French general stayed briefly during the War of Independence, is Louis XVI. In the private chapel, a shrine contains the relics, presented to Don Papiol by a Villanueva convent, of St Constance, a young Roman martyr. The kitchen, faced with 19C ceramic tiles, is spick and span and seemingly ready for the servants to begin work at the hearth.

Workrooms and annexes on the *entresol* and ground floors contain equipment and stores: the stove, olive oil reserve, storeroom, servants' kitchen and the stables.

At the back of the house is a secluded garden.

Castillo de la Geltrú. — *Open 10am to 1pm and 4 to 7pm; closed Sunday and holiday afternoons; 70pts; ticket also valid for the Balaguer Museum.*

The old Catalan seignorial mansion has been restored and converted into a museum in which are displayed an angular 12C Hispano-Moorish bronze mortar, a 13C carved wood altarpiece from Toledo and 17 and 18C Catalan ceramics.

Balaguer Museum (Museo Biblioteca). — *In the Avinguda Balaguer, opposite the station. Open 10am to 2pm and 4 to 7pm; closed Sunday and holiday afternoons; ticket also valid for the Castillo de la Geltrú.*

This museum includes, among its antiquities, a small Egyptian mummy with all its funerary possessions and, among its 17-20C paintings, an *Annunciation* signed by El Greco.

4 The Cantabrian Coast

Although historically and administratively the Basque Country, the Asturias and Cantabria are distinct regions, they are described in this section because geographically and from a tourist point of view they form one with the provinces of Cantabria.

The Asturias and Bilbao are names which conjure up images of coal, heavy industry, a black country, but in reality the mining areas are limited and clearly defined: in the Nalón and Caudal valleys near Oviedo and around the mouth of the Nervión. Everywhere else, with one exception, the land is green being well watered by fine rains from the Atlantic; this exception is the Álava Plain, reminiscent of the Meseta in aridity and flatness.

Mountains and sea. — The Tertiary Era mountain chain bordering the northern edge of the Meseta runs through each of the Cantabrian coastal provinces. The **Basque Mountains,** secondary limestone ranges abutting the Pyrenees foothills, rise to 1 500m - 5 000ft; the **Cantabrian Cordillera,** further west and including the **Picos de Europa,** to more than 2 500m - 8 000ft. It is after the impressive Cordillera barrier that Cantabria Province has come to be known as La Montaña and it is these ranges and the Basque mountains which make the region so full of contrast and delight — snow-capped peaks within 50km - 30 miles of the Atlantic, mountain torrents rich with salmon and trout, dark gorges, sunlit slopes...

The **middle land** is hilly, sandwiched between the mountains and the sea; roads wind along river valleys, bordered by lush meadows, cider apple orchards, fields of maize and beans. Dairy produce is a major source of livelihood, particularly in Cantabria Province, maize the principal crop in the Asturias as can be seen by the number of barns - **hórreos** (illustration p 111) — outside any village. In the Basque country, farming is mixed with large white homesteads (caseríos) standing in their own domains on the hillsides.

The **coast** is lined by low cliffs, cut by inlets or rías narrower than those of Galicia. The most extensive sand beaches are in the Cantabrian area.

The men of the region and their history. — Cantabria's role of mountain refuge goes back to Palaeolithic times — the limestone caves afforded shelter against the elements in the earliest epochs; later, the mountains provided sanctuary from invading conquerors and for those unsuccessful in revolt. The local people are still proud that their Asturian and Cantabrian ancestors were never subdued by the Romans; that it was their region which nurtured the Spanish monarchy; that the Basques as early as the 9C were hunting whales off the coast of Greenland and that, in the 16C, many had joined the explorers and conquerors of the New World. This journeying across the Atlantic has continued, the fruits being visible in many a village where the fortune of the returned native appears as a fine house, known as the **Casa del Indiano.** Industrialisation now provides local employment and attracts men from other parts of Spain. In rural areas, however, peasants still wear the traditional beret and clogs (clogs with three points, known as **madreñas** in Asturias) and can still be seen leading their cows back at dusk for milking or driving solid wheeled carts.

The prehistoric caves. — In the Chipped Stone or Upper Palaeolithic Age (40 000 to 10 000 BC) a region extending over southwest France (see Michelin Green Guide Dordogne in English) and along the Cantabrian coast as far as Avilés was inhabited by an independent people who closely resembled one another in their way of life and artistic expression and are known as the Franco-Cantabrians. There are more than 20 caves containing traces of habitation by Franco-Cantabrians in Cantabria alone, the most important after **Altamira,** being around Puente Viesgo (**El Castillo,** La Pasiega, Las Chimeneas, Las Monedas), Ramales de la Victoria (**Covalanas,** La Haza, Collalvera, Sotarriza), Ribadesella (**Tito Bustillo),** and Santander (Santián, El Pendo).

Wall decoration (line engraving and painting) achieved its climax in the Altamira bison. Other caves decorated only with animal outlines which, nevertheless, reveal an outstanding knowledge of animal physiology (bison at El Castillo, deer at Covalanas). The forms frequently appear shot with arrows or surrounded by geometrical motifs which have given rise to the theory that the drawings were described as simulative magic to bring luck in hunting.

The **personal and decorative art** of these cave dwellers surpassed that of Chipped Stone man elsewhere. Quantities of arrowheads, needles and barbs of carved bone have been discovered as well as necklaces of pierced animal teeth and batons made from antlers and delicately carved into animal profiles (horses, stags, fish). The finds from the **El Pendo** caves dating from c 8 000 BC, are now in Santander Prehistory Museum.

Pre-Romanesque Asturian Art. — The Asturian Kingdom, which was Spain's Christian refuge in the 9C, evolved as a result of history, a style of architecture which owed far more to the canons of Christian art from Byzantium than to those of Islam, which were to influence the whole of southern Spain. The Asturian school, more progressive than the Visigothic began with the great Tioda, architect to King Alfonso II (791-842) and reached its zenith under Ramiro I.

From the start Asturian church **architecture** followed the precepts of the Latin basilica in stonework and rectangular plan with a narthex, a nave and two aisles separated by rounded arches, a vast transept and an east end, again divided into three. Frescoes decorated the walls. Only the lateral chambers, sacristies, existed in Visigothic churches. Greater elevation came with the introduction, from the east, of wall buttresses; windows were increased in number and height (Santullano, p 118).

Decoration inside again borrowed from the east in the motifs carved on capitals and stone window tracery (claustra). Under **Ramiro I** (842-850), ornament became both rich and original. Not everything was new: old Corinthian capitals, medallions and pyramid shaped capitals of eastern appearance were incorporated but were well employed and elegantly linked with carved motifs designed to outline and emphasize blind arcades and adorn columns and capitals (Naranco, Lillo, p 118). Later, under Alfonso III (866-910), Moorish influence did penetrate the area as can be seen in the claustra, strapwork, horseshoe shaped arches and window surrounds (alfiz, p 16 — Valdediós, p 127, Priesca, Gobiendes, p 111). **Gold and silversmiths** in the 9 and 10C produced rich treasures, many of which may be seen in the Cámara Santa in Oviedo Cathedral.

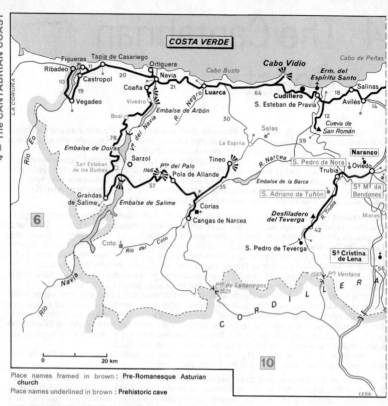

Place names framed in brown : Pre-Romanesque Asturian church
Place names underlined in brown : Prehistoric cave

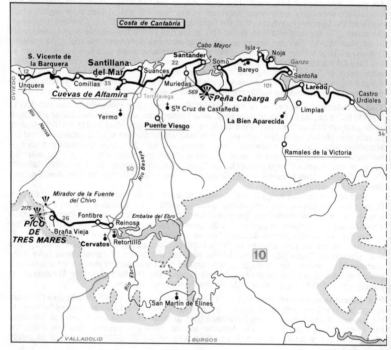

Natural resources for industry. — The mining of iron ore in Cantabria and Vizcaya (Biscay Province) and coal in the Asturias since the end of the 19C, has fostered the development of heavy industry in the region none of which can be equalled in the country.

The mines in southern **Asturias** which provide over 60% of the nation's pit coal and 25% of its anthracite are located principally in the Nalón, Caudal and Aller Valleys, south of Oviedo. The coal produced is being used in ever greater quantities locally to smelt iron mined in the region and in the León mountains, in the large steelworks which now exist in Gijón, La Felguera, Mieres and Avilés. Development on such a scale of heavy industry has brought in new industries: carbochemistry, engineering, shipbuilding, glass and ceramics.

While the mineral wealth of the **Montaña** (iron around Castro Urdiales and Santander) plus capital accumulated from the fishing industry and wool and wheat produced in Castile, enabled heavy industry to be established long ago on a considerable scale, today it is zinc (23 % of national production) from the Reocín and rock salt from Cabezón de la Sal and Polenca, which have attracted new chemical industries to Torrelavega (Solvay and SNIACE manmade fibres).

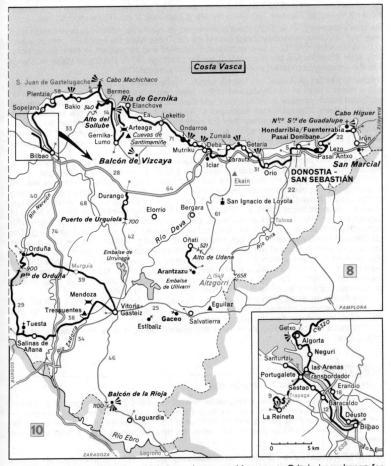

Vizcaya or Biscay Province, which formerly exported iron ore to Britain in exchange for coal, is now self-sufficient in fuel and has developed large steel works (Vizcaya Blast Furnaces) and a dependent metallurgical industry.

The light industries now to be found throughout the Basque Country — engineering, automobiles, papermaking, textiles — are centred in Eibar (fire-arms).

Folklore and tradition. — The Nortenõs or northern folk, active and hardworking, have kept alive many racy traditions and an animated folklore. **Romerías in Asturias** are accompanied by the high sharp tones of the *gaïta* or local bagpipes as are all the many ceremonies which honour cowherds, shepherds, sailors and others performing the most ancient and traditional labour. Among the most typical festivals are those of the *vaqueiros* (cowherds) at Aristébano *(18km - 11 miles south of Luarca)* at the end of July and of the shepherds in the Lake Enol area on 25 July. Cider is the Asturian drink and the festival at Nava in mid-July provides the setting for the ritual pouring of the local *sidra* in a cascade at arm's length from pitcher to glass.

The **Basque country,** unique in so many ways including its *euskara* language of unknown origin, has equally original customs. Every procession is headed by singers and dancers — men dressed in white with red girdles and the famous red berets, perform round dances accompanied by *zortzicos* (singing), *txistus* (flutes) and the *tamboril*. The most solemn, the *aurresku,* is a chain dance performed after mass on Sunday, when the leader invites a girl to join the group. Other dances introduce brooms *(itsas-dantza),* apple baskets *(sagar-dantza)* and ribbons as the figures represent daily tasks from sweeping to apple harvesting and weaving. There is also a local sword dance *(espata-dantza).*

The Basques greatly enjoy contests of skill and strength unknown elsewhere in Spain. There are *aizkolari* or woodcutters who axe the trunk on which they are standing, *palankari* or weightlifters and pairs of oxen competing over the distance they can drag a 3-ton boulder. Every game from pole throwing to the marathon provides the Basque with the opportunity to demonstrate his strength or dexterity and even his intellect for there are contests also for *bersolaris* or poets.

The overriding Basque passion, however, is **pelota.** The game has many variations: it is played between four men on an enclosed court with a net scoop, *chistera* or *cesta punta,* a wooden bat or *pala* or simply like fives, with the hand, a *mano.* Every village has its court and team and at Markina in Vizcaya there is even a Pelota University. Finally there is a Basque tradition of *traineras* or regattas in which boats from every harbour along the coast may be found competing.

Bolos or skittles is played in villages and towns throughout **Cantabria Province.** Also worthwhile is the festival of the sea — Folía — at San Vincente de la Barquera on the Sunday after Easter.

ALTAMIRA Caves ★★ CUEVAS DE ALTAMIRA (Cantabria)

Michelin map 442 fold 4

Open 10am to 1pm and 4 to 6pm; closed 25 December and 1 January. The visit includes three museums and a film on Altamira and the stalactite caves (cueva de las estalactitas).
To visit the cave with paintings write in advance for permission to: Centro de Investiga-ciones y Museo de Altamira, Santillana del Mar (Cantabria). Number of visitors limited.

The cave's discovery. — In 1879 the archaeologist, de Sautuola, noticed rock paintings on a cave roof which he eventually dated as prehistoric. These were the first such paintings ever to be discovered and there was widespread disbelief and scepticism in their authenticity. Only after 20 years and the discovery of similar paintings in the Dordogne Valley in France was the amazing pictorial art of Palaeolithic man fully recognised.

Prehistoric painting technique. — The pigments, chiefly natural ochre (yellow, red or brown with a mineral base of iron oxide) and carbon black, were powdered and mixed with animal fat, blood serum or some other lubricant and then daubed on the smoothest walls with one or more fingers. The technique employed at Altamira and Lascaux is more sophisticated, however, the artists first engraved their subjects in outline on the rock and then filled in the cut with black pigment to give a firm edge to their colourwork; the modelling of the animal bodies is varied by tinting and stump drawing with the aid of pads of moss, fur and other materials.

Utensils and bones discovered in the first cave, which consisted of a kitchen and room, indicate that the inhabitants lived at the cave mouth to take advantage of the daylight.

The route underground follows the old river course. Black outlines and very ancient engravings dating back to approximately 25 000 BC, the Aurignacian Age at the beginning of the Upper Palaeolithic Period, are scattered on the rock face. The finest paintings, however, are near the entrance in a chamber named by a Frenchman, the Sistine Chapel of Quaternary Art. The frescoes in this cave, particularly on the **ceiling ★★,** show bison with extraordinary realism and in full colour, asleep, couched, stretching and galloping. The cavities and excrescences of the rock face have been used to indicate the swelling muscles and hollows in the bodies of the great animals as they stampede. Other beasts include a wild boar running at speed, a primitive horse, red in colour and low standing in which, a doe has been inscribed. The drawings are of considerable size — such as the doe at the far end of the cave on the left — 2m - 6ft 6 ins long, though the average is nearer 1.60m - 5ft. There is an excellent copy of the ceiling in the Archaeological Museum *(p 208).*

The cave's art dates from the end of the Magdalenian Period, 15 000 - 12 000 BC. The floor level has been lowered to make the paintings easier to see and protect — for this reason also the temperature is kept constant at 14 °C - 57 °F.

The stalactite caves, 100 yards from the painted caves, is beautifully decorated with concretions.

AVILÉS (Asturias)

Michelin map 441 fold 7 — Pop 86 584

The life of this once small conservative town of arcaded streets, seignorial mansions and many churches on the left bank of a deep *ría* — called itself the Athens of the north — and living peacefully off fishing and minor local industries, was transformed when the far bank of the inlet was taken over to build what has become one of Spain's most important steelworks.

ENSIDESA Steelworks (Empresa Nacional Siderúrgica). — This important industrial complex (blast furnaces, rolling mills, coking ovens etc.), can been seen in all its magnitude from the bridge across the *ría.* Built between 1950-1957, it is now being reconverted.

Beyond the urban centre a modern steelworks is presently under construction; it will have a liquid steel capacity of 2.5 million tonnes. By-products will provide resources for the power station and chemical works. These products arc exported out of Avilès and Gijon.

The BASQUE Coast ★★ (Guipúzcoa, Vizcaya)

Michelin map **442** folds 6 to 8

The massive sweep of the Bay of Biscay (a corruption of the Basque, Vizcaya), is lined by rocks and steep cliffs, creeks and small estuaries. Fishing villages nestle in the inlets below green hills. Only Cape Machichaco juts far out into the Atlantic.

From San Sebastián to Bilbao
180km - 112 miles — allow one day

7km - 4 miles from San Sebastián bear right into the Bilbao road (N 634).

Aguinaga. — Elver *(angulas)* fish farming town.

Orio. — The fishing village at the end of the long Oria estuary has a picturesque old quarter behind the church. Orio is known less for its industries than for its oarsmen *(arraunalaris)* who are among the best in the Basque country.

As the road rises, look back at Orio; farther on there is a good **view★** forward of Zarautz.

Zarautz. — The resort has been fashionable since Queen Isabel II made it her summer residence in the 19C. The town is sited at the centre of an amphitheatre of hills on a small plain open to the sea. Garden surrounded villas line the vast beach; two **palaces** stand in the town's old quarter: the 16C property of the Marquess of Narros from which corner watch-towers look out over the beach and the Luzea Tower, on the Plaza Mayor with its mullioned windows and a corner balcony.

Beyond Zarautz, the road, which rises to a picturesque **corniche section★★** overlooking the sea, has sometimes to be closed in stormy weather as waves break over it. Getaria Rock, known as "the mouse" — *el ratón* — soon comes into sight.

Getaria. — Getaria, is a fishing village known particularly along the coast for its *chipirones* or squid and its rock — *el ratón*, or San Antón Island to which it is linked by a narrow breakwater road (car turning point on the island). From the rock you can see Zarautz. Fishermen sailed from Getaria harbour to hunt whales long ago; navigators set out for the Indies; **Juan Sebastián Elcano** sailed with Magellan and after the navigator had been murdered in the Philippines, brought his ship home, the only navigator to survive and the first actually to circumnavigate the world (1522). A narrow street, lined with picturesque houses, leads to the 13-15C Church of Our Saviour. The chancel rests on an arch beneath which an underground alley passes, from which one can see into the crypt. Inside is a Flamboyant Gothic gallery.

Zumaia. — *Description p 130.*

Iciar. — The fortress-like church contains a Plateresque altarpiece in dark wood with, at its centre, a smiling 12C Romanesque Virgin, attired in a sumptuous mantle.

On the way to Deba there are several good views of the coast.

Deba. — Deba is a fishing port and resort with a good beach.
The Church of Our Lady of the Assumption, conceals beneath the porch in its fortified front, a Gothic portal decorated with extremely lifelike statues. The cloister galleries with intricate tracery would be graceful but for the austerity of the columns. A niche in a north chapel in the church contains a 13C tomb decorated with a frieze of Christ and the Apostles.

There is a splendid **view★** of the coast from the **corniche road★** as it circles the promontory closing the Deva estuary and, increasingly, of Mutriku's enclosed **site★** as you drop down into the village.

Mutriku. — Massive new buildings are diminishing the picturesqueness of this fishing village where tall houses overlook the harbour from the slopes of Mount St Nicholas.

Two belvederes afford **views★** of Saturrarán beach, a wild strand at the foot of an immensely tall cliff and Ondarroa, which you see first from a road bend.

Ondarroa. — Ondarroa extends on a spit of land between a hillside, and a loop of the Río Artibay. The church, upstanding like a ship's prow at one end, the closely grouped Basque houses with white walls and washing at the windows, the encircling river... make an attractive **picture★**. Canning and fish salting provide employment.

The coast between Ondarroa and Lekeitio has been planted with pines and the road is pleasant although with few views until you round a point and **glimpse★** Lekeitio, its beach and the Island of San Nicolás, joined to the mainland at low tide.

Lekeitio. — A deeply indented bay at the foot of Mount Calvario, divided by San Nicolás Island, serves as the harbour for Lekeitio's long standing fishing industry. The town is a resort with good sand beaches. The 15C Church guarding the harbour has three tiers of flying buttresses and a tall baroque belfry. Inside, in the 3rd south chapel, is a beautiful small Flamboyant Gothic **altarpiece★** of the Road to Calvary; in the north ambulatory chapel is a statue of Our Lady the Ancient, patron of the town.

Ea. — Miniature harbour between two hills at the end of a quiet creek.

After Ea, the road becomes a vantage point from which you look out over the bay and pine covered hills scattered with large Basque farmhouses.

Elanchove. — A peaceful village off the main road. Fishermen have used the bay for centuries as a natural harbour and built their houses overlooking the water, against the steep side of Cape Ogoño (300m - 1000ft).

Once beyond **Playa de Laga,** a vast expanse of rose-coloured sand circling the foot of Cape Ogoño, you can see along the coastline, the peaceful waters of **Guernica Riá★**, Ízaro Island, the white splodge of Sukarrieta town on the far bank and Chacharramendi Island.
The resort of **Playa de Laida,** on the *ría*, is popular with Guernicans.

Arteaga. — A nearby castle, battlemented in imitation of a mediaeval fortress, was once the residence of Eugénie de Montijo, future wife of Napoleon III.

Santimamiñe Cave. — *3km - 2 miles. Description p 114.*

Gernika. — *Description p 114.*

Two viewpoints built beside the road at the mouth of the inlet before you reach Mundaka, enable you to take a last look back along its still waters.
As the road descends, you get a magnificent **view★** of Bermeo.

The BASQUE Coast★★

Bermeo. — Bermeo is the most important inshore fishing port on the Cantabrian Coast. The fishermen's quarter, still crowded onto the Atalaya Promontory overlooking the old harbour, the Puerto Menor, was protected by the ramparts of which traces remain, and the grim granite Ercilla Tower (now a fishermen's museum). St Euphemia's was a church where kings and overlords formerly swore to uphold Biscay privileges *(p 114)*.

Sollube Pass★ (Alto del Sollube). — *5km - 3 miles.* From the road up to the low pass (340m - 1 116ft) there is a good view of Bermeo's semicircular site.

Machichaco Lighthouse. — *2km - 1 mile.* From slightly left of the lighthouse there is a good view west along the uneven coastline.

The road rises in a *corniche* to a **viewpoint★** overlooking the **San Juan de Gaztelugache** headland on which stands a hermitage, the goal of a local *romería* each midsummer's, St John's day. Below, waves have hollowed the rocks into flying buttresses.

Bakio. — A seaside resort with a gently sloping beach now in full development.

There are extensive views from the **corniche road★** to Arminza. From the belvedere there is an interesting **view★,** of the coast, Bakio, the valley farmlands and wooded hinterland.

Arminza. — The only harbour along a wild section of high, inhospitable coast.

Gorliz. — Attractive beach resort at the mouth of the Río Butrón. **Plentzia** nearby *(2km - 1 mile),* an oyster farming centre, is also a resort.

As you leave Plentzia you will see how it lies within a river loop.

Sopelana. — Good beach.

Getxo. — The town is known for its golf course, which is skirted by a **sea promenade.** From the road up to the course there is an interesting view of the Bilbao inlet *(local map p 105)* and on the far bank, Santurtzi and Portugalete. The panorama is even better after dark when you get the flare of the blast furnaces against the night sky.

Algorta and, even more, **Neguri,** Bilbao's residential suburbs on the *ría's* right bank, provide a total contrast to the industrial development along its left shore. Beautiful houses halfway up the hillside overlook the sea; pleasure boats lie at anchor in El Abra Bay at the mouth of the Nervión; the **Las Arenas** beach, though not on the sea, is nearby.

The road continues through the Catholic university town of Deusto and along the foot of Mount Archanda beside the Deusto Canal to Bilbao.

BILBAO (Vizcaya) P

Michelin map 442 fold 6 — Pop 433 030
See town plan in the current Michelin Red Guide España Portugal

Bilbao, capital of Vizcaya Province, 11km - 7 miles from the sea at the end of the Nervión estuary, stands at the centre of a vast industrial area. It occupies a position of economic importance not only in Vizcaya, where it accounts for 80% of industrial output, but also in the national economy, in which it considerably exceeds what might be expected of it as the sixth largest city in Spain.

The old city, which was founded in the 14C, is built up against the mountain, the modern **El Ensanche,** erected last century, extends away beyond the far side of the Paseo del Arenal.

The August Semana Grande with bullfights and Basque *pelota* championships is one of Bilbao's major attractions.

Bilbao was the birthplace of the philosopher **Miguel de Unamuno** (1864-1936) *(p 22).*

Greater Bilbao. — Since 1945 Greater Bilbao has included all the towns between Galdakao and Basauri and the sea. Population density is high on the heavily industrialised left bank, low on the open, richer residential right bank.

The port and local industries. — Bilbao is the largest port in Spain (1985: 28,6 million tons). Since, however, only ships of less than 4 000 tons can navigate the *ría,* quays were constructed at the end of the 19C on the Abra at the *ría* mouth; Punta Lucero and Punta Galea can accomodate ships of 500 000 tons. Bilbao, for centuries a Castile wool port, grew prosperous with the advent of local industry in the 19C: blast furnaces were constructed, rich mineral deposits in the province exploited, iron and steelworks established.

The 20C has seen expansion, and the inauguration of new works (chemicals, fertilisers) and at **Somorrostro,** to the west, of an oil refinery with an output of 8 million tons in 1984. Shipbuilding, traditional to the area, now includes tanker construction.

■ SIGHTS *time: 3 hours*

Fine Arts Museum★ (Museo de Bellas Artes). — *Open 11am to 1pm (2pm Sundays and holidays) and 4.30 to 8.30pm; closed Sunday and holiday afternoons and Monday mornings.*
The museum is housed in two buildings in the **Doña Casilda Iturriza Park,** and divided into two sections.

Fine Arts Museum★ (Museo de Bellas Artes). — *Open 10am to 1.30pm (2pm Sundays and holidays) and 4 to 7.30pm; closed Sunday and holiday afternoons, and all day Monday.*
The museum is housed in two buildings in the **Doña Casilda Iturriza Park.**

Ancient Art★. – *Old building, ground floor.* The right wing's first three galleries contain Flemish Primitives: *The Usurers* by Quentin Metsys, *Pietà* by Ambrosius Benson and a *Holy Family* by Gossaert. In the 4th gallery are: 15C Manises ceramics and Romanesque paintings and sculpture — 13C Crucifixion from the Catalan school and two beautiful fragments of frescoes *(Noah's Ark and Descent from the Cross)* from Urgel Cathedral.
The galleries 5 to 8 display Spanish Romanesque and Gothic paintings: Jaime Huguet, Bartolome Bermejo, Pedro Serra and from the Master of Lanaja, *Pentecost* and *Dormition of the Virgin,* in which the carefully painted faces reflect Flemish influence.
Gallery 9 contains 17C Flemish paintings: Van Dyck, Teniers the Younger, "Hell" Bruegel.
Gallery 10 is devoted entirely to 16 and 17C Italian painting. While galleries 11 to 14 house the Spanish Classical painters: Valdés Leal, Carreño, El Greco *(Annunciation, St Mary Magdalene, St Francis),* Ribalta, Morales, Velázquez (portrait of Philip IV), Zurbarán *(St Isabel, St Catherine* and *Mother and Child* — his last dated work), and Ribera with one of his most outstanding canvases, *Martyrdom of St Sebastian.*

In the left wing, gallery 16, presents three maliciously truthful Goyas': *Martin Zapater*, the writer *Fernandez de Moratín* and *Maria Luisa*. In the next two galleries are 19C Spanish paintings. In gallery 19 Gauguin's *Breton Lavander Pickers* can be seen as well as works by Mary Cassatt, Nonell, Serusier, etc...

Basque Art. — *Old building, 1st floor*. Galleries 20 to 30 house the great Basque painters: Regoyos, Echevarria, Iturrino, Arteta, Tellaeche and Zuloaga.

Contemporary Art. — *New building*. Works by Spanish (Solana, Vázquez Díaz, Gargallo, Blanchard, Chillida, Tapies etc...) and foreign (Kokoschka, Léger, Vasarely, Bacon etc...) artists are represented.

Basque Archaeological Ethnographical and Historical Museum (Museo Arqueológico, Etnografico e Histórico Vasco). — *Open 10.30am to 1.30pm and 4 to 7pm; closed Sunday afternoons, all day Mondays and holidays and 31 July and 23 August.*

The museum is in an old monastery in which coats of arms, tombs, carved stonework and the primitive animal-like idol of Mikeldi may be seen.

At the foot of the steps admire the copy of the Durango Crucifix (the original is in Madrid).

Basque decorative arts are displayed on the 1st floor: statuary and superbly carved wooden furniture. An interesting exhibit of Basque traditions — ceramics, arts and crafts, fishing — can be found on the 2nd floor.

On the top floor is an immense relief model of the Vizcaya Province.

Begoña Sanctuary. — *You can drive up along the San Sebastián road (Avenida de Zuma la Cárregui) but it is easier to take the elevator from the Calle Esperanza Ascao (open 7am to 2pm and 4 to 9pm; 9pts).*

There is an interesting view of Bilbao from the upper terminus footbridge. *On leaving the public garden take the 2nd street to the right for the sanctuary.*

The church contains in a silver *camarín* in the chancel, the venerated figure of the Virgin of Begoña, patron of the province.

■ **BILBAO RÍA**
14km - 9 miles. See p 108 for a description of the right bank from Bilbao to Getxo.

The massive steelworks, at the feet of the mineral rich mountains, are the true feature of this left bank.

Baracaldo. — The Biscay Blast Furnaces (Altos Hornos de Vizcaya), the second largest in Spain after ENSIDESA *(p 106)*, are at Baracaldo and Sestao; production now runs at 2 million tons of laminated steel per annum.

Sestao. — A dockyard town.

Portugalete. — The town, already more residential in character, is also a fishing port. To go to the Las Arenas beach on the far bank, cross the inlet by the famous **transporter bridge** built in 1893 — the silhouette has appeared in every picture of the *ría* since that date! *Fare: 7pts per person plus 35-40pts for the car.* The crenellated so called Salazar Tower near the church dates back to 1379.

La Reineta. — *9km - 6 miles.* From Portugalete make for Trapaga from where you can either continue by car or take the funicular to the village of La Reineta, perched at the top of the mineral bearing mountains which continue southwest into the **Encartaciones** region. Just before the village there is an amazingly interesting **view**★ of the *ría* from one end to the other against its industrial background. Opposite is Santurce Hill with Serantes Fort at the top (446m - 1 463ft).

Santurtzi. — Santurtzi is the kingdom of the sardine — there is even a song about it entitled *Las Sardinas de Santurce.* Eat them grilled at the roadside — delicious!

CANTABRIA, The Coast of ★ (Cantabria)
Michelin map **442** folds 4 to 6

The number and quality of the beaches along this stretch of the Cantabrian coastline draw holidaymakers in the thousands: the expanses of sand are not wide but they are long, gently sloping, swept clean by the changing Atlantic tide and sheltered from sea breezes by low promontories. River mouths are protected by tongues of sand and provide particularly safe sea bathing. Santander and Comillas are especial favourites with Spanish holidaymakers; Laredo, San Vicente de la Barquera and Noja with foreigners.

From Castro Urdiales to San Vicente de la Barquera
171km - 106 miles — allow one day

From the *corniche* road to the east of Castro Urdiales there are good views of the indented coastline. Beyond **Mioño,** which stands in its own small creek, one begins to see the houses bearing coats of arms so characteristic of the province and for which Santillana del Mar is especially well-known.

Castro Urdiales. — Castro Urdiales' **site**★ is spectacular, the beach and harbour lying at the back of a wide bay ringed by mountains, whilst the old town (Flavióbriga), which dates back to the time of the Romans, clusters on a promontory around a ruined castle and a tall Gothic church.

The town, although still living mainly off fishing, fish canning and shipping iron ore, is turning more and more to tourism. Annually the first Friday in July there are battles of flowers and a parade of floats beneath illuminations as fireworks explode in a spectacular celebration known as the Coso Blanco.

Laredo★. — *Description p 115.*

The road to Santoña crosses a curious marshland made up of several small *rías*.

Santoña. — This fishing port at the foot of the Ganzo, commands an estuary mouth which has become narrower on account of sand drifting from Laredo beach.

The town's strategic position brought about its selection as a military headquarters by the French in the Peninsular War and resulted in the construction of the massive fort still standing at the end of the quay which today commands a good view of Laredo.

The Church of Our Lady of the Harbour, which was remodelled in the 18C, in addition to a Gothic nave and twin aisles, has interesting Romanesque features including carved capitals (one in the south portal shows a monk pulling at a mule's tail) and an old font.

Between Santoña and Santander, the N 634 turns away from the coast which makes access difficult to the good beaches around Noja.

Noja. — Noja itself has a vast beach in a bay which, at low tide, bristles with small reefs. To the east, beyond a headland, lies another beach, the Nueva Berria and to the west yet another, the beautiful Ris beach, distinguished by offshore rock islets and fast developing into a major resort.

Isla. — The beach faces onto a small estuary.

Bareyo. — Turn left beyond the bridge towards the church. The small **Church of Santa María** *(to visit apply at the 2nd house on the left in the village; 25pts)* stands on a slope overlooking the Ría de Ajo. Though remodelled it retains interesting features from its original Romanesque design including slender, moulded and festooned arches and historiated capitals in the apse and beautiful capitals at the transept crossing which is covered by vaulting in the form of a dome. The nave has been refashioned in the Gothic style. The font, is probably Visigothic.

3km - 2 miles beyond Ajo, you get your first view of Santander, the Magdalena headland and the Cabo Menor or Lesser Cape which is dotted with white villas.

Somo. — The huge beach ending in the **El Puntal** tongue of sand is popular with the citizens of Santander. There is a regular motorboat service between the provincial capital and the resort *(125pts Rtn).*

Peña Cabarga★★. — *4km - 2 1/2 miles.* A road with a 16% gradient - 1 in 6 — leads to the summit (alt 569m - 1 867ft) on which stands a monument to the Conquerors of America and Seamen Adventurers of Castile. The tower platform overlooks the bay, Santander and the surrounding countryside; go to the top, however, *(lift: 10am to 8pm, 50pts)* for a really splendid circular **panorama★★.**

Santander★. — *Description p 125.*

Alternative route by Suances. — *15km - 9 miles.* Good beach facing directly onto the long Besaya Estuary.

Santillana del Mar★★ and Altamira Caves★★. — *Descriptions pp 126 and 106 respectively.*

Comillas. — Comillas is an old and popular seaside resort: it is picturesque; it has a delightful Plaza Mayor and a minute fishing harbour; it has a local beach and easy access to the extensive sands at Oyambre — 5km - 3 miles west. The town was a royal residence in the time of Alfonso XII, the home of the Spanish court during the season. Buildings which catch the eye include, in the vast park surrounding the Neo-Gothic residence of the Marquess of Comillas, a freakish pavilion by Gaudí and, overlooking the sea from the crown of the hill, the Papal University *(closed).*

San Vicente de la Barquera★. — This resort has an unusual site and a vast beach. Old houses give the place its character and arcaded porticoes give individuality to the Plaza Mayor. The church of Our Lady of the Angels at the top of the partially fortified hill, has two Romanesque portals and Gothic aisles. The bridge of 28 arches which spans the *ría* is another of the town's picturesque features. If you are continuing to Unquera, look back after a few minutes for a pleasing **view★** of San Vicente.

COSTA VERDE ★★★ (Asturias)

Michelin map **441** folds 5 to 10

The coast from Unquera to Vegadeo is rocky but goes in an almost straight line due west except for where Cape Peñas, west of Gijón advances far out to sea. The shore is lined by low cliffs, interrupted by frequent sandy inlets; the estuaries are narrow and deep and although they are known locally as *rías,* bear little resemblance to those in nearby Galicia.

Three ports in this area handle Asturian coal and ore: San Esteban de Pravia, Gijón and Avilés. Other local ports are mostly small and go in for catching and canning fish. Many are picturesque, their houses clinging to or built into a cliff face, lining a small sheltered bay or spread along the banks of an estuary.

A plateau, never more than 20km - 12 miles wide follows the line of the shore, its far side bordered continuously by high mountain ranges.

THE EASTERN COAST ★★

From San Vicente de la Barquera to Gijón
141km - 88 miles — about 5 1/2 hours

A succession of small sandy creeks, isolated but accessible, marks this stretch of coast.

San Vicente de la Barquera★. — *Description see above.*

Pindal Cave. — *2km - 1 mile from Pimiango by a narrow, winding road. Open 10am to 1pm and 4 to 7pm; closed Mondays; 100pts, Tuesdays free. In winter apply at the big house at the end of Pimiango village (signpost).* A path leads to a cave in a cliff overlooking a creek. Fine calcareous needles carpet the roof while the far end of the right wall is decorated with late Palaeolithic animal engravings and outlines in red pigment. Further on, on the right, in a rock hollow, is the outline of an elephant with the heart clearly depicted, probably from the Aurignacian period.

La Franca. — A good beach in a cliff encircled bay just outside the village.

Vidiago. — In this locality the idol of Peña Tu, a megalithic monument, is decorated with carved reliefs and paintings dating from the Bronze Age.

Llanes. — A small spiny lobster fishing port and quiet resort. The cliff top **Paseo de San Pedro** affords a good view of the old, once fortified town, the rampart ruins and castle, the squat Church of Sta María, and some intriguing rock formations on the beach. If you can, be there for the festival of St Rock (16 August) to see the dances in brilliant local costume.

Celorio. — Just north lies a vast sand beach dotted with patches of grass.

Barro. — The beach is sheltered by rock headlands.

Cuevas del Mar. — The village, reached by way of Nueva, has an attractive beach enclosed by cliffs pitted with caves accessible at low tide.

Ribadesella★. — *Description p 122.*

El Fito Belvedere (Mirador)★★. — *2km - 1 mile from Caravia bear left into the Gobiendes road; turn left at the crossroads.* Good views along the coast (La Isla beach and the offshore islet) during the steep ascent are outclassed when you reach the El Fito Belvedere *(1km - 1/2 mile south of Collado de Santa Cruz),* by a **panorama★★** of the Picos de Europa and the coast. On the return, stop at **Gobiendes,** where the 10C Santiago Church is perched on a mound above the road. *(Apply at the house next door).* Note before entering, the two pairs of apsidal windows, and inside the twisted columns crowned by old Corinthian capitals.

La Isla. — *Hórreos* stand beside the houses in the small village built on a rock headland close to the roadside. The vast bay is lined with beaches separated by rocks, one of which, lying offshore, gave the village its name.

(After Ed. Alce photo, Oviedo)

Hórreo

Turn off the main road into the Lastres road.

Lastres. — Lastres is a typical fishing village built against the side of a steep cliff between the beach and the harbour. It is known for its clams.

Priesca. — *2.5km - 1 1/2 miles.* The church of San Salvador was built in 921 like that at Gobiendes but is heavily restored. In the chancel are capitals resembling those at Valdediós *(p 129).*

Villaviciosa. — *Description p 127.*

THE WESTERN COAST★
From Gijón to Ribadeo — *181km - 112 miles — allow one day*

This part of the coast is more indented and steeper. The plateau, west of Cudillero, ends in an almost unbroken cliff wall at the sea's edge; the only exceptions to the small estuary beaches are the expanses of sand at Gijón, San Juan de Nieva and Salinas.

Leave Gijón by ③ on the plan. Turn right after 8km - 5 miles — into the Luanco road. The summer bungalows on the headland on the right make up **Perlora.**

Candás. — Fisherfolk in this village are deeply devoted to their statue of Christ, protector of Candás seamen for generations. The figure with long black hair in St Felix Church, *(at the top of the village; open during services)* standing above a sumptuous baroque altar, is said to have come from Ireland in the 16C.

Luanco. — Luanco harbour lies at the back of a bay sheltered by the Punta de la Vaca. It has a small beach, a sea promenade and a maritime museum *(open 11am to 1pm and 3 to 7pm — 4 to 6pm in winter; closed Mondays)* exhibiting models of ships.

As you arrive in Avilés, there is an amazing view of the ENSIDESA industrial complex from the bridge over the canal.

Avilés. — *Description p 106.*

Salinas. — This resort is expanding rapidly. From the rock islet of La Peñona *(pathway)* you can see the **full extent★** of the beach, one of the longest on the Costa Verde.

San Román. — *13km - 8 miles from Soto del Barco.* The walls of the cave overlooking San Román are decorated with engravings and paintings thought to be 15 000 years old. *Temporarily closed.* On the right wall are outlines of bulls, bison, goats. There is also a wounded stag with head upraised and on a sort of chapel *(camarín)* wall at the end of the main chamber, a beautifully modelled yellow horse.

San Esteban de Pravia. — Coaling port for the inland mines.

Bear left towards Luarca, then right for the Espíritu Santo Hermitage. As the road climbs there are glimpses through the eucalyptus trees of the Nalón Estuary or Ría de Pravia and of waves, lapping the immense San Juan de la Arena beach.

Espíritu Santo Hermitage★. — Extensive **view★** west along the coastal cliffs.

Cudillero★. — The unassuming fishing village, surrounded by steep hills, makes an attractive **scene★** from the end of the jetty with tall houses on the hillsides, white cottages with brown tiled roofs leading down to the small harbour between two rock points and a foreground of fishing boats, masts and nets drying in the sun.

Concha de Artedo. — Superb beach.

Cape Vidio★★. — *2km - 1 mile beyond Soto de Luiña, turn into the headland road which ends at the lighthouse.* The **views★★** along the austere coastline extend east to Cape Peñas and west to Cape Busto.

Three kilometres - 2 miles after the Oviedo fork, look out for a picturesque glimpse of Bozo beach on the Esba Estuary.

Luarca★. — Luarca has a remarkable **site★** at the mouth of the winding Río Negro. The town, which includes seven bridges spanning the river, has a sheltered fishing harbour and a beach on the far side of a high cliff. It is distinctively attractive with white houses with slate roofs and the lighthouse, church and cemetery grouped at the end of the estuary on the headland once occupied by a fort. A path to the top bears left round the lighthouse, circles the church and returns to the harbour, affording as it does so an interesting **view★** of Luarca and the harbour.

Puerto de Vega. — *3km - 2 miles north.* Minute, well sheltered crawfish and lobster harbour with an attractive live preserve.

Navia. — A new town and fishing port on the right bank of the *ría.* A road follows the bank to a belvedere, dedicated to the Great Seaborne Discoverers overlooking the inlet, from where there is a pleasant view of the *ría.*

COSTA VERDE★★★

At the end of the bridge the left fork goes up the Navia Valley *(description p 115)*.

Ortiguera. — *4km - 2 1/2 miles from Navia*. Take to the right the road to Ortiguera, a humble fishing village adorned by the occasional house built by a returned "Indiano" *(p 103)*. The lighthouse commands an attractive view of the coast and Navia beach.

Tapia de Casariego. — The fishing village is at the end of a promontory in a deep bay, its scattered houses, most unusually, separated by fields.

Figueras. — *2km - 1 mile*. From the river port of Figueras you can see Castropol and Ribadeo, both beautifully situated overlooking the Eo inlet.

Shortly beyond Barres there is another view of Ribadeo, Castropol and the inlet.

Castropol. — Castropol, the most westerly port in Asturias lies along a **promontory** at the centre of a *ría* which marks the boundary with Galicia. The quiet village with an all white square faces Ribadeo, its Galician counterpart.

Vegadeo. — The town at the inland end of the *ría* is known for its fair at Whitsun.

Ribadeo. — *Description p 150*.

COVADONGA (Asturias)

Michelin map **441** fold 9 — *Local map p 120*

Covadonga, a famous Spanish shrine and landmark in Spanish history, stands in a suitably grand **setting★★** on a flattened ridge at the centre of a lush green basin, surrounded by the Picos de Europa. The approach road takes you through the valley to the lakes *(see below)*. **Mount Covadonga** and the Peña Santa ranges to the southeast are now a National Park and Animal Reserve *(no hunting)*.

The cradle of the Spanish monarchy. — The Muslims followed up the defeat of the Visigothic King Roderic at Guadalete in 711 by the capture of his capital, Toledo, and the occupation of most of the peninsula. **Pelayo,** a tribal leader claiming descent from the Visigothic kings, fled to the Picos de Europa where he organised a revolt (718). When in about 722, the Emir Alçama sent a small military company from Córdoba to wipe out the rebellious force, Pelayo and his supporters won a resounding victory against the Muslims at Covadonga. Christians everywhere gained new heart and determined to re-establish a national monarchy; the Asturians elected Pelayo who set up his court at Cangas de Onís thereby making Asturias the cradle of the Spanish monarchy and forever after a symbol of resistance.

■ **SIGHTS** *time: 3/4 hour*

Santa Cueva. — The Cave of Our Lady, Cova Dominica, is dedicated to the Virgin of the Battlefield. On an enamelled altar is the deeply venerated 18C statue of the Virgin, patron of Asturias, known as the "Santina" and the centrepiece of a major procession on 8 September. Behind the altar is a modern copper and enamel panel with the stylised figures of the Asturian kings and at the side, the tombs of Pelayo, who died in 737 AD, and Alfonso I.

Basilica. — The Neo-Romanesque basilica built between 1886 and 1901, is preceded by an esplanade on which stands a bronze statue of Pelayo beneath the Cross of Victory; the supposed original cross is in the Cámara Santa in Oviedo *(p 116)*.

Treasury (Tesoro de la Virgen). — *Open 10am to 2pm and 4 to 8pm; closed from November to March except Saturdays Sundays, holidays and the day before holidays; 30pts*. The gifts offered to the Virgin include the magnificent **crown★** with more than 1 000 diamonds.

EXCURSION

The road to Lakes Enol and Ercina★★. — *12km - 7 1/2 miles. It is wiser to make the drive in the morning as mist is liable to fall in the afternoon*. The road is steep. Looking back there is a wide panorama which includes Covadonga and the basilica.

After 8km - 5 miles you reach the **Mirador de la Reina★★** from where there is a picturesque view of the succession of rock pyramids which go to make up the Sierra de Covalierda.

Beyond the pass, two rock cirques formed by *hoyos (p 119)*, provide beautiful settings for **Lakes★ Enol and Ercina** (alt 1 232m - 4 043ft). Wild horses graze the local pastures; the lakes have been stocked with trout *(fishing by permit only!)*.

On 25 July there is a great and crowded Shepherd's Festival at Lake Enol when the men, in glowing red costumes to the accompaniment of *gaita and asturianadas*, perform the *danza prima*.

DURANGO (Vizcaya)

Michelin map **442** fold 7 — Pop 26 101

The small industrial town stands on the River Ibaizábal. The old ramparts, pierced by a gateway rebuilt in the 18C, can be seen near St Anne's Church. San Pedro, in the centre of the town, is 17C and has an amazingly large west door. In Holy Week the main square becomes the setting for a Passion Play.

EXCURSIONS

Urquiola Pass★ (Puerto de Urquiola). — Alt 700m - 2 297ft. *11km - 7 miles south*. The magnificent **drive★** climbs through the Basque Mountains, where the slopes are scattered with attractive white farmhouses, before descending through undulating countryside.

Elorrio. — *9km - 6 miles east*. This small, ancient town in which several houses are emblasoned with coats of arms, possesses a collection of 15 and 16C Crucifixes unique in the Basque country. The one at the town's west entrance is decorated with a frieze of people, the one at the east with a twisted column. The Church of Our Lady of Holy Conception, which is typically Basque with thick round pillars and star vaulting, contains an exuberant Churrigueresque altarpiece.

FUENTERRABÍA HONDARRIBIA (Guipúzcoa)

Michelin map **442** fold 8 — Pop 11 276

Fuenterrabía, now a popular seaside resort and large fishing port, was for centuries the target of attack by the French on account of its strategic position on the frontier. The old stronghold with its steep streets built on a mound commanding the Bidasoa is still encircled by ramparts.

As a reminder of its history, annually on 8 September, Fuenterrabía celebrates whole heartedly or "en alarde" a festival to Our Lady of Guadalupe who is said to have delivered the town from a two month siege by the French in 1638.

On the old town's outskirts, near the harbour, is the Marina, a bustling fishermen's quarter with its characteristic wood balconies.

■ **OLD TOWN** *time: 1 hour*

Puerta de Santa María. — The gate through the 15C ramparts, is surmounted by the town's arms and twin angels venerating Our Lady of Guadalupe.

Calle Mayor. — The narrow main street is picturesquely lined with old houses with wrought iron balconies and carved wood cornices.

Santa María. — The impressive Gothic edifice, remodelled in the 17C when the tower was baroquised, is supported round the apse by massive buttresses. It was in this church that the proxy wedding was held which preceded by six days the solemnisation in France of the marriage of Louis XIV and the Infanta María Teresa (June 1660) *(p 114)*.

Emperor Charles V's Castle. — Sancho Abarca, King of Navarre in the 10C, according to legend, was the founder of this key strongpoint of Navarre. Charles V restored it in the 16C; now it has been transformed again — this time into a *parador*.

EXCURSIONS

Cape Higuer★. — *4km - 2 1/2 miles north. Leave Fuenterrabía by the harbour and beach road.* Turn left and as the road climbs, you will get a good **view★** of the beach, the town and quayside and from the end of the headland, the French coast and town of Hendaye.

Jaizkibel Road★★. — *West of Fuenterrabía.* The **drive★★** is glorious at sunset. Five kilometres - 3 miles from the Chapel of Our Lady of Guadalupe there is a lovely **view★** of the mouth of the Bidasoa and the French Basque coast. The road overlooks the sea as it rises through pine trees and gorse to reach the Jaizkibel Hostal at the foot of a 584m - 1 916ft peak and a belvedere with a superb **view★★** *(viewing table)*. The road down to Pasai Donibane affords **glimpses★** of the indented coastline, the Cantabrian Cordillera and the three mountains which dominate San Sebastián, Ulía, Urgull and Igueldo.

Pasai Donibane★ and Pasai Antxo. — *Description p 118.*
The road skirts the bay formed by the Oyarzun before reaching San Sebastián.

Lezo. — The 17C church of Santo Christo contains a Crucifix before which women pray for "health, wealth and a good husband" *(salud, dinero y buen marido)*.

GIJÓN (Asturias)

Michelin map **441** fold 8 — Pop 255 969
See town plan in the current Michelin Red Guide España Portugal

Gijón is a lively city at the back of a wide bay on the Costa Verde. It has been partly rebuilt and much enlarged since the Civil War when it was badly damaged, and now fans southwards far beyond the original town site on the small Santa Catalina headland. This juts out at a fair height into the bay between two inlets which serve as harbour and beach, the latter, the Playa de San Lorenzo, so vast that Gijón lays claim to the title of seaside resort. The Semana Grande, celebrated on about 15 August, is a brilliant tourist event.

East of Cape Torres *(6km - 4 miles north)* is the coaling port of **El Musel,** the major outlet for the Asturian mines and sixth in Spain in general cargo traffic. Industry is now concentrating in its vicinity.

Jovellanos. — Gijón was the birthplace of Jovellanos (1744-1811), one of Spain's most eminent 18C men of letters.

He was a poet, reformer, liberal economist and author of a treatise on agrarian reform, politician and on the orders of Godoy, prisoner for seven years in Bellver Castle, Majorca. On his release he joined the Junta Central of 1808 against the French. He founded the educational institute which bears his name in his native town to further his belief in the need for a progressive education for all.

The port. — Gijón port was transformed by the construction at the end of the 19C, of a direct railway line inland to the coal mines. Docks had to be built at El Musel to handle the traffic which soon outstripped the capacity of the original port. The new docks were also built large enough to berth the then consequential trans-Atlantic passenger liners. The annual total traffic through the port is some 13 million tons of which 33% is coal. Present economic policy is to use regional resources (coal and iron) to the maximum in the local steelworks at **Veriña** *(4km - 2 miles west)* and develop, again where possible with local resources, the spinning, engineering (tractors and motorcycles) and shipbuilding industries which have recently joined the traditional glass and ceramic industries in the region.

San Lorenzo beach. — The long curved arc of sand on the far side of the headland, is edged by an esplanade banked with flowers and punctuated by tall luxury flats.

The Fishermen's Quarter (Cimadevilla). — *About 3/4 hour.* The quarter's secretive narrow streets swarming with minute bars or *chigres* and houses, rising high up the Santa Catalina hillside, is worlds apart from the wide avenues and high rise constructions of the new Gijón.

East of the quarter are Roman baths dating from the time of Augustus. Part of the not very big but well preserved **hypocaust** is on view *(to visit telephone in advance (985) 34-63-13; open 10am to 2pm — 1.30pm Sundays - and 4 to 8pm; closed Sunday and holiday afternoons and all day Monday)*.

To the west on the Plaza del Marqués stands the 17C **Revillagigedo Palace.** Branching off this same plaza is the Calle Corrida, the main street of the city. Further on, from the north breakwater of the fishing harbour you can see *(telescopes)* the shipping activity at El Musel.

EXCURSION

Universidad Laboral. – *At Somió: 4km - 2 1/2 miles by* ① *on the town plan.* This institution which might be compared to a college of advanced technology and agriculture, was inaugurated in 1939. The complex and grounds, dominated by a 120m – 394ft high tower, cover nearly 4 1/2 ha – 11 acres and include, besides faculty buildings, courtyards, sports facilities, workshops, library and an elliptical church. 4 000 students, are taught to relate technical training to the social sciences.

Universidades Laborales are increasing in number; the majority are sited near provincial capitals.

GUERNICA GERNIKA (Vizcaya)
Michelin map 442 fold 7 – Pop 17 836

Guernica is a new town, small and sparkling at the end of the Oca estuary. The climate is mild. From its appearance it would seem to have forgotten the day when it was the victim of one of the most tragic events of the Civil War and came to symbolise to the world of that time the horror of aerial bombing: when on 26 April 1937 a German air squadron bombed the open town and local inhabitants who had come to the market, killing more than 2 000 in just 3 hours. Picasso expressed his anguish at the event in his painting, *Guernica,* which now hangs in the Casón del Buen Retiro in Madrid.

The town, rebuilt in the traditional style, is the proud possessor of a magnificent covered *pelota* court with a seating capacity of 3 000. Basque *pelota* matches are currently played; *on Saturdays, Sundays, Mondays and holidays at 4.30pm and 31 July in the evening.* The spectacular *cesta punta* style (*i.e.* using the scoop racket) is played the most.

The Tree of Guernica. – In the Middle Ages, Guernica was one of the towns where the local lords would assemble in parley in the shade of a tree: in addition the Guernica oak was one of the four places – the others were Bilbao, Bermeo and Larrabetzu – where newly created Lords of Biscay came to swear that they would respect the local *fueros* or privileges. Guernica was, on this account, visited in 1483 by Queen Isabel, who dressed in Biscay costume for the occasion. In 1876 Biscay lost its *fueros* as a penalty for having sided with the Carlists – but the Tree of Guernica, nevertheless, remains the symbol of liberty to every Basque.

Casa de Juntas. – The building contains the provincial library and archives, also the council chamber (Sala de Juntas) which serves on occasion as a chapel and in which the local notables (Junteros), representatives of the Biscay provinces General Assembly meet periodically.

Open 10am to 7pm (6pm 1 October to 31 May); Sundays and holidays 10am to 2pm and 4 to 7pm (6pm 1 October to 31 May).

Walk around the building to see the famous **Tree of Guernica** or rather its descendant: the present oak, which is a seedling of the original, was planted in the 19C only. The remains of the thousand year old tree are preserved in the small round temple.

EXCURSIONS

The Biscay Balcony★★. – *18km - 11 miles south.* The so-called balcony is a remarkable **viewpoint★★** overlooking the mountainous Biscay landscape: a marquetry of vividly contrasting green fields and dark pinewoods. Dropping down from the pass, if you look northwards, you can just see the sea and Guernica Ría.

Santimamiñe Cave. – *5km - 3 miles north. Bear right after 3km - 2 miles.* Wall paintings and engravings, discovered in 1917 in this mountainside cave, date back to the Magdalenian Period and with the interesting archaeological deposits since analysed, prove that it was inhabited for a period of nearly 30 000 years.

Open 10.30am to noon and 4 to 7pm (5.30pm in winter); closed Sunday and holiday afternoons and all day Monday; time: 1 hour.

Two skeletons were discovered near the entrance. Most of the paintings, protected by a moist patina, are in a small and somewhat inaccessible chamber. The walls are decorated with charcoal drawings of horses, bears, stags and goats. The most important group is on the ceiling and shows six bison standing round a horse. To the right two bison stand upright in apparent confrontation.

A walk through the long gallery will bring you to splendid, and in several instances flame-coloured, **limestone concretions★.**

The times indicated in this guide
when given with the distance allow one to enjoy the scenery
when given for sightseeing are intended to give an idea of
the possible length or brevity of a visit.

IRÚN (Guipúzcoa)
Michelin map 442 fold 8 – Pop 53 445

Irún, largely destroyed by fire in the Civil War, has been rebuilt with wide avenues which bustle with all the activity of an international frontier town.

The town's main festival on 30 June celebrates, as does that of Fuenterrabía *(p 113),* a victory over the French – in this case in 1521 *(see below).*

Pheasant Island. – The island in the River Bidassoa, which marks the frontier, has been the setting of several historic events including, in 1615, the simultaneous passage in opposite directions of Elizabeth of Bourbon to marry Philip IV of Spain and Anne of Austria, daughter of Philip III of Spain to marry Louis XIII and in 1659 the signing of the Treaty of the Pyrenees which in turn brought Philip IV's daughter, María Teresa, to Paris as the bride of Louis XIV *(p 115).*

■ THE SAN MARCIAL HERMITAGE★★

3km - 2 miles east. Leave Irún by the Behobia road and turn into the first right after the Palmera factory; bear left at the first crossroads. A narrow road in poor condition leads to the hilltop (225m - 740ft), the scene of two Spanish victories against the French. The first in 1521 was won, according to legend with the aid of St Martial, the second, in 1813, with that of the English.

During Wellington's final campaign, after the Battle of the Pyrenees (July 1813), Spanish forces under General Manuel Freire, defeated Marshal Soult's army at Irún, hastening the French retreat through the Pyrenees which was to mark the end of the Peninsular War. The **panorama★★** from the hermitage terrace includes Fuenterrabía, Irún, San Sebastián in the distance, and Hendaye (right).

LAREDO ★ (Cantabria)
Michelin map **442** fold 5 — Pop 12 278

Laredo still has a crowded old town of narrow paved streets leading to its church on the hillside which also protects its fishing boat harbour. The residential quarter, built at the turn of the century on the west side of the town is being transformed and extended towards the point by the construction of high rise buildings. Life in the town is also changing with its success as a resort — the population of approximately 12 000 multiplies to the astonishing figure of 100 000 at the height of the summer season. On the last Friday in August it holds its most popular festival, a battle of flowers.

EXCURSION

Limpias; La Bien Aparecida★. — *9km - 6 miles south. Turn left at Colindres.* This pleasant road skirts the Asón.

Limpias. — The fishing village on the banks of the River Asón is known for a miracle which occured there in 1919. In the chancel of the local church is the deeply venerated Crucifix said to have shed tears of blood, a wonderfully carved baroque figure, vigorous and at the same time pathetic, believed to be by Juan de Mena.

La Bien Aparecida★. — A winding uphill road *(4km - 2 1/2 miles)* marked by a Calvary, leads to the baroque sanctuary of Na Sa la Bien Aparecida. Veneration of this Virgin as patron of Cantabria province dates back to 1605. **Panorama★** of the Asón Valley.

NAVIA Valley (Asturias)
Michelin map **441** fold 6

The Navia, which rises in Galicia in the Sierra de Cebreros, crosses several steep volcanic ridges before flowing into the Cantabrian Sea. The wild, enclosed valley is divided by three dams, in which the high mountains stand reflected.

From Navia to Cangas del Narcea — *134km - 83 miles — sharply winding roads; allow 1/2 day. Restaurants and petrol stations are few and far between.*

In Navia, take the Grandas de Salime road along the far bank of the *ría* across which you can see Navia's white houses at the water's edge.

Coaña. — The circular foundations remain of a few houses from the Celtic village built on a mound. *Guided tours: 200pts.*

For a striking **panorama★★** of the **Arbón dam,** built just above a giant bend in the river, pause at the belvedere.
Shortly after Vivedro, there is a **panoramic view★★** extending from a loop in the river course in the foreground, to the Navia Ría mouth in the far distance.
The **juncture★★** of the Navia and the Río Frío is impressive as you look down on it from a giddy height.
Beyond the bridge across the Frío, the road returns to the Navia which it follows to Miñagón. The *hórreos (illustration p 111)* you see from the road are the same rectangular shape as those in Galicia. The descent beyond **Boal** brings you down to the level of the Navia, where 3km - 2 miles further on, the valley is blocked by the high **Doiras dam and reservoir;** the overflow is impressive.
The small village perched on a hillside on the far bank from San Esteban, surrounded by the steepest slopes, all of which are cultivated, is called **Sarzol.**

Grandas de Salime. — Large agricultural town.

Salime Dam. — There are vantage points from which to see the height of the dam, its crest and the power station. The road continues through a desert landscape to the **Puerto del Palo,** an open pass at an altitude of 1 146m - 3 760ft.

Pola de Allande. — Village in a green valley below the Sierra del Palo.

The road twists for some distance through wild gorges before it reaches the Puente del Infierno, the bridge over the rushing Narcea torrent, a favourite haunt of trout and salmon.

Corias. — An originally Roman bridge links Corias built on either bank of the Narcea. The **monastery,** re-erected in severe Neo-Classical style after being burned down in the 19C, was founded in the 11C and occupied for 800 years by Benedictines. There are ornate Churrigueresque altars in the church.

Cangas de Narcea. — Cangas, gateway to the upper Narcea Valley, is a meeting place for trout fishermen, excursionists and hunters. There is a relatively easy road from the town to León by way of the Leitariegos Pass (alt 1 525m - 5 003ft). A road to the right of Leitariegos leads to a small mountain lake.

Tineo. — *30km - 18 1/2 miles from Cangas by way of Corias.* The town perched 673m - 2 208ft up the mountainside affords an immense **panorama★★** to the southeast.

OÑATE OÑATI (Guipúzcoa)

Michelin map **442** fold 7 — Pop 10 770

Oñate with its seignorial residences, monastery and old university, is content now to sit back in its hollow in the fertile Udana Valley. Twice during the First Carlist War the town served as Don Carlos' headquarters and finally it was its fall to General Espartero which forced the Carlists to sign the Vergara Convention of 1839 *(p 127)*.

The road east to the **Udana Pass (Alto de Udana:** 521m - 1 709ft) affords a panoramic view of Oñate nestling in the valley and the distant Udala and Amboto peaks.

Old University. — *To visit apply at the town hall.* The university, now administrative headquarters of Guipúzcoa, was founded in 1542 by a native prelate of Oñate and closed early this century; it was the only university in the Basque country and had considerable cultural prestige. The gateway by the Frenchman, Pierre Picart, is surmounted by pinnacles and crowded with statues among which may be picked out the founding bishop at the centre and Sts Gregory and Jerome (right and left respectively). The exuberant decoration reappears at the corner of each tower and again in the exceedingly elegant two storey *patio*.

Town Hall (Ayuntamiento). — The fine 18C baroque edifice was designed by the son of Martín de Carrera, architect of the Mondragón town hall *(11km - 7 miles away).* At Corpus Christi the square becomes the setting for strange, religious inspired dancing.

St Michael's (San Miguel). — The Gothic church facing the university was remodelled in the baroque period. A Renaissance chapel off the north aisle, closed by beautiful iron grilles, contains an interesting gilded wood altarpiece and the marble tomb of the founder of the university. The golden stone cloister exterior with gallery tracery, arches and statue niches is Isabeline Plateresque in style.

EXCURSION

Arantzazu★. — *9km - 6 miles south.* The **road★** follows from above, the course of the Río Arantzazu which flows through a narrow gorge. Arantzazu Sanctuary is perched at an altitude of 800m - 2 624ft in a mountain **setting★** facing the highest peak in the province, Mount Aitzgorri (1 549m - 5 082ft). Dominating the church is an immense campanile 40m - 131ft high built like the towers framing the façade, with diamond faceted stone symbolising the thornbush (*Arantzazu* in Basque) in which the Virgin appeared to a local shepherd in 1469.

The present building dates from 1955 only. A statue of the Virgin, patron of the province, stands at the centre of a huge wooden altarpiece painted by Lucio Muñoz.

The singing of the friars may be heard at services during the Arantzazu solemn celebrations on 9 September, in Holy Week and on Sundays at 11am.

OVIEDO P (Asturias)

Michelin map **441** folds 7 and 8 — Pop 190 123

Oviedo, the economic and cultural metropolis of the Asturias is a modern town built on a mound at the centre of a fertile, green basin, with the added attraction of a large park at its centre. It developed in the 18C with the establishment of an arsenal and expanded rapidly in the 19C as the coal basin began to be exploited. It is a university town with a College of Mining Engineering. The old town round the cathedral remains a total contrast to that of the modern city, including as it does along its narrow streets many ancient seignorial mansions.

The capital of the Kingdom of Asturias (9-10C). — All that the Muslims left of the small city built by Fruela I (722-768) around a Benedictine monastery on a hill named Ovetum, was a pile of ruins. Fruela's son, Alfonso II (791-842), transferred the court from Cangas de Onís and Pravia where it had been previously to Oviedo. He rebuilt the town, encircling it with ramparts and embellishing it with religious buildings of which only traces remain — the Cámara Santa, the east end of San Tirso Church, Santullano. His successor, Ramiro I (842-850) continued the royal patronage and built a splendid summer palace which remains, in part, on the slopes of nearby Mount Naranco.

But in 914, with the extension of the kingdom's boundaries southwards, Don García (1035-1054) transferred the court to León. The Asturias-León Kingdom existed briefly from 1037 to 1157 and then in 1230 was finally incorporated in Castile. Recognition of a sort returned to the old kingdom in 1388 when the heir apparent to the Castilian throne took the style, Prince of Asturias.

The Two Battles of Oviedo: 1934 and 1936-37. — Insurrection broke out in the Asturian mining area on the morning of 5 October 1934. The following day Oviedo was seized by the miners who set up a provisional revolutionary committee in the city despite their not having control of the barracks, the prison, the governor's palace and other strongpoints. On 11 October regular forces arrived and the committee disbanded. Insurgent miners, however, continued to give battle in the city until the 15th — during the fighting the Cámara Santa was destroyed, the University set on fire, the Cathedral damaged.

In July 1936 when the Civil War broke out, the Oviedo garrison went over within a week to the generals, while the province generally supported the government. Fighting continued throughout 1937 resulting, inevitably, in considerable destruction.

■ THE OLD TOWN *time: 1 1/2 hours*

Cathedral★ (BYZ). — The cathedral, a characteristically Flamboyant Gothic edifice, was begun in the 14C with the construction of the cloister, and completed in the 16C with that of the porch and massive 80m - 262ft south tower, which is lightened above its rich lower decoration by a delicately pierced spire (restored after the Civil War). Three Gothic portals pierce the asymmetrical façade. The doors, which are considerably later, are panelled in 18C walnut; shown at the centre door is Christ *(on the left)* and St Eulalia in a cornfield *(on the right)*.

Interior. — The tall windows surmounting the triforium, the façade and transept rose windows, have the wavy line tracery typical of Flamboyant Gothic. The open vista down the nave enhances the 16C **altarpiece★** of wood, carved with scenes from the Life of Christ. The side chapels were profusely ornamented in the baroque period. On the left on entering, is the 17C Chapel to St Eulalia, overly ornate but containing in a massive baroque shrine the mortal remains of the patron saint of Asturias.

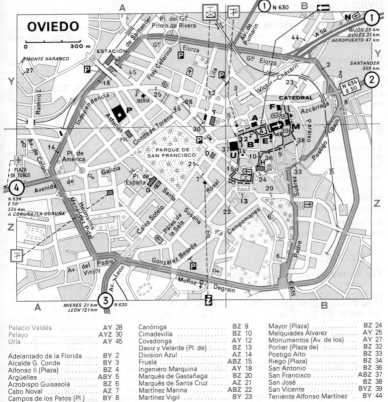

Palacio Valdés	AY 28	Canóniga	BZ 9	Mayor (Plaza)	BZ 24
Pelayo	AYZ 30	Cimadevilla	BZ 10	Melquiades Álvarez	AY 25
Uría	AY 45	Covadonga	AY 12	Monumentos (Av. de los)	AY 27
		Daoiz y Velarde (Pl. de)	BZ 13	Porlier (Plaza de)	BZ 32
Adelantado de la Florida	AY 2	Division Azul	AZ 14	Postigo Alto	BZ 33
Alcalde G. Conde	BY 3	Fruela	ABZ 15	Riego (Plaza)	BZ 34
Alfonso II (Plaza)	BZ 4	Ingeniero Marquina	AY 18	San Antonio	BZ 36
Argüelles	ABY 5	Marqués de Gastañaga	BZ 20	San Francisco	ABZ 37
Arzobispo Guisasola	BZ 6	Marqués de Santa Cruz	AZ 21	San José	BZ 38
Cabo Noval	AZ 7	Martínez Marina	ABZ 22	San Vicente	BYZ 39
Campos de los Patos (Pl.)	BY 8	Martínez Vigil	BY 23	Teniente Alfonso Martínez	BY 44

The **Chaste King's Chapel** — Alfonso II was known as El Casto — off the north transept, stands on the site of the original church and is the pantheon of the Asturian kings. The decoration inside the gate is late Gothic. In the embrasures are the figures of the Pilgrim St James, Sts Peter and Paul and Andrew and, in the covings, the 12 old musicians; at the pier stands a delicate Virgin and Child. In the chapel lie the illustrious Asturian kings.

Cloister. — *40pts*, 14C. On the way look at St Leocadia's Chapel, decorated outside with blind arcades and covered inside with cradle vaulting. The chamber, which corresponds with the Cámara Santa crypt *(see below)*, contains an altar, tombs from the time of Alfonso II and an unusual small stone aedicule which may have been a tabernacle. The cloister has intersecting pointed arching and delicate tracery in the bays.

Cámara Santa★★. — *Guided tours 1 June to 30 September 9.30am to 1pm and 4 to 7pm; the rest of the year 10am to 1pm and 4 to 7pm; 40pts. Access through the south transept.* The Cámara Santa was built by Alfonso II early in the 9C as a shrine for a coffer containing holy relics brought from Toledo on the fall of the Visigothic Kingdom; it was remodelled in Romanesque times and destroyed in an explosion in 1934; the rebuilt chapel contains most of the original works of art.

Six groups of apostles at the entrance form a series of stylised **statue columns★★** which are among the most masterly sculptures of 12C Spain. The head of the Christ figure over the entrance is also remarkable — the artist was obviously influenced by the Door of Glory in Santiago Cathedral which is not surprising because the Cámara Santa was often a stop for the pilgrims before going onto Santiago. Column capitals illustrate the marriage of Joseph and Mary, the Holy Women at the Tomb and lion and wild boar hunts.

The **treasury★★** in the apse, includes ancient gold and silver plate, the **Arca Santa** in the centre, the famous Cross of Victory *(p 112)*, a 12C travelling altar closed by twin doors with ivory inlay (deteriorated) and a Gothic diptych of the Passion, carved in ivory — a dog gliding beneath the ass's legs at the entrance to Jerusalem, Judas purloining fish at the Last Supper.

Cathedral Square (Plaza de Alfonso II) (BZ **4**). — On one side of the cathedral is a walled garden with low reliefs carved in homage to the Asturian kings. Before the west door in the main square stand, on the north side, the 17C **Valdecarzana Palace** (BY **A**) and, at the far end, the oldest house in Oviedo, the 15C **Casa de la Rúa** (BZ **B**).
Walk south round the cathedral. Note in passing the **San Tirso** east window (BZ **E**) — all that remains of the 9C church. The existence of the Moorish *alfiz (p 16)* in a building of that date remains a mystery.

Archaeological Museum (BYZ **M**). — *Open weekdays 10am to 1.30pm and 4 to 6pm; Sundays and holidays 11am to 1pm; closed Mondays 1 January, Good Friday, 21 September and 25 December.*

Local prehistoric finds, coins, medals and finely made and carved objects of wood, including old musical instruments, are on view in the upper cloister.

Romanesque steles are collected in the *entresol* galleries. Two galleries opening off the 15C Plateresque cloister at ground level contain pre-Romanesque art. Humble fragments and reproductions provide striking evidence of the delicate sophistication of monumental decoration in the Asturian period: there are altars such as that of Naranco surmounted by its original stone, reconstructions of chancel screens, low reliefs often showing Byzantine influence, column bases from San Miguel de Lillo, pierced bays inlaid in walls...

The imposing façade next to the museum fronts the 17 and 18C **Monastery of San Pelayo** (BY **F**). By way of the Calle Canóniga and the Calle de San Antonio, make for the Calle de Cimadevilla, which leads through an arch in the town hall to the Plaza Mayor.

OVIEDO

Plaza de Daoíz y Velarde (BZ 13). — Oviedo market is held on this square and in the adjoining picturesque, enclosed square. To the south is the baroque palace of the Marquess of San Feliz.

Old University (BZ U). — The austerely fronted building was completed in the 17C. The Classical court, although restored, still has much of its former style.

Plaza de Porlier (BZ 32). — Among the fine palaces on the square are the Toreno, dating from 1673 (now a library) and the Camposagrado, a harmonious 18C edifice now the seat of the Audiencia Territorial (note the spread eaves).

■ ADDITIONAL SIGHTS

Santullano (BY N). — *Open 10am to 1pm and 4 to 6pm.* The Church of San Julián de los Prados or Santullano, in a small shaded square, is an outstanding example of Asturian art of the first half of the 9C with its porch, nave and twin aisles, wide transept and at the east end, three chapels vaulted in brick. Traces of frescoes remain on the walls. Two unusual grey marble pilasters, finely carved with plant motifs, flank the chancel and rise to form a triumphal arch. There is a Romanesque Crucifix in the north chapel. Outside, the east end is typical with a window with a triple arcade and *claustra* (some restored).

Former Principality's Hospital (Antiguo Hospital del Principado) (AY P). — Now a hotel, the façade of the former hospital is emblasoned with a baroque **coat of arms**★.

EXCURSIONS

The Mount Naranco Sanctuaries★. — *4km - 2 miles northwest by the Avenida de los Monumentos.* Of the summer palace built by Ramiro I *(p 103)* on the south side of the mountain, there remain the former audience chamber now the Church of Sta María and the Royal Chapel, San Miguel. *Guided tours 1 May to 15 October 9.30am to 1pm and 3 to 7pm; the rest of the year 10am to 1pm and 3 to 5pm; closed Sunday and holiday afternoons; 100pts.*

Santa María del Naranco. — The building is attractive, possessing harmonious lines: it is square, two storeyed, supported by grooved buttresses and lit by vast bays. On the upper floor two *miradors* open off the great saloon covered by cradle vaulting. Exterior and interior decoration have been cleverly adapted to architectural necessity and are often similar in style: clusters of slender twisted columns adorn the pillars; the *mirador* capitals are Corinthian, those abutting the walls polygonal; the arch ribs descend to the squinches on fluted pilasters and discs decorated minutely in Byzantine style. The *mirador* **panorama**★ includes Oviedo and on the horizon, the Picos de Europa.

San Miguel de Lillo. — The chapel was truncated when the east end was remodelled in 17C. The narrowness of the aisles accentuates the height of the walls in which several *claustra* type windows remain. The delicacy of the interior carving is a delight: on the door jambs are identical scenes in relief of a consul, surrounded by dignitaries, presiding over contests in an arena.

El Carbayo★★. — *25km - 15 1/2 miles southeast. In Ciaño at the Rosario Felgueroso Park bear right by the church* (sadly deteriorated Romanesque portal) *and right again across the railway.* Beautiful **panoramas**★★ open out from El Carbayo and Otoñes, villages of the Asturias mountains, the Nalón Valley, invaded by the industrial towns of Sama de Langreo and La Felguera, and on a clear day, of the Cantabrian coastline.

Teverga. — *43km - 27 miles. Leave Oviedo by* ④. *In Trubia, bear left for Proaza.* **Trubia,** an industrial town which has manufactured armaments since 1794, stands at the juncture of the Nalón and Trubia Rivers. The road follows the latter which, after Proaza, enters a narrow rift. As you emerge glance back for a **view**★ of the cleft dividing the Peñas Juntas cliff face. Beyond the Teverga fork the road penetrates the enclosed **Teverga Defile**★.

Leave the Puerto Ventana road on your left.

The **Collegiate Church of San Pedro de Teverga** is at the end of La Plaza village. The church, which is late 12C, has had a porch and tower added. The architecture is an obvious continuation of the pre-Romanesque Asturian style. The building includes a narthex, a tall narrow nave and a flat east end, originally three chapels. The narthex capitals are carved with stylised animal and plant motifs: those in the nave include a bear (left) and a lion (right). A museum *(closed temporarily)* off the plain rustic cloister contains liturgical objects and mummies.

███ PASAJES PASAIA (Guipúzcoa)

Michelin map ███ fold 8 — Pop 20 696

Pasajes, in fact, comprises three villages around a sheltered bay connected with the open sea only by a narrow channel; **Pasai Antxo** is a trading port and port of call for ships going to Africa and lies at the back of the bay; **Pasai Donibane**★ and the larger **San Pedro** are squeezed on either side between the mountains and the harbour and are both deep sea fishing ports, processing cod in the town. On occasion the Pasajes' catch has been the greatest on the Cantabrian coast and 4th in value of any port in Spain.

Pasai Donibane★. — Leave the car on the esplanade at the entrance to the village and walk along the one and only narrow street which winds between houses and beneath arches and from which you will catch glimpses of boats and landing stages.

Victor Hugo's house. — *No 63 in the main street.* The poet lived in this house overlooking the harbour in 1843.

Plaza de Santiago. — The main square, framed by tall houses with wooden balconies is particulary picturesque from the water — take a motorboat from San Pedro.

Where the street circles a church, there is a view of the mouth of the bay.

The lighthouse path *(about 3/4 hour Rtn)* passes ancient fortifications.

The main throughroutes are clearly indicated on all town plans.

PICOS DE EUROPA ★★★ (León - Asturias - Cantabria)

Michelin map **441** folds 9 and 10

The Picos de Europa, the highest range in the Cantabrian Cordillera (Torre Cerredo: 2 648m - 8 688ft), stand massed between Oviedo and Santander, some 30km - 20 miles from the sea.

Gorges, cut by swift torrents, have circled and divided the Primary limestone formation into **three blocks:** the **western** or Covadonga Massif, the **central** or Naranco de Bulnes Massif and the **eastern** or Andara Massif. Awe-inspiring clefts, flowed through by streams alive with fish abut the high peaks, jagged with erosion and always snow-capped. The south face is less steep and looks out over a less abrupt but harsher landscape.

Besides the traditional occupations of **cabrales** making — a "blue" ewes' milk cheese — and stock raising, there is mining in the area. The **Liébana,** around Potes, has a mild climate sheltered from the northwest winds and grows walnuts, cherries and medlars as well as maize and even grapes on sun exposed slopes.

The Picos de Europa are made up of a restricted hunting reserve (Reserva Nacional de Los Picos de Europa) and a National Park (on the western block) *(see Covadonga p 112).*

It is possible to drive right round the range and, in places, to penetrate to the heart of the massif. Jeep tracks through the mountains to the mines and power stations, can be used to get to huts and refuges from which one can go climbing or walking. Jeeps can be hired in Arenas de Cabrales, Sotres de Cabrales, La Hermida, Espinama, Potes and Cosgaya.

THE LA HERMIDA DEFILE ★★

From Panes to Potes

27km - 17 miles — about 1 hour (excluding an ascent of the Fuente Dé)

The outstanding feature of the drive is the **ravine★★** which extends either side of a basin containing the hamlet of La Hermida and is some 20km - 12 miles long in all.

The gorge is narrow and so dim as to be bare of vegetation; the Deva has sought out weaknesses in the rock wall so that its course swings like a pendulum.

Na Sa de Lebeña. — *To visit ask Señora García at the first house in Lebeña village.*

The small 10C Mozarabic church stands surrounded by poplars at the foot of tall cliffs. The belfry and porch are later additions. The semicircular vaulting over the three aisles rests on horseshoe shaped arches decorated with beautifully carved Corinthian style capitals.

Potes. — Potes is a delightful village in a pleasing **site★** set in the hollow of a fertile basin against a background of the pointed crests of the central massif. From the bridge there is a view, reflected in the Deva, of old wooden houses and the austere 15C Infantado Tower restored to serve as the town hall.

Fuente Dé★★. — *25km - 15 1/2 miles.* The road follows the Deva through a mixed landscape of mountain woods and meadows. Finally it reaches the wild rock cirque where the river rises (behind the *parador*).

Jeep tracks from Espinama hamlet to the Aliva refuge continue across the Picos de Europa to Poncebos and Tresviso.

The Fuente Dé Parador is at 1 000m - 3 300ft. Nearby is the starting point of the cable-car which travels a further 800m - 2 625ft to the terminal at the top of the sheer rock face. *(Cable-car: 9am to 8pm (10am to 1pm and 3 to 6pm in winter); Rtn fare: 450pts).*

On the way up you may see wild chamois *(hunting restricted)* and from the terminal, the **Mirador del Cable★★,** a splendid panorama including the Upper Valley of the Deva and Potes, and the peaks of the central range. A path, circling the Peña Vieja, brings you to the Aliva refuge *(open June to September).* The effect of erosion on the upper heights of karstic limestone are spectacular, producing long stony plateaux and huge sink holes, known as **hoyos.**

Sto Toribio de Liébana Monastery. — *Approach along a narrow road on the right - signposted.*

The monastery now occupied by Franciscans, was founded in the 7C and grew to considerable importance in the following century when a fragment of the True Cross, brought from Jerusalem by Turibius, Bishop of Astorga, was placed in its safekeeping. A *camarín (access through the cloister)* now contains the fragment in the *lignum crucis* reliquary, a silver gilt Crucifix. The monastery was also the house of **Beatus,** the 8C monk famous for his **Commentary on the Apocalypse** *(p 97).* The church, transitional Romanesque in style, has been restored to its original harmony.

There is a **view★** of Potes and the central chain from the belvedere at the road's end.

THE SAN GLORIO PASS ★

From Potes to Oseja de Sajambre

117km - 73 miles — about 3 hours

The road crosses the green, poplar planted, Quiviesa Valley, then begins an ascent through mountain pastures. 10km - 6 miles beyond Bores, a series of serpentine bends afford a changing panorama on your left. The drive up to the San Glorio Pass is through a silent, very lonely countryside.

San Glorio Pass. — Alt 1 609m - 5 279ft. A track leads north *(1 hour Rtn)* to near the Peña de Llesba, a magnificent **viewpoint★★** for the highest crests: to the right is the east range, to the left the central massif with its steep south face dominating the Fuente Dé.

The peak in the left foreground is the Coriscao (2 234m - 7 330ft).

The scenery remains austere until you come to the village of **Llánaves de la Reina,** tucked into the opening of the **Yuso Gorge** which is spectacular for its rock colouring.

Pandetrave Pass★★. — An ascent through the high mountains brings you to the pass (1 562m - 5 124ft) and a **panorama★★** of the three ranges with, in the right foreground, the Cabén de Remoña and Torre de Salinas, both part of the central massif, and in the distance, lying in a hollow, the Santa Marina de Valdeón.

The road continues beside the Yuso before turning to cross the harsh landscape of the range's south face.

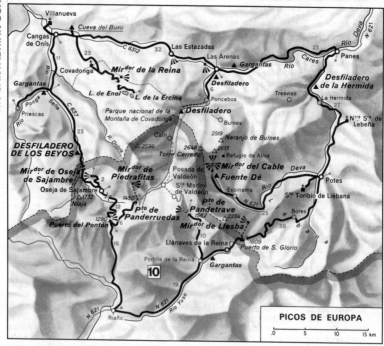

PICOS DE EUROPA

.0   5   10   15 km

Panderruedas Pass★★. — *1/4 hour on foot Rtn.* The narrow winding road through the woods, after 3km - 2 miles reveals wonderful limestone escarpments and ends amidst mountain pastures at an altitude of 1 450m - 4 758ft. Walk up the path to the left to the **Mirador de Piedrafitas** from where there is an impressive **view★★** of the immense cirque which closes the end of the Valdeón Valley. To the northeast can be seen the Cerredo, which at 2 648m - 8 688ft — is the highest peak in the range *(viewing table)*.

Pontón Pass★. — Alt 1 280m - 4 200ft. From the pass you will get a picturesque **view★** of the Sajambre Valley.

The descent begins with tight serpentine bends between elm trees in full view of the western range; it continues as a spectacular *corniche* (tunnels) during which you see the formidable rock wall through which the Sella has hollowed a course.

THE SELLA DEFILE★★★
From Oseja de Sajambre to Cangas de Onís
34km - 21 miles - about 1 hour

Mirador de Oseja de Sajambre★★. — *2km - 1 mile.* There is an awe inspiring **view★★** from the *mirador* of the Oseja de Sajambre basin with the Niaja rock spike at its centre rising to 1 732m - 5 683ft, and of the Los Beyos defile opening between walls of broken rock strata.

The Los Beyos Defile★★★. — The defile, 10km - 6 miles long cut by the Sella through the exceptionally thick layer of limestone, is too precipitous for anything other than an occasional tree to have gained a hold on its sides.

Ponga Gorges★. — *7km - 4 miles.* The Ponga River has cut a wild gorge through to the Sella, almost blocking its own course in some places with fallen rocks.

Cangas de Onís. — An elegant Romanesque hump-backed bridge across the Sella lies west of the town. Sta Cruz Chapel, rebuilt after the Civil War, was erected also west of the town in Contranquil to celebrate the victory of Covadonga. It houses the region's only dolmen of which one stone is engraved.

Villanueva. — *2km - 1 mile from Cangas along the Arriondas road.* At the end of the village stands the Benedictine Monastery of San Pedro which, when it was erected in the 17C, enclosed within its walls an existing Romanesque church. Of this there remain the apse and an elegantly decorated side portal — note on the left the capitals illustrating the farewells of King Favila and his apparently sad end, being devoured by a bear.

Inside *(to visit apply at the monastery)* there are further capitals to be seen in the apse and at the triumphal arch. Imaginatively ornamented stone modillions decorate the apse exterior.

THE CARES GORGES★★
From Cangas de Onís to Panes — *55km - 34 miles — about 1 hour*

In the villages, many of the granaries which form an integral part of the Asturian landscape are decorated with heavy, deep gold coloured corn cobs.

El Buxu Cave (Cueva). — *2km - 1 mile east of Cangas, take the first road on the left. Open (only 25 people are admitted daily) 10am to 12.30pm and to 4 to 6.30pm; closed Mondays and November; 100pts, Tuesdays free.* The cave in the cliff face contains charcoal drawings and rock engravings dating back to the Magdalenian period. There are a stag, horse and bison scarcely larger than a handspread, and red lines and smoke trails.

The road to Covadonga and the lakes★★. — *Description p 112.*

Covadonga. — *Description p 114.*

As you come out of Las Estazadas village there is a **panorama★★** which is both close and widespread of the rock wall which ends the Río Casaño Valley.
From a belvedere on the right, shortly after Carreña de Cabrales, there is a glimpse of the fang-like crest of the **Naranjo de Bulnes** (2 519m - 8 264ft). A monument commemorates the first ascent in 1904.

Arenas de Cabrales. — Arenas, as its name suggests, is the main production centre for *cabrales,* the "blue" ewes' milk cheese. The road now, for a while, skirts the River Cares.

Upper Cares Valley. — *6km - 4 miles and then there is the possibility of a long walk.* The Poncebos road leads south, through a pleasant **cleft★**. After the small Poncebos Reservoir a track *(accessible only on foot, 6km - 3 1/2 miles Rtn — allow 3 hours)* abandons the Cares and continues to the mountain village of Bulnes (760m - 2 493ft).
Leave the car at Poncebos. Here you can hire a car with chauffeur, who will then meet you at Caín (hiring possibilities at Caín).
From Poncebos to Caín *(11km - 7 miles on foot-allow 3 1/2 hours)* a path follows the Cares, plunges down into the **defile★★** before reaching the foot of the central massif. Once picked up at Caín, the hired car takes you back to Poncebos on a track which goes by the Mirador del Tombo leaves, at Posada de Valdeón, the Cares Valley and connects with a surfaced road at Sta Marina de Valdeón.

Beyond Arenas the **gorges★** are green with moss and even the occasional tree. Narrow hump-backed road bridges and fragile looking footbridges span the emerald waters of the river.

PUENTE VIESGO ★ (Cantabria)
Michelin map 442 fold 4 — Pop 2 497

The caves (El Castillo, Las Chimeneas, Las Monedas, La Pasiega) hollowed out of the limestone mountainsides all round Puente Viesgo provide ample proof of their habitation in prehistoric times.

El Castillo Cave★. — *Open 10am to 12.15pm and 3 to 6pm; closed afternoons from 1 November to 31 March and all day Monday; time: 1/2 hour; 250pts.*

Excavation has revealed successive floor levels corresponding to each period in the Palaeolithic Age. It was in the final period (Aurignacian to Magdalenian) that the cave dwellers began painting and engraving the walls, the designs, outlines only, numerous — 750 have been counted — but sometimes incomplete, are widely scattered and some are difficult to get to. Many remain enigmatic, particularly the hands dipped in ochre which have been pressed against the walls to form negatives and were thought, perhaps, to symbolise man's superiority or to possess magical powers. Of the almost 50 discovered only 3 are right hands.

The meaning between parallel lines and point alignments also remains obscure. The parallels may refer to weapons or traps for catching animals, the others to animal tracks heading for the traps or they may even be a rough map of the snares.

Castañeda. — *6km - 4 miles.* Construction began at the end of the 12C on the **Church of Santa Cruz de Castañeda** in the small and smiling valley through which the Pisueña runs. The squat stone building, from which outlines of the square belfry and lantern scarcely stand out, was formerly a collegiate church. The unusually deep doorway is given considerable elegance by a simple decoration of alternate convex and concave covings.

Inside *(to visit apply at the white house a little further on the left side of the road),* although the original Romanesque ground plan has been complicated by Gothic additions, the central area has retained its primitive design : main nave in centre, cupola on squinches. The capitals are somewhat roughly carved with naive figures in the round.

RAMALES DE LA VICTORIA (Cantabria)
Michelin map 442 fold 5 — Pop 2 437

Ramales, at the confluence of the Asón and the Gándara on the eastern border of Cantabria province, is a good excursion centre.

Covalanas Caves. — *3km - 2 miles. Open 10am to 1pm and 3.30 to 7.30pm; closed Mondays; 125pts. In winter apply at Plaza de José Antonio, 5, in Ramales ☎ 64 61 69.*
The caves *(clearly signposted)* are remarkably **situated★** in a cliff overlooking the Gándara Valley (they are visited with an acetylene lamp). The principal chamber contains Palaeolithic wall paintings in red, in a somewhat elongated style, mostly of does together with a few cattle. The contours are, in most cases, indicated with dotted lines — perhaps to save paint!

The adjoining cave has beautiful limestone concretions.

SPAIN : The Michelin Regional Map Series (1 : 400 000)

When choosing your lunchtime or overnight stop
use the above maps as all towns listed in
the Red Guide España Portugal are underlined in red.

When driving into or through a town
use the map as it also indicates all places with
a town plan in the Red Guide España Portugal.

Common reference numbers make the transfer from map to plan easier.

REINOSA (Cantabria)

Michelin map 442 fold 4 — Pop 13 172

Reinosa, built on the southern slopes of the Cantabrian Cordillera, in the vast depression formed by the Ebro Basin, really belongs to the Castilian landscape with its vast expanses of tableland and cereals. In the 18C its situation on the road linking Castile with the port of Santander encouraged commercial development. It has since become primarily industrial (heavy engineering for the navy and merchant shipping and the construction of electrical motors). It is becoming a tourist centre as it is near a reservoir lake and winter sports resort (Alto Campoo).

EXCURSIONS

Retortillo. — *5km - 3 miles south of the C 6318.* All that remains in the small church of the Romanesque period are the oven vaulted apse and the triumphal arch with two finely carved capitals showing warriors against a background of acanthus leaves *(to visit apply to Sr. Ramón González at the house in the centre of the village).* Quite close are the ruins of a villa which stood in the Roman city of **Juliobriga.**

Cervatos★. — *5km - 3 miles south by the N 611 (signpost).* The former **collegiate church★,** which is in an unusually pure Romanesque style, is remarkable for the richness and fantasy of its carved **decoration★.** The portal tympanum is meticulously patterned though little pierced. There is a frieze of lions back to back while varied and audacious figures decorate the cornice modillions and those beneath the capitals of the south apsidal window. Inside there are harmonious blind arcades in the apse and, again, the carving on the capitals and the consoles supporting the arch ribs is both dense and sophisticated with entangled lions, flying eagles, plant motifs and strapwork. The nave was raised with diagonal ribbed vaulting in the late 14C.

Tres Mares Peak★★★. — *26km - 16 miles. Take the Alto Campóo road.*

Fontibre. — Paths lead to the source of the Ebro *(signposted),* a small greenish pool beneath poplar trees. The greatest Iberian river rises at 881m - 2 890ft and remains only a modest stream until joined by the Río Híjar.

Braña Vieja. — A recent small and sunny winter sports resort set amidst the bare heights of the **Alto Campoo.**

Tres Mares Peak★★★. — *Access by chairlift: 8.30am to 5pm in winter; 250pts Rtn. It is a good idea to walk down to the Mirador de la Fuente del Chivo on the return.* The peak (2 175m - 7 136ft), one of the summits of the Peña Labra Sierra, got its name as the source of three rivers which flow from it to three different seas (sea: *mar* in Spanish) — the Híjar, tributary of the Ebro which flows into the Mediterranean; the Pisuerga, tributary of the Duero, which flows into the Atlantic and the Nansa, which flows directly into the Cantabrian Sea. From the crest there is a splendid circular **panorama★★★,** north of the Nansa and the Cohilla Dam at the foot of Mount Cueto (1 517m - 4 977ft), and circling right, of the Ebro Dam, the Peña Labra Sierra, the Cervera de Pisuerga Dam and the León mountains; due west, is the central range including the 2 618m - 8 589ft - Peña Vieja, and linked to it by a series of high passes, the eastern range which includes the Peña Sagra (2 042m - 6 699ft). In the foreground is the eroded mass of the Peña Labra (2 006m - 6 582ft).

Mirador de la Fuente del Chivo. — *At the end of the road.* Bird's-eye view of the Nansa.

RIBADESELLA ★ (Asturias)

Michelin map 441 fold 9 — Pop 6 688

The town and port of Ribadesella, built on the right side of the estuary, took its name from its site on the Sella (*riba:* river bank). Opposite, a holiday resort has been established in the rounded bay.

Crowds come on the first Saturday in August every year to see international kayak races down the Sella, enthusiasts can even follow the boats down the course in a train run especially for the occasion on the track which parallels the river downstream from Arriondas. Arrival at Ribadesella is followed by a *romería.*

Tito Bustillo Cave★. — *Guided tours 1 April to 30 September 10am to 1pm and 3.30 to 6.30pm; closed Mondays; 125pts.*

The junction of three chambers selected for decoration by the Palaeolithic inhabitants of 20 000 BC (between the end of the Solutrian and the middle of the Magdalenian Periods) lies at the end of some 500yds of galleries hung with wonderful stalactites and beyond (on the right) a moraine mass blocking a prehistoric dwelling chamber.

On the large **wall of paintings★** a few animals — a horse, two stags, a doe, another stag and a horse — precede the smoothest area of rock, a sort of low ceiling where, in the hollows of the stone, there are animal outlines 2m - 6 1/2ft long. The dark silhouettes are often emphasised by an engraved line, the inner areas coloured red or ochre.

SAN IGNACIO DE LOYOLA Monastery (Guipúzcoa)

Michelin map 442 fold 7

An immense monastery was erected by the Jesuits in the 18C around the Loyola family manorhouse near Azpeitia. It has since become an important pilgrimage where large crowds attend the solemnities held annually on St Ignatius day (31 July).

During the first week in August the International Festival of Romantic Music is held.

The Soldier of God. — **Ignatius of Loyola** was born in 1491 (died 1556) in Loyola Castle of an old family of the lesser nobility. He was bred to arms. It was while recovering from wounds contracted at the siege of Pamplona *(p 181),* that he heard the call of God and 8 months later, in 1522, left the Loyola mansion to go on pilgrimage to Arantzazu and Montserrat. He next withdrew to a cave near Manresa (Catalonia) where he began to write his **Spiritual Exercises.** In 1523 he set off in pilgrimage to Jerusalem from where, before returning to Spain, he journeyed to Paris (1528) and London (1530). After further wanderings and attendance at various universities, he and the compatriots he had met in Paris, Diego Laínez and Francis Xavier *(p 185)* were ordained (1537) and repaired to Rome.

In 1540, the pope recognised the **Society of Jesus** which Loyola had conceived and of which he had drawn up the constitution and was subsequently elected the first vicar-general.

Ignatius of Loyola was canonised in 1622 at the same time as Francis Xavier and Teresa of Ávila.

Santa Casa. — *Closed 12.30 to 3.30pm. Audio equipment recounting the saint's life is available at the entrance.*

The basement casemates of the 15C tower are all that remain in original guise of the Loyola manorhouse. The rooms in which Ignatius was born, convalesced and converted have been transformed into profusely decorated chapels. *Dioramas at the end of tour.*

Basilica. — The basilica by the Roman architect, Fontana, is more Italian than Spanish in style. It is circular and surmounted by a vast cupola (63m - 118ft high) by Churriguera.

SAN MARTÍN DE ELINES (Cantabria)
Michelin map 🔢 folds 4 and 5 — 6km - 4 miles east of Rúerrero

A 12-13C collegiate church, contemporary with the one at Castañeda *(p 121)*, stands in this small village in the Ebro Valley.

Cross the Ebro and bear right in the village. To visit apply at the presbytery near the church.

The cloister, which has the unexpected appeal of certain rustic buildings, contains several Mozarabic tombs.

The church itself is Romanesque with windows in the apse, emphasised by a frieze of plant motifs (identical with the one inside), a small circular belfry abutting the south wall and modillions decorating the roof cornice. Beyond the chancel is a fine oven vaulted apse enhanced by blind arcading.

SAN SEBASTIÁN ★★★ DONOSTIA (Guipúzcoa) 🅿
Michelin map 🔢 fold 8 — Pop 175 576 (known as Donostiarras after the Basque name for the town).

San Sebastián, placed like a jewel in the beautiful **setting**★★★ of its scallop shaped bay, the Bahía de la Concha, has for centuries been known both abroad and in Spain as the Pearl of the Cantabrian Coast. The modern city is nestled between Mounts Urgull and Igueldo.

The town grew in mediaeval times from a fishing harbour to a trading port and, much later, into an industrial town (east of Urumea). Later still it gained a reputation as an international resort of high fashion, patronised by the Spanish royal family; it has now become one of Spain's most elegant and frequented summer resorts.

The resort. — Two vast sand beaches follow the curve of the bay: La Concha, and beyond the promontory, the fashionable Ondarreta. Behind are gardens, promenades and tall apartment blocks.

Historically San Sebastián's recognition as a resort began in 1889 with the construction to designs by an English architect, Selden Wornum, of the Miramar Palace (Y) *(in summer gardens open to the public).*

The summer calendar includes international jazz and film festivals, a Semana Grande (in August), Basque festivals with folklore festivities, golf and tennis tournaments, racing, regattas, clay pigeon shooting contests etc.

A gastronomic capital. — A feature of this city where one eats well and copiously and where there is a Gastronomic Academy, are the "Sociedades Recreativas" or good food clubs. They number about 30 and have well furnished club houses in the old part of the town where members (men only) prepare excellent meals in the club kitchens which they then consume, accompanied by cider or the local *chacolí* wine.

■ THE OLD TOWN (CIUDAD VIEJA) *time: 2 hours*

San Sebastián was born at the foot of Mount Urgull and there, between the harbour and the mouth of the Urumea, you can still see the old city. Although, in fact, it all dates only from last century — the original was devastated by fire in 1813 — the narrow streets have considerable character. The area comes alive at the evening aperitif hour *(8 to 8.30pm)* when everyone crowds into the bars and small restaurants round the Plaza de la Constitución to pick at shellfish, crustaceans and *chipirones* (squid).

Plaza de la Constitución (Z 9). — The square is lined with houses with tall arcades and numbered balconies — a reminder of the days when they served as ringside seats when bullfights were held in the square.

Sta María (Z B). — The church has a strikingly exuberant late 18C portal. The vast sober interior highlighted by numerous baroque altars.

San Telmo Museum (Z M¹). — *Open 10.30am to 1.30pm and 3.30 to 7pm; closed Monday mornings; 50pts.*

The museum is in an old 16C monastery. The Renaissance cloisters contain Basque stone funerary crosses carved in the Iberian traditional style and dating for the most part between the 15 and 17C. The former chapel, now a conference hall, was decorated by José María Sert in vigorous camaieu style painting with events from Basque history.

On the 1st floor, off the cloister gallery — where there is an interesting ethnographic display including a Basque interior — there are rooms with paintings by Zuloaga *(Torerillos en Turégano)*, Ortiz Echagüe and artists of Spain's Golden Age (Ribera, El Greco, Carreño). Displayed in another gallery are headdresses worn by local women until the mid-18C. The headdresses, said to be of oriental influence, were made by bands of cloth wrapped over a framework.

On the 2nd floor is a large collection of Basque paintings.

Paseo Nuevo (YZ). — The wide **corniche** promenade almost circles Mount Urgull and affords good **views,** of the open sea and the bay. At the end is the **Sea Palace** (Y), an oceanographic museum (skeleton of a whale captured in the bay in 1878), an aquarium and a Seafaring Museum (models, different displays concerning the great Basque sailors (Churruca, Elcano). *Open 10am to 1.30pm and 3.30 to 8pm; closed Mondays; 75pts, children 40pts.*

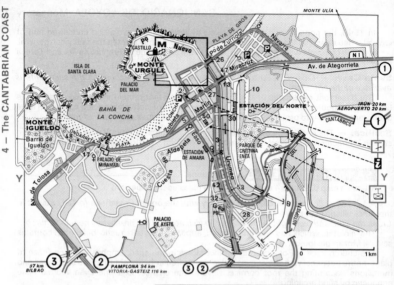

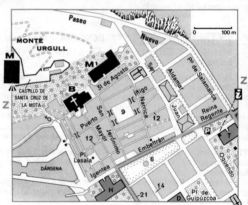

Mount Urgull. — The mound is now a public park and the fortress crowning it, the **Castillo de Sta Cruz de la Mota (YZ M),** a **military museum.** *Park open 7am to 1 hour after sunset - climb difficult, reckon 1/2 hour. Museum temporarily closed.* The artillery galleries on the ground floor include mortars, cannon (some of which were found in the roadstead) and armour; on the 1st floor are 15 to 18C swords and pistols, chased and inlaid with mother of pearl. From the upper terrace *(access from the 2nd floor)* there is a good **panorama★★** of the town, the monuments below and the Concha Bay.

EXCURSIONS

Mount Igueldo. — *4.5km - 3 miles. Access by funicular (50pts Rtn); by car, follow the Concha beach and, after the tunnel, bear right.* The road to the lighthouse climbs to the summit *(toll: 50pts per person)* where there are an amusement park, hotel and restaurant. There is also a splendid **panorama★★★** of the sea, the roadstead, the Island of Santa Clara and San Sebastián, at the centre of the mountain cirque *(telescopes).*

Mount Ulía★. — *7km - 4 miles. Follow the Avenida de Ategorrieta and before reaching the summit and descending to San Sebastián, take the first road on the right.* While driving to the top via a series of hairpin bends there are good **views★** of the town in its setting. The Mount Ulía Restaurant is on the far side of the park at the top *(footpath).*

SANTA CRISTINA DE LENA Church ★ (Asturias)
Michelin map 🔟🔟🔟 folds 7 and 8

4km - 2 miles south of Pola de Lena near Vega del Rey, take the signposted road to the viaduct; walk up the very steep path (1/4 hour) immediately to your left. To visit apply at the house on the right.

The Church of Santa Cristina de Lena is built to pleasing proportions in golden stone. It stands on a small rock spike from which there is a **panoramic view★** of the industrial but, nevertheless, green Caudal Valley. The little building, which is later than those on Mount Naranco, has a Greek cross plan unusual in the Asturias, but the traditional stone vaulting remains, with blind arcades, in which the columns have pyramid shaped capitals emphasised by a cord motif, sculpted modillions extending the arch ribs and turned columns in the choir.

The nave is separated from the raised choir by an iconostastis in which the superimposed arches increase the impression of its being equally balanced on either side. The chancel low reliefs are Visigothic sculptures in a new setting.

*The **Michelin Regional Map Series** is revised regularly.*
These maps make the perfect travelling companion.

SANTANDER ★ (Cantabria) ℗

Michelin map **442** fold 5 — Pop 180 328
See town plan in the current Michelin Red Guide España Portugal

Santander, capital of La Montaña province, extends along the north shore of a great bay closed by the narrow Magdalena headland and the sandy Somo point. Behind the headland lies the older residential quarter of El Sardinero.

To the natural advantages of a beautiful site and extensive sand beaches, the city has added excellent facilities and entertainments, thus becoming one of Cantabria's most sophisticated resorts.

The cataclysm of 1941. — A tornado struck Santander on the afternoon of 15 February 1941: the sea swept over the quays; fire started in the centre of the town and burned throughout the night, engulfing 40 streets and hundreds of houses — 20 000 were left homeless; all communications with the outside world were lost but incredibly no one died.

The new town. — Reconstruction was undertaken to a street plan of blocks of no more than 4 or 5 storeys; space was allocated to gardens beside the sea and promenades such as the **Paseo de Pereda** which skirts the passenger boat harbour, the small fishing boat harbour and finally the pleasure boat harbour (Puerto Chico). The heart of the town, is the **Calvo Sotelo Avenue** with its shops and cafés and just north of it the porticoed square, the **Plaza Porticada,** which is the setting each August for the international festival of drama, music and dance.

The port. — The port developed from the natural advantage of the immense sheltered anchorage.

Trade, which began with Castilian wool and wheat, for which it was a major outlet, diversified over the centuries as local industries developed, particularly steel, chemicals and shipbuilding.

Because the bay was, unfortunately, congested with sandbanks, a canal was dug to make the passage clear for the ships to the **Astillero** quays.

■ MONUMENTS *time: 2 hours*

Cathedral. — *Open 9.30am to 12.30pm and 5.30 to 8.30pm.*

The edifice at the top of the mound looks more like a fortress, even after the rebuilding following the 1941 tornado. Only the 12C crypt *(access through the south portico)* with its three low aisles separated by solid cruciform pillars remained unscathed. To the right of the ambulatory is a stoup which is obviously a Muslim ablutionary bowl and is even decorated with Cufic characters.

Underneath the north aisle Roman ruins were discovered in 1983.

The Gothic cloister, like the main building, is considerably restored.

Menéndez y Pelayo Library. — *Calle Rubio. Guided tours (time : 20 min) 9am to 1pm; closed Saturdays, Sundays and holidays.*

Marcelino Menéndez y Pelayo (1856-1912), Spanish and universal savant, had a passion for books from his earliest years and amassed a fabulous library. Among the collection of nearly 45 000 volumes left by the philosopher to his native town, are many works and manuscripts by great Catalan authors.

The library has been extended and is now an even richer source of bibliography than when bequeathed.

The learned man's house, the **Casa Museo** opposite, gives a clear picture of his modest way of life.

Fine Arts Museum (Museo Municipal de Bellas Artes). — *Open 10am to 1pm and 5 to 9pm (8pm 1 October to 30 June); closed Sundays and holidays.*

On the 2nd floor, on the right is a portrait of *Ferdinand VII,* which the city commissioned Goya to paint. Also by Goya are a series of his *Disasters of War* etchings and some of his *Caprichos.* There is a Zurbarán — *Mystic Scene* — in a gallery on the right. Contemporary paintings, however, are the museum's speciality: landscapes by Agustín Riancho, genre paintings — *The Ragpickers (Los Traperos)* — by the vigorous José Gutiérrez Solana (1886-1945) and the realistic Ricardo Bernardo — *The Flutists (Los Piteros).*

Prehistory Museum★ (Museo Provincial de Prehistoria y Arqueología). — *Open 9am to 2pm (noon Saturdays); closed Sundays and holidays.*

The museum in the basement of the Diputación consists principally of finds excavated in the prehistoric caves in the province (particularly El Castillo and El Pendo).

The richest period is the late Palaeolithic Era from which there are bones engraved with animal silhouettes and more importantly **batons★** made of horn and finely decorated for a purpose still unknown. The best specimen, made from an antler, was discovered at El Pendo.

Among the Neolithic axeheads, note the particularly high polish on those of diorite.

Three large steles indicate the apogee of the Cantabrian culture (Bronze Age).

Finally one gallery is devoted to traces and remains of the Roman occupation. The finds are mostly from Juliobriga *(p 122)* and include coins, bronzes and pottery figurines.

■ EL SARDINERO★★

At the end of the 19C the Spanish royal family took to sea bathing at Santander, making both pastime and town highly fashionable. The town went so far as to build a summer palace *(the gardens close at 8pm)* on the Magdalena Point for Alfonso XIII — now the International University annexe. Summer visitors have the choice of several beaches along the promontory, along the south side of the Magdalena headland and, bordering El Sardinero, three areas divided at high tide by tongues of land brilliant with flower gardens but when the tide recedes, linked by a long sand bank.

Water sports, theatrical and other entertainments, the casino and golf (18 hole course at Pedreña, across the bay) are supplemented in July by further spectacles, including the great St James' festival of bullfighting and throughout August by a festival of drama, music and dancing.

International University. — The "university" has been established in the premises of the Santander University.

The "university" holds summer courses for Spanish and foreign students; some lectures are given in the Magdalena Palace.

SANTANDER★

EXCURSIONS

Cape (Cabo) Mayor. — *7km - 4 miles north.* Cabo Mayor, or Great Cape lighthouse commands not only a wide sea horizon but also a good view of the bay and coastline.

Muriedas. — *7km - 4 miles south. Take the Burgos road.*
The house of Pedro Velarde *(p 200),* hero of the War of Independence, has been restored and is now an **ethnographic museum (Casa de Velarde, Museo Etnográfico de Cantabria).** *Open 11am (10am October to June) to 1pm and 4 to 7pm (6pm October to June); Sundays and holidays 11am to 2pm; closed Mondays.*
A typical, Cantabrian gateway opens onto grounds in which may be seen a *hórreo (p 103)* from the Liébana region and a Cantabrian stele. The 17C residence contains furniture, utensils and tools from all parts of the province. Mementoes of Velarde are displayed in his former bedroom and another large room on the first floor.

The main shopping streets are indicated
at the beginning of the list of streets,
which accompany town plans.

SANTILLANA DEL MAR ★★ (Cantabria)

Michelin map **442** fold 4 — Pop 3 884

The village, which is astonishingly well preserved and highly evocative of long ago, grew up around a monastery, sheltering the relics of St Juliana, who suffered martyrdom in Asia Minor-the name Santillana is a contraction of Santa Juliana.
Throughout the Middle Ages, the monastery was famous as a place of pilgrimage and was particularly favoured by the grandees of Castile. In the 11C it became powerful as a collegiate church; in the 15C, the town, created the seat of a marquisate, was enriched by the erection of fine seignorial mansions *(casonas)* from which subsequently many a great Castilian line was to spring.
Today there is nothing pretentious in what is once more just a small community inhabited largely by farmers who at nightfall return with their beasts up the main street to age old houses, stables and cow byres.

■ **SIGHTS** *time: 1 1/2 hours*

The village has two principal roads, both leading to the collegiate church. Between the two lies a network of communicating alleys. Most of the noblemen's residences, which date from the 15, 16 and 17C, have plain façades of massive rough stone, almost all have wrought iron balconies or wooden galleries *(solanas)* and the majority sport a crest.

Calle de Sto Domingo. — **Villas House,** now an inn *(mesón: open July to the end of September),* is distinguishable by its semicircular balconies; the device on the armorial bearings shows an eagle with spread wings pierced by an arrow and the motto "A glorious death crowns life with honour".
Turn left at the fork into the Calle de Juan Infante.

Plaza de Ramón Pelayo or **Plaza Mayor.** — The **Gil Blas Parador,** the old Barreda Bracho residence, is named after the hero of the novel by the 18C French writer, Lesage.

Borja-Barreda Tower (15C). — The tower, facing the Calle de Juan Infante, has a pointed arched doorway and is altogether extremely elegant.

Calle de las Lindas. — In spite of its name, which means the Street of Beautiful Women, the street and its houses are severe in appearance and more in keeping with the character of the two towers which also stand upon it and, dating from the 14 and 15C, are amongst the town's oldest buildings.
As you come in sight of the collegiate church, you will see on the right, the **Casa de los Hombrones,** named after the two outsize knights supporting the Villas coat of arms on which the family motto appears *(hombrones: tall men).*

Calle del Río. — This street is called after the stream which runs down its centre, fills a drinking fountain and disappears through an arch beneath **Quevedo House.** The Quevedo crest is surpassed only by the magnificent bearings on the nearby **Cossío House.**

Collegiate Church Square. — The **Abbot's House** sports three coats of arms, the central crest incorporating the arms of all the city's great families of the time.

Las Arenas Square. — The much restored but still impressive **Velarde Tower** behind the Collegiate Church, was originally the keep of the 15C palace.

Collegiate Church★. — *Tour : 3/4 hour.* The church dates from the 12 and 13C. While the design of the east end is pure Romanesque, that of the west to some extent lacks unity, although the harmonious placing of the windows and towers and the golden colour of the stone make it fit in well with the overall architecture of the square. Above the portal, which was remodelled in the 18C, is a niche with a statue of St Juliana.

Interior. — The vaulting of the nave was reconstructed at the end of the 13C when it was given intersecting ribs, but that above the transept and apses is original. The aisles and apses are out of alignment, the cupola again, unusually, is almost elliptical, the pillar capitals formalised.
St Juliana's memorial sarcophagus, a 15C sculpture, stands at the centre of the nave; in the choir a 17C Mexican beaten silver altarfront opens to reveal Romanesque stone figures of **four Apostles★** carved with a Byzantine sense of hierarchy. The 17C Hispano-Flemish **altarpiece★** has the original polychrome wood predella which is carved to show the Evangelists in profile.

Cloister★. — *Open 15 June to 15 September 9am to 1pm and 4 to 8pm; the rest of the year 10am to 1pm and 3 to 6pm; closed 28 June, 16 August and Wednesdays 15 September to 15 June; 75pts - ticket also valid for the Regina Coeli Convent.*

The late 12C cloister with Virginia creeper trailing where the Romanesque east gallery once stood, nevertheless, remains robust, elegant, appealing even. Each pair of twin columns is covered by a capital carved by a master craftsman. Though plant and strapwork motifs predominate in the south gallery, the **capitals★★** which do illustrate a scene, often in allegory, are very expressive: look out for Christ and six of the disciples, Christ's baptism and the beheading of John the Baptist, Daniel in the Lions' den.

Regina Coeli Convent. — *On the other side of the village.* The **Diocesan Museum (Museo Diocesano)** now occupies the restored 16C convent of the Poor Clares. *Same opening times as the collegiate church's cloister* On display are popular religious art objects found in the province.

There is a coat of arms at the end of the street on the fine 18C **Casa de Los Tagle.**

VERGARA BERGARA (Guipúzcoa)
Michelin map **442** fold 7 — Pop 15 759

This busy industrial town (textiles), watered by the Deva, still has a few old houses with attractive fronts. The first Carlist War, fought largely across the length and breadth of Guipúzcoa Province, ended at Vergara on 31 August 1839 with the now famous **El Convenio de Vergara** between the Carlist General Maroto and the liberal General Espartero. During the seven year war nearly 270 000 had been killed.

St Peter of Ariznoa. — Beneath the Churrigueresque gallery in the vast 17C church stands a sculpture of *Christ in Agony,* carved in 1622 by Juan de Mesa, follower of Montañés. Inside the church there is also a Ribera painting of the *Nativity* in which the faces of the Virgin and Child are beautifully serene in total contrast to the figure on the Cross.

VILLAVICIOSA (Asturias)
Michelin map **441** fold 8 — Pop 15 703

It was in Villaviciosa that the future **Emperor Charles V,** accompanied by a full escort of Flemish courtiers, landed in 1517 to take possession of his newly inherited kingdom. Excitement ran high amongst the villagers as they saw the princely armada sailing up the long *ría* to their harbour — an error in navigation actually as the ships intended anchorage was Santander! They arranged a *corrida* in his honour, but he remained displeased and retained but sour memories of his first contact with his Spanish subjects.

Of the town with its narrow streets, today's visitor will remember **Santa María Church** on the Plaza Mayor, its west front decorated with a Gothic rose window, its Romanesque portal flanked by slender statue columns. The paired windows in the aisles have an attractive Mudejar decoration. Not far away is a picturesque enclosed square.

EXCURSIONS

Amandi. — *1km - 1/2 mile south along the Infiesto road.* The bell gable of the **Church of San Juan** can be picked out as it stands perched on a mound at the centre of the village. Though remodelled in the 18C the church still has its 13C portal and apse in which the decoration★ shows a high degree of sophistication. Inside the **apse★,** the frieze from the façade reappears to follow in a winding ribbon the concave curves of the intercolumniation.

Tazones. — *12km - 7 1/2 miles. Take the Gijón road; turn right for Tazones.*

Church of San Andrés de Bedriñana. — *2km - 1 mile Rtn.* The church retains from the Asturian period just one minute Mozarabic *claustra,* which is, moreover, very artistically carved.

As the road rises there are views of the *ría,* and, on the far bank, of a large cider mill — cider is the most widely drunk alcoholic beverage in the Cantabrian region.

El Puntal. — The village with its small pleasure boat harbour, pinewood and beach is popular with Villaviciosans. As you leave there is a view of the *ría* mouth and **Rodiles beach,** overlooking both sea and river.

Tazones. — Attractive fishing village at the end of a sheltered bay.

Valdediós★. — *9km - 6 miles. Take the Oviedo road and after 7km - 4 miles turn right in the village of San Pedro down a fairly steep hill.*

In the one valley are a monastery and a small Asturian church both full of character, the latter also possessing an ancient charm.

The **monastery** cloister has three superimposed galleries dating from the 15, 17 and 18C.

In the 13C Cistercian Church (Santa María) intersecting ribbed vaulting has been introduced over the aisles. **San Salvador** *(open 10am to 1pm and 4 to 5pm; 50pts),* which was consecrated in 893 and is known locally

(After Ed. Pardo photo, Oviedo)

Valdediós

as "El conventín" or the little monastery, dates from the end of the period of Asturian art. The raised nave is abutted by narrow aisles; the capitals at the triumphal arch are decorated with the Asturian cord motif. The side portico was intended to serve as a covered walk or cloister; the strapwork capitals, arcaded windows and artistically sculpted *claustra* all show Mozarabic influence.

VITORIA ★ GASTEIZ (Álava) P

Michelin map **442** fold 7 — Pop 192 773

Vitoria, capital of the largest of the Basque provinces, lies at the centre of the **Llanada alavesa,** a vast cereal covered plateau closer by far in appearance to the plains of Castile than the green hills of the Cantabrian coast. The town has developed rapidly this century around the hill on which in 1181, Sancho the Wise, King of Navarre, founded a walled city. Today it is a city of business, trade and industry — food processing, chemicals, engineering and agricultural machinery manufacture. It is also the capital of the manufacturing of playing cards and is famous, since the 18C for its chocolate truffles. The modern quarters around the Calle Dato, provide a lively contrast, to the old town.

Among the local amenities are a river beach just beyond the northern outskirts of the town (Gamarra) and two vast reservoir lakes at Urrunaga and Ullívarri where there is fishing and a variety of water sports are offered.

The August Virgen Blanca festival is picturesque and includes a unique custom: everyone lights a cigar as the "angel" descends from the belfry of St Michael's.

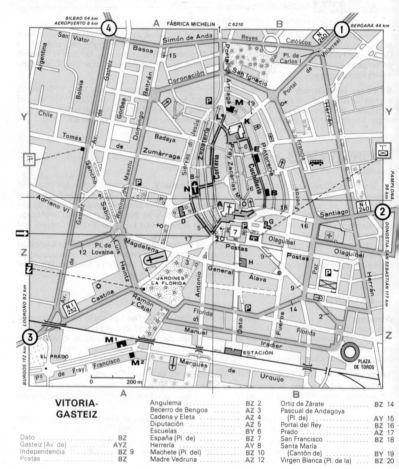

VITORIA-GASTEIZ

Dato	BZ	Angulema	BZ 2	Ortiz de Zárate	BZ 14
Gasteiz (Av. de)	AYZ	Becerro de Bengoa	AZ 3	Pascual de Andagoya (Pl. de)	AY 15
Independencia	BZ 9	Cadena y Eleta	AZ 4	Portal del Rey	BZ 16
Postas	BZ	Diputación	AZ 5	Prado	AZ 17
		Escuelas	BY 6	San Francisco	BZ 18
		España (Pl. de)	BZ 7	Santa María (Cantón de)	BY 19
		Herrería	AY 8	Virgen Blanca (Pl. de la)	BZ 20
		Machete (Pl. del)	BZ 10		
		Madre Vedruna	AZ 12		

■ THE OLD TOWN *time : 1 1/2 hours*

Seignorial houses with balconies and frontages bearing family coats of arms stand grouped round the cathedral, their doorways marking the concentric streets which intercommunicate by steps called after different trades.

Plaza de la Virgen Blanca (BZ 20). — The square, on which stands the Church of San Miguel, presents the classic view of Vitoria, of house fronts, each with one or more balconies, framing the massive monument at the square's centre which commemorates Wellington's decisive victory at the Battle of Vitoria on 21 June 1813, after which King Joseph and 55 000 of his men fled north of the Pyrenees. The square communicates with the nobly ordered 18C **Plaza de España** (BZ 7).

San Miguel (BZ A). — A jasper niche in the porch exterior of this church contains the polychrome statue in late Gothic style of the Virgen Blanca, patron of the city. Enter through the late 14C doorway. The tympanum illustrates the life of St Michael as does the 17C chancel altarpiece carved by Hernández (17C).

Plaza del Machete (BZ 10). — The square lies at the back of the **Arquillos,** a tall arcade which links the upper and lower towns. A niche at the east end of San Miguel Church formerly contained the *machete* or cutlass, on which the procurator general had to swear to uphold the town's privileges or *fueros*.

Cuchillería (Cutlery Street) (BY). — The **Casa del Cordón** (no 24 on the right) (BY B), which dates principally from the 16C, contains a room with a fine 13C Gothic ceiling. It is named after the Franciscan cord decoration round the pointed arch doorway. At no 58, there is the fine emblasoned façade of **Bendaña Palace** (BY E), constructed in the 15C and possessing a beautiful Renaissance staircase inside.

St Mary's Cathedral (BY K). — 14C. The north wall still has a fortified appearance. The west door is covered by Gothic vaulting in which the ribs radiate with sunburst effect from behind large statues. A polychrome Virgin and Child stands at the pier. The tympana over the 14C Gothic doorways illustrate the lives of the saints most venerated in Spain, namely Lawrence, Ildefonsus, James (right portal) and Nicholas and Peter (left portal).

Inside, in a chapel off the south aisle, there is a striking portrayal of the martyrdom of Saint Bartholomew. One of the pillar capitals between the nave and the south aisle shows a bullfighting scene — a carving unique in a church even in Spain! In the south transept are a Plateresque altarpiece in polychrome wood and a painting by the 17C artist, Carreño, of the Immaculate Conception; in the north arm, an interesting Descent from the Cross after the Van Dyck school and a polychrome stone tympanum from the original church. A decorative Plateresque funerary stone can be seen inlaid into the wall of a chapel near the entrance.

Correría (ABY). — In a street punctuated by bars, taverns and restaurants, the **Portalón** (BY L) stands out as a 15C building flourishing bold and restored to its original commercial style with old utensils much in evidence, also a stable, wagon, cellar and winepress.

Archaeological Museum★ (**Museo de Arqueología**) (BY M). — *Open 11am to 2pm and 5 to 7pm; closed Sunday and holiday afternoons and Monday all day.*

A pillar found at Zurbano, northeast of Vitoria, flanked by two columns clasped by weird human and animal forms and a funerary stele entwined by a vine, stand amidst Roman statuary at the museum's entrance.

On the 1st floor are Roman finds principally from Iruña *(see below)* although the contemporary **knight's stele★** (2nd floor) with highly stylised decoration, also from Iruña, is thought to be aboriginal. The Celtiberian finds from La Hoya and several dolmens, particularly that from Eguilaz, also make interesting displays.

Walk along the Correría and up steps to the right to the **Herrería** or Iron Foundry Street (AY 8).

San Pedro (AY N). — Contained on the church's Gothic **portal★** embrasures, are finely carved statues of the Apostles on bases depicting each one's martyrdom. The fate of St Peter appears on the upper register of the tympanum.

Found in the chancel are beautiful bronze recumbent funerary figures in the Plateresque style.

■ ADDITIONAL SIGHTS

Fine Arts Museum (AZ M¹). — *Open 11am to 2pm and 5 to 7pm; closed Saturday Sunday and holiday afternoons and Monday all day.*

On the first floor landing are interesting wood reliefs from Erenchun and two panels of a triptych by the Antwerp school; in the galleries to the left are a triptych by the Master of Ávila, a *Descent from the Cross* by a Flemish school painter, a series of five 16C reliquary busts influenced by the Rhenish school and notably, in the end galleries, paintings by Ribera of *St Peter* and *St Paul* and a graceful *Immaculate Conception* by Carreño. Ribera's painting of the **Crucifixion★**, formerly in the Diputación, is now held by the museum.

The scenes of the Journey to Calvary originally from Salinas, on the ground floor, are remarkably realistic.

Museum of Arms and Armour (**Museo Provincial de Armería**) (AZ M²). — *Same opening times as the Fine Arts Museum.*

Located in a modern building the diverse and interesting collection includes: prehistoric axes, a 19C pistol, 15 to 17C **armour** and even two Japanese suits of armour!

EXCURSIONS

Gaceo★ ; Salvatierra; Eguilaz. — *Leave Vitoria by ② on the town plan.*

Gaceo★. — Superb **Romanesque frescoes★** decorate the chancel of Gaceo church. The south wall shows hell in the form of a whale's gullet, the north, the life of the Virgin with the Crucifixion at the centre and Christ in Majesty above. On the roof are scenes from the life of Our Lord.

Salvatierra. — Cutting through this old town is a noble main street, fronted by houses with flower filled balconies supported on carved consoles and emblasoned with wonderful family crests.

Eguilaz. — A massive **dolmen** from the Basque country stands before the village. Other local finds are now in the Vitoria Archaeological Museum.

Estíbaliz Sanctuary. — *10km - 6 miles east. Leave Vitoria by ②, the N 1. Turn off early into the Estella road, C 132, and after 4km - 2 1/2 miles bear left (signpost).*

The cave sanctuary, supervised by the monks from a Benedictine monastery, is a popular pilgrimage with the Basques of Álava. From the 10C, in fact, the Estíbaliz Virgin has been brought into the chamber to preside over all sessions of the provincial assembly and judicature.

The building is in the transitional Romanesque style; inside, the capitals at the transept crossing are carved in relief in the Silos style *(p 244)*. The Romanesque statue of the Virgin has been restored.

Tour west of Vitoria. — *111km - 69 miles: Leave Vitoria by the Calle Tomás de Zumárraga.* **Mendoza Castle** *(to visit apply to the caretaker, whose house is nearby)*, a fortress with embrasures, a stout outer wall lacking battlements but flanked by four towers, soon comes into view. Now the property of the Dukes of Infantado and much restored, it contains a photographic record of the coats of arms of all the nobility of the province. The towers command an interesting view of the plateau.

The village possesses one of the few pilories *(picota)* still in existence in the region. It bears the armorial crests of the Mendoza, Castile and León and also a set of iron hooks.

Trespuentes. — Pass before the church to see in its attractive setting the originally Roman bridge of 13 arches, which spans the Zadorra. The hill on the far bank marks the outskirts of the town of **Iruña**, where numerous Roman finds have been made (Vitoria Archaeological Museum). A second, but less impressive, Roman bridge exists at Villadas, further south.

Follow the N1 for 1.5km - 1 mile. Turn right towards Pobes.

Salinas de Añana. — The saltpans rising in tiers up the hillside next to the village, produce a most unusual effect — the mineral has been precipitated from the waters of the Muera since Roman times.

The church contains a Flemish picture of the Annunciation with sensitively painted faces *(to visit ask the priest)*. At Easter all the salt makers walk in procession to the church.

Tuesta. — The Romanesque church, dating from the 13C, was remodelled in the 18C and has since been restored. *To visit ask the priest*. The doorway has a pointed arch and a decoration of archivolts and carved capitals, one of which shows a man killing a boar (left). Above there is a group of the Epiphany modelled in the round. The nave ends in an oven vaulted apse. Note the appealing naïve wood sculpture of St Sebastian *(north wall of the nave)*, the lovely 16C Virgin and the carved capitals.

Take the N 625 on the right. Once over the **Orduña Pass** (900m - 2 953ft), which is in Burgos Province, a beautiful **panorama★** opens up of the lush hollow in which Orduña town nestles; in the distance are Amurrio and the Basque mountains *(belvedere)*. The descent to the plain is far from direct, down a serpentine road.

Orduña (Vizcaya Province). — In Sta María Church, which stands in a street leading east out of the Plaza Mayor, there is a picturesque Flemish altarpiece dedicated to St Peter to be seen in the 3rd chapel off the south aisle, behind the grilles.

Return to Vitoria by way of Murguía.

Rioja Balcony★; Laguardia. — *45km - 28 miles south*. The **panorama★** from the Rioja balcony belvedere, south of the Herrera Pass (1 100m - 3 609ft), is incredibly extensive, particularly along the length of the Ebro Valley, flat, brown and almost arid in appearance apart from the winding silver thread of the river's own course. The view is particularly striking if you come to it, of course, from the north.

Laguardia. — You see the town immediately as it stands perched high and is still, in part, ringed by ramparts, towers and fortified gateways. The towns people, in the midst of these mediaeval surroundings, are actively concerned with the rapid development of the Rioja wine trade. Cellars open directly onto the narrow streets which in autumn are heady with the smell of grape marc.

The parish church of Sta María de los Reyes contains interesting polychrome sculptures. Beneath the modern porch is a massive doorway by the late Gothic school responsible for most of the church entrances in Vitoria at the end of the 14C. The Apostles in the embrasures are somewhat mannered and already decadent in style with over large but, nevertheless, expressive faces.

The central altarpiece, inside, is 17C.

YERMO (Cantabria)
Michelin map 442 fold 4

The Church of Sta María in Yermo is a delightful 12C Romanesque building of rose and gold stone. The west door, between billet-moulding decorated windows, has a pointed arch and a tympanum on which St George is vigorously slaying the dragon. The action is continued on the obverse, although the dragon, by this time, appears fatally wounded. The cornice modillions, like those at Cervatos *(p 122)*, display man's deadly sins in a most realistic fashion. Inside *(to visit ask at the house behind the church)* there are interesting capitals at the triumphal arch and statues from the original, 9C church.

ZUMAYA ZUMAIA (Guipúzcoa)
Michelin map 442 fold 7 — Pop 7 700

Zumaya lies below wooded hills at the mouth of the Urola and is both a fishing port and a seaside resort with two good beaches.

Villa Zuloaga. — *No 3, with the large gateway near the Santiago beach at the entrance to the town. Open 15 April to 15 September Thursdays, Fridays, Saturdays and Sundays 4 to 8pm; 100pts.*

The house is built on the site of an inn on the pilgrim way to Santiago de Compostela. It belonged to the painter, Ignacio Zuloaga (1870-1945) and since his death has been transformed into a museum.

Zuloaga, uninfluenced by his contemporaries, the Impressionists, loved brilliant colours and strong forms, and showed his love of his native land in an unvarying choice of realistic and popular themes.

His personal collection of paintings, also on show, included an El Greco, the *Vision of St John in the Apocalypse*, a Goya portrait of *General Palafox*, hero of Saragossa *(p 71)* and signed paintings by Zurbarán and Morales.

San Pedro. — The 15C church contains two remarkable triptychs in chapels off the aisles on either side of the nave. One is by a Flemish painter and shows the Journey to Calvary (south side), the other is of St Christopher and takes the form of a Flamboyant Gothic gilded low relief (north aisle).

Above the doors framing the high altar are delicately carved minute reliefs of the Descent from the Cross (right) and the Flagellation (left).

Join us in our never ending task of keeping up to date.

Send us your comments and suggestions, please.

**Michelin Tyre Public Limited Company
Tourism Department
Davy House - Lyon Road - HARROW - Middlesex HA1 2DQ.**

5 Extremadura

The region's name, a heritage from the Reconquest period, has a ring of isolation — "the land beyond the River Duero". Traditionally pastoral and far from the centres of Spanish life and economy, Extremadura is also separated geographically from the sea, to the south by mountains, to the west by foreign territory. Modern methods of stock raising and the development of high yield crops have, stoped the need to emigrate which since the Middle Ages had sent the men of the province to the ends of the earth.

The landscape. — Extremadura forms part of the Meseta, here a crystalline schist and granite Hercynian platform, levelled off at about 400m - 1300ft between the limestone Sierras de Gredos and the Peña de Francia to the north and the Sierra Morena to the south. The austere landscape of vast plateaux affords grazing in winter for sheep but lies deserted all summer when the beasts are driven into the hills. Cork provides a subsidiary crop. Pig keeping is traditional — Montánchez sausages are known all over Spain and more than one Extremaduran far from home, has been called a *choricero* or sausage-maker.

The population is concentrated along the river courses, particularly the Alagón and the Guadiana, where alluvial soil and irrigation enable a variety of crops to be grown: tobacco, cotton, wheat and market-gardening. The **Tierra de Barros,** the rich and fertile red clay area around Almendralejo, is one of Spain's major cereal and vine regions.

The climate generally is not extreme, although, lacking the modifying influence of the Atlantic, the summers can be baking hot.

The age of the great adventurers. — Nearly all the *conquistadores* were sons of Extremadura: **Cortés** *(p 137)* was born in Medellín, **Pizarro** and **Orellana** *(p 139)* in Trujillo, **Balboa** *(p 137)* in Jerez de los Caballeros, **Pedro de Valdivia** (founder of Santiago, Chile in 1541) and **Hernando de Soto** in the province of Badajoz. They and their less famous fellows who sailed to the Americas, were bowing to economic necessity but, to an even greater extent, following a longstanding tradition. Throughout the 13C a warlike and courageous nobility had held the breach and fought the Wars of the Reconquest — the military orders of Alcántara and Santiago were both founded in this period in the province, inspiring a deep religious fervour in the warlike knights wherever they might be fighting including such other parts of Spain as Granada where they particularly distinguished themselves in the siege.

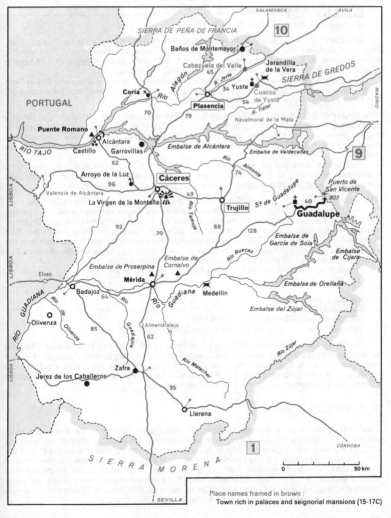

Place names framed in brown :
Town rich in palaces and seignorial mansions (15-17C)

Commerce was disdained and left to the people of the north. The knights began to look for wars abroad: Italy first, then the "Indies" so rich in promise compared to 15C Extremadura which had insufficient food even for its own sparse population. Immense domains remained uncultivated except for sheep grazing the land, where the all powerful guild of shepherds of transhumant stock, the *Mesta*, had seized control of the land. From nearby Portugal at this time too, came tales of legendary kingdoms and fabulous riches to inspire young adventurers, noble and commoner alike, to sail the oceans. So proud *hidalgos* set out: many found a hardship even worse than that they had left behind; many more died; but a few returned and of that few some were rich as princes... Extremadura, then, lost much of its young manhood, but gained from those who returned the lovely mansions which still give charm and character to its old towns and cities.

Spain's Mystical Painters. — Luis de Morales, "the Divine" (*c* 1509 - 1586), studied in Seville, but worked most of his life in Extremadura and Portugal. Isolation made his style somewhat stiff and mannered. However, in favourite compositions such as the *Virgin and Child, Pietà* and *Ecce Homo,* he portrayed deep but restrained emotion in a way which perfectly conveys Spanish and Portuguese mystical belief. The inner purity of the resigned expressions of his figures is deeply moving.

Francisco Zurbarán (1598-1664), born at Fuente de Cantos, studied in Seville. He was influenced by Ribera, but had a vigorous and at the same time, serene style which was original. The **painter of religious** is best known for his monastic portraits executed at the request of such orders as the Carthusians of Jerez and the Hieronymites of Guadalupe. The figures, robust inside their bulky habits, have a calm strength; the serious and reserved faces appear lit from within; the characters seem a compromise, perhaps like his own, descending as he did from a Basque father and Extremaduran mother. His palette found as full a scope in the white habits and serious spiritual visages as it did in the brilliantly coloured clothes and delicate flesh tints of the young girl saints in the pictures now in the Seville Fine Arts Museum *(p 58)*.

The Badajoz Plan. — The Badajoz Plan of 1952 was Spain's first regional development plan. It set out to control the flow of the Guadiana by a series of dams - the Cíjara, García de Sola, Orellana and Zújar — and thus conserve some 3 800 million cubic metres of water - 835 909 million gallons; to irrigate 130 000ha - 500sq miles of countryside; encourage afforestation; develop high yield crops such as maize, sunflowers, market gardening and animal foodstuffs; attract 9 000 peasants to the area and establish them on 4 to 5ha - 10 to 12 acre smallholdings in their own farmhouses or in new villages and, finally, to construct power stations to provide energy for new food processing factories. How the landscape and way of life of the rural community have been transformed since the plan has been implemented can be seen as you travel the N V from Badajoz to Mérida.

ALCÁNTARA (Cáceres)

Michelin map **447** fold 11 — Pop 2 317

In a countryside of ancient shale rocks through which the River Tagus has cut a course, Alcántara watches still over the old bridge which once brought it renown and from which it took its name: Al Kantara is the Arabic for bridge. The castle of the Knights of Alcántara is now in ruins and not much more remains of their 16C monastery.

In 1580 the then Duke of Alba, in a little known skirmish, routed Portuguese forces from the ravines around Alcántara, thus helping to establish Philip II of Spain and his successors firmly for a while on the throne of Portugal (1580-1640).

The Order of Alcántara. — The Knights of St Julián Pereiro, after successfully defending Alcántara fortress against attack by the Moors in 1218 changed the name of their order to that of the town. Like the other **great orders of chivalry** in Spain — Calatrava, Santiago and Montesa - the Order of Alcántara was thus created to free the country from the Moors in the 12C.

Each order, founded as a military unit under the command of a master, lived in a community according to the Cistercian rule, always prepared for combat and capable of withstanding long sieges in their fortresses. They played a major role in the Reconquest.

The Roman Bridge★. — *2km - 1 mile northwest of Alcántara on the road to Portugal.*
The magnificent construction was thrown across the Tagus slightly below the juncture with the Río Alagón, by the Romans in the time of the Emperor Trajan in 106 AD. Drystone masonry keeps poised the massive granite blocks which make up its 194m length and 70m high central arch - 637 and 230ft. Man has wreaked more damage than floodwaters over the years so that the bridge has had to be repaired many times on its ancient foundations. The small temple at one end and central triumphal arch are both Roman.
The dam upstream is part of the Tagus River development plan.

BADAJOZ P

Michelin map **447** fold 20 — Pop 114 361
See town plan in the current Michelin Red Guide España Portugal

Badajoz is the capital of Spain's largest province which is 21 757 km^2 in area - 8400sq miles. Situated on the left bank of the Guadiana near the border with Portugal, it was a battleground for so long that only now, as a result of the Guadiana Valley development scheme, is it emerging economically. Souvenirs of its warrior past remain in the Moorish fortress, narrow mediaeval streets and massive ramparts.

HISTORICAL NOTES

The tribulations of a frontier town. — Badajoz, in Roman times a modest town dependent on Mérida, capital of the province of Lusitania, was itself promoted capital in the 11C, of the Moorish kingdom or *taifa (p 38)* which reached to the Atlantic. At the end of the 16C the city had become a key position in every war engulfing the peninsula: the Wars of Succession between Spain and Portugal, the European Wars of Succession, the Spanish War of Independence or Peninsular War, when both enemy troops (under Soult) and allies (under Wellington) besieged, attacked, pillaged the town and enacted bloody reprisals — a sorry tradition maintained even in the Civil War of 1938-39.

Manuel Godoy. — **Manuel Godoy Álvarez de Faria** (1767-1851), son of a provincial nobleman, left his family at 17, for Madrid where he enlisted in the Guards. He rapidly took the fancy of Queen María Luisa who assisted him to a meteoric career in politics: by 1792, at 25, he was prime minister. The Spanish Grandees and more particularly the heir to the throne, Prince Ferdinand VII, detested the upstart intriguer; at court the whisper went that Godoy's smile was worth more than Charles IV's promise and the common people, seeing how his wellwishing neutrality enabled French troops to make free everywhere, accused him of being in Napoleon's pay. After the Aranjuez uprising *(p 191)*, when his house was sacked and he was maltreated personally by the mob, Godoy followed the royal family into exile at Bayonne where he performed his last service to Charles IV by drawing up the act of abdication under which power was handed over to the Emperor Napoleon. He died, unknown, in Paris in 1851.

■ **SIGHTS** *time: 3/4 hour*

If possible approach Badajoz from the north so as to be able to fully appreciate the fortified site and the majestic entrance afforded by the alignment of the **Palmas Bridge,** a Herreran style granite structure, and the 16C crenellated **gateway** of the same name. The fortress ruins are accessible by car — gardens have been planted within the yellow ochre stone walls.

Driving in the centre of the town is difficult as the streets are narrow.

Cathedral. — The cathedral, built in the 13C in the Gothic style and considerably remodelled at the Renaissance, is consequently full of contrasts: it has a fortress type tower and a delicate Plateresque decoration of friezes and window surrounds.

Inside, at the centre of the nave and masking the general view, is an impressive raised chancel for which the stalls were carved in 1557.

In the sacristy to the right of the sanctuary hang six fine, though faded, 17C Flemish tapestries.

BAÑOS DE MONTEMAYOR (Cáceres)

Michelin map **447** fold 13 — Pop 790

Even in the time of Trajan and Hadrian, it was customary when riding along the Vía Plata from Salamanca to Mérida, to stop and take the waters at Baños de Montemayor. The town on the ledge dividing the Sierras de Gredos *(p 233)* and Peña de Francia *(p 223)*, has a dry and sunny climate and with the sulphurous waters still gushing at 42 ºC - 105 ºF remains a spa resort, treating respiratory illness and skin disease.

Houses in the old part of the town have the wooden balconies typical of Spain's *sierra* regions.

For historical notes on the country see pp 9-10.

CÁCERES ★★

Michelin map **447** fold 21 — Pop 71 852

Within its mediaeval walls, Cáceres encloses a group of Gothic and Renaissance seignorial mansions which, in their identity and historic atmosphere, have no equal in all Spain. It was in this city, still threatened by the Moors, that in 1170 the military Order of Santiago was founded and, not long after, charged with safeguarding pilgrims on their way to Santiago de Compostela.

Cáceres is now the capital of an agricultural province which is expanding its cereal acreage and increasing its herds of cattle and swine and flocks of sheep. The local livestock market fairs at the end of May and in September are the biggest in Extremadura.

■ **OLD CÁCERES ★★ (Cáceres Viejo)** *time: 1 hour*

Route marked on the detailed plan. An evening visit (groups only) is highly recommended.
Once inside the walls flanked by towers, now heavily restored, you are in a quarter bathed in dreams of past glories. No ostentation, no decorative flourishes demean the appearance of these residences of the noblemen of the 15 and 16C, for the mansions were built in the semblance of their owners, the Ulloas, the Ovandos and the Saavedras, proud warriors all, who in their fight against the infidel — Moor or American Indian — won more in prestige than in wealth. The long golden brown walls are usually of rough stone, minimally decorated with a narrow fillet around the windows or a sculptured cornice. All, however, in a place of pride, bear a coat of arms. The fortified towers which once stood guard over the mansions and proclaimed their owners' self esteem and power were lopped on the command of Isabel the Catholic in 1477.

Pass beneath the **Star Arch (Arco de la Estrella)** (A **A**) to follow a narrow path at the foot of the ramparts *(adarve)* incorporated long ago into the abutting houses. The **Golfines Upper Palace (Palacio de los Golfines de Arriba)** (A **B**) and the mansion opposite have attractive *patios*.

Walk down the typical Calle Ancha to see the **Commander of Alcuescar's House** (A **E**) which has a tall Gothic tower, finely carved decoration surrounding the windows and an unusual corner balcony.

St Matthew's (San Mateo) (A **F**). — The church's high nave, begun in the 14C, was abutted in the 16C, in accordance with the practice of the time, by a *coro alto* resting on a stout arcade with basket vaulting. The interior is bare except for the baroque altarpiece and chapels where the tombs of members of noble families bear decorative heraldic devices.

Continuing round the church by the north wall you come, in succession, on two interesting 15C towers both of which have lost their battlements but retained unusual parapets — they are respectively the **Silver Tower (Torre de la Plata)** (A **K**) and the **Sun House (Casa del Sol)** (A **L**) which owes its name to the elegant crest of the Solís family boldly carved over the arch.

CÁCERES

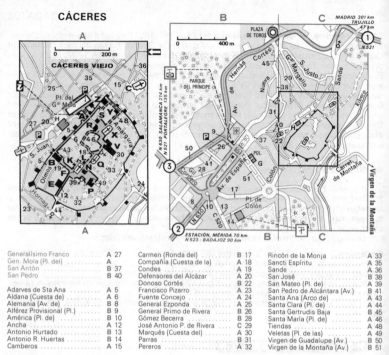

Storks' House (Casa de las Cigüeñas) (**A N**). — *Not open to the public.* The house, now occupied by the military, proudly sports a battlemented tower - the only one to escape the late 15C lopping. It also has a *patio*, decorated with low arches resting on dainty pillars, and a well with a wrought iron wellhead.

The Weather Vane House (Casa de las Veletas) (**A P**). — *Open 10am to 1.30pm and 5 to 7pm (4 to 6pm 1 October to 31 March); closed Monday and Tuesday afternoons and all day Sundays and holidays; 200pts.*

The mansion was built over an 11C **Arabic cistern**, once part of the *alcázar* and still fed by a trickling stream of water from the roof and sloping square outside. It is covered by five horseshoe shaped arches supported on granite capitals with carving which is unfortunately scarcely noticeable. The plain façade, emblasoned with baroque family crests, precedes a small **provincial museum** of archaeology and ethnology.

Pass before the imposing 18C Jesuit College (**A Q**) to bear left briefly into the silent and austere **Cuesta de Aldana.**

Plaza Santa María★ (**A 46**). — This elongated, irregularly shaped square forms the monumental heart of the old city; rising on all sides are attractive golden ochre façades, some with noble lines.

The front of the **Mayoralgo Palace** (**A R**) now restored, has elegant paired windows; the **Bishop's Palace** (**A S**) has a 16C bossaged doorway with, medallions of the Old and New Worlds on either side, (left and right respectively) which are interesting as a rough indication of the world as it was known at this period.

Lower Golfines Palace★ (Palacio de los Golfines de Abajo) (**A V**). — This rich residence, twice honoured by visits by the Catholic Monarchs, has a rough stone façade, Gothic in style with the Mudejar traits characteristic of civil architecture of the late 15C. The paired window derives from the Moorish *ajimez,* while the fillet, delicately framing the two windows and the door, recalls the *alfiz (p 16).*

To lighten the face, a Plateresque frieze with winged griffons was added to the top of the central area in the 16C; medallions and the Golfines coat of arms — a *fleur-de-lys* and a tower — complete the decoration.

Santa María (**A X**). — This nobly styled church, completed in the 16C, serves as the city cathedral. The three Gothic aisles of almost equal height, have lierne and tierceron vaulting from which the ribs descend into slender columns engaged around the main pillars. At the high altar (16C), the carved retable, which is dark and difficult to see but worth the effort, has particularly elegantly draped figures.

Continue along the Calle de las Tiendas, which is full of character and ends at the foot of the **Armourers' Tower (Torre de los Espaderos)** (**A Y**). Although brutally truncated like all the others at the end of the 15C, it retains impressive battlements which give some idea of the scale of the original construction. At the corner turn left and follow the street at the foot of the ramparts back to the Arco de la Estrella.

As you pass the **Toledo-Moctezuma Mansion** (**A Z**), look at the unusual, domed, flanking tower, with the upper part built of brick. The mansion *(under restoration)* was erected by one of the town's most famous sons, Juan Cano de Saavedra, with the fabulous dowry brought him by his wife, none other than the Aztec princess, Montezuma's daughter (Spanish: Moctezuma).

■ ADDITIONAL SIGHT

St James' (Santiago) (**A C**). — *Closed temporarily, restoration in progress.*

This Gothic church (rebuilt in 16C), by tradition the birthplace of the Order of the Knights of St James, is of particular interest for its **altarpiece** carved by Alonso Berruguete in 1557. Scenes of the life of Christ surround a vigorous, finely portrayed St James Matamore or Slayer of the Moors *(p 152).* The high reliefs have the narrow faces and elongated bodies characteristic of the great Valladolid sculptor.

EXCURSIONS

The Mountain Virgin (Virgen de la Montaña). — *3km - 2 miles east.* A 17C sanctuary, built on a hill cloaked in olive trees, shelters the famous statuette which is the goal of a picturesque *romería* held on the first Sunday in May.

From the esplanade, overshadowed by a monumental figure of Christ, there is a **view★** across the Extremadura plain with, in the foreground, old Cáceres, clearly divided into quarters, and below, new Cáceres spreading out westwards.

Garrovillas. — *36km - 22 miles northwest along the N 630.* In this typical Extremadura town, the Plaza Mayor is lined by arcades in which, in a delightful artless way, fantasy has run rife with every pillar askew!

Arroyo de la Luz. — *20km - 12 miles west. To find the church of Asunción, take a bearing on the tower and proceed always along the widest street.* The Gothic nave of this 15 - 16C church has recently been restored.

The altarpiece is worth looking at for the 16 **pictures★** and 4 medallions which compose it and which were, in fact painted on the spot by the Divine Morales *(p 132)* between 1560 and 1563. The complete, almost multiple work by this artist whose paintings are so scattered, provides, therefore, an opportunity to appreciate more fully than usual his gentle and noble style.

CORIA ★ (Cáceres)
Michelin map **447** fold 12 — Pop 10 361

Coria, at the centre of the tobacco region, overlooks the Alagón Valley here carpeted with olive and oak trees. The city, once the Roman township of Caurium, still contains walls and gateways rebuilt in the Middle Ages on the ancient foundations.

Cathedral★. — The cathedral, a Gothic edifice embellished in the 16C with an elegant Plateresque decoration, was, later, crowned with a baroque tower and given a sculptured frieze to further emphasise the height of its walls.

Inside, the single tall aisle has a vaulting decorated with lierne and tierceron ribs which are typical of the region. Note, in the *coro,* the outstanding wrought iron grilles and Gothic stalls. Massive numbered stones, laid as a pavement, cover burial vaults - those over occupied vaults are carved with family crests.

GUADALUPE ★★ (Cáceres)
Michelin map **447** fold 23 — Pop 2 765

Suddenly before you as the road climbs, there is Guadalupe. At the centre of this perfect **picture★** is the deep ochre coloured stone monastery, bristling with battlements and turrets. Below, at the feet of its austere ramparts, clusters the minute old village.

The **village★** is attractively picturesque at close quarters, particularly in spring when flowers bring colour to the balconies of the whitewashed houses closely lining the narrow, twisting alleys; in summer these are well shaded by the steeply pitched brown tile roofs. The traditional craft of copper smelting is still very much alive.

Patron of "All the Spains". — The first sanctuary is believed to have been erected following the discovery of a miraculous Virgin by a cowherd in 1300. Alfonso XI, having invoked this Virgin of Guadalupe, as she was known, shortly before his victory over the Moors at the **Battle of Salado** (24 October 1340) - as a result of which the Moroccans never again attempted a major invasion - had built a grandiose monastery for the Hieronymites. The pilgrimage centre, richly endowed by rulers and deeply venerated by the people, exercised a great influence in the 16 and 17C when it became a famous area of craftsmanship - embroidery, gold and silversmithing, illumination - and more importantly, situated as it was at the heart of the Kingdom of the Conquistadores, the symbol of the **Hispanidad** - that community of language and civilisation which links the Spanish of the Old and New Worlds. Documents authorising the expedition which discovered America were signed here; Christopher Columbus named a West Indian island after the shrine; the first American Indians converted to Christianity were brought to the church for baptism; Christians freed from slavery came in pilgrimage and left their chains as votive offerings...

Solemn processions are held on 12 October, celebrated as the day of the Hispanidad *(p 49).*

■ THE MONASTERY ★★ *time: 1 1/4 hours*

Guided tours 9.30am to 1pm and 3.30 to 6.30pm; 100pts.

The monastery, abandoned in 1835, was taken over by Franciscans in 1908 and restored.

The kernel of the building dates from the Gothic period, late 14 - early 15C, but with rich donations, numerous additions were made in the 16, 17 and 18C. If the resulting plan appears confused, it is because the monks had to crowd ever more buildings within the perimeter. The monastery contains artistic treasures of great value.

Façade. — 15C. The façade, golden in colour, exuberant in its Flamboyant Gothic decoration, overlooks a picturesque square from the top of a flight of steps. It is confined between two tall, crenellated towers of rough stone like the sombre defensive walls on either side. Moorish influence, characteristic of Mudejar Gothic *(p 14),* can be seen in the exaggeratedly sinuous ornament in imitation of Moorish plasterwork. Bronze reliefs on the 15C doors illustrate scenes from the lives of the Virgin and Christ.

Church. — 14C. The church was one of the first of the monastery buildings to be erected but in the 18C arbitrary additions were made such as the pierced balustrade above the nave to take votive lamps in honour of the Virgin. An intricate iron grille wrought at the beginning of the 16C by two famous Valladolid ironsmiths, closes the sanctuary which is ornamented with a large Classically ordered retable carved by the two 17C sculptors, Giraldo de Merlo and Jorge Manuel Theotocopuli, son of El Greco.

GUADALUPE★★

Mudejar Cloister. — 15C. The monastery cloister is of remarkable size with two storeys of horseshoe shaped arches and a **lavabo★** constructed and faced in the original brick and multicoloured tiles. In the former refectory, now an **Embroidery Museum★★** (Museo de Bordados), are ancient copes and altarfronts, richly decorated and finely stitched in the local tradition which goes back to the 14C.

Chapterhouse (Sala Capitular). — Opening onto the delightful 15C cloister, the chamber contains mediaeval antiphonaries and richly illuminated books of hours, a 16C triptych by the Flemish school (possibly Isenbrandt or Benson) of the Adoration of the Magi and, in a case apart, the series of small **paintings★** by Zurbarán which originally adorned the predella of the sacristy altarpiece.

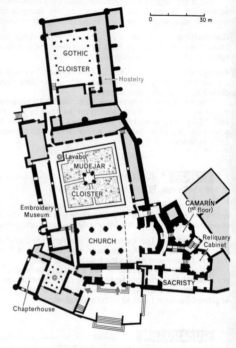

Sacristy★★ (Sacristía). — 17C. The sacristy is a magnificently successful combination of Classical style architecture and highly ornate baroque decoration. The unexpected harmony and rich colouring set off to perfection Zurbarán's well known series of **paintings★★** in his serene yet forceful style, executed between 1638 and 1647, of the monastery's most illustrious priors.

Camarín★. — 18C. The chapel-like room where the Virgin of Guadalupe rests is known as the "Camarín" (1). Riches of every description abound: jasper, gilded stucco and marble and precious wood marquetry frames for nine canvases by the Neapolitan artist, Luca Giordano (1632-1705). The Virgin herself sits on a modern enamelwork throne (1953), a small figure carved in now darkened oak, almost obscured beneath a richly embroidered veil and mantle. The sumptuous crown, worn only in solemn processions, may be seen in the Reliquary Cabinet (Relicario).

Gothic Cloister (Claustro gótico). — *In the hostelry; admission free.* The cloister was built in the 16C in an elegant Flamboyant Gothic style to serve as a dispensary for the four hospitals then in the monastery's care.

EXCURSION

San Vicente Pass (Puerto de San Vicente). — *40km - 25 miles.* The **road★** to the pass lies across the Las Villuercas mountain ranges. During the climb *(8km - 5 miles)* beyond the Guadarranque Valley, there are wonderful **views★** of green mountain ranges, their jagged crests aligned like the waves of the sea in the wild, moorland landscape.

The San Vicente Pass opens the way across the Altamira Sierra to the Meseta where the horizontal lines of the tableland are broken only by the far away heights surrounding Toledo.

Respect the life of the countryside
Go carefully on country roads
Protect wildlife, plants and trees.

JARANDILLA DE LA VERA (Cáceres)

Michelin map **447** fold 13 — Pop 3 144

Jarandilla occupies a pleasantly wooded site overlooking the fertile Vera plain, now largely given over to growing tobacco and red peppers, which are dried and ground locally in the town.

The old feudal **castle** (15C) has been converted into a *parador.* In 1556 its then owner, the Count of Oropesa, opened its door to the Emperor Charles V who remained his guest for three months while the palace apartments were being completed at Yuste.

■ YUSTE MONASTERY

12km - 7 1/2 miles southwest. Guided tours (time: 1/2 hour) 9.30am to 1pm (1.30pm Sundays and holidays) and 3.30 to 6.30pm (3 to 6pm in winter). Sundays and holidays closed between noon and 1pm; 75pts.

In 1556, when **Charles V** had grown weary of power, he abdicated and retired to this modest Hieronymite monastery. Even after 400 years the serene atmosphere, particularly of the surrounding countryside, makes one understand why the great emperor chose this retreat in which to pass his last years. (He died on 21 September 1558).

The monastery which was devastated during the War of Independence, has been partially restored. Charles V's small palace is open and one sees the dining hall, the royal bedroom built to adjoin the chapel so that the emperor could hear mass without having to rise, the Gothic church with fine panelling and woodwork in the chancel and, lastly, the two cloisters, one Gothic, the other Plateresque.

JEREZ DE LOS CABALLEROS (Badajoz)
Michelin map 447 fold 29 — Pop 10 102

Jerez stands proudly in a fortified position on a hillside, its exuberantly baroque decorated belfries and towers pointing to the sky. On the summit is the even more ornate San Bartolomé, façade and belfry faced with painted stucco, glass paste mosaics and *azulejos*.

The town's name, tradition and atmosphere stem from the Knights Templar — Caballeros del Temple — to whom the town was given by Alfonso IX of León on its recapture from the Moors in 1230. It is also the birthplace of the *conquistador,* **Vasco Núñez de Balboa** (1475-1517) who crossed the Darien Isthmus (now Panama) and in 1513 discovered the Southern Sea (the Pacific Ocean).

MEDELLÍN (Badajoz)
Michelin map 447 fold 22 — 8km - 5 miles west of Don Benito — Pop 2 468

Medellín Castle, commanding its hilltop since the Middle Ages, and the 17C bridge, over the Guadiana River, with its statue of the *conquistador,* Hernán Cortés, will be your first landmark.

Cortés, who was born in 1485, was the first Spanish explorer to dream of colonising the Americas. Until then lands had been conquered but never settled; their gold, silver and minerals had been exploited, their products bartered. He was determined to conquer the Aztec Empire and, on disembarking in Mexico in 1519 gained a foothold, took the title *poblador* (empire builder) and solemnly burned his eleven boats. By 1521 he had vanquished Montezuma and his successor and installed himself in the Aztec capital, Mexico City. Charles V heaped him with honours but gave him no power. He discovered Lower California (1536) before returning to Spain where he died, forgotten, in 1547.

MÉRIDA ★ (Badajoz)
Michelin map 447 fold 21 — Pop 41 783

In 25 BC the Roman governor of Augustus founded, in this uncolonised landscape, the township of **Emerita Augusta**. It was well situated on the Guadiana River and at the junction of major Roman roads between Salamanca and Seville, Toledo and Lisbon, and was soon promoted capital of Lusitania.

The Romans lavished upon it temples, a theatre, an arena and even a 400m - 437yd racecourse *(circo),* now overgrown. Two Roman bridges still span the rivers Albarregas and Guadiana where an adjoining quay was also constructed. Water for the colony was brought by means of two **aqueducts** (ABY), the San Lázaro and Los Milagros, of which a few elegant brick and stone arches remain. From the aqueducts the water was fed into two artificial lakes, the Cornalvo and Proserpina, north of the town.

■ **THE ROMAN MONUMENTS** *time: 1 1/2 hours*

Leave the car on the esplanade in front of the theatre.
Open 9am to 8.30pm (6pm 1 October to 31 March); 150pts.

Theatre ★★ **(Teatro Romano)** (BZ). — The theatre was built by Agrippa, Augustus' son-in-law in 24 BC, after the great theatres in Rome. A semicircle of stone tiers afforded seating for 6 000, the front row being reserved for high dignitaries; a pit held the chorus or crowd players; a high stage wall was decorated during Hadrian's reign (2C AD) with a covered colonnade and statues. Behind the stage, overlooking the gardens is a portico where the audience could walk during intervals. Drystone construction only, secures the great blocks of granite (seen in the vaulting of the passageways which lead to the tiers).

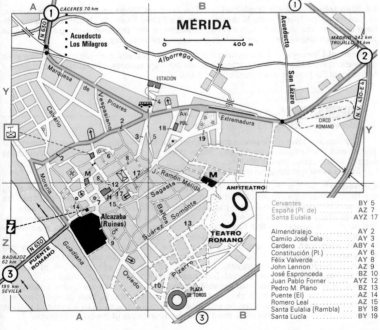

MÉRIDA★

Arena★ (Anfiteatro) (BZ). — The arena, which also dates from the 1C BC held, it is estimated, 14 000 spectators for the chariot races run round its course and the naumachia or mimic sea battles performed when the amphitheatre had been especially flooded. The steps to the audience seats and the *vomitoria,* the great covered passageways through which the crowd left, can still be seen but apart from those reconstituted on either side of the east *vomitorium* (right coming from the theatre), the tiers have disappeared. Round the chariot course is a wall crowned by a cornice which protected the front row of spectators — usually notables — from wild beasts when there were gladiatorial contests. The open ditch in the centre presumably contained arena machinery and workshops.

Patrician Villa (Casa romana del Anfiteatro). — *Below the arena.* Of this rich villa, built in the 1C AD with a peristyle and atrium, only the pavements and bases of the walls with traces of painted decoration, remain. Part of the piping, which brought water from the San Lázaro aqueduct to the villa's private baths, is also still visible.

The pavements and **mosaics** are in remarkably good condition, those in the passages clearly showing intricate geometrical motifs, those in the living rooms the same theme more fancifully executed. There is also a beautiful mosaic, called *Autumn,* depicting grape treading.

National Museum of Roman Art (BYZ **M**). — *Open 10am to 2pm and 4 to 6pm; closed Sunday and holiday afternoons and all day Monday; 200pts.*

The exhibits displayed on the three floors of this modern building are Roman sculpture, mosaics, coins, pottery, bronze objects and glassware. Note in particular the sculptures which come from the *forum* and theatre.

■ ADDITIONAL SIGHT

Alcazaba (AZ). — *Open 8am to 1pm and 4 to 7pm; October to March 9am to 1pm and 3 to 6pm; closed Sunday and holiday afternoons; 75pts.*

The Moors built this fortress in the 9C to defend the 792m - 866yd **Roman bridge★** across the islet strewn Guadiana River. Inside the walls is a most interesting cistern dug to the same depth as the bed of the river from which the tank was kept filled by infiltration. For the decoration of their own particular building the Moors took Corinthian capitals and delicately sculptured Visigothic marble friezes from former buildings or ruins; they vaulted the stairway in the Roman manner with great blocks of granite from the nearby theatre.

OLIVENZA (Badajoz)

Michelin map **447** fold 19 — Pop 9 837

Five centuries as a Portuguese town have left their mark in atmosphere, appearance and architecture on Olivenza.

It is one of the few places in Spain where the **Manueline style** can be seen — that specifically Portuguese architecture of the early 16C, contemporary with the reign of King Manuel (1495-1521). Marking the transition from Gothic to Renaissance this style brought to late Gothic, decorative features which were at the same time Renaissance, Moorish and maritime (sailors knots, ropes, anchors, scales, globes and armillary spheres).

The War of Oranges. — At the end of the 13C, Olivenza was given in dowry to King Denis of Portugal. In 1801 it was ceded to Spain to avert the Alentejo invasion, begun by Godoy's troops *(p 133),* becoming a major conflict between the two nations. The skirmish, the prelude to the bloody battles fought over the same ground in 1811 by Wellington and Soult, left no other souvenir than the story of Godoy's futile gesture of sending oranges to Queen María Luisa from trees at the foot of the Elvas ramparts *(see Michelin Green Guide Portugal - English edition).*

Castle. — The castle was constructed in the early 14C during the reign of King Denis.

St Magdalene's (Santa Magdalena). — The brothers Diego and Francisco de Arruda, architects of the Hieronymite Monastery and the Belem Tower in Lisbon, are believed to have designed the church's Manueline nave. The lierne and tierceron vaulting supported on twisted pillars clearly dominates the baroque sanctuary by its very elegance.

Municipal Library. — The doorway is a delightfully graceful example of Manueline style decoration: included in the adornment are two armillary spheres, symbol of the discoveries of the great Portuguese navigators of the 15 and 16C.

PLASENCIA ★ (Cáceres)

Michelin map **447** fold 13 — Pop 32 178

The regional town of Plasencia stands on a hill at the meeting point of central limestone *sierras* and the Extremaduran plateau. Below flows the River Jerte, circling the mountains rugged with massive granite boulders.

Storks season in the town from February to July.

Cathedral★. — The church, begun in the 13C, had its east end removed and replaced at the Renaissance by a chevet of bold architectural design. Presently the nave and apse are separated by a wall and serve as the parish Church of St Mary and cathedral respectively.

Enter the cathedral by the north door which has a typically Plateresque appearance. Inside, the tall pillars, the fine ribs extending into network vaulting, illustrate the mastery of the famous architects responsible: Juan de Álava, Diego de Siloé, Covarrubias.

The **altarpiece★** is decorated with statues by the 17C sculptor Gregorio Fernández; the **choirstalls★** were carved in 1520 by Rodrigo Alemán — look on the backs and misericords of the lower row for scenes, on the right, from the Old Testament, and on the left, of everyday life: hairdressing, an old-style *corrida* (2nd misericord left of the central canopy).

A door in the south aisle, near the stalls, opens onto the part of the Gothic building still containing older, Romanesque elements. There are cloisters with finely carved capitals, a chapterhouse in which the dome on squinches is disguised outside by a pyramid shaped, round tile covered belfry, and lastly there is the shortened nave of the original church.

Old Quarter. — The streets around the cathedral and the Plaza Mayor are interestingly lined by noble façades and houses with wrought iron balconies.

Start from the Cathedral Square and leaving on your right the **Deanery (Casa del Deán)** with its unusual corner window and balcony, make for the Gothic **St Nicholas' Church,** facing a mansion with a beautiful façade. Continue straight ahead to the **Mirabel Palace** *(visit possible)* which is flanked by a massive tower. A passage beneath the palace, from which you get a view to the right of a majestic two tier *patio,* leads to the **Calle Sancho Polo** and the more popular quarter near the ramparts where there are stepped alleys, white painted houses and washing hanging from the windows — a scene typical in fact of villages further south. Turn right for the **Plaza Mayor,** a square surrounded by porticoed but otherwise dissimilar buildings, which is the bustling town centre.

*The **Maps, Red Guides** and **Green Guides***
are complementary publications.
Use them together.

TRUJILLO ★ (Cáceres)

Michelin map 🔢 fold 22 — Pop 9 445

The modern town gives little idea of the originality and charm of the old town, built on a granite ledge higher up the hillside. This was hastily fortified by the Moors in the 13C against attack by the Christians and, as the centuries passed, had superimposed on its Arabic appearance in the 16 and 17C, noble mansions built by the *Indianos (p 103).*

The nursery of the Conquistadores. — "Twenty American nations", it is said, "were conceived in Trujillo". Accurate or not, it is certainly true that the city can claim to have given its name to three cities in Latin America and fathered numbers of conquerors and colonisers of the New World: **Francisco de Orellana** who left in 1542 to explore the legendary country of the Amazons; **Diego García de Paredes,** nicknamed on account of his Herculean strength, the Samson of Extremadura, and most famous and fabulous of all, **Francisco Pizarro** (1475-1541), the conqueror of Peru. This swineherd, who married an Inca princess, followed what had been Cortés' policy in Mexico *(p 137)* of seizing and executing the ruler, in this case the Emperor Atahualpa, plundering his riches and occupying his capital, Cuzco (1533). The early discovery of the Potosí silver mines made Peru the most important colony in the Spanish Empire but an implacable rivalry between Pizarro and his companion in arms, Almagro, brought the death first of Almagro in 1538 and then of Pizarro, murdered amidst untold riches in his own palace. Rivalries notwithstanding, the conquest of Peru brought Spain precious metals and jewels by the ton, thus introducing a totally new element in the economy of Europe at the end of the 16C.

■ SIGHTS *time: 1 1/2 hours*

The old quarter of Trujillo is less austere than Cáceres *(p 133),* the mansions generally having been built later in the 16 and 17C, and decorated with arcades, loggias and corner windows. The widespread use of whitewash on house fronts and the more steeply inclined narrow streets evoke a countrified atmosphere. Those visiting Trujillo in late spring or at any time throughout the summer will hear the flapping wings and see the outline of many a high perched stork.

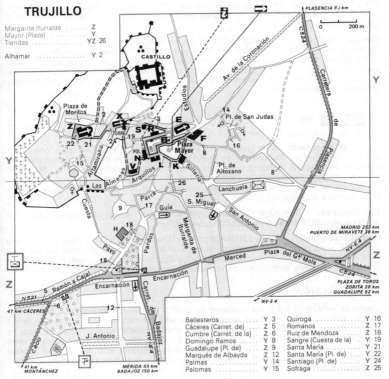

TRUJILLO

Margarita Iturralde .... Z
Mayor (Plaza) .... Y
Tiendas .... YZ 26
Alhamar .... Y 2

Ballesteros	Y 3	Quiroga	Y 16
Cáceres (Carret. de)	Z 5	Romanos	Z 17
Cumbre (Carret. de la)	Z 6	Ruiz de Mendoza	Z 18
Domingo Ramos	Y 8	Sangre (Cuesta de la)	Y 19
Guadalupe (Pl. de)	Z 9	Santa María	Y 21
Marqués de Albayda	Z 12	Santa María (Pl. de)	Y 22
Palmas	Y 14	Santiago (Pl. de)	Y 24
Palomas	Y 15	Sofraga	Z 25

TRUJILLO ★

Plaza Mayor★ (Y). — This square is worth examining in detail for its irregular shape and different levels linked by wide flights of steps and the great variety of seignorial mansions overlooking it. It evokes a way of life long gone and at night is positively theatrical.

(After Ed. Pergamino photo, Montornés del Vallés)

Plaza Mayor

Equestrian statue of Pizarro (Y B). — 1927. Bronze by the American sculptors, Charles Runse and Mary Harriman.

San Martin (Y E). — 16C. Granite walls enclose a vast nave chequered with funerary paving stones. The south parvis served in the past as a public meeting ground.

Dukes of San Carlos' Palace (Y F). — 17C. Now an enclosed convent. The tall granite façade, decorated in the transitional Classical baroque style has a corner window surmounted by the double headed eagle crest of the Vargas. *Ring at the door.* A nun takes you to see the two storey circular, arched inner court and the vaulted chambers below.

Marquess of Piedras Albas' Palace (Y K). — The Renaissance loggia has been accommodated into the original Gothic wall.

Marquess de la Conquista's Palace (Y L). — The palace was built by Hernando Pizarro, the *conquistador's* brother. It has an exceptional number of grilled windows, a Plateresque **corner window★**, added in the 17C with, on the left, the busts of Francisco Pizarro and his wife, and on the right Hernando and his niece, whom he married. Above is the family crest.

Former town hall (Y N). — 16C. Three tiers of Renaissance arcades from a nearby *patio* have been reconstructed to form the façade.

House of Chains (Y R). — The chains are said to have been brought by Christians freed from Moorish serfdom.

Alfiler Tower (Y S). — The so-called needle tower is a Mudejar belfry.

Take the passage beneath the left arcade of the old town hall.

Orellana Pizarro Palace (Y V). — 16C. Beautiful Plateresque upper gallery.

Santiago Church (Y X). — The 13C Romanesque belfry and the tall seignorial tower stand on either side of the Santiago Arch, one of the town's seven original gateways. In the church's 17C renovated nave there is a most expressive Crucifixion.

Santa María★ (Y Z). — 13C. *If closed apply at the house to the right of the steps below the church.*

This Gothic edifice, in which the network vaulting was reconstructed in the 15C, is the pantheon of Trujillo's great men. In the *coro alto,* lit by a wide rose window, are the two stone seats in which the Catholic Monarchs sat during mass when in residence in the city. The 24 panels of the Gothic **retable★** at the high altar are attributed to Fernando Gallego. From the top of the belfry there is a delightful view of brown tile roofs, the Plaza Mayor arcades and the castle.

Castle (Castillo) (Y). — The castle stands out prominently from the granite ledge from which the blocks were hewn with which it was itself constructed. The massive crenellated curtain wall is reinforced by numerous heavy square towers. Above the keep the patron of Trujillo, the Virgin of Victory, can be seen still in vigil; the human guards of long ago must have commanded the surrounding countryside from the battlements which now look down only on the town's main square.

ZAFRA (Badajoz)

Michelin map **447** fold 30 — Pop 12 902

A mediaeval **castle** stands guard at the entrance to this white walled town, one of the oldest in Extremadura. Flanked by nine round towers crowned by pyramid shaped merlons, it was once a Moorish *alcázar;* it was rebuilt in the 15C and transformed in the 16C before being re-equipped this century as a *parador.*

Zafra's cattle fairs are famous locally, especially the St Michael's Fair (Feria de San Miguel) during the week of 5 October.

The squares. — The huge 18C **Plaza Mayor,** lined with arcades, and the adjoining and much smaller 16C **Plaza Vieja** form an attractive precinct.

Candelaria Church. — *Open 10.30am to 1pm (11am to 12.30pm Sundays and holidays) and 7 to 8.30pm (6 to 7.30pm in winter).* The 16C church in transitional Gothic-Renaissance style can be identified by its massive red brick belfry. In the shallow south transept there now stands a recently authenticated and cleaned altarpiece by Zurbarán painted in 1644.

EXCURSION

Llerena. — *42km - 26 miles southeast by road N 432.* The **Plaza Mayor** of this modest country town is one of the most monumental in all Extremadura. On one side stands the Church of Our Lady of Granada in which the composite façade is brought into harmony by the colourful interplay of white limestone and brick; above, the delicacy of two superimposed arcades crowned by an equally delicate balustrade contrasts with the mass of a great baroque belfry. A pomegranate — *granada* in Spanish — decorates the escutcheon on the tympanum over the main door.

6 Galicia

This isolated region, four-square to the Atlantic, is far from the traditional or travel poster image of Spain that everyone knows: granite shores, *rías* or inlets cutting deep into the coastline and the sea with its influence on the life of the people and the climate, which is mild and damp, producing a countryside of green hills and valleys, enclosed fields and woodlands (the region provides 25% of Spain's timber: pine, chestnut and eucalyptus)... It is all the more reminiscent of Wales, Ireland, Brittany or the west of Scotland; and there is even a cultural resemblance for the Celts have left their imprint in the legends of the Holy Grail, in an accursed town drowned at the bottom of a *ría* and in the crosses to be seen in many villages. Bagpipes are the native instrument. Only the language is an exception and has no Celtic strain, Galician being a language of Roman origin.

The Calvary
at Eiroa

Geography. — The territory of the four Galician provinces is, for the most part, an ancient peneplain granite massif which was torn away and resettled by a later, differently orientated, mountain folding. It is in a rift caused by such massive disturbances that the Upper Miño has its course. Although peaks on the plain rise to 2 000m - 6 562ft — the Peña Trevinca on the Castile border is 2 124m - 6 968ft — the average amounts to less than 500m - 1 640ft. Landscape being a matter of scale, the Galician countryside appears one of hills and mountains.

The climate is modified by the sea and there are few extremes. The yearly average is 13 °C - 55 °F; oranges are grown along the Vigo inlet. Rain is plentiful and the province is proverbially the wettest in Spain, although the interior towns like Orense have three dry months each year and as a result have a totally different economy to the coastal towns.

The interior. — This primarily agricultural region, poorly adapted to modern needs, is the worst hit in Spain by people leaving the land either to go to other parts of the country or emigrate. The farms are small, the walled fields minute, the terrain undulating — all these factors hinder maximum exploitation. Land division was traditional until recently under the *foros* system whereby property which could not be divided and sold, was let for an advance payment to a farmer who sublet to tenant farmers producing what is known as the *minifundio*. Farming is mixed with maize as the staple and potatoes, rye, grapes and pasture as secondary crops. The Miño Valley, nevertheless, is known for its wines (El Ribeiro del Avia, harsh and full-bodied and the sparkling Rosal from the A Garda area) and Orense province exports good quality beef, although only in small quantities as cows are kept to work in the fields as well as for milk.

Problems of communication have prevented industry from establishing itself where there is an excessive labour force; there has, therefore, been a drift to the coast to the more heavily industrialised areas of Spain such as Catalonia and the Basque country and even abroad. It is the men only who go, returning, when they have earned enough money, to the smallholding husbanded meanwhile, by the old folk, the wives and children.

The Atlantic seaboard. — As the economy based on the sea has developed so the coastal population has increased until now Pontevedra and La Coruña provinces have a higher average density per km² than any other in Spain and the Rías Bajas in particular, the highest for any rural area with more than 300 to 400 per km² - 777 to 1 036 to the sq mile.

Galician fishing ports, with Vigo and Corunna as the major centres, are Spain's most important, accounting for more than 25% of the national catch. Deep sea trawlers come back heavily loaded with cod, sardines and tunny and inshore boats with molluscs and crustaceans, which for the most part are used for canning and export.

Industry, which is developing with the power supplied by the hydro-electric installations of the interior, is, at present, principally fish canning and papermaking. Shipbuilding is also important. Finally there are prosperous cargo ports at Vigo and Corunna.

History. — The name Galicia, from the same root as Gaul and Wales, is Celtic in origin for it was the Celts who, in about the 6C BC, occupied the region, constructing fortified defenses or **castros** (traces unearthed).

After the Roman period, during the Barbarian invasions, the country was overrun by the Suevians, the Visigoths and, much later in 730, the Moors who remained only briefly. Galicia was then incorporated in the Kingdom of the Asturias, the fount of Christianity in Spain, then began the epic saga, the goal interrupted only by invasions of the Northmen and the brutal campaign of Al Mansur *(p 55)*, of the Pilgrimage to St James of Compostela *(p 152)*.

From the 15C, overseas trade developed rapidly; in 1720 Corunna was granted the privilege of trading with America — a right previously only held by Cádiz and Seville and not extended to other ports until 1778. This was a sumptuous era when brave men *(indianos)* voyaged to the colonies and returned with vast riches and booty.

Folklore and Gastronomy. — The rural character and isolation of the province have resulted in its keeping much of its originality; even in town women carry on their heads their purchases from market in big chestnut baskets; on country roads, yoked cows, their heads protected with an old skin against flies, draw carts with squeaking solid wheels; long barns or **hórreos** stand grouped outside the villages, raised high on stone piles against damp and vermin, their ridge roofs tiled and protected by holy crosses *(illustration p 111)*.

Streets and squares in the towns are lined with houses with *solanas* — corbelled balconies glazed to protect one from the wind while getting the sun. Sometimes, as in Corunna, the glazing covers virtually the whole house front and entire streets appear to be glass fronted. Totally different are the Galician **pazos** or manorhouses where the usually sober lines are relieved by a doorway, a coat of arms, a balconied window and square towers at either end of the main façade.

Place names framed in brown : Renaissance or baroque monastery
Place names underlined in brown : "Pazo"

Festivals are an occasion for dancing in local costume to the **gaita** or local bagpipe, or to drums and castanets. The dances, which are lively, occasionally have a jigging rhythm: the **muñeira** or miller's wife's dance you will see everywhere; **sword dancing** reserved for men only is often seen in the Rías Bajas area; and the **Redondela,** which is also prevalent in the region.

Wild horses run free in the Groba Mountains between Bayona and A Garda. Once a year they are rounded up and corralled for branding at local *curros* or rodeos when there is always a festival. The most picturesque *curros* are those of La Valga, near Vigo *(2nd Sunday in June)* and Torrona near Oia *(1st Sunday in June)* and Mougas *(2nd Sunday in May).*

The Galician coast is famous for its dishes of freshly caught fish, in particular its shellfish and crustaceans *(mariscos)* — scallops *(vieiras)*, mussels *(mejillones)*, limpets *(percebes)* and large prawns *(gambas, langostinos)*. The most popular local dish is the **caldo gallego,** an excellent hot-pot with meat and vegetables.

BAYONA ★ BAIONA (Pontevedra)

Michelin map 441 fold 12 — *Local map p 151* — Pop 9 702

Bayona, at the mouth of the Vigo *ría* or inlet faces out across its vast bay towards the Atlantic but is protected from ocean storms to the north and south by the Monte Ferro and the Monterreal rock promontories. It was into Bayona that the *Pinta* sailed in 1493 with news of the discovery of the New World *(p 49)* and it was to this port that many ships returned throughout the 16 and 17C with gold and precious jewels as well as trade from that New World and elsewhere. Today, the harbour sees mainly pleasure boats as the town turns more and more to tourism.

Monterreal. — *75pts.* Monterreal was circled by a defence wall in about 1500 and a massive castellated fort built upon it slightly later. It later became the governor's residence and has now been converted into a *parador,* surrounded by pine and eucalyptus woods.

A walk round the **battlements★** *(about 1/2 hour)*, rising sheer above the rocks, affords commanding views of the bay, Monte Ferro and the Estelas Islands, the horizon and the coast south to Cape Silleiro.

EXCURSION

The Baiona - A Garda Road★. — *30km - 20 miles.* The coast between the two towns is flat and desert-like although indented by the sea. A fishing village, Oia, breaks the horizon, its houses grouped round the baroque façade of the former Cistercian monastery of Santa María la Real *(private property).*

On the far side of the road are the outlying slopes of the green hills in which the wild horses roam and where the *curros* are held on certain Sundays in May and June *(see above).* Ask at the town hall for exactly when and where.

A Garda. — This small village at the extreme southern end of the Galician coastline, owes much of its prosperity to emigrants returned from Puerto Rico. South *(3km - 2 miles)*, rising between the town and the mouth of the Miño and dominating both from its 341m - 1 118ft is the **Monte Santa Tecla★**. On a clear day climb to the belvederes near the geodesic column and the television mast for the **view★★** which includes the river below marking the Portuguese frontier and beaches extending southwards. The wooded slopes of the mound itself are interesting archaeologically since they bear traces of habitation by man from the Bronze Age to 3C AD. A round hut with a thatched roof such as must have stood on the mountainside, has been reconstituted on the side. Actual finds (knapped flints, stone carvings, pottery) are in a museum at the mountain top *(to visit apply to the caretaker; 50pts).*

BETANZOS ★ (La Coruña)
Michelin map 441 fold 3 — Pop 11 385

Betanzos, a onetime port now silted up, but still most attractive at the end of its *ría*, was also once the flourishing market for the rich Las Marinas Valley when this provided wheat for the whole La Coruña province. At the centre of the town stand a substantial reminder of this former prosperity and importance in the form of three Gothic churches remarkable for their pure lines and rich ornament. The precincts with steep streets and old houses with glazed balconies maintain the old world atmosphere.

Sta María del Azogue★ (of the Market). — The church dates from the 14 and 15C and has a gracefully asymmetrical **façade,** given character by a projecting central bay pierced by a rose window and a portal with sculptured covings. Niches on either side contain archaic statues of the Virgin and the Archangel Gabriel symbolising the Annunciation. Inside, the three aisles of equal height, beneath a single timber roof, make for spaciousness.

San Francisco. — This Franciscan monastery church, in the form of a Latin cross embellished with a graceful Gothic chevet, was built in 1387 by Count Fernán Pérez de Andrade, Lord of Betanzos and Puentedeume. It is chiefly remarkable for the numerous tombs aligned along its walls, the carved decoration on its ogive and chancel arches and the wild boar sculptured in the most unexpected places.

Beneath the gallery to the left of the west door is the monumental **sepulchre★** of the founder, supported by a wild boar and a bear, his heraldic beasts. Scenes of the chase adorn the tomb's sides; his hounds lie couched at his feet, while at his head an angel greets his soul.

Santiago. — The tailors' guild built this church in the 15C on higher ground than the others. The interior resembles Sta María. Above the main door, is a carving of St James "Matamore" or Slayer of the Moors, on horseback. The 16C town hall abutting the chevet, is embellished with an arcade and sculptured coat of arms.

The maps and plans are orientated with north at the top.

CELANOVA (Orense)
Michelin map 441 fold 13 — Pop 7 518

In 936 St Rosendo, Bishop of San Martín de Mondoñedo *(p 150)*, founded a monastery on this site which, since it was on the pilgrim route from Portugal to Santiago, grew greatly in size and importance over the centuries.

This late 17C monumental **church** displays a façade with hints of Classicism. The coffered vaulting is decorated with geometrical designs, the cupola with volutes. An immense altarpiece (1697) occupies the back of the apse and an organ the north wall of the nave.

The baroque **cloister★★**, begun in 1550 to plans by a monk from Celanova, and only completed in the 18C, is among the most beautiful in Galicia: light and shade contrast brilliantly in the interplay of lines and ornamental relief of the original design.

The galleries and majestic staircases have been recently restored. *Enter by the college door on the market square and apply to the caretaker.*

St Michael's Chapel (San Miguel) was one of the monastery's earliest buildings (937). It is in good condition and, therefore, all the more interesting as a rare example of the Mozarabic style.

EXCURSION

Sta Comba de Bande. — *26km - 16 miles along N 540 (going south). At the exit to Sta Comba bear right into a dirt road for 600m - 660yds. Apply at the parish house, beside the church.*

The small 7C Visigothic **church★** overlooks a lake. Inside, the plan is that of a Greek cross, lit by a lantern turret. The apse is square and is preceded by a horseshoe shaped triumphal arch resting on four pillars with Corinthian capitals. Pure lines and perfect wall masonry add a rich quality to what would anyway be a unique building.

CORUNNA ★ LA CORUÑA - A CORUÑA P
Michelin map 441 fold 3 — Pop 232 356

The site of Galicia's principal city is a rocky islet, linked to the mainland by a narrow strip of sand. The lighthouse stands to the north, the shell shaped harbour to the south and along the west side of the isthmus, in the dryest climate in all Galicia, the highly popular Riazor beach (annual rainfall 790mm or 3 1/4 ins).

Corunna, is the capital of Galicia and one of Spain's eleven garrison towns. It is above all, however, an important oil port, although other industries, especially food canning, have made it a significant trading port.

A CORUÑA
LA CORUÑA

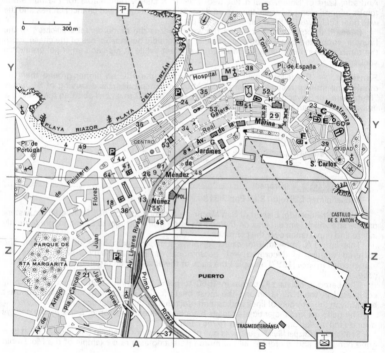

HISTORICAL NOTES

The town was already well developed in Roman times as can be seen from the so-called **Hercules Tower** (X), the only lighthouse to be built in the 2C AD and still functioning. It was originally surrounded by a ramp which Charles III transformed into an interior staircase in 1790 when he altered the building to its present square shape. There is an interesting view of the town and the coast from the top.

The city walls date back to the 13C although they were constantly being rebuilt until by the 18C they formed a complete defence system to which was then added the San Antón fort (BZ). At the centre in the **San Carlos** gardens (BY) *(open 9am to dusk)* where General Sir John Moore lies buried (born in 1761 in Glasgow and died in 1809 *p 145*)

The Invincible Armada. — It was from Corunna that Philip II's Armada finally set sail on 22 July 1588 — one year after Drake had destroyed his first fleet in Cádiz harbour *(p 36)* and some weeks after the king's second fleet had mustered at Lisbon (then Spanish), and after boldly setting out, been forced into the northern harbour by the strength of the gales. Philip, ostensibly to punish Elizabeth for the execution of Mary, Queen of Scots, but principally to prevent her further support of the Protestant rebels in the Low Countries and perhaps even to reassert his claim to the English throne, directed his ships to pick up an invasion force off the Low Countries.

The fleet of 130 men of war manned by 10 000 sailors and transporting 19 000 soldiers was, however, harassed from the start by the smaller more manœuvrable English ships and dogged by bad weather.

Hawkins and Drake among others, seized prizes; no *rendez-vous* was effected off Flanders; raging storms drove the ships off course; 63 ships and more than 15 000 men were lost as the battered fleet rounded Scotland and Ireland before limping back to Corunna. The defeat marked the end of Spanish sea power.

The Postscript. — One year later, in 1589, Elizabeth sent Drake with 30 ships and 15 000 men under Norreys to attack the Spanish and Portuguese coasts in an attempt to establish the Portuguese pretender Dom Antonio. The invaders fired Corunna but the town was saved by **María Pita** who seized the English standard from the beacon where it had been planted and gave the alarm. A plaque on her house *(Calle Herrerías No 24)* (BY **C**) recounts her bravery; a square (BY **29**) in the town is also named after her.

19 and 20C. — In 1809, Marshal Soult in the Battle of Elviña led Napoleon's forces to a decisive victory over the English then under the command of Sir John Moore who was mortally wounded during the encounter.

Throughout the latter years of the 19C, during the period of the frequent liberal uprisings, Corunna consistently supported the insurgents and in consequence suffered severe reprisals. The town was captured early by the Nationalist forces in the 1936-1939 Civil War.

The town is also proud of being the birthplace of the poet **Rosalía de Castro** (1837-1885), who so successfully expressed Galician melancholy.

■ SIGHTS

Three distinct quarters mark Corunna's expansion: the City (Ciudad) and the town centre on the isthmus, the business and commercial centre with wide avenues and shopping streets (Calles Real and San Andrés) and the Ensanche (X) to the south, built up with warehouses and industry.

The City (Ciudad) (BY). — The City is the original town with narrow cobbled streets and small peaceful squares at the northern end of the harbour.

Santa María del Campo Collegiate Church (BY **E**). — A 15C Calvary stands in the small square between a richly baroque house and Santa María Church which has, beneath its rose window, a Gothic portal (13 or 14C) and a tympanum carved with the Adoration of the Magi.

Santiago (BY **F**). — The church's three apses, which overlook the Plaza de Azcárraga, and the north door are Romanesque, the west door with its figures of St John and St Mark against the piers and the massive arches supporting the timber roof above the nave are Gothic. Inside is a beautifully carved pulpit.

Plazuela de Santa Bárbara (BY **60**). — The small shaded square, closely surrounded by old Corunna houses and the high walls with iron grilles at the windows of the Sta Bárbara convent, is a peaceful spot. On summer evenings concerts are given (mainly chamber music).

A late 14C lintel above a doorway is carved to show dead men's souls being weighed before Christ, the Father, St James, St Francis and St Dominic.

Avenida de la Marina★ (BY). — The avenue and its continuation, the Paseo de la Dársena, are lined by typical tall Corunna houses with glazed balconies at every storey.

Méndez Núñez Gardens (BY). — The gardens (Jardines), planted with a great variety of flowering trees, lie between the harbour and "Los Cantones" (Cantón Grande and Cantón Pequeño) in a bustling quarter of the town.

EXCURSION

Cambre. — *11km - 7 miles. Leave by the N 550, ② on the plan, going towards Betanzos. Turn right after the bridge over the Río Mero.* The 12C Romanesque country church of **Sta María★** has a lovely façade, divided into three sections corresponding with the nave and two aisles inside. Multilobed arches, emphasising the windows on either side, show Moorish influence as do the buttress capitals. The tympanum is carved with the Holy Lamb in a medallion supported by angels. The pure style interior has a feature often found in churches on the Santiago pilgrim route *(p 14)*, an apse circled by an ambulatory with five radiating chapels.

FERROL (La Coruña) _____
Michelin map 🔳 fold 3 — Pop 91 764

The town, which dates back to the Middle Ages and retains charming streets from that period at its west end around the port, became important in the 18C when King Ferdinand VI and King Charles III took advantage of its strategic position on a deep *ría* to make it a major Spanish naval base — constructing forts at the entrance to the narrow 6km - 4 mile channel which is its only approach. It was also well placed (favourable winds) for trade with America.

The symmetry of the 18C can be seen in the town plan. The front, hidden by a high wall, is now the naval dockyard. *To visit the dockyards apply to Exmo. Sr. Almirante - Jefe del Arsenal Militar; the tour is conducted weekdays 4 to 6pm; holidays 10am to 7pm.* The yards lie to the east and west of La Graña; industry is developing on the town outskirts.

LUGO 🅿 _____
Michelin map 🔳 fold 4 — Pop 73 986

Lugo, when under the Romans, had been a provincial capital and a major road junction; it was burned down by the Moors in 714 and by the Norsemen in 968. It remained a battleground until last century, trying in vain to resist Napoleon's armies and becoming a centre of insurrection throughout the period of the *pronunciamientos*. Now, peacefully at the heart of an agricultural region specialising in cheese production, the town has taken on new life, building wide shopping streets such as the Reina and Santo Domingo while also preserving a distinguished old quarter around the cathedral.

6 – GALICIA

Town walls★ (Murallas) (YZ). — The massive schist walls which have encircled the heart of the town since Roman times, have been many times repaired and razed to a uniform 10m - 33ft, yet remain a continuous perimeter over 2km - 1 mile long through which one can only enter by one of the rare city gates. The sentry path can be reached by steps at the gates.

Cathedral★ (Z A). — Lugo's position on the Camino Francés or French pilgrim road to Santiago *(p 152)* explains the evident French influence in the Romanesque parts of the church. It is, however, a heterogeneous edifice for it was remodelled in the Gothic period and received additions in the 18C: the Chapel of the Wide Eyed Virgin at the east end has a baroque rotunda, marked at its upper level by a stone balustrade, and contrasts with the north door where a 15C porch shelters a Romanesque **Christ in Majesty★**. The figure is above a capital curiously suspended in midair and carved with the Last Supper.

Inside, the Romanesque nave is roofed with cradle vaulting and lined with galleries, a feature common in pilgrim churches. Immense wooden Renaissance altarpieces are found at the end of the transept — the south one is signed by the sculptor Cornelis de Holanda (1531). A door in the west wall of the south transept leads to a small but elegant cloister.

Sta María (Z 26) and del Campo Squares (Z 4). — The 18C episcopal palace (B), facing the north door of the cathedral on the delightful Sta María Square, is a typical *pazo*, one storey high with smooth stone walls, advanced square wings framing the central façade and decoration confined to the main doorway, a coat of arms and wrought iron balconies. Picturesque alleys, criss-crossing behind the palace, lead to the small Plaza del Campo, lined by old houses and with a fountain at its centre.

Provincial Museum (Y M). — *Open 10am to 2pm and 4 to 7pm; closed Saturday afternoons as well as Sundays and holidays all day.*

Folk displays include a country kitchen *(see below Sta Eulalia de Bóveda).* The Roman town of Lugo is represented and there are displays of coins, and in the San Francisco cloister, altars and sarcophagi.

EXCURSION

Sta Eulalia de Bóveda. — *15km - 9 miles southwest. Leave by ③ on the plan and follow the Orense road for 4km - 2 1/2 miles then bear right towards Friol; turn left after 2km - 1 mile and right after 7km - 4 miles.* The palaeo-Christian monument discovered at the beginning of the century, excavated in 1924 and consisting of a vestibule (today open to the sky) and a rectangular chamber with a basin and round arched niche, continues to intrigue archaeologists. Frescoes of birds and leaves, doubtless of Christian origin, can be seen on the walls. *To visit apply at the house opposite weekdays 10am to 2pm and 4 to 6pm; Sundays and holidays noon to 2pm.*

Europe on a single sheet:
Michelin Map no 920

MEIRA Sierra ★ (Lugo)
Michelin map 441 fold 5

The Ribadeo - Lugo road, the N 640 *(86km - 53 1/2 miles),* is particularly attractive between A Pontenova-Villaodriz and Meira where it crosses the Meira Sierra. The road rises in a *corniche* above an enclosed, wooded valley through which flows a trout stream tributary of the Río Eo. **Views** across the mountains are pinpointed by low square flint houses. **Meira** itself has a 13C church remarkable for the length of its nave of nine bays.

MONDOÑEDO ★ (Lugo)
Michelin map 441 fold 5 — Pop 6 988

The low slate covered houses and wide golden stone cathedral façade of Mondoñedo rise out of the hollow of a lush, well cultivated valley as you drive along the Villalba road. The streets of the **old town** are lined with stylish white walled houses ornamented with armorial bearings and wrought iron balconies in contrast to those in the multilevel cathedral square which is bordered by arcades and *solanas*.

Cathedral★. — The façade, framed in the 18C by twin baroque towers, retains, at the centre, the original (13C) three great Gothic arches, portal and rose window.

The interior is transitional Romanesque with the walls setting off the works of art: a series of late 14C frescoes one above the other (below the extraordinary 1710 organ) illustrate the Massacre of the Innocents and the life of St Peter; the rococo retable at the high altar and the ambulatory chapels where, notably, the altarpiece of the Holy Relics enshrines a piece of the True Cross. A polychrome wood statue of the Virgin in the south ambulatory is known as the English Virgin since the statue was brought from St Paul's Cathedral, London to Mondoñedo in the 16C. Off the south aisle is the emblasoned burial niche of Bishop Juan Muñoz who gave the church its present façade.

The **cloister** is 17C.

Museum★. — *Open 1 July to 15 September 11am to 1pm and 4 to 7pm; noon to 1pm the rest of the year; access by the south ambulatory.*

The museum, rich in statues, altarpieces and paintings (Bayeu, Seville School), also displays 16, 17 and 18C furniture and liturgical objects and a 13C Gothic drawing room.

*When looking for a pleasant, quiet and well situated hotel consult the current **Michelin Red Guide** España Portugal.*

ORENSE OURENSE Ⓟ

Michelin map **441** folds 13 and 14 — Pop 96 085

From ancient times, Orense — the name is said to come from the legendary gold believed to exist in the Miño Valley — has been famous for its waters which pour out at 65 ºC - 150 ºF — from three springs, **Las Burgas** (AZ **F**). The town today is a busy commercial centre. Spanning the river beside the modern bridges is the **old bridge (puente romano)** (B), which dates from the 13C when it was rebuilt on the Roman foundations.

Orense developed originally around the springs: not far away, along the twisting stepped streets is the **old town** (AYZ) with its buildings and squares:

Plazuela de la Magdalena (AZ **23**). — In the square, at the central cross, Mary Magdalene weeps. The Sta María la Madre Church (**S**) dates from 1722.

Plaza del Trigo (AZ **40**). — The *plaza* is a parvis to the cathedral south door.

Plaza del Hierro (AY **17**). — The fountain comes from Osera Monastery *(p 148).*

Cathedral★ (AY **B**). — 12 - 13C. The west face is now shut in by houses and entry is, therefore, through the transept. The south door, in the Compostelan style, lacks a tympanum, but is profusely decorated with carving on covings and capitals; the north door has two statue columns and beneath a great ornamented arch, a Deposition framed by a Flight into Egypt and statues of the Holy Women.

OURENSE-ORENSE

		Capitán Eloy .... AY	José Antonio .... AY
		Cardenal Quiroga ...... AY 9	Lamas Carvajal .... AY 20
		Ceano .... AY 10	La Paz .... AY 21
Bedoya .... AY		Doctor Marañón .... AZ 16	Mayor (Plaza) .... AZ
Calvo Sotelo .... AY		General Franco .... AYZ	Santo Domingo .... AY 39

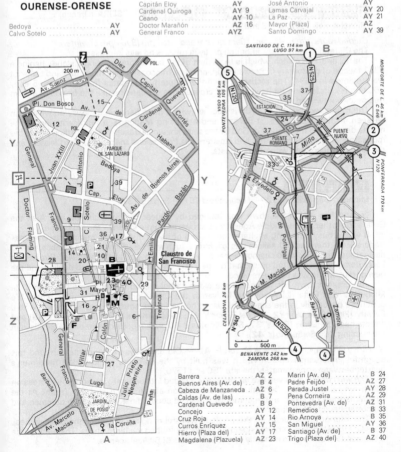

Barrera .... AZ 2		Marín (Av. de) .... B 24	
Buenos Aires (Av. de) . B 4		Padre Feijóo .... AZ 27	
Cabeza de Manzaneda . AZ 6		Parada Justel .... AY 28	
Caldas (Av. de las) ... B 7		Pena Corneira .... AZ 29	
Cardenal Quevedo ..... B 8		Pontevedra (Av. de) ... AZ 31	
Concejo .... AY 12		Remedios .... B 33	
Cruz Roja .... AY 14		Río Arnoya .... B 35	
Curros Enríquez ...... AY 15		San Miguel .... AY 36	
Hierro (Plaza del) .... AY 17		Santiago (Av. de) ..... B 37	
Magdalena (Plazuela) . AZ 23		Trigo (Plaza del) ...... AZ 40	

ORENSE

The high altar is surmounted by an ornate but interesting Gothic retable (early 16C) by Cornelis de Holanda. The 16 and 17C Chapel of Holy Christ (Santísimo Cristo), decorated with incredibly exuberant sculpture, opens off the north transept. The Romanesque triple arched **Paradise Door★★ (Pórtico del Paraíso)** at the west end, illustrates the same theme as the Santiago Door of Glory, but has kept its bright mediaeval colouring; the central arch shows the 24 Old Men of the Apocalypse; the pierced tympanum above is 16C like the narthex vaulting.

A door in the south aisle opens onto the 13C chapterhouse, now the **episcopal museum** *(open 11am to 1.30pm and 3.30 to 6.30pm; closed Sunday and holiday mornings; 25pts)*. Church plate, statues and copes are displayed, some, like the 12C travelling altar, are very ancient.

Archaeological and Fine Arts Museum (AZ M). — *Open 10am to 1pm and 5 to 8pm; closed Sunday and holiday afternoons and all day Monday.*

The finely emblasoned façade overlooking the Plaza Mayor belongs to the former episcopal palace, now a museum. Inside are regional (old kitchen, Lugo pottery), archaeological (Roman, pre-Roman and prehistoric specimens) and fine arts departments *(1st floor:* Romanesque Virgins and Crucifixes, baroque altarpieces and a remarkable early 17C, carved wood, **Stations of the Cross★).**

San Francisco Cloister (AY). — *Ask at the former monastery, now a barracks, to see the cloister.*

The slightly horseshoe shaped arches rest on slender, paired columns to which a diamond and leaf decoration add simple sophistication.

EXCURSION

Ribas de Sil Monastery★ and Sil Gorges★. — *65km - 40 miles Rtn — about 2 1/2 hours plus 1/2 hour sightseeing. Leave by ③ on the plan; turn left after 6km - 3 1/2 miles into a stony road going north to Luintra; 18 km - 11 miles on is a signpost to the monastery.*

San Esteban de Ribas de Sil Monastery★. — The monastery appears suddenly in a majestic **setting★,** spread over a great spur, against a background of granite mountains, deeply cut by the Sil. The church's Romanesque east end remains, as do the three cloisters, built to grandiose proportions largely in the 16C, although one still has Romanesque galleries surmounted by elegant low arches.

Sil Gorges★. — *Return on the downhill road on the left towards the Sil (do not take the signposted turning to the Embalse de San Esteban).* Two dams, one vaulted the other a buttressed type, control the waters of the Sil which flows through deep gorges. Scattered over the slopes are vineyard encircled villages of houses with large tiled roofs. At the second dam, without leaving the left bank of the river, turn into the San Pedro dam road (signposted: Embalse de San Pedro) which joins the C 546; bear left for Orense.

OSERA Monastery of Santa María la Real ★ OSEIRA (Orense)

Michelin map **441** folds 13 and 14

Guided tours (time : 45 min) 10am to 1pm and 4 to 7pm (3 to 6pm in winter).
The Cistercian monastery, although partly in ruins, is no less impressive.

The 12 and 13C **church,** which is the oldest of the conventual buildings, stands behind a 1637 façade of customary Cistercian simplicity. The frescoes in the ambulatory and transept were painted in 1694. The **sacristy★,** once the chapterhouse, dates from the late 15 early 16C and is outstanding for its vaulting of crossed ribs descending like the fronds of a palm tree onto four twisted columns.

The monastery façade of 1708 is adorned with a huge baroque doorway on which can be seen, in the upper part, St Bernard and a Nursing Madonna, a representation of the mystic devotion to the Mother of God by the saint known as Jesus' foster brother. Inside the monastery are a grand staircase, two cloisters, the **Processional and the Medallion Cloisters,** and the **courtyard** decorated with portrait busts.

PONTEVEDRA ℙ

Michelin map **441** fold 12 — *Local map p 151* — Pop 65 137

Legend has it that the town was founded by Teucer, son of Telamon and Ajax the Greater's brother. In the Middle Ages it was known as Pontis Veteris - the old bridge.

It was a busy port lying sheltered at the end of its *ría;* fishermen, merchants, overseas traders lived there as did sailors and explorers such as **Pedro Sarmiento de Gamboa,** skilled navigator of the 16C, wise cosmographer and author of *Voyage to the Magellan Straits.* The Lérez delta, however, silted up so that by the 18C Pontevedra had begun to decline and the new port at Marín was taking its place.

The present town has respected the old, a kernel tucked into the area between Calle Michelena and Calle del Arzobispo Malvar to the Calle Cobián and the river, where life continues peacefully in the shadow of glazed house fronts, squares occasionally set with a Calvary **(Plaza de la Leña** Y **20, del Teucro** Y **45, de Mugártegui** Y **27** or **Pedreira** Y **33)** and streets near the Lérez **(Real** Y **37, San Nicolás** Y **40)** which come to life on market days in the bustling **Calle Sarmiento** (Y **42).**

St Mary Major★ (Sta María la Mayor) (Y A). — Old alleyways and gardens surround this delightful Plateresque church which was built by the mariners' guild in the fishermen's quarter between approximately the late 15C and 1570.

The **west front★** is carved like an altarpiece, divided into separate superimposed areas on which are reliefs of the Dormition and Assumption of the Virgin and the Trinity. At the summit is the Crucifixion at the centre of a pierced coping finely carved with oarsmen and fishermen hauling in their nets.

The interior presents an on the whole successful mingling of Gothic (notched arches), Isabeline (twisted small columns) and Renaissance (ribbed vaulting) styles. The back of the west façade is covered in minutely carved low reliefs of Biblical scenes.

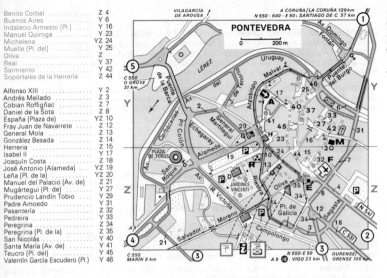

La Peregrina Church (Z E). — The cult of the Pilgrim Virgin began in Galicia in the 17C. This unusual church, erected at the end of the 18C, has a narrow, convex façade and a spacious plan, combining a cross and a rotunda.

San Francisco (Z F). — The church's Gothic façade looks onto the gardens of the Plaza de la Herrería. To the right of the chancel lies the recumbent statue of Don Payo Gómez Charino, Lord of Rianjo, who in 1248 took part in the Reconquest of Seville.

Museum (**Museo Provincial**) (Y M). — *Open 11am to 1.30pm (1pm in winter) and 5 to 8pm (7.30pm in winter); closed Sunday and holiday afternoons; 100pts, free Sundays and holidays, including admission to Santo Domingo ruins (lapidary museum) and the Casa Fernández López (modern Galician painting exhibitions).*
  The major part of the museum is in two fine 18C mansions, linked by an arch, on the Plaza de Leña. In the first are prehistorical and pre-Roman collections (notably the Celtic Golada treasure); in the second, maritime exhibits including the cabin of Admiral Méndez Núñez and the officers' mess below decks from the *Numancia (access by the hatchway)* which he commanded in 1866 at the Battle of Callao during the war against the former Spanish colonies in the Pacific. When told that it was folly to attack a port so well defended — Callao is Peru's chief seaport — the admiral replied "Spain prefers honour without ships to ships without honour". On the museum's upper floor are an interesting antique kitchen and examples of 19C Sargadelos pottery.

Sto Domingo Ruins (Z R). — *Same opening times as the museum.*
  Only the church's Gothic east end remains, its tall bays overgrown with ivy. Arranged inside is a lapidary museum of Roman steles, Galician coats of arms and tombs. There are artisan's tombs showing the tools they used and tombs of noblemen.

EXCURSIONS

Coto Redondo Mirador★★. — *14km - 9 miles by* ③ *on the plan. Leave Pontevedra by the Vigo road; after 6km - 4 miles bear right towards the Lago de Castiñeiras from where signs will take you to Coto Redondo.*
  The hill climb through pine and eucalyptus woods, with occasional good views, is pleasant. From the *mirador* the **panorama**★★ extends over both the Pontevedra and Vigo Rías separated by the Morrazo peninsula.

Caniza Road★★. — *61km - 38 miles by* ② *on the plan.* The C 531 follows a course alternately through green and smiling valleys where the road is bordered by trees and shrubs, or along *corniches* and crestlines with views of the valleys below. At every hilltop there is a vast **panorama**★★ of the silent heath and broom covered heights of Galicia's ancient granite massif.

Rías Bajas★★. — *Description pp 150-151.*

PUENTEDEUME PONTEDEUME (La Coruña) _____
Michelin map **991** fold 3 — Pop 8 459

  This picturesque small town at the end of the Ares Ría, was the cradle of the illustrious Counts of Andrade who numbered amongst them Fernán Pérez the Good, a great builder who was buried at Betanzos *(p 143)* in 1397 and Fernando, hero of the wars against Italy of the early 16C. The Andrade imprint remains in the square keep near the river, last vestige of a 14C palace, and in the ruins of a 13C castle on a height to the east.
  A remarkably long bridge in the town spans the Eume. The Cabañas sand beach, on the right bank, is enhanced by a backdrop of pinewoods.

EXCURSIONS

Caaveiro Monastery. — *14km - 9 miles east. Leave the city on the Betanzos road and soon after bear left on a road along the river with beautiful views. Leave the car beyond the small bridge and continue on foot through the wood (10 minutes).*
  St Rudesind (Spanish - San Rosendo) selected this outstanding **site** on a rock spur overlooking the junction of the Eume and the Sesín. The church's Romanesque apse and fortified door emblasoned with a coroneted coat of arms, have remained intact amidst the overgrown ruins.

PUENTEDEUME

San Miguel de Breamo Church. — *7km - 4 1/2 miles southwest. Take the Betanzos road and just before Campolongo at El Barro take the first road on the right; 300m - 328yds farther on bear left; continue on this road 2km - 1 mile.* The church, built at the end of the 12C and still well preserved, stands isolated at the centre of a clearing. The style is pure Romanesque; the plan that of a T, onto which three apses have been grafted.

Monfero Monastery. — *21km - 13 miles southeast.* The baroque church is recognisable by its chequered façade. The **cloister,** with beautiful vaulting and hanging keystones was partly designed by Juan de Herrera. The upper storey is 18C. *To visit apply to the vicar.*

RÍAS ALTAS ★ NORTH COAST (Lugo, La Coruña) _____
Michelin map **440** folds 1 to 5

The numerous *rías* along the Galician coast, like the sea lochs of Scotland, the *fjords* of Norway and the *abers* of Brittany, are inlets made by the Atlantic into the coastline.

From Ribadeo to Corunna — *240km - 149 miles — about 4 hours*

Although indented, the coast is generally low-lying. The rocks, bare and smooth, the squat houses, their slate roofs weighted with stones against high winds, give the impression that the climate must be grim — yet holiday-makers arrive with the fine season, attracted by the scenery and small sandy creeks where fishermen haul in their boats.

Ría de Ribadeo. — After a headlong course (salmon fishing), the Río Eo slackens its pace where it forms the border between Galicia and Asturias, to wind gently between the widespread green banks of its lower valley.

All along the *corniche* **road**★ from Ribadeo to Vegadeo there are **views**★ of the *ría* and the valleyed Asturian countryside, commanded by Castropol, on its advanced rock spur.

Ribadeo, a coastal trading port last century, is now an important regional centre.

Ría de Foz. — Not far from Foz *(2.5km - 1 1/2 miles south of the Foz-Barreiros road)* and standing almost alone on a height, is the **Church of San Martín de Mondoñedo**★, once part of a monastery of ancient foundation and an episcopal seat until 1112 when this was transferred to Mondoñedo *(p 146).*

The church has a timber roof. Its style is archaic Romanesque and, most unusually in this region, shows no sign of Compostelan influence. The east end, decorated with Lombard bands, is supported by massive buttresses; inside, the capitals on each side of the three apses are naïvely carved.

Foz itself is a busy, small port with a coastal fishing fleet. It has two good beaches divided by a headland **cliff**★ which rises 15m - 50ft above the waves.

Ría de Viveiro. — Sea, countryside and mountain combine in a varied landscape; the roads are shaded by pines and eucalyptus.

Nicomedes Pastor Díaz, 19C politician and poet, sang of this coastline of white sand beaches and lofty headlands.

All **Viveiro** retains of its town wall is its Charles V Gateway, emblasoned above its stone arch with the emperor's arms and enhanced in Renaissance style by surrounding figures in relief and slender watch turrets. San Francisco, a Gothic church in the town, has effectively decorative lancets in the apse. Summer transforms this fishing port into a resort to which, at the end of August, visitors come from all Galicia for the local Naseiro Romería when Galician songs and tunes on the *gaita* precede and follow religious ceremonies. On the last day fish freshly caught and fried, known as *cabezudas,* are eaten by everyone in the open air.

Porto do Barqueiro. — A picturesque fishing village (speciality: crawfish) where the white walled houses with rough slate roofs rise attractively up the hillside.

Ortigueira. — Ortigueira, surrounded by green hills and with quays bordered by well kept gardens, might almost be taken for a lakeside town in Switzerland.

Ferrol. — *Description p 145.*

Pontedeume. — *Description p 149.*

Corunna★. — *Description p 143.*

From Corunna to Cape Fisterra — *144km - 89 1/2 miles — about 3 hours*

Malpica de Bergantiños. — A picturesque harbour well sheltered by the San Adrián Cape.

Camariñas. — A village famous for its pillow-lace *(encajes).*

Cape Fisterra (Cabo Fisterra) Road★. — From the attractive harbour town of Corcubión and even more beyond Fisterra village, the *corniche* **road**★ looks down on Cape Fisterra Bay, enclosed by three successive mountain chains.

The lighthouse on the headland, which so long marked the world's most westerly point, commands a fine **panorama**★.

RÍAS BAJAS ★★ WEST COAST (La Coruña, Pontevedra) _____
Michelin map **440** folds 11 and 12

The Rías Bajas, a coastline well supplied by the sea (crustaceans) and with deep inlets affording safe anchorages, is Galicia's most privileged and attractive region.

MUROS Y NOIA RÍA★
From Muros to Ribeira — *71km - 44 miles — about 2 1/2 hours*

The *ría*, with few towns beside it, is especially delightful for its rural scenery; the wooded **north bank**★★ is particularly attractive.

Muros is a seaside town with a harbour and typical local style houses; **Noia,** a small town with a shaded main square.

Looking out to sea is the Gothic Church of **San Martín**★ with a magnificently sculptured portal and rose window.

AROUSA RÍA
From Ribeira to A Toxa — *97km · 60 miles — about 2 hours*

The Arousa Ría, at the mouth of the Río Ulla, is the largest and most indented of the inlets.

Ribeira. — A large fishing port.

Mirador de la Curota★★★. — *10km · 6 miles from Puebla del Caramiñal.* Admired at a height of 498m · 1 634ft is a magnificent panorama of the four inlets of the Rías Bajas. During clear weather the view extends from Cape Fisterra to the Río Miño.

Padrón. — It was to this village that the legendary boat came which brought St James to Spain *(p 152)*. The boat's mooring stone can be seen beneath the altar in the parish church beside the bridge *(raise the altarcloth and turn on the light, on the left)*. An attractive tall lime avenue borders the Sar. Padrón is also where the poet Rosalía de Castro *(p 145)* lived and died.

Vilagarcía de Arousa. — A garden bordered promenade overlooking the sea gives the town the air of a resort. The **Vista Alegre Convent,** founded in 1648, bestrides the Cambados road out of town. Square towers, coats of arms, pointed merlons produce a *pazo (p 141)* like appearance.

Lobeira Mirador★. — *4km · 2 miles south.* Take a signposted forest path *(2km · 1 mile)* at Cornazo through the pines. From the *mirador* there is a view of the *ría.*

Cambados★. — At the town's northern entrance is the magnificent **Plaza de Fefiñanes★,** lined on two sides by the emblasoned Fefiñanes *pazo,* on the third by a 17C church with lines harmonising with the *pazo* and on the fourth by a row of arcaded houses.

A Toxa★. — A sick donkey abandoned on the island by his owner and later recovered cured, was the first living creature to discover the health- giving properties of the spring on A Toxa. The stream has run dry but the pine tree covered island in its wonderful **setting★★** remains an ideally restful place. The A Toxa - Canelas **road★** affords a succession of views of deserted sand dunes and secluded rock enclosed beaches.

PONTEVEDRA RÍA★
From Sanxenxo to Hío — *63km · 39 miles — about 3 hours*

Sanxenxo. — A true holiday resort with one of the best climates in Galicia.

Combarro★. — A fishing village with its houses with glazed balconies, *hórreos* and Calvaries.

Pontevedra. — *Description p 148.*

Marín. — Headquarters of the Naval Academy and sheltered harbour town.

From Portocelo to Bueu, the pine bordered road overlooks a series of beaches.

Hío. — The village at the tip of the Morrazo headland, has one of Galicia's most famous and most intricately carved Calvaries.

VIGO RÍA★
From Hío to Bayona — *78km · 48 1/2 miles — about 2 hours*

The *ría,* protected inland by hills and out to sea by the Cies Islands, is remarkably sheltered; in addition, by Domaio, where the steep and wooded banks draw together and the narrow channel is covered in mussel beds, it becomes really beautiful. From Cangas and Moaña you can see Vigo on the far side of the inlet.

Vigo. — *Description p 156.*

Panxón. — *2km · 1 mile west of the C 550.* Fishermen's cottages at the foot of Monte Ferro make up a small village overlooked by a Neo-Byzantine style church.

Playa América. — At the end of the bay, garlanded by a ribbon of fine sand, modern high rise blocks announce the development of a popular and elegant resort.

Baiona★. — *Description p 142.*

SAN ESTEBAN Dam ★★ SANTO ESTEVO (Orense)
Michelin map **441** fold 14

A succession of beautiful lakes appear along the length of the Sil River *(see Sil Gorges p 148).* By a picturesque **route★** from Castro Caldelas (15C castle) to Monforte de Lemos one reaches the San Esteban Dam. From the top of the retaining wall is a glorious view of the steep vine covered slopes through which runs the Sil.

The main car parks are indicated on the town plans.

SANTIAGO DE COMPOSTELA ★★★ (La Coruña)

Michelin map **441** folds 2 and 3 — Pop 93 695
See map of built-up area in the current Michelin Red Guide España Portugal.

In the Middle Ages Santiago de Compostela attracted pilgrims from all parts of Europe; it remains, several hundred years later, one of Spain's most remarkable cities, with old quarters, churches, conventual buildings and an air at once ancient, mystical and lively.

Legend and history. — The Apostle James the Greater, known as the Thunderer on account of his temper, crossed the seas, so the legend goes, to convert Spain to Christianity. His boat was cast ashore at the mouth of the Ulla *(p 151)* and he preached for seven years throughout the land before returning to Judaea where he fell an early victim to Herod. His disciples, forced to flee, returned to Spain with his body which they buried near the earlier landing place. Invasions by the Barbarians and later the Arabs caused the grave to be lost to memory.

St James Matamore

Early in the 9C a star is believed to have pointed the grave out to some shepherds. In 844 Don Ramiro I was leading a handful of Spaniards in a bold attack on the Moors grouped at **Clavijo** near Logroño, when a knight in armour mounted on a charger and bearing a white standard with a red cross upon it, is said to have appeared on the battlefield. As he beat back the infidels the Christians recognised St James, surnaming him from that time "Matamore" or Slayer of the Moors. The Reconquest and Spain had found a patron saint.

During the crusade the Lord of Pimentel, it is said, had to swim across a *ria*. He emerged from the sea covered in shells which were then adopted as the pilgrim symbol.

■ THE WAY OF SAINT JAMES (Camino de Santiago)

Michelin maps **441** folds 2 to 20 and **442** folds 7 to 20

The relics of St James discovered early in the 9C soon became the object of a local cult and then of pilgrimage. In the 11C devotion spread abroad until a journey to St James' shrine ranked equally with one to Rome or Jerusalem, particularly perilous since the invasion of the Holy Land by the Turks. St James had a particular appeal for the French who felt united with the Spanish in face of the Moorish threat but English, Germans, Italians and even Scandinavians made the long pilgrimage travelling for the most part through France along the routes organised to a considerable degree, by the Benedictines and Cistercians of Cluny and Cîteaux and the Knights Templars of the Spanish Order of the Red Sword who assured the pilgrims' safety in northern Spain, provided them with funds and flagged the route with cairns. Hospitals and hospices in the care of the Hospitallers received the sick, the weary and the stalwart who travelled almost all in the pilgrims' uniform of heavy cape, eight foot stave with a gourd attached to carry water, stout sandals and broad-brimmed felt hat, turned up in front and marked with three or four scallop shells. A Pilgrim Guide of 1130, the first "tourist" guide ever written, probably by Aimeri Picaud, a Poitou monk from Parthenay-le-Vieux, describes the inhabitants, climate and customs of different countries, the most interesting routes and the sights on the way — the pilgrim in those days was in no hurry and frequently made detours which took weeks or months to complete, to visit a sanctuary or shrine. Churches, therefore, both on and off the way, benefited, as did the associated towns, from the pilgrims who numbered between 500 000 and two million a year.

Of those who "took the cockleshell", the English, Normans and Bretons often came part of the way by boat *(see Parson's Quay in the Michelin Green Guide England: The West Country)*, disembarking at Soulac and following the French Atlantic coast south through Bordeaux to the Pyrenees, or they landed directly in Spain at Corunna, on the north coast or in Portugal. The pilgrims were, in fact, the first passengers ever — previously everyone on board ship having been either crew or soldiery. Mediterranean pilgrims landed in Catalonia and Valencia and crossed the peninsula. The land routes through France began at Chartres, St Denis and Paris, and joining at Tours, continued south to Bordeaux, at Vezelay and Autun to go through Limoges and Perigueux and at Le Puy and Arles.

With the passage of time, however, the faith that made people set out on pilgrimages of the scale of that of Santiago began to diminish: those seeking gain by trickery and robbery, and known as false pilgrims, among whom was the poet Villon, increased; the Wars of Religion, when Christians fought amongst themselves, reduced the faithful even more. Finally in 1589 Drake attacked Corunna *(p 145)* and the bishop of Compostela removed the relics from the cathedral to a place of safety. They were lost and for three hundred years the pilgrimage was virtually abandoned. In 1879 they were found once more, recognised by the pope and the pilgrimage recommenced. In Holy Years, when the feast day of St James (25 July) falls on a Sunday, there are jubilee indulgences and up to two million pilgrims once more visit the shrine.

THE WAY OF SAINT JAMES

0   50 km

The Way in Spain. — The diverse ways through France to Santiago came together to cross the Pyrenees and continued through northern Spain as two routes only — the Asturian, which until the 15C was considered extremely dangerous because of possible attack by brigands and a more southerly route known as the *Camino Francés* or French Way from the number of French pilgrims who followed it and the French monks in the hospices and hospitals along it. It became marked over the centuries by churches and monasteries in which French architectural influence is obvious. Each step on the Way to Santiago will be found described in the province through which the road section passes *(see index)*. Three towns in Galicia are associated with the pilgrimage.

Cebreiro. — Cebreiro is on a windswept height not far from the 1 109m - 3 638ft Piedrafita Pass. The town's unusual drystone and thatched houses *(pallozas)* go back in construction to ancient Celtic huts. *(In one of them there is an ethnographic museum.)*

Still offering shelter to the traveller is an inn beside the small 9C mountain church where pilgrims venerated the relics of the miracle of the Holy Eucharist which took place in *ca*1300. One day, it is said, in spite of a gale, a believer came a long way to hear mass in the church. "What a fool" thought the priest "to travel so far for a piece of bread and little wine". Immediately, to the confusion of the nonbeliever, the bread was turned to flesh and the wine to blood. The holy relics are preserved in silver caskets presented by Isabel the Catholic and may be seen with the miraculous chalice and paten. *To visit apply to the priest.*

Portomarín. — The village of Portomarín had stood for centuries beside a bridge spanning the Miño when modern civilisation required the construction of a dam at Belesar. Before the old village was drowned, however, the church was taken down and re-erected stone by stone on the new site. This **church★** of the Knights of St John of Jerusalem is square in shape, fortified and ornamented with massive supporting arches and Romanesque doors with delicately carved covings. At the west door Christ appears in Majesty accompanied by the 24 old musicians of the Apocalypse.

Vilar de Donas. — *6.5km - 4 miles east of Palas de Rei.* The church, slightly off the main road, is entered through a Romanesque portal. Lining the inner walls are the tombs of Knights of the Order of St James, slain in battle against the infidels. Delicately drawn 15C **frescoes★** still decorate the apse, illustrating Christ in the firmament with St Paul and St Luke on his left and St Peter and St Mark on his right and elsewhere, less distinctly, the faces of the elegant young women who gave the church its name — *donas* (in Galician).

■ CATHEDRAL★★★ (V) *time: 2 hours*

The present cathedral, built upon the same site as the first basilica erected over the apostle's tomb shortly after its discovery and that of Alfonso III destroyed by Al Mansur in 997, dates almost entirely from the 11, 12 and 13C. It is unique in all Spain in being able to be seen from *plazas* on all sides. In 1386 John of Gaunt, who was married to Constance, the daughter of Pedro the Cruel of Seville, invaded Galicia and had himself crowned King of Castile and León in this cathedral.

Obradoiro façade★★★. — This baroque masterpiece by Fernando Casas y Novoa has adorned the cathedral entrance in magnificence since 1750. The central area, richly sculptured and given true baroque movement by the interplay of straight and curved lines, rises to what appears almost to be a long tongue of flame. The upward triangular lines are emphasised by high flanking towers, slender and slightly in recess but sumptuously ornate.

Old Cathedral (Catedral Vieja). — *Open 1 March to 30 September 10.30am to 1.30pm and 4 to 7.30pm; the rest of the year 11am to 1.30pm and 4 to 6pm; closed Sunday and holiday afternoons; 150pts - ticket valid for the cathedral treasure and the museum.*

A crypt which lies beneath the flight of steps before the Obradoiro façade, was constructed in the 11C to support the present cathedral nave on the uneven ground. The style is Romanesque with carved capitals and columns.

Interior. — Behind the baroque façade stands the Romanesque cathedral much as the crowds of pilgrims must have known it in the Middle Ages. The **Door of Glory★★★** (1), a 12C Romanesque wonder carved by Master Mateo, leads from the narthex to the nave. On entering, exhausted pilgrims placed their hands upon the central pillar in token of safe arrival — a gesture which, repeated myriad times, has left finger marks upon the stone. The statues of this triple doorway are beautiful as a composition and in detail, for the master used his art to give variety of expression and styles.

The nave and transept, complete with aisles, are plain but incomparably majestic. Galleries open onto the aisles through twin bays beneath a supporting arch. At major festivals a huge incense burner, the *botafumeiro (displayed in the library)* is hung from the transept dome keystone and swung to the eaves by eight men pulling on a rope — a spectacular performance!

The sanctuary is immensely rich but not necessarily to everyone's taste.

The high altar (2), surmounted by a sumptuously apparelled 13C statue of St James, is covered by a gigantic baldachin. (Pilgrims mounting the stairs behind the altar are going to kiss the saint's mantle.) Beneath the altar a crypt (3) has been built into the foundations of the 9C church which contained St James's tomb and now enshrines the relics of the saint and his two disciples, St Theodore and St Athanasius.

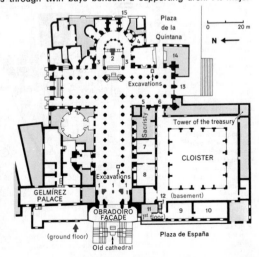

SANTIAGO DE COMPOSTELA★★★

Particularly beautiful among the cathedral's many outstanding features, are the wrought iron grilles and vaulting of the 1521 Mondragón Chapel (4) off the ambulatory, and the Renaissance doors to the sacristy (5) and cloister (6).

The treasure (7 - pieces by the 16C goldsmith Antonio de Arfe) and Reliquary Chapel (8), both on the right of the nave, are good examples of Plateresque interiors.

In 1946 excavations were undertaken in the cathedral beneath the nave and south transept *(visit authorised for experts only; apply at the chapterhouse)*. In addition to the expected foundations of earlier churches, a Roman and Suevian necropolis was discovered and the tomb of Bishop Theodomir, all of which confirmed that the derivation of the name Compostela was not from Campus Stellae (field of the star), as some thought, but from *compostela*, the Latin for cemetery.

Museum. — The library (9), where the *botafumeiro* is displayed, and chapterhouse (10), hung with 18C Madrid **tapestries,** are on the ground floor; on the first floor are five galleries with **tapestries★★** (11) after Goya and Bayeu and a 16C *Life of Achilles*. An archaeological **department** (12), two floors below ground, displays finds from the excavations.

Cloister★. — The plain cloister is crowned by a pierced balustrade with pinnacles.

Goldsmiths' Door★★ (Puerta de las Platerías) (13). — Every square inch of this beautiful Romanesque doorway, with its double arch, is carved in low relief with individual scenes closely juxtaposed as at Sangüesa and Leyre. The **clock tower** (14), on the right, was added at the end of the 17C. To the left, stands the Treasure Tower.

■ OLD TOWN★★ *time: 1 1/2 hours*

Plaza de la Quintana★★ (VX). — Left on leaving the cathedral by the Goldsmiths' Door is this *plaza* made so lively by the bustling of the lingering students. It is bordered at the cathedral's east end by the **Casa de la Canónica (R)** the former canon's residence with a plain but rhythmic arcade and a monastery, whose windows barred by beautiful old wrought iron work, embellish an otherwise austere construction.

Further along, the **Holy Door★** (Puerta Santa) (15 — *see plan of cathedral p 153*) designed by Fernández Lechuga in 1611 and opened only in Holy Years, incorporates all the statues of the prophets and patriarchs carved by Master Mateo for the original Romanesque chancel or *coro.* At the top of a large flight of stairs is the **Casa de la Parra,** House of the Bunch of Grapes **(P)** a fine late 17C baroque mansion.

San Martín Pinario Monastery (V). — The façade overlooking the Plaza de la Inmaculada and the cloister (16-18C) behind, are colossal in style with massive Doric columns in pairs rising from the ground to the roof.

The monastery church which opens onto the Plaza San Martín, on the other hand, has a front composed and as ornate as a Plateresque altarpiece. The interior consists of a surprisingly wide single aisle covered by coffered cradle vaulting. It is lit by a Byzantine style lantern without a drum. The high altar retable, in the most ornate Churrigueresque manner, is by the great architect Casas y Novoa (1730). On either side are baroque pulpits canopied by cottage loaf shaped sounding boards.

Gelmírez Passage (V 32). — Through this passage bordered by imposing edifices one arrives at the Plaza de España.

Plaza de España★★ (V). — The size of the square and the architectural quality of its surrounding buildings make it a fitting setting for the cathedral.

To the left, and in line with the cathedral façade, is the **bishop's palace (Palacio Gelmírez) (A)** *(open 1 April to 30 September 10am to 1.30pm and 4 to 7pm; 75pts.).* 12C and Gothic style apartments are open, including the vast, more than 30m - 98ft long, **synod hall★** with sculptured ogive vaulting. Carved in high relief on the ceiling bosses are scenes from the wedding banquet of Alfonso IX of León.

SANTIAGO DE COMPOSTELA

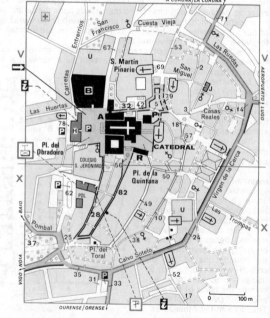

The **Hospital of the Catholic Monarchs** (Hostal de los Reyes Católicos), **(B)** founded by Ferdinand of Aragon and Isabel of Castile as a pilgrim inn and hospital and now a luxurious hotel, presents a **façade**★ adorned with an unforgettable Plateresque doorway which extends to the full height of the building. The hospital's plan of a cross within a hollow square, which affords four *patios,* was common to hospitals of the period. At the centre of the cross is a chapel lit by a lantern on exposed ribs. The dome's beautifully carved supporting columns and the fine mid - 16C gilded wrought iron grille are simply exquisite. *The patios only are open 10am to 1pm and 4 to 7pm.*

Opposite the cathedral is the severely Classical 18C façade of the former Raxoy Palace by the French architect Charles Lemaur (today, the building serves as town hall and Presidency of the Xunta de Galicia-**H**). The square's south side is occupied by San Jerónimo College, a 17C building with an archaic 15C style gateway.

Stroll along the busy **Calle del Franco** (left of the College - **X 28**) where lined up on each side of the street are colleges (such as Fonseca with its Renaissance doorway) boutiques and cafés.

Return to the cathedral by the Puerta Fajera and the **Rúa del Villar** (**X 82**) bordered by arcaded and old houses. Parallel to the Rúa del Villar, the **Rúa Nueva** (**X 49**) also evokes an atmosphere of days past...

■ ADDITIONAL SIGHTS

Santa María del Sar Collegiate Church. — *Calle Castron D'Ouro* (**X 17**). *Open 10am to 1pm and 4 to 6.30pm; closed Sundays; 25pts, including admission to the museum.*

This 12C Romanesque church appears anachronistic by the addition in the 18C of its buttresses. The force of the latter, however, is not superfluous when one looks inside at the astonishing "overflow" of the pillars caused by the pushing down of the vaulting. The only cloister gallery to remain abuts the church and is exceedingly elegant with small raised, paired, **arches**★ richly decorated with carved floral and leaf motifs.

Paseo de la Herradura (**X 37**). — *Acces by the Calle del Pombal.* The wooded hill, once a fairground, makes a pleasant walk with a good **view**★ of the city and the cathedral.

EXCURSION

Pazo de Oca★. — *25km - 16 miles south by road N 525. Garden open 9am (10am in winter) to 1pm and 4 to 8pm (3 to 6pm in winter); 100pts.*

Behind the grey stone *pazo* with its crenellated tower, lies an amazing **garden**★★ in which terraces covered with rust coloured lichen, descend to a water lily pool and to a silent lake on which a stone boat floats idly, where shrubs cast dark shadows...

SOBRADO DE LOS MONJES Monastery

SOBRADO DOS MONXES (La Coruña)

Michelin map **101** fold 3

Sobrado is one of Galicia's vast monasteries, built between the Renaissance and baroque periods. It is badly weatherworn but is in process of restoration by the Cistercian community now living within its walls *(open 10.15am to 3.30pm and 4.15 to 6.45pm; 50pts).*

Preoccupation with size brought a certain severity in the decoration of the church façade. The interior, on the other hand, displays a wealth of imagination in the design, in particular, of the transept cupolas, the sacristy, the Rosary Chapel and the Medallion Cloister.

Of the monastery's mediaeval buildings, there remain a kitchen with a monumental chimney, a chapterhouse and the Mary Magdalene Chapel.

TÚY TUI (Pontevedra)

Michelin map **101** fold 12 — Pop 14 975

Túy was founded by Diomedes, son of the Homeric Hero, Tydeus, according to legend; discoveries on Mount Alhoya confirm at least that a settlement existed on the spot in ancient times. The Romans made it an important township and it became an episcopal seat; Witiza, penultimate Visigoth king, chose it for his residence. It was sacked by invading Arabs and Northmen but arose with renewed vigour to face its strategic rival on the far side of the river, Valença do Minho, in the mediaeval wars between Castile and Portugal.

Since 1884, when a bridge was constructed across the Miño, the town has served as a gateway to Portugal.

Don José Calvo Sotelo, fellow statesman of Primo de Rivera from 1925 to 1930 *(p 12),* was born in the town.

■ SIGHTS

The cathedral, crowning the hill and commanding the river, stands poised above the emblasoned houses and narrow stepped streets of historic Túy.

Cathedral★. — The low-lying church, fringed with crenellations, flanked with towers, still resembles the fortress it was for so long. It was consecrated in 1232 having been built, for the most part in Romanesque Gothic, a style perfectly suited in its simplicity to its military role. The Romanesque north door, marked only by arches cut into the wall stone, is almost austere. In contrast the west front is adorned with a 14C porch which, while remaining defensive in character, is highly decorative with tiers-point arches preceding a richly sculptured **portal.** The tympanum, beneath the chiselled covings, glorifies the Mother of God; above is an Adoration of the Magi and Shepherds and above again the towers of the heavenly Jerusalem rendered ethereal by the interplay of mass and void. The transept plan of three aisles is Compostelan and is found only in these two churches. 16 and 18C additions were confined to the chapels.

The choirstall carvings recount the life and miracles of St Telmo, patron of Túy.

The sentry path over the wide cloister galleries, soberly decorated in Cistercian style, commands good **views** of the river valley.

San Telmo Chapel. — A Portuguese style reliquary shrine has been erected below the cathedral's east end on the site of the house of **San Pedro González Telmo**, a Portuguese Dominican who lived in Túy and died in *ca*1240. Pilgrims visit the alcove in the crypt where the saint died *(entrance: Rúa do Corpo Santo)*.

San Bartolomé Church. — The flat Neo-Classical façade hides one of the oldest churches in Galicia. It dates back largely to the 10C and has a basilical plan of three aisles ending in equal apses. The capitals are pre-Romanesque. The church's site away from the centre of the town is, at first, surprising since from 1069 to 1225 it served as the cathedral but in fact it indicates Túy's original location. *If closed apply to the monastery (Monjas Hospitalarias in Calle Sarabià)*.

Santo Domingo Gardens. — The view from the Gothic church's gardens picturesquely includes Túy hill, crowned by the cathedral, and the river flowing below.

VERÍN (Orense)

Michelin map **441** fold 24 — Pop 9 983

Verín, built between the wide vine covered slopes of the Támega Valley (viñedos del Valle), was already well-known in the Middle Ages; today it lies off the main road, is lively and picturesque with narrow paved streets, houses with glazed balconies, arcades and embossed coats of arms.

Springs rise in the neighbourhood and spa and bottling activities are to be found at **Fontenova** *(take the Vilardevós road and bear first right; free entry to the bottling factory)* and further on at **Cabreiroa, Sousas** and **Villaza**.

Monterrei Castle. — *6km - 4 miles west. Take the* parador *road.*

Monterrei Castle played an important part throughout the Spanish-Portuguese wars, having been strategically built on the frontier for the purpose. It was more than a castle since included within the perimeter were a monastery, a hospital and a town. It was abandoned in the 19C with only a few peasants now living within its walls.

The approach is up a narrow lime avenue from which there is a full **panorama★** of the valley below. *To visit, ask at the house opposite the castle.*

To enter the castle you pass through three defence walls, the outermost dating from the 17C. Inside, at the centre, stand the square 15C keep and the 14C Lady's Tower; the palace courtyard is lined by a three storey arcade and is less austere. The 13C church has a **portal★** delicately carved with a notched design and a tympanum of Christ in Majesty between the symbols of the Evangelists.

VIGO (Pontevedra)

Michelin map **441** fold 12 — *Local map p 151* — Pop 258 724
See town plan in the current Michelin Red Guide España Portugal

Vigo the most important fishing port in Spain is also a large industrial city due to its role as a foreign-trade zone — canning, shipbuilding, metallurgy, and engineering.

Vigo dates back to Roman times. From the 16 to 18C its active commercial trade with North America — authorisation by Charles V in 1529 — attracted English and Turkish corsairs to its waters *(see below)*. In 1589 Drake had attacked the harbour and sacked the town. In the 19C modern Vigo was born; rapidly it has become with Corunna *(p 143)* one of the largest cities in Galicia.

Vigo's **setting★** is outstanding both for its beauty and its maritime advantages. The town, garlanded with pinewoods and gardens, is built in an amphitheatre round the south bank of the deep roadstead, guarded at its entrance by the Cies Islands. The old town and fishermen's quarter are unusual; the Alcabre, Samil and Canido sand beaches, south of the town are very popular.

In the 15 and 16C English buccaneers frequently raided the harbour in search of treasure from the galleons returning with riches from the Spanish colonies.

Treasure laden ships. — In 1701 both English and French corsairs off Vigo surprised ships bringing treasure from the Americas to Philip V of Spain, grandson and candidate of Louis XIV.

In 1702 the Spanish sought protection from the French and a naval escort for their gold, silver and spice laden ships; however, when at the end of their passage the Spanish found themselves intercepted by a combined British and Dutch fleet under Sir George Rooke and the Duke of Ormonde, they turned down the French proposal of seeking shelter in La Rochelle, so sure were they that the French would levy an indemnity, and insisted on continuing on to Vigo. They were destroyed. The treasure seized, it is said, amounted to more than a million pounds and of the galleons not captured many sank to the bottom of the bay from which they have never been raised.

In 1709 Vigo was again taken by the British in the unofficial privateering war which flared eventually in the action of Jenkins Ear.

Castro Castle. — Castro hill behind the town is crowned by a castle fort which commands a magnificent **view★★** of Vigo and the bay.

Mirador La Madroa. — *6km - 3 1/2 miles. Leave Vigo on the road to the airport; after 3.5km - 2 miles bear left (follow signs for "Parque Zoológico"); leave the car in the esplanade in front of the zoo and climb up through the pine forest (50m).* Splendid **view★★** of Vigo and the ría.

*The times indicated in this guide
when given with the distance allow one to enjoy the scenery
when given for sightseeing are intended to give an idea of
the possible length or brevity of a visit.*

7 The Levant Region

The Spain of the huertas. — The Levant region, although largely mountainous, owes much of its richness and originality to its littoral plain, its beauty to the contrast between the grey mountain barrier on the horizon and the lush greenness of the *huertas* in the foreground. The alluvial plain in this southeast corner of Spain stretches from the coast respectively to the Iberian Cordillera, in the north and the Baetic Cordillera in the south. The shore swings round in three great bays, the Gulf of Valencia edged by the **Costa del Azahar** and two further south (Alicante and Murcia), bordered by the **Costa Blanca.** Dunes, often planted with sand retaining pines, offshore sand bars, pools and lagoons (Albufera, the Mar Menor) mark the sea's edge, interrupted, here and there, by rock promontories. By far the largest of these is **Cape La Nao,** actually the northern end of the Baetic Cordillera; others, onetime promontories, such as the hill on which Sagunto stands, have become embanked by alluvial soil, transforming what in Roman times were flourishing ports into inland towns.

The climate of mild winters and hot windy summers is typically Mediterranean except that in this area it is dryer than average. Such rain as there is, falls in autumn and spring in sudden downpours: the rivers flood, bringing alluvial soil down the dry courses *(ramblas)*. Originally this region was both Mediterranean (olive, caroub and almond trees and vines) and steppe-like. However, irrigation — *acequias* — has transformed the countryside into a landscape of **huertas** or intensively cultivated, lush dark green citrus orchards. Around Valencia itself, to the north, are market gardens producing vegetables and flowers; south of the city, beyond the gardens, lie the rice fields of the La Albufera area which, like those around Guardamar (La Mata, Torrevieja), have been cultivated since the Middle Ages and produce the rice used in *paella*, the speciality of the province of Valencia. Further south are the famous **palm groves** of Elche and Orihuela.

Irrigation is controlled on the Valencia *huerta* by a longstanding institution called the Water Tribunal *(p 171).* The *huerta* areas are prosperous and densely populated.

Industry is based on local ports and mineral deposits (lead, zinc, copper and silver) giving rise to metallurgy (Valencia, Alicante), steel (Valencia, Sagunto), paper (Alcoy), shoes (Elda, Vall de Uxó) and toys (Ibi). At **Escombreras** 3.6 million tons of oil were refined in 1985.

The meeting point of many civilisations. — The region has always drawn men to it: Palaeolithic man lived in the caves which abound and left rock paintings, evidence of his daily life; the Phoenicians, established at Cádiz, came east and inland as far as Murcia in their search for metals; the Carthaginians made the Levant their fief until driven out by the Romans. Following the fall of Sagunto, which brought on the Second Punic War, the Romans remained for several centuries until first the Visigoths then the Arabs arrived. The Reconquest brought about the establishment of a Kingdom of Valencia which in the 13C was attached to the crown of Aragon. At the same time the Kingdom of Murcia, extending to Orihuela, and part of Albacete, were linked to Castile. Though so long ago, these events remain evident in the language, with Valencia using a dialect of its own and Murcia speaking Castilian with the addition of many Arabic words (the Arabs, of whom there were a great many in Murcia were only expelled in 1609).

The population has always been markedly independant although subject continually to outside influences. Factions, *germanías*, rose in Valencia against the Emperor Charles V; rebels joined the side opposing Philip V in the War of Succession; the Republican Government sought refuge in the region in November 1936 and again in 1939 (from late 1937 to early 1939 Barcelona was the seat of the government; *p 80).*

The baroque gaiety of Levant art. — Art in the Valencia region, so lively in prehistoric times and in later Iberian sculpture (Cerro de los Santos, La Alcudia), had famous exponents in the Gothic period *(p 170)* and during the Renaissance in Fernando de Llanos, Fernando Yáñez de la Almedina, Juan Vicente Macip (c 1475-1550) and Juan de Juanes (c 1523-1579; *p 170).* The acclaim won in the first part of the 17C with serious works by Ribalta (1555-1628) and Ribera (1591-1652; *p 166)* had given way, by the 18C, to a natural gaiety: baroque decoration spread over palace and church façades, doorways, altarpieces; plaster stucco was applied lavishly to disguise Gothic lines; baroque domes, faced with brilliant, glazed tiles, brought a truly Levantine touch to the Spanish Levant. Spain's major baroque sculptor, Francisco Salzillo was born in Murcia (1707-1783; *p 167).*

Popular joy is expressed in the great local festivals which also provide the occasion for wearing local costume. The Valencia "Fallas" in March are a fabulous institution, emulated, perhaps somewhat palely, by the "Fogueres" of Alicante. The creation for the festivals of giant pasteboard figures, which after the parade are set alight amidst noisy rejoicings beneath sparkling fireworks, enables citizens to indulge their taste for display, satire, caricature and exuberance.

Lastly there are the Moros y Cristianos festivals — the one at Alcoy is the best known — when Moors and Christians fight again.

(After MTTC photo, Madrid)

Murcia - The Cathedral façade

ALCOY (Alicante)

Michelin map **445** fold 18 — Pop 65 908

Alcoy's **site★** at the confluence of the Serpis, Molinar and Barchell Rivers has an incredible mountain setting. The approach from the south, over the **Carrasqueta Pass★** (1 024m - 3 360ft) is very impressive as you round the hairpin bends which take you from the plain to the plateau level of the town. From the Cristina Bridge, in the town, there is a bird's-eye view down to the Callosa de Ensarriá road, another approach.

Alcoy owes its size to industrial development, powered by abundant water supplies not needed for agriculture in so infertile an area. Textiles, paper, agricultural industrial machinery, canning (anchovy stuffed olives) are the principal industries.

Moors and Christians. — The Levant was virtually one huge battlefield throughout the Reconquest. Recaptured cities dreaded the reappearance of the Moors and so when, in 1276, Alcoy, which had been liberated 32 years earlier by James I of Aragon, found itself besieged by the Moor, Al-Azraq, it believed its deliverance could only be by the intervention of St George! In gratitude it still celebrates in the end of April the miraculous relief in the spectacular Moros y Cristianos festivals. For three days, processions march along the beflagged streets and round the walls of a cardboard castle before enacting a fierce conflict won, inevitably, by the Christians.

ALICANTE ★ P

Michelin map **445** fold 21 — Pop 251 387

Alicante has always been enjoyed for its remarkable, luminous skies — the Greeks called it Akra Leuka - the white citadel, the Romans Lucentum - the city of light. The town lies below two hills, which could be easily fortified, and has a natural harbour within a wide bay. It was favoured by the Ancients as it is by the 20C: lying close to the vast beaches of El Postiguet, La Albufereta and San Juan, it has become the tourist capital of the **Costa Blanca** (p 163).

The town prospers through its port which handles produce from the surrounding *huerta* (wine, almonds, dessert grapes) and Murcia. Industry has also recently begun to expand (metallurgy — particularly aluminium — and chemicals).

On 24 June, Alicante gives itself over to the joys of the Fogueres festival (p 157).

■ MAIN SIGHTS time: 2 hours

Follow the route marked on the town plan p 160.

Explanada de España★ (BCZ 7). — This is by far the most pleasant Alicante promenade with its wavy multicoloured marble pavement and magnificent palms providing deep shade as you sit or walk beside the pleasure boat harbour.

Cross the Plaza de Gabriel Miró to the Rambla Méndez Núñez, a bustling main street in the modern area. Continue along the Calle Mayor into the old town and the cathedral.

San Nicolás Cathedral (CY A). — *Open during services.* The church's title of cathedral, which it shares with Orihuela, goes back only to 1959, but its aged foundation dates back at least to the time a mosque stood on the site. The present building is 17C; the nave, in Herreran style, is reminiscent of the Escorial and is dominated by a well proportioned cupola. To the right of the entrance is a fine polychrome Crucifix.

Ayuntamiento (CY H). — The beautiful baroque façade in golden stone is flanked by two towers. A richly decorated rococo chapel, ornate Romantic saloon and the meeting hall are open to visitors (open 9am to 3pm, ask the gate keeper).

Santa María (CY B). — The church with the 18C baroque façade, characteristic of the region, stands in a picturesque square in the old town, just below Santa Bárbara Castle. Once a mosque like San Nicolás, it was rebuilt in the 14C and has since been altered several times inside, particularly in the 17C when the nave was enlarged and the sanctuary disfigured by heavy rococo decoration. Near the entrance is a painting on wood of John the Baptist and John the Apostle by Rodrigo de Osona the Younger, also a graceful Renaissance marble font.

Place names framed in brown : **Huerta capital**
Place names underlined in brown : **Mediaeval ramparts or castle**

Castillo de Santa Bárbara (CY). — *Open 9am to 9pm (7pm 1 October to 31 March; 8pm April and May). Lift charge: 75pts Rtn; 45pts by car (car park: 45pts) ticket valid for lift from halfway to the top.*
Go up by lift and walk back down the path, either all the way (good views) or to the halfway stop.
The fortress originally built, it is said, by the Carthaginian, Amílcar Barca in the 3C BC, stands in a remarkable strategic position on Mount Benacantil. It has played a major role in every warlike episode in the city's history, particularly in the bitter Aragon-Castile disputes of the 13C.

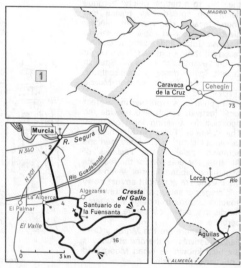

The upper parade ground, the Plaza de la Torreta *(at the lift terminus)*, is overlooked by ancient buildings. A platform on a rock spike near the remains of the keep, commands a **view★** of the old town and its churches, the modern town and the harbour.

The lower perimeter is 16C *(lift halfway point)* and the lowest of all, 18C *(where the path up begins)*.

■ ADDITIONAL SIGHT

Castillo de San Fernando (BY). — The fortifications constructed during the War of Independence, have been turned into public gardens from which there is a good view of the town.

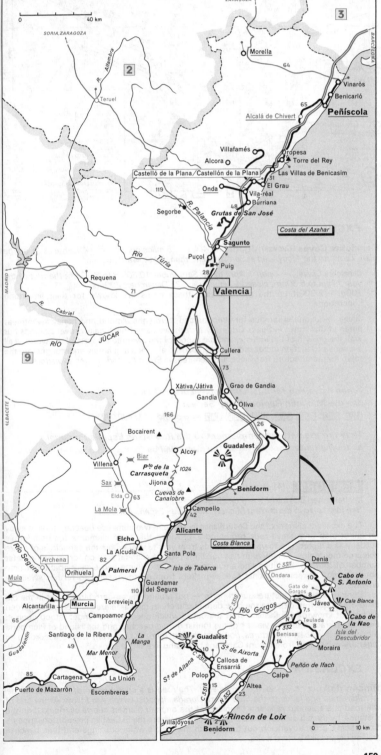

ALICANTE

0   400 m

(Map of Alicante with street labels including: CASTILLO DE SAN FERNANDO, Padre Mariana, Av. de Alcoy, PLAZA DE TOROS, San Carlos, Cuesta de la Fabrica, Vázquez De Mella, Pl. Sta Teresa, Cap. Segarra, San Vicente, Av. Benito Pérez Galdós, Pintor Gisbert, Av. de Salamanca, CASTILLO DE STA BÁRBARA, ASCENSOR, Mola, Pº Federico Soto, Goded, Gerona, San Francisco, Av. de Maisonnave, ESTACIÓN, Av. de Aguilera, Oscar Isabel, Reyes Católicos, Portugal, Av. de Ramón y Cajal, PARQUE DE CANALEJAS, PUERTO, Churruca, Espla, Av. de Loring, Av. de Elche, ESTACIÓN, Pl. Puerta del Mar, PLAYA DEL POSTIGUET, PLAYA ALBUFERETA)

N 330
N 340
168 km ALBACETE
415 km MADRID
81 km MURCIA
24 km ELCHE
12 km AEROPUERTO
Av. Catedrático D. Soler
N 330

Alfonso el Sabio (Av. de)	BY 2
Constitución (Av. de la)	BY 6
Mayor	CY 10
Mendez Núñez (Rambla)	BYZ 12

Calderón de la Barca	BY 4
Calvo Sotelo (Pl.)	BZ 5
España (Explanada)	BCZ 7
Jorge Juan	CY 8
Juan Bautista Lafora (Av. da)	CY 9
Padre Vendrell (Av.)	AZ 13
Poeta Carmelo Calvo (Av.)	BY 14
Ramiro (Pas.)	CY 16
San Fernando	BCZ 17

EXCURSION

Canalobre Caves (Cuevas); Jijona. — *40km - 25 miles north. Leave Alicante by* ① *on the plan. Turn into the Alcoy road at San Juan and then right towards Busot.*

Canalobre Caves. — *Open 1 April to 30 September 10.30am to 8.30pm; the rest of the year 11am to 6.30pm; closed 1 January and 25 December; 200pts.*
700m - 2 300ft up the mountainside, these caves are known for their limestone concretions.

Jijona. — Jijona is famous for almonds and *turrón,* the almond and honey sweetmeat eaten at Christmas in Spain. Originally *turrón* was made from locally grown almonds but with the growth of the industry and the export of the sweet to all parts of the world at all seasons production increased considerably and almonds and honey are brought into the town for manufacture from several other areas in Spain *(factories open to visitors).*

When travelling for business or pleasure in Spain
use the **Michelin Regional Map Series:**
441, **442**, **443**, **444**, **445**, **446**, **447** *at a scale of 1: 400 000.*

They are the perfect complement to the **Red Guide España Portugal**
as towns underlined in red on the maps will be found in the guide.

BENIDORM (Alicante)

Michelin map **445** fold 21 — Pop 25 544
See town plan in the current Michelin Red Guide España Portugal

The excellent climate of the **Costa Blanca** *(p 163)* and two immense beaches curving away on either side of a small rock promontory, provided the basic elements for Benidorm's success as a resort. The town now expands from year to year within the semicircle of ochre coloured mountains, as new high rise buildings provide accommodation for an ever greater number of tourists. Facilities and amusements in the daytime and exceptional night time entertainment attract additional holiday-makers from nearby resorts to further swell the crowds.

Benidorm itself is picturesque in parts — not around the modern blocks, but in the old fishermen's quarter, close to the blue domed church. In the same area is a pleasant garden on a point known as **El Castillo,** after the castle which once, but no longer, stood upon it. From the terrace there are **views★★** of the tourist dotted beaches and the Island of Plumbaria *(accessible by boat: departures hourly: 10am to 8pm; 300pts Rtn)* which, according to legend, was severed from Mount Campana by Roland in a single stroke.

EXCURSIONS

Rincón de Loix★★. — *2km - 1 mile east. The road is a continuation of the Avenida del Mediterráneo and leads to the Club Sierra Dorada signpost which you follow. At the end of the road is a splendid* **panorama★★** *of the orchard planted* huerta *overlooked, in the distance, by the tall* sierras, *and along the coast to where the El Castillo promontory appears like a ship's prow advancing out to sea with the town's white buildings and twin beaches trailing behind like a stern wake.*

Guadalest★. — *28km · 17 miles northwest.* Driving inland, the small valleys, the vegetation, which includes all sorts of fruit trees from citrus to medlars, give the illusion of an earthly paradise.

Polop. — Almost every village in this hilly countryside has a picturesque setting. Polop itself is on a mound encircled by mountains which attracts those who prefer hinterland greenery to the intense heat found along the coast.

Callosa de Ensarriá. — The small agricultural centre of this fertile region.

Take the Alcoy road.

As you approach the *sierras,* the last foothills of the Baetic Cordillera chains which plunge into the sea at Cape La Nao, the landscape becomes more arid but the views more extensive, the mountains more magnificent.

Guadalest★. — Guadalest stands out, facing across the terraced valleys of olive and almond trees, towards the harsh limestone escarpments of the Sierra de Aitana. The **site★** is impressive with the village forced, in self-defence, half-way up a ridge of rock, a natural strong-point accessible only through an

(After Casa Sánchez photo, Alicante)

Guadalest

archway cut in the stone. Little remains from the past for in 1744 an earthquake shattered the rock and wrecked the fortifications. Walk round the **Castillo San José** to see the view which includes the green Guadalest reservoir with its reflections of the surrounding mountain crests, the sea and the amazing site of the old village.

CARAVACA DE LA CRUZ (Murcia)

Michelin map 445 fold 22 — Pop 20 231

Caravaca lies around the foot of a hill crowned with castle ramparts. In May each year, the town celebrates the miracle which took place within its walls in 1232. Then, it is said, a priest named Chirinos was celebrating mass before the Moorish king who had taken him prisoner, when the Cross, which had been missing from the altar, suddenly reappeared; the Moor was moved to immediate conversion and the Cross, always believed to be part of the True Cross, became an object of even greater popular veneration. It was stolen shortly before the Civil War.

Santa Cruz Church. — *To visit apply to the sacristan.* Make for the Castillo where the 15C (restored) ramparts enclose the church which for so long sheltered the Holy Cross *(Santa Cruz).*

The 1722 doorway in local red marble has a surprisingly bold baroque character. *Estípites* or inverted balusters and delicately twisted pillars, more harmoniously ordered than at Vinaròs *(p 162)* add to the vertical character without detracting from the robustness and, in fact, give the entrance something of a Latin-American appearance. Inside there is a strictly Herreran elegance. The Museum of Painting houses canvases (unfortunately in poor condition) by the Master of Caravaca who was influenced by Leonardo da Vinci. These works originally formed part of the altarpiece. From the top of the building there are interesting views of the town and surrounding countryside.

CARTAGENA (Murcia)

Michelin map 445 fold 26 — Pop 172 751

Cartagena, which is uniquely situated at the back of a deep bay sheltered by promontories (Sierra del Algarrobo), is today a major naval base and commercial port. It has prospered for centuries from the export of ores mined inland — lead, iron and zinc.

It was in 223 BC that the settlement was captured by the Carthaginians who enlarged the community into a town which then took the name of its new inhabitants. It developed rapidly under the Romans (traces of the *forum* have been discovered beneath the Plaza de los Tres Reyes); was neglected in preference for Almería by the Arabs and Murcia by the Christians who also removed its bishopric. It returned to favour, however, in the reign of Philip II who fortified the surrounding hilltops and that of Charles III who established an arsenal within its walls.

The construction recently of an oil refinery at Escombreras *(p 157),* 9km - 6 miles away has brought it renewed prosperity.

Near the Plaza del Ayuntamiento is the old submarine (1888) invented by a native of the city — Lieutenant Isaac Peral.

Make your way to the top of the former **Fort Concepción,** now a public garden (Parque Torres), for a good general view of the harbour and the bay. The ruins are those of the Romanesque cathedral destroyed in the Civil War.

Amazing processions take place in the city in Holy Week.

Crafts...
A list of local crafts will be found on p 23.

CASTELLÓN DE LA PLANA   CASTELLÓ DE LA PLANA P

Michelin map **445** fold 9 — Pop 126 464
See town plan in the current Michelin Red Guide España Portugal

Castellón lies at the centre of a *huerta* so unendingly flat that it is known locally as La Plana, the Plain. The town, which originally stood on a cliff a little distance to the north, was moved to its present site in the 13C. It suffered considerably during the Civil War and its Gothic cathedral, apart from the 16C belfry, has been entirely rebuilt. Opposite is the town hall with its elegant 17C façade.

El Grau. — The port of El Grau — the word means landing place — 5km - 3 miles away has been built up as the sea outlet for Castellón's oranges, *azulejos,* furniture, textiles and rope soled shoes. With an immense beach, it is now being developed as a resort.

COSTA DEL AZAHAR (Castellón, Valencia)

Michelin map **445** folds 6, 9, 12, 15 and 18

The coastline, named after the blossom of the orange trees which grow right to the edge of the wide beaches of fine sand, is bathed in almost perpetual sunshine. *Sierra* foothills protect it from the harsh winds of the Meseta to its west.

From Valencia to Vinaròs — *159km - 99 miles - about 1 day*

North of Valencia the coast, which lies constricted between the mountains and the sea, is somewhat hilly. Sand and pebble beaches alternate and tourist development is negligible. Orange groves flourish, growing within a few yards of the sea.

Leave Valencia by ① on the map.

Puig. — The **Monastery of Sta María,** occupied by religious of the Order of Mercy, overlooks the village. *Ring at the side door after the arch. Open 10am to 1pm and 4 to 7pm; 50pts.* The monastery's foundation in the 13C was accompanied by the miraculous discovery in 1237 of a 6C Byzantine style marble low relief of the Virgin which had lain hidden in the earth beneath a bell since the barbarian invasion. James the Conqueror chose the Virgin as patron of the Kingdom of Valencia and ordered the construction of a church and convent in her honour. The church, rebuilt in the Gothic period, was again remodelled in the 18C — the Gothic vaulting, however, has recently been freed of its stucco overlay. The Byzantine Virgin is to be seen at the high altar. The present convent was built between the 16 and 18C; Valencia school paintings are displayed in the 18C cloister.

Take the N 340.

Puçol. — Agricultural centre of the *huerta.*

Sagunto★. — *Description p 170.*

San José Grottoes★ (Grutas). — *17km - 11 miles. 9km - 5 1/2 miles beyond Sagunto bear first left to Vall de Uxó, from where there are signposts, indicating the "Grutas".* The caves *(open 10am (11am Mondays and Tuesdays) to 1pm and 3 to sundown; 275pts, children 125pts)* have been hollowed out by an underground river along which you go by boat for 1 200 yds, seeing on the way beautifully illuminated concretions and extraordinary, eroded shapes.
The tour ends pleasantly with a brief walk.

Turn right at Nules onto the C 225.

Burriana. — Small industrial and agricultural town with a busy port.

Vila-real. — *5km - 3 miles northwest.* The town lies at the centre of an extensive orange growing *huerta.* The immense **parish church,** flanked by an octagonal tower, contains in the sacristy *(to visit apply to the priest)* six paintings vividly depicting the life of the Apostle James by the talented Italian Renaissance painter, Pablo de San Leocadio.

Onda. — *14km - 9 miles by the C 223.* The ruins of the Castle of Three Hundred Towers still dominate the small town. Although Onda is known for its pottery, the ware, principally *azulejos,* is utilitarian compared to that of **Alcora** *(17km - 11 miles north)* which has been famous since the 18C for the rococo decoration applied to its ceramics. The **Natural Science Museum (El Carmen)** *(open 9.30am to 2pm and 3.30 to 8pm (7pm October to February; 7.30pm March to the end of May); closed Mondays (not holiday Mondays) and 20 December to 6 January; 225pts)* stands by the town's southwest exit. The museum displays mammals, fish, reptiles, birds...

Castellón de la Plana. — *See description above.*

Villafamés. — *25km - 15 1/2 miles by C 238 and CS 814.* There is a lovely view of this charming town with its cobblestone streets from the castle ruins. The **Contemporary Art Museum** (Museo Popular de Arte Contemporáneo — *open 11am to 1pm and 3 to 7pm - 8pm in July, August and September; 50pts)* is located in a 15C palace, it displays a number of works of art by such artists as Miró, Chillida, Barjola, Serrano, Genovés, etc...

Las Villas de Benicasim. — Benicasim is now in full development as a resort. From the hill on which the seawater cure hotel stands, you can see right over the bay and the *huerta.*

Oropesa. — A village perched on a hillside above a popular beach.

After 43km - 26 1/2 miles bear right.

Peñiscola★★. — *Description p 169.*

Benicarló. — Small fishing village. The church's baroque doorway is interesting.

Vinaròs. — Big fishing port. The 18C church has a baroque west door.

From Valencia to Oliva

73km - 45 miles — allow 1 day — part of the itinerary on local map p 176

This stretch of coast is particularly popular being, apart from the area around the Cullera lighthouse, a 30km - 50 mile ribbon of fine, pale sand stretched along the sea's edge. The excellent beaches have attracted along its coast the modest development of small seaside resorts, the villages in the past were built inland for greater security from raiders. Most resorts are accessible only along dead end roads through orange groves.

Leave Valencia by ② on the map.

Rice fields appear just south of Valencia. As you approach El Saler you will see the pines planted on the dunes to hold the sand and keep it from silting up La Albufera.

El Saler. — This sand beach near Valencia is ripe for development.

For 2km — 1 mile the road follows the coastline and skirts the Albufera.

La Albufera. — La Albufera is Spain's biggest lagoon — the name in Arabic means small sea. The vast expanse of fresh water in the lagoon is divided from the Mediterranean by an offshore sand bar known as the Dehesa. This is cut by three channels: El Perellonet, El Perelló and the manmade Sueca, through which the fresh water drains into the sea. Since the 13C peasants have profited from the flatness of the land and abundant water to grow rice.

Eel are fished in the lagoon and wildfowl, particularly duck, are shot for sport *(hunting restricted)*. The lake, its people, and atmosphere are unique, especially as night falls. Rent a boat at El Perellonet *(to the east)* or at Silla *(to the west)*.

El Palmar. — The El Palmar road *(3km - 2 miles)*, on the right, is the only carworthy road leading right to the shores of La Albufera.

The village contains several **barracas** or small cottages with whitewashed walls and ridge roofs thatched with rice straw or rushes, formerly the home of *huertanos* or peasants working on the *huertas*. As well as *paella* another local dish is *all i pebre* or eels, from the lagoon, fried in garlic and pepper sauce (*all*: Valencia for garlic; *pebre*: green pepper).

El Perelló. — This fishing port controls Albufera's main outlet to the sea.

Las Palmeras. — Large tourist development close to a good beach.

Cullera. — Cullera is a small harbour at the mouth of the Júcar, which is now being developed with high rise blocks particularly towards the lighthouse headland. The Nuestra Señora del Castillo Hermitage, near the castle ruins, commands a **view**★ of the seaside resort, the old town, the nearby *huerta* and the distant ricefields. *Walk from the Plaza de la Iglesia or go by car along the winding road from the Plaza de José Mongrell in the new part of the town (ignore two roads on the right).*

Coming out of Cullera continue along the main road.

Gandía. — *Description p 165.*

Oliva. — Oliva, the last town in the province of Valencia, lies just under 3km - 2 miles from its, nevertheless, popular beach.

COSTA BLANCA (Alicante, Murcia, Almería) ————————————

Michelin map **445** folds 18, 21, 24, 26, 27 and 29

The southeast coast of Spain, in complete contrast with the nearby Meseta, enjoys a hot dry climate with no rain at all in summer and less than anywhere else at other times. Physically it is a coastline buttressed at intervals by the *sierras* and cut by dry estuaries, formed on the rare occasions when a river may have rushed in flood to the sea. Resorts are developing apace beside the beaches of gleaming sand under the luminous skies of the White Coast or Costa Blanca.

From Alicante to Denia
136km - 84 1/2 miles - allow 1 day — part of the itinerary on local map pp 158-159

This part of the coast is very picturesque with vast beaches divided by headlands. These points multiply as you approach **Cape La Nao** *(p 164)* until the coastline becomes a series of delightful, sand- bottomed creeks.

Leave Alicante by ① on the plan; follow the coast road.

La Albufereta. — The resort at the neck of this promontory which encloses Alicante Bay to the north, has a rocky beach overshadowed by high rise apartment blocks.

San Juan. — The resort north of Cape Huertas, with its long beach of fine sand, is popular with Madrileños and is expanding rapidly.

Campello. — Small fishing village. *Here you return to the main road.*

Villajoyosa. – This is a small port with a church built into its mediaeval ramparts and colour washed houses lining one side of its palm shaded seafront promenade.

Benidorm. — *Description p 160.*

Altea. — Altea, white walls, rose coloured roofs and glazed blue tile domes, rises in tiers up a hillside overlooking the sea — a symphony of colour and reflected light, below the grey cliffs of the Sierra de Bernia. The small fishing village, rapidly developing into a seaside resort, remains highly picturesque, as you will discover if you wander along the alleys up to the church, and from higher still, look down over the village to the sea and the distant, upstanding Peñón de Ifach.

The Sierra de Bernia **road**★ twists and turns before crossing the spectacular Mascarat Ravine *(barranco)* in the mountain hinterland to Cape La Nao.

Calpe. — The **Peñón de Ifach,** rising (332m - 1 089ft) so boldly and unexpectedly from the sea and in shape not unlike the Rock of Gibraltar, provides Calpe with a distinctive **setting**★. The sand bar between the rock and the shore forms twin beaches, which are now separated by high rise blocks with accommodation for the tourists, who flock to the small port, where some of the locals still live by fishing and work at the nearby saltpans.

A path leads to the top of the Peñón *(about 1 hour's walk)* from which, as you climb, you will get interesting views along the coast, of Calpe and the saltpans, of the dark mountain chains, and northwards of the precipitous coast as far as Cape La Nao.

Moraira. — *14km - 8 1/2 miles. Leave Calpe by the north.* The small narrow **road**★ to Moraira winds through the Mediterranean landscape, offering glimpses of pleasant half-hidden villas and, below, of minute sandy creeks. Moraira, sheltered by a promontory complete with an aged tower, is the only village along this little frequented, virtually secluded stretch of coast. *Return to the main road through Teulada (8km - 5 miles).*

Gata de Gorgos. — This small village produces tanned goods, which can be bought from roadside stalls.

Jávea. — Jávea, formerly a fishing port at the mouth of the Jalón, is now a growing resort, its high rise buildings advancing each season ever closer to Cape La Nao. On a mound a little way from the sea, the old quarter remains closely grouped around the fortified Gothic church. Down by the harbour, in the new quarter, is an attractive modern church, the Sta María del Loreto, with the sweeping lines of a ship's hull.

Cape La Nao★. — The climb affords views over Jávea at the feet of the Sierra del Mongó, before you enter pinewoods relieved only by villas standing in individual clearings. **Cape La Nao** is always considered to be the eastern outpost of the Baetic Cordillera chain although in fact the formation continues under the sea to reappear as the Island of Ibiza. The **view★** south from the point is beautiful along the indented coastline to the Peñón de Ifach. The shingle bottomed creeks such as La Granadella (south) or Cala Blanca (north) are excellent for underwater swimming.

Cape San Antonio★. — From near the lighthouse on the headland, a last foothill of the Sierra del Mongó, there is a good **view★** over towards Jávea

(After P. Roy, Explorer photo)

Cape La Nao

and Cape La Nao. Continue along the rocky coast through Las Rotas (villas are going up everywhere amidst the coastal pines) to Denia.

Denia. — An old fort watches over Denia, a fishing and seaport, now a flourishing seaside resort. The town claims to have been founded by Phoceans from Asia Minor and named Dianium by the Romans after the community's temple to Diana.

From Alicante to Águilas — *232km - 144 miles - allow 1 day*

Spain's sandiest shores lie between Alicante and Cape Palos. The coast, backed inland by sand dunes and punctuated by shallow lagoons, affords few natural harbours. Tourist resorts, even today, are widely separated and visitors few, apart from the area around the Mar Menor. Further south the sand beaches give way, in places, to sheltered creeks but even these are not crowded.

Leave Alicante by ② on the map.

Los Arenales del Sol. — A resort profiting from its proximity to Alicante to develop rapidly.

Santa Pola. — The village is known for its restaurants which serve fresly caught fish. Boats leave the harbour *(400pts Rtn)* for the **Island of Tabarca** (Roman remains). Salt flats surround the Vinalopó Delta in the vast and shallow Santa Pola Bay.

Guardamar del Segura. — Guardamar lies near the mouth of the Segura, at the centre of beaches extending beyond the horizon in either direction. Pines, palms and other trees, planted thickly on the dunes not only hold the sand but act as a windbreak.

Torrevieja. — Torrevieja lives off fish, salt and tourists. Hotels are rising rapidly along the indented coastline to the north of the town; salt is harvested after it has crystallised in the natural lagoon saltpans at Torrevieja and La Mata.

Campoamor. — An attractive small seaside resort with fine sandy beaches.

Turn left at San Pedro del Pinatar.

Mar Menor. — The Mar Menor, or Little Sea, is a saltwater lagoon divided from the open Mediterranean by the **Manga,** a sand bar 500m - 1 640ft wide which extends northwards for 20km - 12 1/2 miles from the eastern end of the rocky Cape Palos headland. Almond trees planted in the lowlying hinterland, with here and there a palm or a windmill, add beauty to the landscape of the area which, with good sailing and water skiing facilities on the lagoon, is promised an ever increasing tourist industry. Pontoons with changing cabins line the sea's edge where there is no natural beach in the flourishing resort of **Santiago de la Ribera,** seat of the Air Academy.

La Manga del Mar Menor *(by way of El Algar).* — This elongated seaside resort, developing along the lagoon sand bar is interestingly futuristic architecturally with small houses on piles and luxurious high rise apartment blocks. The enclave is reached by a road which runs to just beyond the bridge over the channel.

La Unión. — Small lead and zinc mining town. Raw materials are shipped through Portman. Held the second or third week in August is the regional folklore festival del Cante de la Minas.

Cartagena. — *Description p 161.*

Puerto de Mazarrón. — The harbour lies in a well sheltered position in the vast bay edged by pleasant, sandy beaches. Houses are being erected in considerable numbers on the nearby hillsides.

The road beyond the small market and mining town of Mazarrón, cuts across the Sierra del Contar, planted here with caroub trees, to reach Águilas.

Águilas. — The town, built on either side of a rock promontory, dates back only to 1765 when Count Aranda, minister to Charles III, enlarged the harbour and restored the castle. The castle summit *(reached up steep paths)* commands a good panorama.

ELCHE ★ (Alicante)

Michelin map 445 folds 20 and 21 — Pop 126 873
See town plan in the current Michelin Red Guide España Portugal

The name Elche is synonymous with palm trees now as it has been ever since the Phoenicians planted groves on the east side of the town hundreds of years ago. The word derives from the Roman, *Illicis,* but the palms and the square white walled, flat roofed, houses produce a Moorish effect — from the bridges over the Vinalopó there are typical views of the ochre houses standing on the site of the old ramparts of which only the Altamira Palace (on the left), onetime *alcázar,* remains. From the 1 to 17 August there are performances of the Elche Mystery *(14 and 15 August inside the basilica)* a mediaeval verse drama recounting the Dormition, Assumption and Coronation of the Virgin. Further festivities take place the 28 and 29 December.

The Palm Grove★★. — The grove, which is by far the most extensive in Europe, numbers even today more than 100 000 trees.

The trees flourish in the mild climate, with the aid of a remarkable irrigation system. Dates are cut in winter from female trees and the fronds, after blanching, from the male trees for Palm Sunday processions and decorations. Cereals and vegetables are grown beneath the trees outside the city limits.

Huerto del Cura★★. — *Open 9am to 9pm; closed Mondays; 100pts.* The *huerto* is a garden of vivid flowers planted beneath particularly magnificent palm trees, including the Imperial Palm, said to be 150 years old.

Municipal Park★. — Located in a beautiful garden established in the Palm Grove is the Museum of Local Handicrafts (Museo de la Artesenía de la Palma - *open Saturdays and Sundays 11am to 1.30pm).*

Santa María Basilica. — The monumental 17C church, designed from the first as a setting for the mystery play, has an interesting baroque portal by Nicolás de Bari.

La Alcudia. — *2km - 1 mile towards Dolores.* The museum *(open 10am to 1pm and 4 to 7pm; closed Mondays; 100pts)* contains archaeological finds, discovered in the city ruins, which date from the Iberian and Roman periods. It was in Alcudia, in 1897, that the mysterious Dama de Elche was discovered *(p 208).*

GANDIA (Valencia)

Michelin map 445 fold 18 — Pop 48 494
See town plan in the current Michelin Red Guide España Portugal

Gandía lies at the centre of a *huerta,* watered by the Serpis and the Bernisa, which produces oranges in quantities. These are exported by the ton from **El Grao de Gandía,** 4km - 2 1/2 miles away, which also handles the town's other industrial products. A seaside resort is developing north of the harbour.

The Borja fief. — The Duchy of Gandía was given in 1485 by Ferdinand the Catholic to the Borjas. The name of this family - Borgia in Italian - acquired its notoriety when in 1492 the Duke, Rodrigo, Bishop of Valencia, became pope, taking the name Alexander VI. He was a remarkable politician but is chiefly remembered for his scandalous private life and as the father of a notorious family including the beautiful but treacherous Lucretia and Caesar — served as a model for Machiavelli's *Prince* — who for political ends had his brother murdered.

However, the fourth duke and great-grandson of Alexander VI, born at Gandía in 1510 was to redeem the family name. He served nearly 20 years as equerry to Queen Isabel at the court of the Emperor Charles V; and on her death in 1539, after having opened her coffin and seen her decomposed body he resolved that if his own wife should die, he would devote himself to God. His wife did indeed die (1546) and he joined the Society of Jesus as a preacher and was ordained in 1551, but soon, despite himself, became third vicargeneral (1565). He left his duchy in the hands of his son while he established the Jesuits throughout western Europe and dispatched missionaries to the Americas. He died in Rome in 1572 and was canonised **St Francis Borja** in 1671.

Former Palace of the Borjas (Palacio del Santo Duque). — *Guided tours (45 min) weekdays May to September 10 and 11am, noon and 5,6 and 7pm; the rest of the year 11am, noon, 4.30 and 5.30pm; Sundays and holidays 10 and 11am, 50pts.*

The mansion in which St Francis was born in the 16C, now a Jesuit college, underwent considerable modification between the 16 and 18C. Only the *patio* remains Gothic in appearance and typical of those along the east coast of Spain.

The tour includes richly decorated apartments with painted or coffered ceilings, *azulejos* and marble pavements. Several rooms have been converted into chapels — one contains the "miraculous" Crucifix, said to have announced to the future saint the imminent death of his wife, another has interesting 16C frescoes.

The last room off the golden gallery has a beautiful floor, a Manises mosaic of the four elements.

Join us in our never ending task
of keeping up to date.

Send us your comments
and suggestions, please.

Michelin Tyre Public Limited Company
Tourism Department

Davy House - Lyon Road - HARROW - Middlesex HA1 2DQ.

JÁTIVA XÀTIVA (Valencia)

Michelin map 📖 fold 18 — Pop 23 755

Játiva, set amidst vine covered hillsides spiked with cypresses, can be seen from a distance because of the crenellated ramparts which ring the two highest hills. The town itself spreads out below. The town was the birthplace of Pope Calixtus III (1455-1458) and Pope Alexander VI *(p 165)* and in 1591 of the painter, José Ribera.

El Españoleto. — José Ribera studied in Valencia, probably with Ribalta before going to Italy where he travelled for a time before settling in Naples in 1616. Lo Spagnoletto, or the Little Spaniard, as Italians called him for his diminutive stature, became accredited to successive Spanish viceroys of Naples, notably the Duke of Osuna, and won early and equally widespread fame in Italy and Spain. A robust and realistic style, reminiscent of Caravaggio in its technique of chiaroscuro, characterises his early work: the religious figures, the monks and saints, have a somewhat coarse energy; the faces are portrayed with painstaking detail; the composition emphasises the dramatic, often dwelling on the atrocious such as the flayed arm in the *Martyrdom of St Bartholomew* (Prado). The later works, however, more serene and in mellower colours, reveal a different and surprisingly sensitive artist.

■ SIGHTS *time: 2 hours*

San Félix Church. — *Access from a signposted path, "Castillo", from the Plaza del Españoleto. Open 10am to 1pm and 4 to 7pm.*
A magnificent group of Valencia **Primitives★** hangs in the Gothic hillside chapel. At the entrance is a white marble **stoup★**, hollowed out of a former capital.

Castillo. — *To visit apply to the caretaker; closed Mondays.* What remains of the castle — it was dismantled under Philip V — stands on the site of the original town. It commands a vast panorama of the old town separated from the modern by the Alameda de Jaume I, and of the *huerta* which extends all the way to the sea.

Collegiate Church. — *Open 9.30 to 11.30am and 7 to 8.30pm.*
The monumental 16C edifice was remodelled in the 18C and has since been restored following a fire during the Civil War.
The Plateresque façade opposite fronts the municipal hospital.

LORCA (Murcia)

Michelin map 📖 fold 26 — Pop 60 627

Lorca lies at the foot of a low mountain range crowned by a rectangular fortress in the fertile valley of the Guadalentín. It is the agricultural market and main centre in the particularly arid southwest corner of the province of Murcia.

"Blancos" and "Azules". — Lorca is one of the cities of Spain where Holy Week is celebrated with full traditional panoply. Sumptuous embroideries, the pride of a local artisanship that is old and famous, adorn the *pasos;* Biblical and Imperial Roman characters in full costume join penitents in long processions, the brilliant colours of the former contrasting with the sombre robes of the latter. Finally, friendly rivalry between the White and Blue Brotherhoods encourages magnificence and solemn dignity.

Casa de los Guevara. — *The house, now the tourist office, is in the Calle Lope Gisbert. The* patio *is open 10am to 1pm and 4 to 6pm; closed Saturday and holiday afternoons and Sundays.*
The doorway, unfortunately in not very good condition, is, nevertheless, a good example of baroque sculpture (1694). Admire the decorated *patio.*

Plaza de España. — *Access by the Calle Prim.*
The square is surrounded by the fine baroque façades of the **town hall,** the palace, now the local **law court** *(juzgado)* and the **Collegiate Church of San Patricio.**

Castillo. — *A road leads from the square to the outer wall.*
The stony path circling the second perimeter commands good views of the town and the wide Guadalentín Valley. Of the fortress itself two towers remain, the rough stone Espolón and the keep, known as the "Torre Alfonsina".

MORELLA (Castellón)

Michelin map 445 fold 6 — Pop 3 337

Morella has an amazing **site★**: 14C ramparts, punctuated by towers, form a mile long girdle round a 1 004m - 3 294ft high hill on which the town has been built in tiers. Crowning the rock summit are the ruins of a mediaeval castle.

The "Maestrazgo". — Morella lies at the heart of the mountain region which was the fief *(maestrazgo)* of the Knights of Montesa, a military order founded in 1316 by James II of Aragon. The order, which had its seat at San Mateo *(40km - 25 miles east of Morella)* as of 1317, fortified all villages in the region so as to better fight the Moors. Each community at the foot of its castle was given much the same appearance with a main square approached by large doorways and narrow streets lined by balconied houses. Most occupy attractive sites and standing as they do in insolated, strongpoint positions, have retained considerable authenticity and character.

St Mary Major Basilica★. — *Open 10am to 2pm and 3.30 to 6pm (5pm in winter); 75pts.*
The basilica is one of the most interesting Gothic churches in the Levant. It has two fine portals: the 14C Apostle Door and the later, Virgin's Door with a pierced tympanum. The unusual raised Renaissance *coro* at the nave centre, has a spiral staircase magnificently carved by a local artist (Biblical scenes) and a delicate balustrade with a frieze illustrating the Last Judgment. The sanctuary was sumptuously decorated in baroque style in the 17C and an elegant organ loft introduced into the nave in the 18C.
There is a small museum (beautiful Valencian Descent from the Cross, 14C Madonna by Sassoferrato).

Castillo. — *1/4 hour climb. Access through the San Francisco Monastery.*
On the way up there are good **views★** of the town, the 13-14C monastery ruins, the 14-15C aqueduct and the rippling lines of the surrounding *sierras*.

MURCIA ★ P

Michelin map 445 fold 23 — Pop 288 631
See map of the built-up area in the current Michelin Red Guide España Portugal

Murcia lies on either side of the Segura, at the centre of a fertile *huerta*. The city, founded in the reign of Abdu'r-Rahman II in 831 as Mursiya, was finally captured in 1266, during the Reconquest and was soon sufficiently secure for the pope to transfer the episcopal seat to it from Cartagena, a city always vulnerable to pirate attack.
Up to the 18C Murcia prospered from agriculture and silk weaving; today, it is a university town and commercial and industrial centre (fruit canning etc.), expanding by wide avenues and walks (Paseo del Malecón) from the original kernel of mediaeval streets.

Two famous 18C sons of Murcia. — **Francisco Salzillo** (1707-1783), the son of an Italian sculptor and Spanish mother, is the last famous name in Spanish polychrome wood sculpture. *Pasos,* or processional groups, were his speciality although single figures and all other types of carving abound among the 1 800 works attributed to the artist and of which one or more examples are to be seen in almost every church in the province.
The other notable 18C Murcian was the statesman, Don José Moñino, **Count of Floridablanca** (1728-1808), minister to Charles III and IV. If Murcia owes him much, Spain owes him more, for it was by his counsel that the country's economy was put on its feet.

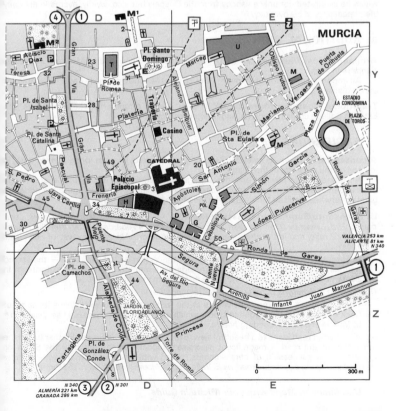

MURCIA★

The Murcia Festivals. — Murcia Holy Week processions are particularly solemn: on the morning of Good Friday, penitents in robes of mauve and stockings embroidered in the style of the peasants of the local *huerta,* bear, in procession through the town, the eight Salzillo *pasos* from the Church of Jesus.

In contrast, the week after Easter is given over to the Spring Festival when, amidst general rejoicing, there are fancy dress parades, processions of floats and finally a Burial of a Sardine, to symbolise the end of Lent.

■ MAIN SIGHTS *time: 3 hours*

Cathedral★ (DEY). — The original edifice, erected in the 14C, is camouflaged outside by Renaissance and baroque additions.

The **façade★,** with an arrangement of columns and curves as successful architecturally as decoratively, is a brilliant example of baroque. One side is flanked by an impressive belfry completed in the 18C. The interior, beyond the entrance which is covered by a baroque cupola and matches the façade, is preponderantly Gothic, apart from the 16C **Capilla de los Junterones** *(4th south chapel)* which has a rich Renaissance decoration. The **Capilla de los Vélez** *(off the ambulatory)* is sumptuous late Gothic with splendid star vaulting and wall decoration which clearly includes Renaissance and Mudejar motifs. In a gallery to the left is a skeleton! The sacristy, approached through two successive Plateresque doors with outstanding panels, is covered by an unusual, radiating dome. The walls are magnificently panelled with Plateresque carving below and baroque above.

The interesting carved stalls (1567) in the chancel *(coro)* are from an old Castilian monastery.

Museum. — *Go through north transept; open 10am to 1pm and 4.30 to 7pm; 50pts.*

At the entrance is a Roman sarcophagus showing Apollo and the Muses. The treasure, in the chapterhouse, includes monstrances and the crowns of the Fuensanta Virgin, while in the side chapels are Salzillo's **St Jerome★** from the Ñora Monastery and a 14C altarpiece by Barnaba da Modena of St Lucy and the Virgin.

Belfry. — *Same opening times as the museum; closed Mondays; 35pts.*

At the top there is an interesting **panoramic view★** of Murcia and its *huerta,* ringed by mountains.

In the cathedral square is an Italianate **bishop's palace,** with an elegant cloister.

Calle de la Trapería (DY). — One of the most sumptuous **Casinos** in Spain was built in the late 19C in this main street through the old quarter. Its comfort, elaborate decor and general atmosphere, give it much the style of a 19C London club — with the same rule of men only!

On the palm tree shaded **Plaza de Santo Domingo** can be seen the east end of the church of the same name (**E**); the baroque west face, never completed, overlooks the Plaza de Romea.

Salzillo Museum★ (CY M). — *Open 9.30am to 1pm and 4 to 7pm (3 to 6pm in winter); closed Sunday and holiday afternoons, 1 May and 14 September; 75pts, Sundays free.* The museum possesses many of Salzillo's masterpieces including the eight polychrome wood sculptures of *pasos* carried by the Brotherhood of Jesus in the Holy Week processions *(see above).* They stand in the side chapels of the Church of Jesus, where the deep emotion on the faces in the Last Supper and Christ's Arrest and the majesty of St John and the Angel in the Agony in the Garden groups can be clearly seen.

There are also in the museum countless numbers of the artist's terracotta figurines in which he illustrated not only episodes from the Gospels but also, vividly, events in the daily life of peasants of his own day.

■ ADDITIONAL SIGHTS

Archaeological Museum (DY M[1]). — *Open 9am to 2pm; closed Mondays as well as Sundays in August; 75pts.*

An important collection of Hispano-Moorish (12-14C) and Spanish (17 and 18C) ceramics are on display.

Traditional Costume Museum (DY M[2]). — *Closed temporarily.* The museum in San Esteban College contains regional and foreign costumes.

EXCURSIONS

Alcantarilla. — *9km - 6 miles by ③ on the plan.* A **Huerta Museum** *(open 9am to dusk)* is located on the outskirts of the village.

An ethnographic pavilion provides background information while outside are orange trees and market gardens, white *barracas* or rustic dwellings of another age and a *noria,* the giant waterwheel devised for irrigation by the Moors.

La Fuensanta Sanctuary; Cresta del Gallo★. — *Round tour 32km — 20 miles. Local map p 158. Leave by ② on the plan. Turn left towards La Alberca shortly after the railway (1km - 1/2 mile) and left at the canal and turn right before Algezares by way of Fuensanta (signposted).*

La Fuensanta Sanctuary. — The Sanctuary of the Virgen de la Fuensanta — the sacred fountain is the goal of a popular pilgrimage each autumn during the first fortnight in September. There is a good view of the *huerta* from the church terrace.

Continue on the road via "Cresta del Gallo" (signposted).

Cresta del Gallo★. — From a belvedere at the foot of the peak which takes its name of Cock's Comb from the jagged red rocks which outline its crest, there is a vast **panorama★** of Murcia and its surrounding *huerta.*

A non-surfaced road leads to a beautiful **view** *(5km - 3 miles)* of the *huerta.* Further on, on the other side of the road, a magnificent **panorama★** suddenly opens out over the Sierra de Columbares, a succession of bare summits, pitted with craters. *After a 5km - 3 miles descent you reach a surfaced road via El Valle and La Alberca which leads to Murcia.*

Use Michelin Maps with your Michelin Guide.

ORIHUELA (Alicante)
Michelin map 445 fold 23 — Pop 49 851

Life is peaceful amidst the many churches in the town of Orihuela which lies along the banks of the Segura, at the foot of a deeply scored hill. The river provides water for the abundant orange and lemon trees of the *huerta* and for the **palm grove**★ which is best seen from the N 340.

Orihuela, although attached to the Kingdom of Valencia in 1304, has always naturally been a part of Murcia of which it was the capital under the Visigoths and the Arabs. In the 16C it was made an episcopal see and for two centuries it was a university town, until the 18C, when it was supplanted by the city of Murcia itself.

Sto Domingo College. — *Near the Alicante Gate at the north end of the town.* The so-called college, now the diocesan school, housed Orihuela University from its foundation in the 16C until it ceased to exist in the 19C.

The sober Renaissance façade conceals two cloisters — a large one, restored since the Civil War, and a Herreran style, two storey court known as the University Cloister. The vast 18C church has coloured frescoes in the nave, rich rococo stucco mouldings in the chancel and transept.

El Salvador Cathedral. — *In the Calle Ramón y Cajal.* The cathedral, which has shared its title since 1959 with Alicante, was erected in the 14 and 15C in the Gothic style. The South or Chain Door is Gothic but the North or Annunciation Doorway is later and elegantly Renaissance. The three aisles inside have Gothic vaulting with occasional, highly original spiral ribs.

In the museum *(open 10.30am to 1pm; apply to the tourist information centre)* is Velázquez' painting of the *Temptation of St Thomas Aquinas;* a *Christ* by Morales and a *Mary Magdalene* by Ribera.

The 18C bishopric facing the cathedral has a delightful cloister.

Santiago Church. — *The church stands in a shaded square beyond the town hall, going towards Murcia.* It was built by the Catholic Monarchs for the Order of Santiago — the sovereigns' emblems and St James figure prominently on the Gothic portal.

In the Gothic interior note the side chapels: statues attributed to Salzillo — the Holy Family is outstanding. The legacy of the Knights of Santiago may be seen in the silver treasure in the **museum** *(temporarily closed).*

You will find an index at the end of the guide
listing all subjects referred to in the text
(monuments, picturesque sites, points of interest,
historical or geographical items, etc.).

PEÑISCOLA ★★ (Castellón)
Michelin map 445 fold 6 — Pop 3 077

Peñíscola, a peninsula (from which the name derives) closely built up now with cubic, white walled cottages to the foot of the austere stone castle at the summit, was the final refuge of the mediaeval antipope, **Benedict XIII.**

A resort is developing on either side of the neck of the promontory, beside the vast sand beaches.

Pope Luna. — In 1394 the Aragon Cardinal Pedro de Luna was elected successor to the antipope Clement VII by the French cardinals in conclave at Avignon. It was a dubious heritage, however, as his predecessor had never succeeded in establishing his claim. The withdrawal of the support of King Charles VI of France and of St Vincent Ferrer, the accusation of heresy by the Councils of Pisa (1409) and Constance (1416), in no way diminished the self styled Benedict XIII's conviction of his right. He considered the proposal that he should abdicate and help to heal the schism, inadmissible and, in the face of general hostility, sought refuge in the fortress on Peñíscola. There he remained until he died in 1422, a nonagenarian, tenacious as ever, who even named his own successor! (This prelate had little stomach, however, and soon abdicated in favour of the Rome elected Martin V).

The old city★★. — The village within the ramparts, which date from the reign of Philip II, has narrow twisting streets *(closed to cars)* amusing to wander along.

Castillo. — *Open 1 June to 30 September 9.30am to 8.30pm; 9am (10am April and May) to 1pm and 4 to 6pm (5pm April and May) the rest of the year; closed 1 January and 9 September;* 100pts.

The castle, built by the Templars in the 14C, was modified by Pope Luna whose coat of arms, which includes a crescent moon in allusion to his name, can be seen on one of the gates.

Grouped round the parade ground are the church, a vast hall with pointed vaulting and a free standing tower containing the conclave room and the study of the learned antipope who, among his many acts, confirmed in six bulls the foundation in 1411 of St Andrew's University in Scotland *(see Michelin Green Guide to Scotland)* and promulgated the Statutes of Salamanca University.

View★ of the village from the castle terrace.

REQUENA (Valencia)
Michelin map 445 south of fold 11 — Pop 18 152

Requena is a commercial town in the heart of a vineyard area. The old town perched on a mound, still has considerable character with narrow streets, old houses and straddling arches.

The two churches, **San Salvador** and **Santa María** (where the stone is sadly weatherworn) have interesting Gothic doorways. Inside Santa María there is appealing *azulejos* decoration.

SAGUNTO ★ (Valencia)

Michelin map 445 fold 12 — Pop 52 759

Sagunto, with its back against a wide hill, crowned by the ruins of an ancient citadel is surrounded on its other three sides by a *huerta*, watered by the Río Palancia. The port 5km - 3 miles away handles the export of oranges and import of coal for the large local steelworks, using iron brought from Aragon.

A legendary siege. — Sagunto, like Numantia *(p 248)*, has a place in Spain's heroic history. In 218 BC the Carthaginian general, Hannibal, besieged Sagunto, then a small seaport allied to Rome — the harbour and surrounding countryside have since silted over. Sagunto was abandoned by Rome, and the inhabitants, seeing only one alternative to surrender, lit a brazier. They fed the fire until the flames were high, then women and children, the sick and the old, threw themselves into the furnace while soldiers and menfolk made a suicidal sortie against the enemy. The event marked the opening of the Second Punic War. Five years later Scipio Africanus the Elder rebuilt the city which became an important Roman and, later, Visigoth, town.

The ruins★. — *Cross the old quarter to the ruins. Ruins and museum open 10am to 2pm and 4 to 7pm (6pm in winter); closed Sunday and holiday afternoons and all day Monday; 150pts.*

The Theatre. — The Ancient Roman theatre on the hillside has been restored.

The Acropolis. — Ruins and remains can be seen superimposed and juxtaposed of ramparts, temples and houses built by Iberians, Phoenicians, Carthaginians, Romans, Visigoths, Arabs... In 1811, in the War of Independence, the French General Suchet besieged the town, leaving major works on the west side to mark yet another period in Sagunto's history. A vast **panorama★** spreads out on all sides from the Acropolis — the town, *huerta*, Palencia Valley, the sea.

EXCURSION

Segorbe. — *33km - 20 1/2 miles northwest by the N 234.* The town, an episcopal see since Visigoth times, has a remodelled Neo-Classical cathedral, chiefly important for its **museum** in which are a number of altarpieces painted by the Valencia school. *Open 11am to 1pm and 5 to 7pm; closed Sunday and holiday afternoons; 100pts.*

There are several paintings by **Juan Vicente Macip** who remained attached to the Gothic style although he was greatly influenced by the Italian Renaissance style *(Adoration of the Kings)*. His son **Juan de Juanes** *(p 176)*, however, took up with a certain charm the favourite themes of Leonardo da Vinci — note his *Ecce Homo.* Several works displayed are attributed to Rodrigo de Osona the Elder or his son. A *Last Supper*, said to be by Jacomart aided by Juan Reixach, is especially notable for its portraiture. In the treasury there is a magnificent 15C marble bas-relief of a Madonna by Donatello. The chapterhouse within the Gothic cloister is beautiful.

VALENCIA ★★ P

Michelin map 445 folds 12 and 15 — Pop 751 734

Valencia, the capital of a fertile agricultural province of the same name, is a prosperous industrial centre with shipyards, metallurgical and chemical plants, furniture and textile factories. The produce and those products exported by sea from this, Spain's third largest city, are handled at the nearby, bustling port of **El Grao.**

The modern city is swathed round the old, its wide avenues encircling the fortified gates, old churches and narrow streets lined with Gothic style houses.

Valencia and its history. — The city, founded by the Greeks, passed successively into the hands of the Carthaginians, the Romans, Visigoths and Arabs. In 1094 it was reconquered by the Cid *(p 216)* who was created Duke of Valencia but lived only five years in the city before dying there in 1099. The Moors recaptured it three years later and held it until 1238 when it was once more retaken, this time by James the Conqueror, who declared it the capital of a kingdom which he allied to Aragon. Valencia then enjoyed 150 years of prosperity until the 15C when, like Catalonia and Aragon, it began to decline. A silk renaissance in the 17C renewed its fortunes.

Prosperous or not, Valencia has been involved over the past two centuries in every war and insurrection in Spain. In 1808 it rose under the leadership of a Father Rico against the French and set up an independent city government; in 1812 it was retaken but held only briefly by Suchet after the French victory over the English at Albufera; in 1843 it rose under **General Narváez** to restore the regency of María Cristina of Naples; finally in the Civil War the city became in March 1939 after the fall of Catalonia, the last refuge of the Republican forces, only ceasing all resistance at the end of the month on the 30th following the fall of Madrid.

Bombing during the Civil War destroyed or damaged many buildings in the old town.

Art in Valencia in the 15C. — Valencia knew a brilliant period, both economically and artistically, in the 15C due to the patronage of Don Fernando de Antequera, elected King of Aragon by the Caspe Commission in 1412. (Among Valencia's own envoys to the Commission was the future Saint, Vincent Ferrer).

Examples of the 15C architectural flowering are to be seen in the palaces, city gates, the cathedral, the Lonja and the contemporary Gothic mansions in the old city and in the sculptures adorning entrances and portals as at St Martin's.

In painting several artists won renown: **Luis Dalmau,** influenced by Flemish painting, who evolved a Hispano-Flemish style; Jaime Baco, known as **Jacomart,** and his fellow, **Juan Reixach** who were both influenced by Flanders and Italy and the **Osonas,** father and son, who again showed Flemish austerity in their work.

Valencia craftsmen of the 15C were also outstanding in the decorative arts: wrought iron, gold and silversmithing, embroidery and especially in ceramics, for which special centres were established at Paterna and Manises *(p 173)*.

The Valencia huerta. — The city lies along the banks of the River Turia at the heart of a fertile countryside known locally as La Huerta. On this expanse, watered by an irrigation system laid down by the Romans and improved by the Arabs, are the millions of orange trees which produce the fruit for which the whole region is famous.

These are beautiful in April when in blossom and in November when they are brilliant with fruit. The *huerta* also grows vegetables and fruit for the city. South of Valencia are the paddy fields of La Albufera *(local map p 176)*, brilliant, at times with the green of young riceplants.

Since the Middle Ages disputes in the *huerta* have been settled by the Water Tribunal: every Thursday at 10am, representatives of the areas irrigated by the eight canals, accompanied by an *alguazil*, meet before the Apostle Door of the cathedral; the offence is declared, judged and sentence pronounced immediately (a fine, deprivation of water) by the most senior judge. The proceedings are oral and there is no appeal.

The *huerta* has found its place in literature in the realistic, dramatic novels of **Vicente Blasco Ibáñez (1867-1928):** *La Barraca* (The Cabin), *Entre Naranjos* and *Cañas y Barro* which describe the life of the fisherfolk and ricegrowers of the Albufera.

The Fallas. — Valencia holds a week long carnival every year during the week preceding 19 March. The custom goes back to the Middle Ages when on St Joseph's day, the carpenter's brotherhood, one of the town's traditional crafts, burned their accumulated wood shavings in bonfires known as *Fallas* (from the Latin *facula* or *fax:* torch). The name became synonymous with a festival for which, in time, objects were made solely for burning — particularly effigies of less popular members of the community! In the 17C single effigies were replaced by pasteboard groups or floats produced by quarters of the town — rivalry is such that the figures are fantastic in size, artistry and satirical implication. Prizes are awarded during the general festivities which include fireworks, religious and flower processions, *corridas* etc., before everything goes up in the fires or *cremá* of the evening of 19 March.

■ THE OLD TOWN *time: 3 1/2 hours not including the Ceramics Museum*

Follow the route marked on the plan on pp 174-175.

Cathedral★ (EX A). — The cathedral stands on the site of a former mosque. Although construction began in 1262, the major part of the building dates from the 14 and 15C. The Gothic style was completely masked in the late 18C by a Neo-Classical renovation which has been recently removed.

The early 18C west face, which is elegant in spite of being narrowly confined, is in imitation of the Italian baroque style (by a German architect). The lower relief is by Ignacio Vergara, who with Esteve, executed the Assumption of the tympanum. Abutting the façade is the **Miguelete★,** or Micalet as the Valencians call it, a tall Gothic octagonal tower with pierced upper bays, apparelled in a delicate Flamboyant tracery. The south door, the Puerta del Palau, is Romanesque, the north, the **Apostle Door,** Gothic, decorated with numerous, but timeworn sculptures. The Virgin and Child surrounded by angel musicians, now at the tympanum, stood against the pier until this was removed in the 16C; the figures beneath the rose window are the Doctors of the Church. The windows in the beautiful Flamboyant Gothic lantern above the transept crossing are of alabaster.

Sanctuary. — The high altar retable, painted early in the 16C by Fernando de Llanos and Yáñez de la Almedina, illustrates the Lives of Christ and the Virgin in a style markedly influenced by Leonardo da Vinci.

Ambulatory. — Behind a beautiful balustrade at the back of the high altar there is an alabaster relief of the Resurrection (1510). Opposite is the 15C Virgen del Coro in polychrome alabaster and, in a chapel, a Crucifixion attributed to Alonso Cano.

Chapel of the Holy Grail or chapterhouse *(1st right on entering)*. — The chamber, which in the 14C served as a reading room, has elegant Flamboyant vaulting. Behind the altar, twelve alabaster low reliefs by an Italian sculptor half encircle a magnificent small purple agate cup, said to be the Holy Grail (the vessel traditionally used by Our Lord at the Last Supper and in which a few drops of his blood are said to have fallen). The cup, according to legend, was brought to Spain in the 4C and belonged first to the Monastery of San Juan de la Peña *(p 70)* then to the crown of Aragon which in the 15C, presented it to the cathedral.

Museum. — *Access through the Holy Grail Chapel. Open 10am to 1pm and 4 to 6pm; closed Sunday and holiday afternoons and December to February; 50pts.*

(After N. Thibaut, Explorer photo)

Valencia — The Cathedral

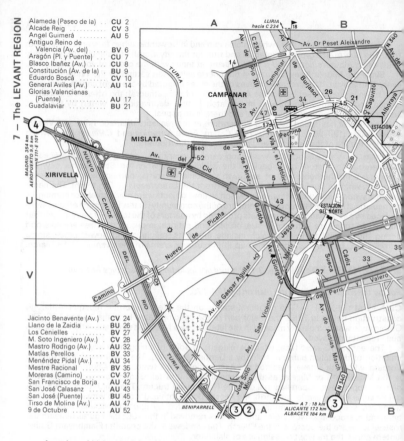

A series of Valencia Primitive altarpieces precedes a painting by Zurbarán, a Virgin by Correggio and an *Ecce Homo* by Juan de Juanes. The treasury includes several very rich pieces, the most magnificent being a monumental custodial made since the Civil War. In the St Francis Borja Chapel are two large paintings by Goya of the saint exorcising a dying man and bidding farewell to his family on entering the Church.

Ascent of the Miguelete. — *Open 10am to 1pm and 4.30 to 6pm; 75pts.* From the top there is a bird's eye view of the cathedral roofs and the town with its countless glazed ceramic domes.

Nuestra Señora de los Desamparados (EX B). — Beneath the church's cupola stands the venerated statue of the patron of Valencia: the Virgin of the Abandoned *(desamparados)*

Palacio de la Generalidad★ (EX W). — *Apply for permission to visit. Open weekdays 9am to 2pm.*

This fine 15C Gothic palace to which one tower was added in the 17C, and a second, identical with the first, in the 20C, was, until the reign of Philip V (who suppressed the *fueros* in 1707) the meeting place of the Valencia Cortes. Like those of Aragon and Catalonia, this Cortes was charged with the collection of the "general" tax, so-called since no one escaped paying it. The name remains.

You enter an attractive Gothic *patio* before ascending to the first floor to see the oratory (altarpiece by the local 16C painter, Juan Sariñena), the Royal Hall (portraits of the Valencian Kings) and the Cortes' Grand Council Chamber. The *azulejos* frieze and the caissoned ceiling are 16C; the Churrigueresque gallery was an 18C addition. Several of the 16C portraits are of members of the Cortes (which only sat twice, neither time in this hall!) and the Water Tribunal. More remarkable still are the two golden saloons in the 17C tower, each with a wonderful gilt and multicolour *artesonado* **ceiling★**. The second contains an amazing sculpture, typical of the Valencian artist Benlliure, of Dante's Inferno (1927).

Calle de Caballeros (EX). — Some of the houses along the main street of the old town have kept their Gothic *patios* (nos 22, 23).

San Nicolás (EX C). — *Access along the Calle Abadía.* This, one of the town's oldest churches, has been completely renovated in the Churrigueresque style. Among the 16C paintings are an altarpiece by Juan de Juanes *(chapel to the left on entering)* and a Calvary by Osona the Elder *(by the font).*

Follow the Calle de la Bolsería.

Lonja★ (EX E). — *Open 10am to 2pm and 4 to 6pm; closed Mondays, holidays and Sunday afternoons.*

The present building was erected at the request of the Valencia silk merchants in the 15C (from 1483 to 1498) to replace an earlier commercial exchange similar to those of Barcelona and Palma. The prosperity which required a larger building was well reflected in the style of the new edifice: Flamboyant Gothic.

The Lonja, topped by a notched roof ridge, has an impressive Gothic entrance. The left wing, divided by a tower from the entrance, is crowned by a gallery decorated with a medallion frieze. The old commercial silk **hall★** is lofty, with ogival arches supported on elegantly twisted pillars; the walls are pierced with bays filled with delicate tracery.

A staircase from the Orange Tree Court leads to the Maritime Consulate (law court). *If closed apply to the caretaker.* The late 15C **ceiling★**, from the old town hall, is made up of carved and gilded beams supported by consoles sculpted with human and fantastic animal figures.

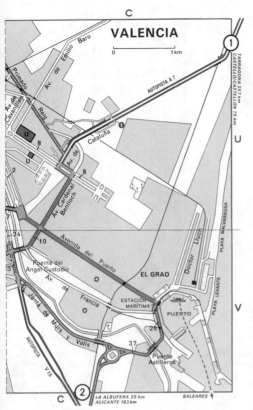

Iglesia de los Santos Juanes (DEX F). — This vast church, near the local market, with its single aisle is a good example of the transformation often effected in the 17 and 18C by the application of exuberant Churrigueresque stucco to Gothic interiors. The impressive south face dates from 1700. The church was badly damaged by fire in the Civil War.

Return to the cathedral square (Plaza de Zaragoza) by the Plaza del Collado.

As you pass the **Church of Santa Catalina** (EXY K) look up at its architecturally successful 17C baroque belfry.

Follow briefly the Calle San Vicente Mártir a bustling shopping street in the modern quarter.

San Martín (EY L). — The west door is decorated with a bronze group by the Flemish Gothic school, which illustrates St Martin dividing his cloak.

Ceramics Museum★ (Museo Nacional de Cerámica) (EY M[1]). — *Open 10am to 2pm and 4 to 6pm; closed Sunday and holiday afternoons and Mondays, Maundy Thursday, Good Friday and Christmas Day; 200pts.*

The old Palace of the Marquess de Dos Aguas has an amazing Churrigueresque façade: the alabaster doorway, carved by Ignacio Vergara in the 18C after a cartoon by the painter, Hipólito Rovira, shows two burly atlantes pouring water *(agua)* from amphorae in illustration of the marquess' name.

The painter, who died mad, covered the façade with frescoes which were destroyed in the 19C.

Nearly 5 000 ceramic exhibits dating from the Iberian period to the present, make up the collection, which was donated in large part by a great amateur, González Martí.

Most of the pieces on display were made locally. The oldest, going back to the 13C are from **Paterna** *(6km - 4 miles north of Valencia)*. The green and white ware, in which brown manganese streaks can be seen, and the alternative blue and white, were supplanted in popularity in the 14C by lustreware from **Manises** *(p 175)*. This, in turn, fell from favour in the 17C, when the colours of Talavera ceramics *(p 213)* were found more pleasing, and became all the fashion.

In the 18C potteries were set up at Alcora *(p 162)* and the craft was revived locally in Valencia and the surrounding area. Manises has resumed production and is now manufacturing on a fairly large scale.

On the 1st floor are galleries showing Alcora maiolica, Oriental porcelain and *socarrats* or the tiles which, in the 14 and 15C, were used locally to face the areas between beams in ceilings.

On the 2nd floor is a gallery with Picasso ceramics; a Valencian kitchen has been set up, and in other rooms Paterna ware and Manises lustre dishes and plates are displayed.

On the ground floor is the 18C carriage of the Marquess de Dos Aguas.

The Patriarch or Corpus Christi Collegiate Church★ (Colegio del Patriarca) (EY N). — This former seminary, founded by the Blessed Juan de Ribera, Archbishop of Valencia and Patriarch of Antioch, dates back to the 16C. The *patio*, which is architecturally harmonious has, at the centre, a statue of the founder by the modern sculptor, Benlliure. The seminary is characterised by the *azulejos* friezes, some in a relief known as *de diamante,* which colour all the lower walls.

In the south chapel hang six 15C Flemish tapestries; in the north, walls and vaulting are entirely covered with frescoes by Matarana.

The **museum** is in the Rectorial saloon and adjoining rooms on the 1st floor. *Open Saturdays, Sundays and holidays 11am to 1pm; 50pts.* The interesting collection of 15 to 17C pictures includes paintings by the Valencia Primitives, by Juan de Juanes, Caravaggio, Van der Weyden (beautiful triptych) and finally Ribalta, Morales and El Greco (one of the many versions of the *Adoration of the Shepherds*).

Facing the college is the **University** (EY U), the buildings grouped round a vast Ionic quadrangle *(entrance in the Calle Universidad).*

Make for the Plaza San Vicente Ferrer and then the Calle Palau.

Casa de los Almirantes de Aragón (FX P). — This 15C house preserves, as a symbol of its former noble status, a Gothic entrance arch *(zaguán)* and *patio.*

Almudín (EX M[2]). — This 14 to 16C granary with popular style frescoes covering the walls and 19C *azulejos* altar, is now a **palaeontology museum** *(open 10am to 1pm and 4 to 6.30pm; closed Mondays, holidays and Sunday afternoons).* It displays, among other items, antediluvian skeletons discovered in Argentina by the Valencian, José Rodrigo Botet.

In the nearby Plaza Beltrán, the house located at no 1 or the **Casa de Escribá** (FX R) has a Gothic *patio.*

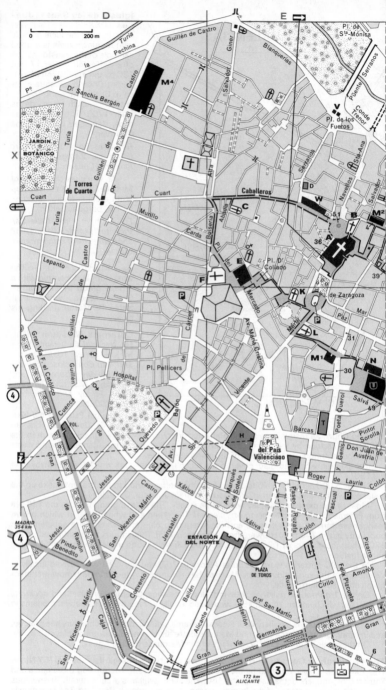

■ ADDITIONAL SIGHTS

Plaza del País Valenciano (EY). — This bustling square in the centre of modern Valencia, with the town hall overlooking it on one side, is famous for its brilliantly spectacular flower market.

Santo Domingo Monastery (FY S). — *Apply at the sentry post.* The church of this 16C monastery was considerably remodelled in the 17C. The 15C **Royal Chapel★**, in which the groined Gothic vaulting without ribs is an architectural masterpiece, contains the tombs surmounted by recumbent statues, of the 17C Marquesses of Cañete. A part, including the great Gothic cloister and chapterhouse, is now occupied by the army.

Jardines del Real (FX). — The royal gardens have become Valencia's major park. The Royal Bridge, the **Puente del Real** and the Puente del Mar are both 16C, the former being decorated at one end with niches containing modern copies of earlier revered statues of St Vincent Ferrer and St Vincent the Martyr of Saragossa.

Fine Arts Museum★★ (Museo Provincial de Bellas Artes) (FX M³). — *Open 1 October to 30 June 10am to 2pm and 4 to 6pm; the rest of the year 10am to 2pm; closed Sunday and holiday afternoons and all day Monday, 1 January, Good Friday and Christmas Day; 200pts.*

1st floor. — 15 to 19C painting. The most interesting are the Primitives. Countless altarpieces prove the vitality of the Valencia school of the 15C — among the many are Jacomart, Reixach, the Elder and Younger Osonas and many anonymous artists such as the authors of

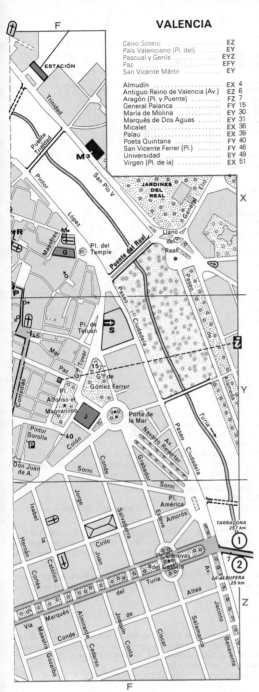

VALENCIA

the Flemish influenced retable of San Martín (gallery 25) or that of Fray Bonifacio Ferrer (gallery 27). In gallery 30 there is a triptych by Hieronymus Bosch (1450-1516), *Los Improperios* — the Mocking of Christ — of which the original centrepiece is in the Escorial Monastery. Representing the Renaissance are Juan Vicente Macip and Juan de Juanes *(p 170)*, Yáñez de la Almedina, Fernando de Llanos, Fray Nicolás Borrás, a Valencian and Morales (Calvary). Tenebrism (term applied to paintings in dark tones) made its first appearance in Spain at the beginning of the 17C in the works of Ribalta and came to full fruition in those of José de Ribera whose *St Sebastian* and *St Jerome* can be seen hanging next to a canvas by El Greco. In the same period first Juan Sariñena acquired local repute then the baroque Valencia artist, Espinosa. One gallery is devoted to Goya and in one room there hangs, all alone, the self-portrait of Velázquez. Finally come the 19C academic painters of whom Vicente López, again a native of Valencia, is the most famous.

2nd floor. — Displayed on this floor are 19 and 20C works of art. Note the Valencian artists Francisco Lozano (gallery 67), Joaquín Sorolla (gallery 66), Ignacio Pinazo (galleries 71 and 72) and Antonio Muñoz Degrain (galleries 73 and 75).

3rd floor. — 19 and 20C historical painting.

Ground floor. — Iberian and Moorish archaeology; Romanesque, Gothic and Renaissance sculpture; contemporary born sculptors, notably José Capuz and Mariano Benlliure.

Serranos Towers★ (EX V). — *Under restoration; temporarily closed.* The towers, now considerably restored, but, nevertheless, a good example of late 14C military architecture, guarded one of the few entrances to the much beleaguered mediaeval city. The defensive features all face outwards, the architects, obviously, and rightly, never having considered the possibility of treachery from within. The battlements have massive, flowing lines, the ornament over the gateway a light delicacy.

Prehistory Museum (Museo de Prehistoria) (DX M⁴). — *Open 10am to 2pm and 4 to 6pm; closed Mondays and Sunday afternoons; inquire locally for holidays.* Exhibits include reproductions of the Levant region, cave paintings, amphorae and pottery, among which, in the Iberian department, are vases from the former village church in San Miguel de Liria, decorated with contemporary scenes in red.

Cuarte Towers (Torres de Cuarte) (DX). — Massive gateway towers (15C).

EXCURSIONS

Manises. — *8km - 5 miles by ④ on the plan.* Manises, a small industrial town, has long been known for its ceramics *(p 175)*. The pottery workshops are open to visitors.

La Albufera; the Huerta. — *Round tour of 105km - 65 miles. Leave Valencia by ② on the plan. Description to Cullera p 163.*
On leaving Cullera, follow the Sueca road. You will find yourself driving for miles through the ricefields which extend south of the Albufera.

Sueca. — Main centre in the Albufera.
Take the Albalat de la Ribera road which follows the course of the Júcar.

VALENCIA★★

The narrow road leaves the ricefields to wind between two irrigation canals on the edges of intensively cultivated orange groves.

At Algemesí turn into the Guadasuar road.

The road, bordered by lush green orange trees, crosses the Río Magro, a tributary of the Júcar. *At Guadasuar make for L'Alcudia.*

Between L'Alcudia and Carlet proper, peach and apricot orchards alternate with orange groves.

Take the Alginet road at Carlet to bring you on to the main road.

Alginet. — The local countryside is more sparingly irrigated and for a time vines replace citrus trees which, however, reappear further north, dominating the centre of the *huerta.*

Turn right for Silla.

Silla. — Ricefields east of the town make you aware that you are once more in the Albufera region. Boats can be hired in the town to sail on the lagoon.

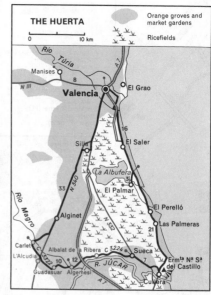

North of Silla are the local market gardens which supply fresh produce to Valencia.

VILLENA (Alicante)

Michelin map **445** fold 20 — Pop 28 279

In the Middle Ages the region of Villena was a powerful feudal domain owing allegiance to the Kingdom of Castile. It was guarded by outpost strongholds, perched in every case upon a rock mound: Chinchilla, Almansa, Biar, Sax and La Mola. In the 15C the new masters of Villena, the Pachecos, constructed the keep.

Among the castle's mediaeval owners were two well-known men of letters: in the 14C the fabulist, Don Juan Manuel *(p 187)*, and, in the 15C, **Henry of Aragon,** sometimes known as the Marquess of Villena, who was both poet and magician (1384-1434).

Archaeological Museum. — *On the Santiago Church Square.*

The museum is in the town hall which has an 18C façade.

The jewel of the collection is an Iberian period solid gold **treasure★** *(to visit apply at the Policía Municipal).*

Santiago. — *If closed, enter through the Chapel of the Holy Sacrament.* The vaulting in this 15-16C church is supported in an unusual way upon spiral pillars which continue above the carved imposts as turned engaged columns. The overall effect gives the nave great individual elegance.

Castillo. — *To visit apply at the Policía Municipal in the town hall.* Cross the two perimeters and two brick vaulted chambers to reach the top of the keep which commands an extensive panorama.

EXCURSION

Bocairent. — *26km - 16 miles northeast.* The church in this small market town where **Juan de Juanes** died (1579) has an interesting **museum** *(temporarily closed)* with several paintings by the artist — known as the Spanish Raphael — and his school (*Last Supper* by Marçal de Sax, of the 14C Valencia school, also a Sorolla).

The church plate includes a monstrance attributed to Benvenuto Cellini. A nearby chapel is decorated with 18C frescoes.

8 Navarre

Habitat and landscape. — Navarre is a province of sharp contrast with no transition between the lush mountain pastures and dry, but fertile plains.

The Navarre Pyrenees. — The mountains, watered by rain from the Atlantic, rise regularly from the 900m - 2 953ft of Mount La Rhune in the west to the 2 504m - 8 225ft of the Pic d'Anie in the east, both peaks actually just over the French border.

West of Roncesvalles, the likeness to the Basque provinces is clear with the countryside divided into small areas of pasture and maize, villages extending along valley courses and the houses, russet tiled and whitewashed with stone quoining.

East of Roncesvalles, the enclosed valleys are more mountainous in character. Stone houses with steeply pitched slate roofs give a clear idea of the harshness of the climate; trees, principally beech, cover the upper slopes — the Irati Forest (Bosque de Irati), which extends into France, is a particularly beautiful example on a grand scale. **Limestone sierras,** the Andía, Urbasa, Navascués and Leyre, mark the line where the mountains drop to the Ebro Basin, their arid, stony slopes facing south and quenching every emerging river course (Lumbier and Arbayún Valleys) but hiding behind them dense beech and pinewoods. The pilgrim route to Santiago lay south of these *sierras* as can be seen from the artistic heritage which still marks the trail.

The plain. — The plain, out of the path of the moist Atlantic winds, is mostly dry. In its clay soil and tall brick houses it resembles neighbouring Aragon.

Cereals predominate in the **Cuenca** or Pamplona Basin, while around Estella, the landscape changes to one of olive groves and vineyards. Aridity increases as you approach the **Ribera** or Ebro Valley; troglodyte dwellings appear in the neighbourhood of Caparroso and Arguedas. While the western Ribera, a continuation of the well-known Rioja *(p 236)*, is the wine growing area of Navarre, the eastern part, around Tudela and now well irrigated, has become a prosperous horticultural region growing and canning asparagus, haricot beans, artichokes and peppers.

Major dates in Navarre's history. — Navarre was the territory of the **Vascons,** ancestors of the Basques. They were not overcome by the Romans but were forced to retreat before the Visigoths to the northern Navarre and present Basque provinces and Gascony. Its history begins with the eviction of the Moors from Pamplona at the end of the 8C by Charlemagne and the subsequent struggle by the Kings of Navarre against the Carolingians who wished to retain Navarre as a buffer kingdom between the empire and the Saracens.

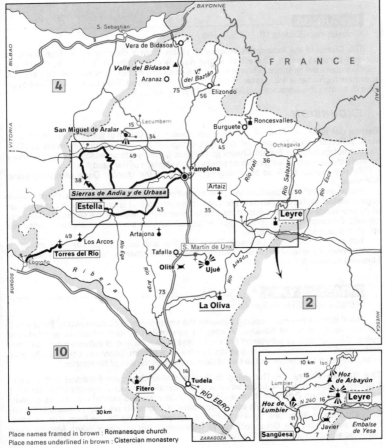

Place names framed in brown : Romanesque church
Place names underlined in brown : Cistercian monastery

Sancho III the Great (1004-1035) dreamed of unifying Christian Spain and his rule did, in fact, extend from León to Catalonia but on his death the division of the kingdom between his four sons caused the inevitable end of his dream. Navarre found itself between Castile and Aragon which annexed the kingdom for some years before it became drawn into the French political orbit.

Thibaud I of Champagne, called on to succeed his uncle, Sancho the Strong, who died leaving no heir, initiated the **French dynasties** of Champagne, France, Evreux, Foix and Albret, which were to occupy the throne of Navarre from 1234 to 1512. Crises in the succession and the hostility of the local nobility to foreign rulers produced a permanent state of unrest; nevertheless, and perhaps on account of this very disturbed atmosphere, the period proved to be Navarre's golden age artistically, particularly the reign of **Charles III**, the Noble (1387-1425), the great builder of churches and castles.

In 1512 the French lines ended with the flight of the Albrets before the Duke of Alba who seized Navarre for Ferdinand of Castile. When subsequent kings from Henri IV to Charles X proclaimed themselves King of France and Navarre they were, in fact, referring to the French part of the former kingdom as Basse-Navarre in French and Ultrapuertos or Beyond the Passes in Spanish (capital: St-Jean-Pied-de- Port).

In the 19C Carlism had many adherents in Navarre, monarchist by tradition and strongly Catholic. Volunteers, *requetés*, in their numbers enlisted in the forces of Don Carlos who issued his first proclamation at Elizondo in 1834. His grandson, Carlos María, also pretender to the crown, set up his headquarters in the final years of the struggle in Estella (1872-76). It was in the same spirit that Navarre *requetés* fought on the Nationalist side in the Civil War.

Mediaeval Art. — Navarre, as the first leg in Spain of the French pilgrimage route to Santiago, the *Camino Francés (p 153)* became endowed with a large number of **Romanesque buildings** — churches, monasteries, funerary chapels. From the 11 to the 13C the most diverse and the richest artistic traditions converged on the kingdom ultimately elaborating a composite Romanesque style so finite that it remained the local style for a very long time. To the façades composed as "vast carved pages", reminiscent of many church and cathedral fronts to be seen along the pilgrimage routes through Aquitaine and central France, was added a Moorish touch by the addition of domes and cupolas and occasional multilobed covings and, even more importantly, originality and unity from the vigour of style of local Navarre sculpture. With the arrival of the French upon the throne in the 13C, influence from north of the Pyrenees became paramount. Several monastic foundations were entrusted to the **Cistercians** who erected magnificent transitional style churches still, however, profoundly Romanesque in concept.

The reign of Charles III saw the arrival at last of Gothic, a style characterised by high walls with few openings and unostentatious decoration. **Mural paintings** were used to cover the vast expanses of bare wall in palaces and churches — fragments in Pamplona Museum give a good idea of the technique.

Folk dancing and traditional games. — The mountain people keep up an ancient folklore tradition of Basque origin *(p 106)*. Every procession is accompanied by a frenzied troupe of dancers and singers in the famous red beret. The *jota* is danced on the plain, as in Aragon, but to a different time and tune. Trials of skill and strength among woodsmen and weight lifters always draw a crowd while every village has its *pelota* players and some also a skittle team. The greatest Navarre festival will always be the Pamplona "Sanfermines" *(p 182)*.

Los ARCOS

Michelin map 442 fold 18 — Pop 1 466

The **Church of the Assumption** (Asunción), visible from a distance by its high tower, is Spanish baroque inside. The effect in the nave is overwhelming: stucco, sculpture and painting cover every space, while at the centre of all this clutter rises sombre, stiff and still above the high altar, a 14C statue of the Virgin carved in wood. The cloister with Flamboyant bays illustrates the elegance and lightness of 15C Gothic.

EXCURSION

Torres del Río★. — 7km - 4 1/2 miles southwest. The **Church of the Holy Sepulchre★** is an unusual Romanesque building, tall in height, octagonal in plan and dating from about 1200. Its resemblance to the Eunate Chapel *(p 184)* has given rise to speculation that it is also a funerary chapel with its lantern turret serving as the lantern of the dead.

To see inside, apply at the house to the left of the church: Doña Mercedes López Martínez.

Inside, vertical lines predominate: the magnificent Mudejar inspired, star shaped **cupola** is geometrical perfection; sparse, complementary decoration is provided in the disposition of minute windows at the points of the star, a frieze of modillions and a series of historiated capitals. Opposite the oven roofed apse, which contains the altar and an ancient Crucifix, is a spiral staircase to the round tower.

The open countryside between Torres del Río and Logroño *(21km - 13 miles)* is characterised by alluvial terraces which run one into the other as they line the banks of the Ebro and its tributaries.

BIDASSOA Valley ★

Michelin map 442 folds 8 and 9

The Bidassoa has cut a course between the lower foothills of the western Pyrenees in the northwest corner of Navarre. Villages lie surrounded by lush meadows and fields of maize; the river and its tributaries are the habitat of salmon and of salmon-trout, the latter prepared in the Navarre manner is stuffed with a slice of ham. Shoots of doves on the wing in migration are held between the end of September and the end of November.

The Baztán Valley. — The valley, in fact, is that of the upper Bidassoa and includes fourteen villages which, in accordance with an ancient communal system often found in valleys of the High Pyrenees, form a single administrative and judicial unit. Maize growing and cattle raising are the valley's economic mainstay. The roads are hilly, particularly the one from Elizondo to Pamplona by way of Irurita, Berroeta and the Velate Pass. The so called English Road from the Otsondo Pass to Gorramendi got its name when Marshal Soult retreated along it hotly pursued by Wellington.

Elizondo. — Elizondo, the capital of the Baztán is a favourite residential town with the many *Indianos* or *Americanos,* as Basques who go to Latin America to make their fortunes and then return home, are known. Most houses sport a coat of arms.

The "Cinco Villas". — As you descend towards the mouth of the Bidassoa, you enter the ancient confederation of the Cinco Villas or five delightful towns of **Aranaz, Yanci, Echalar, Lesaca** and **Vera de Bidasoa.** Many of the house façades are decorated with armorial bearings; deep eaves shelter wooden balconies with delicate balustrades. Behind lies an upper floor, often used as a granary and from which peppers can sometimes be seen hanging out to dry.

The Bidassoa enters a narrow cleft in the granite, the Endarlaza Gorge, and continues through the Basque country to the sea, marking the frontier between Spain and France.

ESTELLA ★★

Michelin map ▨▨▨ north of fold 18 — *Local map p 183* — Pop 13 086

Estella, a town spread over rising slopes on either side of the Río Ega, is divided into parishes which have grown in size without losing their local character. The nobility of the brick and rough stone façades recalls the destiny intended for this city selected in the 12C by the Kings of Navarre as their centre; in the 19C, after a fierce battle on the **Montejurra** *(5km - 3 miles south),* Estella was taken over by the Carlists. The first Sunday in May they gather to commemorate this day. It was the city's situation, however, on the pilgrim road to Santiago which brought it its artistic buildings.

"Estella la Bella". — Such was the name pilgrims gave the town in the Middle Ages when they stopped to venerate Our Lady on the Hill before continuing to Santiago. The modern church stands on the site on which, according to tradition, on 25 May 1085, shepherds, guided by falling stars, found a statue of the Virgin. Of the town's many mediaeval hospitals, the leper hospital of St Lazarus became the most famous. In the 11C a colony of freemen, many of them French, came to help populate the city.

■ SIGHTS *time: 2 hours*

Plaza de San Martín. — The square was originally at the heart of the freemen's parish, bustling with comings and goings to shops and inns; today nothing disturbs the still small square but perhaps its splashing fountain overlooked from one side by the emblasoned 16C front of the **former town hall** and, from the west corner, by the **Palace of the Kings of Navarre,** one of the oldest lay buildings in all Spain (12C).

San Pedro de la Rúa. — The church, which is still, remarkably, in part 12 and 13C, stands facing the royal palace on a cliff spur formerly crowned by the city castle.

The **portal★,** at the top of a monumental flight of steps, pierces the north wall. The doorway's originality, with capitals and covings richly sculptured, lies in its tiers-point scalloped arch, Caliphate influenced. Similar doorways can be seen in Navarre at Puente la Reina and Cirauqui *(p 184)* and in the Saintonge and Poitou regions of France. Inside are three Romanesque apses, with, at the centre, a column of intertwined serpents. To the left, a baroque chapel contains a relic of St Andrew, the pride of the church since 1270!

A door in the second bay in the south aisle leads to the cloister.

The Romanesque **cloister★** lost two galleries when the nearby castle was blown up in the 16C. The loss becomes all the more regrettable as one discovers the skill and invention of the masons who carved the remaining capitals: the north gallery series illustrates scenes from the lives of Christ and Sts Lawrence, Andrew and Peter, while plant and animal themes enliven the west gallery where the architect unexpectedly included a group of four obliquely angled columns.

Church of the Holy Sepulchre (Santo Sepulcro). — The church, which stands on the pilgrim road, the Rúa, is remarkable for its portal which is purely Gothic. Superimposed above the door are the Last Supper, the three Marys at the Holy Sepulchre and Hell and Calvary. The niches which frame the doorway contain somewhat mannered figures of saints.

St Michael's (San Miguel). — This church, on the far bank stands in a quarter lived in at the end of the 12C by natives of Navarre and still mediaeval in atmosphere with its narrow streets. The **north portal★,** obscured by a porch, seems almost to have been designed as a challenge to the "foreigners" on the opposite river bank.

Tympanum. — Christ appears surrounded by the Evangelists and other personages.

Covings. — Starting from the centre the sculptures in the covings show guardian angels, the Old Men of the Apocalypse, prophets and patriarchs, and scenes from the Gospels, martyrs and saints.

Capitals. — The capitals illustrate from left to right, the childhood of Christ and two hunting scenes — note the dignity of facial expression throughout.

Walls. — Upper register: eight statue columns of the Apostles; lower register: two **high reliefs★★,** the most accomplished and expressive of the doorway showing, on the left, St Michael slaying the dragon and weighing souls, here represented as young children, and on the right, the three Marys coming from the Sepulchre. The noble bearing, the elegance of the draperies, the serenity of the angels, the anxiety of the women bringing the news of the empty tomb, make the carving a masterpiece of Romanesque art.

■ IRACHE MONASTERY★

3km - 2 miles south. There has been a Benedictine monastery on this site since the 10C. Irache, a major halt on the Santiago pilgrim road, was a Cistercian community before becoming a university in the 16C, under the Benedictines (which closed in 1833). *Open weekdays 10am to 2pm and 5 to 7pm (4 to 6pm in winter); Saturdays and Sundays 9am to 2pm and 4 to 7pm (6pm in winter); closed Mondays.* The cloister, in a somewhat cold Renaissance style is decorated with bosses and capitals illustrating the life of Christ and St Benedict.

Church★. — The pure Romanesque style apse lies directly in line with the original intersecting ribs of the nave vaulting. At the Renaissance the dome on squinches was reconstructed and the *coro alto* added to the original structure. The main façade and most of the conventual buildings were rebuilt in the 17C.

179

FITERO ★

Michelin map **442** fold 18 — Pop 2 186

Fitero, a small spa, was known in the Middle Ages for its Cistercian monastery of **Santa María la Real★,** founded in the 12C by monks from Escaladieu Abbey in the Pyrenees. The first abbot, **Raimundo,** brought the abbey early fame when he created the Order of the Knights of Calatrava *(p 193).* The church *(to visit apply to the parish priest),* although possessing pointed arches, remains strongly Romanesque in spirit; the transept is well ordered, the decoration uncomplicated or befittingly Cistercian. A beautiful 13C **chapterhouse** opens off the cloister, rebuilt in the 16C and now in poor repair. The abbey treasure, rich in ancient reliquary coffers is in the presbytery.

LEYRE Monastery ★★

Michelin map **442** folds 19 and 20

A splendid **panorama★★** opens out at the end of a steeply winding approach road, over the manmade Lake Yesa; on all sides are marl hills, their limestone crests forming majestic ramparts while in the Leyre Sierra, itself, great walls of mixed ochre coloured stone and local rock hang suspended, halfway up the ridge face.

The Abbey of San Salvador of Leyre had established itself by the early 11C, as the uncontested spiritual centre of Navarre; Sancho III, the Great and his successors made it their pantheon and gave their blessing to the erection of a church which, with its crypt, was to be one of the greatest works of Romanesque art in Spain (consecrated: 1057). Bishops of Pamplona were, by tradition, former abbots of Leyre which held dominion over some 60 villages and 70 churches and monasteries. In the 12C, however, when Navarre was joined to Aragon, the royal house neglected Leyre in favour of San Juan de la Peña *(p 70);* in the same period the Pamplona bishops sought greater authority and instituted a lawsuit which considerably reduced both the finances and the prestige of the old monastery. Finally in the 19C the monastery was abandoned.

In 1954, however, a Benedictine community from Silos returned to restore the 17 and 18C, conventual buildings which have now been converted into a hostelry.

East End. — Three apses of equal height with the nave wall surmounted by a turret and a further square tower with treble windows, make a delightful group. The beautiful smoothness of the walls and the total absence of decoration indicate the construction's great age.

Crypt★★. — The crypt, built in the 11C to support the Romanesque church above and to the same ground plan, looks even older, so roughly robust and archaic is its appearance. The vaulting is high enough but divided by arches with enormous keystones or, in some cases, double ribs, descending on massive capitals, incised only with the simplest lines. Unusually these capitals stand on shafts of unequal height, practically at ground level.

The Crypt

Church★. — In the 13C when the Cistercians rebuilt the church's central aisle to include a bold Gothic vault they, nevertheless, retained the first bays of the earlier Romanesque church. The three aisles which have come down to us intact have cradle vaulting with double ribs springing throughout from equal height, the decorative elegance arising from engaged pillars and finely designed capitals and the appeal of massive blocks or rough hewn stone beautifully assembled. In the north bay a wooden chest contains the remains of the first Kings of Navarre.

West Portal★. — 12C. The portal's rich decoration has won for it the name of Porta Speciosa. Carvings occupy every available surface. On the tympanum are archaic statues — Christ *(in the centre),* the Virgin and St Peter *(on His right)* and St John *(on His left);* the covings are alive with monsters and fantastic beasts. Above, the spandrels show *(on the right)* the Annunciation and the Visitation.

LUMBIER and ARBAYÚN Defiles ★

Michelin map **442** folds 9 and 19

In Navarre, as in Aragon, the valleys of the High Pyrenees have a north-south axis, debouching suddenly upon the Jaca depression after cutting through the last chains of limestone foothills. During this final mountain passage the drop in level is very sharp and the rivers, the Irati and Salazar, flow through deep, narrow canyons.

Hoz de Lumbier. — The gorge cut by the Irati through the Leyre Sierra foothills between Lumbier and Liédena is a bare 5km - 3 miles long and so narrow that it appears at either end as a mere crack in the cliff face. By car, bear right, off the south approach into Lumbier into a road along the river bank which joins the N 240 south of Liédena. Along the N 240 is a belvedere from which there is a good **view** of the gorge.

Hoz de Arbayún. — The Río Salazar is so steeply enclosed within the limestone walls of the Sierra de Navascués that the road has to diverge from the river course and the only way to see it is by going to the viewpoint north of Iso. From there, is a splendid **view★★** of the end of the canyon where the bare cliff walls are clad, at their base, in a dense green vegetation from the heart of which pours the sparkling stream.

OLITE ★

Michelin map **442** fold 19 — Pop 2 829

Olite, the preferred residence of the Kings of Navarre in the 15C, the "Gothic town" as it is known, lives always in the shadow of its castle which has all the appearance and size of a mediaeval city. The San Martin de Unx road affords a good general view.

Fortress of the Navarre Kings★. — *Open 10am to 2pm and 6 to 8pm (4 to 6pm in winter); 100pts.*

It was Charles III, the Noble, who gave orders in 1406 for the castle to be built. Being French — a Count of Evreux and native of Mantes — explains why the architects came from north of the Pyrenees to help design the fortress which, therefore, emerged with foreign style fortifications a transition between the massive stone constructions of the 13C and the royal residences of the late 15C. Behind the fifteen or so towers marking the perimeter were hanging gardens; within were inner halls and chambers, brilliantly decorated by Moorish craftsmen with *azulejos*, painted plasterwork, coloured marquetry ceilings. The plan is now confused, so many times has the building been altered and devastated. Restored areas have been converted for use as a *parador*.

Santa María la Real. — The church is the former chapel royal. An atrium of slender multilobed arches precedes the 14C **façade★**, a beautiful example of Navarre Gothic sculpture *(p 14)*. The only figurative carving on the portal is on the tympanum which illustrates the lives of the Virgin and Christ. A retable above the high altar frames a Gothic statue of Our Lady.

St Peter's (San Pedro). — The church façade below the attenuated Gothic spire has a somewhat disparate appearance. The depth of the splayed covings framing the 12C portal, contrasts with the cylindrical columns which form the base. Eagles on either side symbolise, right and left respectively, Gentleness and Violence.

A stone, carved in the 15C to represent the Trinity, stands in the north aisle.

La OLIVA Monastery ★★

Michelin map **442** fold 19

La Oliva was one of the first Cistercian monasteries to be erected by French monks outside France during the lifetime of St Bernard (1090-1153). The monastery's influence was considerable in the Middle Ages when it spread the Christian word far beyond the confines of Spain. The buildings, now stripped of treasure and trappings, retain the beauty of the pure Cistercian style.

Open 9am to 8pm (6pm 1 October to 31 March).

Church★★. — Late 12C. Apart from a triangular coping and the turret added in the 17C, the church front remains bare and is, therefore, a perfect setting for the interplay of lines of the **portal** and two rose windows. The interior is suprisingly deep with pillars and pointed arches lined with thick polygonal ribs in austere Cistercian style.

Cloister★. — Late 15C. The arches appear exceptionally light in this cloister where Gothic additions were grafted onto an older construction without thought of style or even malfunction as can be seen by the arch descenders which, in part, obscure the entrance to the 13C **chapterhouse.**

PAMPLONA ★ 🅿

Michelin map **442** fold 9 — *Local map p 183* — Pop 183 126

Pamplona commands two major frontier roads, to the Roncesvalles Pass and the Velate Pass, and since very early times has been the most important city of the Spanish Pyrenees. Of the period when it was capital of the kingdom of Navarre and a fortified city, it has conserved, around the cathedral, a quarter of old houses lining narrow streets and ramparts to the north and east overlooking the Río Arga. Modern quarters of wide, straight avenues, lined by luxurious blocks (**Paseo de Sarasate**) (AY 38), and arcaded squares decorated with fountains and ornamental boulders (**Plaza del Castillo**) (BY), have been developed, extending the southern periphery. Finally, a wide green belt of parks and gardens (**La Taconera**) (AY), rings this now prosperous looking city and its large private university.

On a lighter note Pamplona is also known for its caramels and its famous *feria.*

(After Marín photo, San Sebastián)

Sanfermines

PAMPLONA★

The "Sanfermines". — The festival of St Firminus is celebrated with joyous ardour from 6 to 14 July each year by citizens and visitors alike in a carefree atmosphere perfectly described by Hemingway in **Fiesta (The Sun also Rises).** Visitors pour in doubling the town's population and crowding the great evening bullfights. The most spectacular and the event most prized by "Pamplonés", however, is the **"encierro"** or early morning *(around 8am)* bull running, through the palisaded streets, of the beasts selected to fight in the evening.

Historical notes. — Pamplona goes back to Roman times and is said to have been founded by Pompey who, tradition has it, gave the town his name. In the 8C the Moors occupied the town briefly before being expelled with the help of Charlemagne, who, however, took advantage of the weakness of the native forces to dismantle the city wall. In revenge the people of Navarre took part in the historic massacre of Charlemagne's rearguard in the Roncesvalles Pass. In the 10C Pamplona became the capital of Navarre; in the late 14 early 15C it reached the peak of its power under Charles III the Noble, who endowed it with a fine Gothic cathedral. Throughout the Middle Ages, the city was troubled by disputes between the citizens of the old quarter — the Navarrería — who supported an alliance with Castile, and the freemen who lived on the city outskirts and favoured the retention of the Navarre crown by a French line. Navarrería was destroyed in 1277 by a French expeditionary force on pretext of reprisal; in 1512, the town was captured, on behalf of Ferdinand the Catholic, by the Duke of Alba, who with local support, was thus able to prevent the titular monarch, Jean d'Albret, from entering his capital. In 1521 Henri d'Albret, Jean's successor, tried unsuccessfully to retake the town. During the struggle a young Castilian army officer, Ignatius Loyola *(p 122),* was wounded and fell — a stone marks the spot on the pavement in San Ignacio Avenue, opposite a commemorative basilica.

■ SIGHTS *time: 2 hours*

Cathedral★ (BY). — The present Gothic cathedral was built in the 14 and 15C over an earlier Romanesque edifice whose only remains (doorway and cloister capitals) are now in the Navarre Museum. At the end of the 18C, Ventura Rodríguez reconstructed the west front in the baroque and Neo-Classical style then fashionable.

The nave, only two tiers high, has wide arches and windows and, with plain ribbing and great bare walls, the unadorned appearance typical of Navarre Gothic. Before the intricate wrought iron grille closing the sanctuary, stands the alabaster **tomb★,** commissioned in 1416 by Charles III the Noble, founder of the cathedral, for himself and his queen. The reclining figures were carved by Janin Lomme. There is a late 15C Hispano-Flemish altarpiece in the south ambulatory chapel.

Cloister★ (A). — 14-15C. The cloister has a fragile appearance, with elegant Gothic arches surmounted, in some cases, by gables. Sculptured tombs and doors add interest; note the Dormition of the Virgin on the tympanum of the cloister door which is almost baroque in expression.

PAMPLONA

Conde Oliveto (Av. del)	AZ 6		Principe de Viana (Pl. del)	BZ 26
Cortes de Navarra	BY 8		Reina (Cuesta de la)	AY 27
Cruz (Pl. de la)	BZ 9		Roncesvalles (Av. de)	BY 28
Carlos III (Av. de)	BYZ	Esquiroz	AZ 12	Sancho el Mayor	ABZ 29
Chapitela	BY 5	Estafeta	BY 13	San Fermín	BZ 30
García Castañón	ABY 14	Juan de Labrit	BY 16	San Francisco (Pl. de)	BZ 31
San Ignacio (Av. de)	BYZ 34	Leyre	BYZ 17	Sangüesa	BZ 33
Zapatería	AY 42	Mayor	AY 20	Santo Domingo	AY 36
		Mercaderes	BY 22	Sarasate (Paseo de)	AY 38
Amaya	BYZ 2	Navarrería	BY 23	Taconera (Recta de)	AY 39
Ansoleaga	AY 3	Paulino Caballero	BZ 25	Vínculo (Pl. del)	AYZ 40

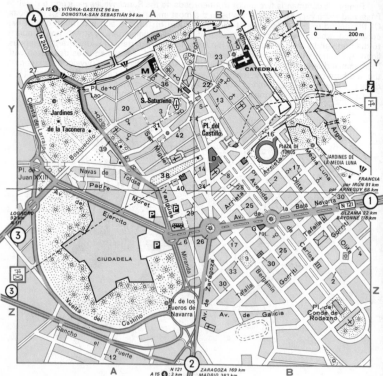

Off the east gallery, containing beautiful 14C star vaulting, is the Barbazán Chapel, so-called after the bishop who had it constructed to contain his tomb. On the south side is the "Precious Doorway", a key piece in the sculpture of the period with tympanum and lintel beautifully carved with scenes of the life of the Virgin and, on either side of the door, two statues together forming a fine Annunciation.

Diocesan Museum. — The museum is in the old refectory and adjoining kitchens, which date from 1330. In the refectory, a lofty hall with six pointed arches, the reader's rostrum is decorated with an enchanting unicorn chase — a legendary beast which only a damsel might approach.

The square kitchen, quartered by fireplaces, has a central lantern — rising to 24m - 79ft at its apex.

The museum *(open 16 May to 15 October 9am to 2pm; 100pts)* displays religious objects including polychrome wood statues of the Virgin and Christ from all parts of the province.

On leaving the cathedral follow the narrow Calle del Redín to the ramparts where a small bastion, now a garden, commands a view of the fortified Zumalacárregui Gate (on the left) and an old wall and further away, a bend in the Arga River and Mount Cristóbal.

Navarre Museum★ (AY M). — *Closed temporarily.*

The museum has been built on the site of a 16C hospital of which the Renaissance gateway has been preserved.

The galleries 1 to 3, on the left as you enter the courtyard, contain Roman lapidary exhibits such as funerary steles, inscriptions and **mosaic★** pavements from 2 and 4C villas. The mosaics are principally geometric and often in black and white — gallery 3, however, contains an illustration of Theseus and the Minotaur.

The Romanesque period (gallery 4) is represented by archaic 10C reliefs from Villatuerta and more importantly by **capitals★** from the former 12C cathedral of Pamplona on which an unknown artist carved three Biblical scenes — the Passion, the Resurrection and the Story of Job — with a care for detail only equalled by his mastery of composition and brilliance of imagination.

On the second floor are Gothic and Renaissance paintings. The first three galleries, reconstituted as the interior of the Palace of Oriz, are decorated with 16C monochrome painted panels depicting the story of Adam and Eve and the wars of the Emperor Charles V. The following galleries display fragments of **mural paintings★** from different periods and all areas of the province: Artaíz (13C), Artajona and Pamplona (13 and 14C), Gallipienzo (14 and 15C), Olleta (15C). The apparently diverse collection has common characteristics — the unobtrusive emphasis on face and feature, the crowds, the sideways stance — passed down from French miniaturists and well exemplified in Juan Olivier's refectory mural, painted in 1330 (gallery 24).

Before leaving, look at the great mosaic from the Liédena Villa (2C) in the courtyard.

St Saturninus (San Saturnino) (AY). — This composite edifice at the centre of a tangle of narrow streets in the old quarter has a mingled architecture of Romanesque brick towers, 13C Gothic porch and vaulting and numerous later additions.

Inside, in a chapel opposite the main door, is a Gothic group of sculpture of the Flemish school.

EXCURSIONS

Andía and Urbasa Sierras★. — *Round tour of 169km - 105 miles — about 3 hours.* The pleasure of this tour lies in driving through beechwoods and, as you rise to the top of a pass, getting a wide view over the countryside. Visits to religious buildings erected along the Santiago pilgrim road add still further interest *(allow an extra 2 1/2 hours for Iranzu and Estella).*

Leave Pamplona by ④ on the map, the San Sebastián road; turn left immediately after the bridge over the Arga.

The road goes first to Echauri then rises, *corniche* style, to the pass (840m - 2 756ft), affording, just before the top, an extensive **view★** of the winding Valley of the Arga.

At the N 111, turn right.

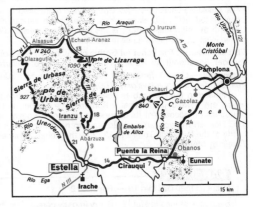

Iranzu Monastery. — *Signposted from the N 111.* This Cistercian monastery, built at the end of the 12C in lonely isolation in a wild **gorge★** is now a college. Restored to its former prime, it is a good example of the Cistercian transitional style from Romanesque to Gothic in which robustness and elegance combine. The cloister bays, where they have not been given a later florid Gothic fenestration, are typical, with Romanesque blind arcades, oculi and wide relieving arches. The church, with somewhat primitive vaulting, has a flat east end decorated with a triplet, or three windows, symbolising the Trinity, a feature found in many Cistercian churches.

Lizarraga Pass Road★. — On emerging from the tunnel (alt 1 090m - 3 576ft) pause briefly before beginning the descent through woods and pastures, at the **viewpoint★** overlooking the green Ergoyena Valley.

Continue to Echarri-Aranaz where you turn left into the N 240 to Olazagutía and then left again towards Estella.

PAMPLONA★

Urbasa Pass Road★★. — The fairly steep climb between great free standing boulders and clumps of trees has a beautiful wildness in total contrast to the wide and lushly wooded valley which follows. Beyond the pass (alt 927m - 3 041ft) tall limestone cliffs add character to the landscape before the road enters the series of gorges through which flows the sparkling Río Urenderra.

Estella★★. — *Description p 179.*

The return to Pamplona is along the Santiago Pilgrim Road now the N 111.

Ciraugui★. — The village's alleys lined by steps, are closely crowded by houses, their lower walls whitewashed and pierced by rounded doorways, their upper fronts adorned with iron balconies, and further embellished with coats of arms and carved cornices. At the top of the village *(difficult climb)* stands the Church of San Román with a 13C multilobed main **portal**★ similar to that of San Pedro de la Rúa in Estella *(p 179)*.

Puente la Reina★. — The venerable hump-backed bridge which spans the Río Arga and gives the town its name, has been trodden by countless numbers of pilgrims to Santiago. It was here that the two major French pilgrim roads, after crossing the Pyrenees by the Roncesvalles and Somport Passes respectively, met to continue together along the final stage. At the entrance to the town, coming from Pamplona, a bronze pilgrim stands where his fellows foregathered, who had travelled the *caminos (p 152)*.

The wide N 111 circles the old town outside whose walls stands the **Church of the Crucifix** (Crucifijo). The porch communicated with the pilgrims' hospice. A second nave was added to the existing 12C main aisle in the 14C and now contains the famous Y-shaped Cross with the profoundly expressionist **Christ**★ carved in wood and said to have been brought from Germany by a pilgrim in the 14C.

Walk along the narrow but extremely elegant main street, the Calle Mayor, fronted by houses of golden brick and carved wood eaves, to the **bridge.** On the way you will see **St James'(Santiago)** church with its **portal**★ *(p 14)* crowded with by now almost effaced carvings. Inside, the nave, rearranged in the 16C, was decorated with altarpieces and two statues placed facing the entrance: St James the Pilgrim, in gilded wood, and St Bartholomew.

Eunate★. — *5km - 3 miles east.* The origin of this **Romanesque chapel,** so harmonious in proportion and design remains unknown. The finding of human bones supports the theory of the building having been a funerary chapel on the pilgrim road like that of Torres del Río *(p 178)* on the Castile-Navarre border. The outside gallery, now exposed, formerly led to adjoining buildings and was used by the pilgrims as a shelter.

Artaíz. — *23km - 14 miles southeast.* The small Romanesque church on a wooded mound, has a remarkable, advanced and seemingly detached **doorway.** The embrasure capitals, the stylised lions in the spandrels and, even more, below the cornice, the modillions, carved with figures, and the intermediary metopes, illustrating the mass, Christ in hell and the feast at Dives' house, all demonstrate a rare craftsmanship by some unknown mediaeval mason.

RONCESVALLES

Michelin map **442** fold 9

Roncesvalles has come down to us rather as a heroic epic than as the geographical pass, known to countless mediaeval pilgrims or the site where, in 778, the Basques of Navarre massacred the rearguard of Charlemagne's army as Roland was leading it back through the Pyrenees to France. The late 12 early 13C **Poem of Bernardo del Carpio** describes Bernardo as a national hero who sought only with his Basque, Navarre and Asturian companions in arms to avenge the Frankish invasion of Spain; the early 12C **Song of Roland,** the first French epic poem, on the other hand, glorifies the heroic but ultimately despairing resistance of a handful of courageous Christian knights — Roland and the twelve peers of the Empire — against hordes of Saracen fanatics brought to the field by the traitor Ganelon.

Ecclesiastical Buildings. — This vast, grey walled, mass of buildings with bluish zinc roofs, dating back to the 12C appears hidden by dense vegetation. The buildings served formerly as an important pilgrims' hostelry with a funerary chapel, square in plan, now the Chapel of the Holy Spirit and a collegiate church rich in relics.

Royal Collegiate Church. — This Gothic church, inspired by those of the Ile-de-France, was consecrated in 1219, since when it has been repeatedly and unfortunately, restored. Beneath the high altar canopy is the pilgrimage's *raison d'être* a Virgin and Child in wood, plated in silver, made in France in the 13 or 14C.

Chapterhouse. — The beautiful Gothic chamber, off the cloister, contains the tombs of the founder, Sancho VII, the Strong (1154-1234), King of Navarre and his queen.

Museum★. — *Open 1 June to 30 September 11am to 1.30pm and 4 to 6pm; the rest of the year Sundays and holidays only; 100pts.*

Housed in the old stables, the museum contains fine pieces of ancient plate; among which are a Mudejar casket, a Romanesque gospel, a 14C enamelled reliquary which, doubtless on account of its chequered design, is known as Charlemagne's chessboard, a 16C Flemish triptych, an emerald, said to have been worn in his turban on the day of the battle of the Navas de Tolosa in 1212 by the Sultan Miramamolín el Verde and a lovely *Holy Family* by Morales.

SANGÜESA ★

Michelin map **442** fold 19 — Pop 4 572

Sangüesa stands in arable country (mostly cereals), on the left bank of the River Aragón. It still seems to guard the bridge which in the Middle Ages brought her prosperity and valuable works of art.

Sangüesa and the pilgrimage. — Fear of the Moors compelled Sangüesans to live until the 10C on the **Rocaforte** mound; by the 11C, however, the citizens had been persuaded by the Kings of the Reconquest to come down and defend the river bridge. Alfonso I of Aragon, the Battler, built a castle on the east bank and granted a *fuero* or charter to the town which he peopled with freemen from all parts of Europe and which soon comprised six parishes and eleven hospices.

Sangüesa reached its climax at the end of the Gothic period when, in contrast to the fortified residence constructed by Carlos, Prince of Viana (1421-1461), unfortunate heir to the throne of Navarre, prosperous citizens began to erect elegant residential mansions.

The former **palace of the Prince of Viana,** now the town hall, still stands in its own grounds. Through the gateway is the façade, flanked by two imposing battlemented towers.

The main street, the former **Rúa Mayor,** which continues in a straight line from the bridge and formed part of the pilgrim road, is lined with comfortable brick houses with the classical upper gallery protected by deep carved wood eaves. Some windows still have rich Gothic or Plateresque surrounds. In the second street on the right coming from the bridge can be seen the baroque front of the **Vallesantoro Palace,** protected by monumental overhangs carved with imaginary animals with men's, horses' and lions' heads.

Santa María la Real★. — This former royal chapel, begun in the 12C, was completed in the mid - 13C with the construction of the south portal, the octagonal tower and its spire.

South Portal★. — The portal, begun in the late 12C and modified in the 13C, is so crowded with sculpture that one stands amazed at the number of subjects depicted and the variety of ways in which they have been illustrated. At least two artists worked successively on the masterpiece: the Master of San Juan de la Peña who came from Aragon in the 12C, and in his severe style, carved the superimposed arched gallery. A second was a certain Leodegarius, a Burgundian of whom little else is known, apart from his name which he carved on one of the embrasure statue columns.

The **statue columns,** already Gothic, derive, but with a more marked sense of tradition, from those at Chartres and Autun. From left to right can be seen: Mary Magdalene, the Virgin, the mother of St James, St Peter (?), St Paul (?) and a rare portrayal of Judas Iscariot hanged.

On the **tympanum,** God the Father at the centre of angel musicians receives, at his right, the chosen but with down-pointing left arm reproves the sinners — note the suggestion of drama in the Last Judgment conveyed by the upright stance of the fortunate and the contortions of the damned. In a corner is St Michael weighing souls.

The **covings** swarm with geometric and animal motifs and figures: the second innermost shows the humbler trades clogmaker, lutemaker, butcher...

The **spandrels** have been used unusually as space for disparate but, nevertheless, vigorous sculptures.

The older **upper arches** show God surrounded by the symbols of the four Evangelists, two angels and the twelve disciples.

Interior. — Darkness makes the capitals of the pillars in the nave difficult to see but what can be more easily discerned are three semicircular Romanesque apses decorated with graceful blind arcades and a beautiful dome on squinches built in the 13C influenced in design by the Gothic style.

■ JAVIER CASTLE

7km - 4 miles east. **Francis Xavier,** patron saint of the Navarre, was born here in 1506. At 22 he met his Basque compatriot, Ignatius Loyola, in Paris, then formulating the principles of the Society of Jesus *(p 122).* Xavier was sent by the Portuguese who had very considerable and well established commercial interests with the Far East, as a missionary first to Goa and then to Japan. There, it still being a hundred years before the country was to close her shores to foreigners, he was well received and made some 200 000 converts from Buddhism. Xavier left Japan, where he is still greatly revered, in 1551, and died the following year. He was canonised in 1622.

Castle. — *Guided tours 9am to 1pm and 4 to 7pm;* Son et Lumière *performances June and July, Saturdays, Sundays and holidays 10.30pm; August 10pm and September 9.30pm.*

The fortress, birthplace of the saint, was in part destroyed by Cardinal Cisneros in 1516. The visit includes the Guardroom, the Oratory, which contains a 13C Christ in walnut and an unusual 15C fresco of the Dance of Death, the Great Hall and the saint's bedroom (among the oldest parts, 10-11C of the castle).

■ SAN MIGUEL DE ARALAR Church ★

Michelin map 442 fold 8 – 15km - 9 miles southwest of Lecumberri

Turn right off the Pamplona road shortly after Lecumberri into a road which passes through forests of beech trees as it crosses the **Sierra Aralar.** From the church a wide view opens out across the Araquil Valley and, beyond, to the rock escarpments of the Andía Sierra. The Romanesque church encloses a small independent chapel with a tiled saddleback roof which some declare to be 8C, some late 12C.

It was here that in the 18C was found a magnificent gilt and enamel **altarfront★★,** *(not on display)* now considered one of the major works of European Romanesque goldsmithry. The bronze gilt plaques highlighted with enamels, cabochon and faceted precious stones, have been assembled into a small altarpiece although it is not known whether this was the original design. The enamel panels, both *cloisonné* and *champlevé,* are outstanding for their brilliance and variety of colour and the delicacy of the arabesque and foliage motifs. Only the heads of the figures portrayed are in relief, each with a lively and individual expression. The quality of the work makes its origin most likely late 12C Limousin.

■ TAFALLA

Michelin map 442 folds 18 and 19 — Pop 9 863

Today Tafalla is a market town at the heart of a cereal growing region; in the days of Charles III, the Noble, at the turn of the 13-14C, it was the site of a fortress palace.

Santa María. — *On the Estella road out of Tafalla take the first road on the right after passing under a bridge.*

Inside are a baroque organ loft and large 16C **altarpiece★** by the Basque sculptor Juan de Ancheta who also carved those in Jaca cathedral and the Seo of Saragossa.

The narrow streets around the north and east sides of the church are full of character and very typical.

EXCURSION

Artajona. — *11km - 7 miles northwest.* The massive **fortified enclave** known as the Cerco de Artajona, its walls flanked by square towers and amongst the most impressive in Navarre, can be seen from afar.

In the middle of the 12C it was occupied by the Templars; subsequently a French bishop of Pamplona donated to the Church of St-Sernin in Toulouse the Gothic Church of **San Saturnino** which, with its imposing, stoutly buttressed, ochre stone nave, stands high in the wind on the summit. The tympanum in the west door is carved in the French style to illustrate the life of the saint. Inside, at the end of the great nave, the gold of the 1497 altarpiece still gleams; the 14C murals which once covered the apse, however, are now in the Navarre Museum, Pamplona *(p 183).*

Local people have abandoned the Cerco, grouping their houses at the foot of the hill round a modern church. A white arch at its east end spans the picturesque Calle de San Juan, lined with biscuit coloured, sometimes emblasoned, stone houses.

TUDELA ★

Michelin map **442** fold 19 — Pop 24 629

Tudela is the great agricultural centre of the "Ribera" *(p 177).*
The town became known in the 9C when the Moors made it a dependency of the Córdoba Caliphate. It was freed only in 1119 but remained tolerant towards the Moslems until early in the 16C, which is the reason for the size of the Moorish quarter, the Morería, and the predominance of old brick houses in the Mudejar style.

St Anne's feast day (26 July) is celebrated annually, as at Pamplona *(p 181),* with several days of great rejoicing, including morning *encierros* and afternoon bullfights.

Cathedral★. — *Open 9am to 1pm and 5 to 8pm.*
The cathedral, begun late in the 12C continued building until the mid - 13C, so that the edifice emerges as an excellent example of the transitional Romanesque-Gothic style derived from the Cistercian tradition and common throughout Spain.

The Last Judgment Doorway★. — The portal, difficult to see through lack of space, presents nearly 120 groups of figures illustrating the Last Judgment. The horrors of hell are depicted with relish! The capitals above the small columns tell the story of the Creation (left) and of Adam and Eve (right).

Interior. — The nave appears Romanesque in its elevation and Gothic in its vaulting and tall windows. The transept is spacious. Excepting around the chancel and a few chapels, which are baroque, the church is rich in Gothic works of art including early 16C choirstalls, the retable at the high altar, the stone reliquary statue of Byzantine appearance dating from about 1200 of the White Virgin, the **Chapel of Our Lady of Hope★** with its several 15C masterpieces, including the sepulchre of a chancellor of Navarre, the central, 15C altarpiece and on the right wall, the St Catherine altarpiece with, on the central panel, a delicate portrait of the young martyr.

Cloister★★. — *25 pts.* 12-13C. Harmonious yet small, this cloister reveals Romanesque arches resting alternately on groups of two or three columns with historiated capitals. These, apart from the ones at the corners which have formal animal and plant motifs, relate scenes from the New Testament and the lives of the saints in a style inspired by the carvings of Aragon.

Ajimeces (p 16) and a door of the mosque which once stood on the site have been preserved in two of the gallery walls.

St Nicholas'. — When the church in the old quarter was rebuilt in the 18C a tympanum of Romanesque origin was placed in the façade built of brick in the Mudejar style.. The composition of the tympanum and the gentle expression on the faces of the seated figure of God the Father holding his Son and surrounded by the symbols of the Evangelists, recall the style of Master Mateo, creator of the Santiago Cathedral Door of Glory *(p 153).*

UJUÉ ★

Michelin map **442** fold 19 — Pop 329

Ujué, perched on a summit overlooking the Ribera *(p 177),* remains, with tortuous streets and picturesque façades, much as it was in the Middle Ages. A *romería* procession, dating back to the 14C, sets out annually on the Sunday after St Mark's Day *(25 April),* when penitents dressed in black capes and bearing a Cross gather from far and wide to implore the mercy of the Virgin of Ujué.
For a guided tour, ring at the presbytery facing the church.

The fortress. — The church towers, always used for military purposes, command a view which extends to Olite, the Montejurra and the Pyrenees. Lofty walls and a covered watch path circling the church still exist of the mediaeval palace.

The church. — A Romanesque church was built on the site at the end of the 11C. In the 14C, Charles II, the Bad, undertook the construction of a Gothic church but work must have been interrupted for the Romanesque chancel remains to this day.

In the central chapel, a wooden Romanesque statue, plated in silver, is the venerated Santa María la Blanca.

9 Madrid Castile-La Mancha

Madrid-Castile-La Mancha, comprising the provinces of Madrid, Albacete, Cuenca, Ciudad Real, Guadalajara and Toledo, lies south of the Central Cordillera, at the hub of the peninsula; it is high, flat, seemingly parched and arid, swept by biting winds, snow, hostile in the brazen heat. But it has a fascination all its own — the mystery of infinite horizons, umber colouring, windmills... Clear vibrant light... It was not by chance that that most characteristic of Spanish heroes, Don Quixote, came from Castile-La Mancha.

And it was here, nevertheless, that Philip II set the new capital of Spain, Madrid.

The tilted tableland. — The south Meseta, which comprises Madrid-Castile-La Mancha, is a vast tableland watered by two large rivers: the Tagus, which cuts a deep cleft through the limestone Alcarria and the idly flowing Guadiana. The landscape is flatter than that of Castile and León where the upper Tertiary sediment is less homogeneous, the average altitude is lower — 500-700m compared to 800-1 000m (1 640-2 226ft; 2 624-3 280ft). Despite such physical advantages, however, the climate is even drier, the summers heavier, particularly in La Mancha.

The **Toledo Mountains,** bare, eroded and virtually uninhabited, cut across the region, dividing the Tagus basin from that of the Guadiana; other ranges ring the borders: the Central Cordillera, the north (Gredos and Guadarrama Sierras), the Sierra Morena the south and to the northeast the **Serranía de Cuenca,** a limestone massif pitted with sinkholes and cut by defiles.

Beyond, further north is the **Alcarria,** where the Tagus and its tributaries flow through deeply eroded clefts, peopled by the occasional village. On the upper mountain slopes in this area grow the aromatic plants — thyme, rosemary, lavender, marjoram from which a delicious local honey is produced.

The land of border castles — "castillos". — Whereas elsewhere by the 12C, cities had been founded and were enjoying communal rights, Castile and León, south of Toledo was a no-man's land between Christian and Muslim territories, pinpointed only by castle fortresses — *castillos* — which in time gave the province its name. At the start of the Reconquest defence was entrusted to the Military Orders of **Calatrava, Santiago** and **San Juan** who in return were granted vast sheep grazing terrains. This resulted in the development, because of the climate, of a transhumant cycle (Mesta, *p 247*) between the Iberian Cordillera at one season and Madrid-Castile-La Mancha and Extremadura at the other. Elsewhere land was cultivated by small communities giving the region the character which it has to this day in which towns, frequently with the atmosphere of overgrown villages, centre, as in northern Spain, on picturesque and at times even grand, **Plaza Mayor.**

Later in history a second line of fortifications was constructed along the frontier between the Kingdoms of Aragon and Castile. The principal **strongholds** — Sigüenza, Molina de Aragón, Belmonte, Alarcón — were given in apanage to the great feudal families of which some, such as that of the Marquess of Villena-Pacheco, served the royal interest little or not at all as they advanced their own power and fortunes.

The "secano" system of agriculture. — The land lacks water and there is no irrigation: *secano* means un-irrigated land in Spanish as opposed to *regadío* or well irrigated.

Cereals, olive trees and vines, however, can be grown: vines cover the ground of La Mancha, olive groves relieve the landscape; there are whole fields of saffron.

The manmade lakes of the Sea of Castile will, in time, regenerate vast areas for afforestation and cultivation. Pines are already being extensively grown for timber in the northern parts of Cuenca.

Mineral wealth. — The mineral resources of the region have brought on the establishment of an important industrial complex at **Puertollano.** It is a centre of petro-chemical industry and its by- products.

A large part of the mercury from **Almadén** is exported.

Local crafts. — There are active craftsmen and women still in southern Castile. Women make **hooked** and **pillow lace** in the villages of Ciudad Real Province *(see under Almagro).* Toledo Province maintains its tradition of **ceramics;** blue and yellow ware from Talavera, green and yellow from El Puente del Arzobispo; also **embroidery** in Lagartera, **damascene** in Toledo *(p 214),* **pottery** in La Mancha (Mota del Cuervo, Consuegra).

ALARCÓN ★ (Cuenca)
Michelin map **444** fold 25 — Pop 271

Alarcón crowns a mound of brown earth almost encircled by a loop in the Júcar River. The town fortress stands at the ravine's edge, pale, square, guarded by two lines of fortifications and adding considerably to the melancholy beauty of the **site★★.**

Alarcón, meaning Alaric's town, was founded by the son of a Visigothic ruler in the 5C. On its reconquest from the Muslims, it was ceded to the Knights of Santiago and eventually came into the hands of **Infante Don Juan Manuel** (1282-1348) who wrote many of his cautionary tales while living there *(p 21).* As the property of the Marquess of Villena in the 15C, the castle became the symbol of feudal arrogance against the crown.

The Alarcón Dam, 3km - 2 miles away controls the Júcar's impetuous flow.

The village. — Roughcast obscures many a stone house front in the modest country village.

The parish Church of **Sta María** (restored), possesses an elegant Renaissance west door and, at the end of a vast Gothic nave, a composite 16C carved altarpiece.

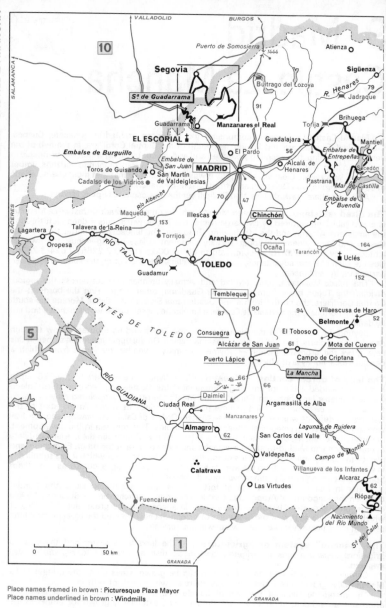

Place names framed in brown : Picturesque Plaza Mayor
Place names underlined in brown : Windmills

ALBACETE P

Michelin map 444 folds 25 and 26 — Pop 117 126
See town plan in the current Michelin Red Guide España Portugal

The province of Albacete is like an arid Castilian promontory jutting into the fertile greenery of the *huerta* country; the provincial capital itself appears typical of La Mancha *(p 210)*, facing out over the flat, cereal covered plain (Al-Basite signified "the plain" to the Arabs). Today the town is known for its manufacture of knives and scissors. It suffered considerably in the Republican siege of July 1936 when the cathedral was set on fire (burnt area now rebuilt).

Albacete Museum. — *Open 10am to 2pm and 4 to 7pm; closed Sunday and holiday afternoons and all day Monday; 200pts.*
This museum erected in the municipal park, the Parque de Abelardo Sánchez, houses the rich finds from the province's prehistoric sites and its many Iberian and Roman antiquities — note the minute amber and ivory dolls discovered in the Roman necropolis at Ontur (Michelin map 444 north of fold 35).

EXCURSION

Chinchilla de Monte Aragón. — *14km - 8 1/2 miles southeast.* Chinchilla, perched on the side of an oblong shaped mound below its old castle walls, consists of a network of narrow streets in which lie hidden many an elegant Gothic and Renaissance façade. The mansions of which these form part, are an indication of the town's prosperity when it was the stronghold of the Marquess of Villena. In 1833 the town became, for a time, the provincial capital before being superseded by Albacete.
The **Plaza Mayor** is modest but delightful, overlooked by the 18C festooned, ochre coloured **town hall** with a pediment bust of Charles III, by a wooden pillared arcade and by the great bare side wall of the Gothic-Renaissance Church of **San Salvador.**

In contrast the buttresses at the east end are delicately ornamented and inside it contains a boldly designed Plateresque apse.

The **Lonja** front is surmounted by a gallery; the adjoining town hall side wall is 16C.

Chinchilla still practises its traditional craft of pottery.

ALCALÁ DE HENARES

(Madrid) —————————————

Michelin map ▨▨▨ fold 14 or ▨▨▨ fold 18 — Pop 142 862

The city of Complutum in the fertile Henares Valley was large and important in Roman times; after the Reconquest it came under the archbishops of Toledo, one of the greatest of who, Cardinal Cisneros, founded a university in the town in 1498, which brought him great renown since it became famous for its language teaching and in 1517, published the first Polyglot Bible or Biblia Complutensis with parallel texts in Hebrew, Latin, Greek and Chaldean. In 1836 the university was transferred to Madrid.

The Civil War annihilated Alcalá's architectural and artistic riches; proximity to Madrid has brought modern industrial development. The city, once again has a university. The traditional delicious sweetmeats *(almendras garrapiñadas)* are made by the Poor Clares whose convent is by the University.

Alcalá was the birthplace of Cervantes, Catherine of Aragon, daughter of Ferdinand and Isabel and first wife of Henry VIII, and the Spanish architect, Bustamante *(p 15)*.

The adventurous storyteller. — **Miguel de Cervantes Saavedra** was born in Alcalá in 1547. His adventures began in his mid-twenties, when after four years in Italy, he enlisted and found himself at the Battle of Lepanto (1571) during which he was wounded; in 1575 he was captured by the Turks, taken off to Algeria as a slave and rescued only after five years. On his return to Spain he wrote a pastoral novel, *La Galatea* (1585) and various works before, in 1605, he published the first part of *Don Quixote (p 210)*. It was immediately an immense success — an English translation appeared in 1612, a French in 1614 — but brought Cervantes little actual cash. He continued writing: humorous stories of adventure and intrigue, comedies, *entremeses* or one act prose farces, novels and the second part of *Don Quixote* (1615). He died a relatively poor man, on 23 April 1616 — the same day as Shakespeare.

Don Quixote is a brilliant idea: an elderly gentleman sets out as a doubty knight errant in search of adventure and to redress wrongs in the terms of the storybooks he loves; he is accompanied by his simple but astute squire. The confrontation and interaction of enigmatic relationships, of the ideal and the real, the true and the illusory, reveal the meditations of a man of 58 deeply involved in philosophy and life.

Old University (Colegio de San Ildefonso). — *Guided tours (time: 40 min) 15 July to 15 September 11am to 1pm and 6 to 8pm; the rest of the year Saturdays and Sundays only 11am to 1pm and 4 to 6pm; 50pts.*

The beautiful **Plateresque façade★** (1543) by Rodrigo Gil de Hontañón, stands on the small San Diego Square close by the Plaza de Cervantes. The **Patio Mayor,** known as the Santo Tomás de Villanueva *patio,* with its 3 floors has a certain dignity: at the centre is a well-head with a swan motif, the emblem of the Cisneros. A museum was installed on the first floor.

Cross the Philosophers' Patio to reach the delightful **Three Languages Patio** (1557) where Latin, Greek and Hebrew were taught. In a small room, the **Paraninfo,** formerly used for examinations and degree ceremonies is now the setting for the solemn opening of Alcalá University terms. The decoration includes a gallery delicately ornamented in the Plateresque style and an *artesonado* ceiling.

San Ildefonso. — This 15C chapel adjoining the Old University, houses the **mausoleum★** of Cardinal Cisneros. It is a richly sculpted work by Fancelli and Bartolomé Ordóñez. Note the *artesonado* ceiling.

Plan your own itinerary by looking at the map of the most outstanding sights (pp 4-5).

ALCALÁ DEL JÚCAR ★ (Albacete)

Michelin map 🔢 fold 26 — Pop 1 797

The village has a **site**★ equally magnificent by day or night. It has been built between its castle tower and church into the very face of the cliff which is circled below by the Júcar.

A walk through the steep alleys *(no cars allowed)*, though tiring, is well worthwhile. Most of the dwellings hollowed out of the living rock possess, at the far end of long passages, balconies overlooking the opposite side of the cliff! One of these dwellings, the Masagó, can be visited *(Sundays and holidays only 9am to 2pm and 4 to 10pm; closed afternoons in winter; 50pts)*.

ALCARAZ (Albacete)

Michelin map 🔢 folds 24 and 33 — Pop 1 808

Alcaraz stands isolated upon a clay soil mound at the centre of the *sierra* of the same name. The city, which grew rich manufacturing carpets, retains a Renaissance character marked by the style of Vandelvira who was born there in 1509 *(p 49)*.

Calle Mayor. — The main street, off which run steep, stepped alleys, is fronted by old houses of settled ease. The simple lines are broken only by two heraldic style warriors and, in the square, by a doorway (Puerta de la Aduana) with delicate Plateresque decoration.

Plaza Mayor. — Among several elegant, porticoed buildings overlooking the square are the 18C **Lonja** which abuts the clock tower, the 16C **Pósito**, a former municipal granary and the **town hall** also 16C and emblasoned with a coat of arms. The 15C **Church of the Holy Trinity** has a Flamboyant Gothic portal but a Renaissance baptistry. Inside is a museum of sacred art. A path leads, beneath two arches, to the cemetery from which there is an attractive view.

EXCURSION

Source (Nacimiento) of the Río Mundo. — *62km · 39 miles south. Take the Riópar road.* The road passes through a wooded valley to emerge onto the Sierra de Alcaraz. **Riópar** is known for its bronze foundry (works of art).
5km · 3 miles from Riópar, bear right for Siles. After 6km · 4 miles a road leads off to the left to the Cueva de los Chorros. The Río Mundo, a Segura tributary, rises in a bubbling spring, half hidden by vegetation in a cave at the foot of the steep Sierra del Calar.

ALMAGRO ★ (Ciudad Real)

Michelin map 🔢 fold 22 or 🔢 fold 26 — Pop 8 364

Almagro, once the main stronghold of the Knights of Calatrava *(p 187)* became, for a time in the 18C, the provincial capital but was later displaced by Ciudad Real.

It is known for its aubergines and lace.

Women can be seen sitting in groups in the street in the villages along the Almagro Valdepeñas road and in nearby **Moral de Calatrava** and **Aldea del Rey** as they ply their pillow lace bobbins at breathtaking speed.

Plaza Mayor★. — The square is one of the most unusual in Castile. It is oblong in shape with a continuous colonnade framing two sides, supporting two storeys separated by bands of white masonry and illuminated by an unbroken series of small paned windows all with green surrounds. Since the 16C, no 11 has served as the **Corral de Comedias★**, one of the courts where the earliest Spanish plays were performed. *Open 9am to 2pm and 4 to 9pm.* The court's wooden porticoes, oil lamps, well and scenery wall form an interesting rust and white composition. *The Festival of Modern Theatre takes place during St Bartholomew festival (24 to 28 August) and during last fortnight in September the International Festival of Classical Theatre occurs.*

The town alleyways. — Leave the square on the left by the Calle de la Nuestra Señora de las Nieves; continue along the Calle de las Bernardas and the second left, which skirts a Dominican convent with a fine crest. Along the cobbled streets are whitewashed houses and the grand sculptured doorways of monasteries and convents.

Former Calatrava Monastery (Antiguo Convento de Calatrava). — There is an attractive Plateresque staircase off the restored cloister.

ALMANSA (Albacete)

Michelin map 🔢 fold 27 — Pop 20 331

Almansa, once the Moorish Al-Manxa, is a city of the plain, swathed around the foot of a lofty limestone spike crowned by a mediaeval castle. Its claim to fame lies in its association with the Battle of Almansa of 1707, won by the Duke of Berwick (illegitimate son of James II of England who became a Marshal of France) against the British and their allies, to assure the Spanish throne for the Bourbon King, Philip V.

Asunción Church. — The church, although completely transformed in the Neo-Classical period, remains interesting for its monumental Renaissance portal attributed to Vandelvira.

The nearby seignorial mansion, the **Casa Grande**, has a fine 16C doorway with armorial bearings supported by twin giants. Inside is a *patio* with superimposed galleries.

Castillo. — The 15C ramparts (restored) perched precariously along the rock ridge, command the plain and now make a pleasant walk *(apply to the guard)*.

EXCURSION

La Vieja Cave (Cueva). — *22km · 14 miles northwest by Alpera.* Most prehistoric caves in this part of Spain are up cliffs and, therefore, difficult to reach, and, also, being open to the sky, are weatherworn. This one, however, still has clearly visible paintings *(to visit apply in the morning at Alpera town hall - ayuntamiento)*. Elongated outline figures of men hunting stags with bows and arrows can be seen, typical of Levant cave painting. One figure, possibly the chief, has a plumed headdress, the women long robes.

ARANJUEZ ★ (Madrid)

Michelin map **444** fold 13 or **447** fold 17 — Pop 35 936

Aranjuez appears at the centre of the Castilian plain (particularly if you approach from the south) like an oasis, green with shrubs and grass and leafy avenues around the royal palaces.

The shaded walks described by writers, sung by composers (Joaquín Rodrigo : *Concierto de Aranjuez*), painted by artists (the Catalan, Santiago Rusiñol, *p 97*) and where Bourbons strolled in the 18C are now popular with Madrileños. On 30 May, Aranjuez celebrates the feast day of San Fernando with popular festivities and a bullfight.

A royal town. — The Catholic Monarchs enjoyed staying in Aranjuez in the residence (14C) of the Grand Master of the Knights of Santiago. The Emperor Charles V contented himself with enlarging this domain. His son Philip II, however, called on the future architects of the Escorial, to erect a new palace surrounded by gardens.

Under the Bourbons the town became one of the principal royal residences and was considerably embellished. All went well until it was suddenly devastated by fire, rebuilt in 1748 and then again badly burned. Most of the palace was reconstructed once more including the present frontage. Ferdinand VI built the town to a gridiron plan; Charles III added two wings to the palace and Charles IV erected the delightful, Labourer's Cottage.

The Aranjuez Revolt (El motín de Aranjuez). — In March 1808, Charles IV, his queen and prime minister, Godoy *(p 133)* were at Aranjuez where they were making preparations to flee, on 18 March, first to Andalusia then to America on account of Godoy having, in effect, allowed Napoleon's armies free passage to Portugal through Spain the year before. In Portugal, the French were fighting the Portuguese who were strongly supported by the British. The Spanish people, however, had objected to the passage of the French and Godoy had counselled his king to follow the Portuguese royal house into exile.

On the night of 17 March, Godoy's mansion was attacked by followers of the heir apparent, Prince Ferdinand; Charles IV disowned his minister and was compelled to abdicate in favour of his son. This was not enough, however, Napoleon summoned both to Bayonne and made both abdicate in his own favour (5 May).

These machinations and negotiations and the presence of a French garrison in Madrid stirred the Spaniards to the revolt of 2 May 1808 *(p 200)* which marked the beginning of the War of Independence.

■ ROYAL PALACE★ and the ISLAND GARDEN

Guided tours of the museums 10am to 1pm and 3.30 to 6.30pm (3 to 6pm in winter); the gardens are open 10am to sunset; closed Tuesdays, 1 January, 1 and 30 May, 4 or 6 September, 25 December and afternoons of 24 and 31 December; 400pts.

Royal Palace★ (Palacio Real) (A B). — This Classical style palace of brick and stone dates from the early 18C. In spite of many modifications it retains considerable unity of style and symmetry. The court of honour overlooking a vast outer square, is framed by the main building with wings at right angles on either side; domed pavilions mark the angles and arches the ends of each wing and the entrance. The apartments have been left as they were at the end of the 19C.

The grand staircase was designed by the Italian, Giacomo Bonavia during the reign of Philip V — the bust of *Louis XIV* by Coysevox recalls the French king's close parentage and protagonism for his grandson.

Throughout Brussels' tapestries decorate the walls, Madrid manufactured Persian style carpets warm the floors and there is a general air of the luxury of the period. In María Luisá's apartments, in an antechamber, are paintings by the Neapolitan artist Luca Giordano, and in

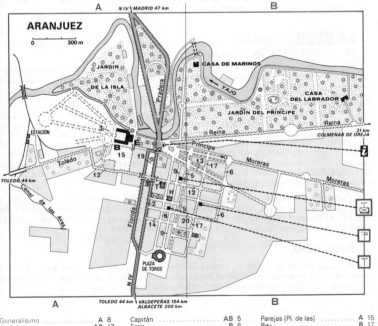

the music room, a piano presented by Eugenia de Montijo, the future Empress Eugénie, to Isabel II. The chapel has frescoes by Bayeu (1792) and a statue of the Virgin carved by the Valencian, Maella. The **throne room,** above crimson velvet hangings and rococo furnishings, has a ceiling painted with an allegory of monarchy — ironically it was in this room that Charles IV signed his abdication in March 1808.

The **Porcelain Saloon★★,** a former audience chamber, is gracefully rococo with white, garlanded porcelain tiles brightly illustrating in coloured high relief, scenes of Chinese life, exotica (lower walls) and children's games (the corners). The carved and painted wood doors, the chandelier, the marble pavement, enhance the effect of the tiles made in the Buen Retiro Factory in Madrid in 1763. In the king's apartments a music room precedes the smoking or Arabian Saloon — a diverting reproduction of the Hall of the Two Sisters in the Alhambra. A Mengs Crucifixion hangs in the bedroom; in the Infantes' Saloon the walls are covered by 200 small pictures delicately painted on rice paper with Oriental style motifs. Even the royal guardrooms is hung with paintings by Giordano.

Museum of Royal Robes. — *Temporarily closed.* The court dress of sovereigns up to the time of Charles II is displayed in the museum. Starting with the reign of Ferdinand VII the royal attire is authentic: the royal mantle worn by the queens of the early 19C is in the 7th gallery; in later rooms are the robes of the great military orders, the service uniforms of Alfonso XII and XIII and members of the present royal house.

Parterre★ (A E). — A formal garden, laid out by the Frenchman, Boutelou, in 1746, extends along the palace's east front.

The Island Garden (Jardín de la Isla) (A). — The informal garden, which dates back to the time of Philip II, is on an artificial island in a bend in the River Tagus. Cross the canal which once drove mill wheels, to reach the park with its fountains.

■ THE PRINCE'S GARDEN★

To visit the Labourer's Cottage; 200pts; the Sailor's House; 100pts.

The Prince's Garden★ (Jardín del Príncipe) (B). — The garden is more a park, landscaped beside the Tagus by Boutelou in 1763 for the future Charles IV. Within its bounds were a model farm, greenhouses with tropical plants and stables for exotic animals.

The Labourer's Cottage★★ (Casa del Labrador) (B). — The so-called cottage, named ironically after the workhouse which originally stood on the site, stands in the Prince's Garden and is a Versailles type Trianon built by Charles IV in a Neo-Classical style similar to the palace. The brick and stone building comprises two floors and an attic. The wrought iron grille and balustrade surrounding the courtyard entrance are surmounted by 20 Carrara marble busts. The interior is an excellent example of luxurious 18C decoration: there are Pompeian style ceilings, embroidered silk hangings, doors of solid mahogany, marble pavements, furniture and lamps, canvases by Brambilla, clocks and porcelain.

The billiard room on the first floor has a ceiling illustrating the Four Elements by Maella and magnificent embroidered silk hangings of views of Madrid.

The statue gallery includes authentic Greek busts, statues and inlaid in the marble pavement, Roman mosaics from Mérida; the French clock at the gallery centre incorporates a reproduction of Trajan's column. In the María Luisa room are remarkable hangings made up of 97 small pictures of Spanish towns. The centre of the ballroom is now occupied by a deep green malachite table and chair, a present given by the Czar Alexander III to Charles IV. The Platinum Room or Gabinete de Platino, has walls decorated with gold, platinum and bronze inlays; in the ante-room is a bird carved from a single piece of ivory.

The Sailor's House★★ (Casa de Marinos) (B). — The building houses the royal vessels of six sovereigns: Isabel II, Charles IV — the outside was painted by Maella — Alfonso XII — the ships is of mahogany *(caoba)* — María Cristina — the ceiling is painted to resemble a woven hanging — Alfonso XIII and Philip V, whose *falúa*, is richly carved.

BELMONTE ★ (Cuenca)

Michelin map **444** fold 24 — Pop 2 811

Monumental gateways and a length of the massive perimeter which linked town and castle remain to give an idea of Belmonte's past; it was the native town of the 16C prose writer **Fray Luis de León** *(p 240).*

Castle. — *Open 10am to 2pm and 5 to 7pm; closed 24 to 28 August; 100pts.*

The hexagonal fortress, flanked by circular towers, was constructed in the 15C by Juan Pacheco, Marquess of Villena, as part of the defences of his vast domain. It was subsequently abandoned, until the 19C when it was restored, although it lost all its furnishings. In 1870 the castle court was disfigured by a dark red brick facing, apparently to the taste of the then owner, Eugenia de Montijo. All that remains in the empty rooms are beautiful Mudejar **ceilings★** — the audience chamber is outstanding — and delicately carved stone window surrounds. Follow the curtain walls to the pyramid stepped merlons to command a view of the austere La Mancha countryside.

Old Collegiate Church. — *If closed, apply to the parish priest.* In the church are a collection of 15, 16 and 17C polychrome wood **altarpieces** executed in a local high relief style. The 15C **choirstalls★,** originally in Cuenca cathedral, are carved from unpolished wood to illustrate, very realistically, scenes from Genesis and the Passion.

EXCURSION

Villaescusa de Haro. — *6km - 4 miles northeast.* The parish church *(apply to the parish priest)* includes an early 16C **Chapel of the Assumption★,** closed by a wrought iron screen of original design. The Plateresque style is clearly apparent in the chapel.

Respect the life of the countryside
Go carefully on country roads
Protect wildlife, plants and trees.

CAÍDOS, Valle de los ★★ (Madrid)

Michelin map 🗺 fold 3 or 🗺 fold 7 — *Local map p 199*

The Valle de los Caídos, the Valley of the Fallen, is a spectacular monument to the dead of the Civil War in a beautiful setting deep in the Guadarrama Mountains. The valley, formerly the Cuelgamuros, is splendid with granite outcrops and pine trees.

Open 10am to 7pm in summer — 9.30am to 6.30pm in winter; closed afternoons of 1 and 6 January and 25 December and all day 17 July and 10 August. Toll: 150pts per car, more than two passengers: 300pts.

The Juanelos. — The monolithic columns at either side of the road entrance were designed as part of an arch by Juanelo Turriano, clockmaker to the Emperor Charles V.

Basilica★★. — The basilica was hollowed into the base of a massive granite spike, crowned by an immense Cross. The west door in its austere granite façade, is crowned by a *Pietà* carved by Juan de Ávalos. At the entrance is a fine wrought iron screen with 40 statues, in metal, of the Spanish saints and soldiers. The 262m - 860ft nave (St Peters', Rome: 186m - 610ft; St Paul's, London: 152m - 500ft) is lined with chapels between which have been hung eight copies of 16C Brussels' **tapestries** of the Apocalypse. Above the chapels' entrances are alabaster copies of the most famous statues of the Virgin in Spain. A **cupola★,** 42m - 138ft in diameter, above the crossing shows in mosaic the heroes, martyrs and saints of Spain approaching both Christ in Majesty and the Virgin. On the altar stands a painted wood figure of Christ Crucified against a tree trunk by the sculptor, Beovides; at the foot is the funerary stone of José Antonio Primo de Rivera, founder of the Falangist Party, and that of Franco. Ossuaries contain coffins of 40 000 people from both sides in the Civil War *(in the crypt: not open).*

The Cross★. — The Cross is 125m - 410ft high (150m - 492ft including the plinth), the width from fingertip to fingertip, 46m - 150ft. The statues of the Evangelists around the plinth and the four cardinal virtues above are proportionally gigantic. There is a good view from the base *(access: north side by funicular: 100pts Rtn; closed 2 to 4pm).*

The great building showing Herreran influence on the far side of the valley from the basilica, is a Benedictine monastery, seminary and social studies centre *(not open).*

CALATRAVA Castle-Monastery ★ (Ciudad Real)

Michelin map 🗺 folds 30 and 31 or 🗺 fold 35

Calatrava Castle, a crumbling ruin, its walls lofty spikes crowning a high hill, still gives a feeling of awe. It conveys, as no other **site** the lonely ordeals undergone by the Knights of the Reconquest *(p 132).*

In the mid - 12C the **Campo de Calatrava,** east and south of Ciudad Real, was the scene of unceasing warfare between Christians and Muslims. The old Calatrava Fortress, built originally by the Moors on the banks of the Guadiana, was captured and abandoned by the Templars, before being taken over by Raimundo, Abbot of Fitero *(p 182).* A soldier before he became an abbot, he installed a garrison in the castle where in 1158 he founded the Order of Calatrava, the first of Spain's military orders. Al Mansur, however, captured the castle which remained in Muslim hands until the victory of Las Navas de Tolosa (1212) when the knights regained control of the region. They determined to build a new fortress in an impregnable position: it was completed by 1217.

The fortress. — *7km - 4 miles southwest of the Calzada de Calatrava, turn right into a 2.5km - 1 mile long surfaced uphill road. Apply to the watchman.*

There are three stout perimeters, the second actually built into the rock and the whole construction amazingly massive.

The church, restored, has fine brick vaulting, described as swallow's nest in design. The ruins of Salvatierra Castle are visible from the fortress towers.

CHINCHÓN ★ (Madrid)

Michelin map 🗺 fold 13 or 🗺 fold 18 — Pop 3 900

It is to the **Countess of Chinchón** that the west owes quinine. The countess, wife of a 17C viceroy of Peru, was cured of fever by an Indian medicament prepared from tree bark; having proved the remedy she brought it back to Europe. In the 18C Linnaes, the Swedish botanist, named the bark bearing tree chinchona, in the vicereine's honour.

The large parish church stands on the **Plaza Mayor★,** the uneven but picturesque square of Chinchón which comes to life during the summer bullfighting season.

Chinchón is known for its aniseed spirit which is now distilled in the old castle.

CIUDAD REAL Ⓟ

Michelin map 🗺 folds 21 and 22 or 🗺 fold 26 — Pop 51 118

The town, founded in 1255 by Alfonso X, the Wise, as Villa Real, a strongpoint from which to control the growing power of the military orders in the region, was elevated to the status of Royal City — Ciudad Real — in 1420. The expulsion of the last of the Moors in the 17C and its temporary loss of position to Almagro (1750-1761) as capital of La Mancha proved fatal to its wellbeing.

West of the town is the probable site of the Battle of **Alarcos** of 1195 when Alfonso VIII's forces were routed by the Almohad horsemen and the line of the Reconquest was forced back to the Tagus, leaving Toledo and Cuenca under threat until the brilliant Christian victory of Las Navas de Tolosa (1212).

Puerta de Toledo. — The Mudejar style gateway on the north side of the town is a relic of the 14C town wall.

Cathedral. — 16C. The spacious effect of the single aisle is enhanced by the bare walls; the retable at the high altar, in scale with its surroundings, is adorned with 17C statues whose tall forms recall Berruguete.

St Peter's. — Gothic elegance has been retained in the façades of the 14C church. In a south chapel, the Coca family chapel, there are a 15C Flemish school stone altarpiece and a 16C recumbent figure sculpted in alabaster in the Plateresque style.

CONTRERAS Dam ★ (Cuenca, Albacete)

Michelin map **444** folds 17 and 26 or **445** fold 11

The Madrid-Valencia road runs along the crest of the massive Contreras Dam built at the threshold of the Cabriel Valley. As you cross there is a spectacular **view★** back over the reservoir, downstream into the valley course and, in the lower foreground, of the picturesque old road with its many serpentine bends.

CUENCA ★★ P

Michelin map **444** fold 16 or **445** fold 7 Pop 41 791

Cuenca lies at the heart of a boulder strewn, hilly province of the same name between the richer Levant plains and the Castilian Meseta. The relative isolation of the provincial capital should not discourage the would-be visitor for the surrounding countryside is unusual and the town itself has an old quarter in a uniquely spectacular **setting★★**.

Holy Week processions are considerably enhanced by the site: at dawn on Good Friday the ascent to Calvary is enacted along the steep alleys to the accompaniment of drums. A festival of sacred music is also held throughout Holy Week in the Church of San Miguel (**A**).

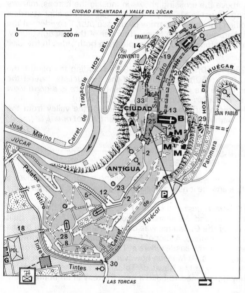

CUENCA

Alfonso VIII	2
Alonso de Ojeda	3
Andrés de Cabrera	5
Angustias (Bajada a las)	7
Cardenal Paya (Pl.)	8
Carmen (Pl. del)	12
Colegio San José	13
Descalzos (Pl. de los)	14
Fray Luis de Léon	18
Júcar (Ronda del)	19
Julián Romero	20
Mosén Diego de Valera	23
Obispo Valero	24
Pío XII (Pl. Mayor de)	25
Pósito	
Puente de San Pablo	29
Puerta de Valencia	30
San Nicolás (Pl.)	33
Trabuco	34

> For maximum
> information
> from town plans
> consult the key p 30.

■ THE OLD TOWN ★★ (Ciudad Antigua) time: 2 1/2 hours

The quarter stands on an advanced cliff top, surrounded, on three sides, by a precipice. The narrow streets are fronted by houses which are very tall for lack of ground space.

Go through an arch in the 18C town hall and park in the main square (Plaza Mayor de Pío XII). Follow the route marked on the plan.

Cathedral★ (**B**). — The cathedral, Gothic in design, Renaissance in decoration, suffered a partial collapse of its west front in 1902. The 13C nave is contemporary French and Norman in architectural style. Among the edifice's most outstanding features are a 15C triforium, 16C altarpieces, wrought iron **screens★** and, off the north aisle, a 16C **Knights' Chapel** in which, besides an iron screen, there are 15C tombs and panels by the late 15C painter Yáñez de la Almedina.

Treasury★. — *Open 11am to 1.30pm and 5 to 7pm (4.30 to 6pm in winter); 50pts.* The **door★** to the chapterhouse was carved by Berruguete. Inside, copes, 16C paintings and tapestries form a small museum.

Part of the treasury has been transferred to the **Diocesan Museum** (**M²**; *open 11am to 2pm and 4 to 6pm - 8pm Saturdays; closed Sunday and holiday afternoons and all day Monday; 100pts*). Among its key pieces are two El Greco paintings, *The Calvary* by Gerard David, a 14C Byzantine reliquary and a Limoges enamel crozier.

The Hanging Houses★ (**Casas Colgadas**) (**M**). — *Walk along the cathedral south wall.* Among these 14C houses are a restaurant and a museum. Go through an arched passage beside the *mesón* to the San Pablo footpath from which one can see the houses overhanging the rock face.

Museum of Abstract Art★. — *Open 11am to 2pm and 4 to 6pm (8pm Saturdays); closed all day Monday and certain holidays and Sunday afternoons; 100pts.* One of the hanging houses forms a setting for the works by Spanish painters.

(After FITER photo, San Hilario Sacalm)

Casas Colgadas

Cuenca Museum★ (M[1]). — *Open 10am to 2pm and 4 to 7pm; closed Sunday and holiday afternoons and all day Monday; 75pts.*

The first floor displays prehistoric objects. The second floor, the most interesting exhibits: sculpture, ceramics and numismatics found in the Roman excavations of Segóbriga, Valeria and Ercavica (in gallery 10 a Roman kitchen-cellar has been reconstructed). On the third floor are works of art by contemporary Cuenca artists.

Turn back to the cathedral and along Calle San Pedro; bear first left for the Plaza San Nicolas from which steps lead off beneath a stone arch to the Plaza de los Descalzos.

Plaza de los Descalzos (14). — A Franciscan monastery and hermitage, known as the Virgin in Anguish, stands in the quiet, tree-lined square.

Return to the Calle San Pedro. Go left by the polygonal Church of San Pedro (C), into an alley on the left which ends at the edge of the Júcar Ravine. Good view!

Come back to the church and this time skirt the Huécar Cliff by walking down Calle Julián Romero. This delightful alley brings you back to the cathedral.

EXCURSIONS

The "Hoces" (Ravines). — *Town plan p 196.* Roads which parallel the river on either side as it circles the bottom of the precipitous rock spur, afford amazing views of those incredible houses.

Hoz del Júcar. — The Júcar is the shorter and more enclosed ravine. Poplars stand reflected in the green river waters below the ochre coloured cliff.

Hoz del Huécar. — *Round tour of 15km - 9 miles.* The Huécar course swings from side to side between less steep abutting slopes as it drains a small valley where market-gardening is found. The Cuenca houses, seen from below appear to defy gravity.

Turn left at the end of the ravine by the signpost "Carretera pintoresca", a serpentine road, and left again for the San Jéronimo Monastery (Convento). Shortly afterwards, in a right bend, there is a remarkable **vista★** of the valley's tall pillars of grey rock and, in the distance, of the Cuenca houses. Enter the old town by one of the gateways.

Serranía de Cuenca★. — *81km - 50 miles.* Leave Cuenca in the Ciudad Encantada direction continuing past the Hoz del Júcar (see above). At the end of a winding road along the right bank, cross the Júcar.

Devil's Window (Ventano del Diablo). — *4km - 2 1/2 miles beyond the bridge, on the left.* The vantage point commands an impressive view of the **Júcar Gorges★.**

Turn right in the pinewood to the Enchanted City.

Enchanted City (Ciudad Encantada). — *Admission: 40pts.* The rock chaos is the result of erosion in a deep stratum of limestone; great boulders have been isolated from the mass and strangely carved by the elements. A marked footpath leads *(1 hour)* through the dreamlike landscape in which the two major features are the crossing of the "toboggan slope" and the "sea of stones" *(mar de piedras).* 2km - 1 mile away is the **Mirador de Uña** *(bear left at the fork)* from which there is an open view of the Júcar, dominated all along its course by tall cliffs and, in the distance, Uña and its lake.

As the road skirts the water's edge there are **views★** of the manmade Lake Toba against a background of pine covered mountain slopes and bare rock crests.

Tragacete. — A meeting place for hunters and trout fishermen, the village (alt 1 283m - 4 209ft) lives off stockraising and lumber from the local pinewoods.

Source of the Cuervo★ (Nacimiento del Cuervo). — *12km - 7 miles. Take the surfaced, signposted road on the village outskirts; leave the car just before a bridge (12km - 7 miles).* A narrow footpath climbs *(1/4 hour)* to the early **falls★** of the Cuervo which rises amidst rocks and mossy grottoes, hidden by greenery.

Las Torcas★. — *21km - 13 miles. Leave Cuenca south on the town plan, take the road to Teruel and after 7km - 4 miles bear left (signposted).* The road crosses a pleasant pine forest where the old-looking "torcas" can be seen. These deep crater-like openings caused by underwater springs can at times reach spectacular proportions — note the Torca del Lobo.

ESCORIAL Monastery ★★★ Monasterio de EL ESCORIAL (Madrid)

Michelin map **444** fold 3 or **447** fold 7 — *Local map p 199*

San Lorenzo de El Escorial was an insignificant village on a foothill (1 065m - 3 494ft) of the Sierra de Guadarrama when Philip II selected it as the site for his monastery-palace. Today hundreds of thousands of tourists come to gaze at the massive building, a monument to the king who commissioned it, the architect, Juan de Herrera, and 16C Spain.

St Lawrence, patron of the town and monastery, is celebrated annually on 10 August.

Historical notes. — On 10 August 1557, St Lawrence's Day, Philip II's forces beat the French at St Quentin in Flanders. In thanksgiving the king decided to erect and dedicate to the saint, a monastery which would be consigned to the Hieronymites and would also incorporate a royal palace in which he would live and a royal pantheon in which he would be buried. The project, supervised personally by Philip, was a stupendous one-there are nearly 1 200 doors, 2 600 windows; it required 1 500 workmen but it was completed in 21 years (1563-1584) which is why the building has an exceptional unity of style.

Reaction to sumptuous ornateness fashionable in Charles V's reign produced from the architects a sober monument with clean cut, majestic lines. The general designs of the first architect, Juan de Toledo, were followed, after his death in 1567 by his assistant Juan de Herrera, who, however, is responsible for the final overall elegance.

It is said that the monastery by its gridiron plan recalls St Lawrence's martyrdom. It measures 206m X 161m - 676ft X 528ft and is built of grey granite — the austerity of the stone serving to emphasise, if anything, the severity of the architecture. When the king commanded an increase in height to accommodate a larger community of religious, Herrera took the opportunity to position the rows of windows asymmetrically to lessen the monotony of horizontal lines which, otherwise, are only relieved by the pointed corner towers. The edifice finally has the grandeur of a great palace, the austerity of a dedicated monastery.

ESCORIAL Monastery★★★

(After Spanish National Tourist Office photo)

Escorial Monastery

TOUR

Guided tours (time: 1/2 day) 10am to 1.30pm (1pm for the Prince's Pavilion) and 3.30 to 7pm (6pm in winter); closed Mondays, 1 January, 1 May, 10 August, 10 or 11 September and afternoons of 24, 25 and 31 December; 300pts.

One hour before closing time tickets are only delivered for the Royal Apartments, the Royal Pantheon, the Chapterhouses and the Library (125pts.); 1/2 hour before closing time no tickets are sold.

The church is open 9am to 1.15pm and 3.30 to 6.45pm (3.30 to 5.45pm in winter).

Royal Apartments★★ (Palacios). — While Philip II and the Spanish Habsburgs remained on the throne, the Escorial was a place of regal splendour: the king resided in apartments encircling the church apse, other royal apartments extended around the Mascaroon Courtyard. The Bourbons, who, in fact, preferred the palaces of La Granja, El Pardo and Aranjuez to the Escorial, when, nevertheless, in residence occupied suites on the north side of the church. The palace took on renewed glory in the 18C in the reigns of Charles III and IV but lost its position as a centre of court life again later.

A staircase built in the time of Charles IV goes up *(3rd floor)* to the **Bourbon apartments.** These are sumptuous with Pompeian ceilings and fine **tapestries★.**

The hangings include many made in the Royal Tapestry Works in Madrid after designs by Spanish artists, notably Goya as in the series which follows from especially commissioned cartoons on popular subjects and pastimes. In later rooms are Flemish tapestries — a *Neptune* (from the Telemachus series) and several in spirited style after Teniers.

In the Battle Gallery there are frescoes: on the south wall, of the Victory at Higueruela in the 15C against the Moors and on the north wall, the victory at St Quentin against the French.

The austerity of **Philip II's apartments** *(2nd floor)* is all the more striking after the luxury of the Bourbon rooms. Those of the Infanta Isabel Clara Eugenia, like those of her father comprise a suite of relatively small rooms in which the principal decoration derives from dados of Talavera ceramic tiles.

The king's bedroom, where he died, aged 71 in 1598, is directly off the church. A communicating door allowed him to walk in at any time in the early years and at the end, when he was dying of gangrene caused by advanced gout, to be present during services and contemplate the high altar from his bed. The paintings in the apartments include Hieronymus Bosch's *Haywain* (part of the Seven Deadly Sins' triptych) and a portrait of the king in his old age by Pantoja de la Cruz. Facing the gardens and the plain, the throne room is hung with 16C Brussels' tapestries, the Portrait Gallery, which follows, with royal portraits.

Finally one is shown Philip's sedan chair in which he was carried when no longer able to walk.

New Museums★★ (Nuevos Museos). — The museum assembles works of art, particularly paintings but also including tapestries and other items previously dispersed throughout the monastery.

In the basement. The paintings include a Patinir: *St Christopher*, a Bosch *Ecce Homo (Los Improperios)* in satirical vein and a panel of his Garden of Delights *The Creation* (replica of painting in the Prado) which is again ironic and also highly imaginative. The *Moneychanger and his Wife* is by the Fleming, Marinus and there is a beautiful triptych attributed to the Flemish painter, Gerard David.

A room devoted to another Fleming, Michel Coxcie (1499-1592), precedes the 16C Venetian School which the king greatly admired, particularly Titian, created Court Painter in 1533 by the Emperor Charles V. The Titian gallery affords a panorama of the artist's religious pictures and includes such outstanding works as an *Ecce Homo*. In the 4th Gallery there is another major Titian, the *Last Supper*, with, all around paintings by followers and successors: Tintoretto, Veronese (a gold tinted *Annunciation*), Bassano and Reni. The 5th Gallery contains Ribera *(p 166)* paintings including *Jacob grazing Laban's sheep*, an *Entombment* and *St Jerome Penitent* — all with the artist's characteristic style of portraying especially vivid faces.

Finally come the great galleries of Spanish 17C painting centring on the Velázquez painting of *Joseph's Tunic*.

The **architectural museum** in the vaulted basement outlines the monastery's construction in biographies of the principal men involved, including craftsmen, account books, Herrera's designs, tools, materials and techniques.

On the ground floor. Surrounded once more by paintings, note in particular El Greco's **Martyrdom of St Maurice and the Theban Legionary★**, commissioned by Philip II but too original in composition, too acid in colouring, to suit his taste and never hung by the king. Nevertheless, this picture of the martyrdom of the legionary who refused to sacrifice to the gods, and of St Maurice trying to convince his companions that he should be executed in the other's place, is now considered one of El Greco's greater works. To be seen, in addition, in these galleries are a sober and expressive Van der Weyden *Calvary* and a copy by Coxcie of Van der Weyden's *Descent from the Cross* (original in the Prado). There is also a beautiful 16C Brussels tapestry.

Ground floor

0   50 m

Tour route

Mascaroon Courtyard

Sanctuary — ROYAL PANTHEON

NEW MUSEUMS

Sacristy

ROYAL APARTMENTS

CHURCH

The Evangelists'

Courtyard

CHAPTERHOUSES

Tickets

ENTRANCE

THE KINGS' COURTYARD

COLLEGE

MONASTERY

Entrance   LIBRARY

Finally there are five works in one gallery by El Greco, demonstrating the artist's powerful effect. One picture, the *Vision of Philip II,* a rare royal portrait by the artist, who anyway was no royal favourite, shows the king meditating on paradise while at prayer.

Church★★. — The plan in the form of a Greek cross and even the edifice's entire conception owe much to St Peter's, as Juan de Toledo had worked for a period under Bramante in Rome. The nave is immense. Four colossal central pillars, each with a girth of 30m - 100ft, support a cupola which rises 92m - 302ft high. The frescoes in the nave vaulting were painted by Luca Giordano under Charles II's reign. Wide, shallow, red marble steps lead to the sanctuary where the dominating feature is the massive high altar **retable** (one of nearly 50 in the church) designed by Herrera. It is 30m - 100ft tall and is composed of 4 registers of jasper, onyx and red marble columns, separating Italian paintings of the Lives of Christ and the Virgin and statues by Leone and Pompeo Leoni of the Doctors of the Church (bottom), the Evangelists, Sts Andrew and James and finally, at the top, Peter and Paul on either side of Calvary. The tabernacle is also by Herrera. To the left and right of the altar are the royal stalls with, at their back by Pompeo Leoni, the funerary figures at prayer of Charles V and his Queen, Isabel of Portugal, their daughter María and her two sisters, their son Philip II and three of his wives including Mary Tudor, and his son, Don Carlos. The door at the end on the right is the one communicating with Philip II's room.

In the north aisle (on the back of the 1st pillar) is the painting of the *Martyrdom of St Maurice* by Romulo Cincinnato, which Philip II preferred to that of El Greco's.

The Kings' Courtyard★ (Patio de los Reyes). — One of the three Classical gateways in the palace's principal façade opens onto this courtyard which serves as parvis also to the majestic west front of the church. The façade was intended to repeat the design of the main gate but the pinnacles were replaced by the unfortunate statues of the Kings of Judea after which the court is, in fact, named.

Royal Pantheon★★ (Panteón de los Reyes). — Access is through the Evangelists Courtyard in which the walls are painted with frescoes of the Lives of Christ and the Virgin by Tibaldi (east wall) and his followers, and down a narrow marble and jasper staircase.

The chapel which was begun in 1617 in the reign of Philip III was completed in that of Philip IV. It lies exactly beneath the high altar in the church and is octagonal in shape. Deep rectangular niches contain 26 identical baroque sarcophagi in dark grey marble decorated with jasper pilasters with bronze capitals; in these lie the mortal remains of Spanish monarchs from the time of the Emperor Charles V (the only exceptions are Philip V and Ferdinand VI who are buried respectively at La Granja and in Madrid and the shortlived Amadeus of Savoy buried in Italy). The kings and Isabel II are on the left, the queens whose sons succeeded to the throne and Queen Isabel's consort, Francis of Assisi, on the right. The massive but cold richness is emphasised by a great Genoese chandelier crowded with decorative cherubs.

The Prince's Pantheon (19C) includes not only princes — many of them young children but also princesses and queens whose children did not succeed to the throne.

Chapterhouses★ (Salas Capitulares). — The former chambers, good sized rooms with ceilings painted by Italian artists with frescoes of grotesques, are now a museum of art.

The gallery on the right contains canvases by Navarrete (1526-1579), one of the artists summoned by the king to work at the Escorial and sometimes known as the Spanish Titian. On the left, the most interesting painting is a *Holy Trinity* by Ribera. In the next gallery is a display of magnificent sacerdotal robes of the 16-18C, executed by the Convent of Guadalupe school, ivories (Gothic diptych: French 14C) and liturgical objets including a mitre covered with plumes by Mexican Indians.

Library (Biblioteca). — *2nd floor.* Philip II took an especial pride in the library which soon numbered 10 000 volumes. It survived a fire in 1671 and the ravages of Napoleon's army and is now a public library of 40 000 books and some 2 700 manuscripts dating from the 5-18C. The gallery is 54m - 177ft long and richly decorated; the shelving, designed by Herrera, is of exotic woods; the ceilings, sumptuously painted by Tibaldi, represents the liberal arts: reading from the end you see Grammar, Rhetoric, Dialectic, Arithmetic, Music, Geometry, Astronomy, with Philosophy and Theology at each end.

In the cases, on the marble tables, are precious manuscripts (starting from the far end): 5C text of St Augustine, finely illuminated *Cantigas de Santa María,* a poem by King Alfonso the Wise, autographs of St Teresa and an 11C Beatus.

ESCORIAL Monastery★★★

THE PRINCE'S PAVILION★ (Casita del Príncipe)

Southeast along the road to the station. Vehicle toll: 50pts. Same opening times as the monastery.

The Casita del Príncipe stands in its own grounds, the Prince's Gardens, which lie east of Philip II's apartments, and it is, of course, minute compared to the palace. It was built at the end of the 18C by Juan de Villanueva for the Prince of Asturias, the future Charles IV. He took the greatest personal interest in its decoration which explains its air of sophisticated luxury. Although the best paintings have all been removed to the Prado, the house itself remains a delight with painted Pompeian style ceilings (Maella, Vicente Gómez), silk hangings, canvases by Luca Giordano, a mahogany and marble table in the dining room, clocks, carpets, chandeliers and porcelain from the Buen Retiro Factory.

EXCURSIONS

Upper Pavilion (Casita de Arriba). — *3km - 2 miles southwest; on the road to Ávila. Same opening times as the monastery.* This hunting lodge, also by Villanueva, is a modest replica of the Prince's Pavilion. It was built for his younger brother, the Infante Gabriel, who visited it mainly to indulge his passion for music. The interior has been refurnished in the style of the period; the first floor was arranged as apartments for Prince Juan Carlos before his accession to the throne.

Philip II's Seat (Silla de Felipe II). — *7km - 4 1/2 miles. Acces by narrow roads either from the golfcourse or beyond the Casita de Arriba.* You arrive at a chaos of broken rocks where four seats appear to have been hollowed out. Legend has it that Philip II used to sit in one of these contemplating the erection of the monastery - and making alterations to the plans. The **view**★★ of the surrounding countryside as well as of the palace, is remarkable.

GUADALAJARA P

Michelin map **444** fold 5 — Pop 56 922

The town of Guadalajara, capital of the province of the same name, which has been greatly influenced by its proximity to Madrid, is virtually its industrial satellite.

The town, founded in Iberian days, became the fief of the **Mendozas** in the 14C, a name famous in Spanish history. It includes among its members López de Mendoza, **Marquess of Santillana** (1398-1458), poet and author of the pastoral *Serranillas* and his son, **Cardinal Pedro González de Mendoza** (1428-1495), the grey eminence of the Catholic Monarchs; it was a Mendoza, the second Duke of Infantado who, in the 15C, constructed the palace at the north entrance to the town.

Palace of the Duke of Infantado. — The edifice is a masterpiece of civil architecture of the time of the Catholic Monarchs. The interior decoration formerly rivalled in magnificence that of the façade and *patio*, with beautiful coffered ceilings, panelling and tiles.

Francis I of France, captured at Pavia in 1525, was received with such pomp at the palace on his way to imprisonment in Madrid as to displease the Emperor Charles V. Philip II married Elizabeth of Valois within its walls in 1559.

In 1936 bombs aimed at nearby barracks hit the building and very largely destroyed it. It has been restored and houses the provincial archives and fine arts museum; the diamond stonework of the façade is once more complete but 17C windows detract from the effect; the beautiful upper gallery with paired windows beneath ogee and corbelled loggias is now also complete. Restoration work is in progress on the once magnificent two storey *pátio* with its characteristically low Isabeline arching *(p 15)*.

EXCURSION

Sea of Castile; Brihuega. — *Round tour of 165km - 102 1/2 miles — allow 1 day — map* **444** *folds 5, 6, 14 and 15*

Pastrana. — This delightful town once a ducal city, retains memories of the **Princess of Eboli,** favourite of Philip II, whose ambition proved her undoing. Although her husband retained the title of Duke of Pastrana, she, on falling from favour, was confined to Pastrana Palace. This stands on the main square, the plain front is of rough hewn stone. The square is lined on all sides except the north, by a portico. Walk up to the late Gothic **collegiate church** founded at the end of the 16C by the dukes as their pantheon *(open 11am to 1pm — 1 to 3pm Sundays and holidays — and 4 to 6pm; 100pts).* In the treasury are 4 **tapestries**★ woven in the 15C in Tournai after cartoons by Nuno Gonçalves which illustrate the capture of Arzila and Tangier by Alfonso V of Portugal in 1471. Although damaged they reveal the 15C Portuguese painter's mastery of composition, love of detail (armour and costume) and talent for portraiture.

Take the Almonacid de Zorita then the Sayatón roads.

Sea of Castile (Mar de Castilla). — The series of **artificial lakes** along the course of the Tagus form a vivid green inland sea which brings alive the landscape of brown rocks, umber soil and silver grey of the occasional olive grove. The undertaking was accomplished by the Madrid Electrical Union (UEM) which, since 1946, has constructed dams, power stations and the three vast reservoirs of **Entrepeñas, Buendía** and **Bolarque** — the first two linked by an overflow tunnel and with a capacity of 2 500 million m^3 or sufficient water to irrigate 100 000 ha - 550 000 million gallons and 250 000 acres. The power stations produce 250 million kWh a year. Near Almonacid de Zorita, the nuclear power station produces 1 milliard kWh annually. The hydraulic undertaking besides its part in regional industrial development, affords, as a local by-product, expanses of water which offer relaxation and water sports — a tourist potential already being exploited.

The surrounding of the **Buendía** *(15km - 9 miles south of Sacedón)* and **Entrepeñas dams and lakes** have been landscaped and include shaded gardens and viewpoints; the northern shores of Lake Entrepeñas have been left wild: the landscape is hilly, the views more extensive. The ascent to **Mantiel** affords splendid views of the whole complicated reservoir — *pantano* — undertaking divided by a wooded promontory.

Via Durón continue to Brihuega.

Brihuega. — The town, which is on the Alcarria Plateau *(p 189),* descends in tiers along the edge of the Tajuña depression to a site which looks particularly steep when seen from the south. Romanesque church roofs in near ruined condition can be seen half-hidden above white houses; the streets are narrow and often steep; on Sta María Square remains of the town walls stand romantically cloaked in ivy. The town's small restored Church of **San Felipe** *(to visit apply to the priest)* has a harmonious transitional Romanesque-Gothic nave.

The annual Virgen de la Peña Festival (16 August) is the occasion for a spectacular release of bulls through the streets and adjoining fields!

The Duke of Vendôme won a victory during the War of Spanish Succession on this spot in December 1710 and a second at Villaviciosa to the northeast, which did much to secure Philip V the throne of Spain.

GUADARRAMA, Sierra de ★ (Madrid)

Michelin map **444** folds 3 and 4 or **447** folds 7 and 8

The Sierra de Guadarrama is a minor chain in the Central Cordillera, and less high than the Sierra de Gredos *(p 235)* of which it is a continuation (Peñalara, its highest point has an altitude of 2 430m - 7 970ft). It, nevertheless, provides a barrier for Madrid Province in the northwest.

The range is part of the Hercynian massif uplifted by Tertiary earth movements. The countryside comprises granite and gneiss outcrops, steep slopes covered up to halfway by evergreen oaks and pinewoods but above, near the crests which show traces of glaciation, is Lake Peñalara, its waters covering the bottom of a glaciary basin. The upper heights are rich in streams which pour down to fill the province's many reservoirs.

The Guadarrama Sierra is a green oasis in the Castilian desert close to Madrid — so close that you can even see the range's snow-capped peaks from the capital. These are also visible on the far side of the range from Ávila and Segovia. Mountain and rural resorts have developed in the sierra to which Castilians flee in summer from the torrid heat of the Meseta: the **Escorial** *(p 195),* **Guadarrama, Cercedilla,** the last two doubling with **Navacerrada** and **Los Cotos Passes** as ski resorts.

From Manzanares El Real to Guadarrama
138km - 85 1/2 miles - allow 2 days excluding visits to Segovia and Escorial Monastery

Manzanares el Real★. — The 15C **castle★** *(open 10am to 2pm and 5 to 8pm - 3 to 6pm 1 October to 30 May; closed Mondays and holidays; 70pts)* is considerably enhanced by its setting against the background of the Sierra de la Pedriza *(see below).* To the south lies the somewhat melancholy manmade Lake Santillana. The fortress itself is well proportioned, the austerity of its lines relieved by bead mouldings on the turrets and the Plateresque decoration applied to the south front.

Sierra de la Pedriza. — *3km - 2 miles.* This granite massif, foothill to the Sierra de Guadarrama, which presents by turns a chaos of rose rock, ravined cliff face and ruiniform screes, is popular with rock climbers, particularly in the Peña del Diezmo area (1 714m - 5 624ft).

Miraflores de la Sierra. — Attractive view from a belvedere on the village outskirts.

Morcuera Pass. — As you reach the pass (1 796m - 5 893ft) an extensive view which includes the El Vellón reservoir, opens to the south.

A descent through bare moorland brings you to the wooded Lozoya depression. In the distance by Lozoya town, can be seen the Pinilla Dam and Lake supplied by the Angostura River, a well known trout stream.

El Paular★. — The first Carthusian monastery to be founded in Castile stands amidst green elms and pines in the Lozoya Valley. It dates back to 1390 and during its long history had suffered many depredations before being restored by the Benedictines. More recently, the conventual buildings around the picturesque pillared cloister, have been converted for use as an early *patio* to the church which includes two Flamboyant Gothic portals by Juan Guas — one opens onto another cloister with the ogee arches typical of Late Gothic. The church *(guided tours weekdays noon, 1 and 5pm; Sundays and holidays at 1pm and 4 to 6pm; closed Thursday afternoons)* disfigured in the 19C at the time of the *"desamortización",* contains a delicate Gothic screen and a magnificent 15C alabaster **altarpiece★★,** illustrating the Lives of the Virgin and Christ and which from its care for the picturesque and for detail in costume and bourgeois interiors, is certainly Flemish. In contrast, the Sagrario Chapel, behind the high altar, is decorated in exuberant baroque.

199

GUADARRAMA, Sierra de★

The road continues through dense pinewoods.

Los Cotos Pass. — Alt 1 830m - 6 004ft. The pass is the terminus for mechanical hoists for skiers. From the upper terminus of the Zabala teleseat *(200pts one way, 225pts Rtn)* excursions may be made in summer to Lake Peñalara *(15 minutes)*, the Dos Hermanas summit *(1/2 hour)* and the Peñalara, the highest point *(3/4 hour)*.

Navacerrada Pass★. — Alt 1 860m - 7 102ft. There is a **view★** from this pass on the borders of two Castiles, of the Segovian plateau and the line of the valley, hidden beneath dense pines, through which the road to Madrid runs. The pass is now a popular winter sports resort; it is linked by train to Cercedilla.

The serpentine descent through the pines is refreshing.

La Granja de San Ildefonso★. — *Description p 247.*

Segovia★★. — *Alternative route 11km - 7 miles. Description p 245.*

Riofrío★. — *Description p 247.*

Guadarrama Pass (Alto de los Leones). — Alt 1 511m - 4 958ft. *Since 1963 it has been possible to cross the Sierra de Guadarrama at all seasons through the road tunnel, 2.8km - 1 1/2 miles long. Accessible only from the motorway (toll: 255pts to San Rafael).* The old pass road *(gradient up to 9% -1 in 11)* is picturesque, particularly on the southern slope; the pass itself commands a fine **panorama★** and from each bend there are new **points of view★** of the *sierra* foothills and the Castilian plain. The slopes are dotted with sanatoria and attractive summer homes.

Guadarrama. — Country resort at the foot of the massif.

Valle de los Caídos★★; Escorial Monastery★★★. — *11km - 7 miles. Description pp 193 and 195.*

The towns and sights described in this guide
are shown in black on the maps.

MADRID ★★★ P

Michelin map 🔢🔢🔢 fold 13 or 🔢🔢🔢 fold 17 — Pop 3 188 297

Madrid stands at the very centre of Spain and, at 646m - 2 120ft, is the highest capital city in Europe. It was made the capital by decree of Philip II in the 16C but progress was slow and difficult until the 19C when momentum began to gather. Madrid today is a modern city with a recognised international status.

New residential areas have been enlarging the metropolis at an ever increasing rate since the turn of the century and more particularly since the end of the Civil War; the quarters are cut by wide through roads, notably the north-south artery which, at the city's centre, incorporates the Paseos del Prado, de Recoletos and de la Castellana, where open air cafés line the shaded sidewalks.

A major artery on its own is the **Gran Vía** (KLX), fronted by shops, banks, hotels and cinemas and, in the evening, crowded with strollers and people sitting at cafés beneath the coloured electric signs. Madrid also has a subway.

But there is another Madrid, a city apart with little to do with concrete, neon lights and the new fangled, yet still very much a part of the capital — it is the old Madrid of concentric, narrow streets, steps and vaulted alleys.

Of the writers born in the city (Lope de Vega) or those who went there to live (Cervantes), **Pérez Galdós** (1843-1920), a Canary Islander, gave the metropolis the greatest place in his work, leaving as a result a vivid picture of Madrid society in the 19C.

Fortune's Wheel. — Madrid's site, inhabited by prehistoric man, was for many centuries only a small settlement. It became a centre when the Moors erected a fortress on the site which they named Majerit; in 1083 the fort was captured by the King of Castile, Alfonso VI, who as he entered the town, discovered a statue of the Virgin by a granary *(almudín)*. The town mosque was converted into a church which was dedicated to the Virgin of the Almudena, also declared the city patron. From the 14C Spanish sovereigns came regularly to Madrid: the Catholic Monarchs made a solemn entry in 1477 and inaugurated the construction of the Monastery of San Jerónimo el Real; the Emperor Charles V rebuilt the Muslim fortress, the Alcázar; Philip II decreed it capital of Spain in 1561 in place of Valladolid. At the end of the 18C the building programme was inaugurated which was to provide many of today's public monuments.

Madrid, and even more its citizens suffered cruelly in the Civil War.

Two days after the uprising of 18 July 1936, the Republicans attacked the barracks and captured the city. Troops then arrived from Seville and began the siege which was to last 2 1/4 years or until the end of the war — from 6 November 1936 to 28 March 1939.

El Dos de Mayo. — In 1808, the French under General Murat had been occupying Madrid for two months, when on 2 May crowds gathered before the palace to prevent the departure of the queen and her children for Bayonne *(p 191)*. Murat ordered his soldiers to fire. The Spaniards, led by **Pedro Velarde** rose in revolt: citizens marched to Monteleón Park, where Captain **Daoíz** gave them arms from the munitions depot, and fought in the streets until they were utterly beaten and the heroes of the hour, Velarde and Daoíz had been killed. Murat restored the order but in every region revolts broke out which presaged the War of Independence.

Goya boldly depicted the night of uprising and atrocity and the dawn fusillade on Príncipe Pío hill in two paintings: the 2 May and the 3 May — *El Dos de Mayo, El Tres de Mayo* — both in the Prado.

LIFE IN MADRID

Life in Madrid is extremely pleasant, relaxed, unhurried; the air is dry and mountain clear. Like capitals everywhere, the city is the national melting pot: there are people from every region and seemingly few old Madrid families. Restaurants specialise in, Madrileño cooking serving **cocido madrileño** (Madrid hotpot), **callos a la madrileña** (tripe) or dishes from provincial Spain or France, Italy, China... Madrid, in other words, is not a purist haven steeped in local colour.

5pm is the time to go shopping in the large stores around the Puerta del Sol, the area also where craftsmen can still be found, and in the fashionable shops on the Calle Serrano, a favourite with Madrid women who end the afternoon in a tea shop (Spanish: *cafetería*) eating cakes and drinking chocolate or coffee... Before dinner, idle your way to the quarter crossed by the Calle de la Cruz (near the Puerta del Sol) or to the Calle de Cuchilleros (near the Plaza Mayor) where there are hundreds of small bars busy serving **tapas** *(p 26)*, **vino blanco** and **Manzanilla** (dry sherry). Dinner is eaten very late and is followed by a stroll through the streets, a drink at a pavement café or entertainment that ends only in the small hours — every type of entertainment exists in Madrid from the *tablado flamenco* to the *avant-garde*.

Madrid has pure air which traffic is beginning to pollute a little. In summer the heat can be exhausting and Madrileños who are neither bullfighting enthusiasts nor passionate supporters of Real Madrid (football team), make every effort to leave at least for brief periods. Lakes, mountains (skiing in winter), royal palaces, museum towns such as Toledo and Segovia, invite...

■ THE OLD TOWN (La Ciudad Antigua) *time: 2 1/2 hours*

Make your tour, if possible, either first thing in the morning or at the end of the afternoon when the churches will be open.

Plaza Mayor★. — The vast square was the heart of old Madrid, the setting for the greatest religious ceremonies, including *autodafés*, and royal occasions and proclamations — a tournament was held on it in 1623 in honour of the future Charles I of England; today it is an oasis of quiet, faintly rustled on Sundays by a market, held beneath the porticoes, selling stamps, coins, medals and cigar bands. The *plaza* attracts crowds in summer when the festivals of yesteryear — tournaments, dramas — are played out upon the large central area.

On the north side flanked by Herreran towers stands, where a bakery (panadería) once was, the re-erected Casa de la Panadería. The 17C equestrian statue on the square centre is of Philip III.

Pass through the **Cuchilleros Arch (A)** to the street of the same name fronted by very tall houses and, like its continuation, the Cava de San Miguel, crowded with typical small restaurants and eating houses — *mesones* and *tabernas*. *Cavas* were originally the ditches or moats on the outer side of mediaeval ramparts.

By way of the quiet Plaza del Conde de Barajas, make for the Plaza de San Justo or Puerta Cerrada, an old city gate. Continue along the Calle San Justo.

San Miguel Basilica (Iglesia Pontificia) (B). — The church is a surprising 18C construction, typically Italian baroque in style, with a convex front embellished with statues. The low relief above the door shows the Spanish saints, Justus and Pastor, to whom the basilica was previously dedicated. The interior is graceful and elegant with an

Cava San Miguel	9	Gómez Mora	40
Cebada (Pl. de la)	10	Príncipe Anglona	65
Conde de Barajas (Plazuela del)	15	Puñonrostro	68
		Ribera de Curtidores	77
Cordón	17	San Javier (Pl. de)	84
Cuchilleros	23	San Justo	87

oval cupola, vaulting on intersecting ribs, supplely designed cornices and abundant stuccowork.

Pass along the north wall of the church to the Plaza de la Villa.

Plaza de la Villa. — Historic buildings frame the square, which has at its centre a bronze statue of Álvaro de Bazán, hero of Lepanto, by Mariano Benlliure (1862-1927). On the east side is the **Lujan Tower (Torre de Los Lujanes) (C)** where Francis I was held prisoner after the Battle of Pavia; a small Gothic side door has been preserved. Next door is the **Hemeroteca.** Inside is a lovely Gothic banister and in the vestibule are two Renaissance tombs. On the west side is the **City Hall (Ayuntamiento) (H)** designed by Gómez de Mora. Its *Patio de Cristales*, Goya Gallery and Audience Chamber are open to visitors *(weekdays 9am to 2pm)*. Adjoining the City Hall by an arch is the **Casa de Cisneros (E)**, inside of which is a gallery of tapestries. This house, which belonged to the archbishop's nephew retains, from its 16C construction, one fine window overlooking the Plazuela del Cordón.

Plazuela del Cordón. — The cord decoration surrounding the entrance to the very large Casa de los Alfaro recalls that it was once a bishopric. Isidor, future patron saint of Madrid, lived as a husbandman in the corner house, the **Casa de Juan de Vargas (Y)**. Go down the steps on the right to take a look at the **Plazuela de San Javier (84)**, a glimpse of old Madrid.

Return to the Calle del Cordón and cross over the Calle de Segovia.

San Pedro (K). — The church's 14C Mudejar tower is one of only two to exist in Madrid (the other is at San Nicolás).

Go along the Calle del Príncipe Anglona to the Plaza de la Paja, to look down on the fountain in the Plaza de la Cruz Verde.

Capilla del Obispo★ (N). — *Closed for restoration.* The Gothic chapel completed in the 16C in the time of the Archbishop *(obispo)* of Plasencia, contains a splendid altarpiece of polychrome wood in which Berruguete's pupil, Francisco Giralte, illustrated the Lives of Christ and the Virgin. Against the south wall is an alabaster tomb, in the Plateresque style, of the bishop at prayer against a setting outstanding for its detail. The tombs of his parents, founders of the chapel, which flank the altarpiece, were carved by the same hand.

MADRID★★★

San Francisco el Grande. — *Restoration work in progress. Guided tours 11am to 1pm and 5 to 8pm (4 to 7pm in winter); closed Mondays and Fridays; 50pts.*

The wide 18C Neo-Classical front by Sabatini is only slightly less imposing than the interior crowned by a 33m - 108ft wide cupola. Contemporary artists, of whom one was the young Goya, were commissioned in 1781 to decorate the six chapels off the nave. He painted his (the first north chapel) with a picture of St Bernardino of Siena preaching before the King of Aragon.

In the *antesacristía* or chapterhouse sacristy are Plateresque stalls from the former El Paular Monastery *(p 199)*.

The Torre de Madrid skyscraper on the Plaza de España is visible from the parvis.

Walk along the Carrera de San Francisco and the Cava Alta to the Calle de Toledo.

Calle de Toledo. — A lively street not far from El Rastro.

San Isidro Cathedral. — The 17C edifice with a massive, austere façade, surmounted by twin towers, was a Jesuit church until last century when it was raised to the status of cathedral.

You can visit the Neo-Classical cloister of the college.

Plaza de la Provincia. — The red building on the square is the Ministry for Foreign Affairs; inside is an elegant 17C cloister *(apply for permission to visit)*.

Atocha (Ronda de) .... BM 3
Ciudad de Barcelona
  (Av.) .... BM 12
Delicias (Pas. de las) .... BM 24
General Ricardos .... ABM 39
Infanta Isabel (Pas.) ..... BM 42
Manzanares (Av. del) ..... BM 48
Raimundo Fernández
  Villaverde .... BL 69

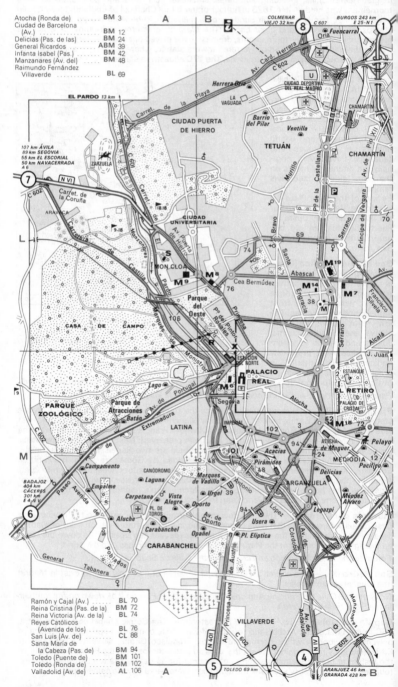

Ramón y Cajal (Av.) ...... BL 70
Reina Cristina (Pas. de la) BM 72
Reina Victoria (Av. de la) BL 74
Reyes Católicos
  (Avenida de los) .... BL 76
San Luis (Av. de) .... CL 88
Santa María de
  la Cabeza (Pas. de) .... BM 94
Toledo (Puente de) .... BM 101
Toledo (Ronda de) .... BM 102
Valladolid (Av. de) .... AL 106

■ MONUMENTS

Royal Palace★★ (Palacio Real) (KY). — *Guided tours (time: allow 1/2 day) weekdays 9.30am to 12.45pm and 4 to 6.30pm (3.30 to 5.15pm October to April); Sundays and holidays 10am to 1.30pm; closed 1 and 6 January, 1 May, 24 June and 24 and 25 December all day as well as on state occasions; inclusive ticket: 400pts.*

The 18C palace is also known as the East Palace (Palacio de Oriente) after the Plaza de Oriente, before its east front.

On this square stands a bronze equestrian statue of Philip IV cast by the Florentine, Tacca from a design by Velázquez, and claimed by many to be the finest piece of sculpture in Madrid.

The Alcázar, reconstructed by the Emperor Charles V *(p 200)*, was burnt to the ground in 1734. Philip V replaced it by the present edifice designed by the Italians, Juvara and Sachetti.

It forms a quadrilateral on a high bossaged base, overlooking the Manzanares. The south face has a decorative pedimented entrance fronting an impressively designed, deep, porticoed forecourt (Plaza de la Armería). A white stone balustrade crowns the walls, austerely punctuated with pilasters and Doric columns. In contrast to the impressive but impersonal exterior, the interior is sumptuous.

State apartments and chapel (Palacio y Capilla). — *Limited ticket including the private apartments: 150pts.*

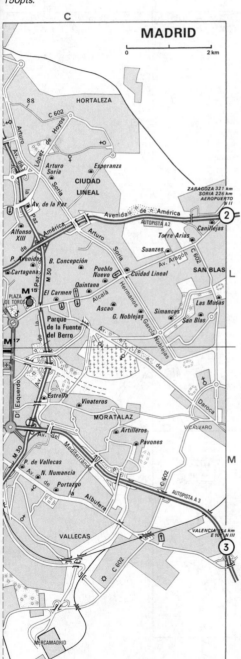

MADRID

The former royal apartments are now used for official guests.

A grand staircase leads to the **apartments of Charles III** (1716-1788) in which the Ambassador's Audience Chamber has a ceiling painted by Mengs, Goya portraits of Charles IV and Queen María Luisa hang in the antechamber and there is a rococo decoration in the **Gasparini Salon.**

In the apartments of Francis of Assisi, consort of Isabel II, which follow, note the *peineta* chairs in the yellow salon, so called because the backs are shaped like the tall combs *(peineta)* worn in Andalusian women's hair. After the immense Alfonso XII banqueting hall comes a music room, converted to house the extensive collection of clocks founded by Charles III in 1770.

The **apartments of Queen María Cristina of Habsburg** (1858-1929), mother of Alfonso XIII, are now a museum of **tapestries★** where the interest lies in the furnished interior as a whole since everything dates from the second half of the 19C, the so-called Isabel II style. There are also numerous royal portraits on the walls. A wonderful crystal chandelier made at La Granja *(p 247)* enhances the first room; a Pompeian style decoration in low relief stuccowork, the sumptuous Mirror Room.

Private apartments (Habitaciones particulares). — The suite of 22 rooms in the advanced south wing remains much as the last occupants, Alfonso XIII and Victoria Eugenia, grand-daughter of Queen Victoria, left them to go into exile in 1931.

The **throne room★** is resplendent with crimson velvet hangings and a fine Tiepolo painted ceiling of the Spanish monarchy.

Museum of painting, embroidery, porcelain and fine crystal (Museo de pinturas, bordados, porcelanas y cristalería). — *Limited ticket: 100pts.*

The museum in the former apartments of Princess Isabel of Bourbon, sister of Alfonso XII, on the first floor, displays the palace's most precious decorative items. Among the pictures are a portrait of the *Duke of Burgundy* attributed to Van der Weyden, a *Road to Calvary* by Hieronymus Bosch, several Rubens, some good Italian paintings, four canvases by Goya including an interesting picture of the War of Independence, a Velázquez portrait of the *Count of Olivares*, a *St Paul* by El Greco, several Zurbaráns and two delightful small Watteaus.

The museum also contains interesting displays of beautiful embroideries and services of fine porcelain.

Library, Numismatic and Music Museums (Biblioteca y Museos de medallas y música). — *Limited ticket: 100pts.*

The library created by Philip V, now contains 150 000 volumes and includes rarities both old and new: the book of the Valle de los Caídos, manuscripts including that of the conquest of Peru, an incunabulum of 1459...

The numismatic collection of coins and commemorative medals dates from the 16C to the present. The music museum in the final gallery contains magnificent old instruments (several Stradivarii), two royal pianos, two guitars — one inlaid with mother of pearl, the other with precious woods.

Royal Pharmacy (Real Farmacia). — *Limited ticket: 100pts.*

The distillation room where medicaments were concocted and the glass and porcelain apothecary jars stand neatly arranged in rows.

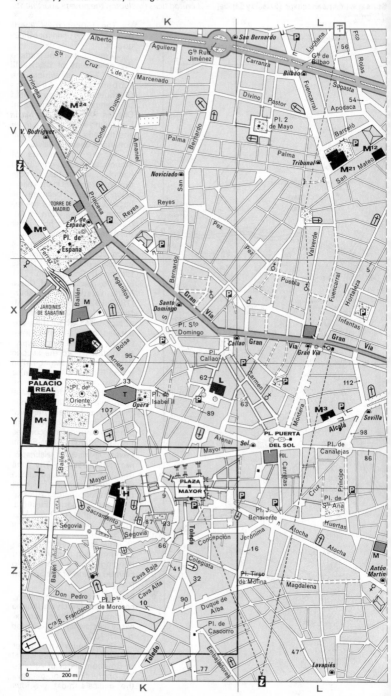

Armoury★ (Real Armería) (KY **M⁴**). — *Limited ticket: 100pts. Entrance west side of the Plaza de la Armería.*

The collection of arms and armour made by the Catholic Monarchs, the Emperor Charles V and Philip II, remains considerable despite pillage on 2 May 1808, and a fire in 1884. Mainly 15 to 17C pieces, including Charles V's suit of decorated armour, are on the ground floor while in the basement is the vaulted hall where arms from the reigns of Philip II, III and IV and Japanese, Turkish and Moorish weapons are on display.

Carriage Museum★★ (Museo de Carruajes Reales) (BM **M⁶**). — *Closed Mondays; limited ticket: 100pts. Leaflet.* A pavilion erected in 1967 at the centre of the former **Campo del Moro** winter garden houses the old royal horse-drawn carriages, most of which date from the reign of Charles IV, the late 18C. The vehicle in carved black ebony, the only carriage to survive the palace fire of 1734, although made in the 17C, is always claimed to have belonged to Juana the Mad (d 1555); the litter was the one used to transport the sick Emperor Charles V to Yuste *(p 136)*. There are carriages in the Charles IV style — one with gilded panels *(tableros dorados),* another described as being made of shells *(de concha)* — and one with a coronet, presented by Napoleon. The monogram on the late 18C "crested" carriage belonged to María Luisa Teresa, Queen to Charles IV.

The coronation coach, which was built in the 19C for Ferdinand VII, still bears marks of the assassination attempt made on Alfonso XIII and his bride, Victoria Eugenia, May 1906.

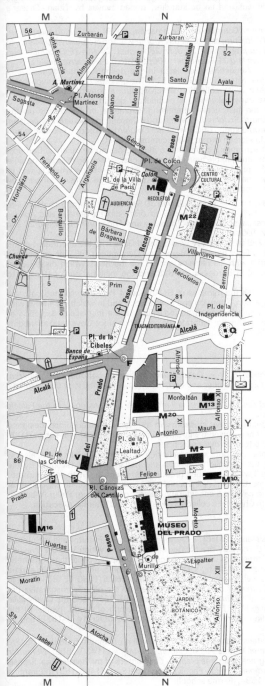

MADRID

Alcalá	LMY
Arenal	KY
Carmen	LY
Fuencarral	LVX
Gran Vía	KLX
Hortaleza	LVX
Mayor (Calle, Plaza)	KYZ
Montera	LY
Preciados	LY 63
Puerta del Sol (Pl.)	LY
San Jerónimo (Carrera de)	LMY 86
Augusto Figueroa	LMX 5
Cava San Miguel	KZ 9
Cebada (Pl. de la)	KZ 10
Conde de Romanones	LZ 16
Cuchilleros	KZ 23
Estudios	KZ 32
Felipe V	KY 33
Grafal	KZ 41
Lavapiés	LZ 47
Marqués de Villamagna	NV 52
Mejía Lequerica	LMV 54
Nicasio Gallego	LMV 56
Postigo de San Martín	KY 62
Puerta Cerrada (Pl.)	KZ 66
Ribera de Curtidores	KZ 77
Salustiano Olózaga	NX 81
San Justo	KZ 87
San Martín	KY 89
San Millán	KZ 90
Santa Bárbara (Pl.)	MV 91
Santo Domingo (Cuesta de)	KX 95
Sevilla	LY 98
Vergara	KY 107
Virgen de los Peligros	LY 112

Drive through Spanish towns using the plans in the **Michelin Red Guide España Portugal.** Features indicated include:

throughroutes and by-passes, new streets, car parks and one-way systems.

All this information is revised annually.

MADRID★★★

Descalzas Reales Convent★★ (KY L). — *Guided tours (time: 1 1/2 hours) 10.30am to 1pm and furthermore on Tuesdays, Wednesdays and Thursdays 4 to 6pm; closed Mondays, the afternoon of 31 December and all day 1 and 6 January, in Holy Week the Wednesday to Saturday, 1 May and 24 and 25 December; 100pts with Convent of the Incarnation.*

It was Joanna of Austria, daughter of the Emperor Charles V, who founded the convent of Poor Clares in this palace in which she was born. For two centuries it served as a retreat for those nobles who wished to live apart from the world. The nobility heaped gifts upon the order which has now put its riches in religious art on display in buildings abutting the conventual cloister.

There is a magnificent grand staircase to the upper cloister gallery. On this floor, where each chapel is more sumptuous than its precedent, note the recumbent figure of Christ by the 16C sculptor Gaspar Becerra. In the *antecoro* converted into a museum are precious ornaments and liturgical objects; in the *coro* itself, a somewhat mannered *Mater Dolorosa* by **Pedro de Mena** (17C) and in the former nuns' dormitory, twelve 17C **tapestries★★** after cartoons by Rubens of the Apotheosis of the Eucharist. On the *entresol* are a series of rooms with portraits of the royal family. Among the religious works, particularly, is a *St Francis* by Zurbarán. In the sacristy are wonderful sculptures by Pedro de Mena — a *Dolorosa* and an *Ecce Homo* — and by Gregorio Fernández *Magdalen in Torment*. In the reliquary gallery there is an impressive selection of finely engraved boxes and chests.

The main picture gallery is rich in paintings by Bruegel the Elder *(Adoration of the Magi)*, Isenbrandt, Gérard David, Rubens and an outstanding signed canvas by Titian, *Caesar's Pence*.

Convent of the Incarnation★ (Convento de la Encarnación) (KX P). — *Guided tours (time: 1 hour) 10.30am to 1pm and 4 to 6pm; closed all day Monday, 1 and 6 January, 25 March, in Holy Week Wednesday to Saturday, 1 May, 27 July, 28 August, 24 and 25 December and afternoons on Sundays, holidays and 31 December; 100pts with the Descalzas Reales.*

The convent occupied by Augustinas Recoletas in the delightful small square, was founded by Margaret of Austria, wife of Philip III in 1611. The generosity of each successive Spanish monarch may be seen in its collection which retains a considerable number of interesting works of art. The early galleries are particularly rich in paintings of the 17C Madrid school and include the historically interesting *Exchange of Princesses on the Bidassoa in 1615 (p 114)*, a Ribera, *St John the Baptist* and a Carreño *Immaculate Conception*. There is a noteworthy polychrome statue of *Christ at the Column* by Gregorio Fernández and by the same sculptor, in the cloister, an expressive recumbent Christ.

The **reliquary gallery★** is a sumptuous room with a painted ceiling by Vicencio Carducci and nearly 1 500 relics in every imaginable type of precious casket: among the most notable are the Lignum Crucis and the phial containing the blood of St Pantaleon which is said to liquify each year on 27 July. The 18C church is impressed with the transitional baroque Neo-Classical style of Ventura Rodríguez.

San Antonio de la Florida (BL R). — *Open 1 July to 30 September 10am to 1pm and 4 to 7pm; the rest of the year 11am to 1.30pm and 3 to 6pm; closed Sunday and holiday afternoons, as well as Wednesdays, 1 January, Thursday and Friday in Holy Week, 29 and 30 May, 25 December all day; 100pts.*

The chapel was built in 1798 by Charles IV who ordered Goya with the decoration of the cupola. The fresco was done by Goya between August and December 1798. The chapel also contains the tomb of the artist with his remains except for the head, which disappeared mysteriously between his burial in Bordeaux in 1828 and the exhumation for transfer to Madrid in 1888.

The cupola **fresco★** illustrates the miracles of St Antony of Padua performed before a crowd vividly realistic in expression, attention and indifference and in which, as always with Goya's crowds, each figure is the portrait of an individual; it is a marvellous depiction of Madrid society. Angels less than angelic, decorate the squinches since Goya used as models the beautiful women of 18C Madrid!

■ MUSEUMS

The Prado★★★ (Museo del Prado) (NZ). — *Open Tuesdays through Saturdays 9am to 7pm; Sundays 9am to 2pm; closed 25 December and certain holidays; 400pts, with the Casón del Buen Retiro.*
Goya's works of art and all of the 18C painting will most likely be transferred to the Palacio de Villahermosa (MY V).

The Prado is one of the world's great museums. In the Neo-Classical edifice, designed by Villanueva as a natural science museum but since 1819 the home of more than 6 000 works of art, hang nearly all the former royal collections.

The museum is, therefore, not only supremely rich in Spanish painting but also in Flemish works collected by the Catholic Monarchs and Italian pictures favoured by the Emperor Charles V and Philip II who summoned great painters such as Titian and Tintoretto to come and work at their court. Almost all Spanish monarchs, whether distinguished or inept in other ways, appear to have had considerable talent for collecting: Philip IV bought many pictures in London when Charles I's collection was auctioned after his execution.

First floor

Flemish Primitives and the Renaissance (15-16C). — Among the Flemish Primitives is the noticeable interest in interiors (*St Barbara* by the Master of Flemalle) to which Van der Weyden (1400-1464) added great richness of colour, a sense of composition and the pathetic *(Descent from the Cross, Pietà)*. Memling's (c1430-1494) works are noticeably serene *(Adoration of the Kings)*. The weird imaginings of **Hieronymus Bosch** (1450-1516) (known in Spain as El Bosco) in the *Garden of Delights* are followed by the equally imaginative but smooth and misty land and seascapes of Joachim Patinir (1485-1524) and the vividly alive and crowded scenes of Bruegel the Elder (1525-1569), *Triumph of Death*. Typical of the German school are outstanding figure and portrait paintings by **Dürer** (1471-1528) and by Cranach, a hunting scene.

Italian School (15-17C). — The Italian school is particularly well represented from the 15C. Fra Angelico's (1387-1455) spiritual Gothic *Annunciation*, Mantegna's (1430-1506), *Dormition of the Virgin*, and Botticelli's graceful figures precede the painters of the **Renaissance: Raphael** (1483-1520) *(Portrait of a Cardinal, The Holy Family)*, Andrea del Sarto (1486-1531) (Florentine school) and Correggio (1489-1534) (Parma school).

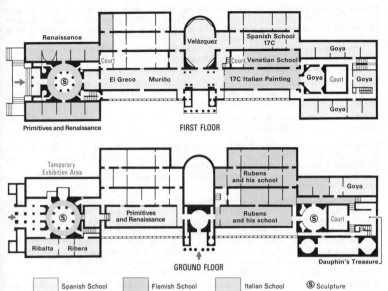

FIRST FLOOR

- Renaissance
- Court
- El Greco
- Murillo
- Primitives and Renaissance
- Velázquez
- Court
- Venetian School
- 17C Italian Painting
- Spanish School 17C
- Goya
- Goya
- Court
- Goya
- Goya
- Goya

GROUND FLOOR

- Temporary Exhibition Area
- Primitives and Renaissance
- Ribalta
- Ribera
- Rubens and his school
- Rubens and his school
- Goya
- Court
- Dauphin's Treasure

☐ Spanish School   ☐ Flemish School   ☐ Italian School   Ⓢ Sculpture

Owing to the current reorganisation of the museum, certain galleries may be closed and the hanging arrangements of certain works of art may be changed.

The triumph of colour comes with the three great Venetians: **Titian** (1490-1576) whose subtle touch could be put to portraiture (wonderful portrait of the Emperor Charles V - *illustration p 12*) or epic works of vast size; **Veronese** (1528-1588), with fine compositions beautifully highlighted and **Tintoretto** (1518-1594) who excelled in golden flesh tones.

Spanish School (late 16-18C). — The large central gallery, in which hang major works by the great masters of Spain's **Golden Period,** opens with portraits of the court of Philip II by two court painters, Sanchez Coello, pupil of the Dutchman Antonio Moro, and his disciple, Pantoja de la Cruz. An artist inspired by Caravaggio is **El Greco** *(p 217)*. Among his paintings in the Prado are the portraits of a *Gentleman with his Hand on his Breast*, his religious pictures over a period of years from the early *Trinity* to the portrayal, with ever mounting passion and devotion of the *Adoration of the Shepherds*. Realism continues with **Zurbarán** but coupled with serenity; a departure from his more usual paintings of religious appears in the strikingly wordly portrait of *St Casilda* and in the series intended for Buen Retiro Palace of the *Labours of Hercules*. **Murillo's** *(p 55)* typically smooth Immaculate Conceptions, fluttering with realistic cherubim, contrast with his genre portraits.

The Prado possesses the greatest pictures of Spain's greatest painter: **Velázquez** *(p 55)*. There are portraits of kings and queens, figures at court and humble folk, brilliant in themselves and always set against harmonious backgrounds *(Baltasar Carlos)*, mythological scenes illustrated with totally human characters *(The Forges of Vulcan,* the *Topers)* and history impressively recorded *(The Surrender of Breda - Las Lanzas)*. Finally there are the later works, among them two world masterpieces — *The Spinners (Las Hilanderas)* and the *Maids of Honour (Las Meninas)* — once seen, never forgotten.

Further pictures by the 17C masters are represented by the works of Mazo, disciple of Velázquez, Carreño de Miranda (royal portrait painter greatly influenced by Velázquez) and Alonso Cano, who like Murillo, paints Immaculate Conceptions.

Spanish painting maintained its supremacy in the 18 and 19C with **Goya** *(p 64)*. Portraits, royal and incredibly unflattering (the *Family of Charles IV)* and individual likenesses, of obvious friends including his brother-in-law, *Bayeu* (the picture in the Prado is from memory as it was painted after the sitter's death), of women (the *Maja Nude,* the *Maja Clothed*), show his total mastery and reveal, besides that of the sitters, much of his own personality.

Some forty of Goya's tapestry cartoons painted in oils between 1775 and 1791 for weaving at the Royal Tapestry Works, give a colourful picture of popular life in 18C Madrid. The War of Independence affected Goya deeply; bitterly he recorded his thoughts and comments in the big *2 May and 3 May* (1814) canvases.

Flemish School (late 16 and 17C). — Notable in the collection are the religious paintings of Ambrosius Benson, the portraits of personalities at the court of Philip II by the Dutchman, Antonio Moro (16C), the delightful series on the Five Senses by "Velvet" Bruegel the Younger (17C) and his and David Teniers the Younger's popular scenes.

Rubens, that most baroque of painters, inspired by the epic canvases of the Venetians, renewed Flemish art in the 17C, as can be seen from the many canvases in the museum which are from the royal collections. Of the same period are works by **Van Dyck** and Jordaens and the animal painters, Snyders and Paul de Vos.

Dutch School (17C). — There are two Rembrandts among other Dutch paintings by Hobbema (landscapes) and Metsu (interiors).

French School (17 and 18C). — The French are represented by Poussin landscapes and canvases by Claude Lorrain and by the later, 18C, delights of Watteau.

One gallery is devoted to the great baroque colourist, **Tiepolo,** continuator of the Venetian school who came to Spain to work especially for Charles III.

Ground floor

Painters of Spain's Golden Period. – **Ribalta** paints his religious figures realistically using chiaroscuro (influenced by Caravaggio), thus inaugurating a new style in Spain. **Ribera** is personified by his masterpiece, *The Martyrdom of St Bartholomew,* in which the artist uses chiaroscuro to accentuate the horror of the event.

MADRID★★★

Spanish primitive and Renaissance painting (15 and 16C). — Among Gothic painters, **Bermejo** stands out (*St Dominic of Silos Enthroned,* with his rich gold costume) as do **Pedro Berruguete** *(St Dominic before the Inquisition)* and **Yáñez de la Almedina** whose figures *(St Catherine)* have much of the grace of those of Leonardo da Vinci.

The paintings of Macip and his son, Juan de Juanes *(p 176)* elegant, delicate and colourful, precede those of the "**Divine" Morales** *(p 132)* whose example in the Prado is the most accomplished of his many portrayals of his favourite theme of the *Virgin and Child.*

Goya. — On display are the brutal *Disasters of War* (1808) etchings and *La Tauromaquia.* The following gallery exhibits the so-called' Black Paintings (1820-1822) with which Goya had decorated his country home, the Quinto del Sordo.

Sculpture. — The **Dauphin's Treasure**(basement)which belonged to Louis XIV, includes the precious objects now displayed near Greek and Roman sculpture in marble and bronze.

Archaeological Museum★★ (Museo Arqueológico Nacional) (NV M^{22}). — *Open 9.15am to 1.45pm; closed Mondays and 1 January, Thursday and Friday in Holy Week, 1 May, 25 December as well as other holidays (inquire locally); 200pts.*

Housed in the same building are the National Library and galleries *(entrance: Paseo de Recoletas)* displaying contemporary art.

Prehistoric Art and Archaeology★. — *Galleries 1-18.* The art of the Upper Palaeolithic Age is represented with the reproduction of the Altamira Cave in the garden. The arrival of metal on the Iberian peninsula (around the middle of the 3rd millenium BC) coincides with the development of the Los Millares culture which has left interesting female-shaped idols.

The galleries that follow are devoted to the Bronze Age (2nd millenium BC): the said Bell-Beaker and El Argar cultures. Exhibited in gallery 6 is the treasure fished out of the Riá Huelva. From the megalithic culture in the Balearic Islands note the Costix bulls.

The remaining galleries contain objects from Egypt and Greece (vases).

Iberian and Classical Antiquities★★. — *Galleries 19-26.* Two Iberian galleries reveal clearly the origin of local techniques and the artistic influence of the Phoenicians, the Greeks and the Carthaginians *(p 12).* The second gallery, where the influence of Carthage is obvious, shows sculpture at a high peak of artistic expression: standing out from the greatest Iberian sculptures is the **Dama de Elche** *(p 165),* a polychrome stone head, in sumptuous head-dress and corsage, mysterious and imposing in expression. In the same gallery are the **Dama de Baza,** a realistic goddess figure of the 4C BC and the woman bearing an offering discovered at Cerro de los Santos. Other galleries illustrate Spain's adoption, when under Roman domination, of the invader's techniques and later how she developed a Hispanic Palaeochristian art which incorporated ideas from Christian Africa and Byzantium.

Mediaeval and Renaissance Decorative Art★. — *Galleries 27-35.* In this department are the magnificent votive crowns of Guarrazar dating from the Visigothic period *(p 215)* and the incomparable art of Muslim Spain including ivory caskets. Romanesque tombs and capitals, Gothic sculpture in subsequent galleries, continue to show deep Moorish influence even after the Reconquest, until finally the Renaissance brought in that of Italy (bronzes, furniture).

The Bourbon period. — *Galleries 36-40.* The building or re-modelling of royal palaces in the 17, 18 and 19C encouraged the decorative arts, particularly ceramics (Talavera *p 213*) and crystal work (La Granja *p 247*).

Lázaro Galdiano Museum★★ (BL M^{7}). — *Open 10am to 2pm; closed 1 January, Thursday, Friday and Saturday in Holy Week, 1 May, all August, 1 November, 25 December as well as Mondays; 100pts.* The museum in the Neo-Classical mansion is a bequest to the nation by an art lover, José Lázaro Galdiano. The **collection of enamels and ivories★★★** *(ground floor),* traces the evolution of enamelling from Byzantium to 16C Limoges; equally outstanding are the mediaeval gold and silver work, the Italian Renaissance jewellery and

(After National Archaeological Museum photo, Madrid)

Visigothic votive crown

other art objects (Leonardo da Vinci - Crucifix). The collections on the 3rd floor encompass embroideries, fans, weapons and 17C portraits; the 2nd floor is entirely devoted to painting, starting with Spanish (Pedro Berruguete, the Master of Astorga) and Flemish Primitives (Quentin Metsys - *Crucifixion*) and Spain's Golden Period which includes works by El Greco, Ribera, Zurbarán and Murillo. The English school is well represented with pictures by several artists including Gainsborough, Reynolds, Romney, Constable and Bonington. There are canvases by the Italians, Francesco Guardi and Tiepolo, and also paintings from Goya's Black Period. The 1st floor has walls hung with Flemish Primitives and Spanish masters - Morales, Murillo, Carreno and Sánchez Coello .

Casón del Buen Retiro★ (NY M^{10}). — *Same opening times as the Prado Museum.*

This annexe to the Prado Museum is divided into two sections:

19C Spanish Art. — *Entrance via Felipe IV, no 13.* An interesting overall view of 19C Spain. On the ground floor are portraits by Vicente López and José del Madrazo and sculptures by Benlliure and Alvarez Cubero. Upstairs genre painting is exemplified by such artists as Alenza, Lucas, Esquivel, F. de Madrazo, Rosales and Fortuny, while landscapes and canvases demonstrating the artistic styles of the early 19C are represented by Haes, Sorolla, Regoyos and Rusinol.

Guernica and the Picasso Donation. — *Entrance via Alfonso XII, no 28.* Surrealism, cubism and expressionism combine in Picasso's famous composition in black and white, *Guernica* (1937), inspired by an episode in the Spanish Civil War *(p 114).* Until 1981 in the Museum of Modern Art in New York City, the work of art is now displayed in the Casón ballroom (ceiling frescoes by Luca Giordano). Accompanying this main work are a series of studies showing the evolution of this famous canvas.

The Americas Museum★ (Museo de América) (BL M⁸). — *Closed temporarily.* Outstanding are the **Pre-Colombian department★** — Peru and particularly Mexico (stele from Palenque, Mayacalendar...) and gallery of **Hispano-American and Philippine crafts★.**

Waxworks Museum★ (Museo Colón) (NV M¹). — *Open 10.30am to 2pm and 4 to 9pm; 400pts, children: 200pts.*
Wax figures from Spanish history and contemporary celebrities in realistic setting.

Army Museum★ (Museo del Ejército) (NY M²). — *Open10am to 2.30pm; closed Mondays; 50pts.*
A wide range of weapons and equipment (some 27 000 objects) are displayed in the vast rooms of the Buen Retiro Palace (built in 1631): armour (16C), flags, tapestries, paintings, guns, swords... Among the most interesting note a piece of the cross that Christopher Columbus had when he landed in the "New World", the famous "Tizona" sword belonging to El Cid as well as letters written by Napoleon, Nelson, Blake and Wellington.

Museum of Contemporary Spanish Art★ (AL M⁹). — *Open 10am to 6pm (3pm Sundays); closed Mondays and holidays; 150pts.*
This museum contains 20C Spanish painting and sculpture (about 600).

Cerralbo Museum (KV M⁵). — *Open 10am to 2pm and 4 to 7pm; closed Sunday afternoons, Mondays, holidays and August; 200pts.*
In this former residence of the Marquess of Cerralbo are furniture, a collection of arms and armour, tapestries, porcelain, ceramics and **paintings★.** These include a *St Francis* by El Greco in the chapel, and in the long gallery, canvases by Ribalta, Herrera the Younger, Tintoretto, Titian, Ribera, Zurbarán and Van Dyck.

San Fernando Royal Academy (Real Academia de Bellas Artes de San Fernando) (LY M³). — *Being installed; only 1st floor open. Open 9am to 7pm (2pm Sundays, Mondays and holidays); 200pts.*
There are notable works by two painters especially in this large and varied collection: Zurbarán's portraits of six monks and Goya's *Burial of the Sardine* and a *Self-Portrait.* Also exhibited are master drawings by Spanish and Italian artists of the 15 to 17C.

Romantic Museum (Museo Romántico) (LV M¹²). — *Open 10am to 6pm (2pm Sundays and holidays); closed Mondays and holidays; 200pts.*
An evocative collection of late 19C furniture and painting — the Romantic Period — left by the Marquess of La Vega-Inclán to the nation.

National Museum of Decorative Art (NY M¹³). — *Open weekdays 10am to 3pm (5pm 1 October to 30 June); Sundays 10am to 2pm; closed Mondays and holidays; 150pts.*
Furniture, and decorative folk art from the 16 to 19C.

Sorolla Museum (Museo Sorolla) (BL M¹⁴). — *Open 10am to 2pm; closed Mondays, August, 1 January, Thursday and Friday in Holy Week, 1 May, 1 November, 25 December; 150pts.*
The works of the Valencian Joaquín Sorolla y Bastida (1863-1923) are exposed in his home.

Bullfighting Museum (Museo Taurino) (CL M¹⁵). — *Open 9am to 3pm; 10am to 1pm Sundays and holidays in bullfighting season; closed Mondays and Saturdays; 50pts.*
This museum, in honour of the great toreadors, abuts on the **Las Ventas Bullring,** which, with a seating capacity of 22 300, is the largest in Spain.

Lope de Vegás House (Casa Museo de Lope de Vega) (MZ M¹⁶). — *Open only Tuesdays and Thursdays 10am to 2pm; closed holidays and 15 July to 15 September; 75pts.*
A skilful reconstruction of most of the Spanish Golden Age dramatist's house (d 1635).

The Mint and Coin Museum (Fábrica Nacional de Moneda y Timbre) (LM M¹⁷). — *Open 10am to 2pm; closed Sundays and holidays.*
Roman, Spanish and foreign coins.

Ethnological Museum (Museo Etnologiá) (BM M¹⁸). — *Open 10am to 2pm and 4 to 7pm; closed Mondays all day and Sunday and holiday afternoons; 100pts.*
The exhibits are predominantly from the Philippines with a few mummies from Incan civilisations and the Canaries.

Natural Science Museum (Museo de Ciencias Naturales) (BL M¹⁹). — *Open 15 June to 14 September weekdays 9am to 2pm; the rest of the year 9am to 2pm and 3 to 6pm; Sundays and holidays 10am to 2pm; closed certain holidays, inquire locally; 30pts.*
Geology, mineralogy and zoology departments.

Maritime Museum (NY M²⁰). — *Open 10.30am to 1.30pm; closed Mondays, August and certain holidays, inquire locally; 5pts, Thursdays free.*
Juan de la Cosa's map of 1500 on which America is shown for the first time, is on display.

Municipal Museum (LV M²¹). — *Open 10am to 2pm (3pm Sundays) and 5 to 9pm; closed Sunday afternoons and Mondays and holidays all day.*
The museum is in a former hospice for which Pedro de Ribera carried to the extreme the rococo ornamentation of the **main doorway★** the black stone against the red brick façade giving full emphasis to his every extravagance. The same exuberance reappears in the niches he designed for the **Toledo Bridge** (BM **101**) to contain statues of San Isidro and Sta Mariá de la Cabeza. A series of rooms, recently opened, contains objects (documents, paintings, models...) illustrating Madrid's history and cultural life.

■ OTHER SIGHTS

El Retiro★★ (BM). — The park originally formed the grounds of a palace built in the 17C by Philip IV of which only the building containing the Military Museum and the Casón del Buen Retiro remain, in the same way that the nearby church is all that is still standing of a Hieronymite monastery. The Retiro or Madrid Park (130ha - 321 acres) is beautiful with dense clumps of tall trees (La Chopera at the south end), elegant, formal flowerbeds (El Parterre at the north end), avenues, vistas, fountains even statues, temples, colonnades and a lake. The main avenue, the Paseo de la Argentina, flanked by statues of former sovereigns (originally intended for the palace) leads to the **Great Lake** (Estanque) in which the monument to Alfonso XII stands reflected. Not far away, near the Palacio de Cristal, are a pool and grotto.

MADRID★★★

Casa de Campo★ (AL). — *From Paseo del Pintor Rosales there is a cable-car; 260pts Rtn.*
The park, largely replanted by Philip II, extends around a central lake *(boating)* and was, for centuries, a royal hunt.

Amusement Park (AM). — *Inquire locally for opening times: ☎ 463-29-00; closed Mondays; 90pts, children 50pts.*

Zoo★★ (AM). — *Open 10am to sunset; 250pts, children 170pts.* There are some 2 000 animals, grouped by continents.

University City★ (Ciudad Universitaria) (ABL). — The extensive complex of 20C architecture set in its own grounds comprises the buildings of the University of Madrid — Alcalá (Universidad Complutense) and the Polytechnic Institute of Engineering. The city stands on a hillside immediately overlooking the wooded Pardo range and beyond, the Sierra de Guadarrama. Also among the city's buildings are the **Moncloa Palace** (AL S), the official residence of the Prime Minister, the **Americas Museum★** *(p 209)* and the **Museum of Contemporary Art★** *(p 209).*

Puerta del Sol (LY). — The actual Puerta del Sol or Sun Gate disappeared in the 16C but the name remains. A small monument illustrates the city's coat of arms: a bear and an arbutus tree.
In front of the Presidencia de la Comunidad de Madrid stands the Kilometre 0 point from which all the main roads of Spain radiate and distances are measured.

Plaza de España (KV). — The stone monument to Cervantes, the bronze figures of Don Quixote and Sancho Panza in the square, appear overwhelmed by the size of the latest skyscrapers: the Torre de Madrid and the Edificio España.
Starting from the square and leading to the University City is the Calle Princesa, bordered by open air cafés.

The Cibeles Fountain (Fuente de la Cibeles) (NXY F). — The most famous fountain in Madrid and perhaps all Spain, is the Cibeles, the Greek goddess of fertility who rides her chariot at the junction of the Paseo del Prado, the Alcalá and the Paseo de la Castellana. She was the creation, like the nearby Alcalá Arch, of Charles III in the 18C.

Alcalá Arch (NX Q). — Constructed by Sabatini to celebrate the triumphant entrance of Charles III in Madrid.

West Park (Parque del Oeste) (ABL). — This delightful landscaped garden extends across slopes overlooking the Manzanares. The rose garden, La Rosaleda *(below the Casa de Campo cable-car station),* is a delight in June and the Paseo del Pintor Rosales among the most welcome of the avenues bordering the park as it is lined with open air cafés.
Nearby is the Príncipe Pío Hill on which stands the 4C BC **Temple of Debod** (BLM X) rescued from drowning when the Aswan Dam was constructed. Note the hieroglyphs on the interior walls.

El Rastro. — *Detailed plan p 201.* The Madrid flea market is open on Sunday mornings and holidays *(until 2pm)* in a street named the Ribera de Curtidores and in the neighbouring byways.

La Fuente del Berro Park (CLM). — A small park near the centre of the city.

Royal Tapestry Factory (Real Fábrica de Tapices) (BM Z). — *Open 9.30am to 12.30pm; closed Saturdays, Sundays, holidays and August; 25pts.*
A display of Goya tapestry cartoons precedes a visit to the factory where tapestries and carpets are still woven by the same methods as were employed from the 18C onwards in the making of furnishings for the royal palaces.

Avoid visiting a church during a service.

La MANCHA (Ciudad Real, Toledo, Cuenca, Albacete)
Michelin map **444** folds 22 to 26

La Mancha, a Tertiary aggradation, a high tableland of infinite horizons, is bone dry — the Arabic word for parched earth is *manxa* — but it ripples with cereals under *secano* cultivation *(p 187),* lies clouded with purple when the fields of saffron come into bloom and is striated with perfectly aligned olive trees and vines.
The inhabitants congregate in large villages of white walled houses along straight streets and in wine trade towns such as Alcázar de San Juan and Daimiel.
The famous local cheese, the *queso manchego,* is now also manufactured elsewhere.

The wine harvest. — La Mancha is Spain's largest single wine area with over a million acres of vineyards — 450 000ha: 5 million hectolitres. The stock, widely spaced in square vineyards, produces a wine of low alcoholic content, mostly white, which the Spanish consider an everyday table wine — a *vino común* or *corriente.* Only wines from Valdepeñas *(p 220)* and Manzanares are brand named *(appellation contrôlée).* **Daimiel** is known for its cooperative, **Tomelloso,** said to be built over a wine vat, and for the *coñacs* (brandies) distilled in quantity from local white wine. Dessert grapes now also form part of the local agricultural economy.

In the steps of Don Quixote. — Looking at this flat, austere landscape, shimmering, phantasmagoric in its infinity, it is immediately obvious why Cervantes chose it as the setting for the wanderings of the ingenious Hidalgo Don Quixote de la Mancha *(p 189).* The windmills around **Mota del Cuervo** and **Campo de Criptana** easily become transformed, in the mind's eye, into enormous giants, which the Knight of Rueful Countenance on his nag, Rossinante, felt compelled to charge with rusted lance, so fevered was his imagination by romances of chivalry, so convinced was he of his mission as knight errant sent to right wrongs and injustice. Cervantes described the knight's mirages whereby men and objects became malevolences and whereby he felt compelled to combat at no matter what cost and despite the waverings of his faithful squire, Sancho Panza. The novel, of course, provided a portrait and commentary on contemporary life and, in addition, took on the epic quality which has made it live for three centuries. Whether or not Argamasilla was the birthplace of Don Quixote — a title it disclaims — many other places on the plain do claim to be the site of the knight's many exploits.

■ MANCHEGAN VILLAGES

Alcázar de San Juan. — The large market town gets its name from the Moorish castle, a stronghold of the Order of St John, although in fact it dates back considerably further, to the 1 and 2C AD as can be seen by interesting Roman mosaics uncovered near the castle keep, known as Don Juan of Austria's Tower *(apply at the town hall)*.

Argamasilla de Alba. — The Cueva de Medrano *(apply at the town hall near the church or at the Calle Cervantes, 8)* is the modest lodging in which Cervantes is said to have stayed while writing the opening chapters of *Don Quixote*.

Consuegra. — From the hill, spiked with windmills, and the ruins of a 12C castle, there is an attractive view of Consuegra standing in the plain, the Church of San Juan rising conspicuously above the white houses with rose tiled roofs. The castle was once a stronghold when Consuegra was the seat and priory of the Knights of San Juan — the Spanish branch of the Knight's Hospitallers of the Order of St John of Jerusalem. Today the town is best known for its potters or *alfares* (studios along the Madridejos road).

(After MTTC photo, Madrid)

Consuegra windmill

Ruidera Lakes. — *Description p 212.*

Puerto Lápice. — According to local tradition it was at one of the inns of this village that, in a fantastic scene, Don Quixote was dubbed knight by the innkeeper.

El Toboso. — El Toboso of all Manchegan villages, has perhaps most completely kept its ancient character. It was here that the knight discovered the damsel of his dreams, the peerless Dulcinea, daughter of a labourer, possessor of all earthly virtues.

Dulcinea House, at one end of the village, is furnished in the local style *(open 10am to 2pm and 4 to 7pm; closed all day Monday and Sunday afternoons; 75pts)*. In the town hall are rare editions of the romance including translations.

■ MOLINA DE ARAGÓN (Guadalajara)
Michelin map 🟦🟦🟦 fold 24 or 🟦🟦🟦 fold 23 — Pop 3 795

Of the **Moorish ramparts** which at one time linked fort and town, only crumbling bricks remain; of its period in the 12C as a county capital, even less, but of the 13C wall erected by the Christians a short distance from the town to protect the massive keep known as the **Tower of Aragon,** there is ample to remind one of Molina's unenviable role in the Middle Ages as a disputed strongpoint between warring Aragon and Castile.

■ EL PARDO (Madrid)
Michelin map 🟦🟦🟦 folds 4 and 13 or 🟦🟦🟦 folds 8 and 17

The town, encircled by hills covered by an evergreen oakwood known as the Bosque del Pardo, surrounds the former palace of the same name.

King Juan Carlos I lives 5km - 3 miles to the southwest in Zarzuela Palace.

Pardo Palace★ (Palacio de El Pardo). — *Guided tours 10am to 1pm and 3.30 to 6.30pm (3 to 6pm in winter); closed Sunday afternoons, Tuesdays all day, certain holidays and during Official Visits; 100pts.* The palace was built by Philip III (1598-1621) at the site of Philip II's palace (1556-1598) which had been destroyed in a fire in 1604 and remodelled in 1772 by Sabatini. For a long time the palace was the residence of the Head of State; Franco lived there 35 years.

As you walk through the reception rooms and private apartments you will see an ensemble of elegant furniture, chandeliers, clocks and Sevres porcelain; more than 200 tapestries hang on the walls. Some are 17C Brussels but the majority are 18C tapestries from the Royal Tapestry Factory *(p 210)* after cartoons by González Ruiz, Bayeu, Van Loo, and of course Goya. In the chapel are paintings by Lucas Jordán.

The Prince's Pavilion (Casita del Príncipe). — *Same opening times as the Palace; 60pts.*

The pavilion, erected in 1772 by Juan de Villanueva for the future Charles IV as a gift for his wife, María Luisa, though it has lost its parkland setting, remains a richly decorative artefact. The small rooms rival one another in sophistication: the vestibule with coloured marbles and stucco, the dining room with Talavera silk hangings and upholstery, the Fable Cabinet with embroidery inspired by the tales of Samaniego.

The Quinta. — *Same opening times as the Palace; 60pts.*

The former residence of the Duke of Arcos became crown property in 1745. Inside, elegant early 19C wallpaper embellishes the walls.

Capuchin Monastery (Convento de Capuchinos). — *Signposted entrance.*

The church *(closed between 1.30 and 4.30pm)* which contains several 17C paintings, is known particularly for a statue now in an adjacent chapel, originally commissioned in 1605 by Philip III from Gregorio Fernández in Valladolid. The polychrome wood figure, which turned out to be a masterpiece, shows **Christ Recumbent★**.

PRIEGO (Cuenca)

Michelin map 444 folds 15 and 16 or 445 fold 4 — Pop 1 183

This Alcarria village *(p 187)* commands the entrance to the Escabas Ravine.

Hoz de Beteta★. — *37km - 23 miles by C 202.*

San Miguel de las Victorias. — *Turn left outside Priego (3km - 2 miles).* The old convent, built in an outstanding **site★★** on a terrace directly overlooking the mouth of the Escabas Ravine, contains a collection of baroque statues by Carmona (Christ at prayer, saints). *Apply to the priest.*

The **Escabas Ravine** continues for several miles along its deeply cleft course.

Hoz de Beteta★. — The ravine, which begins 6km - 4 miles beyond Cañizares is wild.

Beteta. — The small mountain village clings to the top of a rock spike.

RUIDERA Lakes Lagunas de RUIDERA (Ciudad Real, Albacete)

Michelin map 444 folds 23 and 24 or 445 fold 16

A dozen lakes, now established as a national park, at the centre of the **Campo de Montiel** provide water for the many headstreams of the Guadiana River. The biggest expanse is **Colgada Lake** which is becoming a summer resort.

SAN MARTÍN DE VALDEIGLESIAS (Madrid)

Michelin map 444 fold 12 or 447 fold 16 — Pop 4 786

The old market town still retains from the 14C, a castle which belonged to the all powerful Constable of Castile, Álvaro de Luna. The ramparts are particularly impressive from the parish church, one of those which gave the valley its name, Val de las Siete Iglesias, valley of the seven churches.

EXCURSIONS

Lake (Pantano) San Juan. — *6km - 4 miles.*
As the road descends there are attractive **views★** of the narrow part of the Alberche Reservoir where the banks are deeply indented and pine trees come down to the water's edge. The area is popular with Madrileños *(water sports facilities).*

Toros de Guisando; Burguillo Reservoir★ (Ávila Province). — *16km - 10 miles. Take the Ávila road and after 4km - 2 1/2 miles bear left.*
The Bulls of Guisando, as they are called, four rudimentarily carved figures in granite stand *(2km - 1 mile along the road)* in an open field. Their origin is unknown. They are, however, obviously ancient and remain an enigma in spite of the possible theory that they represent a Celtiberian idol or a Roman boundary-mark.
Continue along the Ávila road.
The **Burguillo Reservoir★**, a manmade lake on the River Alberche, provides a fine setting for water sports enthusiasts amidst hills covered with a sparse vegetation.

Aldea del Fresno. — *28km - 17 miles southeast of Navas del Rey.*
Located west of Aldea del Fresno is the Reserva El Rincón one of the largest nature reserves in Spain. *For opening times inquire locally: ☎ 862-06-57; closed Mondays; 350pts, children 250pts.*

SPAIN: The Michelin Regional Map Series (1: 400 000)
You may pick out at a glance
   the motorways and major roads for a quick journey
   the secondary or alternative roads for a traffic-free run
   the country lanes for a leisurely drive
These maps are a must for your holidays.

SIGÜENZA ★ (Guadalajara)

Michelin map 444 fold 6 — Pop 6 656

Sigüenza, descending in tiers from its hilltop, is dominated by its imposing cathedral fortress and fortified castle *(parador).*

The old town. — The Plaza Mayor, which extends from the south wall of the cathedral, is lined along another side by an arcaded gallery and opposite by the façade of the town hall and a sober fronted building marked by a top heavy balcony. There are Romanesque doorways and stylish mansions in the narrow streets off the square.

Diocesan Museum. — *Open 1 April to 6 January 11.30am to 2pm and 5 to 7.30pm; the rest of the year Saturdays, Sundays and holidays only 11.30am to 2pm and 4 to 6.30pm; 75pts.* Among the treasures are sculptures by the 16C Italian, Pompeo Leoni (Room C), a *Pièta* attributed to Luis de Morales and an Immaculate Conception by Francisco de Zurbarán (Room E) and a fiery Elijah attributed to the 18C sculptor, Francisco Salzillo (N).

Cathedral★★. — *Time: 1 hour. Apply to the sacristan 11am to 1pm and 4 to 8pm (6pm in winter).*
The nave, begun to a Cistercian plan in the 12C, was only completed in 1495, the end of the Gothic period; the ambulatory and cloister are slightly later. The roof and transept dome were rebuilt after damage in 1936.
The façade appears that of a fortress as it stands flanked by crenellated towers and powerful buttresses until you notice the great rose and Romanesque windows with their old glass.
The nave with sober lines and high vaulting supported on massive pillars graced by slender engaged columns, conveys an impression of solid strength.

North aisle:

(1) **Doorway**★ decorated with Renaissance pilasters, Mudejar arabesques and Gothic cusping;
(2) 15C **triptych** by the Castilian school.

North transept. — **A sculptured unit**★★:

(3) 16-17C **jasper doorway** opening onto the cloister of multicoloured marble.

(4) 16C **Sta Librada altar** designed by Covarrubias as a retable with the central niche containing an altar surmounted by painted panels of the martyrdom of the saint and her eight sisters, all born, according to legend, on the same day;

(5) 16C **Sepulchre of Dom Fadrique of Portugal:** an Italian Renaissance monument adorned successfully with Plateresque decoration.

Sanctuary (Presbiterio). — A beautiful wrought iron grille encloses two alabaster **pulpits**★, one Gothic (6), the other Renaissance (7); the altarpiece is 17C; the walls have been embedded with tombs.

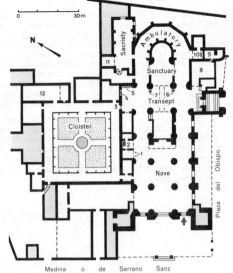

(8) **The Donzel Chapel.** — The **Donzel tomb**★★ was commissioned by Isabel the Catholic for her young page, Don Martín Vázquez de Arce, who died at the gates of Granada in 1486. The figure, considered a major work of sepulchral art in Spain, shows the youth reclining on one elbow, reading serenely; it is incredibly realistic and unlike any other Spanish funerary monument. In the centre of the room is the mausoleum of the Donzel's parents.

The annexe (9) is hung with 15C Castilian paintings.

Ambulatory. — There is a 16C wooden **Crucifix**★ at the back of the chapel (10).

Sacristy. — The sacristy by Covarrubias has a **ceiling**★ which is an amazing profusion of heads and roses between which peer thousands of cherubim; the panelling and woodwork of doors and furniture are delicately carved in ornate Plateresque.

The 16C Reliquary Chapel (11) is covered with a **dome**★.

Cloister. — The cloister in 16C Gothic style is embellished with Plateresque doors opening on chapels, one of which (12) is hung with 17C Flemish tapestries.

EXCURSION

Atienza. — *31km -19 miles northwest.* Atienza is a typical Castilian village built at the foot of a castle of which only the keep remains proudly upright on its rock. The modest, porticoed, Plaza Mayor is attractively mediaeval. The town once had seven churches but since the Civil War all that remains of interest are the Churrigueresque altarpiece in the parish church on the square *(Plaza Mayor),* and the surprising rococo chapel in the small Holy Trinity Church *(Iglesia de la Trinidad, near the cemetery),* given by Philip V to the village in recognition of its support in the War of Succession.

TALAVERA DE LA REINA (Toledo) —————————————————

Michelin map ▨▨▨ fold 11 or ▨▨▨ fold 15 — Pop 64 136

The name Talavera, like that of Manises and Paterna, has been associated since the 15C with the **ceramic tiles** used to decorate the lower walls of palaces, mansions and chapels. Talavera *azulejos* were always recognisable by their blue and yellow designs; today tiles have been largely replaced by the manufacture of domestic and purely decorative ware such as plates, vases and bowls. Green indicates that an object was made in **El Puente del Arzobispo,** a small village *(34km - 21 miles southwest)* which now specialises in the mass production of pottery drinking jars - *cacharros. Studio workshops (Artesanía Talaverana) at the west end of Talavera are open to visitors (9am to 1pm and 4 to 8pm).*

The Prado Virgin Hermitage. — *At the entrance to the town coming from Madrid, just after the park.*

The church, which is virtually an *azulejos* museum, gives a good idea of the evolution of the local style. The oldest tiles, dating from the 14 to 16C, yellow coloured and with geometric designs are in the sacristy *(access through the north door);* 18 to 20C tiles with blue or even narrative designs are in the church proper and the portal.

EXCURSION

Oropesa; Lagartera. — *32km - 20 miles west.*

Oropesa. — Two churches and a castle rise above the town which is made up of noble houses still sporting their coats of arms and with windows decorated with ironwork. The **castle** retains its proud bearing of 1366 and still commands the village from its curtain walls (view); the annexes were built in 1402 and are now a *parador.* In the stairwell a plaque recalls that it was Count of Oropesa, **Francisco de Toledo,** Viceroy of Peru from 1569 to 1581, who had won renown for his liberal laws in favour of the Indians.

Lagartera. — This village has been known for several centuries for the embroidery worked by its women who, dressed all in black, sit in summer at their front doors or in a forecourt and in winter at the first floor windows of their houses. They embroider long skirts and vivid coloured bonnets in peasant style, tablecloths and subtly toned silk hangings with scatterings of flowers — every cottage has its own display.

TOLEDO ★★★ P

Michelin map **444** fold 12 or **447** fold 16 — Pop 57 769

Toledo stands out against the often luminously blue Castilian sky: a golden biscuit city rising from a granite eminence, encircled by a steep ravine filled by the green waters of the River Tagus. It is as spectacular as it is rich in history, buildings, art... every corner has a tale to be told, every aspect reflects a brilliant period of Spanish history when the cultures of east and west flourished and fused: one is constantly aware of this imprint of Christian, Jewish and Moorish cultures which productively co-existed during the Middle Ages.

Within its **walls,** the city shelters beautiful sights amidst winding old **streets** which provide a spectacular setting for the Corpus Christi procession *(p 24).*

Toledo **damascene** (black steel inlaid with gold, silver and copper wire) has been renowned for centuries; equally reputed are Toledo braised partridge and marzipan!

The site★★★. — The city's incomparable site can be seen particularly well from the Circunvalación Road for 3.5km - 2 miles parallels, on the far bank, the almost circular loop of the Tagus which flows all the way round from the Alcántara to the St Martin Bridge *(p 219).* It is worth, also, going out to the belvederes on the surrounding heights covered by extensive olive groves *(cigarrales)* in which white houses stand half concealed for truly memorable views of the city as it lies couched between the Alcázar and the Monastery of St John of the Kings.

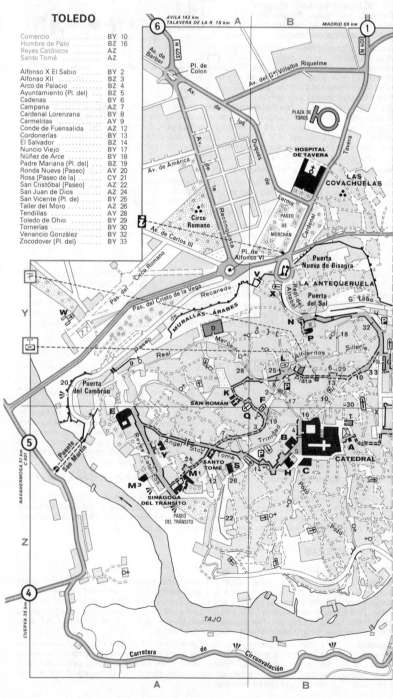

TOLEDO

Comercio	BY	10
Hombre de Palo	BZ	16
Reyes Católicos	AZ	
Santo Tomé	AZ	
Alfonso X El Sabio	BY	2
Alfonso XII	BZ	3
Arco de Palacio	BZ	4
Ayuntamiento (Pl. del)	BZ	5
Cadenas	BY	6
Campana	AZ	7
Cardenal Lorenzana	BY	8
Carmelitas	AY	9
Conde de Fuensalida	AZ	12
Cordonerías	BY	13
El Salvador	BY	14
Nuncio Viejo	BY	17
Núñez de Arce	BY	18
Padre Mariana (Pl. del)	BZ	19
Ronda Nueva (Paseo)	AY	20
Rosa (Paseo de la)	CY	21
San Cristóbal (Paseo)	AZ	22
San Juan de Dios	AZ	24
San Vicente (Pl. de)	BY	25
Taller del Moro	AZ	26
Tendillas	AZ	28
Toledo de Ohío	BY	29
Tornerías	BY	30
Venancio González	BY	32
Zocodover (Pl. del)	BY	33

Roman town to Holy Roman city. — The Romans, appreciating the site's advantage strategically and geographically at the centre of the peninsula, fortified and built up the settlement into a town which they named Toletum. It passed, in due course, into the hands of the Barbarians, and in the 6C to the Visigoths who ultimately made it a monarchical seat. The Visigoths, defeated at Guadalete in 711 (p 11), abandoned the town to the Moors who incorporated it in the Córdoba Emirate, until the successful revolt of the *taifas* in 1012 raised it to the position of capital of an independent kingdom. In 1085 Toledo was conquered by Alfonso VI of León.

Two years later, when the king removed his capital to it from León, the city with its mixed Moorish, Jewish and Christian communities began to prosper richly. It is to Alfonso VII, whose coronation as emperor took place there, that Toledo owes its title of imperial city. The Catholic Monarchs gave it the Monastery of St John and only found the city pall when compared to Granada, reconquered under their own aegis in 1492. Charles V had the Alcázar rebuilt. Also during his reign the city took part in the Comuneros' Revolt (p 245) led by Juan de Padilla, a Toledan. Progress was halted in 1561 when Philip II named Madrid as Spain's capital, leaving Toledo as the spiritual centre, the seat of the primacy. The events of 1936 within and without the Alcázar (p 216), brought it briefly into the limelight of history.

Toledo and the Visigoths. — Toledo played a key role during the Visigoth supremacy in the peninsula which began in 507. By 554 they had made it their capital and Councils of State, which had met in Toledo as early as 400, were resumed; that of 589, following upon the conversion of King Reccared two years previously, established the Visigoth hegemony and the religious unification of Spain. The Visigoths, torn by internal strife, however, were unable to resist the Moors and abandoned Toledo in 711; it took Pelayo and a small band of Christians to reinstate the dynasty (p 112).

Toledo and the Jews. — Toledo would appear to have been by far the most important Jewish town in Spain: in the 12C the community numbered 12 000. Under **Ferdinand III** (1217-1252), a tolerant monarch who encouraged the intermingling of the races which brought about a cultural flowering, the city developed into a great intellectual forum. This wellbeing reached its climax under his son **Alfonso X, the Wise** (1252-1284) who gathered round him a court of wise Jews and, in the main, was their friend though not above extracting massive fines and taxes from them! Jewish prosperity and immunity, suddenly and brutally ceased in 1355 with a pogrom instigated by the supporters of Henry IV of Trastamara, in 1391 when the faithful at the synagogue of Sta María la Blanca were massacred at the behest of **St Vincent Ferrer** and finally in 1492 with the Catholic Monarchs' decree of expulsion.

Mudejar art in Toledo. — Toledo, which for centuries had numbered citizens of different races and religions, became the ideal setting under Christian rule for the development of the Mudejar style (p 14).

Moorish art (the use of brick in construction, of sculptured plaster and *azulejos* in decoration, of *artesonado* ceilings) inspired architects and appears not only in palaces (Taller del Moro), but also in synagogues (Tránsito, Sta María la Blanca) and churches. Thus in the 13 and 14C most Toledan churches were given Romanesque semicircular **east ends** and blind arcades with variations unknown elsewhere; bricks were used in place of stone and **belfries** squared and decorated until they appeared strongly reminiscent of minarets. The edifices have a nave and two aisles — a Visigothic influence — tripartite apses — a Romanesque souvenir — and wood vaulting carved in the Moorish style.

El Greco. — Domenico Teotocopulos, the Greek — El Greco — one of the great figures in Spanish painting, was born in Crete in 1541. After an apprenticeship painting icons, he went to Italy where he worked under Titian and Tintoretto and studied Michelangelo before journeying to Spain in 1577 and settling in Toledo where he remained until he died in 1614. Although he didn't always succeed in pleasing Philip II he found favour and fortune with Toledans. His work, with its acquired Italian techniques, retained considerable Byzantine influence which appeared as a lengthening of forms — a mannerism which increased as the painter aged; a recurring feature in illustrated scenes was the division of the canvas into two — earth and heaven — demonstrating El Greco's belief that this life was but preparation for an exalted hereafter. The supernatural is a constant preoccupation, figures convey an intense spiritual inner power — all is seen with the eye of the visionary and portrayed sometimes by means of apparent distortion, by brilliant, occasionally crude colours, often by violent, swirling movement so that some pictures have the aspect of hallucinations. But the portraits by contrast are still, the colours deep, expressions meditative in religious, watchful in the worldly.

TOLEDO★★★

■ MAIN SIGHTS *time: allow one day*

There is something to see and enjoy at every step in Toledo. Walking along the maze of arrow, winding lanes you pass churches, old palaces and houses.

Alcázar (CYZ). — *Open 9.30am to 7pm (6pm in winter); closed 1 January, 28 September and 25 December; 100pts.*

The Alcázar, destroyed and rebuilt so many times, stands, massive and proud as ever, dominating all other buildings in the city. It was Charles V who decided to convert the 13C fortress of which the Cid had been the first governor, into an imperial residence. The conversion was entrusted first to Covarrubias (1538-1551) and subsequently to Herrera who designed the austere south front. The construction was damaged and restored twice during the wars of the 18 and 19C but this was nothing as compared to the shelling of 1936 which left the fortress in ruins. Reconstruction has restored the Alcázar to its appearance at the time of Charles V — an innovation is the Victory Monument by Ávalos in the forecourt. You see the bullet-marked underground galleries which sheltered 600 women and children and the two babies born there during the 8-week Republican siege, and the office above in which Colonel Moscardó was ordered by phone to surrender or see his son shot. His son died on 23 August; the Alcázar was relieved on 27 September.

Casa de la Hermandad (BZ A). — A late 15C building which was formerly a prison.

Cathedral★★★ (BZ). — *Open weekdays 10.30am to 1pm and 3.30 to 7pm (6pm in winter); Sundays and holidays 10.30am to 1.30pm and 4 to 7pm (6pm in winter); combined ticket to visit the treasury, chapterhouse and sacristy: 200pts.*

Construction, like that of Burgos Cathedral, began in the reign of Ferdinand III (1227) under Archbishop Rodrigo Jiménez de Rada. Unlike other churches in the vicinity, the design was French Gothic but as building continued until the end of the 15C, plans were modified and the completed edifice presents a conspectus of Spanish Gothic, although considerably masked by additions. The church, nevertheless, remains of outstanding interest for its sculptured decoration and numerous works of religious art.

The **Clock Door** (Puerta del Reloj), in the north wall, is the old entrance, dating from the 13C although modified in the 19C. The west front is pierced by three tall 15C portals of which the upper registers were completed in the 16 and 17C: at the centre is the **Pardon Door** (Puerta del Perdón), crowded with statues and crowned with a tympanum on which the Virgin presents St Ildefonsus with a chasuble. The harmonious tower is 15C; the dome, which replaces the second tower, was designed by El Greco's son in the 17C. In the south wall, the 15C **Lion Door** of Flamboyant Gothic style and designed by Master Hanequin of Brussels and decorated by Juan Alemán was flanked in 1800 by a Neo-Classical portal. *Enter by a door, left of the façade, which opens onto the cloister.*

The size and robust character of the cathedral rather than its elevation are what strike one as one gazes at the roofs over the five unequal aisles and the great supporting pillars. A wonderful collection of stained glass (1418-1561) colours the windows; magnificent wrought iron grilles enclose the sanctuary, *coro* and chapels.

Sanctuary. — The sanctuary, the most sumptuous part of the church, was enlarged in the 16C by Cardinal Cisneros. The immense polychrome **retable★★**, carved in Flamboyant style with the Life of Christ depicted in detail on five registers, is awe inspiring in its way; the silver statue (1418) of the Virgin at the predella, far more comprehensible. On a pillar to the left is the shepherd who guided the Christian army to victory at Las Navas de Tolosa in 1212 and another on the right, is the Moor, Abu-Walid, who interceded before Alfonso VI on behalf of the Christians who destroyed the mosque. The marble tomb of Cardinal Mendoza *(p 198)* in Plateresque style on the left is by Covarrubias. The recumbent figure is the work of an Italian.

"Coro". — A series of 14C high reliefs and wrought iron enclosed chapels form the perimeter of the *coro* which is itself closed by an elegant iron screen (1547). Within are magnificent 15 and 16C walnut wood **choirstalls★★★** of which the lower parts were carved by Rodrigo Alemán (c1495) to recall, in 54 beautifully detailed and picturesque scenes, the conquest of Granada; the 16C upper parts are by Berruguete (left) and Juan de Borgoña (right). The central low relief, the Transfiguration, in alabaster is also by Berruguete. The pipes of a sonorous organ dominate the central area, occupied by two bronze lecterns and a Gothic eagle lectern. The 14C marble White Virgin is French.

Treasure (Tesoro). — A Plateresque doorway by Covarrubias opens into the chapel under the tower. Beneath a Granada style Mudejar ceiling admire the splendid 16C silver-gilt **monstrance★★** by Arfe, which, although it weighs 180kg and is 3m high — just under 400lbs and 10ft high is paraded through the streets at Corpus Christi. The custodial, at its centre, is fashioned from gold brought from America by Christopher Columbus. There is also a Bible given by St Louis of France to St Ferdinand (Ferdinand III of Castile 1199-1252, father of Eleanor, wife of Edward I of England).

Mozarabic Chapel. — The chapel beneath the dome *(open only during Mozarabic mass at 9.45am)* was erected by Cisneros to celebrate mass according to the Visigothic or Mozarabic ritual.

Ambulatory (Girola). — The double ambulatory, surmounted by an elegant triforium with multilobed arches, is bordered by seven apsidal chapels separated by small square chapels. The vaulting is a geometrical wonder of alternating triangles and rectangles.

There is little room behind the sanctuary to step back for a good look at the **Transparente** (1732), that contentious but famous work of Narciso Tomé which forms a baroque island in the Gothic church. Often illuminated by the sun's rays which pour through an actual hole in the ambulatory roof (made to allow light to fall on the tabernacle), the Transparente appears as a vast wall of swirling forms more dreamlike than real: beneath a parabolic arch in an ornamental framework of angels, sculptures in full relief can be distinguished of the Virgin and the Last Supper. In the **Chapel of St Ildefonsus,** there are tombs, of which the one in the centre of Cardinal Gil de Albornoz (14C) is the most notable. The **Chapel of St James** (Santiago) was erected, on the site of an earlier Chapel to St Thomas of Canterbury, by Count Álvaro de Luna, Constable of Castile, as a family mausoleum.

Chapterhouse. — An impressive Mudejar ceiling and two Plateresque carved walnut wardrobes in an antechamber and remarkable Mudejar stucco doorways and panels, precede the chapterhouse where there is a particularly beautiful multicoloured **Mudejar ceiling★**. The walls, painted by Juan de Borgoña (d c1533) are hung with portraits of former archbishops including two by Goya painted in 1804 and 1823.

Chapel of the New Kings (Capilla de los Reyes Nuevos). — The work of Covarrubias, the Plateresque chapel contains the tombs of the Trastamara line (the kings and queens) of the 14-15C, Henry II, John I, Henry III and his Queen, Catherine of Lancaster, daughter of John of Gaunt, and John II.

Sacristy. — The first gallery, with its vaulted ceiling painted by Luca Giordano, includes a powerful group of **paintings by El Greco★** of which *El Expolio* (the Saviour stripped of his Raiment), painted soon after the artist's arrival in Spain, is outstanding. A forerunner of many other New Testament scenes, it conveys a dominating, exalted personality, set against the swirling folds of robes in vivid, often acid tones, which establish a rhythmical movement, akin to baroque, on the canvas. Also among the collection is one of El Greco's series of portraits of the Apostles. Works by other artists in the sacristy include a remarkable portrait of *Pope Paul III* by Titian, a *Holy Family* by Van Dyck, a *Mater Dolorosa* by Morales and the *Taking of Christ* by Goya which displays to advantage his skill in composition, in the use of light and portraying individuals in a crowd. There is also one of Pedro de Mena's (17C) most characteristic and famous sculptures, *St Francis of Assisi (in a glass case).* In the vestiary are portraits by Velásquez *(Cardinal Borja),* Van Dyck *(Pope Innocent XI),* Ribera and Titian. In the old laundry are liturgical objects dating back to the 15C.

Cloister (Claustro). — The architectural simplicity of the 14C lower gallery contrasts with the bold mural decoration by Bayeu of the Lives of Toledan saints.

Cathedral Museum's New Galleries (Nuevas Salas del Museo Catedralicio). — *Open 10.30am to 12.30pm and 4 to 6pm; closed Mondays; 50pts.*

Recently installed in the treasurer's house, these galleries display works by Caravaggio, El Greco, Bellini and Morales as well as 15 and 16C chasubles and gold and silverplate.

Ringing the square before the cathedral are the 18C **Archbishopric** (Palacio Arzobispal) (BZ **B**), the 17C **Town Hall** (BZ **H**) with its Classical façade and the 14C **Law Courts (Audiencia)** (BZ **C**).

St Thomas' (Santo Tomé) (AZ). — *Open 10am to 1.45pm and 3.30 to 7pm (6pm in winter); closed 1 January and 25 December; 75pts.*

The church, like St Romanus *(p 218),* has a distinctive 14C Mudejar tower. Inside is El Greco's famous painting **The Burial of the Count of Orgaz★★★** (El Entierro del Conde de Orgaz), executed in about 1586 for this church. The interment is transformed by the miraculous appearance of St Augustine and St Stephen waiting to welcome the figure from earth, symbolised by a frieze of figures in which, as he highlighted faces and hands and painted vestments with detailed Biblical references, El Greco made every man an individual portrait — he is said to have painted a self-portrait in the sixth figure from the left.

The El Greco House and Museum★ (Casa y Museo del Greco) (AZ M¹). — *Open 10am to 2pm and 4 to 7pm; closed Sunday afternoons and Mondays and holidays all day; 75pts.*

El Greco moved into a house in 1585 similar to this attractive 16C Toledan **house.** In the first floor studio hang a *St Peter Repentant* (Lágrimas de San Pedro), a version of the painting in the cathedral and, in what would have been the artist's workroom, a signed *St Francis and Brother León.* In the **museum** (first floor) are an interesting View and Plan of Toledo (including a likeness of his son and different in other ways from the version in the Prado) and the complete series of individual portraits of the Apostles and Christ — a later and more mature series than that in the cathedral. In the domestic **chapel,** which has a multicoloured Mudejar ceiling, the picture of *St Bernardino of Siena* in the altarpiece is by the artist; the *Crowning of Thorns* is Hispano-Flemish.

El Tránsito Synagogue★★ (Sinagoga Del Tránsito) (AZ). — *Same opening times as the El Greco House.*

Of the eight synagogues of the old Jewish quarter (Judería), this and Sta María la Blanca are the only ones to remain. Money for its construction was provided in the 14C by Samuel Ha-Levi, treasurer to King Peter the Cruel. In 1492 it was transformed into a church and dedicated soon afterwards to the Dormition (Tránsito) from which it gets its name.

It appears from the outside as an unpretentious small building but inside an amazing **Mudejar decoration★★** covers the upper part of the walls and all the east end. Above the small rectangular hall is an *artesonado* ceiling of cedarwood; just below, beneath multifoil arches resting on slender alabaster columns, are 54 elegant windows covered with a lacelike, and in places, pierced stone tracery. Below again runs a frieze, decorated at the east end with *mocárabes (p 16)* and on the walls with inscriptions in Hebrew to the glory of Peter the Cruel, Samuel Ha-Levi and the God of Israel. The three arches at the centre of the east wall are surmounted by a panel in relief of roses surrounded by magnificent strapwork and, at either side, by inscriptions describing the synagogue's foundation.

The adjoining rooms, at one period a Calatrava monastery, have been converted into a **Sephardic Museum (Museo Sefardí)** displaying tombs, robes, costumes and books. Several are presents from Sephardim or descendants of the Jews expelled from Spain in 1492.

Santa María la Blanca Synagogue★ (AZ Y). — *Open 10am to 2pm and 3.30 to 7pm (6pm in winter); closed 1 January, Holy Friday and 25 December; 40pts.*

This was the principal synagogue in 12C Toledo; in 1405, however, it was given to the Knights of Calatrava who transformed it into a church and gave it its present name. Subsequent vicissitudes, including modification of the east end in the 16C, left the Almohad-style mosque incredibly unharmed so that restoration has been possible and the hall appears as before with five tiered aisles, separated by 24 octagonal pillars supporting horseshoe shaped arches. The plain white of the canted pillars and arches is relieved by stone capitals intricately carved with pinecones and strapwork. Above, the decoration is equally outstanding. The polychrome wood altarpiece is 16C.

St John of the Kings Monastery★ (San Juan de los Reyes) (AZ E). — *Open 10am to 1.45pm and 3.30 to 7pm (6pm in winter); closed 1 January and 25 December; 50pts.*

The monastery was erected by the Catholic Monarchs in thanksgiving to God for their decisive victory over the Portuguese at Toro in 1476. The overall architecture is typically Isabeline, that style which includes in the Flamboyant Gothic style, touches of Mudejar and even Renaissance art, particularly in this case since construction continued until the early 17C. The exterior is somewhat austere despite the ornamented pinnacles and stone balustrade which crown the edifice and, in the latter instance, circles the octagonal lantern. Covarrubias designed the north portal during the later stages of construction, including in the decoration, the figure of John the Baptist flanked by Franciscan saints. The fetters on the façade were taken from Christian prisoners freed from the Muslims in Andalusia.

TOLEDO★★★

Cloister. — Although restored, the cloister remains extremely attractive with Flamboyant bays and the original Plateresque upper galleries (1504) crowned with a pinnacled balustrade. The upper gallery has Mudejar *artesonado* vaulting.

Church. — The church, rebuilt after being fired by the French in 1808, has the single wide aisle typical of Isabeline churches; at the crossing are a dome and lantern. The **sculptured decoration★** by the church's Flemish architect, Juan Guas, provides a delicate stone tracery *(cresteria)* which at the transept forms twin tribunes for Ferdinand and Isabel. The transept walls are faced with a wonderful frieze of royal escutcheons, supported by an eagle, the symbol of Saint John — the monastery was constructed by the monarchs before the capture of Granada with the idea that it would be their burial place, hence the monograms, crests and repeated ornamental allusions. Other decorations include Mudejar *mocárabes* on the transept oven vaulting and heads in picturesque high relief on the triumphal arches. The original altarpiece has been replaced by a 16C Plateresque retable.

Not far away are a Visigothic palace and gateway, which were once part of the town perimeter (rebuilt in the 16C). The **Puerta del Cambrón** (AY) is named after the *cambroneras* or hawthorns which grew around it.

Turn left out of the Calle Santo Tomé into the quaint Travesía del Campana alley.

Before you, in the small shaded Plaza del Padre Mariana, stands the monumental baroque façade of **San Ildefonso** (BYZ **F**) and higher up, that of **San Pedro** (AYZ **Q**).

St Romanus★ (Iglesia San Román) (AY). — *Open 10am to 2pm and 4 to 7pm; closed Sunday and holiday afternoons and Mondays, 1 January and 25 December all day; 150pts including admission to the Santa Cruz Museum.* The church at the highest point in the town, has a fine upstanding Mudejar tower closely resembling that of St Thomas'. The inside of the 13C Mudejar church has been transformed into a **Visigothic Museum** (Museo de los Concilios y de la Cultura Visigoda) which clearly demonstrates, from its collection of fragments from monuments of the short-lived capital, the importance of the period in Spanish history. The three aisles divided by horseshoe shaped arches are reminiscent of Santa María la Blanca; the walls, however, are covered with frescoes of the raising of the dead and the arch intrados with the pictures of the Evangelists. The apse was remodelled in the 16C when a cupola was built over it by Covarrubias. Note the 18C altarpiece. Visigothic bronze jewellery and votive crowns, richly jewelled with cabochon stones like that of Guarrazar *(p 208)*, steles, fragments from capitals, balustrades from the choir and pilasters decorated with geometric motifs or scrollwork, are original but in the mainstream of art whereas the purpose of the rare 6C representation, on a door jamb, of the moon, which is obviously symbolic, remains a mystery *(3rd gallery along)*.

The Plateresque doorway opposite belongs to St Clement's Monastery (AY **K**).

In the Plaza San Vicente, note the Mudejar east end of St Vincent's (BY **L**) before continuing up the Calle de la Plata with its houses with carved entrances.

Plaza del Zocodover (BY 33). — This bustling triangular square is the heart of Toledo.

Sta Cruz Museum★★ (CY M^2). — *Open 10am to 7pm (2pm Sundays and holidays); closed Mondays, 1 January and 25 December; 150pts including admission to San Romanus.*

Cardinal Pedro González de Mendoza, Archbishop of Toledo, died before fully realising his ambition to build a hospital for the sick and orphaned but his project was completed by Queen Isabel. There were two architects as there had been two patrons before the Plateresque buildings were finished: Enrique Egas and Covarrubias, who was responsible for the **façade★**. On the gateway tympanum Cardinal Mendoza kneels before the Cross supported by St Helena, St Peter, St Paul and two pages; on the arches are the cardinal virtues while above two windows frame a high relief of St Joachim and St Anne.

The museum which is large but well arranged, is known for its **collection★** of 16 and 17C pictures which includes **18 paintings by El Greco★**.

Ground floor. — In the 1st corridor are 16C Flemish tapestries, **Primitive paintings★**, and the Astrolaba or Zodiac tapestry, woven in Flanders in the mid - 15C for Toledo Cathedral, which fascinates still by its originality and modern colouring. The 2nd corridor is devoted to the reign of Charles V: note the *Ascension* and *Presentation in the Temple* by the Master of Sigena. In the 3rd corridor hangs the pennant flown by Don Juan of Austria at the Battle of Lepanto (1571) with before it a 17C Crucifix. There is also the retable by Martinez Castañeda of the Dormition of the Virgin; in the last corridor is a *Christ at the Column* by Morales.

1st floor. — In the first gallery are studies of Christ by El Greco's pupil, Luis Tristán, and a remarkable altarpiece of the Visitation for which Berruguete carved the principal scenes — Calvary, the Visitation. The next wing includes two interesting Riberas: the *Descent from the Cross* and the *Holy Family at Nazareth* in which the specialist in tenebrism showed himself also to be a master of light and delicacy, particularly in his portrayal of the Virgin. The *Mater Dolorosa* and *Ecce Homo* statues of Pedro de Mena (17C) are wan and lifeless, the *Dolorosa* of the Juan de Mena school (17C) more baroque. The next corridor is devoted to El Greco with gentle portraits of the *Virgin* and *St Veronica*, a version of the *Expolio* later than that in the cathedral *(p 217)* and including a greater emphasis on the *Holy Women*. Typical of the same artist in its division into an earthly and an exalted plane, is his *Coronation of the Virgin* with the added original touch of St John's presence at the scene. The most famous picture in the collection is the **Altarpiece of the Assumption★** which dates from 1613, the artist's final period. The figures are particularly elongated, the colours rasping. The last corridor is hung with six 16C Brussels tapestries illustrating the life of Alexander the Great. There is also a *Crucifix* by Goya. The **Plateresque patio★** has bays with elegant lines complemented by the openwork of the balustrade and enhanced by beautiful Mudejar vaulting and, even more, by the magnificent staircase by Covarrubias. Adjoining rooms house an **archaeological museum.**

Puerta del Sol (BY). — The Sun Gate in the town's second perimeter is a fine 14C Mudejar construction of an earlier date with two circumscribing horseshoe arches. At the centre a later low relief shows the Virgin presenting San Ildefonso with a chasuble. At the top, the brick decoration of blind arcades incorporates an extraordinary sculpture of two girls bearing on a platter the head of the chief *alguazil* of the town, who was condemned for their violation. Go through the Visigothic Valmardón Gate (**N**) and the garden adjoining the Cristo de la Luz to reach the top of the Puerta del Sol *(apply to the caretaker)* from which there is an interesting view of the city buildings.

Cristo de la Luz (BY **P**). — In 1000 AD the Arabs erected a mosque on the site of a ruined Visigothic church; in the 12C this mosque was converted into a Mudejar church. Legend has it that the church was named Christ of the Light because when Alfonso VI was making his entry into Toledo, the Cid's horse in the royal train, suddenly knelt before the mosque in which, inside a wall, a Visigothic lamp was discovered lighting up a Crucifix. Three series of arches of different periods, superimposed blind arcades, a line of horizontal brickwork surmounted by Cufic characters, make up the façade. Inside, pillars, for the most part Visigothic, support superimposed arches, similar in design to those in the mosque in Córdoba. Nine domes, each different, rise from square bays.

■ ADDITIONAL SIGHTS

Taller del Moro (AZ S). — *Open 10am to 2pm and 4 to 7pm; closed all day Monday and Sunday and holiday afternoons; 75pts.*

This workshop *(taller)*, used by a Moslem as a collecting yard for building material for the cathedral is, in fact, an old palace.

The Mudejar decoration can still be seen in rooms lit by small grated windows, interconnected through slightly horseshoe shaped openings ornamented with *atauriques* or Almohad style stucco.

Victorio Macho Museum (Casa-Museo de Victorio Macho) (AZ M³). — *Temporarily closed.*

The house is now a museum, where the sculptor (1887-1966) returned to end his days after years in Argentina. There are beautiful views of the Tagus from the garden.

St James on the Outskirts (Santiago del Arrabal) (BY X). — *Open 7.30 to 10.30am (8am to 2pm Sundays and holidays) and 5 to 8.30pm.*

This beautifully restored Mudejar church contains the ornate Gothic Mudejar pulpit from which St Vincent Ferrer is said to have preached. The altarpiece is 16C.

Convent of the Conception (Convento de la Concepción) (CY Z). — Only the Chapel of San Jerónimo *(ask the porter)* can be visited; it is notable especially for its Mudejar dome which is an interesting combination of Renaissance and Moorish styles.

Hospital de Tavera★ (BY). — *Open 10.30am to 1.30pm and 3.30 to 6pm; closed 1 January and 25 December; 150pts.*

The hospital, founded in the 16C by Cardinal Tavera, was begun by Bustamante in 1541 and completed by González de Lara and the Vergaras in the 17C. The building is now a school except for certain **apartments★** rearranged in 17C style after the Civil War by the Duchess of Lerma.

Pictures in the immense dining saloon include portraits of the *Emperor Charles V* by Titian and the *Infanta Clara Eugenia* by Coello; the hospital archives contain some volumes bound in leather by Moorish craftsmen. The El Greco painting of the *Holy Family* is arresting, the portrait of the Virgin perhaps the most beautiful the artist ever painted with St Joseph, in the background, depicted with a particular attention. In an adjoining room is Ribera's portrait of the *Bearded Woman* (a peasant from Calabria). The reception hall contains a magnificent El Greco, the **Baptism of Christ★**, more mature than the version in the Prado.

Also by El Greco is a portrait of *Cardinal Tavera* which, although painted from a death mask, is intensely alive, and paintings of his favourite saints, *Saint Peter* and *Saint Francis,* together with a small sculpture of *Christ Revived* which clearly bears his imprint. In the duchess' bedroom are a precious Gothic style ivory Crucifix and a painting by Tintoretto of the *Birth of the Messiah.*

The consecutive Renaissance *patios* by Covarrubias form a gallery to the church *(under restoration)* which has a Carrara marble portal by Berruguete who also carved the tomb of Cardinal Tavera in the nave. The retable at the high altar was designed by El Greco.

Old Bisagra Gate (Puerta Antigua de Bisagra) (BY V). — This gate in the former **Muslim ramparts,** is the one through which Alfonso VI made his entry to the city in 1085.

New Bisagra Gate (Puerta Nueva de Bisagra) (BY). — The gate, which now consists of two towers and an intermediary courtyard, was rebuilt by Covarrubias in 1550; massive round crenellated towers, facing the Madrid road, flank a giant imperial crest.

Alcántara Bridge (CY). — The 13C bridge ends respectively to west and east in a Mudejar tower and baroque arch. On the far side of the Tagus, behind battlemented ramparts, the restored 14C **Castle of San Servando,** an advanced strongpoint in mediaeval times, can be seen.

A plaque on the town wall by the bridge recalls the escape through a window of **St John of the Cross** (1542-1591) from his monastery prison nearby.

St Martin's Bridge (AZ). — The mediaeval bridge rebuilt in the 14C following damage by floodwaters is marked at its south end by a crenellated tower; the north end is 16C.

Cristo de la Vega (AY W). — The Church of Christ of the Vega, formerly St Leocadia, stands on the site of a 7C Visigothic temple, the setting of early church councils and, according to legend, the apparition in the 7C of St Leocadia before St Ildefonsus and the king.

Although considerably modified in the 18C, it still has a fine Mudejar apse. Inside *(apply to the caretaker)* a modern Crucifix now stands in place of the one around which many legends had gathered including the one in which the figure offered an arm to a jilted girl who had come to seek comfort.

Roman circus (Circo Romano) (AY). — The circus in the public garden shows by its size the status of the Roman city of Toletum.

EXCURSIONS

Guadamur. — *15km - 9 miles. Leave Toledo by ⑤ on the plan, bearing left into the Navahermosa road.* The **castle** overlooking the village was built in the 15C and restored in the late 19C.

The apartments, occupied for a period by Queen Juana the Mad and her son, the future Emperor Charles V, have been furnished with Spanish period furniture; *(apply to the porter: open only on the 10th, 20th and 30th of each month 10am to 2pm and 4 to 7pm; 3 to 6pm in winter; 50pts).*

TOLEDO★★★

Illescas. — *33km - 21 miles. Leave by ① on the plan.* In the La Caridad Convent Church are five El Greco **paintings★** including in the north and south transepts, a portrait of St Ildefonsus writing at the dictation of the Virgin and the Virgin of Charity; in the sacristy *(temporarily closed)* are an Annunciation, Nativity and Coronation of the Virgin.

The splendid Mudejar tower that you can see, is on the parish church.

Tembleque. — *56km - 35 miles. Leave by ③ on the plan.* The 17C **Plaza Mayor★**, at the heart of this uniformly white village is a very large quadrilateral, framed by a graceful three storey portico in which the lowest arches are of stone, the upper of wood. An unusual cobweb style roof crowns one of the square's entrances which was certainly once used as a bullring.

UCLÉS Monastery (Cuenca)

Michelin map ₄₄₄ folds 14 and 15 — Pop 501

Uclés Monastery stands massive and golden, crowning a fortified mound overlooking the village. *Apply at the* porteria *or porter's lodge.*

Although construction began in the early 16C in the Renaissance Plateresque style, the monastery is reminiscent, on a reduced scale, of the Escorial since the architect of all its major features was **Francisco de Mora** (1560-1610) Herrera's only disciple. Two successful baroque sculptures are immediately evident: the courtyard fountain and the main gate where the pediment decoration recalls that from 1174 to 1499 Uclés belonged to the Order of Santiago.

The ramparts command an extensive panorama.

VALDEPEÑAS (Ciudad Real)

Michelin map ₄₄₄ folds 22 and 23 — Pop 24 946

Valdepeñas, which stands at the southern tip of the vast wine growing area of La Mancha, produces a good light table wine.

The town is a stopping place on the Madrid-Andalusia road, its life and activity centring particularly on the **Plaza de España,** where colour washed houses rise above a shady portico. In complete contrast, on one side, stands the Late Gothic façade of the Church of the **Assumption (Asunción),** with a harmonious tower, a Plateresque upper gallery and inside, an early 17C altarpiece combining sculpture and painted panels.

The Invencible Cooperative winestore *(102 Calle Raimundo Caro Patón)* which processes the grapes of 900 cultivators and is the town's largest **winery,** is open to visitors. Production amounts to 240 000 hectolitres — 5.28 million gallons — of which 70% is white wine. The picturesque old terracotta vessels of last century are being replaced by 5m high - 16ft — concrete vats capable of containing 16 000 litres - 5 500 gallons.

The Victory Monument hill north of the town makes a good lookout over the vine covered plain.

EXCURSIONS

Las Virtudes. — *24km - 15 miles south. Turn left after Santa Cruz de Mudela.* The village claims that its bullring is the oldest in Spain (1641). It is square and is blocked along one side by the wall of the 14C Sanctuary of Our Lady of Holy Virtue which inside has a Mudejar ceiling over the nave and a Churrigueresque altarpiece.

San Carlos del Valle★. — *22km - 14 miles.* The small village of San Carlos has a delightful 18C **Plaza Mayor★** in which, amidst the colourful brick houses, a former hospice, no 5, has a stone entrance and a typical *patio (if closed apply at the police station).*

Overlooking all is the baroque village church, crowned importantly by a dome and four lantern turrets.

10 Castile and León — La Rioja

This region comprises Castile (the provinces of Ávila, Burgos, Segovia, Soria, Palencia and Valladolid), León (provinces of León, Zamora and Salamanca) and the province of La Rioja, which are linked geographically and historically.

The landscape. — Castile and León-La Rioja correspond, except in the northeast, with the area of the Duero Basin. This is centred 1 000m - 3 280ft up on the northern Meseta, a plateau ringed by the **León Mountains,** part of the Galician Hercynian range, to the northwest, by the **Cantabrian Cordillera** upraised by the Alpine folding and which exceeds 2 500m - 8 200ft in the Picos de Europa to the north, by the **Iberian Cordillera,** the same formation and though less high still rising to 2 000m - 6 560ft in the Demanda and Urbión Sierras to the east and, finally, by the **Central Cordillera** (Guadarrama, Gredos and Peña de Francia Sierras) to the southeast. The forested mountain slopes, cut by leaping torrents, make a landscape of ravines and lakes.

The Meseta's Tertiary sediment resists erosion in different ways so that the region includes wide valleys descending in tiers punctuated with rock spikes, narrow defiles, gently undulating hills. These variations notwithstanding the aspect is of a sparsely populated plateau with only occasional villages breaking the infinite horizons *(illustration p 7)*.

Cereals provide the agricultural mainstay; wheat between the Pisuerga and Cea Rivers, in the **Tierra de Campos** with its red brick villages, wheat and rye elsewhere for cattlefeed. Only the southwest peneplains are used to graze livestock — sheep on smaller holdings, fighting bulls on ranges of up to 500ha - 1 235 acres.

The Reconquest consolidated. — The small kingdom of the Asturias was the first to resist the Muslim advance of the 8C; from there resistance spread south. In the 10C León became the capital of the free Christian area, known as the Kingdom of León and extending to the River Duero. It was at this time that the Upper Ebro Valley, an area coveted equally by the Moors and the Kingdom of Navarre and, therefore, bristling with fortresses *(castillos)* declared its independence and established itself as a separate entity, the County of Castile *(p 233)*.

Sovereignty was shortlived, however, for in 1037 a single ruler united the adjoining kingdoms *(p 228)* and from 1230 they were linked permanently. The Christian advance, after having fortified their lines along the Duero, crossed the Central Cordillera and reached the Tagus (capture of Toledo : 1085), consolidating the reconquered territory by erecting first one *(p 247)* and then a second *(p 225)* line of fortifications from which the region was given the name of "land of castle" or Castile.

Gastronomy. — Castilian specialities are : roast lamb *(cordero asado)* and suckling pig roasted on a spit *(cochinillo tostón* or *tostado),* fresh ewes' milk cheese (in Burgos) and the traditional *cocido* or chick pea hotpot.

La Rioja is known for its wine *(p 238)*.

ÁGREDA (Soria)

Michelin map 𝟒𝟒𝟐 fold 18 — Pop 3 638

Ágreda was a strongpoint on the Castile-Aragon frontier. To the south lie the **Moncayo Mountains** (2 313m - 7 587ft maximum).

Sister María de Ágreda, confidant and religious adviser to the politically weak but art loving Philip IV (1621-1665), founded the Convent of the Conception in the town.

St Michael's. — The church, rebuilt in the 15C, has a crenellated Romanesque tower and inside, a Renaissance retable of painted panels which, with traces of the Mannerist style, depict scenes of the Passion, of Genesis and the life of St Michael.

AGUILAR DE CAMPOO (Palencia)

Michelin map 𝟒𝟒𝟐 south of fold 4 — Pop 6 883

The landscape in this region at the northern edge of the Meseta is broken by limestone escarpments thrust up by the folding which formed the Cantabrian Cordillera. It is from its position on one of these high outcrops that Aguilar **castle** has withstood time as it looks down on the old town which still possesses rampart gateways with pointed arches, in some cases surmounted by a carved figure or crest, and mansions emblasoned with coats of arms.

Sta María la Real Monastery. — *On the edge of the town towards Cervera de Pisuerga.* The transitional Romanesque Gothic building is known for the historiated capitals in its church and for its cloister and chapterhouse. *Under restoration, however, open for visits 10am (11am Sundays) to 2pm and 4 to 8pm (6pm Saturdays and Sundays).*

St Michael's Collegiate Church. — The church at the end of the long, porticoed, Plaza de España, shelters within its vast Gothic aisles two fine mausoleums : the first, 16C of the Marquesses of Aguilar praying, the second, in the north apsidal, carved in a surprisingly realistic manner, of the archpriest García González.

EXCURSIONS

Aguilar Reservoir. — *2.5km - 1 1/2 miles west.* Summer water sports centre.

Olleros. — *6km - 4 miles south along the Palencia road.* Santos Justo y Pastor Church *(apply at the bar: 25pts)* was hollowed out of the cliff face in Romanesque times.

ALBA DE TORMES (Salamanca)

Michelin map 🔲🔲 fold 38 or 🔲🔲 fold 5 — Pop 4 106

Only the massive keep still stands of the proud castle of the Dukes of Alba in this once famous mediaeval town which boasts of possessing the mortal remains of St Teresa of Ávila who died in 1582 in the Carmelite Convent she had founded.

Turn left immediately after the bridge over the Tormes and climb to the square; on the left is St John's, on the right an alley down to the Carmelite Convent.

Carmelite Convent Church. — The body of St Teresa of Jesus or of Ávila, is now enshrined in the high altar; a chapel to the left contains funerary stones from successive tombs of the saint. On one of the stones is carved Teresa's reply when asked if she wished to return to Ávila to die: "Have you no place here for me?" At the end of the church, through a grille, can be seen a reconstitution of the cell in which the indefatigable woman died in 1582.

St John's. — In the Romanesque Mudejar central apse built of brick, stands an unusual 11C sculpture★, taken from an even older altarpiece, which shows Christ and the Disciples, all equally noble in expression and stance.

The times indicated in this guide

when given with the distance allow one to enjoy the scenery

when given for sightseeing are intended to give an idea of

the possible length or brevity of a visit.

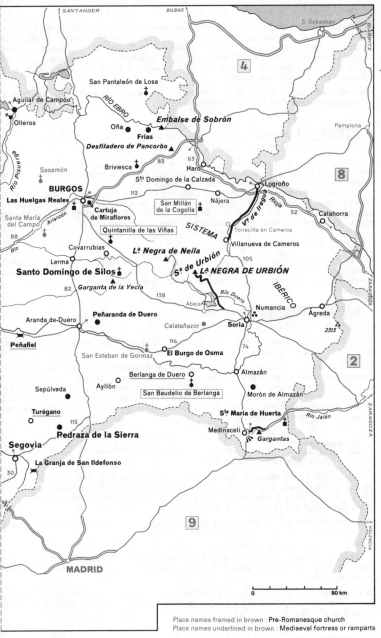

Place names framed in brown : **Pre-Romanesque church**
Place names underlined in brown : **Mediaeval fortress or ramparts**

La ALBERCA ★★ (Salamanca)

Michelin map 𝟒𝟒𝟭 fold 37 — Pop 1 357

La Alberca lies at the heart of the Sierra de la Peña de Francia, at the end of a crystalline chain which divides the Meseta in two. This region, full of character, is an isolated one, traversed by few roads, fewer still of which are surfaced.

This village, in particular, has kept its charm: it has houses built of stone up to first floor level surmounted by overhanging half-timbered upper storeys; twisting streets lead to the Plaza Pública. On Sundays everyone still foregathers upon it, the village elders in white gaiters, black trousers and waistcoats and shirts secured at the neck with a gold buckle. Traditional also in this fervent community, are the celebrations accompanied by songs and age-old dances on 15 August, the Assumption, and the day after, by the performance of the ancient mystery play or "Loa" relating the triumph of the Virgin in face of the devil. Some of the costumes are very old and intricately embroidered.

There is a carved and coloured granite pulpit of the Evangelists in the church.

EXCURSIONS

Peña de Francia★★. — *15km - 9 miles west.* The Peña, a shale spike of 1 732m - 5 682ft and the highest peak in the range can be distinguished easily from a considerable distance. The final section of the approach road is spectacular as cutting through the green rock, it circles the point, affording wide **panoramas★★** of the Hurdes Mountains to the south, the heights of Portugal to the west, the Castilian plain as far as Salamanca to the north and the Sierra de Gredos to the east. There is a Dominican monastery with a dependent hostelry at the summit *(occupied in summer only).*

La ALBERCA★★

Las Batuecas Road★. — The road climbs imperceptibly to the Portillo Pass (1 240m - 4 067ft) *(2km - 1 mile south)* before plunging by means of 12km - 7 miles of serpentine bends into a deep, green valley. It continues, beyond Las Mestas, to the desolate and long isolated **Las Hurdes** region of Extremadura, setting for Buñuel's early film, *Land without Bread* (1932). With new schools, improvement in cereal growing and extensive olive tree planting, the area is being transformed rapidly.

Miranda del Castañar. — *15km - 9 miles east*. The village of narrow alleys has houses with widespread eaves and flower-filled balconies.

ALMAZÁN (Soria)
Michelin map **442** fold 27 — Pop 5 657

The small town, on a height dating back to the Romans, was a renowned fortress which suffered harsh vicissitudes during the Reconquest and still worse, became a prize in the long Castile — Aragon struggle. It retains three fortified gateways.

The late 12C Romanesque **San Miguel Church** on the Plaza Mayor has a Cordoban style **dome★** on squinches and a stone altarfront, illustrating the martyrdom of Thomas of Canterbury. Also on the square is the Classical façade of the 16-17C **Palace of the Counts of Altamira** which, at the back, overlooks the Duero from an elegantly arcaded gallery.

EXCURSION

Morón de Almazán. — *14km - 9 miles southeast*. The Plaza Mayor buildings are dignified by delicate Plateresque decoration, the church tower given elegance by grotesques and finials outlining each tier and in the centre of the square stands a pillory.

ARANDA DE DUERO (Burgos)
Michelin map **442** fold 25 — Pop 27 598

Aranda, a major road and rail junction, rivals Sepúlveda, as the home of the best roast lamb *(cordero asado)* in Castile and León.

Santa María. — The church founded by the Catholic Monarchs at the end of the 15C has a typically Isabeline **façade★** with, above the portal covings, three high reliefs of the Passion on a pediment scattered with crests, roses and the *flechas* crossed with a yoke which was the founders' emblem. A crowning cornice in the style of the Burgos school completes the front. The slightly later carved door panels are in poor condition but Christ's entry into Jerusalem can still be distinguished *(top left)*.

ARÉVALO (Ávila)
Michelin map **447** fold 6 — Pop 6 748

Approaching from the north, the first thing you see is the 14C **castle** with its massive, crenellated keep. It was in this fortress that Isabel the Catholic, who was born in 1451 only 24km - 15 miles away in the Madrigal de las Altas Torres (to the west), spent her childhood. At the right of the fortress wall sections still edge the precipice.

Monumental centre. — The **Alcocer Arch,** a vaulted gate superimposed by an old brick house, opens the way to the quiet, porticoed Plaza Real.
Cross the square and take the street opposite the arch.

This street is straddled by the belfry of **Santa María Church** which has a Mudejar east end. The west front overlooks the **Plaza de la Villa★,** a typical main square and one of the best preserved in Castile.

La Lugareja. — *2km - 1 mile south along the Nava de Arévalo Road*. The unusual Mudejar church with sweeping lines and a complicated blind arcade brickwork decoration stands isolated on a knoll.

ASTORGA (León)
Michelin map **441** fold 17 — Pop 14 040

In Roman times, Asturica Augusta was a major road junction; in the Middle Ages Astorga was famous for its fairs and as a halt on the way to Santiago de Compostela.

Gourmands of every age have relished its *mantecadas* or rolls and its bread which is said "to bulk large in the hand and light on the stomach".

Maragatos Country. — Long ago an ethnic group of unknown origin but possibly of mixed Gothic-Moorish blood, settled in the Astorga area. These Maragatos lived for centuries in the heart of the inhospitable mountain region becoming known as muleteers and characterised as taciturn but honest. They may still be seen occasionally at a religious festival or wedding in their national costume of voluminous black knee breeches, embroidered shirt front and round felt hat and the women in short skirts and slashed sleeves. Jacks in full Maragato dress can be seen striking the hours on the town hall clock on the Plaza Mayor.

Cathedral★. — The church, begun at the very end of the Gothic period (note the forest of buttresses at the east end), progressed towards a highly involved Renaissance style, particularly in the façade which was erected in the 17C; and where the porch low reliefs illustrate specific actions by Christ such as the Expulsion of the Moneylenders from the Temple, the Pardoning of the Adulterous Woman... Above the door is a beautiful Deposition carved in rose limestone.

The nave is large, with upsweeping lines from ribs from the innumerable slender, engaged columns which surround the pillars. Behind the high altar is a 16C **retable★** by three artists named Gaspar — respectively a painter : Gaspar de Hoyos, a sculptor : Gaspar de Palencia and a sculptor in relief : **Gaspar Becerra** (1520-1570), an Andalusian, who after studying in Renaissance Italy, evolved a personal style of humanist sensitivity far removed from the baroque expressionism of the Spanish sculptors.

Diocesan Museum★. — *Open 10am to 2pm and 4 to 8pm; 11am to 2pm and 3.30 to 6.30pm in winter; closed January and February; 125pts, 200pts including admission to the Museum of the Ways to Santiago de Compostela.*

The museum is rich in 11-13C Romanesque statues of the Virgin and in church plate, including a 13C gold filigree Holy Cross Reliquary and a 10C casket.

Episcopal Palace. — This fantastic pastiche of a mediaeval palace was dreamed up by Antonio Gaudí *(p 84)* in 1889. A brilliant interior decoration embellishes several floors which are otherwise taken up with a **Museum of the Ways to Santiago de Compostela** (Museo de los Caminos - *open 10am to 2pm and 4 to 8pm; 11am to 2pm and 3.30 to 6.30pm in winter; closed Mondays in winter; 125pts, 200pts including admission to the Diocesan Museum).* On the ground floor among the mediaeval art with the common theme of the pilgrimage are a 13C equestrian statue of St James in wood and other wood sculptures, painted panels (life of St Martin of Tours) and figures in mediaeval pilgrim costume.

ÁVILA ★★ P

Michelin map **447** fold 6 — Pop 41 735

Ávila, at 1 131m - 3 710ft Spain's highest provincial capital, is situated on one of the plateaux of the Meseta. The Castilian climate at such an altitude is extreme — winters are long and snowy, winds bitingly cold (average temperature in May: 12 ºC - 53 ºF).

"Ávila de los Caballeros". — After the reconquest of Toledo in 1085, Alfonso VI established a **second line of fortifications** south of the Duero *(p 221)* comprising Segovia, Ávila and Salamanca, which he peopled with Christians from Asturias. The Knights of Ávila, hence the town's original name, gained renown as they joined in the recapture of Saragossa in the 12C and Córdoba, Jaén and Seville in the 13C. Ávila itself reached its zenith in the 15C but by the next century had begun to decline as the nobility left to join the imperial court of Charles V at Toledo. The city was at its lowest ebb, when the expulsion of the Muslims in 1609 brought a loss of craftsmen and merchants and its population fell to 2 000. Life ossified for centuries — only relatively recently has the city spread beyond its mediaeval perimeter and even now it remains a traditional centre of Castile and León, living, for the most part, off craftsmanship (woollen blankets and *yemas* or egg yolk sweetmeats).

■ **MAIN SIGHTS** *time: 3 hours*

Follow the route marked on the plan below.

The walls★★. — The walls are complete. They dominate the landscape from afar — particularly from the west, where they overlook the River Adaja and from the Salamanca road, from the spot known as the Cuatro Postes (Four Posts). They are altogether, both physically and atmospherically, one of the most vivid examples extant of mediaeval fortifications: they are battlemented (2 500 embrasures), average 10m in height - 33ft and are punctuated by 88 advanced bastions and towers, including 8 gateways; they enclose an equilateral hexagon of 900m x 450m - 2 953ft x 1 476ft. The greater part dates from the 11C although modifications were made in the 14C.

The sentry path is open.

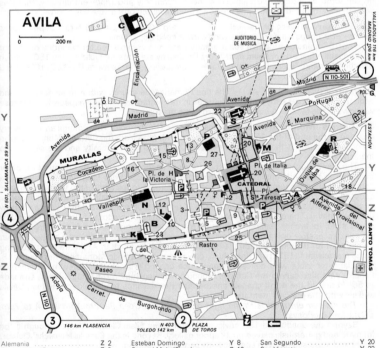

ÁVILA★★

Cathedral★★(Y). — The use of granite in the building's construction, the fortified appearance and inclusion of the **east end**★ as an advanced bastion in the ramparts, even though crowned with a double row of battlements, give the **exterior** an austere appearance which window tracery, a ball decoration along the upper outlines of the tower, buttresses and pinnacles and even portal carvings, do little to mellow.

The 14C north doorway with French Gothic decoration, unfortunately in stone too friable to resist erosion, originally stood in the west front but was removed in the 15C by Juan Guas when he redesigned the main entrance which was curiously remodelled once more in the 18C.

The **interior** is a total contrast to the exterior, the nave having a Gothic elevation, the stone piebald patches of red and yellow and the **works of art★★** everywhere: the **trascoro** (1531) has many beautifully detailed Plateresque statues which blend into a harmonious unit; the **choirstalls** are of the same period; two delicately worked wrought iron **pulpits** — one Renaissance, the other still Gothic but with infillings obviously influenced by Granada stucco.

At the end of the apse, in which the windows are still Romanesque — the cathedral's construction lasted from 1135 to the 14C — is a painted **altarpiece** by Pedro Berruguete and Juan de Borgoña dating from about 1500 with a gilded surround and Italian Renaissance style pilasters. The back and sides of the high altar which face onto the double **ambulatory** are inlaid with five Renaissance sculptured panels: those on the sides show the evangelists and four holy knights (Hubert, George, Martin and James). At the ambulatory centre is the monumental alabaster **tomb★★** of Cardinal Alonso de Madrigal, 15C Bishop of Ávila, nick-named **El Tostado** on account of his dusky complexion, ornamented with the sculptured masterpiece by Vasco de Zarza, of the bishop, a theologian and an abundant writer, writing before a beautiful epiphany.

Museum. — *Open 9am (11am Sundays and holidays) to 1pm and 3 to 7pm (5pm in winter); 50pts, free Mondays.*

Preceding the museum are an **ante sacristy** and a **sacristy★★** (both 13C) which has a remarkable eight rib vaulting, contains a massive 16C alabaster altarpiece and, in place of windows, sculptures in wood in imitation of alabaster of the four scenes of the Passion. In the museum are a head of Christ by Morales, a portrait by El Greco, a monumental Isabeline grille, late 15C antiphonaries and a colossal monstrance 1.70m - 5ft 8 ins high made by Juan de Arfe in 1571.

Valderrábanos Palace (YZ F). — On the cathedral square the former nobleman's residence, now a hotel, has a fine 15C doorway surmounted by the family crest.

St Vincent's Basilica★★ (**San Vicente**) (Y S). — Open 10am to 1pm and 3 to 6pm; 25pts. Access by the south façade. The vast Romanesque basilica, which took from the 12 to 14C to construct, and, therefore, has ogive vaulting, stands on the alleged site of the 4C martyrdom of St Vincent of Saragossa and his sisters, Sabina and Cristeta (an alternative account sites the saint's death in Valencia).

The 14C south gallery with slender columns clustered and ringed, the carved cornice extending the full length of the nave, the tall porch added to the west front and the two incomplete towers, though apparently disparate, yet combine into a harmonious whole. The **west portal★★** is outstanding for the statue columns beneath the richly decorative cornice and covings which seem so lifelike that they might almost be gossiping at the church entrance.

Inside, beneath the 14C **lantern tower**★ is the martyr's **tomb★★,** a late 12C masterpiece under a strange 15C Gothic baldachin with a pagoda shaped canopy. The saint's martyrdom on the tomb is depicted so masterfully, both technically and representationally, that it is sometimes attributed to the same unknown mediaeval sculptor as the west portal.

The Deanery (Casa de los Deanes) (Y M). — *Open 10am to 2pm and 5 to 7.30pm; closed Sunday afternoons, all day Mondays and certain holidays; 200pts.*

The 16C mansion around a sober granite *patio* was constructed for cathedral deans but now houses a fine arts **museum** *(first floor).* On display are large **triptych**★ by the 15C Flemish painter, Memling, Spanish furniture (tables, *bargueños*) and Talavera (17-18C; *p 213)* and Manises ceramics *(p 175).*

St Peter's (San Pedro) (YZ A). — The fine Romanesque church with a triple east end and wide transept shows early Gothic influences in its pointed arching and especially in the rose windows in the façade. A beautiful lantern lights the transept.

St Thomas' Monastery★ (**Santo Tomás**) (Z). — *Off the plan.* The Dominican monastery founded at the end of the 15C and embellished with gifts from the Catholic Monarchs, who on occasion made it their summer residence, was also the university and the seat of the Inquisition.

The **church** façade incorporates the principal decorative motifs to be found on other buildings in the unit: architectural details are emphasised with long lines of balls — a common feature throughout Ávila but here used almost to excess — the yoke and arrows adopted by Ferdinand and Isabel as their emblem since the initials of the Spanish words, *yugo* and *flechas*, recalled their own initials (Y was used in mediaeval times where we now use the initial I). The church, in accordance with Dominican custom of the time, has only a single aisle, its arches resting on clusters of slender columns. A rare feature are the two galleries accessible only from the cloister — therefore, only the monks have access — that on the west for the choir, that on the east containing the high altar. At the transept crossing is the **mausoleum**★ (1512) of Prince Juan, only son of the Catholic Monarchs who died at 19. The alabaster table with delicate Renaissance carving was by the Florentine, Domenico Fancelli who also carved the Catholic Monarchs' mausoleum in the Chapel Royal, Granada *(p 50).* In one of the north chapels another fine Renaissance tomb belongs to Juan Dávila and his wife, the prince's mentors.

The cloister entrance is to the right of the church. Open 9am to 1pm and 4 to 7pm; 50pts, free Mondays.

Beyond the unadorned 15C novices' cloister is the **Silent Cloister**★, small enough to be intimate and generously carved on its upper gallery. Beyond is the **Catholic Monarchs' Cloister**, larger and more solemn with spectacularly bare upper arching.

From the Silent Cloister, stairs lead to the choral gallery containing beautiful 15C Gothic **choirstalls**★ carved with pierced canopies and arabesques; from the same cloister's upper gallery, more stairs go to the high altar gallery where one can see in detail Berruguete's masterpiece in high relief, the **St Thomas Aquinas retable★★** (c1495).

■ THE ÁVILA OF ST TERESA *time: 3/4 hour*

Ávila was the birthplace of St Teresa of Jesus (1515-1582), one of the greatest mystics of the Catholic Church (her visions greatly affected her contemporaries) and an indefatigable protagonist for reform. Living at a time when the Reformation was gaining adherents throughout Western and Central Europe and the monastic orders, grown rich in power and possessions, were relaxing their discipline, she succeeded in widely reestablishing the strict observance of the Carmelites, gaining converts and founding 17 convents herself. Her letters are famous, particularly those to her spiritual director, **St John of the Cross** (1542-1591), as are her mystical writings and her autobiography. She was canonised in 1622 and made a Doctor of the Church in 1970.

Convent of St Teresa (La Santa) (Z B). — *Open 8am to 1.15pm and 3.30 to 8.30pm.* Adjoining the convent church, built in the 17C on land once owned by her parents, is a profusely ornate baroque chapel erected on the site of the bedroom in which Teresa was born *(access: north transept).*

Convent of La Encarnación (Y C) — *Open 9.30am to 1pm and 4 to 7pm (3.30 to 6pm 1 November to 31 March); closed Tuesdays; 35pts.* The saint entered the convent and remained there 20 years before beginning her reforms.

Convent of San José (Las Madres) (Y R). — This was Teresa's first foundation (1562). The Guillamas Chapel on the north side of the church (1610) contains founders' **tombs★**. A small **museum** *(open 10am to 1pm and 4 to 8pm; 10pts)* houses mementoes of the saint.

■ ADDITIONAL SIGHTS

Polentinos Palace (YZ N). — 1535. The building, now a barracks, has a fine Renaissance decorated entrance and *patio.*

St Secundus Hermitage (Ermita de San Segundo) (Y E). — The Romanesque chapel was built at the foot of the ramparts on the discovery of what were taken to be the mortal remains of St Secundus, disciple of St Peter. The **statue★** of Secundus, first Bishop of Ávila, at prayer, is by Juan de Juni (1572).

Verdugos Palace (Y P). — The Gothic Renaissance palace front, emblasoned above the entrance and window with the family crest, is flanked by two stout square towers.

Núñez Vela Palace (Z K). — The Renaissance palace's features include windows framed by slender columns surmounted by blasons on the façade and a beautiful inner *patio.*

Guzmán Tower (Z L). — The Oñates' palace is distinguished by a massive early 16C corner tower complete with battlements.

AYLLÓN (Segovia)
Michelin map 442 fold 26 — Pop 1 497

Ayllón has retained a section of its ancient ramparts on its south side. Through the gateway is the **Palace of Juan de Contreras** (1497) with a fine Plateresque **entrance★** edged with a Franciscan cord motif. The main square, surrounded on all sides by shady arcades and sculptures or emblasoned gateways, adds considerable style to the village.

BÉJAR (Salamanca)
Michelin map 447 fold 13 — Pop 17 008

Béjar's impregnable **site** is seen to best advantage when you approach the small town (sheets and woollen fabrics) from the northwest: at the feet of the perpetually snow covered Sierra de Béjar, buildings straggle out along a narrow rock platform, formerly defended at the promontory's south end by the ramparts which now only encircle a picturesque old quarter.

EXCURSION

Candelario★. — *4km - 2 1/2 miles south.* Candelario is perhaps a more self-conscious village than many in the mountains, but it is picturesque. The white washed houses with revealed grey stone window surrounds and ties, have flower filled upper galleries of wood beneath spread eaves. The unevenly paved, steep alleys become rushing torrents when the mountain snows melt. On Sundays some women still wear the local costume with its voluminous black velvet skirt and finely embroidered blouse, black shawl edged with green and small headdress perched on top of a curious hairstyle, known as *de zapatilla.*

BENAVENTE (Zamora)
Michelin map 441 fold 28 — Pop 12 509

The town, once the seat of local counts and always well placed at the junction of roads to León and Galicia, was properous in the Middle Ages as is shown by the suffixes to the names of its two principal churches — *Azogue,* a corruption of the Arabic *souk,* the other *Mercado,* and both meaning market. **Pimentel Palace** (now a *parador),* a proud example of restored Renaissance architecture (it was completely burned down except for its tower by Napoleon's army), still commands the fertile Elsa Valley. It has preserved an upstanding 16C Caracol or Snail-shell Tower, quartered by round turrets. From the terrace are views of the valley.

Santa María del Azogue. — The church has a Romanesque exterior and a wide east end with five stepped apses and two side doors decorated in the local style *(p 254).* The interior is Gothic with 13C sculptures illustrating, on the back of the south door, God the Father and Christ Crucified and at the crossing, the Annunciation.

San Juan del Mercado. — The 12C carving in the south portal is an outstanding unit, in particular the tympanum and inner coving which illustrate the voyage of the Magi.

BERLANGA DE DUERO (Soria)
Michelin map 990 fold 27 — Pop 1 565

Berlanga still appears protected in mediaeval fashion with stout ramparts reinforced by advanced bastions below the massive walls of its castle — the town was a Duero strongpoint (p 247). In the monumental 16C **hall church** are two chapels containing Flamboyantly carved and painted altarpieces and two 16C recumbent alabaster statues.

EXCURSION

San Baudelio de Berlanga. — 8km - 5 miles southeast in the village of Casillas.
The small, isolated 11C Mozarabic chapel is highly original: at the centre of the square nave is a massive pillar on which descend the eight flat ribs which support the roof. The gallery on a double line of horseshoe shaped arches, was covered, like the rest of the building, in the 12C with frescoes.

BRIVIESCA (Burgos)
Michelin map 990 fold 16 — Pop 4 855

Briviesca, whose claim to fame is that in 1388 the Cortes here created the title of Prince of the Asturias for the heir apparent to the throne, is a quiet town. It lies at the centre of a narrow plain, on the banks of the River Oca producing traditional praline sweetmeats.

Santa Clara*. — The exceptionally light 16C chapel, tall and elegantly designed as a polygon beneath Gothic vaulting has two acceding bays which give it an overall cruciform plan. The great 1568 **altarpiece*** of wood is baroque at its most extreme.

EL BURGO DE OSMA * (Soria)
Michelin map 990 fold 26 — Pop 4 946

Approaching from the west you can see the tall baroque tower of El Burgo cathedral. The town is 18C with porticoed streets and squares and elegant baroque institutional buildings such as the San Agustín Hospital on the Plaza Mayor.

Cathedral*. — Open 10am to 1pm and 4 to 7pm (3.30 to 6pm in winter); 100pts. The Gothic sanctuary arose in 1232 as a result of a vow by the Cluniac monk, Don Pedro de Osma, to replace the former Romanesque cathedral which had stood on the site. The east end, transept and chapterhouse were completed in the 13C; the Late Gothic cloister and the chancel, embellished with Renaissance decoration, in the 16C; ambulatory chapels were remodelled and the 72m - 236ft tall belfry erected in the 18C.
The Gothic decoration in the late 13C **south portal** includes in the splaying, statues of (left to right) Moses, Gabriel, the Virgin, Judith, Solomon and Esther; on the lintel a Dormition and on the pier, Christ displaying his wounds (late 15C). The interior is remarkable for the elevation of the nave, the finely wrought ironwork **screens** (16C) by Juan Francés, the **retable** of the Virgin by Juan de Juni at the high altar and 16C white marble **pulpit** and **trascoro** altarpiece.
Apply to the archivist to see the other treasures. These include the 13C **tomb of San Pedro de Osma***, an 11C Crucifix with the figure covered with buffalo hide, and the **chapterhouse**. In the museum among the **archives** and illuminated **manuscripts*** are a rich 1086 Beatus Apocalypse (p 97) and a 12C manuscript with the signs of the Zodiac.

BURGOS *** P
Michelin map 990 fold 15 — Pop 156 449

Burgos province, sometimes known as the Shield of Castile, is the largest in the old kingdom; Burgos city stands in a shallow river valley at the centre of a 900m - 2 952ft high windswept plateau. Nevertheless, the malicious saying that summer begins in the city on Santiago's Day — 25 July — and ends on Santa Ana's — 26 July — is a bit exaggerated! The Río Arlanzón flows through the city, its banks lined with avenues and gardens; the slender, openwork cathedral spires rise high into the sky.

"Caput Castellae". — Burgos, repeatedly, devastated in its early years, was founded anew by Diego Porcelos, a Castilian count in the 9C; within 50 years, in 951, it was selected by Fernán González as capital of the then County of Castile (p 233). González' descendants remained faithful to the city which grew in importance with the county's emerging power; a still more glorious prospect opened when in 1037 Ferdinand I united under one crown Castile, León and the Asturias and the new kingdom began to win the series of victories against the Muslims which eventually won back Madrid (1083) and Toledo (1085). At the same time it grew rich on tribute from Moorish princelings.

El Cid's country (1026-1099). — The exploits of Rodrigo Díaz, native of Vivar (9km - 6 miles from Burgos) light up the late 11C history of Castile. The brilliant captain first supported the ambitious King of Castile, Sancho II, then Alfonso VI who succeeded his brother in somewhat dubious circumstances. Alfonso, irritated at Díaz' suspicions and jealous of his prestige following an attack on the Moors in 1081, banished the warrior hero although he was, by then, married to the king's cousin, Ximena. Diáz, as a soldier of fortune, entered service first with the Moorish king of Saragossa and subsequently fought Christian and Muslim armies with equal fervour. His most famous enterprise came when at the head of 7 000 men, chiefly Muslims, he captured Valencia after a nine month siege in 1094. He was finally defeated by the Moors in an exploit at Cuenca and died soon afterwards (1099). His widow held Valencia against the Muslims until 1102 when she set fire to the city before returning to Castile with the Cid's body which was buried first in the Monastery of San Pedro de Cardeña (10km - 6 1/2 miles east of Burgos) before finally being interred in the cathedral in 1921. Legend has transformed the stalwart but often ruthless 11C warrior, the Campeador or Champion of Castile, El Cid (Seid in Arabic), into a chivalrous knight of exceptional valour. The first epic poem **El Cantar del Mío Cid** appeared in 1180 and was followed by ballads and dramas. In 1618 Guillén de Castro wrote a romanticised version of Cid in his **Las Mocedades del Cid** upon which Corneille, in 1636, based his drama Le Cid.

The Gothic city. — In 1492 Burgos relinquished its title as capital to Valladolid but the loss of political involvement appears to have released energy for commercial and artistic enterprises: the town became a wool centre for the sheep farmers of the Mesta *(p 247)*; fleeces were sent for export to Santander and Laredo; architects and sculptors arrived, particularly from the north, and transformed monuments into the currently fashionable Gothic style until plague, floods and other catastrophes, at the end of 16C, followed by the decline of the Mesta, halted everything. In the War of Independence, Burgos regained importance as a French stronghold which successfully resisted a disastrous siege by Wellington in October 1812 only to be blown up by King Joseph as he retreated north in June 1813.

The founding city of the Movimiento Nacional (1936-1939). — It was in Burgos that the Movimiento Nacional set up a provisional government in 1936 against the Republican Government; in Burgos again that General Franco was proclaimed head of government and commander-in-chief of the armed forces in revolt and from La Isla Palace that he proclaimed the ceasefire on 1 April 1939.

■ **CATHEDRAL★★★** (AY) *tour: about 1 1/2 hours*

The cathedral, the third largest in Spain after Seville and Toledo, is a remarkable example of the transformation of French and German Flamboyant Gothic into a style typically Spanish in the natural exuberance of its decoration. Inside, the works of art incline to make it a somewhat grandiose museum of Gothic sculpture, but there are wonderful features.

Ferdinand III laid the foundation stone in 1221 and there followed, under the aegis of Maurice the Englishman, then Bishop of Burgos and recently returned with drawings from France (at that time very much influenced by the Gothic style), the first of the cathedral's two principal building periods which, in the event, correspond with distinct periods in the Gothic style. In the 13C the nave, aisles and portals were designed and erected by local architects, influenced by their northern neighbours. The second period in the 15C saw the erection of the west front spires and the Constable's Chapel *(p 230)* and the decoration of other chapels, this time directly foreign influenced through architects and sculptors from Flanders, the Rhineland and Burgundy gathered round him by the great Burgos prelate, Alonso of Cartagena.

These artists from a Europe in which Flamboyant Gothic was beginning to grow sterile, found new inspiration in Mudejar arabesques and other important elements in Spanish art. **Felipe Bigarny,** the Fleming **Gil de Siloé,** the Rhinelander **Johan of Cologne** were the most outstanding of those gathered in the town: they acclimatised rapidly and with their sons and grandsons — Diego de Siloé, Simon of Cologne and Francisco de Colonia — created virtually a Burgos school of sculpture.

The cloister was erected in the 14C; the magnificent lantern over the transept was rebuilt by Juan de Vallejo in the mid- 16C.

Exterior. — Walking round the cathedral, one becomes aware of how the architects took advantage of the sloping ground (the cloister upper gallery is level with the cathedral pavement) to introduce delightful small precincts and closes cut by stairways.

West front (1). — The ornate upper area with its frieze depicting the kings from the Bible, balustrades and two openwork spires, pinnacled and crocketed, is the masterwork of Johan of Cologne.

Coronería Portal (2). — The statues at the jambs have the grace of their French Flamboyant Gothic originals, although the folds of their robes show more movement; the Plateresque **Pellejería Portal** (3) or Skinner's Door in the adjoining transept wall was designed by Francisco de Colonia early in the 16C.

Continuing round by the east end it becomes obvious that the Constable's Chapel with its ornate but finely balanced Isabeline decoration and lantern with a circlet of crocketed pinnacles is one of the cathedral's later, outstanding additions.

El Sarmental Portal (4). — The covings are filled with figures from the Celestial Court, while the tympanum is an incredible sculpture in which each of the four Evangelists sits in a different position as he writes at his desk.

Interior. — *Open 10am to 1.30pm and 4 to 7pm (6pm in winter); 150pts.* Note the transept door (5) with beautifully carved Gothic style panels.

Transept crossing, choirstalls and capilla mayor★★. — The splendid star ribbed lantern of the transept crossing rises on four massive columns to a height of 54m - 177ft above the funerary stones of El Cid and Ximena, inlaid in the crossing pavement.

The imposing unit (6) of 103 walnut choirstalls, carved between 1507 and 1512 by Felipe Bigarny, shows Biblical stories on the upper, back rows and mythological and burlesque scenes at the front. The handsome recumbent statue of wood plated with enamelled copper, on the tomb at the centre, dates from the 13C and is of Bishop Maurice. The *capilla mayor* (7) altarpiece is a 16C Renaissance work in high relief against an intrinsically Classical background of niches and pediments.

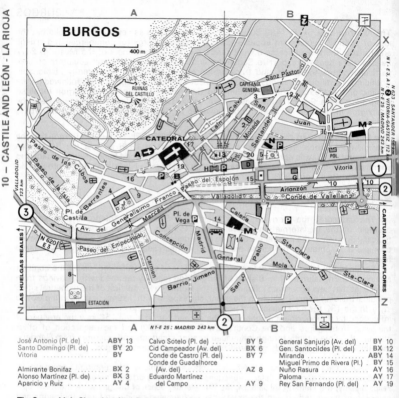

BURGOS

0   400 m

The Constable's Chapel ★★ (del Condestable) (8). — The Isabeline chapel founded by Hernández de Velasco, Constable of Castile, in 1482 and designed by Simon of Cologne, is lit by an octagonal cupola with lacework, star shaped vaulting surmounted by a lantern. All the great early Renaissance sculptors of Burgos cooperated in the subsequent decoration of the walls and altarpiece: at the centre, under their tomb, carved in Carrara marble, lie the constable and his wife and beside them an immense Granada marble funerary stone for the names of their descendants. On the chapel's right side is a Plateresque door to the **sacristy** (1512) (9) where there is a painting of *Mary Magdalene* by Leonardo da Vinci.

Ambulatory ★ (10). — The *trasaltar (p 16)*, carved partly by Felipe Bigarny, includes an extra-ordinarily expressive representation of the Ascent to Calvary.

The Coronería Staircase (11). — The Golden Staircase of pure Renaissance style, majestically proportioned was designed by Diego de Siloé in the early 16C: the twin pairs of flights which rise gradually and form a shallow diamond, are outlined by an ornately elegant gilded bannister by the French master ironsmith, Hilaire.

The chapels. — Every chapel is a museum of Gothic and Plateresque art: Gil de Siloé and Diego de la Cruz cooperated on the huge altarpiece in **St Anne's Chapel ★** (12) which, amidst heavy gilding, illustrates the saint's life and represents a Tree of Jesse with at the base, the Virgin and Child and at the centre the first meeting of Anne and Joachim. At the beginning of the cathedral nave, high up near the roof, is the **Papamoscas** or **Flycatcher Clock** (13), a popular 16C clock with a jack which opens its mouth on the striking of the hours. In the **Chapel of Holy Christ** (14) is a Crucifixion with the figure covered with buffalo hide to resemble human flesh — this example is particularly venerated. The **Chapel of the Presentation** (15) contains the tomb of the Bishop of Lerma *(p 236)*, carved by Felipe Bigarny and the **Chapel of the Visitation** (16), that of Alonso de Cartagena by Gil de Siloé.

Cloister. — *Entrance fee: 150pts.* The cloister erected in the 14C, presents a panorama of Burgos Gothic sculpture with stone, terracotta and polychrome wood figures crowding the galleries. *The Christ at the Column* by Diego de Siloé in the **sacristy** (17), is a supreme example of Spanish expressionism in post 16C Iberian sculpture.

The **chapterhouse** (18) displays, besides 15 and 16C Brussels tapestries of the theological and cardinal virtues, a 15C table with Toledo damascene work, a Van Eyck diptych, a Memling Virgin and Child and above, a Mudejar *artesonado* ceiling with ivory inlays.

St Catherine's Chapel (19) contains manuscripts and documents (the marriage contract of El Cid). Note the 15C carved and painted consoles showing Moorish kings paying homage to the King of Castile. The **St James Chapel** (20) contains church plate and liturgical objects.

■ ADDITIONAL SIGHTS

Burgos Museum ★ (BY M¹). — *Open 10am to 1pm and 5 to 7pm; closed Saturday, Sunday and holiday afternoons and all day Monday; 200pts.*

Prehistoric and Archaeological Department (Casa de Miranda). — Housed in a Renaissance mansion (elegant *patio*), this section contains finds discovered in the province covering the Prehistoric to Visigothic periods. Note the Roman funerary steles and the rooms devoted entirely to the Romain site of Clunia.

Fine Arts and Contemporary Art Department (Casa de Angulo). — *Under restoration.* Gothic and Renaissance funerary sculpture. On the **tomb ★** of **Juan de Padilla,** Gil de Siloé has beautifully rendered the countenance and robes of the defunct.

Also exhibited are two works of art from the Monastery at Silos: an 11C **Hispano-Moorish casket ★**, delicately carved in ivory in Cuenca and highlighted with enamel plaques and a 12C **altarfront ★** in beaten and enamelled copper. Equally notable are a 16C Flemish painting of *Christ Weeping* and a 15C gilded wood altarpiece from the Church of Mercy. . .

Santa María Arch★ (Arco de Santa María) (AY B). — The gateway defending a bridge of the same name and the city walls, dates from the 14C. In the 16C it was modified and embellished with statues of the famous: Diego Porcelos, flanked by two semi-legendary judges said to have governed Castile in the 10C, below, and Count Fernán González *(p 233)* with the Emperor Charles V and El Cid, above, (centre, left and right).

San Nicolás (AY A). — *Open daily 7 to 8.15pm; Mondays 9am to 9pm; Sundays and holidays 9am to 1.30pm and 5 to 6pm.* The **altarpiece** carved by Simon of Cologne in 1505, is both large and ornate with more than 465 figures in scenes, above, of the Virgin crowned at the centre of a circle of angels, St Nicholas surrounded by events from his life — note the voyage by caravel to Alexandria — and below, a back view of the Last Supper.

Casa del Cordón (BY N). — Presently under reconstruction and housing the Caja de Ahorros (savings bank), the palace of the Constables of Castile was built in the 15C. Still decorating its façade is the thick Franciscan cord motif which gave the palace its name. It is interesting historically as the place where Columbus was received by the Catholic Monarchs on his return from his second voyage to America and also where Philip the Fair died suddenly of a chill after a game of *pelota*, reducing to despair his already much disturbed wife, Juana the Mad.

Plaza José Antonio (ABY 13). — This delightful circular main square, typically lined by a portico, is the setting for all public festivities (Corpus Christi, *p 27*).

Marceliano Santa María Museum (BX M²). — *Open 10am to 2pm and 5 to 8pm; closed Sunday afternoons and all day Monday; 25pts.* The museum, built in the ruins of the former Benedictine Monastery of San Juan, displays 150 Impressionist type canvases by the Burgos painter Marceliano Santa María (1866-1952).

Las Huelgas Reales Convent★ (AY). — *1.5km - 1 mile west.* Las Huelgas Reales, originally a summer palace of the kings of Castile, was converted in 1180 into a convent by Alfonso VIII and his wife Eleanor, daughter of Henry II of England. The religious were Cistercians of high lineage; the abbess all powerful; by the 13C the convent's privilege, both spiritual and temporal, extended to more than 50 towns and it had become a common place of retreat for members of the house of Castile and even the royal pantheon.

Rearrangement over the centuries has resulted in a heterogeneous and somewhat divided building in which, although the Cistercian style of the 12 and 13C predominates, there are Romanesque and even Mudejar elements (13-15C) and Plateresque furnishings.

Guided tours (time: 1/2 hour) 11am to 2pm and 4 to 6pm; closed Sunday afternoons and all day Monday; for holidays inquire locally; 100pts.

Church. — The clean lines of the exterior are pure Cistercian. The interior is divided into two by a screen: from the transept, open to all, you can see 17C Beauvais **tapestries** in the central apse and the revolving **pulpit** (1560) in gilded ironwork which enabled the preacher to be heard on either side of the screen. Royal and princely tombs, rich with heraldic devices and historical legend, line the aisles, while at the centre of the nave, between 16C tapestries, and preceding the long line of choirstalls before the **roodscreen**, delicately carved and coloured in the Renaissance style and superimposed by a fine 13C Deposition, is the relatively plain double sepulchre of the founders, Alfonso VIII and Eleanor of England.

Gothic Cloister. — 13-15C. Enough fragments of Mudejar vaulting stucco remain to give an idea of the delicacy of the strapwork inspired by Persian ivories and fabrics.

Chapterhouse. — A trophy from the Battle of Las Navas de Tolosa *(p 31)* and 15C Flemish pictures hang in the historic chamber in which General Franco assembled his government for the first time and the Falange swore loyalty to the new regime.

Materials Museum★. — *Under restoration.* The tombs in the convent, especially that of the Infante Fernando de la Cerda, who died in 1275 (whose tomb was the only one not to be desecrated by French troops in 1809), contained precious fabrics, court dress and regalia, which as displayed, provide a vivid review of royal wear in 13C Castile.

Romanesque Cloister. — Late 12C. Slender paired columns, topped by highly stylised capitals, combine in an elegant cloister. Several rooms in this part of the building, Alfonso VIII's old palace, were decorated by the Moors. In the chapel is a statue of St James with articulated arms, which according to legend, dubbed the princes of royal blood, knights.

Miraflores Carthusian Monastery★ (**Cartuja de Miraflores**) (BY). — *4km - 2 1/2 miles east.* This old royal foundation, confided to the Carthusians in 1442, was chosen by John II as a pantheon for himself and his second wife, Isabel of Portugal. The king died in 1454 and his daughter Isabel, had reigned as queen for many years before the church was completed in full Isabeline Gothic style in 1498 *(details p 15)*.

Church. — *Open 10.15am to 3pm (11.20am to 12.45pm Sundays and holidays) and 4 to 7pm (6pm in winter); closed Maundy Thursday and Good Friday during services.* The sobriety of the façade, relieved only by the buttress finials and the founders' escutcheons, gives no indication of the interior richness. This appears particularly in the apse where the high altarpiece and royal tombs form the outstanding **sculptured unit★★** designed by the Fleming, Gil de Siloé in the last years of the 15C. The polychrome wood altarpiece is the work of Siloé and Diego de la Cruz. The striking design replaces the usual rectangular compartments by a great central circle, outlined by a file of figurines, and inner and outer small garlanded circles, each crowded with Biblical figures.

The royal mausoleum at the centre of the apse is in the form of an eight pointed star on which, amidst an exuberant Flamboyant Gothic decoration of scrolls, canopies, pinnacles, cherubs and armorial bearings, can be seen the somewhat formal royal figures of King John and Queen Isabel. In an ornate recess in the north wall is the tomb of the Infante Alfonso, whose premature death, gave the throne to his sister Isabel the Catholic *(p 245)*. The statue of the young prince at prayer is technically brilliant but impersonal (compare with that of Juan de Padilla, *p 230*).

Also in the church are two Primitive paintings and an Annunciation by Pedro Berruguete (left and right respectively near the altar), a 15C Hispano-Flemish triptych and Gothic **choirstalls★** carved with an infinite variety of arabesques.

*Except where otherwise stated, all recommended itineraries
in towns, are designed as walks.*

CARRIÓN DE LOS CONDES (Palencia)

Michelin map 441 fold 20 — Pop 3 016

Carrión, at the centre of a fertile cereal plain, was once an important halt on the way to Santiago de Compostela. Three interesting buildings remain from that time.

The cruel fate of cruel husbands. — Counts of Carrión, learning of the rich dowries promised to the daughters of Rodrigo, El Cid Campeador *(p 228),* journeyed to Valencia, where at his court they won the girls and celebrated their marriage feasts before returning north. On their way back to Carrión, however, they beat their wives and abandoned them on the road. The Cid, to avenge his daughters, sent knights to Carrión who executed the avaricious counts. The daughters subsequently found better husbands among members of the royal houses of Aragon and Navarre.

San Zoilo Monastery. — This ancient Benedictine monastery dating back to the 11C was rebuilt during the Renaissance. The **cloister★** by Juan de Badajoz has distinctive vaulting with keystones and bosses designed as figurines and medallions.

St James' (Santiago). — The Romanesque façade is quite beautiful with 12C **carvings★** : the portal's central coving is filled with everyday figures at work: (from left to right) the architect with his compass, the barber (or sheep shearer?) with massive scissors, the potter at his wheel, the cobbler... the high reliefs in the upper frieze show early Gothic influence in the figures of the Disciples and Christ in Majesty flanked by the symbols of the Evangelists.

Santa María. — The Romanesque sculptures in the south portal of this old church depict on one of the recessed arches the Old Men of the Apocalypse, Musicians and the Good Shepherd and the three Kings on the frieze.

EXCURSION

Villalcázar de Sirga. — *5km - 3 miles southeast.* The village is grouped round an early Gothic **church★** of vast size, pierced, on its south front, by a carved **door★**, surmounted by a beautiful frieze in two registers. In the south transept are the Gothic **sarcophagi★** of the brother of Alfonso X of Castile, who had him murdered in 1271, and his wife. The costumes worn by the figures are carved with an eye for detail as is the prince's funeral procession.

CIUDAD RODRIGO ★ (Salamanca)

Michelin map 441 fold 36 — Pop 14 776

Ciudad Rodrigo appears high on a hilltop, guarded by the square tower of its 14C Alcázar and mediaeval ramparts and, if you are coming from Portugal, on the far side of the River Águeda spanned by a Roman bridge. After the Moorish invasion it was re-established in the 12C by Count Rodrigo González from whom it takes its name; later it became a fortress on the Spanish Portuguese frontier and finally, in the War of Independence, a stronghold freed from the French after a siege and bloody battle by Wellington in 1812 — a success which brought him the title of Duke of Ciudad Rodrigo and Grandee of Spain.

The ramparts. — The walls constructed on sparse Roman foundations in the 12C, were converted to a full defensive system on the north and west flanks in 1710. There are several stairways up to the 2km - 1 mile long sentry path.

Cathedral★. — The church was built in two stages, from 1170 to 1230 and in the 14C; in the 16C Rodrigo Gil de Hontañón added the central apse. The stiffness of the figures of the Disciples in a gallery in the upper part of the south transept façade is all the more obvious because of the flowing lines of the surrounding blind arcades.
Open 9am to noon (9.30 to 10.30am Sundays and holidays) and 4 to 6pm.
The choirstalls carved by Rodrigo Alemán are Isabeline; the **altar★** in the north aisle Renaissance — the alabaster Deposition, beautifully composed and carved in low relief is by Lucas Mitata. The 13C **Virgin Portal★** (west door), masked outside by a Classical belfry which forms the cathedral narthex, has a line of apostles carved between the columns beneath the splayings and the covings.
The **cloister★** *(50pts)* is made up of diverse architectural styles and includes a Plateresque door in the pure Salamanca style *(p 240),* opening off the east gallery and in the west gallery Romanesque capitals illustrating man's original sin and at the column bases, grotesques symbolising greed and vanity.

Cerralbo Chapel. — The chapel, built between 1588 and 1685 is pure and austere but harmonious in the Herreran style. Adjoining the south side is a quiet square, surrounded by white arcades, the Plaza del Buen Alcalde.

Los Castro Palace (or **Count of Montarco's Palace**). — Not far from the city's north wall on the Plaza del Conde stands the 15C palace's long façade, its off-centre entrance surrounded by an *alfiz (p 16),* flanked by twisted columns.

Plaza Mayor. — Two Renaissance palaces stand on this, the city's lively main square: the first, now the **town hall,** has a façade with two storeys of basket handle arcading forming a gallery and a loggia, the second, the **Los Cueto,** has a decorative frieze separating its first and second storeys.

COCA Castle ★★ (Segovia)

Michelin map 447 fold 7

This fortress is the most outstanding example of Mudejar military architecture in Spain. It was constructed in the late 15C, on the site of a Celtiberian settlement and later Roman town, by Moorish craftsmen for the archbishop of Seville, Fonseca, and consists of three concentric battlemented perimeters, flanked by polygonal corner towers and turrets with at the centre, a massive keep.
It is the epitome of all fortresses, but with the sun mellowing the brick and the interplay of shadows on battlements and watchtowers, it can be attractive as well as awesome. *Open July to September 8am to 3.30pm; the rest of the year 9am to 2pm and 3 to 6pm; closed Saturdays, Sundays and holidays from July to September.* The keep and chapel, which contains Romanesque wood carving, are open.

COVARRUBIAS (Burgos)

Michelin map 442 folds 15 and 16 — Pop 663

The Arlanza Valley, with vineyards upon its slopes and poplars lining the water's edge, narrows to a wooded gorge as you approach the ancient town of Covarrubias. This is still partly surrounded by mediaeval ramparts, guarded by the Doña Urraca tower, strangely shaped like a decapitated pyramid. A Renaissance palace straddles the street to the picturesque **old quarter**, where a large number of the façades of the houses have been restored. The town is the burial place of one of Castile's great historic figures, Fernán González who died in 970.

The awakening of Castile. — In the 10C the kings of Asturias-León set out to quell the growing independence of the counts of Castile. One, however, **Fernán González**, managed to unite several small fiefs into what he considered his kingdom and which, as the new County of Castile, eventually extended from the Cantabrian Sea to the Duero and included what are now the provinces of Cantabria, Álava, Vizcaya, La Rioja, Burgos and Palencia. Castile supported its ruler for over forty years in the campaign to sweep the Muslims south, beyond the Duero, thus casting itself a leading role in the Reconquest and so ultimately in the unification of Christian Spain.

Collegiate Church. — *Guided tours at 10.30am and 1.30, 3.30 and 7.30pm (6.30pm 1 October to 31 May); Sundays and holidays 10am to 2pm and 4 to 8pm (7pm 1 October to 31 May); closed Tuesdays 1 October to 31 May.* The church, with a nave and two aisles and cloisters with ornamental vaulting, makes an impressive Gothic unit, a pantheon worthy of some twenty mediaeval tombs including those before the altar of Fernán González and his wife.

Treasury and museum. — *Open 10am to 2pm and 4 to 8pm. (7pm 1 October to 31 May); closed Tuesdays 1 October to 31 May; 75pts.* A painting by Pedro Berruguete and another by Van Eyck stand out from the collection of Primitives; note especially the 15C Flemish school **triptych** in which the central high relief of the Adoration of the Magi has been attributed to Gil de Siloé; the panels are in the Hispano-Flemish style. There is also a splendid processional cross made by the goldsmiths of Calahorra of the 16C.

FRÓMISTA Church ★★ (Palencia)

Michelin map 441 fold 20 or 442 folds 13 and 14

Many pilgrims on the way to Santiago de Compostela halted at Frómista which afforded a choice of four hospices and the opportunity of making a pious offering at the Benedictine Monastery of St Martin of which only the church remains at the centre of a large square. *Open 10am to 2pm and 4 to 8pm; closed Tuesday mornings and all day Monday.*

The church, erected in about 1066, with beautifully matched rough hewn stone blocks of considerable size, marks a climax in the development of Romanesque architecture in Castile; after earlier essays in Palencia, Jaca and León (St Isidore), it demonstrates the achievement of perfect ordinance in this particular style so that later Romanesque churches throughout Castile were all greatly influenced by it. It suffered a somewhat over zealous restoration in 1904.

Outside, the eye travels over the classic east end, rising from the apsidals up to the apse proper, up again over the transept walls, almost imperceptibly to the cupola squinches and finally to the lantern tower; the decorative features are all there, all equally unobtrusive but perfectly placed: billets outlining the windows, engaged columns, cornices with ornately carved modillions. Inside, the same pure Romanesque lines are apparent in the cradle vaulting, apsidal oven vaults, the dome on squinches, double ribbed arches and indispensable decorative relief of carved capitals.

GREDOS, Sierra de ★★ (Ávila)

Michelin map 447 folds 13, 14 and 15

The Sierra de Gredos, which includes the Almanzor (2 592m - 8 502ft), the highest peak in the Central Cordillera, has dissimilar contours, the north face being marked by glaciary features such as mountain cirques and lakes, the south, a steep granite wall, by eroded clefts. In order to preserve valleys rich with orchards of apples, pears and figs, trout in the Alberche and Tormes Rivers and the *capra hispánica,* a type of mountain goat, which haunts the upper heights, a Reserva Nacional de Gredos has been created.

East to West Crossing — *158km · 98 miles — allow 6 hours*

Piedralaves. — This attractive village is blessed with a good summer climate.

Águila Caves★ (Cuevas del Águila). — *Bear left immediately beyond the village of Rama-castañas and continue for 4km - 2 1/2 miles along the surfaced road. Guided tours (time : 3/4 hour) 10.30am to 1pm and 3 to 7pm (6pm in winter); 225pts.*
A single vast chamber is open to the public. Among many concretions are lovely frozen streams of calcite, ochre crystals coloured by iron oxide and massive pillars still in process of formation.

Arenas de San Pedro. — The village, surrounded on all sides by pines which are tapped for resin, is a centre for climbers and walkers and also trout fishermen. A 14C castle with a tall, square keep, stands proudly beside the torrential stream.

Puerto del Pico Road★. — The road cuts through the centre of the *sierra*. After crossing the delightful village of **Mombeltrán** (15C castle with well preserved exterior) the road rises to a *corniche*, paralleling the old Roman road, which one can see below. From the pass (1 352m - 4 436ft) there is a good **view★** of the mountains and, in the foreground (south), of the Tiétar Valley and, beyond, the Tagus Valley. Beyond the pass the landscape becomes austere with granite boulders crowning the hilltops. The **Gredos Parador** stands out amidst a pine forest in a magnificent **setting★★** and from the terrace is a beautiful panoramic outlook. Beyond Hoyos del Collado there is a **view★** right along the Tormes Valley.

At El Barco de Ávila, still dominated by its old castle, bear left into the N 110.
From the Tornavacas Pass look out for a **view★** of the wide Jerte Valley below.

Cabezuela del Valle. — The village, crowded against the left bank of the Jerte, has a delightful, very steep **main street★** marked at the start by a Calvary.

HARO (La Rioja)

Michelin map **442** fold 17 — Pop 8 581

Haro is a prosperous small town at the centre of the famous "Rioja alta" wine area *(p 236)*. Its prosperous past is recalled by many of its 16 and 18C houses.

St Thomas'. — The south portal of the church (16C) was designed and was as delicately sculptured as a Plateresque altarpiece by Felipe Bigarny. In the Gothic interior the ribs supporting the vaulting sweep down onto clustered columns which divide the nave.

LEÓN ★★ P

Michelin map **441** fold 18 — Pop 131 134

León, which extends along the left bank of the Bernesga and is surrounded on all sides by the Meseta, combines two cities — a dynamic modern metropolis which will continue and even increase in prosperity as the recently discovered iron ore in the Cantabrian Cordillera to the north is exploited, and an ancient city intensely proud of its masterpieces in three different styles of architecture: Romanesque (St Isidore), Gothic (the Cathedral) and Renaissance (St Mark's).

The mediaeval town. — In the 10C, kings of Asturias erected walls around their new capital, built on the site of earlier Roman fortifications; they peopled it with Mozarabs, Christian refugees from Córdoba and Toledo, so that by the 11 and 12C León had become virtually the centre of Mozarabic Spain. The east part of the city records the early mediaeval period clearly in the still evident remains of the rampart walls and houses fronting alleys where peeling roughcast reveals brickwork façades. The most evocative quarter lies between the arcaded Plaza Mayor and the particularly attractive market square (**BZ**).

The modern city. — León is flourishing on the mineral undertakings (iron and coal) and hydroelectric installations now established in its environs (dam on the Esla) and on livestock farming. The city limits are extending westwards as new buildings are erected.

León's artistic tradition has also been maintained: Gaudí erected a Neo-Gothic palace on the Plaza de San Marcelo; Vela Zanetti has decorated several churches with popular frescoes on the city outskirts and Subirachs has a massive bronze at the Virgen del Camino *(p 235)*.

■ SIGHTS *time: 2 1/2 hours*

Cathedral★★★ (**BY**). — *Under restoration*. The cathedral, constructed mainly between the mid -13 and late 14C, is true Gothic in style even to the very high nave with vast windows.

West face. — Flanked by robust but very dissimilar towers although both have steeples — again dissimilar — the façade has a central crocketed and turreted gable, wheel and rose windows and gallery and, at its base, is pierced by three deeply recessed portals separated by unusual, sharply pointed arches. The gently smiling Sta María Blanca (a copy: original in the axial chapel) stands at the pier of the central doorway in which the lintel carries graphic portraits of the blessed and the damned. The left portal illustrates the childhood of Christ, the right, the St Francis door, includes the Dormition and the Coronation of the Virgin.

Generalísimo Franco	BY	9
Ordoño II	AYZ	
Padre Isla (Av. del)	ABY	
Rúa	BZ	
Calvo Sotelo (Pl. de)	AY	2
Caño Badillo	BZ	3
Cartagena	BZ	4
Espolón (Pl. de)	BY	7
General Sanjurjo (Av.)	BY	8
Guzmán el Bueno (Glorieta de)	AZ	10
Independencia	BZ	12
Jose Fernandez (Av. de)	BZ	13
Murias de Paredes	BZ	14
Pendon de Baeza	BZ	15
Puerta Obispo	BY	16
Ramiro Balbuena	AY	17
San Francisco (Paseo)	BZ	19
San Isidoro (Pl. de)	BY	21
San Marcos (Pl. de)	AY	22
San Pedro	BY	23
Santo Domingo (Pl. de)	BY	25
Santo Martino (Pl. de)	BY	26

South face. — The statues decorating the jambs of the central portal are outstanding.

Interior. — The **stained glass windows**★★ — 125 windows and 57 oculi with an area of 1 200m² — 12 917 sq ft are unique in Spain and even endanger the strength of the walls (the last restoration was at the end of last century). The west front rose and the three central apsidal chapels contain the oldest, 13-15C glass; St James' Chapel has glass in which the Renaissance influence is already apparent while those of the nave, which were realised much later, some are even considered modern, illustrate three great themes: flora, minerals (below), and historic personages, heraldic crests (behind the triforium) and, high up, the blessed.

In the *capilla mayor* is a 15C altarpiece in the form of a triptych painted by Nicolás Francés with a left panel vividly illustrating the **Entombment**★. At the foot of the altar is a shrine with relics of San Froilán, the city patron. Several Gothic tombs can be seen in the ambulatory and transept.

The interesting Renaissance **trascoro**★ by Juan de Badajoz, includes four alabaster high reliefs framing the central arch through which there is an appealing view down the length of the nave.

Cloister★★. — *Guided tours 10am to 1pm (2pm Sundays) and 4 to 7pm; closed Sunday afternoons 1 January; 15 August and 25 December; 150pts.*

The galleries are contemporary with the 13-14C nave but the vaulting, with its ornately carved keystones, was added only at the beginning of the 16C. The galleries are interesting with now faint frescoes by Nicolás Francés, Romanesque and Gothic tombs and capitals carved with vividly lifelike scenes. The sheltered north door to the cathedral is dedicated to the figure of the Virgin with the Offering, at the pier.

Museum. — The collection includes a 10C illuminated Mozarabic Bible, a Crucifix carved by Juan de Juni, the Plateresque staircase which formerly led up to the chapterhouse and a 13C sculpture of the Archangel Gabriel, previously at the south portal.

St Isidore★ (BY). — The basilica, built into the mediaeval ramparts, its belfry like a watchtower overlooking the walls, was dedicated in 1063 to Isidore, Archbishop of Seville and Doctor of the Visigothic church, whose body had been brought north for burial since Seville was then under Moorish rule. Of the 11C church there remains only the narthex, erected as a pantheon for the royal house of León — Asturias — Castile. The basilica is 12C.

The **south front** lost its Romanesque design when the east end and transept were remodelled in the Gothic period and a balustrade and pediment were added during the Renaissance. The sculptured decoration of the two portals bears a close resemblance to others on the pilgrim way to Santiago de Compostela.

Royal pantheon★ **and treasury**★. — *Entrance left of the church. Open daily 1 July to 31 August 9am to 2pm and 3.30 to 8pm; the rest of the year 10am to 1.30pm and 4 to 6.30pm; Sundays and holidays 10am to noon, closed 1 January and 25 December; 125pts.*

In the Pantheon, which is one of the earliest examples of Romanesque architecture in Spain, the **capitals**★, inspired by Asturian art *(p 103)*, were the first in Spain to be decorated with scenes from the Gospels (beside profane boxing scenes and grotesques); the **frescoes**★★ (12C) include New Testament, hunting and pastoral scenes and, on the inside of an arch, the tasks of the months.

In the **treasury** are ancient caskets, decorated in 11C Mozarabic style with carved ivory plaques or 12C Limoges enamels, the beautiful **Doña Urraca Chalice**★ comprising two Roman agate cups mounted in the 11C in a gold setting inlaid with precious stones.

Old Monastery of St Mark (Antiguo Monasterio de San Marcos) (AY). — The site has been connected with Knights of the Order of Santiago or St James since the 12C: first as that of the mother house of the soldier friars, protectors of pilgrims on the way to Santiago de Compostela and, three centuries later, as that of the monastery planned by Ferdinand the Catholic, Grand Master of the Order, as being worthy of the dignity and riches acquired by the Knights during the Reconquest. This eventuated in the present sumptuous edifice, erected finally at the height of the Renaissance in the reign of the Emperor Charles V (part of it has been transformed into a hotel).

The 100m - 328ft long **façade**★★, in spite of the addition in the 18C of a baroque pediment, has a remarkable unity in the division of its two storeys by a regular system of windows and niches, friezes and cornices, engaged columns and pilasters. Medallions in high relief, depicting famous people from the Bible, Rome, or Spain. provide additional decoration: Lucretia and Judith support Isabel the Catholic, Trajan and Augustus, Charles V... At the main entrance a baroque ornament depicts the events of St James' life from his slaying of the Moors to his apotheosis at the pediment apex. The church front, blasoned with scallop shells, remains incomplete.

Archaeological Museum★. — *Open 10am to 2pm (1pm Sundays and holidays) and 4 to 6pm; closed Sunday and holiday afternoons and all day Monday; 75pts.* The first gallery, with star vaulting, displays among its items of religious art, the small outstanding, **Carrizo Crucifix**★★★, an 11C Romanesque ivory of great presence and penetrating gaze, with hair and beard formally dressed and loincloth arranged in a manner clearly Byzantine influenced. Through a window can be seen the *artesonado* Renaissance ceiling of the old chapterhouse. The cloister galleries serve as a lapidary museum. The **sacristy**★, a sumptuous creation by Juan de Badajoz (1549), has vaulting on ribs, decorated with scallop shells, ribands and cherubim, which meet in bosses carved as masks.

EXCURSIONS

Virgen del Camino. — *5km - 3 miles by ④ on the plan.* Several churches dedicated to the Virgin of the Way have stood on this site beside the pilgrim road. This latest sanctuary, was erected in 1960, to shelter the presently venerated statue, a baroque *Pietà*. The **façade**★ is decorated with bronze Pentecostal statues, showing the Virgin surrounded by the tall, emaciated but realistic figures of the Disciples, by the Catalan artist, José María Subirachs (b 1927).

San Miguel de Escalada★. — *28km - 17 miles by ② on the plan. Open 10am to 1pm and 4 to 8pm (3 to 6pm in winter).*

Only the church remains of the monastery founded at the end of the 9C by monks expelled by the emirs of Córdoba, but even so it is the largest and best preserved Mozarabic monument to exist in Spain today *(p 14)*. It stands at the centre of a terrace abutting one of a group of surrounding hills.

LEÓN★★

The **exterior gallery★,** built in 1050, has horseshoe shaped arches resting on carved capitals at the top of smoothly polished columns. The main **church★** (under restoration) building is considerably earlier, dating from 913. The nave and two aisles, covered with wooden vaulting, are divided from the apses by a triple arched portico and a balustrade of panels carved with Visigothic (birds pecking seeds, bunches of grapes) and Moorish motifs (stylised foliage).

Valporquero Caves★★ (Cuevas). — 47km - 29 miles north (BY) on the LE 311. Open 10 May to 1 November 10am to 2pm and 4 to 7pm; time : 1 hour; 200pts.

The caves, hollowed out over millions of years by underground streams, are still in process of formation (be careful not to slip on the damp clay paths). The temperature is constant at 7 ºC — 45 ºF. Neutral lighting enables you to see not only the extraordinary shapes of the concretions — there is a stalactite "star" hanging from the roof of the large chamber — but the variety of tones — 35 have been counted — of red, grey and black of the mineral oxide stained stone. The tour ends with a walk along a narrow passage 1 500m - 4 920ft long cut obliquely by subterranean waters through a 40m - 131ft thick layer of soft rock.

LERMA (Burgos)

Michelin map 442 fold 15 — Pop 2 591

The tall, mediaeval ramparts which once protected the city, can be seen more clearly from a distance (on the road from Irún to Madrid, the N 1), than nearer to, when they are masked by buildings.

Philip III's favourite (1598-1618). — The death of Philip II in 1598, brought about a crisis of authority, his successors preferring to devolve their responsibilities of government upon favourites who turned out to be as ephemeral as they were avaricious; counterbalancing their advice with the reverentially Christian Habsburg Kings, but creating a constant struggle for power were the royal confessors. The "reign" of the Duke of Lerma, favourite of Philip III coincided with a period of untold extravagance and corruption: the court, dizzied by celebrations and balls, divided its time between Valladolid and Madrid; the duke, once having feathered his own nest turned his attention to his home town which as a result became one of Spain's rare examples of Classical town planning. In 1618 he was usurped by his son, the Duke of Uceda.

Tour. — Enter the town through the fortified gateway. The narrow cobbled streets are lined with houses, some of which are very old. The quarter containing larger residences and public buildings was ordered by the duke in the 17C to be built higher up. It includes two vast squares, the larger of which is lined on one side by the austere façade of the ducal palace but on two others by stone porticoes above which rise buildings of one further storey built of brilliantly coloured brickwork.

LOGROÑO (La Rioja) P

Michelin map 442 fold 17 — Pop 110 980
See town plan in the current Michelin Red Guide España Portugal

Logroño, on the right bank of the Ebro in country traversed by the old pilgrim road to Santiago de Compostela and at the meeting point of the two Rioja areas, remains a busy provincial capital. It is a manufacturing centre (textiles) and still produces its famous coffee caramels (p 23). Nearby is Clavijo (17km - 11 miles south), the famous battlefield on which Ramiro I beat back the Moors with the aid of St James (p 152) in 844.

La Rioja. — La Rioja, a fertile area in the Ebro Valley called after a tributary, the Río Oja, includes almost all La Rioja provinces besides parts of Alava and Navarre. It divides into two regions, **Rioja Alta** — Upper Rioja — the more mountainous and better watered area which extends from Haro, the principal town (p 234), to Logroño, and **Rioja Baja** — Lower Rioja — which ends at Alfaro and includes a wide valley and the ochre coloured soil and tableland relief which presage Aragon.

The vine has long had pride of place: the first written mention of Rioja wine appears in a document of 1102; it was being exported to France, Flanders and Italy by the 16C. Phylloxera in France in the late 19C brought increased demand, the expansion of vineyards and the arrival of Bordeaux vine growers. La Rioja is now known for its red wine which though light and smooth, has some body.

Lower Rioja, particularly on the Navarre side of the Ribera (p 177), specialises in growing and canning early vegetables: asparagus, artichokes, peppers and tomatoes gross an average of 385 000 tons annually — local canning provides 95% of Spain's asparagus exports. **Calahorra,** an ancient Roman town, birthplace in 1C AD of Quintilian the Rhetorician and the poet Prudentius in 348 is now the region's major commercial centre.

■ SIGHTS time: 1 hour

Cathedral. — The present edifice, with the sweeping vaulting of the 15C, was given a baroque façade in 1742, so that now bare walls contrast with an abundant decoration applied to the towers and the main portal, deeply recessed beneath a coffered semi-dome. Inside, the principal features are the **Chapel of Our Lady of the Angels** (1762) which is octagonal in shape and rococo in ornament (west end of the nave) and the altarpieces, found in the **Kings' Chapel** (1554 — first chapel on the north side) and in **St Ildefonsus' Chapel** (third chapel on the north side).

San Bartolomé. — Events in the life of St Bartholomew are cleverly carved in archaic style in the coving of the small church's early 14C west portal. The pure lined interior (13-14C) is unusually wide but short.

Imperial Church of Santa María de Palacio. — In 1130 Alfonso VII presented the Order of the Holy Sepulchre with his Logroño Palace of which the church remains, though this is now preponderantly 16-18C. It does, however, retain an astonishing early 13C spire, pyramid shaped with every rib outlined with crockets.

EXCURSION

Iregua Valley★. — *41km - 25 1/2 miles south along the N 111 about 3/4 hour.* For 15km - 9 miles the road skirts orchards and market gardens in the Ebro plain, until, near Islallana, appear the first **rock faces★** of the Sierra de Cameros, overlooking the Iregua from a height of more than 500m - 1 650ft. Two tunnels later, the valley narrows, squeezed between massive reddish coloured boulders. It opens out between wooded slopes and narrows again upstream, the torrent running always at the bottom of a deep ravine of yellow and grey rock. The *corniche* road dominates the site of Torrecilla en Cameros before it enters **Villanueva de Cameros,** a picturesque hamlet where the half-timbered houses are roofed with circular tiles.

MEDINACELI (Soria)
Michelin map **442** fold 27 — Pop 1 036

Medinaceli, situated like an acropolis above the Meseta plains, was inhabited in Roman times, as can be seen from the triple **triumphal arch★,** erected in the 2 or 3C AD and visible from the Madrid road. The mediaeval fortified town is now only a quiet village off the main road, with open **views** across the Meseta and south to the Jalón Valley saltmarshes.

Between Medinaceli and Somaén *(13km - 8 miles northeast),* the N II enters the **Jalón Gorges★** between red ochre cliffs rising 200m - 650ft above the river.

MEDINA DEL CAMPO (Valladolid)
Michelin map **441** fold 29 — Pop 19 237

Medina del Campo, a busy agricultural market town and major railway junction.

The vast **Plaza de España** is framed by a 16C church and the emblasoned façades of the old stone slaughterhouse (1562) and the brick town hall (1660) which, on the right, also spans the street into the square. The former Dueñas Palace, now an Instituto Laboral, which has an elegant *patio* with Renaissance arches, stands in Santa Teresa Street.

La Mota Castle★. — *To visit ☎ (983) 80.10.24.* The battlemented brick castle overlooking the town, is flanked at one corner by a massive square keep. It remains as impressive as when it was the frequent residence of Isabel the Catholic — she died there in 1504.

MEDINA DE RIOSECO (Valladolid)
Michelin map **441** fold 29 — Pop 5 018

Medina de Rioseco is one of the major agricultural centres of the **Tierra de Campos,** the granary of Castile. The picturesque narrow main street, the Calle de la Rúa, is shaded along its length by porticoes supported by wooden pillars.

Santa María. — *Open in summer 11am to 2pm and on weekdays 4 to 7pm; in winter Saturdays and Sundays only 11am to 2pm; 100pts.* 15-16C. The central altarpiece was carved by Esteban Jordán. The **Benavente Chapel★** (16C), to the left of the high altar, in all its exuberant decoration over walls and cupola, recalls scenes of the Last Judgment and the Garden of Eden, by Jerónimo del Corral.

Santiago. — *Same opening times as Santa María; 50pts.* The altarpieces in the three apsidal chapels make a spectacular Churrigueresque group.

NÁJERA (La Rioja)
Michelin map **442** fold 17 — Pop 6 192

Nájera, at one end of a bridge on the pilgrim road to Santiago de Compostela, was the capital of the Kingdom of Navarre until 1076 when La Rioja *(p 236)* was incorporated in Castile. Not far away at **Navarrete** in 1367, Peter the Cruel aided by the Black-Prince, vanquished his half-brother Henry II Trastamara. The rivalry between the Spanish brothers continued, dividing Castile, until the death of Peter I in 1369.

Santa María la Real Monastery★. — *Open 1 May to 30 September 9.30am to 12.30pm and 4 to 7.30pm; the rest of the year 10am to 12.30pm and 4 to 6.30pm; 50pts.* The monastery was founded in 1032 by Don García III, King of Navarre.

Cloister★. — The cloister, abutting the strangely purple cliff, has wide, pointed bays each filled with Manueline style stone tracery (1520) to a different arabesque pattern.

Church. — Beneath the gallery, two soldiers bearing the colours of King García and his Queen, Estefanía of Barcelona, guard the entrance to the **royal pantheon★** of princes of Navarre, León and Castile of the 11 and 12C (funerary statues: 16C). At the centre, between the kneeling figures of the founders, is the entrance to the cave where the Virgin was found. The present polychrome figure is 13C. Among the royal sarcophagi (in the side aisle) is the gracefully carved 12C **tomb of Doña Blanca of Navarre★.**

Coro alto★. — Look at the beautiful carving and infinite variety of the misericords and armrests in the **choirstalls★** (1495) and particularly at the central seat on which the founder king is depicted majestically in full armour beneath a delicate canopy.

OÑA (Burgos)
Michelin map **442** fold 5 — Pop 2 053

Oña stands on an uneven **site★** in a valley hollow. The **square** in the village centre, made up of three different levels, is picturesque. The **parish church,** once the St Saviour Monastery Church and founded in 1011 by Count Sancho of Castile as a family pantheon, in consequence, contains in the chancel 11C tombs; it also possesses a 15C Flamboyant Gothic cloister.

PAJARES Pass ★★ (León and Asturias)

Michelin map **441** south of folds 7 and 8

The Pajares Pass, between the provinces of León and Asturias, is the most picturesque road over the western Cantabrian Cordillera. The **road★★** (N 630) approaching the pass from the south follows the course of the Bernesga to La Robla from where it continues directly upwards across several gullies.

Santa María de Arbás Collegiate Church. — *1km - 1/2 mile south of the pass.* The Romanesque church, given a porch and a new vaulting during the Renaissance, has **capitals★** decorating the pillars of the nave, triumphal arch and the apsidal arches, carved with a stylised foliage motif clearly Far Eastern in origin.

The pass.★★ — The pass at 1 379m - 4 524ft makes an excellent point from which to scan the sharply pointed Cantabrian Cordillera. Hoists provide skiers with easy access to the heights.

The *corniche* road down the north side of the mountains is steep in places (gradient : 15% — 1: 6). There are opencast mines on the mountainsides and above the ravine walls.

PALENCIA Ⓟ

Michelin map **441** fold 30 — Pop 74 080
See town plan in the current Michelin Red Guide España Portugal

Palencia is a long narrow north-south town, hemmed in to the west by the Río Carrión and to the east by the railway. It has prospered from coal and anthracite mined in the Cantabrian Mountains to its north and grain grown on the irrigated plains to the south, the Tierra de Campos. Immediately surrounding the town is a green swathe of market gardens, irrigated by the Castilian Canal and its tributaries.

Palencia, which dates back to Celtiberian times, was the seat of Spain's first university, founded by Alfonso VIII in the early 13C.

Cathedral★★. — *Time: 3/4 hour.* Since the 7C a chapel has stood on the site to enshrine the relics of San Antolín, a Visigoth born near Toulouse, martyred by and subsequently, on their conversion, venerated by the Arian Visigoths. The chapel lay forgotten during the Moslem occupation and for long after, until, according to tradition, Sancho the Great of Navarre came upon it while hunting wild boar. The king erected a Romanesque chapel (1034) over the ruins which survives as the crypt to the 14-16C cathedral. The dazzling painted interior is due to Bishop Fonseca who gathered round him in the early 16C a group of highly skilled artists.

Interior★★. — The cathedral's centre is occupied by an incredible assemblage of works of art in all the slightly different styles of the early 16C: Flamboyant Gothic, Isabeline, Plateresque and Renaissance. The **trascoro** provides a spacious setting for sculptures by Gil de Siloé and Simon of Cologne; the central triptych is a masterpiece by Juan of Flanders; the beautiful finely wrought choirscreen at its summit is by Gaspar Rodríguez (1563); the choirstalls are Gothic, the multicoloured organ gallery, above, is dated 1716. The huge, infinitely compart-mented, early 16C **high altar retable** opposite, was carved by Felipe Bigarny, painted by Juan of Flanders and is surmounted by a Crucifix by Juan de Valmaseda. The **Chapel of the Holy Sacrament,** behind the *capilla mayor* is exuberantly Gothic with a rich altarpiece by Valmaseda (1529). To the left, beneath an arch is the sarcophagus of Queen Urraca of Navarre (d 1189).

Museum★. — *Open 9am to 1pm and 4 to 6pm; closed Sunday and holiday afternoons; 100pts.* The museum is to the right of the west door, in the Gothic cloister and dependent rooms. The collection includes a *St Sebastian* by El Greco and a triptych by Pedro Berruguete and four 15C **tapestries★** of New Testament scenes, woven to Bishop Fonseca's commission and with his crest incorporated at the corners.

EXCURSION

Baños de Cerrato. — *14km - 9 miles southeast;* cross the railway at Venta de Baños before turning right towards Cevico de la Torre. The Visigothic Basilica of **St John the Baptist★** (San Juan Bautista) is the oldest church in Spain in a good state of preservation. Its origin is that King Recesvinto decided to build a sanctuary in Baños de Cerrato when taking a cure there in 661. The date is beneath the apsidal arch.
Open 9am to 1pm and 3 to 7pm; closed Mondays.

The aisles are covered with timber vaulting and are separated by horsehoe shaped arches supported on marble columns. The capitals are carved with a stylised foliage motif which includes the long, ribbed leaf which later appeared widely in Asturian art. Note the decorative frieze in the central apsidal chapel.

PANCORBO Ravine ★ (Burgos)

Michelin map **442** fold 16

The Pancorbo Ravine, with impressively massive cliffs, cuts through the Montes Obarenes and was the setting of a rearguard action by the French against Wellington in 1813. From the national Irún-Madrid road, which passes through the defile, Pancorbo village can be seen perched on a **site★,** halfway up an obliquely striated limestone hillside.

PAREDES DE NAVA (Palencia)

Michelin map **441** south of folds 19 and 20 — Pop 3 011

The village was the birthplace of several great artists including **Jorge Manrique** (1440-1479), whose *Coplas* on the death of his father, with reflections on the brevity of life and the vanity of human deeds, remains Spain's most famous elegy, the painter **Pedro Berruguete** (c1450-1504) and his son **Alonso** (c1488-1561), who was primarily a sculptor.

Santa Eulalia. — The church, distinguished by its square, Romanesque inspired, belfry, has a **high altar retable★** which unveils Pedro Berruguete's art style. The **parish museum** in the church *(open 11am to 2pm and 4 to 7pm; 100pts),* possesses mostly 16C items including works by Siloé, Juan of Flanders and both Berruguetes.

PEDRAZA DE LA SIERRA ★★ (Segovia)

Michelin map 🗺 fold 8 — Pop 481

Pedraza, perched on a knoll, has kept much of the atmosphere of a seignorial town as it stands still encircled by mediaeval walls and surveyed by a powerful castle on the crag.

Entering through a fortified gateway one finds oneself in a maze of narrow, steeply inclined alleys, bordered with often crested country style houses. The Plaza Mayor is framed by rustic porticoes superimposed by deep balconies, and a Romanesque bell tower.

PEÑAFIEL ★ (Valladolid)

Michelin map 🗺 fold 24 — Pop 5 238

Peñafiel is dominated by its redoubtable 14C **castle★,** massively constructed at the meeting point of three valleys. Often compared to a ship stranded high on the shore, the fortress consists of two concentric oblong perimeters enclosing a rock spike. This is crowned by a characteristically Castilian square keep (in the second perimeter), reinforced at its summit by machicolated turrets.

In the village, **San Pablo Church** (1324) has a Mudejar east end, and inside, Renaissance vaulting over the Infante Chapel (1536).

The vast **Plaza del Coso,** is equally Castilian in being almost completely ringed by houses with deep balconies from which to watch bullfights held in the square below.

PEÑARANDA DE DUERO ★ (Burgos)

Michelin map 🗺 fold 25 — Pop 821

The **Plaza Mayor★** forms an architectural unit, apart from the palace, of half-timbered houses resting on robust stone pillars; at its centre is a 15C pillory.

Miranda Palace★. — *Open 10am to 1.30pm and 4 to 7pm (3.30 to 6pm in winter).*
Fronting the Plaza Mayor is the noble façade and full style Renaissance entrance of Miranda Palace. Inside, thanks to the work of Francisco de Colonia, is a *patio* surrounded by a two tier gallery. There is also an inner *patio* arch, a grand staircase and saloons with *artesonado* ceilings and monumental fireplaces.

PONFERRADA (León)

Michelin map 🗺 fold 16 — Pop 52 499

An iron bridge built at the end of the 11C across the Sill to help pilgrims on their way to Santiago de Compostela, gave the **Bierzo** capital its name. The area, a subsided basin between the León Mountains and the Galician Massif, closely resembles Galicia.

Local iron mines are bringing a new prosperity to the town.

The Templars' Castle. — *Open 9am to 1pm and 4 to 7pm (3 to 6pm 1 October to 28 February); closed Tuesdays.* The still massive ruins of the battlemented, turreted, machicolated Templar's Castle, close by the main square, command good views of the valley and surrounding mountains.

Santo Tomás de las Ollas. — *1.5km - 1 mile east. Follow the N VI for 1km - 1/2 mile then turn left.* The small 10C Mozarabic church has a most unusual plan in which the single aisle is joined to an oval apse, decorated with horseshoe shaped arches.

PUEBLA DE SANABRIA (Zamora)

Michelin map 🗺 folds 16 and 26 — Pop 1 858

Puebla de Sanabria is a pretty mountain village of houses with stone roofs and white walls, some still emblasoned with family crests, with porticoes or overhanging balconies. In the centre of the village is a late 12C, reddish grey granite church with a west door simply outlined with a large bead motif and guarding it, a stalwart 15C castle with an esplanade which overlooks the Río Tera and the lake.

EXCURSION

Sanabria Valley. — *19km - 12 miles northwest.* The valley, hollowed out northwest of Puebla by glaciary erosion at the feet of the Cabrera Baja and Segundera Sierras, is made delightfully alive by streams running through the light undergrowth — it is a well — known shooting and salmon-trout area. *Follow the road from Puebla towards the lake for 14km - 9 miles before turning right; after 6km - 4 miles bear left.*

San Martín de Castañeda. — There are attractive **views★** of the rushing stream of the Tera and the mountain encircled lake all the way to the Galician looking village of which the first distinguishable sight is the east end of its pure lined 11C Romanesque church.

Sanabria Lake. — The mountain encircled lake, which lies at nearly 1 028m - 3 372ft is used for all types of water sports *(regattas in July).*

QUINTANILLA DE LAS VIÑAS Church (Burgos)

Michelin map 🗺 fold 15 — 23,5km - 14 1/2 miles north of Covarrubias

Ask for a guide in the village at the door marked Turismo *(1km - 1/2 mile).*
The hermitage's great age — it is generally reputed to be 7C Visigothic — makes it interesting archaeologically. All that remains are the apse and transept, built of skilfully bonded blocks of stone. The low relief decoration, which underlines the shape of the walls outside, is unusually appealing. The same foliated scrollwork of bunches of grapes and birds are repeated inside on the keystones of the triumphal arch of which the imposts, on either side, are decorated with symbolic figures.

SALAMANCA ★★★ P

Michelin map **441** folds 37 and 38 — Pop 167 131

Salamanca is a lovely university city of golden stone, narrow streets, large and small squares, splendid buildings and exuberantly rich façades; it is a city of domes and spires, of wealth and a long tradition of learning still youthfully alive.

HISTORICAL NOTES

The tumultuous past. — Iberian in origin, Salamanca was conquered in the 3C BC by Hannibal, flourished under the Romans who built the **Roman bridge (AZ)** across the Tormes, and invaded repeatedly by the Moors. Alfonso VI expulsed the Moors in 1085. It recovered, only to be troubled in the 14 and 15C by rivalry among the 'big' families whose younger members formed factions known as **Los Bandos.** Such was the vendetta spirit that two Monroy brothers of the Santo Tomé Bando were killed by Manzano brothers of the San Benito Bando after an argument at a game of *pelota:* immediate vengeance by their mother, Doña María, and the Santo Tomé faction resulted in the decapitated Manzano heads being triumphantly planted on the Monroy tomb — after which the implacable fury was known as María La Brava or Indomitable. The *bandos* remained active until 1476.

Salamanca was occupied by the French during the War of Independence; when the French evacuated the town, Wellington entered it (June 1812) but within days had moved south to the **Arapiles Valley** where, on 22 July, he won the resounding Victory of Salamanca which proved to be a major turning point in the war.

The University. — The University was founded in 1215 (Oxford University *c*1167) and grew under the patronage of Kings of Castile, high dignitaries and learned men such as Benedict XIII *(p 169).* Its teaching was soon widely renowned (it took part in the reform of the Catholic Church) and by the 16C it numbered 70 professors of studies and 12 000 students.

Among its great and famous members have been the Infante Don Juan, son of the Catholic Monarchs, St John of the Cross and his teacher, the great humanist, **Fray Luis de León** (1527-1591) and **Miguel de Unamuno** (1864-1936), Professor of Greek, University Rector and philosopher of international standing *(p 22).*

The artistic flowering. — In the late 15 early 16C, two major painters were working in Salamanca: **Fernando Gallego,** one of the best Hispano-Flemish artists (much influenced in precision of line and realism by Thierry Bouts) and **Juan of Flanders** (b 1465), who settled in the city in 1504 and whose elegant and gentle work is outstanding for the subtle delicacy of its colours.

In architecture, the 15C also saw the evolution of the original Salamanca *patio* arch, a mixtilinear arc in which the line of the curve, inspired by Mudejar design, is broken by counter curves and straight lines, while the 16C brought decoration to an ebullient climax in pure **Plateresque art** *(illustration p 15).*

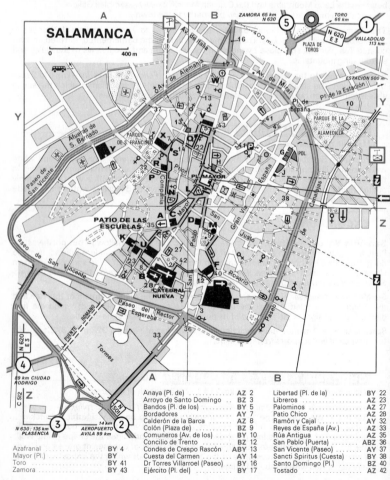

Anaya (Pl. de)	AZ 2	Libertad (Pl. de la)	BY 22
Arroyo de Santo Domingo	BZ 3	Libreros	AZ 23
Bandos (Pl. de los)	BY 5	Palominos	AZ 27
Bordadores	AY 7	Patio Chico	AZ 28
Calderón de la Barca	AZ 8	Ramón y Cajal	AY 32
Colón (Plaza de)	BZ 9	Reyes de España (Av.)	AZ 33
Comuneros (Av. de los)	BY 10	Rúa Antigua	AZ 35
Concilio de Trento	BZ 12	San Pablo (Puerta)	ABZ 36
Condes de Crespo Rascón	ABY 13	San Vicente (Paseo)	AY 37
Cuesta del Carmen	AY 14	Sancti Spíritus (Cuesta)	BY 38
Dr Torres Villarroel (Paseo)	AY 16	Santo Domingo (Pl.)	BZ 40
Ejército (Pl. del)	BY 17	Tostado	AZ 42

Azafranal	BY 4
Mayor (Pl.)	BY
Toro	BY 41
Zamora	BY 43

■ MONUMENTAL CENTRE

Time: 3 hours. Follow the route on the map opposite.

Plaza Mayor★★ (BY). — The square, built for the city by Philip V in gratitude for its support in the War of Succession, is among the finest in Spain. It was designed as a unit principally by the Churriguera brothers: four plain, ground level arcades, circular arched, support the balconied windows of three storeys which rise in perfect formation to a pinnacled balustrade, interrupted only to include on the north and south sides, the pedimented fronts of the Town Hall and Royal Pavilion, the latter distinguished by the bust of Philip V.

Pass through the pavilion into the Rúa Mayor.

The House of Shells★ (Casa de las Conchas) (AZ C). — *Closed due to restoration.* This 15C house with its 400 scallop shells, carved in the same golden stone as the wall and its line of highly decorative Isabeline windows and at ground level, beautiful wrought iron window grilles, composes a timelessly decorative and unique façade. The *patio* has delicate mixtilinear arches, pierced balustrades and, as decoration, sculptured lions' heads and coats of arms.

Clerecía (AZ A). — *Temporarily closed.* This impressive Jesuit College was begun in 1617 and was only finished with the completion of the baroque towers by Andrés García de Quiñones in 1755. Beside the church is a baroque cloister *(entrance: Calle Compañía).*

The Schools' Square★★★ (Patio de Las Escuelas) (AZ). — This small square, off the old Calle Libreros, is surrounded by the best examples of Salamanca Plateresque.

University (U). — *Open daily 9.30am to 1.30pm (1pm in winter) and 4.30 to 7pm (6pm in winter); Sundays and holidays 10am (11am in winter) to 1pm; closed Saturday afternoons 1 November to 28 February, 1 and 6 January, 24 June, 25 December and the first day of term; 50pts; last admission: 20 min before closing time.* The sumptuous **entrance★★★** *(illustration p 15)* of 1534 is a brilliant piece of sculpture, composed for general effect though with the utmost care for detail, as in the goldsmith's art. Above the twin doors, covered by basket handle arches, the carving is in ever greater relief as it rises through three registers to the final pierced frieze and pinnacles, to compensate for the increasing distance from the ground. A central medallion in the first register shows the Catholic Monarchs who presented the doorway; in the second, above crowned escutcheons and medallions, are portrait heads in scallop shell niches; in the third, flanking the pope supported by cardinals, are Venus and Hercules (in square frames) and the Virtues (in roundels).

Off the *patio* are the lecture halls: the Large or Paraninfo Hall, where official functions were held, is hung with 17C Brussels tapestries and a portrait of *Charles IV* by Goya; Master Salinas Hall — **Salinas** (1513-1590) was professor of music — contains two fragments of a predella painted by Juan of Flanders and a 15C portfolio of music; a hall where Fray Luis de León lectured in theology, is as it was in the 16C with the professor's desk beneath a sounding board and scarred students' benches — a luxury in days when students usually sat on the ground. The chapel (1767) where Fray Luis is buried, was formerly the University Library and has a remarkable 15C painted ceiling of which a large part has been removed to the Minorite Schools *(see below).*

The grand staircase rises beneath spread star vaulting, its bannister carved with foliated scrollwork and imaginary scenes and at the third flight with a bullfight.

A gallery on the first floor has its original, rich, coffered ceiling with stalactite ornaments and a delicate low relief frieze along the walls. A still Gothic style door with a fine 16C grille opens into the 18C library which contains 40 000 16-18C volumes of which 3 600 are manuscripts and 400 are incunabula (some of which date back to 11C).

Students' Hospice (U). — The hospice, completed in 1533, has an interesting Gothic entrance where a trefoil arch and escutcheons are contained by a surrounding *alfiz (p 16).*

Minorite Schools (Escuelas Menores) (U). — Standing to the right of the hospital and crowned by the same openwork Renaissance frieze, is the entrance to the Minorite Schools, a Plateresque portal decorated with coats of arms, roundels and scrollwork. The typical Salamanca **patio★** (1428) inside, has lovely lines. The library, on the right as you enter, has a double Mudejar ceiling; the Calderón de la Barca gallery *(p 21),* on the *patio* side, contains the former University Library decoration (transformed into a chapel in 18C — *see above),* including a third of the Fernando Gallego so-called **Salamanca ceiling★** of the constellations and signs of the zodiac — the interest of even this remaining part gives an idea of what the whole must have been like in the 15C.

Salamanca Museum (AZ K). — *Open 1 July to 30 September 9.30am to 2pm; the rest of the year 10am to 2pm and 4 to 6.30pm; Saturdays and Sundays 10am to 2pm; closed Mondays and holidays; 200pts.* Being installed in the Álvarez Abarca House, this museum devotes nine rooms to archaeology and fine arts. In room 1 is a lovely *artesonado* ceiling and a *Deposition* by Morales. As you leave the museum by the Plaza Fray Luis de León admire the elegant Isabeline and Renaissance windows.

New Cathedral★★ (Catedral nueva) (AZ). — Construction, begun in 1513 was largely completed by 1560, although additions continued to be made until the 18C.

The **west front★★** is divided below the windows into four wide bays which correspond to the ground plan. The bays are outlined by pierced stonework, carved as minutely as the keystones in the arches, the friezes and pinnacled balustrades, which mark the Gothic building's horizontal lines. The decoration on the single portal, which in retable style includes scenes such as a Crucifixion, overflows the covings and tympanum.

The pattern of the vaulting, the delicacy of the cornices, the sweep of the pillars, strike one immediately on entering. The eight windows in the lantern are given added effect by a drum on which scenes from the Life of the Virgin were painted in the 18C by the Churriguera brothers who also designed the ornate baroque choirstalls, *trascoro* and organ loft above the stalls on the north side; the south loft is Plateresque (1558).

Old Cathedral★ (Catedral vieja) (AZ B). — *Enter through the 1st bay off the south aisle in the New Cathedral; open in summer 10am to 2pm and 3 to 8pm; in winter 9.30am to 1.30pm and 3.30 to 6pm; 50pts; last admission: 20 min before closing time.*

Fortunately the builders of the New Cathedral respected the fabric of the Old which, nevertheless, is almost totally masked outside by its larger descendant. It was built in the 12C and is a good example of Romanesque, the pointed vaulting being a legitimate, if unusual, innovation; the **lantern** or Cock Tower (Torre del Gallo), with two tiers of windows and ribbing, is outstanding. High up beneath the vaulting, the capitals are carved.

SALAMANCA ★★★

The **altarpiece★★** in the central apsidal chapel was painted in 1445 by Nicholas of Florence and comprises 53 compartments decorated in still fresh colours in vivid detail beneath a Last Judgment in which the dark background adds to the brilliance of the Risen Christ. The Virgin of the Vega at the retable centre, is a 12C wooden statue, plated in gilded and enamelled bronze. Recesses in the south transept contain obviously French influenced 13C recumbent figures and frescoes; the St Martin Chapel *(light at the entrance),* at the west end of the nave, is entirely covered in 13 and 14C frescoes.

Cloister. — The cloister is 18C, earlier Romanesque galleries having foundered in 1755 during the Lisbon earthquake. Adjoining are the Talavera Chapel with a Mudejar dome on carved ribs where the ancient Mozarabic rite was celebrated — the altarpiece is by Pedro Berruguete — the St Barbara Chapel, formerly used for university examinations; in the chapterhouse the **Diocesan Museum,** which contains works by Fernando Gallego (St Catherine altarpiece), and on the floor above, by Juan of Flanders (St Michael altarpiece); and finally, the Anaya Chapel in which are a 15C organ, 16C Gutierre recumbent statues and at the centre, the finely decorated 15C **tomb★★** of Bishop Diego de Anaya.

Leave the New Cathedral through the south transept. From the **Patio Chico** (AZ 28), or Small Square, you can see the Old Cathedral apse and scallop tiling on the Cock Tower.

St Stephen's Monastery★ (Convento de San Esteban) (BZ E). — *Open 9am to 1pm and 4 to 7.30pm (7pm in winter); 50pts.* Gothic and Renaissance styles are mingled in this 16 and 17C building, so that while typically Gothic pinnacles decorate the lateral buttresses, nothing could be more Plateresque in style than the sculpture of the impressive **façade.**

Cloister. — The cloister's features are the prophets' heads in **medallions★** and Rodrigo Gil de Hontañón's grand staircase (1540) which leads to the choir gallery (view).

Church. — The gallery has star vaulting. The central altarpiece by José Churriguera, is crowned by a painting of the *Martyrdom of St Stephen* by Claudio Coello.

Las Dueñas Convent (BZ F). — *Open 10am (10.30am in winter) to 1pm and 4 to 7pm (5.30pm in winter); 40pts.*

The 16C **cloister★★** only is open, but its upper gallery is decorated with profusely carved capitals (characters from the *Divine Comedy* and a portrait of Dante).

Clavero Tower (BZ M). — The tower, all that remains of a castle built in about 1450, stands now alone, a massive polygonal keep, crowned with sentry turrets decorated underneath with Mudejar trelliswork. It houses the municipal museum *(open 10am to 2pm and 4.30 to 7.30pm; 9.30am to 2.30pm the 1st and 3rd Sundays of the month; closed Saturday afternoons, Mondays and the 2nd and 4th Sunday of the month).*

Fonseca Palace (Diputación) (BZ D). — The **patio★** of this Renaissance palace, combines Salamanca mixtilinear arches at one end with a corbelled gallery on the right and an arcade on the left in which the capitals resemble those in the Dueñas Convent.

■ PICTURESQUE QUARTERS *1 1/2 hours walk*

The route (town plan p 240) is along quiet streets, fronted by 15 and 16C houses. Leave the Plaza Mayor by the alley in the southwest corner.

St Martin's (ABY L). — The Romanesque church has a north door with dog-tooth covings in the Zamora style. Note the stairs up to the Plateresque decorated gallery and the former west door, since incorporated in a baroque chapel.

St Benedict's Quarter (Barrio de San Benito). — Surrounding the square, at the centre of which stands the church (AY N), are the mansions of the old noble rival families *(Los Bandos p 240).* The church itself, dating from 1490, was the Maldonado family pantheon.

Church of Immaculate Conception (Iglesia de la Purísima Concepción) (AY P). — The church contains works by Ribera, one of which, the **Immaculate Conception★** over the high altar is very well known.

Monterrey Palace (AY R). — The typical Renaissance palace (1539), has an openwork balustrade crowning a long top floor gallery, between low square corner towers.

Casa de las Muertes (AY S). — The early 16C façade, one of the first examples of Plateresque, is attributed, complete with its somewhat formalised design of medallions, foliated scrollwork and decorative putti, to Diego de Siloé.

Ursuline Convent (Las Úrsulas) (AY X). — *Open in summer 9.30am to 1pm and 4.30 to 7pm; in winter 9.30am to 12.30pm and 4 to 6.30pm; 10pts.*

The 16C church contains the **tomb★** of Alfonso de Fonseca on which the incredibly delicate carved low reliefs are attributed to Diego de Siloé. The **museum** has a beautiful Morales triptych and fragments of an altarpiece by Juan de Borgoña.

Plaza de Los Bandos (BY 5). — María la Brava's house (ABY Q), with an *alfiz* and 15C coats of arms, faces the Renaissance gateway to the Garci Grande Palace (BY V).

■ ADDITIONAL SIGHTS

Fonseca College (AY Y). — *Open 9am to 2pm and 4 to 7pm; 25pts.*

The college was built in the 16C to plans by Diego de Siloé for Irish students. The elegant Gothic **chapel★,** behind a finely carved Plateresque door, contains a vast altarpiece by Alonso Berruguete. The **patio★** is a lovely example of Spanish Renaissance.

St Mark's (San Marcos) (BY W). — The 12C church's round shape was certainly originally designed as protection against possible Moorish attack. Inside are fragmentary frescoes.

EXCURSION

Buen Amor Castle. — *21km · 13 miles by* ⑤ *on the plan then bear right into a signposted private road. Open 10am to 2pm and 3 to 8.30pm (6.30pm in winter); 75pts.* This castle served as the Catholic Monarch's base in the early years when they were fighting supporters of La Beltraneja *(p 245).* Alonso II, Archbishop of Toledo, transformed it into a palace, adding a pleasant Renaissance *patio* as a suitable setting for his mistress! The dining hall has an *artesonado* ceiling.

SAN CEBRIÁN DE MAZOTE (Valladolid)
Michelin map 990 folds 28 and 29 — Pop 280

Approach: 6km - 3 1/2 miles north of Mota del Marqués on the N VI turn right into a surfaced road (5km - 3 miles).

The 10C church, built to a cruciform plan with a nave and two aisles, is a rare Mozarabic structure. The modillions are typical but some of the capitals and the apsidal low reliefs show traces of an earlier, Visigothic style.

SAN MILLÁN DE LA COGOLLA (La Rioja)
Michelin map 990 fold 16 — Pop 298

The tomb of a Berceo hermit shepherd, Millán or Emilian of the Hood *(cogolla)*, who died a centenarian in 574, soon became a local pilgrimage and remained so even under the Muslims. First a church was built in the mountains (Suso), then, in 1053, a monastery, in the valley (Yuso). The Benedictines left in 1835.

Suso Monastery. — *Open 10am to 2pm and 4 to 7pm (6pm in winter); closed Mondays and 26 and 27 September.* The ascent opens up views of the terraced and intensively cultivated Cárdenas Valley. In the church, the cubic apse with big carved corbels is Mozarabic, the chapel hollowed out of the rock, Visigothic — in one is a recumbent 12C statue of San Millán — the Mozarabic east end, comprising two aisles divided by three horseshoe shaped arches and the extensions to the aisles, westwards, Romanesque.

Yuso Monastery. — *Guided tours (time: 1/2 hour) 10.30am to 12.30pm and 4.30 to 7pm (4 to 6pm 1 October to 30 June); closed Mondays; 100pts.* The monastery was erected between the 16 and 18C, in Renaissance style in the case of the church, Neo-Classical and baroque respectively for the portals and sacristy. In the treasury are splendid **ivories★★** from two 11C reliquaries. These were robbed of their gold mounts and precious stones by French soldiers and are now shown as sets of ivory plaques — San Millán's (1067-1080), consisting of 14 Romanesque pieces, is carved with great human expression, San Felices' (1090), 5 pieces, with a distinctly Byzantine sense of hierarchy.

SAN PANTALEÓN DE LOSA (Burgos)
Michelin map 990 fold 6

The picturesque Losa Valley, in the green Cantabrian Cordillera, is enclosed by rock walls in which the strata run obliquely.

St Pantaleón's. — *Leave the car by the roadside and apply at the house marked "Teléfonos".* The Romanesque church of 1207 in a remarkable **site★**, crowning a rock spike above the village, consists of an apse and domed bay, enlarged with Gothic additions. A telamon at the west door has a fishing net over one shoulder while in a coving and around the windows appear unexplained heads and legs.

SANTA MARÍA DE HUERTA Monastery ★ (Soria)
Michelin map 990 fold 28

A Cistercian community settled in this spot in 1162 and in 1179 laid the foundations of the present buildings. Work continued throughout the 13C on the lines of the order's Burgundian monasteries but took on a less austere appearance at the Renaissance. From 1835 to 1930 the monastery stood empty before being reinhabited and restored.

Open 10am to 1pm and 3 to 7pm (6.30pm in winter); closed 11am to noon on Sundays and holidays; 100pts, free Tuesdays.

Hostelry Cloister. — 16-17C. The cloister, which is Herreran in style, opens on the north side onto the monastery's oldest buildings, notably the **laybrothers' hall,** divided down its length by robust pillars, crowned with stylised capitals.

Knights' Cloister★. — 15-16C. The arches at ground level are pointed and plainly elegant, but above and quite amazing in this Cistercian setting, is a gallery added in the 16C, in full Plateresque style with decorations and medallions of apostles, Spanish kings...

Refectory★★. — The refectory is a masterpiece of 13C Gothic with sexpartite vaulting rising 15m - 50ft above the 35m - 115ft long hall. The reader's pulpit can be seen in one wall, also the hatch to the **kitchen** which has a monumental central chimney.

Church. — Exuberant Churrigueresque ornament in the *capilla mayor* and Neo-Classical facings to the pillars, largely conceal the original architecture. Between the narthex and the aisles there is an intricately decorated 18C wrought iron screen.

Coro Alto. — The gallery is beautifully decorated with Renaissance panelling and woodwork including small carved columns between the lower stalls. The Talavera *azulejos* on the floor are very old.

SANTO DOMINGO DE LA CALZADA (La Rioja)
Michelin map 990 fold 16 — Pop 5 544

St Dominic of the Causeway came into being when Dominic, an 11C hermit living beside the Glera, built a bridge across the river and a road *(calzada: road, causeway)*, to help pilgrims on their way to Santiago de Compostela. This done, he converted his hermitage into a hospice and erected a hospital. A town grew up around the halt on the Camino Francés *(p 153)* and in the 14C was considered sufficiently important to be encircled by the ramparts which are still standing.

The roasted cock that crowed again. — A live cock and hen are kept in the cathedral in memory of the miracle said to have occured in Santo Domingo, when a cockerel stood up on a charger after it had been roasted and, fully feathered, crowed aloud to testify before all the innocence of a pilgrim unjustly accused of theft and hanged. He too was found to be alive and duly released; pilgrims still collect the birds' white feathers.

SANTO DOMINGO DE LA CALZADA

Cathedral*. — *Open 9am to 2pm and 4 to 8pm.* The church is Gothic, apart from the ambulatory and some of the apsidal chapels which are Romanesque. A separate baroque tower was added in the 18C. The **saint's tomb,** beneath a 1513 baldachin, is in the south transept, and opposite, is a painted and gilded Gothic creation in the form of a sumptuous cage for the legendary cock and hen.

The **retable*** at the high altar (1538) is Damián Forment's *(p 20)* last work, and in the use of baroque high relief and swirling movement, the human body as a decorative element and the Renaissance ideas, is both original and by far his freest composition.

The St John Baptist Chapel *(2nd off the north aisle)* contains a fine 15C Hispano-Flemish **retable** composed of 24 scenes and 9 statues.

SANTO DOMINGO DE SILOS Monastery ★★ (Burgos)

Michelin map 442 fold 15

The monastery is named after an 11C monk, Dominic, who reconstructed the conventual buildings, erected the previous century by Fernán González, Count of Castile, and demolished by Al Mansur *(p 38).*

These reconstructed buildings, for centuries a halt on the pilgrim way to Santiago de Compostela, were abandoned in 1835, but were reinhabited by Benedictine monks from Poitou, in France, in 1881, who planted the magnificent cypress in the cloister.

The cloister**. — *Apply at the porter's lodge. Guided tours (time: 45 min) 10am (12.15pm Sundays and holidays) to 1pm and 4.15 to 6.45pm (5 to 8pm Thursdays June to September); 75pts.*

The cloister, which is very big for a Romanesque building, comprises two super-imposed, architecturally similar galleries. Careful study of the quite outstanding carved decoration in the ground level arcades reveals that several major sculptors worked on the stone. The first and most original craftsman was primarily a linear artist with a hieratical turn of mind who preferred symbolism to total realism — his work extends along the east and north galleries, capitals nos (**10**), (**11**), (**12**) and (**13**) and the reliefs on the southeast, northeast and northwest corner pillars; the second man was more partial to volume than line and personified his figures; the third,

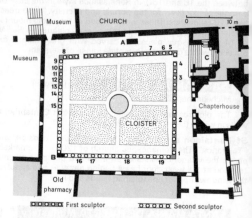

First sculptor   Second sculptor

again a highly skilled mason, carved the southwest pillar (**B**).

The capitals. — The capitals, apart from those which are historiated (**6**, **14**, **15**) or covered with strapwork (**1**, **9**), illustrate a fantastic bestiary which derives from the Mudejar use of animal and plant motifs. The principal themes are:

Harpies: horned (**7**), attacked by eagles and defended by dogs (**4**).

Animals on top of one another: combats between eagles and lions (**5**), birds (**8**); eagles and hares (**18**).

Birds in courtship display: with necks interlaced (**10**), in a perfect curve (**11**), with grimacing monster heads (**19**) and with those of slender gazelles (**2**).

Animals amidst foliage or ensnared by plant tendrils: as a decorative theme (**12** and **3**) and arousing terror in birds (**16**) and stags (**17**).

The low reliefs. — The **northeast pillar** shows the Descent from the Cross and on the upper register, the earth and the moon on the point of being clouded over; on the other face is an original representation of the Entombment and the Resurrection as a single composition.

The **northwest pillar,** concerned with doubts on the Resurrection in the minds of some disciples, shows Christ on the road to Emaus and before St Thomas.

The **southwest pillar** (**B**) is devoted to the Virgin, with, on the left, an Annunciation in which Mary appears crowned by two angels, and on the right, a Tree of Jesse.

The **southeast pillar** is carved almost in the manner of an ivory diptych; on the left is the Ascension, on the right, Pentecost — note the sculptor's invention of having Paul — recognisable by his bald patch — present at both events.

The galleries. — St Dominic's tomb (**A**), surmounted by a 13C sarcophagus carved in high relief, lies in the north gallery; *artesonado* vaulting, overpainted in the 14C, extends over the west gallery. A small **museum** displays some very old pieces, including a chalice of St Dominic's with filigree decoration, an enamel reliquary, a 10-11C manuscript of the Mozarabic rite (the musical notation is now, unfortunately, illegible). The **old pharmacy** has a collection of Talavera ceramic jars each decorated with the monastery crest.

As you leave the cloister look at the fine door known as the Virgins' Door (**C**), flanked by turned columns, which led to the former Romanesque monastery church.

The church. — The present church (1756-1816), which is agreeably proportioned, combines the rounded volume of baroque with the plain grandeur of the Herreran style.

■ YECLA GORGES ★

5km - 3 miles east; time: 10 min.

The "Gorges" are a cleft several hundred feet deep but only three feet wide in places, cut through a layer of grey limestone by a small rushing stream. They can be followed along their full length.

SEGOVIA ★★ P

Michelin map 447 fold 7 — Local map p 201 — Pop 53 237

Segovia has a **site**★★ which has made many compare the city to a ship. Approaching from the east *(① or ② on the town plan)*, the centre of the city, appears perched on a triangular rock at an altitude of 1 000m - 3 280ft. To the left is the Roman aqueduct, to the right are the cathedral domes and spires and further right still at the rock top, the Alcázar, 100m - 328ft above the confluence of the Eresma and Clamores Rivers.

Segovia's **Romanesque churches** are among its greatest treasures. Common architectural features include well rounded apses, frequently a tall square belfry beside the east end and a covered gallery where weavers' or merchants' guilds used to meet.

Historical notes. — Segovia was an important military town in Roman times; under the Moors in the Middle Ages it became a wool town — by the 15C it numbered 60 000 citizens.

Isabel the Catholic, Queen of Castile. — On the death of Henry IV in 1474 many grandees refused to recognise the legitimacy of his daughter, Doña Juana, as **La Beltraneja,** after her mother's favourite, Beltrán de la Cueva. In Segovia in her stead, the grandees proclaimed Henry's half-sister, Isabel, Queen of Castile — thus preparing the way for Spain's unification since Isabel was already married to Ferdinand, heir apparent of Aragon. La Beltraneja, aided by her husband, Alfonso V of Portugal, pressed her claim, but renounced in 1479.

The ''Comuneros''. — The Spanish were considerably incensed at the beginning of Charles V's reign by the emperor's Flemish court and companions, his attempt to impose absolute rule and new taxes. Town forces *(comunidades)* under the leadership of the Toledan, Juan de Padilla and the Segovian, Juan Bravo, rose in revolt but were crushed finally at Villalar in 1521 and the leaders executed in Segovia.

■ TOUR OUTSIDE THE WALLS★ *1 1/2 hours by car*

Follow the route on the inset map on p 246. Views of the city setting, the red Castilian countryside and green river valley.

Start from the Plaza del Azoguejo.

Roman Aqueduct★★★ **(Acueducto romano)** (BY). — This Roman aqueduct is one of the finest still in existence and it is still operating. It is 728m - 2 392ft long, rises to a maximum height of 28m - 92ft in the Plaza del Azoguejo where the ground is lowest and consists throughout of two tiers of arches which are strong yet slender.

San Millán (BY). — The early 12C church stands at the centre of a square which allows a full view of its pure, still primitive Romanesque lines, porticoed gallery with carved capitals and modillions, and an 11C Mozarabic tower.

Alcázar★ (AX). — *Open 10am to 6.30pm (3.30pm 1 October to 31 March); 125pts.*
The mid - 14C building was remodelled in the 15C. The keep, the Torre de Juan II, is flanked by corbelled turrets. Several rooms display mediaeval armoury, period pictures and furnishings. From its windows and terrace is a good view of the lush, green Eresma Valley, the El Parral Monastery and the Meseta.

Santa Cruz Convent (BX C). — The convent pinnacles, the decorated Isabeline entrance and the frieze with the emblems of the Catholic Monarchs, can be seen from the road.

San Lorenzo (AZ A). — The Romanesque church with its unusual brick belfry stands in a square surrounded by corbelled half-timbered houses.

(After MTTC photo, Madrid)

The Alcázar

El Parral Monastery★ (BX). — *Open 9am to 12.30pm (11.30am Sundays and holidays) and 3 to 6.30pm (6pm in winter).*
The church, behind its never completed façade, has a nave rich with carved doors, Flamboyant and Renaissance recesses and a superb altarpiece by Juan Rodríguez (1528).

Vera Cruz Chapel (AX). — *Open 10.30am to 1.30pm and 3.30 to 7pm; closed November, Mondays, 1 and 6 January, 24 June, 25 October and 25 December; 50pts.*
The unusual polygonal building was erected in the 13C either by the Templars or the Knights of the Holy Sepulchre. At the centre are two small rooms, one above the other, entered from a circular corridor, in which the order's secret ceremonies were conducted.

Return to the Plaza del Azoguejo along the Cuesta de los Hoyos.

■ THE OLD TOWN★★ (Ciudad Vieja) *1/2 day on foot*

Streets inside the walls are picturesque with 15-16C Castilian type entrances surrounded by *alfiz (p 19)* and façades decorated with Mudejar and geometric designs.

Plaza del Conde de Cheste (BY 9). On the square stand the palaces of the Marquesses of Moya (B), Lozoya (E), the Counts of Cheste (F) and de las Cabezas (K).

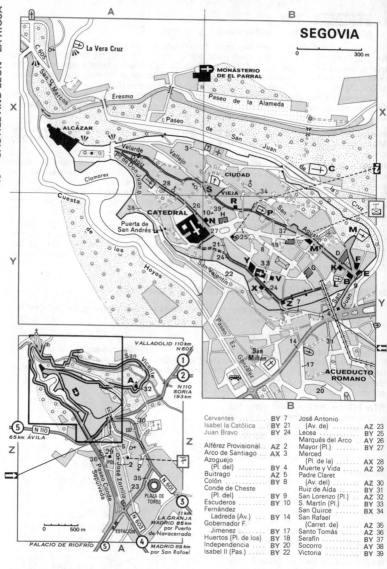

SEGOVIA

San Sebastián (BY L). — Small Romanesque church in a quiet square.

San Juan de los Caballeros (BY M). — The outstanding feature of this Romanesque church is its portico with its carvings of portrait heads, plant motifs and animals. Inside, **Daniel Zuloaga** (1852-1921), an artist who did much to revive Spanish ceramic art, established his studio, now converted into a **museum** *(open 10am to 2pm and 4 to 6pm; closed Sunday and holiday afternoons and all day Monday).*

Fine Arts Museum (Museo Provincial de Bellas Artes) (BY M¹). — *Open 10am to 2pm and 4 to 6pm; closed Sunday and holiday afternoons; 75pts.*
   The 16C house makes a good setting for works of art (Rembrandt engraving).

Holy Trinity Church (Trinidad) (BY P). — Spacious, almost austere, Romanesque church.

Casa de los del Hierro (BY R). — 16C entrance with historiated scrollwork, grotesques.

St Stephen's (San Esteban) (BX S). — One of the latest (13C) and most beautiful of Segovia's Romanesque churches with an unusual six storey tower and spire.
   Velarde and Daoiz Streets (AX) cut through the quiet old cathedral chapter quarter where there are many beautiful doorways.

Casa del Marqués del Arco (BY N). — The mansion has a rich Renaissance *patio*.

Cathedral** (AY). — The beautiful golden stone, the stepped east end, pinnacled and delicately balustrated, the tall tower, bring considerable grace to the massive building, erected during the reign of the Emperor Charles V. The width of the aisles combines with the decorative lines of the pillars and ribs in the vaulting, to make the interior both light and elegant. Among the chapels, which are closed by fine wrought iron screens, the first off the south aisle contains as altarpiece an Entombment by Juan de Juni.

Cloister*. — *Open 1 June to 30 September 10am to 6pm; 10am to 1pm and 3.30 to 6pm the rest of the year; closed 1 January and 25 December; 75pts.* The 15C cloister belonged to the former cathedral, which stood near the Alcázar. When this was destroyed in the 16C during the Comuneros' Revolt, the cloister was transported stone by stone and reerected on the new site. The chapterhouse is hung with 17C Brussels **tapestries*** (stories of Queen Zenobia); the museum displays altarpieces, church plate and incunabula. At the cathedral east end you will see a relief of a horseman.

Plaza San Martín★ (BY 33). — The square at the centre of the old mansion quarter is the most evocative of historic Segovia: on it stand **Juan Bravo's house** (X), with a gallery beneath the eaves, the 14C **Lozoya** mansion tower (V) as a reminder of the family's power in former times and the ornate entrances to big houses. At the square's centre is the 12C **Church of San Martín★**, framed by a covered gallery on pillars with finely carved capitals.

The old 17C **prison** (BY Y) has a decorative baroque pediment.

Casa de los Picos (BY Z). — The house, faced closely with diamond pointed stones, is the most original of Segovia's 15C mansions.

EXCURSIONS

La Granja de San Ildefonso★. — *11km - 7 miles by* ③. La Granja is a little Versailles at an altitude of 1 192m - 3 902ft in the centre of Spain. It was built at the feet of the Sierra de Guadarrama *(p 199)* by Philip V, grandson of Louis XIV, in pure nostalgia.

The palace. — *Illustration p 17. Guided tours (time: 1 1/2 hours) 10am to 1.30pm (2.30pm Sundays) and 3 to 6pm; closed Sunday afternoons, all day Mondays; inquire locally for holidays; 140pts.* Galleries and saloons, faced with marble or hung with crimson velvet, are lit, beneath painted ceilings and gilded stucco mouldings, by ornate chandeliers, made by local workshops which became renowned for chandelier and glasswork in the 18C. A **tapestry museum★★** on the 1st floor contains principally 16C Flemish hangings, notably *(3rd gallery)* eight of the *Honours and Virtues* series, a *Life of St Jerome* and a *Miraculous Catch of Fishes* after a Raphael cartoon.

The gardens★★. — Rocks were shattered and the ground levelled before the French landscape gardeners (Carlier, Boutelou) and sculptors (Dumandré, Thierry) could start work on the 145ha - 358 acre park which is to a great extent inspired by the gardens and parkland of Versailles. The woodland vistas are more natural, however, the rides more rural, the intersections marked by less formal cascades. The chestnut trees brought from France at a great expense, are superb.

The **fountains★★** *(they play 30 May, 25 July, and 25 August at 5.30pm; 60pts)* begin at the Neptune Basin, go on to the New Cascade, a multicoloured marble staircase in front of the palace, and end at the Fama or Fame Fountain which rises in a 40m - 131ft high plume of water.

Riofrío Domain★. — *11km - 7 miles south by* ⑤ *; 20pts per car to enter the park if not visiting the palace.* Riofrío Palace can be seen through the evergreen oaks where deer roam, below the Mujer Muerta (the Dead Woman), a foothill of the Guadarrama Sierra *(p 199)*.

Palace. — *Same opening times as the La Granja de San Ildefonso; 140pts; closed Tuesdays.* Riofrío was planned by Isabel Farnese as the equal of La Granja which she had to vacate on the death of her husband, Philip V. Construction began in 1752 but though it was very big — it measures 84m x 84m - 275ft x 275ft — it never became more than a somewhat pretentious hunting lodge. A Classical grand courtyard and monumental staircase with double flights (24 groups of allegorical statuary) lead to sumptuously decorated apartments.

A **Museum of the Chase** illustrates with paintings (including a Velázquez), man the hunter, from prehistory to the time of the Bourbons. Display of the principal types of game found in Spain.

SEPÚLVEDA (Segovia)
Michelin map ▨▨▨ fold 8 — Pop 1 590

Approaching Sepúlveda from the south you will get a good view of its terraced **site★**.

Leave the car in the town hall square, which is overlooked by the old castle ruins, and walk up to the **Church of San Salvador** from which there is a good view of the town and surrounding countryside. The church itself is typical Segovia Romanesque with a multiple storeyed belfry with paired bays and an east end decorated with a carved cornice. It has one of the oldest lateral doors in Spain, dating from 1093.

SOBRÓN Dam ★★ **Embalse de SOBRÓN** (Burgos)
Michelin map ▨▨▨ fold 6

The lake, formed by the Sobrón dammed Ebro waters, extends back more than 5km - 3 miles between impressive limestone cliffs and affords striking views along its length. **Frías★**, in the distance on its perched site *(19km - 12 miles west)* turns out to be picturesque with old houses, some half-timbered, some with overlapping round tile roofs, fronting cobbled streets, and a castle commanding a **panorama★** of the valley.

SORIA ★ **P**
Michelin map ▨▨▨ fold 27 — Pop 32 039

Poets including the Sevillian **Antonio Machado** (1875-1939), who wrote *Campos de Castilla* (1912), have always sung the praises of Soria, the pure, the mysterious, the warlike even, and of its scenery — the plain scorched and windswept by turns, the mountains on the horizon, the trees and the burnt Siena colour of its stone buildings.

"Soria pura, cabeza de Extremadura". — The city arms symbolise events in the 10C when Soria and its dependent countryside marked the limits (*cabeza:* head, extremity) of Castile in the face of the Muslim conquered south and as such was coveted by both sides. Gradually the Christians constructed a **fortified line** along the Duero reinforced by bastions such as **Berlanga, Gormaz, Peñaranda** and **Peñafiel**.

The Mesta. — In the 13C large scale sheep farmers grouped together to organise the seasonal migration and free passage of their stock across cultivated land. Soria prospered while the Mesta remained powerful in the 16C until 1836 as it commanded one of the five main tracks or *cañada* used by the flocks leaving Extremadura and Castile-La Mancha for the summer pastures of the Cantabrian Cordillera. The sheep farmers as they grew rich, built fine homes in the town, particularly in the **Calles Real** (B), **Caballeros** (A 6) and **Aduana Vieja** (A 2).

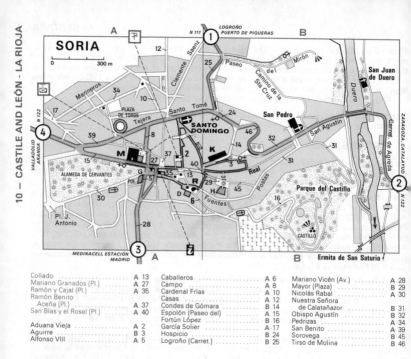

SORIA

0 — 300 m

■ MAIN SIGHTS   *time: 1 1/2 hours*

Monumental Centre. — *from the Plaza Ramón y Cajal.*

San Juan de Rabanera (A R). — San Juan has the most harmonious lines of Soria's Romanesque churches; the **portal,** recalls the events of the saint's life in the capitals on the small columns on the right and on the skilfully composed tympanum. The unusual decoration at the church's east end is repeated inside in the niches in the apse which has Byzantine style vaulting with concave quartering. Also in the church are two interesting Crucifixes — a Romanesque one over the altar and a baroque one in the north transept. There is in addition a graceful Renaissance altarpiece in the south transept.

Palace of the Counts of Gómara (B K). — The long façade, bold upstanding tower and two storey *patio* are a proud example of late 16C opulence.

Santo Domingo★ (A). — The west front is immediately attractive with two tiers of blind arcades and a single heavily carved, central **portal★★.** The overall French air is explained by the fact that the church's founders were Alfonso VIII and his wife, Eleanor of England, also Duchess of Gascony, on either side of the portal. The figures on the tympanum have been carved with great care for detail. The scenes so realistically illustrated include the early chapters of Genesis (on the jambshaft of the capitals), the Old Men of the Apocalypse playing stringed instruments, the Massacre of the Innocents, Christ's childhood, Passion and Death (in ascending registers on the archivolt).

Numantia Museum (Museo Numantino) (A M). — *Closed due to restoration.* Numantia excavation finds and plan *(for details see below).*

San Pedro Cathedral (B). — *Open 10.30am to 2pm and 4 to 7pm.* The light and spacious 16C Gothic church is beautiful; the **cloister★** *(25pts)* is older possessing three Romanesque galleries.

San Juan de Duero (B). — *Open 10am to 2pm and 4 to 7pm; closed Sunday afternoons and all day Monday; inquire locally for holidays; 200pts.* The monastery founded by the Hospitallers of St John of Jerusalem, is on the far bank of the Duero. Only the graceful gallery arcading remains of the 12-13C **cloister★,** but this is unique, the intersecting, overlapping pointed arches owing much to Moorish art. The church contains a small lapidary museum and, what is more interesting, two aediculés, on either side of the apse.

■ ADDITIONAL SIGHTS

Castle park (B). — The lines of the poet, Machado *(p 247),* on the Soria countryside come alive on this hillside: "..., violet mountains, poplars beside green waters..."

San Saturio Hermitage (B). — *Open 1 May to 30 September 10am to 2pm and 4.30 to 9pm; the rest of the year 10.30am to 6.30pm; closed Tuesdays and February.* A shaded path beside the Duero leads to the cave where the holy man sat in meditation. The octagonal chapel built into the rock and covered inside with frescoes is 18C. View.

EXCURSIONS

Numantia ruins. — *7km - 4 miles northeast by ①. Same times and charges as San Juan de Duero (see above).* There are few signs of the events which took place in Numantia in 133 BC. The Romans were in Spain and in 139 BC had thought that after the murder of the Lusitanian chief, Viriatus, their legions would suffer little general opposition, even though they had not gained control of the central Meseta and the 8 000 men of the Arevaci tribe had routed them on five occasions. **Scipio Aemilianus,** who had destroyed Carthage laid siege to Numantia in 134 BC. After eight months the Numantians could resist no more but, unwilling to submit, they burned their city and perished one and all. The present ruins are of the Numantia rebuilt by the Romans in 133 BC. Column shafts show the position of a peristyle in a patrician villa.

Sierra de Urbión★★. — *Roads are liable to be blocked by snow between November and May; inquire before leaving.* It seems surprising that this part of the Iberian Cordillera, which rises at one point to 2 228m - 7 310ft and is so close to the Soria plateau and the flat ochre coloured Ebro Valley, should be hilly and green and filled with streams rushing through pinewoods and meadows. One of these streams is the source of the Duero (910km - 565 miles).

Laguna Negra de Urbión★★★ (Soria). — Alt 1 700m - 5 576ft. *46km - 28 1/2 miles northwest by ④ — about 1 hour. At Cidones bear right towards Vinuesa; continue for 18km - 11 miles before turning into the Montenegro de Cameros road (9km - 6 miles) and finally left into the Laguna road (6km - 4 miles).* The **road★★**, after skirting the Cuerda del Pozo reservoir which is ringed by tall stone cliffs, rocks and evergreen oaks, continues through pines to the **Laguna Negra★★★**. The Black Lagoon is a translucent glaciary lake at the foot of a semicircular cliff over which cascade two waterfalls.

Laguna Negra de Neila★★ (Burgos). — Alt 2 000m - 6 560ft. *About 86km - 53 1/2 miles by ④. At Abejar turn right towards Molinos de Duero; continue to Quintanar de la Sierra where you bear right for Neila (12km - 7 1/2 miles) and then left for Huerta de Arriba; 2km - 1 mile on the left is the road to the Laguna Negra.* From the **road★★** are changing views of the valley and the Sierra de la Demanda.

TORDESILLAS (Valladolid)

Michelin map **441** fold 29 — Pop 6 681

The historic town of Tordesillas, from the south, appears massed upon the steep Duero bank. Its Plaza Mayor has unusual pillars supporting its portico.

The Treaty of Tordesillas (1494). — It was in Tordesillas, in 1494, that Spain and Portugal, under the arbitration of Pope Alexander VI of the Spanish Borja family *(p 165)*, signed the treaty dividing the New World between them. All lands west of a line of longitude 370 leagues west of the Cape Verde Islands were to be Spanish, all to the east, Portuguese — a decision which gave Spain all Latin America except Brazil.

Santa Clara Convent★. — *Guided tours (time: 1 hour) 10am to 1pm and 3 to 7pm (3 to 6pm in winter); closed Mondays and certain holidays; 50pts.* Peter I, the Cruel, converted the palace, built for his father Alfonso XI in about 1350, into a convent where he installed María de Padilla, to whom he may have been secretly married, in spite of Blanche of Bourbon being his queen. For María, who was homesick for the beauty of Seville, the king brought artistic delight to this distant heart of Castile.

Juana the Mad locked herself away here on the death of Philip the Fair in 1506 *(p 231)*.

The **patio★**, with multifoil and horseshoe shaped arches, strapwork decoration and multicoloured ceramic tiles, is well worthy of a Seville palace.

The gilded chapel with a fine Mudejar cupola, exhibits mementoes and works of art including Juana's organ, the spinets of Charles V and Philip II and a 12C altarfront.

The church is on the site of the former throne room; the choir has a particularly intricate *artesonado* **ceiling★★**. In the Saldañas Chapel are the founders' tombs and a 15C retable, originally a travelling altar. Local excavations have revealed Moorish baths.

TORO ★ (Zamora)

Michelin map **441** fold 28 — Pop 9 781

Toro stands beside the Duero at the centre of a vast clay soil plain. Wheat is grown north of the river (Tierra del Pan), vines to the south (Tierra del Vino). It was the setting, in 1476, for Ferdinand's resounding defeat of La Beltraneja's and the Portuguese forces *(p 245)*.

The town's Romanesque churches have sadly deteriorated with age or been unfortunately restored in all too many cases (except for the collegiate church).

Collegiate Church★. — *Apply to the priest; time: 1/2 hour.* Construction began in 1160 with the elegant lantern tower and ended, in 1240 with completion of the portal.

Exterior. — The Romanesque exterior of ascending lines ending in the two tier drum of the lantern tower, flanked by corner turrets, is impressive. The north portal is equally typical. The Gothic **west portal★★**, repainted in the 18C, is the church's great treasure. It is dedicated to the Virgin who stands with the Child at the pier, a posed figure with a youthful face, like those on the jambs and tympanum. More expressively carved are the figures of the Celestial Court on the archivolt and the Last Judgment on the recessed orders.

Interior. — Start beneath the cupola with its two tiers of windows in the drum. The dome was one of the first in Spain to be set on squinches. Polychrome wood statues stand against the pillars at the end of the nave on consoles, one of which is carved with an amusing version of the birth of Eve. In the sacristy the picture known as the Virgin and the Fly, attributed to Fernando Gallego, is especially interesting as it includes what is considered to be the truest likeness of Isabel the Catholic also note the priceless 17C ivory Calvary.

San Lorenzo. — This brick Romanesque church's east end, with its stone base, blind arcades and dog-tooth decoration on the upper cornice, has much of the Mudejar style of Castile and León (Olmedo, Arévalo), influenced by the craftsmen of Toledo. The wooden gallery in the retro-choir is carpentered and painted in the manner of an *artesonado* ceiling.

TURÉGANO (Segovia)

Michelin map **447** folds 7 and 8 — Pop 1 207

This Castilian village has a singular **view★** from its arcaded Plaza Mayor, of a castle dominated by a tall campanile.

Castle★. — *To visit apply to the sacristan.* From the 12C the town and castle were the property of the bishops of Segovia, one of whom Juan Arias Dávila, played a large role in the 15C in the controversy over Henry IV's successor *(p 245)*.

Two of the three perimeters rebuilt in the 15C by Dávila are still standing. They encircle the older 13C church and the later 17C campanile (transported from a nearby church and re-erected). The archaic looking nave has old capitals on the south side.

VALLADOLID ★★ Ⓟ

Michelin map **441** folds 29 and 30 — Pop 330 242
See map of built-up area in the current Michelin Red Guide España Portugal

Valladolid is a university city, an episcopal see — the Holy Week ceremonies are splendid. As one of the former capitals of Castile, it is rich in decorated buildings, and in art. It is also a prosperous modern city (engineering and food production).

Castile's kings frequently resided at Valladolid between the 12 and 17C: Peter the Cruel married there in the 14C, Ferdinand and Isabel in 1469; it was the birthplace of Henry IV, Philip IV and his sister Anne of Austria, mother of Louis XIV. The city was also deeply involved in the 16C Comuneros Revolt *(p 245)*.

The Isabeline style. — The Isabeline style evolved as the ultimate stage before Plateresque. The decorative focus on entrances *(p 14)* produced rectangular panels which eventually extended from ground level to cornice and were compartmented like an altarpiece. Whereas the Salamanca Plateresque fronts *(p 15 and 240)* are outstanding for their considerable sophistication in composition within a confined form, those of Valladolid, being earlier, demonstrate a less developed but more vigorous art.

The Renaissance. — **Santa Cruz College** (BX S), built at the end of the 15C, is one of the first truly Renaissance buildings; the finely carved decoration at the entrance, in fact, is still Plateresque but the stone bossage and window design are of entirely Classical inspiration. The **Palace of the Marquesses of Valverde** (AV P) of 1503 is even decorated with atlantes; the **Capitanía General** (AV N), has a *patio* with finely carved modillions.

The Herreran style. — The influence of the cathedral architect was considerable in the town. His disciples built the churches of **Las Angustias** (BX L) in which, at the end of the south transept, stands Juan de Juni's masterpiece, the **Virgin of the 7 Knives★** (de los 7 Cuchillos), and **San Miguel** (AV K) which contains statues by Gregorio Fernández as well as copies by Juan de Juni and Pedro de Mena. The church also has a **Herreran patio** (AX B) of impressive simplicity *(closed due to restoration)*.

■ MAIN SIGHTS *time: 2 hours*

San Gregorio College★★ (BV). — *Open 10am to 1.30pm and 4 to 7pm; closed Sunday afternoons, all day Monday and certain holidays, inquire locally; 150pts.*

The college, which was founded in the 15C by Fray Alonso of Burgos, confessor to Isabel the Catholic, is the greatest example of the Isabeline style of architecture in Valladolid. The **entrance★★** is unbelievably rich; every fantasy from "savages" to interwoven branches of thorns, is somehow felicitous in its inclusion in the strongly hieratical composition which focuses first on the doorway and then rises to the magnificent heraldic motif above. It is considered that the artist was almost certainly Gil de Siloé.

The college now functions as a **National Museum of Polychrome Sculpture★★★** and as such contains major works by Juan de Juni *(Entombment: illustration p 20)*, Gregorio Fernández, Pompeo Leoni and Pedro de Mena *(Mary Magdalene)* besides an altarpiece by Berruguete designed for San Benito but shown here dismounted. Some of the gallery ceilings are beautiful.

The **patio★★** is a delight.

(After MTTC photo, Madrid)

San Gregorio College - The patio

At ground level tall spiral columns support plain basket handle arches; above, the theme is repeated but with an infinitely delicate, dense decoration: the bays are divided, small columns support smaller arches and in the space above is a lacework tracery. A magnificent balustrade lines the upper gallery; a cornice frieze, evenly interspersed with escutcheons, completes the stonework fantasy.

A **chapel★** *(closed due to restoration)*, designed by Juan Guas, on the far side of a small *patio*, contains an altarpiece by Berruguete, a tomb by Felipe Bigarny and carved choirstalls.

St Paul's (San Pablo) (BV E). — The lower **façade★★** by Simon of Cologne is typically Gothic. The upper façade is later and in a Plateresque arrangement *(p 15)*.

Cathedral★ (BX Q). — *Open weekdays 7am to 1pm and 5.30 to 8pm.*

The cathedral project, commissioned in about 1580 by Philip II from Herrera, was only realised very slowly and was distorted to some degree by the architect's 17 and 19C successors — as in the upper part of the façade, filled with baroque ornament by Alberto Churriguera who also worked on the octagonal section of the tower.

The powerful interior remains one of Herrera's major successes. The **altarpiece** (1551) in the central apsidal chapel, highlighting with gilding and colour the interplay of perspective and relief so that the figures seem almost truly alive, is by Juan de Juni.

Museum (BX M¹). — *Open 10am to 2pm and 5.30 to 8pm; closed Sunday afternoons and holidays; 100pts.* In the old Gothic Church of St Mary Major at the east end of the cathedral, are a 15C altarpiece, two paintings of the Ribera school, two portraits attributed to Velázquez and a great silver monstrance by the master jeweller, Juan de Arfe (16C). In the Chapel of Saint Iñes fragments of Mudejar art are displayed.

VALLADOLID

■ ADDITIONAL SIGHTS

Archaeological Museum★ (AV M²). — *Temporarily closed.*
    This 16C palace, besides archaeological specimens (Etruscan mirror, Roman sculptures), displays an interesting mediaeval collection of 15 and 16C paintings, 13 and 15C frescoes, furniture, carvings and tapestries.

Santa María la Antigua (BX V). — The only Romanesque features in this otherwise elegantly Gothic church, are its tall slender tower, topped by a pyramid steeple, and its portico with triple columns, along the north wall.

St Benedict's (San Benito) (AX F). — The church's generally robust simplicity and massive, monumental porch, give it a fortress-like air (1499).

University (BX U). — Remarkable Churrigueresque entrance.

Cervantes' House (AY R). — *Open 10am to 6pm (2pm Sundays and holidays); closed Mondays; 75pts.*
    The house belonged to Cervantes for the last years of his life and looks much as he knew it with white walls and simple furnishings.

Oriental Museum (AY M³). — *Open daily 4 to 7pm; Sundays and holidays 10am to 2pm; 125pts.*
    Located in a Neo-Classical college (18C) designed by Ventura Rodríguez, the museum houses a collection of Chinese (bronze, porcelain, lacquerware, coins and silk embroidery) and Philippine art (ivory pieces and numerous reminders of the Spanish presence on these islands).

EXCURSION

Simancas Castle. — *11km - 7 miles south by ⑤ on the plan.* The castle was constructed in 1480 by the Admirals of Castille but was purchased by the Catholic Monarchs after the completion of the Reconquest when they determined next to subdue the grandees. This they did in part by preventing them owning or fortifying strongholds. The Emperor Charles V had the castle converted into a repository for state archives which it has remained without interval so that the 8 million documents represent a complete history of 16-20C Spanish administration in a single priceless **collection★.** *Apply in advance by telephoning 59 00 03.*

The main car parks are indicated on the town plans.

ZAMORA ★ P

Michelin map **441** fold 27 — Pop 59 734

Only traces remain of the walls which made Fernando I refer to the city as "wall girded Zamora" and which made it the westerly bastion of the fortified Duero line during the Reconquest *(p 247)*. The town played its part in the repeated struggles for the throne of Castile: in the 11C when Sancho III's sons fought for his kingdom *(p 178)*, and in the 15C, when La Beltraneja unsuccessfully disputed the rights of Isabel the Catholic *(p 247)*.

ZAMORA

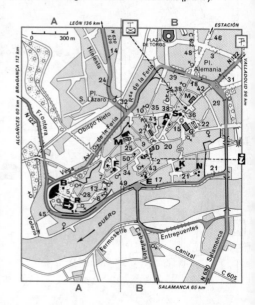

Among the mansions in the old quarter which lies between the quiet **castle** grounds (A B) and the **Magdalena Church** (A F), are several with fine fronts, particularly the **Casa del Cordón** (B E) and the **Casa de los Momos** (B A) which both have Isabeline windows.

Zamoran Romanesque arcnitecture. — The 12C saw a series of originally designed Romanesque churches erected in Zamora province; particular features included portals without tympana, surrounded by multilobed arches and often possessing heavily carved archivolts. The larger churches in Zamora, Toro and Salamanca, also had domes on squinches over the transept crossing. These cupolas were frequently superimposed on drums, pierced by windows which provided considerable light inside. The best examples of the style in Zamora itself, besides the cathedral, are the **Magdalena** (A F), **Santa María de la Orta** (B K), **Santo Tomé** (B N) and **Santiago del Burgo** (B S).

Holy Week. — Zamora's Holy Week solemn celebrations are renowned for the numbers who attend and for the spectacular *pasos* street processions.

On Palm Sunday a children's procession escorts a *paso* of Christ's entry into Jerusalem; on Maundy Thursday evening a totally silent, torchlight procession follows the poignant Dead Christ, sculpture by Gregorio Fernández, borne by white penitents through the streets in imitation of the walk to Golgotha. The **Holy Week Museum** (AB M) *(open 10am to 2pm and 4 to 7pm; 50pts)* contains most of the *pasos* except for the Dead Christ which belongs to the Church of Santa María la Nueva *(opposite the museum)*.

Cathedral★ (A R). — *Time: 3/4 hour.* The architecture of the 12C cathedral outside is a conspectus of different styles: the north front is Neo-Classical in keeping with the square it overlooks; the belfry and graceful Byzantine inspired cupola covered with overlapping flat stone tiles like fish scales, are Romanesque; the south front, the only original part of the structure, is again Romanesque with blind arcades and a door which has unusual covings with pierced festoons.

The aisles inside are transitional Romanesque-Gothic, the vaulting going from broken cradle to pointed ogive. Slender painted ribs support the luminous **dome★** on squinches above the transept. At the end of the Gothic period, master wood carvers and wrought iron smiths entered the church — there are fine grilles enclosing the choir, two Mudejar pulpits (15C) and **choirstalls★★**, decorously depicting Biblical figures on their backs and more hilariously, allegorical and burlesque scenes on armrests and misericords. The cloister is Herreran. The principal exhibit in the **cathedral museum★** is a series of 15C Flemish tapestries *(open 10am to 1.30pm and in addition 4 to 7pm during the summer; 50pts)*.

EXCURSIONS

San Pedro de la Nave. — *19km - 12 miles northwest. Follow the N 122 for 12km - 7 1/2 miles then turn right.*

The Visigothic church, in danger of drowning on account of the damming of the Esla, has been rebuilt at El Campillo *(to visit inquire at the entrance of the village)*.

It is late 7C and is artistically remarkable for the carving on the transept capitals which has a strong sense of composition: Daniel in the Lions' Den, the Sacrifice of Isaac... The frieze, halfway up the wall, is made up of Christian symbols: grapes, doves, etc...

Arcenillas. — *7km - 4 1/2 miles southeast along the C 605.*

Fifteen panels of the life, death and resurrection of Christ from the great Gothic altarpiece designed for Zamora Cathedral by the late 15C artist **Fernando Gallego**, one of the greatest Castilian painters to adopt the Hispano-Flemish style, have been reassembled in the village church.

11 Balearic Islands

The Balearic Archipelago is made up of two pairs of islands encircled by islets: Majorca and Minorca, Ibiza and Formentera, known to the Greeks as the Pityuses or pine lands. The islands, which together form one of Spain's 50 provinces, have a land area of 5 000km² - 1 900sq miles. The capital is Palma de Mallorca; the language, derived from Catalan, Balearic.

Landscape. — The limestone hills, none of which exceeds 1 500m - 5 000ft differ in origin: Ibiza and Majorca are an extension of the Baetic Cordillera, Minorca a part of Sardinia. The lush vegetation produced by the autumn rains is one of the Sunshine Islands' greatest attractions; pines line the sloping, indented shores, providing shade on the beaches close to the water's edge; junipers and evergreen oaks cloak the upper hillsides; almonds, figs and olives, some said to be 1 000 years old, cover the lower slopes and flatlands.

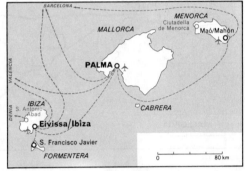

Shipping lines

The three larger islands differ considerably in character, although having the common characteristic of inland tranquillity and coasts seething, in many areas, with bustling tourist activity. Around it all, flows the wonderfully limpid sea.

Historical notes. — The first traces of man on the islands can be seen in the *talayots* (p 261) which date back to the Bronze Age. Much later, Balearic islanders were known as brave and skilful mercenaries in the rival armies of Rome and Carthage. From 902 to 1229 the islands were occupied by the Muslims who left a clear imprint in place names — names beginning with "Ben" - in irrigation — though today windmills have replaced the *norias* or waterwheels — and, most importantly, in the system of agriculture which combines the growing of cereals with that of fruit trees. The Reconquest by the Aragonese in 1229 (pp 61-62), placed the Balearics at the centre of trade in the Mediterranean and brought about a period of prosperity. This ended in the 16C when Spain, by now united, turned its energies to overseas discovery, abandoning its Mediterranean interest to Barbary pirates and the Turks. Evidence of the insecurity felt by the islanders remains in the walls constructed around the towns of Majorca, the watch towers and the fortified towns and churches built on Ibiza.

Since the 18C the Balearics have been involved in all the major conflicts which have convulsed the mainland but without suffering irreparable damage.

THE ISLAND OF MAJORCA ★★★   MALLORCA

Michelin map 🄰🄰🄳 folds 40 to 42

Majorca has an area of 3 640km² - 1 405sq miles — measures some 75km - 46 miles from north to south and 100km - 62 miles from west to east. The population is 561 215. The scenery, the mild climate and hotels, make the island a major tourist centre.

The island's hundred faces. — A relief map of Majorca shows two lines of hills divided by a considerable flat expanse. The fruit trees which cover the island to some extent unify the landscape, which is otherwise extraordinarily varied.

The **Puig Major chain** in the northwest, its crests — none exceeds 1 436m - 4 711ft, running parallel to the coast, its cliffs plunging spectacularly into the sea, forms a solid rock barrier against offshore winds from the mainland. Pines, junipers and evergreen oaks cover the slopes, interspersed here and there by the gnarled and twisted trunks of Majorca's famous 1 000 years' old olives. Villages, perched halfway up hillsides, are surrounded by terraces planted with vegetables and fruit trees.

The central plain is divided by low walls into arable fields and fig and almond orchards; the market towns, with outlying windmills to pump water, retain the regular plan of mediaeval fortress towns.

The heights to the east are pine covered; the coast is rocky, hollowed with wonderful caves and indented with sheltered, sand carpeted, coves.

The short lived Kingdom of Majorca (1262-1349). — James I of Aragon set sail on 5 September 1229 from Salou to recapture Majorca from the Muslims, thinking by so doing, also, to reopen trade routes with Italy. The decisive battle, in which it is said 50 000 died, took place in the Bay of Palma on 31 December 1229. Thirty years later the Conqueror united the Balearic Islands, Roussillon and Montpellier in a single independent kingdom which he presented to his son, James II. He and his successor, Sancho, brought prosperity to the island, founding new towns, building strongpoints and peopling the territory with Catalan immigrants. Nor did it apparently suffer when Pedro IV seized the archipelago in 1343, killing the young prince at Llucmajor, to reunite it to the crown of Aragon. Churches were built, a merchant navy was established which brought local prosperity and a school of cartography founded which rapidly became famous.

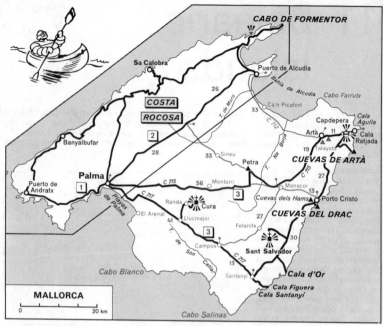

The Majorcan Primitives (14-15C). — Gothic Majorcan painting, characterised by a marked gentleness of expression, was wide open to external influences: the so-called **Master of the Privileges** showed, even in the 14C, a Sienese preference for miniaturisation and warm colours; later, both **Joan Daurer** and the talented **Master of Bishop Galiana** became inspired by Catalan painting; the end of the century saw the assertion of personal characteristics in **Francesch Comes,** whose mannerism was to portray figures with full lips.

In the 15C, artists on the island included some who had studied in Valencia such as Gabriel Moger, the suave Miguel Alcanyis and Martí Torner. The **Master of the Predellas** is distinguishable by his detail, Rafael Moger by his realism. There were also two master painters, both from abroad, **Pedro Nisart** and **Alonso de Sedano,** who, at this time, introduced the Flemish style which was to dominate Majorcan painting in the 16C.

Famous Majorcans and illustrious visitors. — **Ramón Llull,** born in Palma in 1235, is a good example of the cosmopolitan outlook of Majorca in the 13C. A reformed libertine, he became convinced that preaching was preferable to the sword as a method of conversion and so learned foreign languages, studied philosophy, theology and alchemy, before setting out for Africa where he died *(p 257)*, martyred, on his third expedition in 1315. The Doctor Illuminatus, as he was known, was later beatified.

Another of the island's personalities was **Junípero Serra** *(p 261)*.

Among the foreign writers, poets and learned men to visit the island in the 19C, were **Chopin** and **George Sand.** They passed the winter of 1838 in Valldemosa Carthusian Monastery, but the bad weather and local hostility to their unorthodox way of life, left George Sand disenchanted although the beauty of the countryside did evoke enthusiastic passages in her book, *A Winter in Majorca* and Chopin appeared reinspired, if not cured, by the stay. **Robert Graves** (1895-1985) the English poet, novelist and critic lived (as of 1929) and died here. The Austrian Archduke, **Ludwig Salvator** (1847-1915), passed most of his 53 years' stay on the west coast where he compiled the most detailed study ever made of the archipelago. In 1896 the French speleologist, **E. A. Martel** *(p 260)*, explored many of the island's caves.

Economy. — Tourism is the major factor in the economy, with an expanding shoe manufacturing industry second and a rising artificial pearl industry at **Manacor** now finding foreign as well as domestic outlets. The famous maiolica ware, characterised by clear base colours and tin glazing, which originated on Majorca, has been superseded by rustic pottery made principally at **Inca.**

Horticulture supplies the fresh fruit canning and dried fruit industries (tomatoes and figs, and apricots respectively) while 17 000 tons of almonds are shipped to the mainland annually. Inca, Binissalem and Felanitx are wine and Bunyola and Sóller olive oil centres. **Ensaimada,** a light roll dusted with sugar is the tasty, local speciality.

PALMA DE MALLORCA ★★ P
Michelin map 443 fold 41 — Pop 304 422

The visitor who has the good fortune to arrive in Palma by boat, discovers a city spread across the back of a wide bay, its proud cathedral standing guard as in foregone days of maritime glory. Closing the bay westward is the residential, Terreno quarter (AX), where hotels rise before a steep pine covered hill crowned by the squat mass of Bellver Castle.

The harbour. — A seafront promenade, planted with palm and orange trees, the Paseo Sagrera (CZ), leads to the old and new harbours, the latter able to accommodate the largest liners. The old harbour serves both passenger and merchant ships.

The bay. — The bay, protected from north and west winds by the Puig Major range, has a mild climate all the year round. West of the town, hotels have been erected along the indented Bendinat coastline where there is little sand except at the two beach areas of Palma Nova and Magaluf. The coast to the east is less sheltered, being straight, but has mile upon mile of fine sand and is being developed as a series of resorts, the Ca'n Pastilla, Ciudad Jardín and El Arenal, known collectively as the **Playas de Palma.**

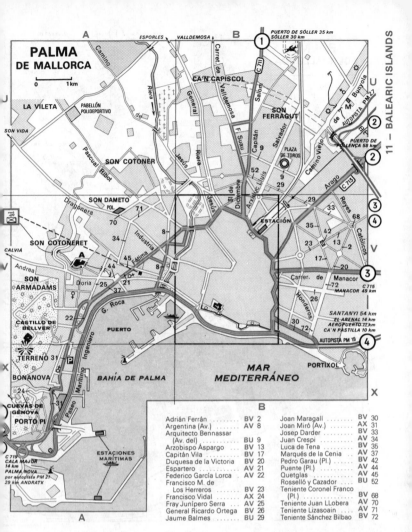

PALMA DE MALLORCA

0   1 km

Adrián Ferrán	BV 2	Joan Maragall	BV 30
Argentina (Av.)	AV 8	Joan Miró (Av.)	AX 31
Arquitecto Bennassar		Josep Darder	BV 33
(Av. del)	BU 9	Juan Crespi	AV 34
Arzobispo Aspargo	BV 13	Luca de Tena	BV 35
Capitán Vila	AV 17	Marqués de la Cenia	AV 37
Duquesa de la Victoria	BV 20	Pedro Garau (Pl.)	BV 42
Espartero	AV 21	Puente (Pl.)	AV 44
Federico García Lorca	AV 22	Quetglas	AV 45
Francisco M. de		Rosselló y Cazador	BU 52
Los Herreros	BV 23	Teniente Coronel Franco	
Francisco Vidal	AX 24	(Pl.)	BV 68
Fray Junípero Serra	AV 25	Teniente Juan LLobera	AV 70
General Ricardo Ortega	BV 26	Teniente Lizasoain	AV 71
Jaume Balmes	BU 29	Teniente Sánchez Bilbao	BV 72

The "Ciutat de Mallorca". — This was the name by which the city was known after its liberation on 31 December 1229 and during its most prosperous period when trade links were forged with Barcelona, Valencia, the countries of Africa and even the kingdoms of northern Europe; Jews and Genoese established colonies in the town, the latter even founding an exchange, and James II and his successors endowed the city with beautiful Gothic buildings. Finally the Aragon policy of expansion in Naples and Sicily, enabled Palma to extend her commercial interests also. Although, during the period of the Great Discoveries, the city was under constant threat from marauding Barbary pirates, embellishment continued with the building of yet more mansions and palaces.

Palma's old mansions. — In the 15 and 16C, the great families of Palma, descended from rich merchants and landed gentry, favoured the Italian style. They constructed elegant residences with stone façades, relieved by windows with Renaissance style decoration. It was only in the 18C that a characteristic Majorcan **casa** appeared with an inner court of massive marble columns, wide shallow arches and incorporating stone steps to a high and graceful loggia. Balustrades of stone or wrought iron completed the decoration. The same families built themselves luxurious summer **villas** north of Palma.

Palma today. — The city in which 43% of the island's population live, has the greatest number of visitors of any town in Spain.

Tourists congregate in and around the **Terreno** (AX) and **Cala Major** *(leave by ⑤)* residential quarters, but the native heart of the city, remains the **Paseo des Born**. This wide *rambla*, known as **El Born** (CYZ 16), follows the course of the Riera River before this was diverted in the 16C to run outside the walls on account of its occasional, devastating floodwaters. The shops selling pearls, glassware and local craftwork — wrought iron, filigree, embroidery — are in the old town east of El Born.

■ **THE SEA FRONT** *time: 1 1/2 hours*

Cathedral★★ (CZ). — More than 300 years were to pass between the laying of the cathedral foundation stone in 1230 and the completion of the west doorway in 1601 ; in that time the walls, closely shouldered by tall buttresses surmounted by pinnacles and turrets, and pinned by a double row of flying buttresses, all in golden Santanyí limestone, rose high above the roofs of the old quarter as the boldly designed Gothic nave took shape.

The west face, shattered by the earthquake of 1851, was rebuilt on conventional Gothic lines around the Renaissance portal which had remained intact. The south door, known as the Mirador, overlooks the sea, the delicate Gothic decoration dating from the 15C preserved beneath a porch. The statues of Saints Peter and Paul on either side prove that Sagrera, architect of the Lonja, was also a talented sculptor. Enter through the north door.

The cathedral is among the largest of Gothic cathedrals with dimensions of 121m x 55m - 397ft x 180ft and a height of 44m - 144ft to the peak of the vaulting above the nave.

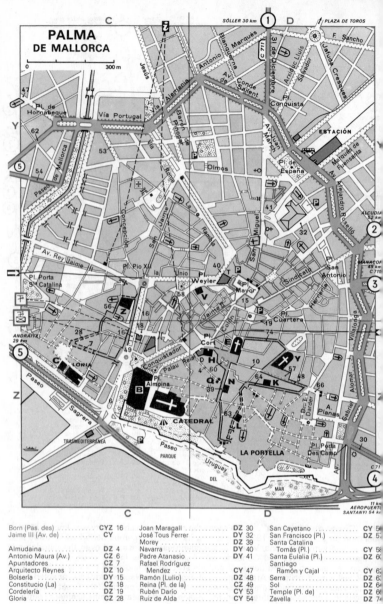

PALMA
DE MALLORCA

The traditional Gothic plan of the nave has been modified to omit the triforium; the massive columns rise directly to the springing of the pointed arches, providing an open view of the considerable area covered by the three aisles. The octagonal pillars on which the vaulting rests are incredibly slender, considering the size of the edifice, and are almost without decoration. A departure has been made from Spanish tradition to provide an uninterrupted interior vista: the choirstalls were removed to either side of the high altar which is surmounted by a most unusual wrought iron baldachin designed by Gaudí. On the north side of the chancel is a richly carved Renaissance pulpit.

Museum. – *Open 10am to 12.30pm and 4 to 6.30pm; closed Sundays and holidays.* 100pts.

The chapterhouses contain the Diocesan Museum, which contains many reliquaries, one of which is the True Cross decorated with precious stones.

La Almudaina (CZ B). – *Open 9.30am to 1.30pm and 4 to 6.30pm (6pm 1 October to 15 May); closed Sunday and holiday afternoons;* 40pts.

This ancient Moorish fortress, dating from the Walis' caliphate, was converted in the 14 and 15C by the Kings of Majorca into a royal palace. Remaining from that time are a graceful Gothic balcony overlooking the sea and, in the *patio,* carved overhanging eaves and a Chapel to St Anne with a 15C altarpiece.

Lonja★ (CZ). – *Open only during temporary exhibitions.*

The designer of this 15C commercial exchange was **Guillermo Sagrera.**

The Lonja's military features are only for appearance sake: the pierced gallery never served as a sentry path, the merlons and turrets are not for defence but decoration. But such devices distract the eye from the inevitable buttresses and the austerity of the outer walls which were further modified by large Gothic windows with delicate tracery. The interior, in which cross vaults outline the pointed arches which descend onto six beautiful, spirally fluted piers, has all the elegance of perfect proportion.

Former Maritime Consulate (CZ C). – The early 17C building decorated with a Renaissance balcony was the meeting place of the Merchant Shipping Tribunal.

THE OLD QUARTERS (Barrios Antiguos) *time: 2 1/2 hours*

The early demolition of the city walls, apart from the section overlooking the sea, enabled the city to expand rather than destroy its old quarter and rebuild on the site.

Walk: east of El Born. — *Allow 2 hours on foot. Start from the Plaza Cort.*

Town Hall (Ayuntamiento) (DZ H). — Carved wood eaves overhang the 17C façade. Inside, on the first floor, is a Van Dyck painting of the *Martyrdom of St Sebastian.*

St Eulalia's (DZ E). — 13-15C. The nave is unusually bare for a Gothic church; behind the high altar is a 15C statue of the Dormition of the Virgin.

St Francis'★ (DZ Y). — 13-14C. A vast Gothic nave lies, behind the façade which was given an extraordinary half-Plateresque, half-baroque decoration when it was remodelled in the 17C. The carved portal tympanum is by Herrera. Inside, the first apsidal chapel on the left is the tomb of Ramón Llull *(p 254)* surmounted by a 15C alabaster statue.

The ground level galleries of the cloister were begun in 1286 and completed in the 14C. Apart from one side of trilobed openings, the architect divided the bays of the remaining galleries into multiple lobes supported on groups of slender small columns which he varied in diameter and number together with decoration on the capitals, to achieve diversity and grace. The ceiling throughout is of painted wood.

Casa Marqués del Palmer (DZ K). — In the middle of the aristocratic Calle del Sol stands the impressive Casa Marqués del Palmer, built in 1556 in stone and now blackened by age. Renaissance decoration around the upper floor windows mellows the austerity of its Gothic wall. The upper gallery, protected by the traditional deep eaves, is a replica of that at the Lonja.

The former old Jewish quarter, **La Portella,** lies close against the town wall.

Moorish Baths (DZ L). — *Open 9am to 2pm and 4 to 8pm (6pm in winter); closed Sunday afternoons and holidays; 25pts.*

The baths are the only relic to remain intact and unrestored from the time of the caliphate in Palma. The baths, beneath the pierced oculi, and Classical dome, supported on eight columns with rudimentary capitals, were used after the Reconquest by Jews and Christians alike. The Roman amphora was discovered in the garden.

Casa Oleza (DZ N). — The inner 17C courtyard is delightfully harmonious with a neatly designed balcony resting on a full, low arch and a well with a wrought iron wellhead.

Turning towards the St Eulalia and Cort Squares, you pass the **Almundaina Arch** (DZ Q), the gate in the Almoravid wall which formerly surrounded the emirs' palace.

Walk: west of El Born. — *Allow 1/2 hour on foot. Start from the Plaza Pio XII (end of El Born).*

Casa de los Marqueses de Sollerich (CY Z). — *Open 11.30am to 1.30pm and 5 to 8.30pm; closed Sundays and Mondays.* The decoration of the front of this 18C residence overlooking the Born, is completed by an elegant loggia; behind this front *(follow the narrow covered way round the building)* is the most perfect **patio★** in Palma, complete with a beautifully proportioned double flighted staircase.

Stop at no 28 in Gloria Street to look at the *patio.*

Apuntadores Street (CZ 7). — Tha Casa Marqués at no 51, has a boldly designed staircase; no 45, was the home of the painter, Ochoa and is now the Mansión del Arte.

INDIVIDUAL SIGHTS AND EXCURSIONS

Casa Berga (DY V). — The mansion almost outside the old quarter dates from 1712 and now houses the law courts. The façade is encumbered untypically with stone balconies but the inner courtyard, although vast, is a characteristic Majorcan *patio.*

Spanish Pueblo★ (AV A). — *Access by Calle Andrea Doria. Open 1 May to 30 September 9am to 8pm; the rest of the year 9.30am to 5.30pm; closed Sunday and holiday afternoons; 200pts.* This model village, where the most typical houses of every region of Spain have been reconstructed, differs from the village erected in Barcelona *(p 80),* in that here the buildings are exact reproductions of actual famous houses or monuments or parts of monuments: the Court of Myrtles from Granada, El Greco's house in Toledo... Craftsmen at work in the alleys and folk dancing and singing in the streets give the village life.

Features of all the major Roman constructions in Spain have been incorporated in the monumental **Congressional Hall** (Palacio de Congresos) which stands facing the village.

Bellver Castle★ (AV). — *3km - 2 miles west. Open 1 May to 30 September 9am to 8pm; the rest of the year 9.30am to 5.30pm; 50pts.*

Bellver Castle, built by the Majorcan kings of the 14C as a summer residence, was converted not long afterwards into a prison, which it remained until 1915. Among those incarcerated was the poet, dramatist and politican **Jovellanos** *(p 113),* known also, at the time, for his progressive system of education. He was released in 1808, just as French officers captured by the Spanish at the Battle of Bailén, arrived.

The castle's circular perimeter, round buildings and circular inner court are highly original; a free standing and again round keep dominates all. The ground floor is peopled by large Roman statues, which with other items (a bequest of Cardinal Despuig) together with finds from excavations on the island are in the **archaeological museum.**

A full **panorama★★** of the Bay of Palma can be seen from the terrace.

Génova Grotto. — *5km - 3 miles southwest. Guided tours (time: 25 min) 10am to 1.15pm and 3 to 9pm; 400pts, children 200pts.* There are good views from the cave approach road of Palma and Calamajor Bay. The grotto itself is a series of small caves where clever lighting displays with almost theatrical effect miniature concretions, in many cases coloured by metal oxides, and some unusual ball-like formations.

The times indicated in this guide
when given with the distance allow one to enjoy the scenery
when given for sightseeing are intended to give an idea of
the possible length or brevity of a visit

The ROCKY COAST ★★★

1 EXCURSION FROM PALMA: VIA BANYALBUFAR★★

141km - 87 miles Rtn - local map below — allow one day

Leave Palma by ⑤ on the C 719.

The deeply indented southwest coast has the highest density of hotels of anywhere on the island. In dream-like settings between two cliffs or beside a deep fringe of pine trees, minute **beaches,** carpeted with fine sands, lead down to the translucent sea. The road, the C 719, passes through residential areas to reach Palma Nova before continuing on a zig-zag course through the pines.

Santa Ponsa★. — Beautiful cove. A promontory divides the site, an attractive small fishing harbour lying to the south and the beach to the north. On the promontory, a Cross, at the far end, commemorates the landing on 12 September 1229 of a great number of James I's troops preparatory to their Reconquest of Majorca from the Muslims.

Paguera★, Cala Fornells★ and Camp de Mar★. — Lovely sandy coves.

The **road★** has *corniche* sections between Camp de Mar and Puerto de Andratx.

Place names framed in brown : Old mansion

Puerto de Andratx. — The small fishing harbour now also used by pleasure craft, lies well sheltered at the back of a narrow roadstead. The town of Andratx, some distance behind the harbour, is scarcely distinguishable against the grey mountain background, dominated by the 1 025m - 3 363ft high Mount Galatzo. The C 710 between Andratx and Sóller is an extremely winding **corniche road★★★,** mostly along the cliff edge which extends all the way to the indented northwest coast. It is shaded along its length by pine trees. Two viewpoints (mirador) have been built beyond Andratx, **Ricardo Roca** and **Ses Animes,** a former watchtower. **Terraces★,** cut into the less steep hillsides right down to the sea's edge, are planted around **Estellencs** with almond and apricot trees and around **Banyalbufar** with tomato plants and vines from which a somewhat sweet red wine is made.

Valldemosa Carthusian Monastery★ (Cartuja). — *Open 9.30am to 1pm and 3 to 6.30pm (5.30pm in winter); closed Sundays and certain holidays; 250pts.* Valldemosa has a pleasant terrace setting amidst olive groves, caroub trees and almond orchards. The buildings are 17 and 18C; in the church are frescoes by Manuel Bayeu; in the sacristy, collections of copes, embroideries and reliquaries. A **pharmacy** was built onto one of the cloister galleries in the 18C. After the departure of the monks in 1835 the monastery was rented out, tenants leasing cells as required! It was here that Chopin and George Sand passed the winter of 1838-1839 *(p 254).* The rooms are decorated with triptychs and paintings. Museum of Ludwig Salvator *(p 254)* mementoes.

The road beyond Valldemosa runs along cliffs more than 400m - 1 300ft high.

Son Marroig. — *Open 10am to 2.30pm and 4.30 to 8pm (5.30pm in winter); 100pts.* The former residence of Archduke Ludwig Salvator includes an exhibition of archaeological finds, furniture and Majorcan work collected by the author and several of his volumes on the Balearic Islands. From the arcaded balcony there is a good **view★** of the locally famous, pierced rock rising out of the sea, the Foradada.

Deià. — The road by-passes the village of red houses perched on a hillside amidst olive and almond trees. All around are higher hills, covered in evergreen oaks and conifers giving it almost a mountain **setting★.** A sharp turn in the village may bring you in full view of the sea; descending you will find a creek with a tiny beach.

Sóller. — The town lies spread out in a wide basin where market-gardens, oranges and olives grow. To the east rise the mountains of the Alfabia Sierra, some 1 100m - 3 600ft high.

Puerto de Sóller. — It lies at the back of an almost circular bay so sheltered that a part is now a submarine base. Puerto itself, with the advantages of a pleasure boat harbour, a sand beach and low mountain hinterland is now the major seaside resort of the west coast. It has a further asset in being within easy access of Majorca's Costa Brava.

From Sóller to Alfabia, the **road★** zigzags up the densely wooded northern slopes of the Alfabia Sierra affording interesting views westwards.

Alfabia Gardens. — *Open 8am to 7pm; closed Sundays, 1 January and 25 December; 100pts.*

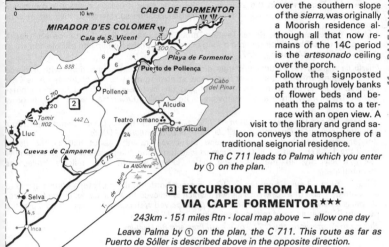

The domain, which is built over the southern slope of the *sierra*, was originally a Moorish residence although all that now remains of the 14C period is the *artesonado* ceiling over the porch.

Follow the signposted path through lovely banks of flower beds and beneath the palms to a terrace with an open view. A visit to the library and grand saloon conveys the atmosphere of a traditional seignorial residence.

The C 711 leads to Palma which you enter by ① on the plan.

② EXCURSION FROM PALMA: VIA CAPE FORMENTOR★★★

243km - 151 miles Rtn - local map above — allow one day

Leave Palma by ① on the plan, the C 711. This route as far as Puerto de Sóller is described above in the opposite direction.

After looking at Puerto de Sóller, return to the C 710 on the left, which runs along the hillside into the heart of the mountains.

Fornalutx. — The mountain village with steep cobbled streets is a little off the road.

The road goes through a long tunnel before following the Upper Valley of the Pareis along a defile which becomes ever more enclosed as it nears the sea and approaches its end at the so-called **Gorg Blau**. The road turns away at Gorch Blau. All this time the landscape is dominated to the west by the impressive **Puig Major** *(military reserve)*.

Sa Calobra Road★★★. — The narrow, magnificent and incredibly boldly planned road, plunges towards the Mediterranean, then windingly ascends through olive groves and evergreen oaks, before, once more, descending, at times vertiginously a weird and desolate landscape of steep, jagged rocks, dominated always by the Puig Major.

Sa Calobra★. — Pleasure boats from Puerto Sóller are often to be seen moored in the rocky creek beside which stand the few houses of Sa Calobra village. North of Sa Calobra the **Pareis River★** appears, pouring limpidly over the beach of round white shingle which lies in its path to the sea. The river bed is accessible along a track (200m - 656ft) which passes through two underground galleries; a 2-3km - 1 1/2 - 2 miles walk along the course in dry weather, but not to be undertaken in the heat of the day, gives an idea of how enclosed the stream is.

1km - 1/2 mile north of the Sa Calobra fork, a **belvedere★** (alt 664m - 2 179ft) gives a good view over a length of the cleft hollowed out by the Pareis. The road then passes through a lovely evergreen oak forest.

Our Lady of Lluc Monastery. — The monastery approach is lined with arcaded, country style buildings which once provided shelter for pilgrims, who still come in numbers to pray before the "Moreneta", a dark wood, Gothic statue in the church. The small ethnological museum in the main building *(1st floor; open 10am to 5.30pm; closed 25 December; 110pts)* contains bronze objects discovered in local *talayots (p 261)*, evidence of a civilisation dating back to 600 to 123 BC on the island. There is also, in the museum, a 14C alabaster statue of the Virgin.

From a pass 5km - 3 miles north of Lluc you can see right across to Pollença Bay, and as you begin to descend, the jagged peaks of the Tomir range to the east.

Pollença. — The town stands between two hills, the **Puig** (333m - 1 092ft) to the east, and a **Calvary** crowned hill to the west *(access by narrow streets or up long cypress bordered steps)*. The low red stone houses open directly on the street through rounded doorways built with massive arch stones.

Cala de Sant Vicent★. — The wide cove is bordered to the east by tall cliffs and to the south by dense pinewoods which grow down to the fine sand beach.

Puerto de Pollença★. — This large resort has a perfect **setting★** in a sheltered bay which between Cape Formentor in the north and Cape del Pinar in the south, provides a vast expanse of calm water for skiing and sailing (moorings for pleasure craft).

The **road★★★** from Puerto de Pollença is highly spectacular, as it twists and turns, rises several times to a high *corniche* and, at one point, follows a narrow, jagged crest, to reach the lighthouse at the tip of Cape Formentor.

It begins with an ascent of the northern slope up hairpin bends through arid country.

Es Colomer Belvedere★★★. — *Access by a stepped path beside a precipice.* The belvedere overlooks an impressive, vertical drop — *viewing table.*

The road cuts over to the southern slope and descends into a valley shaded by evergreen oaks and pines.

Formentor Beach★. — The beach is well sheltered, faces Pollença Bay and is further enhanced by woods and the flowered terraces of the Hotel Formentor.

Once through the tunnel which temporarily hides the Cala Figuera to the north, the landscape becomes arid, the mountain crests impressively high, the valleys deep.

Cape Formentor★★★. — This most northerly point of the island, drops sheer to the sea 200m - 650ft in a formidable rock wall.

Alcudia. — Alcudia, still encircled by 14C ramparts, guards access to the promontory which divides Pollença Bay from that of Alcudia. A prosperous Roman colony once lived in the area around the church, south of the ramparts.

The ROCKY COAST★★★

The **Quay Gate (del Muelle),** which led to the harbour, remains of the early fortified walls, reconstructed and incorporated by the Moors when they strengthened the ramparts, in the 14C. The streets in the shadow of the walls have a certain distinctive mediaeval air as have the town's houses, brightened by Renaissance surrounds to their upper windows.

1.5km - 1 mile south is the **Roman Theatre.** Tombs have been hollowed out in several places among the tiers. Objects discovered during excavations of the Roman site of Pollentia are in the Bellver Castle Museum (p 257).

Puerto de Alcudia. — Alcudia Port has direct passenger boat connections with Minorca and Barcelona. It overlooks a vast bay, while, stretching away to the south as far as Ca'n Picafort, is a narrow sand beach, the longest on the island, bordered by green pinewoods. The marshy hinterland, meanwhile, is being utilised ever more extensively to grow rice.

Campanet Caves★ (Cuevas). — 2.5km - 1 1/2 miles from the C 713. Open 10am to 6pm (5pm in winter); closed 25 December and 1 January; 300pts, children 150pts.
Bouganvilleas and hydrangeas surround the caves' mouth. About half of the caves along the 1 300m path - 1 500yds have ceased formation, their concretions now being totally dry. In the area still water laden, straight and delicate stalactites predominate.

Selva. — 5km - 3 miles from the C 713. A cypress bordered flight of steps adds majesty to the Gothic façade of **St Lawrence's Church** which is relieved by a bell gable. In the first north chapel is a **Calvary★,** a fragment of an altarpiece carved with realism in which the face of the penitent thief has an air of resigned serenity.

Return to Palma along the C 713 by way of Inca and Binissalem.

The CAVES ★★ LAS CUEVAS

Itinerary ③ on local map p 254 — Round tour of 266km - 165 miles starting from Palma — allow one day

Leave Palma by ④, the motorway going east; continue along the C 717.

Cura Monastery★. — The road climbs Randa by tight hairpin bends to the monastery high on the hillside. The buildings have been restored and modernised by the Franciscans who have occupied them since 1913. You may visit (Tuesday to Thursday 10am to 1pm and 4 to 6pm; Friday 10am to 1pm; 50pts) the 17C church, refectory (now a restaurant) and library which possesses manuscripts by Ramón Llull (p 254). From a terrace on the west side of the monastery there is a **panorama★★** of Palma, the bay, the Puig Major chain and, in the northeast, Cape Formentor, the northernmost point on the island.

Cala Figuera★. — Fishing boats lie in the cove; white houses stand amidst the pines which come down to the water's edge.

Cala Santanyí★. — Cove with a good sand beach.

Cala d'Or★★. — Pinewoods surround the creek where, half encircled by massive boulders, limpid waters cover the inlet's gold sand bottom. The site, still off the tourist beat, is one of the most attractive along the east coast.

Sant Salvador Monastery★. — The monastery perched on a mound 500m - 1 600ft above the plain (tight hairpin bends), commands a wide **panorama★★** of the eastern part of the island.
It was founded in the 14C although the church and buildings, now used for pilgrims, were rebuilt in the 18C; the wooden carving of the **Last Supper** in the entrance hall is 17C. In the church behind the baroque high altar is a deeply venerated statue of the **Virgin and Child,** while in the south chapels are three **cribs** set in dioramas and a multicoloured stone **altarpiece** carved in the 14C in low relief with scenes from the Passion.

Porto Cristo. — The fishing village, sheltered by its position at the end of a narrow inlet, has prospered by its proximity to the Drac Caves.

Drac Caves★★★. — Guided tours (time: 1 hour) 10am (11am 1 November to 31 March) to noon and 2 to 5pm; closed 25 December; 350pts.
Four chambers succeed one another over a distance of 2km - 1 mile, their transparent pools reflecting richly decorative concretions. The marine origins of the caves seem unquestionable in spite of their size: the French speleologist, **E. A. Martel** (p 254), who first explored them in 1896, believed that infiltration through the limestone subsidence and faults had caused the cavities in which several pools are slightly salty. Rainfall dissolved the soft Miocene limestone, forming as it did so, countless concretions. In the words of Martel: "On all sides, everywhere, in front and behind, as far as the eye can see, marble cascades, organ pipes, lace draperies, pendants or brilliants, hang suspended from the walls and roof". It is the **roofs,** above all, which are amazing, glittering with countless, sharply pointed icicles. The tour ends with a look at the **Martel Lake,** 177m - 581ft long and limpidly translucent and, finally, a short boat ride.

Hams Caves. — 1 km - 1/2 miles to the left off the Manacor road. Guided tours (time: 45 min) 9.30am to 5.30pm (4.30pm in winter); 445pts. The caves, following the course of a former underground river, communicate directly with the sea, so that the water level in several of the clear small pools, rises and falls with the slight Mediterranean tides. The concretions are delicate and some, such as the stalactites in the **fishhook chamber★** are as white as snow.

Artà Caves★★★. — Guided tours (times: 45 min) 9.30am to 7pm (5.30pm 1 October to 31 March); closed 25 December; 225pts. The caves, magnificently sited in the cape closing Canyamel Bay to the north and accessible by a corniche road, were largely hollowed out by the sea — the giant mouth overlooks the sea from a height of 35m - 115ft. The chambers themselves are impressively lofty and contain massive concretions. The **vestibule** is blackened by smoke from 19C visitors' torches but the following caves are very various and equally impressive, containing the **Queen Column,** 22m - 72ft tall, Dantesque surroundings cleverly highlighted in a so-called **Inferno** and a fabulous decoration of concretions in the **Flag Hall.**

Cala Ratjada. — The Cala Ratjada with its delightful fishing village and pleasure boat harbour, is also a seaside resort on account of the creeks which lie on either side of it. On your way through the pines to the lighthouse you pass two, so far untouched, but 2km - 1 mile further north is the **Cala Agulla,** well known for its sandy beach.

Capdepera. — *Access: to the fortress by car, along narrow roads; on foot up steps.* The remains of a 14C fortress still girdling the hilltop give Capdepera an angular silhouette of crenellated walls and square towers. The buttressed ramparts now enclose only a restored chapel, but it is still possible to walk the old sentry path, **viewing★** the sea and the nearby *calas.* The local cottage industry is basket weaving from palm fronds.

Artà. — A high rock, crowned by San Salvador Church and the ruins of an ancient fortress, distinguish Artà from a distance.
The Artà region is rich in **megalithic remains** *(see below),* particularly *talayots* which sometimes can be seen beyond the low walls dividing the fields.

Petra. — Petra is the birthplace of **Junípero Serra** (1713-1784), a Franciscan who devoted his life to missionary work among the Indians in Mexico and California, where missions he founded grew into settlements and subsequently, the towns of San Diego, Monterey, San Francisco... His home is now a museum.

Return to Palma along the C 715.

THE ISLAND OF MINORCA MENORCA

Michelin map **443** folds 43 and 44

Minorca, the second largest of the Balearic Islands, with an area of 669km^2 - 258sq miles — a maximum length of 48km - 30 miles and 58 727 inhabitants, has, so far remained out of the tourist mainstream.
The windswept plateau, the heaths more akin to a mist enveloped Atlantic countryside, nevertheless, have a certain, if possibly somewhat melancholy charm. The green northwest recalls Cornwall; the south with low stone walls surrounding small fields and trees bent by the wind, the Isles of Scilly. The brilliant whitewashed walls, roofs and dividing walls, however, add southern brilliance to the scene.

The coast. — The north and south coasts are totally different as can be seen immediately from a plane or the highest point on the island, Mount Toro, 358m - 1 174ft high. The north is cut into a saw's edge of *rías* and deep coves, the south is bordered by a high almost straight line of rock cliffs, cut at intervals, by rivers which, over the centuries have produced great beaches of fine sand where they flow into the sea.

The Megalithic monuments. — In the European Bronze Age, the second millenium BC, the Balearics were populated by settlers from the eastern Mediterranean. The cavernous nature of the Minorcan countryside offered natural shelter both for the living and the dead; some of the caves, such as Cala Coves, they even decorated.
Talayots, in the form of great cones of stones possibly covering a funeral chamber and forming, it is believed, the base for a superimposed wooden house, are a feature of the island — more than 200 have been discovered, some surmounted by what appears to be a geodesic column. Where several stood grouped together in a village, they were protected by perimeters and sometimes endowed with a temple with a **taula** or central altar — a fine *taula* dominates the prehistoric site of **Trepuco,** facing the airport.
Other single monuments, **navetas,** take the form of upturned boats and are thought to have been tombs, that of **Els Tudons,** near Ciudadela, probably having been dedicated to Isis, patron goddess of explorers and sailors. The approach to the prehistoric monuments is nearly always along narrow stony tracks. *Close the gates after you.*

Economy. — Cereals are grown and arboreal fruit, particularly figs. The island's relative humidity also enables sheep to be reared, providing the inhabitants with meat, milk for the well known cheese "queso de Mahón", and leather for shoes.
Fornells is known locally for its spiny lobsters which are served with the now famous "mahonnaise" - mayonnaise.

MAHÓN MAÓ
Michelin map **443** folds 33 and 44 — Pop 22 926

Mahón, the capital, lining the end of an enclosed **roadstead** 5km - 3 miles long is most striking when approached from the sea.
Apart from the short period from 1756 to 1763 when the French were in possession, the town was occupied throughout the 18C, from 1708 to 1783 by the British as a key point in their Mediterranean strategy. Many traces of the period remain, particularly in the design of the tall houses with sash windows but without balconies, overlooking the harbour. There are also rocking chairs...
On the north side of the harbour is the San Antonio *finca* — the Golden Farm — where Admiral Nelson lived during a brief stay on the island, and where he put the finishing touches to his book, *Sketches of My Life* (October 1799).

Archaeological Museum. — *Temporarily closed.*
Prehistoric objects, many from local *talayots,* provide the major displays in the museum in the Archive Palace in Plaza de la Conquista.

The harbour. — Walk down the steep Abundance Ramp, which is cut by a majestic flight of steps, alons the quay. From the northside of the roadstead look across the water to the town which you will see typically with the larger houses lining the top of the cliff and the fishermen's huts colour washed cottages, restaurants and shops snug against the foot.

The roadstead. — Closely packed buildings on the south side allow only rare glimpses of the sea and the houses perched on the green hillsides. A road follows the northern, less populous, shore to Fort Mola *(no entry),* affording views of the islands in the roadstead.

EXCURSIONS

San Luis. — *4km - 2 1/2 miles south.* The town, with its streets at right angles, was founded and dedicated to St Louis during the French occupation of the island.

Small seaside resorts are being established south of San Luis at **Cala Alcaufar,** where the houses, a little distance inland, are sometimes flanked by an unusual round tower, at **Binibeca,** where the houses have been built close together in the style of a fishing village and **Punta Prima** where the small sand beach is framed by smooth flat rocks.

Cala'n Porter★. — *12km - 7 miles west.* High promontories protect a narrow estuary inlet, lined by a sandy beach. Houses, thinly scattered, stand perched upon the left cliff and on the plateau beyond the gorge.

Beyond the plateau are ancient troglodyte habitations, the **Cuevas d'en Xoroi,** overlooking the sea from the upper part of the cliffs. Bar *(refreshments obligatory).*

Alayor. — *12km - 7 miles northwest.* This inland town is one of the most consistently white walled and white roofed in the Balearics. There are several shoe factories.

CIUDADELA ★ CIUTADELA DE MENORCA

Michelin map **448** fold 32 — Pop 17 580

Ciudadela, the former capital, has retained the fortifications which stood it in good stead in the 16C against marauding Barbary pirates. The design of its squares, the picturesqueness of the narrow arcaded streets have a certain dignity and give the town, a calm and indefinable charm. The midsummer's day, St John festival, is very old.

The **Plaza de España,** bordered by white arcades, is the heart of the town; beyond, in a quarter of narrow alleys, lined by houses sporting coats of arms, is the 14C fortified Gothic **cathedral** with its single aisle.

The nearer you get to the harbour the more massive the fortifications appear. The **Plaza del Born,** framed by Classical façades and a baroque palace, stands on the site of the former citadel parade ground; the inclined approach to the **harbour** was the fortress counterscarp. Go to the end of the north quay for a view of the walled town.

Cala Santandria. — *3km - 2 miles south.* This is a small sheltered beach in a creek which contains rock caves, some of which served as shelters in prehistoric times.

Cala de Santa Galdana★★. — *22km - 14 miles south.* Tall bare cliffs surround a limpid bay and a fine sand beach, fringed by sweet smelling pines.

FORNELLS

Michelin map **448** fold 33

Fornells harbour lies at the mouth of a deep inlet, surrounded on all sides by bare moorland; the village lives off crawfish fishing as can be seen from the craft bulging with lobster pots moored in the harbour. Taste the delicious crawfish soup, the Caldereta.

Monte Toro. — *11km - 7 miles south. 3.5km - 2 miles from Mercadal.*
From the church crowned summit you can see the indented Fornells Bay to the north, the straight line of the coastal cliffs to the south and Mahón to the southeast.

*When looking for a pleasant, quiet and well situated hotel consult the current **Michelin Red Guide.***

THE ISLAND OF IBIZA

Michelin map **448** folds 39 and 40

Ibiza, third largest of the Balearics has an area of $572km^2$ - 221sq miles, a length of 41km - 25 miles and a population of 60 937. It lies 45 nautical miles southwest of Majorca. The **White Island,** as it has been called, is known for its unique topography and life style. House walls are brilliantly white, roofs flat and terraced, alleys tortuous as an African *souk* and atmosphere similar to that of the Greek Islands — a heritage, in part, from its Carthaginian period.

Ibiza's history dates from when trade began to develop throughout the Mediterranean: in the 10C BC, Phoenicians made the island a staging post for ships loaded with Spanish metal ores returning to Africa; in the 7C BC, Carthage grew all powerful and founded a colony on the island; under the Romans the capital grew in size and prosperity to judge from the necropolis uncovered at Puig des Molins *(p 264).*

Landscape. — Ibiza is a mountainous island where the lines of relief run in various directions, leaving little space for cultivation between the limestone hills which finally plunge into the sea. Among pines and junipers on the hillsides stand the cube-shaped houses of many small villages. The roads do not follow the coastline and the best way to see the island, therefore, is by boat. The shore appears wild and indented, guarded by high cliffs; promontories are marked by rocks out to sea, some standing as high as the amazing limestone needle known as **Vedrá★.**

The cliffs disappear at certain points, to afford sites where smooth rocks provide good underwater swimming or sand beaches, fringed with pinewoods.

Houses on Ibiza. — The individual design, African in character, makes the houses one of the island's most charming features. The cottage, or **casament,** is made up of several white cubes with few windows; each represents a single room and opens off a central common room. The flat roofs are used to collect rain; the arched porches to provide shade and to house crops.

Country churches are equally plain with gleaming white exteriors and dark interiors. The façades are square, surmounted by narrow bell gables and pierced by wide porches.

Folklore and traditional costume. — Ibiza has a live folklore which is uncomplicated and authentic. Older women and many peasant women still wear the long black gathered skirt and shawl. Down their backs hangs a single full plait tied with a bow. At festivals the costume is brightened with fine gold filigree necklaces or **emprendades**. The island dances are performed to the accompaniment of flute, tambourine and castanets, by groups whose skill is demonstrated by the gathering speed at which they can accomplish the steps.

(After MTTC photo, Madrid)

A village church

IBIZA ★★ EIVISSA

Michelin map **443** fold 39 — Pop 25 489

Ibiza's vibrating and colourful beauty should be seen, if possible for the first time from the sea; alternatively take the Talamanca road (② *on the plan*) out of town and after 1km - 1/2 mile turn round and look back, whereupon you will see the old wall dividing the town respectively into the Marina quarter below and the Upper Town, crowned by the cathedral.

The Upper Town★ (Dalt Vila) (Z). — The Upper Town, enclosed by the 16C wall is the heart of the old city and retains even today a certain rustic, mediaeval character. Façades may be crumbling beneath the whitewash and climbing plants but there remain many noble Gothic houses worth looking at particularly for their large *patios*.

Enter the quarter through the **Las Tablas Gateway (YZ A)** and either continue by car up a steep slope to the cathedral square or wander there leisurely on foot through the quiet meandering streets.

Archaeological Museum★ (Z M¹). — *Open 10am to 1pm; closed Sundays and holidays; 100pts, the ticket is also valid for the Necropolis.* The museum provides the visitor with an introduction to a lesser known period of art which had little outside influence and left few remains — the art of Carthage or **Punic art** which flourished from the 7C BC to 3C AD. The contents exhibited in the 4 galleries of this museum were all discovered on the island.

In chronological order, are rough figurines, mostly cast in the fine local clay and believed, in the majority, to be worshipping priestesses or goddesses such as the goddess Tanit. Also on exhibit is jewellery of moulded glass including necklaces and amulets originally from Egypt as well as the two feminine terracotta busts: one coloured and with a Punic countenance, the other a Greek beauty. The museum also contains Punic and Roman coins, vases and amphorae with designs in red on a black background from Greater Greece (southern Italy).

Cathedral (Z B). — The cathedral's massive 13C belfry, which closely resembles a keep but for its two storeys of pierced Gothic bays, totally dominates the town. The nave was rebuilt in the 17C. An ancient bastion before the east end has been converted into a belvedere from which you can get a good **panoramic view★** of the town and harbour.

La Marina (Y). — The Upper Town is silent; the Marina, a network of bustling, crowded, shopping streets.

Open air cafés and bars line the harbour quay.

Sa Penya Quarter★. — The fishermen's quarter, built on a narrow rock promontory at the harbour mouth, is quite different from the rest of the town both by its situation and its almost oriental air. Within the limited space available, cubic white houses overlap and superimpose on one another in picturesque chaos, completely blocking streets in places and compelling them to continue by means of steps cut out of the rock or to end at a cliff edge overlooking the sea.

Aníbal	Y 5	Juan Román	Z 17
Antonio Palau	Y 6	La Carroza	Z 18
José Verdera	Y 16	Obispo Huix	Z 20
Maestro J. Mayans	Y 19	Opispo Torres	Z 22
		Pedro Francés	Z 23
Amadeo	Y 4	Pedro Tur	Z 24
Conde Rosellón	Y 10	Ramón y Tur	Z 25
Cuesta Vieja	Z 12	San Ciriaco	Z 27
General Balanzat	Z 14	Vara de Rey (Pas.)	Y 28

The Necropolis (Z). — *Guided tours at 4.30, 5.15, 6 and 6.45pm; closed Sundays and holidays; 100pts, the ticket is also valid for the Archaeological Museum.* This large Phoenician - Carthaginian necropolis on the side of the **Molins** or **Windmill Mound (Puig des Molins)** was still in use in Roman times. Hypogea or underground vaults, the oldest have been hollowed out of the rock; each contains one or more sarcophagi. In all some 2 000 tombs have been accounted for.

The Punic ceramics found in the tombs are now in the museum.

EXCURSIONS

Ses Figueretes *(1.5km - 1 mile southwest by ③)* **and Talamanca** *(3km - 2 miles northeast by ②).* — These are the capital's two beaches. From the rock promontory dividing the Cala Talamanca from Ibiza harbour, there is a view of the two clearly distinct bays.

Jesús. — *3.5km - 2 miles northeast. Leave by ② on the C 733 and after 2.5km - 1 1/2 miles bear right. To visit apply at the house adjoining the south wall.*

The church's 16C altarpiece shows the Virgin and Child painted in the late Gothic style and angel musicians, at Our Lady's feet, in the Renaissance style.

The Saltpans (Sas Salines). — *8km - 5 miles south.* Near the airport, in the sandy area which forms the southernmost part of the island, are 400ha - 162 acres of saltmarsh. This has been exploited since Carthaginian times and today produces 50 000 tons of salt a year which is shipped from La Canal to the mainland.

SAN ANTONIO ABAD ★
Michelin map 443 fold 39 — Pop 12 331

San Antonio is particularly attractive for two reasons: its light and the harmony of its **bay★**. At the foot of the green carpeted hills, tall buildings emphasise the curve of the bay. The upper part of the town remains old in character with narrow streets and a typical 17C church. There is a large pleasure boat harbour.

Cala Gració. — *2km - 1 mile north.* A lovely, sheltered but minute creek; narrow access.

Port des Torrent and Cala Bassa. — *5km - 3 miles southwest. Both accessible by a poor dirt road.* Port des Torrent is all rocks; Cala Bassa a pine fringed beach.

In this part of the coast the rocks are smooth and separate and just above or just below the water line, providing perfect underwater swimming conditions.

Cala Vadella. — *15km - 9 miles south.* The approach road, frequently along the hillsides, affords views to the right of the string of islets closing the bay and ahead, of the **Vedrá★** rock standing, 382m - 1 253ft high, out to sea. The road ends in a rapid descent to the enclosed, sandy creek of Cala Vadella.

SANTA EULALIA DEL RÍO
Michelin map 443 fold 39 — Pop 13 098

Santa Eulalia stands on the estuary of Ibiza's only river, the Río Balcar, at the centre of a fertile market garden area. Pinewoods and the long **Es Caná** beach 4km - 2 1/2 miles to the north explain its current tourist development.

Puig de Missa. — *Bear right off the Ibiza road 50m after the petrol station (on the left).* The minute, fortified town crowning the hilltop is a remarkable symposium of the island's traditional peasant architecture; the town is a surviving example, in fact, of those easily defended religious hills where, in case of danger, the church served as a refuge.

Cala de Portinatx★. — *22km - 14 miles north.* The last section of the approach road is picturesque as it threads its way between evergreen oaks and almond trees and you look down on the Cala Xarraca. Creeks sheltered by tall narrow cliffs with pine trees fringing the sandy **beaches★**, make Cala de Portinatx one of the island's most attractive areas.

THE ISLAND OF FORMENTERA
Michelin map 443 folds 39 and 40

Formentera, the Wheat Island of the Ancients *(frumentum:* wheat in Latin) lies just over 7km - 3 1/2 nautical miles south of Ibiza. It is the fourth of the Balearic Islands in size with an area of 115km² - 44sq miles and an overall west to east length of 14km - 9 miles although it is in fact really two islets joined by a sandy isthmus. The "capital" San Francisco Javier, the passenger port, Cala Sabina, the saltpans and the dry open expanse on which cereals, figs and almonds and a few vines are cultivated, are on the western islet; the island's 192m - 630ft high "mountain" rises from the **Mola** Promontory on the eastern islet. Rock cliffs and sand dunes alternately line the shore.

4 209 people live on Formentera. The inhabitants arrived comparatively recently, the island having been abandoned in the Middle Ages in the face of marauding Barbary pirates and only repopulated at the end of the 17C. Most of the present population are fishermen or peasant farmers, shipping to Ibiza figs and fish and to Barcelona 10 000 tons of salt a year. The women wear a traditional dress similar to that of Ibiza.

Cala Sabina. — Your landing point on the island is in the main harbour: a few white houses stand between two big lagoons, saltmarshes glisten in the distance on the left.

San Francisco Javier. — Chief and only town on the island. Note its 18C church.

The beaches. — Two sand beaches are being developed: Es Pujols, protected by Cape Punta Prima and Mitjorn, long and open on the south side of the isthmus.

Nuestra Señora del Pilar. — The small village at the centre of the Mola Promontory has a geometrically designed church similar to those on Ibiza only smaller.

Mola Lighthouse. — The road ends at the lighthouse, overlooking an impressive cliff.

12 Canary Islands

The Canary Islands (Michelin map 🔲🔲🔲 folds 31 and 32) lie in the Atlantic, ten times nearer to the coast of Africa than they are to Spain — 115 to 1 150km respectively (70 and 700 miles). The archipelago slightly to the north of the Tropic of Cancer — average latitude 28° — is divided into eastern and western administrative provinces namely, **Las Palmas,** comprising the islands of Grand Canary, Fuerteventura and Lanzarote, and that of **Santa Cruz de Tenerife** with the four islands of Tenerife, La Palma, Gomera and Hierro.

The total area of the archipelago, including the 6 smaller islets, is 7 273km² - 2 808sq miles (Madrid province: 7 995km² - 3 086sq miles); the population totals 1 444 626.

Access:

Air. — Iberia has direct services from the United Kingdom and Spain. Package tours have their own charter flights or special arrangements with commercial airlines.

Sea. — Melia Travel (12 Douer Street, London WIX 4NS, ☎01 409 1884) are the British agents for Compañía Transmediterránea who run passenger lines from Spain to the Canary Islands.

Inter-island services. — There are frequent inter-island air and boat services (the only larger island not accessible by air is Gomera). Enquire locally and book in advance in summer.

The conquerors... — The islands are alluded to in Greek literature, referred to more exactly by Plutarch and described in some detail by Pliny the Elder who named them the Isles of the Blest or the Fortunate Islands. In the age of the great explorers, many landed, none stayed, not even the Genoese, **Lancelloti Malocello** after whom, nevertheless, Lanzarote was named.

The first true expedition to the archipelago took place in 1402 *(p 271)* as a final result of which, after several years' struggle against the native population, **Jean de Béthencourt,** a Frenchman under commission to the king of Spain, and **Gadifer de la Salle,** subdued the islands of Lanzarote, Fuerteventura and to a lesser degree those of Gomera and Hierro. Only at the end of the century was Grand Canary conquered by **Pedro de Vera** (1483) and shortly afterwards La Palma (1492) and Tenerife (1496) by **Alonso Fernández de Lugo,** to bring the entire archipelago under Spain.

The origin of the name Canary is thought locally to derive from a breed of dog discovered by the Romans on the islands and still extant on Fuerteventura. This, it is said, made them name the islands Insula Canum. Later, when the yellow finch, also indigenous, was discovered and named "canary" after the island, the whole archipelago changed to its present name.

...and Guanches. — The island conquerors of the 15C found a native population who, lacking all outside contact, was still living in the Stone Age. The **Guanches,** originally inhabitants of Tenerife and Gomera but later of the other islands also, raised swine, goats and sheep, kept dogs, grew a few crops, lived in caves, dressed in skins and ate meat, cheese and **gofio** or cornbread. Utensils were rudimentary and little decorated.

The people's only sophistication lay in their ,burial procedures when they usually mummified the corpse before wrapping it in fine goatskins and immuring it in a cave or rock cleft. Little is known of the Guanches' racial origin; bones and mummies reveal them to have been of the Cro-Magnon type of man; certain characteristics are typical of the Berbers of North Africa. The presence on the islands of fair skinned, blond inhabitants, has never been explained. Conquest and even more, natural disasters — plague, famine, volcanic eruptions — have left few, if any, pure blooded survivors.

A volcanic archipelago. — Volcanic eruptions would appear to have thrust the islands from the bottom of the Atlantic seabed well prior to the Tertiary era. Two, Gomera and Grand Canary, have the true volcano silhouette and most, with the exception of Fuerteventura and Lanzarote, have hills inland and cliff lined shores. The height of Mount Teide at 3 718m - 12 195ft the highest point in the archipelago, slightly exceeds the local depth of the Atlantic Ocean 3 000m - 1 640fathoms. Erosion and eruptions — the last was on La Palma in October 1971 — continue to modify the island's appearance with lava streams, slag deserts, cone and cinder areas.

The most extensive of these, known locally as **malpaís,** is on Lanzarote.

The Fortunate Islands. — Though snow may cover the highest peaks (Mount Teide) for several months of the year, the coast basks all the year round in a climate which never varies more than between 18 and 30 °C - 65 to 86 °F. (The heat of Africa is modified by the Canary Current.) Rain is virtually unknown, the eastern islands sometimes going without rain for several years. Predominating amidst the vegetation on these islands, therefore, and on the south coastlines of the other islands where they are protected from the wind, the *sotavento,* are xerophils or plants adapted to dry conditions, such as cacti *(cardón)* and **nopals** *(tunera)* or cochineal figs (a type of Barbary fig) so-called as they are favoured by the fly from which the dye was extracted.

The dragon-tree of Icod *(p 277)*

By contrast hillsides with a north aspect exposed to the northeast tradewinds, the *barlovento,* support, in the somewhat humid atmosphere, a flourishing vegetation of laurels and giant brooms on volcanic soil rich in natural minerals and highly fertile.

Irrigation enables a wide variety of plants and crops to be grown and water from the mountain is, therefore, carefully stored in vast cisterns. These supply the banana plantations which now cover much of the northern lowlands on Grand Canary and Tenerife and the tomato fields in the southern areas. In the eastern islands peasant ingenuity has had to make up for the lack of water-gathering peaks *(p 271).*

Relics of the islands original flora can be seen in the thousands of years old dracaena or **dragon-trees** — *(illustration p 265);*

The tree sap was used medicinally by the early Guanches.

The Canary Island's economy is based on agriculture including exports and a limited quantity of fishing. The most fertile land areas are overpopulated, resulting in a steady stream of emigrants leaving for Venezuela. Industry is making a start with the establishment of shipyards in Las Palmas and on Tenerife of a tobacco factory and oil refinery. The latter is supplied by Venezuela, the Middle East and Nigeria and has been producing some 8 000 000 tons of refined oil a year. Finally there is tourism — already a major factor and increasing annually.

A holiday in the Canaries. — Standard time in the Canaries is GMT.

When to go? — In the Canaries it is always springtime; you can bathe all the year round.

The tourist high season, when the hotels are full, is from January to March. If you go in summer it will obviously be hot and the atmosphere heavy but generally you should find it perfectly supportable — be careful, however, of sunburn.

Where to stay? — The south coast on either of the two main islands is recommended for the sunny aspect and the beaches. If you prefer a town atmosphere, go to Las Palmas or Puerto de la Cruz on Tenerife; if you want to escape, go where tourist resources are few — to the peaceful paradises of Gomera or Fuerteventura.

How to book and what to do. — Individual bookings are sometimes difficult, many hotels being occupied by package tours *(especially from 1 November to 30 April).* Enquire early. Excursions to add interest to your holiday, can be made by coach, taxi, local buses and hired cars *(offices at airports and elsewhere on all the islands: details — Spanish Tourist Office p 28).*

GRAND CANARY   (Las Palmas)

Michelin map 𝟿𝟿𝟶 fold 32

The scallop-shaped island of 1 532km² - 592sq miles has as its highest point, the Pozo de las Nieves. Declining heights ring the mountain, their slopes cut by dry ravines, *barrancos,* from which swift streams have been diverted to man-made lakes and irrigation channels. The island relief is more or less uniform but climatically the contrast is extreme between the north — fertile, humid and the kingdom of the banana tree — and the south — a wide expanse of desert only beginning to be cultivated with tomato plants.

The north and west coasts are edged by steep cliffs; the south is swathed in wide, accessible beaches and is being rapidly developed to provide facilities for tourists.

GRAN CANARIA

0   5 km

Las PALMAS DE GRAN CANARIA ★★ P

Local map p 266 — Pop 366 454

Las Palmas was founded in a palm grove in 1478 by Juan Rejón; it is now capital of the province of Las Palmas and with Santa Cruz de Tenerife, one of Spain's major ports. The city is the largest in the archipelago, extending for nearly 10km - 6 1/2 miles southwards from the Guiniguada Ravine northwards to the Isleta Peninsula which forms a natural breakwater to the world famous harbour.

The urban area divides distinctly into two, the old city of **Vegueta,** dating back to the time of the conquest and the **Puerto de la Luz,** built high with tourist hotels and amenities between the harbour and Alcaravaneras Beach (Playa de las Alcaravaneras) on one side and the Canteras Beach (Playa de las Canteras) on the other. Between lies the residential garden city, the **Ciudad Jardín,** beyond the cliff which once bounded the city to the west, and new housing developments.

Gando airport *(30km - 19 miles)* and Las Palmas harbour being on the air and sea routes from Europe to South America, bring the island transit visitors as well as longer staying winter tourists.

Christopher Columbus. — It has been said that, but for the Canary Islands, Columbus might never have discovered America. The Genoese navigator, persuaded that there must be a westerly passage to Asia sought in vain to convince the sovereigns of Portugal, England, Castile and France until, finally, the Catholic Monarchs *(p 49)* granted him a commission and three ships: the *Niña,* the *Pinta* and the *Santa María.* He set sail westwards from Palos in August 1492 but was forced to put into Las Palmas and Gomera for repairs to the *Pinta.* On 12 October 1492 he spied land and set foot for the first time on American soil — in the Antilles Island of San Salvador. In three subsequent voyages he landed each time in the archipelago (at Las Palmas or on Gomera) before going on to discover the other islands of the Antilles (1493), the Orinoco delta (1498) and the shores of Honduras (1502).

■ **VEGUETA** *time: 1 1/2 hours*

Make for the cathedral by way of the picturesque Calle Juan León y Joven (beautiful doorways). Continue on foot as marked on the map.

Cathedral (CZ A). — *Open Mondays to Fridays 6 to 10.30am; Saturdays 7 to 10.30am and 7 to 9pm; Sundays and holidays 7 to 11.30am and 6.30 to 8pm.* The cathedral was begun in the 15C and only completed in the 19C. The façade is strictly Neo-Classical, the interior, however, more Gothic-Plateresque. In the transept are statues by the Canaries' sculptor, **José Luján Pérez** (1756-1815) of St Joseph and the *Mater Dolorosa* (right) and the Virgin and Child (left).

In the treasury is a beautiful monstrance attributed to the Italian goldsmith, Benvenuto Cellini (16C).

Plaza de Santa Ana (CZ 78). — The pleasant palm bordered square is overlooked by the fine façade of the 1842 town hall. The bronze dogs *(see above)* recall the possible derivation of the name of the archipelago *(p 265).*

Columbus' House★ (Casa de Colón) (CZ B). — *Open 9am to 1.30pm (1pm Saturdays and days before holidays); closed Sundays and holidays; 5pts.*

The palace of the island's first governors and where Columbus himself stayed in 1502, now houses a museum in a typical Canaries' setting, of the era of the discoverer.

Nearby is **St Antony's (Iglesia de San Antonio Abad)** (CZ C) on the site of the chapel in which Columbus attended mass. The present church has an elegant baroque interior *(to visit apply at Columbus' House).*

Plaza del Espíritu Santo (CZ 25). — A delightful small square.

Go by the Calle Luis Millares to the picturesque **Plaza de Santo Domingo** (CZ 79).

Canaries Museum (Museo Canario) (CZ M¹). — *Open 10am to 1pm (noon Saturdays) and 3 to 7.30pm; closed Saturday afternoons and all day Sundays and holidays; 100pts.*

A visit, even a brief one, to the first floor galleries, is far the best way to obtain an idea of Guanche ethnography. In a case in gallery 20 is a collection of idols including an unusual figure of a seated woman; in the centre of 21 are *pintaderas* or terracotta seals found only on Grand Canary and whose purpose remains a mystery: were they for tatooing, branding or sealing harvests?

■ **THE MODERN TOWN**

Go by car along the Avenida Marítima del Norte. The avenue on land reclaimed from the sea, now runs the full length of the built-up area.

San Telmo Park (CZ). — The Calle de Triana or Calle Mayor, the main street of the old town, always full of life and bustle, begins by the park. The baroque interior of **San Telmo Church** (CZ E) is full of character.

Doramas Park (AZ). — This large park in the centre of the city encloses the great Santa Catalina Hotel and the **Pueblo Canario,** a Canary Island village created by the painter Néstor de la Torre.

Folk dancing and singing are held in the village *(Sundays 11.45am to 1.15pm; Thursdays 5.30 to 7pm).*

The house of the painter, Néstor de la Torre (1888-1938), is now a **museum** (AZ M²) *(open 10am to noon and 4 to 7pm; Sundays 10.30am to 1.30pm; closed Wednesdays and holidays; 30pts).*

Tartanas or picturesque coaches, start from the Hotel Santa Catalina on sightseeing tours of the town.

Santa Catalina Park (CXY). — The park lies at the centre of the tourist quarter of Puerto de la Luz. Nearby streets are lined with bars, restaurants and nightclubs which overflow at night into the dense crowds.

Las Palmas is a free port and so there are also countless Indian and other stalls and bazaars selling oriental and more particularly duty free goods to the predominantly Scandinavian tourists.

La Luz Castle (Castillo de la Luz) (AY F). — A maritime museum (Museo del Mar) will occupy this fort which in the 16C protected the town from marauding pirates.

The port (AY). — Ocean liners can be seen moored alongside the 3km long - 2 mile Dique del Generalísimo. In 1985 some 14 419 ships called at the port necessitating the construction of an additional dock on the north side of the harbour.

Playa de las Canteras (CX). — Deeply indented and sloping gently this beach sheltered from the waves by a rocky offshore bar, is paralleled by a promenade.

Paseo Cornisa (AZ 15). — End the tour by going to the top of the Paseo Cornisa through the modern Escaleritas quarter for a **view★** of Puerto de la Luz and Isleta.

Pérez Galdós Museum (Casa Museo) (CZ M³). — Open 9am to 1pm (library open 4 to 8pm); closed Sundays and holidays and in July and August.

The house in which the writer, Pérez Galdós (1843-1920; p 200) was born contains souvenirs.

NORTH as far as Agaete

59km - 36 1/2 miles - allow 1 day — Local map p 266

Leave Las Palmas by ③ on the adjoining plan.

Arucas. — Arucas is the third largest town after Las Palmas and Telde on the island.

A narrow road leads from the north wall of the church to the top of the **Montaña de Arucas★★**, a sugar loaf mound from which one can look down on the town of white walled houses set in an apparently limitless green sea of banana trees.

Firgas, 3km - 2 miles off the main road produces a mineral water consumed locally in considerable quantity.

Gáldar. — Gáldar, at the foot of the mountain of the same name was the Guanarteme of Guanche

LAS PALMAS DE GRAN CANARIA

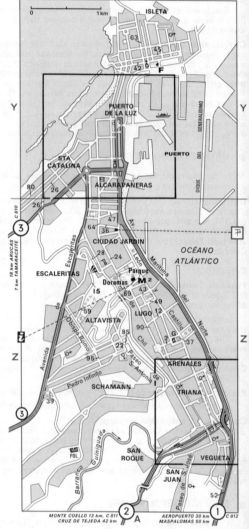

royal court and still has traces of the ancient and largely unknown civilisation. A cave, the Cueva Pintada, discovered in 1881, is decorated with **wall paintings★** of which the significance remains a total mystery. Guanche objects are also displayed. *Closed temporarily. Access from the 3rd road on the right after the main street, going towards Agaete.*

Guancha Necropolis. — *1.5km - 1 mile north of Gáldar along the coast. Take the second road on the right before the church; turn 2nd left then 1st right and continue to the end of the tarmac. Walk 800yds along the path on the right.* Suddenly you will come on a group of circular constructions built of massive blocks of lava rock. This was a Guanche necropolis. Tombs were placed individually in the rock clefts. The most mysterious as it is the most complex is the one farthest to the east. *Other tombs may be seen if you follow the path to the left.*

6km - 4 miles from Gáldar are the **Cuevas de las Cruces,** picturesque natural caverns, hollowed out of the volcanic tufa.

Agaete. — Picturesque, white walled village in the heart of a fertile countryside.

Los Berrazales★. — *6km - 4 miles to the spa hotel.* The **Agaete Valley★** lies sheltered deep in the mountains, carpeted in a lush vegetation.

Puerto de las Nieves. — A small fishing port which in the days when overland transport to Las Palmas was difficult, used also to be a banana port. From the quayside can be seen the locally famous rock point known as the Finger of God, Dedo de Dios, on account of its surprising shape.

PUERTO DE LA LUZ

VEGUETA TRIANA

SPAIN: The Michelin Regional Map Series (1: 400 000)

They show

golf courses, arenas, beaches, pleasure boat harbours, national parks, game reserves, viewpoints, scenic routes, interesting sights.

These maps make the perfect travelling companion.

San Nicolás de Tolentino. — *34km - 21 miles.* A highly spectacular road, which follows the steeply escarped coastline and crosses several ravines, brings you to San Nicolás, a village lying in a fertile basin where sugar cane and tomatoes are grown.
On the return take the coast road once beyond Guía.

Cenobio de Valerón**. — *Open 10am to 1pm and 3 to 5pm; closed Sundays.* In a remarkable site the group of caves in the volcanic rock, protected by a basalt crust, constituted, in Guanche times, a type of convent *(Cenobio)*. In this remarkable setting young daughters of the nobility were instructed, it appears, as vestal virgins *(harimaguadas)*.
On the mountain summit the chiefs met in solemn council or *tagoror*.

San Felipe. — The small fishing village has a remarkable rock setting.

The CENTRE and Cruz de Tejeda

143km - 89 miles — allow one day — Local map p 266

Leave Las Palmas by ② on the map p 268.

Jardin Canario★. — *Open 8am to 7pm (6pm in winter).* A tropical terraced garden built into the cliff face.

Tafira. — Country retreat for the citizens of Las Palmas.

Bandama Belvedere★★ (Mirador). — *Turn left at Monte Coello.* A narrow road *(5km - 3 miles)* leads to the top of the Bandama (569m - 1 867ft) from where there is a remarkable view of the Bandama crater *(caldera)*. This magnificent volcanic basin with eruption formations intact, is carpeted with green crops. From the peak there are also good views of Las Palmas and the island interior.

Santa Brígida. — To the north of the village is a fine avenue of palm trees.

Vega de San Mateo. — Large agricultural market centre (big Saturday and Sunday fairs).

Las Lagunetas. — Attractive view of crops planted in a terraced semicircle.

Cruz de Tejeda★★. — Not far from the *parador* on the 1 450m - 4 757ft pass, is the village of Tejeda in a huge volcanic basin described by Unamuno as resembling a petrified tempest. Standing out from this incredible tormented landscape are the impressive Bentayga Rock, in the centre, and on the left, the Nublo Rock, said to have been worshipped by the Guanches. On a clear day you can see Mount Teide.

Take the Los Pechos road.

Pozo de las Nieves★★★. — From the sometimes snow-capped summit (1 980m - 6 496ft) where the island's meteorological station is situated, there is a vast panorama of the Tejeda countryside and towards the east, of the coast and the sea.

At Cruz de Tejeda turn into the Artenara road. 5km - 3 miles beyond the first crossroads there is an attractive **view★** of the troglodyte village of **Juncalillo** where most of the inhabitants live in caves formed by a lava stream.

Artenara. — The village at 1 219m - 3 991ft is the highest on the island. From the restaurant (Parador de la Silla) in a cave on the way out of the village, there is an interesting **outline view★** of the Bentayga Rock.

Tamadaba Pinewood★★ (Pinar). — The magnificent wood of Canary Pines extends to the edge of a cliff which drops sheer to the sea. *12km - 7 miles from Artenera there is a left turn where a surfaced road leads off; continue along it for 300yds, before parking the car and walking through the pines to the cliff edge.* There you will get a **bird's-eye view★** of Agaete, Gáldar and the coast and of Mount Teide.

Return by the way you came; bear left towards Valleseco.

Zamora Belvedere★ (Mirador). — There is a good **view★**, shortly after Valleseco, of Teror at the end of its small valley.

Teror. — The majesty of the façade of the 18C Church of Our Lady of the Pine Tree (Nuestra Señora del Pino) perfectly befits a town which has such a distinguished air and retains many fine mansions with wooden balconies. Inside the church is the statue of Our Lady of the Pine, the island's much venerated patron which, traditionally, was found in 1481 in the branches of a pine tree. The treasury *(open daily 2 to 4pm; Sundays and holidays 10.30am to 2pm and 3.30 to 6pm; closed August and September; 15pts)* contains the Virgin's embroidered mantle and other riches. An annual pilgrimage assembles the islanders to Teror bearing gifts.

SOUTH as far as Maspalomas

58km - 36 miles — allow one day — Local map p 266

Leave Las Palmas by ① on the map p 268.

Telde. — The city, like Gáldar, was once a Guanche capital. Below the town the Church of St John the Baptist, founded in the 15C, contains a 16C Flemish altarpiece illustrating the Life of the Virgin; above is a figure of Christ, modelled in Mexico of maize leaves and roots by a method now lost.

Walk up the main street and turn right into the narrow Calle E. Navarro.

The street leads to the quiet old world San Francisco quarter.

Cuatro Puertas★. — *Turn left into the road just beyond the shacks on the far side of the crossroads; the poorly surfaced road leads to the top of the Montaña de Cuatro Puertas.* The cave with four openings or doors, *puertas,* was the meeting place of the Guanche Council or Tagoror. The mountain's east face is honeycombed with caves used by the Guanches as burial chambers. Fine view of the sea.

Ingenio. — Centre of traditional embroidery.

Playa de San Agustín. — Large seaside resort.

Playa del Inglés. — The residential area rings a pleasantly flowered shopping centre. The immense beach is edged with golden sand dunes.

Maspalomas. — An oasis, a stately palm grove scattered with well kept villas, a lagoon and surrounding dunes form the unexpected setting of the **Playa de Maspalomas★**.

Mogán. — *37km - 23 miles.* The road, more hilly as it follows the coastline where countless seaside resorts are springing up, goes through the small fishing village of **Puerto de Mogán** before ascending the wild *barranco* to Mogán (776m - 2 545ft).

Alternative road by San Bartolomé de Tirajana★. — *Extra distance 47km - 29 miles.* The climb to San Bartolomé by the **Barranco de Fataga★**, almost a grandiose canyon, is impressively beautiful. The road continues through **Fataga,** a picturesque village surrounded by orchards, before reaching **San Bartolomé** which is magnificently situated in a green mountain circle at the foot of tall grey cliffs, probably the inner walls of an ancient volcano.

The road continues a further 6km - 4 miles to the Cruz Grande Pass from where there is a good view of the mountains before you reach the Nublo Rock. As you leave **Santa Lucía** there is a small Guanche museum *(open 9am to 6pm; 70pts),* containing objects found on a hillside to the east.

LANZAROTE   (Las Palmas)

Michelin map 990 fold 32

Lanzarote with an area of 813km² - 313sq miles is the most unusual of the Canary Islands. Seaside resorts are beginning to be developed along its fine white sand beaches but the usual thing for visitors to do is to go over for a one or two day visit to see its quite outstanding volcanic features.

From the 14C to the present. — The Genoese, Lancelloti Malocello, landed on the island in the 14C but left no trace other than his name. Conquest came in 1402 with the arrival of the Normans, **Gadifer de la Salle** and **Jean de Béthencourt** who met little resistance so that Béthencourt was shortly able to present the island to the King of Castile. Lanzarote then became the base for expeditions to one after another of the other islands but without success until finally, Fuerteventura was also subdued. Béthencourt left Lanzarote in 1416, much mourned by the local inhabitants, to return to his native France. Government of the island was taken over by his cousin, Maciot.

Once the main islands had been conquered, Lanzarote was largely left to its own devices and since its coast was open and mountains low, it became a prey to marauding pirates in search of men and women to sell as slaves... Calamity of a different nature occurred in 1730 in the form of a massive volcanic eruption. Near the village of Timanfaya a flaming mountain range, the **Fire Mountains,** suddenly appeared. For six years the eruption continued until one third of the island was covered in a sea of lava. In 1824 it all began again, this time to the north where a new volcano, Tinguatón, thrust out of the earth's crust and molten lava poured over the southwest. Villagers eventually returned to build new houses and plant crops in the lunar landscape of more than 100 craters, lava fields, the **malpaís** and layers of blackish cinders and pebbles.

In **La Geria,** a fertile pebble area, the peasants have built low semicircular walls to protect from the northeast wind the vines from which they produce an excellent light white wine with a distinctive bouquet, the Lanzarote Malvasia. Everywhere fields are covered in a deep layer of volcanic pebbles, known locally as *picón,* which absorb dew at night and provide humidity by evaporation during the day — there is virtually no rainfall on the island. Another unique feature are the dromedaries which somehow complete the unforgettable landscape.

ARRECIFE
Local map p 272 — 29 502

The capital, founded on a coastal site outlined by offshore reefs (*arrecife* in Spanish: reefs), was further defended seaward by the **St Gabriel Fort** (Castillo de San Gabriel), built in the 16C on an islet connected to the town by a drawbridge.

To visit the main harbour, **Puerto de las Naos** at the north end of the town, walk along the main street, Calle León y Castillo. Turn first right beyond the bend, left at the end, then right.

SOUTHWARDS
Round tour of 105km - 65 miles starting from Arrecife — *Local map p 272*

Janubio Saltpans★ (Salinas). — The sea has entered a disused crater producing myriad contrasts in colour and form — the gleaming white pyramids of salt, the deep blue still water, and geometrically square pans in the semicircular lagoon.

Papagayo Point★ (Punta). — *12km - 7 miles.* The **Rubicón** where Béthencourt originally settled has not developed as he expected: all that now recalls the island's conquest is an old tower standing at the cliff edge. From the point *(access along a poor road)* where there are magnificent rock creeks there are also good **views★** of the Playa Blanca and Fuerteventura.

Los Hervideros. — In the caverns at the end of the tongue of lava, the sea boils (*hervir:* to boil) in an endlessly fascinating spectacle.

El Golfo★. — A lagoon, retained by a sandbank in the crater, is filled with vivid emerald green water; a steep cliff of pitted black rock forms an impressive backcloth.

Fire Mountains★★★ (Montañas del Fuego or **Parque nacional de Timanfaya).** — The range which emerged only in 1730, stands out sometimes red, sometimes black; in a lunar landscape of volcanic cinder and slag.

5km - 3 miles north of Yaiza, dromedaries stand at the roadside *(9am to 1.30pm: 500pts per person)* to take those who want briefly to experience the swaying, jolting movement a little way up the mountainside *(about 15 minutes).* You get a good view of the next crater and Graciosa Island. There is also a footpath to the summit to see the surrounding craters which are impressive.

The volcanoes may be quiescent but their inner fires burn and bubble still. At **Islote de Hilario** the phenomena are spectacular: twigs dropped into a hole in the ground 50cm - 20ins deep catch fire; water poured into a pipe set into the lava, evaporates immediately into steam.

We would suggest you continue by taking the bus ride along a special road through the lava fields *(departures every hour 10am to 2pm and 3 to 4pm; time: 1 hour; 375pts per person. Recorded commentary in several languages)* as you will then get some extraordinary views of the landscape and be taken across craters in the Fire Mountain range.

On the return go and see *(small footpath to the right of the road)* the minute crater known from its shape and the colour of the lava slag upon its walls, as the **Cup of Chocolate (Tacita de Chocolate).**

Return by way of La Geria.

La Geria★★. — La Geria lies between Yaiza and Mozaga a weird landscape of blackish desert pockmarked with craters. Near **Mozaga,** the centre of the island, a monument symbolising Fecundity has been erected in honour of the continuing courage of the peasants of Lanzarote. There is a small ethnographic museum next door.

San Bartolomé. — Winds bring fertilising pollen to this area from the Sahara but their strength is such that crops have to be protected by low straw windbreaks.

NORTHWARDS

Round tour of 85km - 52 1/2 miles starting from Arrecife — Local map below

Guatiza. — One of the island's last windmills still turns in the wind here. Further north around **Mala**, *nopals (p 265)* flourish in the fields.

Los Verdes Cave★★★ (Cueva). — *Guided tours (time: 1 hour); departures hourly from 11am to 6pm inclusive; 275pts.*
At the foot of the Corona Volcano are miles of underground galleries where the Guanches used to take refuge from marauding pirates. The galleries were formed during successive eruptions when lava streams cooled and hardened into dense basalt layers, diverting or allowing subsequent streams to flow around or over earlier flows. There are 2km - 1 mile of galleries at different levels, now illuminated to show the kaleidoscope of colours and shapes in the underground phantasmagoria.

Jameos del Agua★. — *Open 11am to 7pm (3am Tuesdays, Fridays and Saturdays); 275pts; night performance: 600pts.*
The seawater lagoon in a cave in the lava rock is interesting biologically, as being the habitat of a minute, white millenary crab which is born blind and, less esoterically, for the folk dancing and singing which takes place weekly in surroundings now arranged to outstrip any of nature's fantasies.

Del Río Belvedere★★ (Mirador del Río). — At the north end of the island, a steep headland, the **Riscos de Famara,** stands like a ship's prow before the waves. In the 17C major fortifications, including a battery *(batería),* were constructed on the vantage point where a cliff edge belvedere has now been placed. This commands a superb **panorama★★** across the beautifully blue **El Río** sea inlet of Graciosa and its neighbouring islands (Montaña Clara, Alegranza) and, immediately below, of the local saltpans.

Haría. — As on all the islands, the northern end is the most attractive. 5km - 3 miles south of the village there is a fine **view★** from a belvedere of the lush Haría Valley with its hundreds of palm trees. In the distance rises the Corona Volcano.

Teguise. — Teguise, once the island's capital, is the home of the *timple,* a miniature guitar intrinsic to Canary folklore.
Nearby is **Guanapay Castle (Castillo),** built in the 16C on the edge of the volcano of the same name. From the summit there is a vast **panorama★** including Teguise in the foreground and Graciosa Island on the horizon. The village, in a most attractive setting at the foot of an extinct volcano, is Soó.

FUERTEVENTURA (Las Palmas)

Michelin map ▨▨▨ fold 32

Fuerteventura, the largest of the Canary Islands after Tenerife, is also, relatively, the least populous (11 people to km² - 28 to sq mile). It is an arid land, a "skeletal island" in the words of Unamuno, scattered with countless bare crests, mostly extinct volcanoes. Only goats can graze such terrain. Palm trees and numerous windmills, drawing water from the subsoil (tomatoes, cereals), mark the sites of scattered villages.
Fuerteventura, so near Africa, shares its climate; the continent's sand, blown across the sea, gave the island its present form by building up an isthmus, El Jable, between the originally separate islets of Maxorata and Jandía. The endless beaches are also wind borne African sand. African sun is the reason why no Fuerteventura peasant is ever seen without his straw hat with a brim slightly more upturned than those of the natives of Lanzarote.
The island's attractions lie in the beauty of bare landscape, in a shore lined almost along its entire length by immense beaches of white sand or rocks which provide good underwater swimming and, for those who enjoy it, open sea fishing with good catches in the channel between the island and Africa.
On the third Saturday in September everyone goes in pilgrimage to the hermitage of the Virgen de la Peña, near Vega de Río de Palmas.

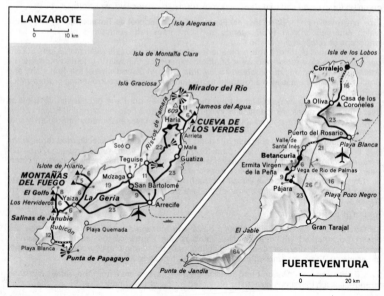

SOUTHWARDS

59km - 36 1/2 miles — Local map p 272

Puerto del Rosario. — This town is the capital (pop 13 878). South of it is the **Playa Blanca.**

Betancuria★. — This spot, hidden away in a valley in the heart of the mountains was chosen, in 1404, by Béthencourt *(p 271)* as the site for the island capital. Access is from the north, along the Santa Inés Valley from which there are good views of the town. Looking south there is an attractive contrast between the wide horizon of bare, rose tinted crests and the village of Vega de Río de Palmas nestling in its green valley-oasis.

From the early conquest years, Betancuria retains, in addition to a certain city style, a ruined Franciscan monastery and an ancient **cathedral** with white walls and a picturesque wooden balcony. *To visit apply at 11 Calle Roberto Roldán.* The three aisle interior contains interesting statues and a sacristy with a fine *artesonado* ceiling.

A small ethnographic museum on the south side of the town displays Guanche exhibits. *The caretaker lives in the house opposite.*

Pájara. — The carvings on the church doorway are obviously Aztec inspired.

Gran Tarajal. — The port, also the second largest town on the island, lies in tamarisk country (*taraje:* tamarisk).

NORTHWARDS

39km — 24 miles — Local map p 272

La Oliva. — Go by way of the path beginning at the back of the church to look at the 18C former governor's house known as the Colonels' House, **Casa de los Coroneles,** now falling into ruin. Not far away on the right is the **Casa del Capellán** or Chaplain's House, a minute, double roofed dwelling in a clearing circled by a dry stone wall. The decorative motifs carved on its door and window are much the same as those on Pájara church *(see above)*.

Corralejo★. — Corralejo is a small fishing village and seaside resort beyond the *malpaís (p 271)*, at the very end of the island. A translucent sea bathes the white sand beaches edged, in the east, by still unspoiled dunes. For underwater swimming take a boat to Lobos Island. Lanzarote can been seen in the distance.

TENERIFE   (Santa Cruz de Tenerife)

Michelin map 🔢🔢🔢 fold 31

Tenerife, the largest (2 053km² - 792sq miles) of the Canaries, gets its name from the Guanche word meaning snow-capped mountain. And this is indeed the most characteristic feature of the triangular shaped island with its long mountain spine, dominated by a gigantic volcanic cone 3 718m - 12 198ft high. This peak, the Teide, the highest Spanish summit, is nearly always snow-capped. Past volcanic activity is everywhere apparent on Tenerife, one of the most spectacular examples being the Cañadas crater which rings the Teide. As in Grand Canary, the south is arid, the north lush with banana trees. Although steep cliffs edge the shore, the major resort of Puerto de la Cruz is at the island's north end, together with one of the finest landscapes in the Canaries — the sea of Orotava banana plantations rippling before the great snow-capped Mount Teide.

SANTA CRUZ DE TENERIFE 🅿

Local map p 277 — Pop 190 784

The town, formerly a small port serving La Laguna, developed in the 19C and has since become the island's maritime and industrial centre. With Las Palmas, it is a port of call for ocean liners and cargo vessels. It has been a free port since 1852. An oil refinery, tobacco and other factories have recently increased local commerce. The **view★** from the harbour breakwater (Puerto) gives a good idea of the town setting with its stepped semicircle of highrise buildings against the background of Mount Teide and the Anaga mountain range.

Church of the Conception (BZ C). — Only a few balconied houses around this 17C reconstructed church remain of the old town. The altarpieces are worth looking at.

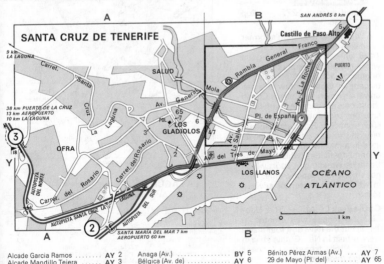

SANTA CRUZ DE TENERIFE

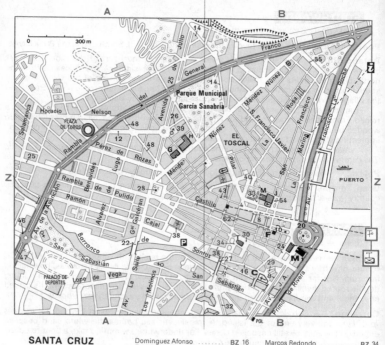

SANTA CRUZ DE TENERIFE

Paso Alto Castle (Castillo) (BY). — It was when attacking the town and castle on 24 July 1797 that Nelson lost both the battle... and his right arm. Among the cannon on view, is one known as the Tiger *(on the right)*, which fired the fatal ball.

Municipal Park (Parque Municipal García Sanabria) (ABZ). — Tropical trees and plants, and a small zoo.

Archaeological Museum (Museo Arqueológico) (BZ M¹). — *Open 9am to 1pm and 4 to 6pm; closed Saturday afternoons, Sundays and holidays all day and afternoons in July and August; 25pts.*

The museum is on the 3rd floor of the 18C El Cabildo Insular Palace *(entrance: Avenida Bravo Murillo).* Examples of the Guanche civilisation on display include, most importantly, mummies in their cave surroundings. On the ground floor *(entrance: from the square)* a model of the island is on display.

Palacio de Carta (BZ F). — This 18C building, now a bank, has an attractive *patio.*

Avoid visiting a church during a service

La LAGUNA

Local map p 277 — Pop 112 635

La Laguna, the island's former capital, was founded by Lugo in 1496 on the edge of a lagoon which has since disappeared. The original quadrilateral plan is still evident in what is now a small university town. At Corpus Christi the streets are carpeted with flowers; on 14 September the Crucifix from San Francisco Monastery, the town's patron, is venerated in a massive procession and general festivities which include Canaries wrestling, a sport which goes back to Guanche times and in which visitors are not advised to join!

Cathedral (Y A). — The Neo-Classical façade was erected in 1819, but the nave and four aisles were rebuilt in Neo-Gothic style in 1905. Rich treasury *(access through transept).*

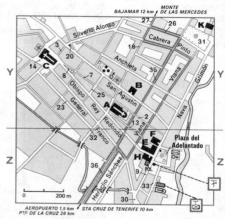

LA LAGUNA

Bishopric (Palacio episcopal) (Y B). — Beautiful stone façade of 1681 and colourful flowered patio.

Church of the Conception★ (Iglesia de la Concepción) (Y C). — The early 16C church is typical of the sanctuaries built at the time of the conquest. In contrast to the sober style of the architecture are an intricate Mudejar ceiling and baroque pulpit and choirstalls.

Plaza del Adelantado (Z). — The town hall **(ayuntamiento)** (H), which has been remarkably restored in the Canaries' style, is open *(entrance: Calle Obispo Rey Redondo)*. Opposite is the old **Convent of Santa Catalina** (E) with its original upper gallery, a local feature now rare but once common enough in the islands.

    Farther on is the 17C **Nava Palace** (F) reminiscent in style of the bishopric; the interior is 18C.

San Francisco Convent (Y K). — *At the end of the Calle Nava Grimón*. The convent church contains, most importantly, at the centre of a typical beaten silver altarpiece, the much venerated 15C Crucifix *(p 274)*.

■ MONTE DE LAS MERCEDES★★

Round tour 47km - 29 miles — Local map p 277. The mountainous Anaga headland is high enough to catch clouds from the north, making the area sufficiently humid for woodlands of tree laurel, giant broom and *fayas*, a local species, to flourish. From the road along the crest there are views of the forest and the meadows of the coastal plain.

    Cruz del Carmen Belvedere★ (Mirador). — Good view of the La Laguna Valley.

    Pico del Inglés Belvedere★★ (Mirador). — A most impressive panorama spreads out below the 1 024m - 3 360ft peak of the entire Anaga headland with all its harmonious small valleys and indented coastline; in the distance rises Mount Teide.

    Puerto El Bailadero★. — Climb to the pass which commands good views either way.

    Taganana★. — As one descends there are magnificent **views★★** of the village's picturesque setting. Go and see the interesting Hispano-Flemish altarpiece in the church *(to visit inquire at no 13 in the square)*.

    San Andrés. — Small fishing village; nearby is the grey sand beach of Las Teresitas.

Returning to Santa Cruz you pass the new harbour installations.

■ PUERTO DE LA CRUZ ★

Local map p 276 — Pop 39 241
See town plan in the current Michelin Red Guide España Portugal

    The mushroom - like growth of Puerto de la Cruz at the heart of the banana region on the north coast, is due not to the fishing on which it once relied (the local name is still "el Puerto": the harbour), but tourism. The sun and Mount Teide look down on an exuberant proliferation of high-rise buildings going up side by side along the rock strewn and reef outlined coast.

    A pleasant **sea promenade★,** lined with souvenir shops and flower hung viewpoints, provides the main attraction of Tenerife's most important resort.

Botanical Gardens★★★ (Jardín de Aclimatación de La Orotava). — *At the town entrance, Carretera del Botánico. Open 9am to 7pm (6pm in winter); closed 1 January, Good Friday and 25 December; 100pts. Booklet available in Spanish only.* The gardens are in a small 2ha - 5 acre setting where trees and flowers, native to the Canary Islands and other less clement parts of the world, flower profusely. Orchid houses add an oriental touch and a rubber plant, nearly 200 years old, which is perched on top of contiguous roots as though on stilts, an air of fantasy. The garden dates back to the 18C when it was established on the orders of Charles III.

EXCURSION

Mirador Humboldt★★★; La Orotava★; Los Realejos. — *27km - 17 miles along the Cuesta de la Villa - La Orotava road.*

Mirador Humboldt★★★. — The belvedere is named after the German naturalist, Alexander Humboldt who visited Tenerife in 1799 and was especially struck by the **Orotava Valley★★★.** This immense depression at the foot of Mount Teide extends all the way to the sea, its dense green carpet of banana trees relieved by water gleaming in the irrigation cisterns and the white buildings of La Orotava town and Puerto de la Cruz.

La Orotava★. — This ancient town still has many houses with picturesque *tea* or Canary pinewood balconies. From the main square you get a delightful glimpse of the old town houses with red tile roofs framed by a dragon-tree growing near a wooden balcony.

Continue on foot to the town hall square where you take a downhill street on the right. The 18C **Church of the Conception** has a graceful baroque façade between flanking towers. The treasury is open *(apply to the priest)*.

Continue round the north wall of the church. Houses with most beautiful balconies line the steeply inclined, paved, **Calle de San Francisco★.** One of the oldest, the **Casa de los Balcones,** has been arranged as a crafts museum. The street ends at a square from which a narrow street on the left leads to the **Botanical Garden,** a modest replica of the garden at Puerto de la Cruz. Nearby, in what was once the Park of the Marquess of Quinta Roja, is a fine upstanding rose red palace which now overlooks the town square.

Every year, the Thursday after Corpus Christi, the streets are strewn with flowers and the main square is decorated with a gigantic variegated sand and pebble picture. On the second Sunday after the feast there is the San Isidro *romería* when everyone from the neighbouring villages who works on the land — St Isidore was a farm labourer — comes in local costume in bullock carts to join in a great procession.

Los Realejos. — Los Realejos is made up of an upper (Realejo Alto) and a lower (Realejo Bajo) village. From the town hall terrace of the upper village, there is a view of the villages along the coast; the nearby church has interesting vaulting. A dragon-tree growing in the cemetery, stands perched on a tall rock spike.

MOUNT TEIDE ★★★

Four roads lead from the coast up to the Cañadas plateau where at 2 356m - 7 730ft a cable-car takes over the ascent to the summit. Each of the approach roads afford different landscapes but all reach their climax in the view of the giant peak itself which, with its tapering snow-capped cone, had a magic for the navigators of old as it has for the inhabitants and tourists of today, whether on Tenerife itself or on a clear day from the neighbouring islands of La Palma, Gomera and Grand Canary.

Access by way of La Esperanza. — The road, the Carretera Dorsal, begins by overlooking Santa Cruz and La Laguna, then, climbing to the crest which divides the island into two, looks down on the north and south coasts alternately.

La Esperanza Woods★. — The road works its way for several miles through dense Canary pinewoods.

Las Raíces. — In the centre of the clearing an obelisk commemorates the alliance of the local military chiefs in July 1936 under General Franco, then Captain-General of the Canary Islands, against the Spanish Republican Government. (Franco was posted to the Canaries in February 1936 after the triumph of the Popular Front.)

Pico de las Flores Belvedere★★ (Mirador). — The belvedere commands an extensive panorama of the north coast and the La Laguna basin.

Viewpoints on the ascent enable one to compare the fertility of the north with the aridity of the south.

El Portillo. — The pass at 2 000m - 6 560ft is the meeting point of the La Esperanza and Puerto de la Cruz mountain roads; it is also the gateway to the mineralogically extraordinary world of Las Cañadas.

Las Cañadas del Teide★★. — Las Cañadas is the name of the ancient fallen in crater area (now a national park), from whose centre at an altitude of more than 2 000m - 6 560ft has surged the more recent Teide Volcano.

At the centre of the crater park, near the *parador,* are the great lava boulders, uncovered by erosion, known as **Los Roques;** at other points stand the **Los Azulejos,** so-called after the ceramic tiles which also glint with the blue-green lustre of copper oxide. Abundant scori or stone debris has been left over the centuries by lava streams as they swept across the surprisingly level basalt rock floor.

Teide Summit★★★. — *Cable-car from 9am to 5pm; 400pts Rtn.*

It takes about 3/4 hour to climb from the cable-car terminal at 3 555m - 11 664ft over loose volcanic scree, past sulphur smoke holes nearly 25m deep and 50m across - 82ft X 164ft to the cone edge. If the weather is clear you can see almost the entire archipelago. In the foreground is the geologically unrelated **Pico Viejo** Crater and all around the Cañadas plateau, ringed by mountain peaks.

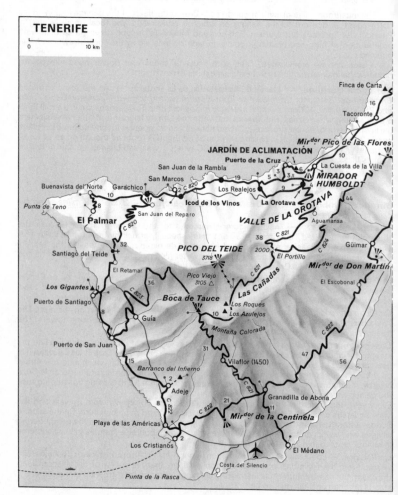

Access by La Orotava★. — The road reveals three distinct zones of vegetation in the island's north: bananas, vines and heaths on the high mountains where the inhabitants live in poor, archaic style. Beyond **Aguamansa,** just beside the road, look out for the huge "daisy", a natural formation in the basalt rock.

Access by Guía. — This more monotonous approach, crosses ancient Pico Viejo lava streams and passes through pinewoods.

Access by Vilaflor. — **Vilaflor** at 1 450m - 4 757ft is the highest town in Tenerife. The road runs directly towards a great reddish cliff face, the **Montaña Colorada,** only turning off at the last moment to circle a pinewood and arrive at the **Boca de Tauce★★** pass which at 2 055m - 6 742ft opens onto the Cañadas de Teide.

Mount Teide from Boca de Tauce

TOUR OF THE ISLAND

246km - 150 miles — allow 2 days — Local map pp 276 and 277

Santa Cruz de Tenerife. — *Description p 273.*
La Laguna. — *Description p 276.*

THE NORTH COAST
Between Tacoronte and Garachico — *48km - 30 miles*

Tacoronte. — Mount Teide comes into view. In the church, the chancel has a Mudejar ceiling.
A great dragon-tree can be seen at the bottom of a small ravine as you leave Tacoronte.

Bajamar. — *13km - 8 miles.* On your way pass the British owned, Canaries style, farm called the **Finca de Carta** *(closed temporarily, due to restoration).* Bajamar is a large seaside resort.

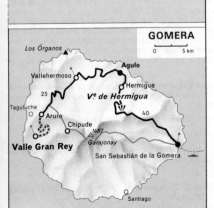

To the south of Tacoronte is La Matanza de Acentejo where Lugo and his troops were roundly defeated by the Guanches in 1495. (Swiftly Lugo took his revenge at a place since named La Victoria de Acentejo.) Unforgettable is the arrival into Puerto de la Cruz.

Botanical Gardens★★★ (Jardín de Aclimatación de La Orotava). — *Description p 275.*

Humboldt Mirador★★★ and La Orotava★. — *Description p 275.*

San Juan de la Rambla. — The **church square★** has character, the church interior, charm.

Icod de los Vinos★. — Icod, in a vine growing area (*vinos:* wines), goes back to the conquest and the **dragon-tree★** *(p 265)* is several thousand years old. This doyen of Canary *dracaena draco* is signposted (Drago) on the edge of the town in the Guía direction. The **San Marcos Church** is interesting as is the adjoining small square, lined with elegant houses.

San Marcos. — *3km - 2 miles north of Icod.* To reach this attractively sited seaside resort in a rocky creek encircled by jagged black cliffs, the road passes through banana plantations.

Garachico. — The only remainders of what before the eruption of 1716, was a major centre in the northern part of the island are a still, old quarter, the **San Miguel Fort (Castillo)** and nearby, a sea promenade built upon the rough pointed rocks. Look back on Garachico from San Juan del Reparo *(p 278).*

El Palmar★★. — *18km - 11 miles from Garachico.* Bear left just before Buenavista village. Beyond El Palmar a small village stands over a volcano chimney.

THE WEST
From Garachico to Los Cristianos
67km - 41 1/2 miles — local map p 276

5km - 3 miles south of Garachico, make a detour of 500yds to the left, at the crossroads, towards San Juan del Reparo for a good **view★** of Garachico, built in a semicircle.

Santiago del Teide. — Picturesque domed church.

El Retamar. — Once past the village, the road descends steadily through lava fields.

Los Gigantes★. — The Teno mountain range ends in a gigantic black cliff.

The several small harbours, which for long have lined the coast, **Puerto de Santiago, Puerto de San Juan...** are now being joined by new, but as yet, small, resorts.

Adeje. — Within walking distance *(2km - 1 mile)* of the village *(off the main road)* is the grandiosely beautiful Hell Valley, **Barranco del Infierno★.**

Playa de las Américas. — The resort marks the start of new hotel developments.

Los Cristianos. — Small fishing village, now one of the largest resorts on the island. A car ferry service to the island of Gomera.

THE SOUTH COAST
From Los Cristianos to Santa Cruz
109km - 68 miles — local map pp 276-277

The inland road is longer *(103km - 64 miles)* and more winding than the motorway *(74km - 46 miles)* but is more picturesque and has several good viewpoints.

Centinela Belvedere★★ (Mirador). — This belvedere, built like a sentinel's post on a rock spike at the sea's edge, commands a vast inland sweep over the farmland plain, scattered with volcanic craters. In the distance, near the red cone of the Montaña Roja, is El Médano, while inland, are the towns of Granadilla, Chayola...

Granadilla de Abona. — A proud, small agricultural town.

El Médano. — *11km - 7 miles.* The quiet resort stands beside a beach, protected from the wind by the remains of the cone of an extinct volcano.

As you leave El Escobonal village glance back over the cultivated hillsides.

Don Martín Belvedere★★ (Mirador). — Walk a short way up the hill opposite the hotel to get a view of the Güimar Rift Valley and the wide variety of crops grown upon its slopes.

Güimar. — A major centre on the south coast.

Candelaria. — The old town of Candelaria is a famous place of pilgrimage. According to tradition two Guanche shepherds found a statue of the Virgin washed up on the beach in 1390; in 1826 this statue was swept away by a storm from the cave in which it had been placed; in 1958 the present monumental basilica was completed as a shelter for the new statue of the Virgin, the patron of the archipelago, venerated particularly by the islanders on 14 and 15 August each year. On the square outside are statues of ten former Guanche chiefs of Tenerife, the Menceyes.

GOMERA (Santa Cruz de Tenerife)

Michelin map 🇩🇩🇩 fold 31

This round island *(local map p 279)* of 378km² - 146sq miles rises steeply to a single mountain mass from coastal cliffs cut by deep ravines. Crowning the range at a height of a 1 487m - 4 879ft is Mount Garajonay. Few traces remain of early volcanic activity apart from the upstanding boulders known locally as *roques* which can be seen occasionally and the basalt cliffs, Los Órganos, only visible from the sea. The fertile red soil is carefully husbanded: hillsides are industriously terraced; irrigation is controlled — the result is bountiful crops of bananas, grapes and tomatoes and a landscape, including also numerous date palms, unique in the archipelago.

San Sebastián de la Gomera. — The capital, at the mouth of a wide valley, is where Christopher Columbus *(p 267)* readied his ships before going on to discover America in 1492. You can follow his route down the main street from the corner house where he took on water (ask to see the well *(el pozo)* in the country courtyard - *patio),* to the **Church of the Assumption** where he heard mass, to the two storeyed white house, a little before the post office *(correos)* where he is said to have slept. In 1488 Doña Beatriz de Bobadilla on the assassination by the Guanches of her husband for the seduction of one of their women, had had to take refuge in the building known as the **Tower of the Count of Gomera** (Torre del Conde). The countess was only delivered from further attack by the arrival of Pedro de Vera who massacred the Guanche men and banished their women from the island. The hill to the east on which the *parador* stands, commands a good view of the town and, on a clear day, of Mount Teide.

Valle Gran Rey★★. — *63km - 39 miles.* As you emerge from the first tunnel, you will see before you the beautiful **Hermigua Valley★★** where white walled houses, palms and banana trees cover the valley floor at the feet of tall cliffs.

Agulo★. — Picturesque setting beside the sea; Tenerife lies on the horizon.

Vallehermoso. — The village lies at the end of a beautiful valley *(hermoso: beautiful).*

Arure. — Take the narrow road to the concrete bridge. From the far side there is a good **panoramic view★** of the village of Taguluche, standing isolated, near the sea.

The road beyond Arure is in very bad condition.

Valle Gran Rey★★. — The ravine, the Barranco del Valle Gran Rey, at the end of which are the village houses, is the most spectacular on the island.

You can return through **Chipude,** an attractive potter's village.

LA PALMA   (Santa Cruz de Tenerife)

Michelin map 𝟵𝟵𝟬 fold 31

La Palma, with an area of 728km² - 281sq miles as green as it is beautiful, has a central mountain range which culminates in a peak of 2 423m - 7 947ft high. A gigantic crater, the **Caldera de Taburiente**, occupies the island centre, the volcano, probably the cause of the island's emergence from the seabed, extends south in a chain of individual peaks, Las Cumbres. These, their sides cloven by deep ravines, drop abruptly to the sea in a roughly indented coastline. Crops grow abundantly in the lowland areas.

SANTA CRUZ DE LA PALMA
Local map p 280 — Pop 16 629

The island capital was founded by Lugo in 1493 at the foot of a tall cliff which is, in fact, a half eroded crater, the Caldereta. In the 16C, with rising cane sugar exports and the expansion of the dockyards, using local hardwood timber cut from the dense inland forests, Santa Cruz was one of Spain's major ports; today it is a peaceful city where mansions with elegant façades and great wooden balconies line the seafront promenade.

5km - 3 miles south lie the black sand and rocks of the Playa de Los Cancajos.

El Salvador Church. — *Open 8.30am to 1pm and 4 to 8.30pm.* The 16C church, on the Plaza de España, has fine **artesonado ceilings★** in the nave and Gothic vaulting in the sacristy. Opposite is the town hall *(ayuntamiento),* a Renaissance style building (16C). Continue to the delightful **Plaza de Santo Domingo,** where the chapel of the former monastery, contains ornate baroque altars *(to visit inquire at the El Salvador Church).*

NORTH as far as Los Sauces
31km - 19 miles — *Local map p 280*

The *corniche* road, from which there are good views of the coast, crosses deep, densely overgrown, ravines *(barrancos).* Note the many volcanic craters.

La Galga. — North of the village, on emerging from a tunnel, the road traverses a particularly rugged **ravine★,** filled with lush vegetation.

Alternative road by San Andrés. — *Extra distance 9km - 6 miles.* A stony road leads to the delightful, forgotten village of **San Andrés.** The local church has a good Mudejar ceiling over the chancel. Further north is the Punta Gorda, a rock point in which a seawater swimming pool, the **Charco Azul,** has been hollowed out. Finally you come to the tiny fishing village of **Espíndola** where the fishing boats are drawn up at the end of the shingle beach into the shelter of a crevice in the cliff face.

Punta Cumplida. — *7km - 4 1/2 miles. 3km - 2 miles before Los Sauces, turn right into a road signposted "Faro", continue along a dirt road.* Below, as you circle the lighthouse, the waves break on the polygonal basalt rock piles.

Los Sauces. — The town, amidst banana plantations, is the great agricultural centre of the north of the island.

Los Tilos★. — *2km - 1 mile.* A detour up the Barranco del Agua brings you to the *tilos* woods, a type of myrtle which covers the ravine in a dense, shiny, greenery.

SOUTH by Los Llanos and Fuencaliente
170km - 106 miles - Local map p 280

After the Santa Cruz Ravine, take the first turning on the left which heads north. Straight ahead is the **Virgin's Ship** (Barco de la Virgen), a boat made of cement and the goal of the Virgen de las Nieves Pilgrimage. The road continues past the foot of the Santa Catalina fort.

Las Nieves. — On a square, shaded by great laurel trees, at the foot of the Pico de las Nieves (the Snowpeak), stands the **Church of Nuestra Señora de las Nieves** and within it the statue of the island's patron. Every five years the figure is led in procession to the boat built in her honour in Santa Cruz.

La Concepción Belvedere★★ (Mirador). — The summit of the Caldereta commands a wonderful **bird's-eye view★★** of Santa Cruz and the coast further north.

A tunnel brings you out on the western slopes of the central mountain chain.

Caldera de Taburiente★★★ (National Park). — *4km - 2 1/2 miles beyond the tunnel take a dirt road on the right towards La Cumbrecita, then follow the signs to La Caldera.* From the **Cumbrecita Pass** (1 833m - 6 014ft) and even more splendidly from the **Lomo de las Chozas Pass,** 1km - 1/2 mile further on, there is a fantastic **panorama★★★** of the Caldera de Taburiente. The Roque de los Muchachos opposite is 2 423m - 7 950ft high. It is here that the Observatorio del Roque de los Muchachos is located and where Great Britain along with 7 other countries have research facilities. The equipment includes two British telescopes: the Isacc Newton, originally at the Royal Observatory in Greenwich *(see Michelin Green Guide to London)* and the William Herschel *(under construction),* the third largest telescope in the world. Standing out from the jagged stone spine dividing the crater floor is a small spike, the Idafe Rock, once sacred to the Guanches.

Los Llanos de Aridane. — This large market town lies at the centre of a vast plain *(llano).*

El Time★★. — From the top of the El Time cliff there is a remarkable **panorama★★** of the Aridane Plain, covered in a sea of banana trees, and the Barranco de las Angustias, an impressive rock fissure which is the only outlet for the waters which accumulate in the Caldera de Taburiente.

Puntagorda. — *14km - 9 miles.* Along the road, in this northwest part of the island, the general beauty of the landscape makes the drive worthwhile.

Puerto de Tazacorte. — *8km - 5 miles.* Small harbour where Lugo landed in 1492.

Puerto de Naos. — The descent, first through the lava fields of 1949 and then the banana plantations, is picturesque. The beach area has been developed into a seaside resort.

San Nicolás. — The lava stream from the Nambroque Volcano, which in 1949 cut the village in two, still scars the landscape.

SOUTH by Los Llanos and Fuencaliente

Fuencaliente*. — Before entering Fuencaliente, look back and you will get a **glimpse*** of the coast through the pines. The sunny village was a spa until 1677 when its hot water spring disappeared during the eruption of the **San Antonio Volcano***. As you circle the volcano you will see the impressive craters of the Teneguía Volcano which only made its appearance in October 1971 and the lava stream which, as it flowed towards the sea, separated the lighthouse from the village. The surrounding area, which is now covered in ash, is cultivated as before.

Belmaco Cave (Cueva). — *5km - 3 miles from the airport fork.*
At the end of the cave are several rocks engraved with enigmatic labyrinthine Guanche inscriptions.

HIERRO (Santa Cruz de Tenerife)

Michelin map **990** fold 31

Hierro, although the smallest of the islands (278km² - 107sq miles), is not the flattest. In shape it resembles a half crater open to the north with a rim more than 1 000m - 3 280ft high (Malpaso 1 501m - 4 925ft).

The far away island, isolated and difficult of access, has few inhabitants but those who do live there speak a remarkably pure Castilian. Apart from fishing off Restinga, the people raise sheep and goats (they make delicious cheeses) and farm and cultivate vines from which they produce an excellent white wine. Banana trees are being planted in the El Golfo region and figs and tomatoes around Timijiraque. It seems probable that, in time, the island with its variety of inland scenery and rocky coast ideal for underwater swimming, will be developed by the tourist trade.

Valverde. — The island's capital stands perched at an altitude of 571m - 1 873ft.

El Golfo**. — This depression surrounded by lofty rock walls is probably an ancient crater. The rim is covered with laurels and giant briars, the floor itself with vines, banana trees and sugar cane; the **Salmor Rocks** in the northeast are known locally because nearby, is the Fuga de Gorreta the habitat of a primeval lizard; **Sabinosa,** to the west, is a spa. Magnificent **viewpoints**** over the crater include the belvedere 1km - 1/2 mile from Guarazoca, that at El Rincón, approached along a track across La Dehesa, and that at Jinama, west of San Andrés.

La Dehesa. — From the track across the arid pastoral domain of La Dehesa, there are **extensive views*** of the south side of the island where the slopes, the colour of fire and pitted with craters, drop sharply towards the still waters of the Atlantic, known around this part of the coast as the "mar de las Calmas". To the east, the **El Pinar** area is covered with a vast and pleasant **pinewood***. In the **Nuestra Señora de los Reyes Hermitage** is the statue of the Virgin which, every fourth year, is led in procession with the Kings (Los Reyes) to Valverde. The cortege is preceded as it crosses each parish by a group of local *danzarines*. **Orchilla Point** was designated by Marius and Ptolemy (2C AD) as lying on the zero meridian which Ptolemy reasoned should run through the Fortunate Islands. Beyond the lighthouse, a beacon for all South America bound vessels, is a wood of sabine trees, conifers with twisted trunks, native only to Hierro.

Tiñor. — The Garoe, a tree venerated by the Bimbaches, stood to the northeast until a storm felled it down in 1610. The tree's leaves collected water by condensation which was then gathered in turn by grateful tribesmen.

Tamaduste. — A large sandbank has dammed the rock creek on which the small seaside resort stands.

INDEX

Buen Amor Castle . . . . . .   *Towns, sights and tourist regions.*

(Granada) . . . .   *Name of the province in which a town is situated.*

Al Mansur, Coro . . . . .   Historic personages described, titles of works and local terms explained in the text.

287

NOTES

MANUFACTURE FRANÇAISE DES PNEUMATIQUES MICHELIN

Société en commandite par actions au capital de 700 000 000 de francs

Place des Carmes-Déchaux — 63 Clermont-Ferrand (France)

R. C. S. Clermont-Fd B 855 200 507

© Michelin et Cie, Propriétaires-Éditeurs 1987

Dépôt légal : 87-1er Trim. - ISBN 2 06 015 213-5 - ISSN : 0763-1383

Printed in France 2-87-50

Photocomposition : S.C.I.A., La Chapelle d'Armentières — Impression : LAZARE-FERRY, Paris 12e no 8816